To my parents,
IRENE and FRANK HAY

CONTENTS

PREFACE

Biomechanics is concerned with the forces that act on a human body and the effects that these forces produce. Physical education teachers and coaches of athletic teams, whether they recognize it or not, are also concerned with forces and effects. Their ability to teach the basic techniques of a sport or physical activity depends largely on their knowledge of the effects they are trying to produce and of the forces that cause these effects. It seems logical, therefore, that physical educators, coaches, and athletes should look to biomechanics for a scientific basis for the analysis of the techniques used in sports. It is the purpose of this book to present such a scientific basis and to demonstrate how it can be used to advantage in the analysis of sports techniques.

Part I is concerned with defining biomechanics, establishing the role biomechanics can play in analyzing sports techniques, and evaluating the importance of a knowledge of biomechanics to the physical educator, the coach, and the athlete.

Part II is devoted to a discussion of basic biomechanical concepts which are of importance in the analysis of the techniques used in sports. Particular emphasis is placed on concepts associated with projectile motion, elastic impact, Newton's Laws and their angular analogues, mechanical energy, center of gravity, buoyancy and flotation, and fluid resistance.

The material is presented so that the reader, in proceeding from the simple to the complex, needs only the information previously given to understand each new concept as it is introduced. For example, unlike many other texts in the field, the discussion of centers of gravity is delayed until the reader has become acquainted with the concepts of force, weight, moment, resultant moment, and equilibrium—concepts that must be understood before a complete understanding of the center of gravity concept can be obtained.

Several important topics, not normally covered in a text of this kind, are considered. Among these are the concepts of impulse, mechanical energy, lift, and drag. The segmentation method of locating the center of gravity of an athlete is also covered in some detail.

Part III contains a detailed analysis of the techniques used in eight major sports—gymnastics, golf, swimming, and track and field among the individual sports; and baseball, basketball, football, and softball among the team games.

The writer of a text of this kind is faced with deciding whether to write a short (and, necessarily, superficial) analysis of a large number of sports or whether to write a longer, more detailed analysis of just a few. The latter course has been chosen in the belief that superficial treatments, by their very nature, rarely contain much of real value and in the hope that the more detailed approach may make the analysis of value to a wide range of readers.

The analysis of the techniques involved in each sport is divided into two parts. The first, entitled Basic Considerations, is concerned with enumerating the basic factors involved in the performance of each technique and with showing how these factors interrelate with one another to produce the desired result. The second part contains a detailed discussion of the techniques themselves with particular emphasis on those areas where there are known to be disagreements among teachers and coaches. Where possible these disagreements are resolved, either by the simple application of the basic concepts of biomechanics or by reference to research findings on the subject. Where further research is needed before a disagreement can be resolved, this fact is drawn to the attention of the reader in the hope that this will not only acquaint him (or her) with the limits of present knowledge in the area, but perhaps also stimulate an appropriate research project in quest of a solution.

This fourth edition contains many changes from the third edition. A few of these are fairly substantial; others, and by far the majority, are relatively minor.

- The section on rebound tumbling, which previously concluded the gymnastics chapter, has been deleted. Product-liability litigation has driven the sport into extinction in the United States and it no longer warrants consideration in a text of this kind. It will, however, be missed by those who had come to recognize the trampoline as a wonderful vehicle for the demonstration of biomechanical concepts.
- Exercises, intended to give readers practice in the application of basic concepts, have been included at the end of each of the first seven chapters. These exercises emphasize, not the mere regurgitation of information committed to memory, but the application of concepts in situations not previously discussed. They are intended to test the reader's ability to use concepts and not merely to recall them.
- Recommended readings have been listed at the end of most chapters. These are intended to serve two purposes—supplemental reading material and reference material. In most of the lists, there are some entries in which the topics discussed in the chapter are discussed again at a similar level. These entries may be considered as supplemental reading material. The lists in Part III (Analysis of Sports Techniques) contain reviews of existing knowledge on a given topic, and classic studies or recent research on a given sport, event or technique. These entries, offered as reference material for further study, often contain some material that is beyond the scope of this text.
- A great deal of research on the biomechanics of sports techniques has been published in the years since the last edition of this book. Where appropriate, major findings from such studies have been included in

the discussion of the techniques concerned. This research activity has been very unevenly distributed among the sports considered in this text. There have been hundreds of studies conducted on the techniques used in track and field and in swimming. There have been a few on the techniques used in baseball, gymnastics, and golf. There have been almost none at all on the techniques used in basketball and football. The changes from one edition of this text to the next reflect these differences in research activity.

- Finally, efforts have been made once again to eliminate errors, to clarify the text and to improve the artwork. In the latter regard, many new figures have been added and many old ones have been modified to better convey the message intended.

Many people have contributed to the writing of this book in one way or another—some by the inspiration, guidance, and opportunities provided the author over the years; some by their direct contributions of artwork, secretarial services, and critical review; and one by her patient acceptance that it all takes time and effort away from other important responsibilities. The author would like to extend his sincere thanks to:

FRANK SHARPLEY, whose unremitting search for biomechanical solutions to technique problems in track and field provided the author with his initial motivation to take up study in this area and whose enthusiasm, energy, and sheer innovative genius continue to be a source of inspiration.

LOUIS ALLEY, for his guidance during the author's years as a graduate student, and for his subsequent efforts to provide the author with every opportunity to pursue his work in this field.

PHILLIP SMITHELLS, who did much to mold the author's philosophy of physical education and athletics and who provided the author with time and facilities to work on the first edition of this book.

BRENDA JOSEPH, who entered the manuscript into computer files, assembled the artwork, and performed a dozen other tasks to prepare it all for publication; CHARMAINE DAPENA, who prepared most of the new artwork for this fourth edition; HOWARD PAYNE, who provided the new photo sequences used in the last two chapters; and ROBERT ETTEMA and RICHARD HINRICHS, for their constructive criticisms of parts of the manuscript.

And finally to my wife HILARY, who patiently suffered the disruption of our life together that this book might be written.

JAMES G. HAY

BIOMECHANICS IN PHYSICAL EDUCATION AND ATHLETICS

The study of any field begins logically with an attempt to obtain a general idea about the content of the field, the uses to which that content might be put, and the importance of a knowledge of the field in various situations. This introductory chapter is devoted to a discussion of these basic questions.

WHAT IS BIOMECHANICS?

For many years, the term *kinesiology* (literally, the science of movement) was used to describe that body of knowledge concerned with the structure and function of the musculo-skeletal system of the human body. Later the study of the mechanical principles applicable to human movement became widely accepted as an integral part of kinesiology. Later still the term was used rather literally to encompass all the sciences that might usefully contribute to the study of human movement. At this point it became clear that kinesiology had quite lost its usefulness to describe specifically that part of the science of movement concerned with either the musculo-skeletal system or the mechanical principles applicable to human movement. Several new terms were suggested as substitutes and *anthropomechanics, anthropokinetics, biodynamics, biokinetics, homokinetics,* and *kinanthropology* all had their proponents. Ultimately, there emerged one term that gained much wider acceptance than any other. That term was *biomechanics*.*

The term *biomechanics* has been variously defined as:

The mechanical bases of biological, esp. muscular activity [and] the study of the principles and relations involved.[1]

The application of mechanical laws to living structures, specifically to the locomotor system of the human body.[2]

. . . the study of the structure and function of biological systems by means of the methods of mechanics.[3]

However, since this book is concerned principally with the application of biomechanics to a quite limited field—that is, to the analysis of the techniques employed by humans in sports—a further and more restricted definition is offered here:

Biomechanics is the science concerned with the internal and external forces acting on a human body and the effects produced by these forces.

WHAT IS THE FUNCTION OF BIOMECHANICS?

The internal and external forces acting on a human body determine how the parts of that body move during the performance of a motor skill. They determine, in short, what is commonly referred to as the performer's *technique*.

There is often a wide range of techniques that might be used for the same purpose in sports and exercise. There are three widely recognized grips that may be used when driving a golf ball; there are numerous variations of the grab start technique that may be used in freestyle, butterfly, and breaststroke events in swimming; there are several different methods that may be used in leading off base in baseball; and so on.

Most of these techniques have been developed by teachers, coaches, and athletes seeking, by trial and error, to improve performances. This, however, is not the only way in which new techniques are developed. The handspring vault with the gymnast going into and out of a piked position during the dismount—the so-called Yamashita vault—was developed quite by accident. Yamashita, the gymnast who first performed it, simply piked to save an otherwise poor handspring vault! New techniques have also been

---

* Although the term *biomechanics* is now used throughout the world—as, for example, in the titles of national and international societies such as the American Society of Biomechanics, the European Society of Biomechanics, and the International Society of Biomechanics—the term *kinesiology* is still used with either its restricted or more general meaning in some parts of North America. The relative merits of the terms *biomechanics* and *kinesiology* have been discussed at some length by Atwater, A. E. (1980), Kinesiology/Biomechanics: Perspectives and trends. *Research Quarterly for Exercise and Sport*, 51:193–218; and by Nelson, R. C. (1980). In J. M. Cooper and B. Haven (Eds.), *Proceedings of the Biomechanics Symposium Indiana University, October 26–28, 1980* (pp. 4–13). Ind.: The Indiana State Board of Health. Readers interested in pursuing the matter further should consult these sources.

developed as the result of scientific analysis. Malmberg[4] has reported, for example, that Soviet scientists have come up with "no less than 1000 [gymnastic] stunts that have never been done before and are presently researching them." The development of one of these—"the reverse hecht (as performed by Tkatchev and Andrianov)"—was claimed to be "the first time [that] science went ahead of the gymnast."

The process of attempting to improve performance by developing new techniques is an ongoing one in most sports. It is especially evident, however, when new rules or new equipment alter the conditions under which the skills involved are performed. Thus, changes to the rules governing the turns in swimming events led to the development of new techniques of turning. The development of the sponge-faced table tennis bat, the fiberglass vaulting pole, and the steel-edged ski led to the development of new techniques or the modification of old ones.

Given these various circumstances, teachers, coaches, and athletes often have difficulty deciding which technique to use. A simple and commonly used "solution" to this problem is to copy the technique used by the current champion in the sport involved. This practice appears to have some merit. Top athletes often try many different techniques over a period of years and adopt the one that seems to produce the best results. In such cases, the technique adopted is likely to be close to the optimum for the motor skill concerned.

The practice of "copying the champion" does have some major limitations, however. In some instances, the champion has succeeded in spite of having a technique that is far removed from the optimum. This is frequently the case in sports where such attributes as speed, strength, and endurance are more important than technique. Thus, for example, the runner in Fig. 1-1 was an Olympic champion and a world-record holder in the 100 m despite obvious flaws in her starting technique.

In those cases where the champion has tried many different techniques and adopted the one that produces the best results, he (or she) is most unlikely to have perfected that technique. Thus anyone who blindly copies the technique of a champion copies not only its desirable features, but also its undesirable ones. This point is well illustrated in the following true

Figure 1-1. Champions often have flaws in their techniques. This figure is taken from a photograph of an Olympic champion and world-record holder starting in a 100-m event. Note that both right arm and right leg are forward.

story—the names have been omitted to protect the guilty! Some years ago, a British athlete met for the first time the Russian world-record holder in his event, a man whom he much admired. After the usual preliminaries, the British athlete said that he had studied the Russian's technique and decided that a certain feature of that technique was largely responsible for his success. He also said that he had worked very hard to incorporate this feature into his own technique. The Russian was much amused by all this. He explained, as diplomatically as he could, that he considered this feature to be the one major fault in his technique—a fault that he had just recently succeeded in eliminating!

In addition to those already mentioned, there are other major weaknesses in the practice of "copying the champion." Champions change frequently, and often the technique used by one is substantially different from that used by the next. The technique used by a champion may be the optimum (or, at least, near the optimum) for a person with the same physical attributes as the champion, and far removed from the optimum for a person less well endowed or less well trained. Adoption of the technique used by the champion may thus be totally inappropriate.

Having once established what technique should be used in a given instance, teachers and coaches are confronted with the task of detecting and correcting faults in an athlete's performance. The greatest difficulty here—even if it is seldom recognized as such—is that of locating the cause of the faults observed. Although it is not too difficult for an experienced eye to detect a gross fault in an athlete's technique (particularly when that technique is well known and widely used), the cause of that fault may be very difficult to locate. One of the reasons is that the cause is often far removed from the effect. (In jumping, tumbling, and diving, for example, effects observed in the air or on landing are almost always caused by faults in the technique of the takeoff or the run preceding the takeoff.) Many teachers and coaches attempt to correct the effect that they have observed and give little or no thought to the underlying cause that has produced it. In general, such attempts are quite ineffectual. The athlete's performance is likely to deteriorate as the teacher or coach adds to the problems instead of helping to resolve them.

All of this raises two obvious and important questions. Given all the weaknesses in the copy-the-champion approach, is there a better way to select the best technique to use in a particular case? How can teachers and coaches improve their ability to locate the causes of the faults they observe?

The answers to these questions lie with the science of biomechanics—a science which provides a sound, logical basis upon which to evaluate the various techniques that might be used in a given case and to connect observed effects with their underlying causes.

A knowledge of motor learning equips teachers and coaches to make sound judgments concerning methods of instruction, length, frequency, nature of practice, and so on. A knowledge of physiology equips them to make sound judgments concerning the amount and type of training to prescribe in a given case. Finally, a knowledge of biomechanics equips them to choose appropriate techniques and to detect the root causes of faults that may arise in their use. In short, just as motor learning may be regarded as the science underlying the acquisition of skills and physiology the science underlying training, biomechanics is the science underlying techniques. (*Note:* It is as well to recognize here that these sciences do not have ready-made answers to *all* the problems that confront teachers and coaches. However, where they are unable to provide an answer immediately, they do offer the means whereby an answer might ultimately be obtained.)

Although many people are interested in sports techniques in one way or another, three groups readily distinguish themselves—physical education teachers, coaches, and athletes. Because each of these groups tends to view sports techniques in a different way, the importance of a knowledge of biomechanics to each of them will be considered in turn.

HOW IMPORTANT IS A KNOWLEDGE OF BIOMECHANICS?

To the Physical Education Teacher.   Physical education (or coeducation) and its aims have been variously described:

> . . . *physical education has been defined as a process through which favorable adaptations and learnings—organic, neuromuscular, intellectual, social, cultural, emotional, and aesthetic—result from and proceed through fairly vigorous activities.*[5]

> *Physical education . . . has as its aim the improvement of human performance, through the medium of physical activities . . .*[6]

> *Physical coeducation means that the learner's individual dimensional needs—physical, intellectual, social, emotional, and spiritual—are satisfied explicitly through all forms of physical activity.*[7]

The seemingly endless array of such statements have at least one thing in common: they all visualize the aims of physical education being realized through the medium of physical activities. It should thus be clear that the success that physical educators achieve must be conditional on their knowledge of this particular medium—the techniques, teaching and training methods involved, and the sciences upon which they are based. It can therefore be stated emphatically that a knowledge of biomechanics (and of motor learning and physiology) is essential to physical education teachers who are not content to limit their effectiveness by making critical judgments based on guesswork.

To the Coach.   The importance of a knowledge of biomechanics to a coach depends to a certain extent on the sport involved. A cross-country coach, concerned primarily with cardiovascular and muscular endurance and only to a very limited extent with techniques, will clearly benefit less from a knowledge of biomechanics than will a coach of baseball, football, gymnastics, or swimming, in all of which techniques play a much larger role.

Another factor here is the level at which the individual is working. The physical education teacher generally works with beginners or near-beginners and so is concerned with the broad fundamentals of sports techniques and the broad biomechanical principles underlying them. The coach, on the other hand, works at increasingly more advanced levels and hence is concerned not only with broad fundamentals but also with precise details. As the level of performance increases, so does the coach's need for a thorough knowledge of biomechanics. At the highest levels of sports in which techniques play a major role, improvement comes so often from careful attention to detail that no coach can afford to leave these details to chance or guesswork. For such coaches, a knowledge of biomechanics might well be regarded as essential.

At this point, there will possibly be some who are inclined to scoff at such a claim and to cite cases of highly successful coaches who have little or no apparent knowledge of biomechanics. Their success merely emphasizes that other things are also important. What is worthy of thought, however, is the level to which the performances of their athletes might rise, if to all these coaches' other attributes was added a knowledge of biomechanics!

To the Athlete. While the importance of a knowledge of biomechanics to physical education teachers and coaches is generally agreed, there is no such agreement on its importance to athletes.

A number of studies have been conducted in an attempt to determine the value of a knowledge of biomechanics in the learning of a physical skill. However, since the subjects of almost all these studies were complete beginners, they shed little light on the importance of a knowledge of biomechanics to the skilled athlete.

Some leading authorities on motor learning have expressed opinions concerning this question:

> As the learner progresses or gets older and more generally experienced, verbal directions and an analysis of movement can help more in increasing the meaningfulness of the skill and in giving new insights into it.[8]

> The experimental literature does not cover the value of mechanical analysis for the advanced student, but empirical evidence seems to indicate somewhat greater value at the higher skill levels.[9]

Thus, although no conclusive evidence is available, it would appear that a knowledge of the biomechanical principles involved might well enhance the performance of an already skilled athlete.

Exercises

1. Identify three sports techniques that were developed by athletes. (*Hint:* Such techniques often bear the names of the athletes who "invented" them.)
   Or: Identify one sports technique that was developed following a change in the rules governing the event or sport.

Or: Identify one sports technique that was developed following a change in the facilities or equipment used in the event or sport.

2. Name one scientific journal that publishes articles on each of the following: (a) motor learning; (b) exercise physiology; and (c) sport biomechanics. Using a standard method for citing a reference, cite one article published in these journals in the last 12 months on each of the following topics: (a) the effects of different methods of instruction on the learning of a motor skill; (b) the effects of training on the structure and/or function of the human body; and (c) the effects of variations in technique on the results obtained in the performance of a motor skill.

Notes

1. *Webster's Third New International Dictionary of the English Language* (1976). Springfield, Mass.: G & C. Merriam Co.
2. *Dorland's Illustrated Medical Dictionary* (1981). Philadelphia: W. B. Saunders Co.
3. Hatze, H. (1974). The meaning of the term "Biomechanics". *Journal of Biomechanics, 7;* 189–90.
4. Malmberg, E. (1978). Science innovation and gymnastics in the USSR. *International Gymnast,* 20: 63.
5. Baley, J. A., and Field, D. A. (1976). *Physical Education and the Physical Educator* (p. 31). Boston: Allyn & Bacon.
6. Bucher, C. A. (1979). *Foundations of Physical Education* (p. 16). St. Louis: C. V. Mosby Co.
7. Melograno, V. (1979). *Designing Curriculum and Learning: A Physical Coeducation Approach* (p. 58). Dubuque, Iowa: Kendall/Hunt Publishing Co.
8. Knapp, B. (1966). *Skill in Sports: The Attainment of Proficiency* (p. 28). London: Routledge & Kegan Paul.
9. Lawther, J. D. (1968). *The Learning of Physical Skills* (p. 101). Englewood Cliffs, N. J.: Prentice Hall.

In general, all motion may be described as translation or rotation or some combination of these two.

TRANSLATION

Translation (or *linear motion*) takes place when a body* moves so that all parts of it travel exactly the same distance, in the same direction, in the same time. One way of deciding whether a body is undergoing translation is to consider the motion of a straight line drawn on the body. If this line remains of the same length and is always parallel to the previous positions it occupied, the body is undergoing translation. A close look at the example of translation in Fig. 2-1 reveals that this criterion is, in effect, the same as the one given earlier—that is, the same distance, same direction, same time criterion. In this example, the line that has been selected is one joining the right shoulder and right hip joints. (Any number of other lines could have

---

* In biomechanics the term *body* is used to refer to both inanimate objects (such as items of sporting equipment) and animate objects (such as the human body or parts of the human body). In this latter regard it is important to realize that it is convenient in some instances to consider the human body in its entirety, and in others to consider it as a system comprised of a series of separate bodies (head, trunk, arm, forearm, etc.).

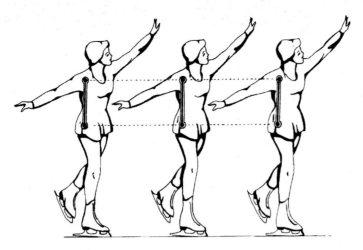

Figure 2-1. Straight-line (or rectilinear) translation.

been selected for the purpose.) The dotted lines—in this case straight and parallel—show the paths taken by the two joints mentioned.

In Fig. 2-2, the motion of the skydiver during free fall is also an example of translation, as successive positions of the line joining his hip and shoulder joints again indicate. This time, however, the path taken by each of these joints is a curved line rather than a straight one. (*Note*: The straight-line and curved-line types of linear motion are frequently referred to as *rectilinear translation* and *curvilinear translation*, respectively.)

Finally, in Fig. 2-3, although the first and last positions shown might suggest that translation has taken place, consideration of the intermediate positions clearly indicates that this is not the case.

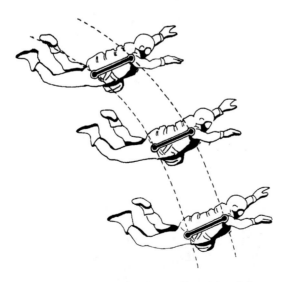

Figure 2-2. Curved-line (or curvilinear) translation.

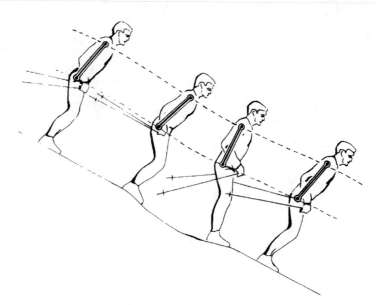

Figure 2-3. Nonlinear motion.

ROTATION

Rotation (or *angular motion*) takes place when a body moves along a circular path about some line in space so that all parts of the body travel through the same angle, in the same direction, in the same time. This line, which may or may not pass through the body itself, is known as the *axis of rotation* and lies at right angles to the plane of motion of the body.

The athlete performing calisthenics in Fig. 2-4 provides an example of angular motion as he raises his legs from the floor to the vertical. The gymnast in Fig. 2-5 provides yet another example, but this time the axis of rotation lies just outside the physical limits of his body—actually, through the center of the horizontal bar on which he is swinging. (*Note:* In both cases the plane of the motion and the axis of rotation are at right angles to each other.)

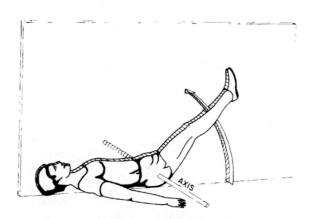

Figure 2-4. Angular motion about an internal axis.

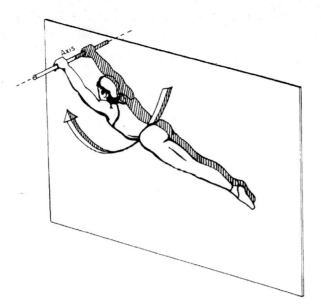

Figure 2-5. Angular motion about an external axis.

**GENERAL
MOTION**

While rotation is a good deal more common than translation in sports techniques, much more common than either is *general motion*, which is some combination of the two. The racing cyclist, for example, translates his upper body as a direct result of the rotary movements of his legs (Fig. 2-6).

In addition to this combining of translation and rotation there is often a combining of several rotations. Consider the action of one of the cyclist's legs (Fig. 2-7). Here there are at least three simultaneous rotations taking place. First, there is the rotation of his thigh about an axis through his hip joint (which is itself translating). Then there is the rotation of his leg about his knee joint, and finally there is the rotation of his foot about his ankle joint. As can probably be imagined, a study of the combined motions of the elements within such a system can become quite complex.

Figure 2-6. General motion—translation and rotation combined.

Figure 2-7. A complex general motion.

1. A playground slide consists of three sections: a long, straight section sloping downward at an angle of about 50° to the horizontal; a medium-length, curved section; and finally, a short, straight section parallel with the ground. A little girl sits at the top of the slide and lets go. Assuming that she keeps her trunk erect and doesn't change the positions of her head, arms, and legs during the descent, what forms of motion does she experience on the way down? If she experiences linear motion at any stage, be sure to specify whether this is rectilinear or curvilinear motion.

2. In a correctly performed squat exercise, an athlete rotates simultaneously about five axes: one axis passes through two joints, the others pass through one joint each. Through which joints do these axes pass? In what directions do these axes lie? Do any of these directions change substantially during the course of the exercise?

Recommended Readings

HAY, J. G., and REID, J. G. (1988). *Anatomy, Mechanics and Human Motion.* Englewood Cliffs, N. J.: Prentice Hall, pp. 109–13 (Human motion).

KELLEY, D. L. (1971). *Kinesiology: Fundamentals of Motion Description.* Englewood Cliffs, N. J.: Prentice Hall, pp. 58–69 (The classification of whole-body motion).

LINEAR KINEMATICS

Kinematics is the branch of biomechanics concerned with describing the motion of bodies. Thus kinematics deals with such things as how far a body moves, how fast it moves, and how consistently it moves. It is not concerned at all with what causes a body to move the way it does. This latter aspect of motion is the preserve of *kinetics*—a complementary branch of biomechanics that will be considered later in this book.

Linear kinematics deals with the kinematics of translation, or linear motion; angular kinematics (see Chap. 4) deals with the kinematics of rotation, or angular motion.*

Distance and displacement are quantities commonly used to describe the extent of a body's motion. When a body moves from one location to another, the *distance* through which it moves is simply the length of the path that it follows. The *displacement* the body undergoes in the course of the

DISTANCE AND DISPLACEMENT

* The concepts introduced in this chapter—and those introduced in the chapter on linear kinetics—apply equally to the translatory motion of a body that also experiences rotation as they do to the motion of one that experiences translation alone. In other words, they are applicable not only to the analysis of linear motion—which, after all, occurs only occasionally in sports—but also to the analysis of the linear aspects of general motion.

same motion is found by measuring the length of a straight line joining its initial and final positions and noting the direction that this line takes. In lay terms, the displacement is a measure of the motion "as the crow flies."

The concepts of distance and displacement are perhaps best understood in terms of an example. Consider the maps of the two marathon courses shown in Fig. 3-1. In both instances, and in accord with long-established tradition, the competitors are required to run the rather odd distance of 42.2 km to complete the race. The displacements they undergo in the process depend on the nature of the course. In the first case shown (the course for the annual Boston marathon), those who finish undergo a displacement of 38.6 km in an ENE direction. In the second case (the course for an Olympic Games marathon), the starting and finishing lines coincide. Thus, although competitors may spend two to three hours running more

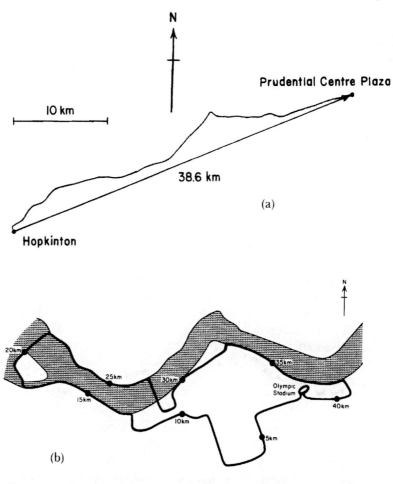

Figure 3-1. The displacement a runner experiences in the process of completing a marathon depends on the nature of the course. In (a), the Boston marathon, the runner's displacement is approximately 38.6 km ENE. In (b), the 1988 Olympic Games course in Seoul, the runner's displacement is 0 km.

than 42 km, the displacement they experience is zero (ignoring any small differences in the position at which they cross the line at start and finish).

When a body moves in a straight line, as in a 100 m dash, the distance over which it travels and the displacement it experiences have the same magnitude, namely 100 m. The two quantities differ, however, in that the displacement must contain reference to the direction of the motion (as well as to its magnitude) whereas the distance is completely defined by its magnitude alone. Thus, a sprinter who runs 100 m in a northerly direction covers a distance of 100 m and undergoes a displacement of 100 m, North.

SPEED AND VELOCITY

The rate at which a body moves from one location to another is usually described with reference to its speed or velocity—two quantities that are generally and wrongly thought to be identical.

The average speed of a body is obtained by dividing the distance covered by the time taken:

$$\bar{s} = \frac{l}{t} \qquad (3\text{-}1)$$

where $\bar{s}$ = the average speed; l = the length of the path (that is, the distance covered); and t = the time.

The average velocity is obtained by dividing the displacement by the time taken:

$$\bar{v} = \frac{d}{t} \qquad (3\text{-}2)$$

where $\bar{v}$ = the average velocity and d = the displacement and, because velocity is a measure of a body's motion in a given direction, specifying this direction.

As with distances and displacements, the magnitudes of the average speed and the average velocity are equal only when the motion is in a straight line and in one direction. Thus, the average speed of a baseball player during his run to first base is the same as the magnitude of his average velocity. A girl who swims 50 m in a 25-m pool also moves in an essentially straight line but, because she reverses direction at the midpoint in her swim, has an average speed and an average velocity that differ markedly from one another. If she completes the swim in say, 30 s, her average speed is

$$\bar{s} = \frac{50\text{m}}{30\text{ s}}$$

$$= 1.67 \text{ m/s}$$

Her average velocity, however, is

$$\bar{v} \;=\; \frac{0 \text{ m}}{30 \text{ s}}$$

$$=\; 0 \text{ m/s}$$

This somewhat surprising result comes about because the swimmer's displacement is zero. (The small difference between her position on the block at the start and in the water at the finish has been ignored.) Thus, while increasingly greater average speeds are needed to break records in swimming, the average velocities generally remain unaltered at 0 m/s.

At this point one might question the value of computing average velocities since they appear to convey very little information of interest. The merits of computing average speeds might also be questioned because, typically, the average speed over an extended distance is a very poor indicator of how that distance was covered. Consider, for example, the world records for the men's 1500 m set by swimmers A and B (Fig. 3-2). The graph showing the average speeds of the two swimmers for the full distance of the event (Fig. 3-2[a]) conveys little more than was already known—that is, one was faster overall than the other. However, when the average speeds for successive 300-m segments of the full distance are considered (Fig. 3-2[b]), the different ways in which the two races were swum begin to emerge. Specifically, it can be seen that A swam the first and last 300 m markedly faster than B and that the two differed relatively little during the middle stages. When this process is continued one step further and the average speeds for every 100 m are considered (Fig. 3-2[c]), an even more detailed comparison becomes possible. This idea of obtaining an ever-clearer picture of what took place by progressively reducing the distance over which times are taken leads directly to the concept of *instantaneous speed*.

The instantaneous speed of a body is equal to its average speed over such a very short distance (starting from the position occupied by the body at the instant in question) that the speed will not have time to change. In similar fashion the instantaneous velocity of a body is defined as its average velocity over such a very short distance that the velocity will not have time to change. Further, as is the case with average speeds and velocities when a body is moving in a straight line, the instantaneous speed of a body is equal to the magnitude of its instantaneous velocity.

Because the instantaneous speed is equal to the magnitude of the instantaneous velocity of a body, the word *speed* is often used in preference to the much longer description. For example, when a body is thrown into the air, it is customary to speak of its "speed of release"—meaning the number of m/s at which it left the hand—rather than of the "magnitude of the velocity of release."

Time and again in sports techniques it is this concept of an instantaneous

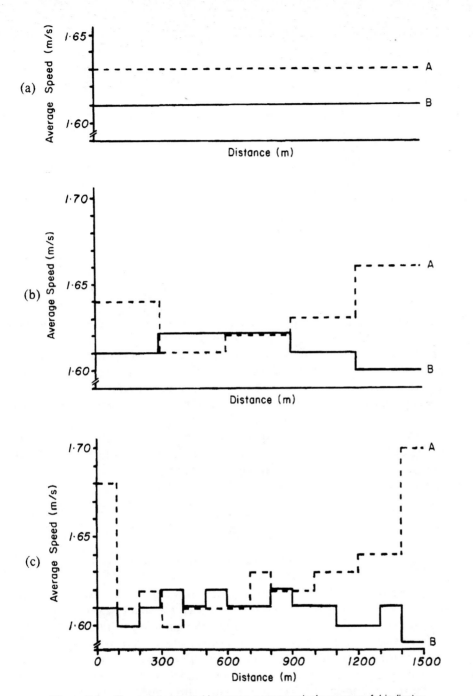

Figure 3-2. The average speed becomes a progressively more useful indicator of performance as the distance (or time) over which it is computed decreases.

speed or velocity (rather than an average value) that is critical. For instance, when an athlete jumps or throws, it is the velocity of the body in question at the instant of takeoff or release that largely determines the final outcome.

(*Note:* [1] Physics and mechanics texts usually define instantaneous speed in terms of a "very short interval of time" rather than a "very short distance." The latter has been used here because it is believed to be a little easier to understand and because measurements of instantaneous speed taken in biomechanics frequently make use of the concept of a "very short distance." [2] When average and instantaneous quantities are represented here in algebraic form, average values are distinguished from instantaneous values by the addition of a line [or bar] above the appropriate letter. Thus, for example, s is used to represent the instantaneous speed and $\bar{s}$ [read "s bar"] the average speed.)

ACCELERATION

In many sports activities the success enjoyed by an athlete is directly related to the athlete's ability to increase or decrease velocity rapidly. The football lineman seeks to build up as much velocity as he can before he makes contact with his opponent. The softball player stealing second base builds up velocity as quickly as possible, to minimize the time available for the defense to react; and then reduces his velocity at the end of the run to avoid overrunning the bag. Basketball players must likewise be able to build up velocity quickly and to "stop on a dime." All of these people, and many more in other sports, are concerned with *acceleration*.

Acceleration (which, like displacement and velocity, necessarily includes a magnitude and a direction) is defined as the rate at which the velocity changes with respect to time. In algebraic form:

$$\bar{a} = \frac{v_f - v_i}{t} \tag{3-3}$$

where $\bar{a}$ = the average acceleration; v_f = the final velocity; v_i = the initial velocity; and t = the elapsed time.

A close look at Eq. (3-3) shows that it is possible to have positive, negative, and zero values for the acceleration. Anytime that v_f is greater than v_i, the numerator of the right-hand side of the equation will be positive and the acceleration itself will be positive. Conversely, when v_i is greater than v_f, the numerator and the acceleration are both negative. Finally, when v_f and v_i are equal, there has obviously been no change in the velocity and hence, by the very definition of acceleration, this latter must be zero.

All of this presents no problems when the motion takes place in a straight line and in one direction. Under such circumstances, it is customary to speak of negative acceleration as *deceleration* or *retardation* or just plain "slowing down." As an example, the base runner (Fig. 3-3) starts from a position of zero velocity and then undergoes positive acceleration until he

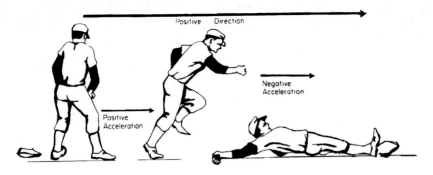

Figure 3-3. Positive and negative acceleration in running between bases.

is close to second base. He then experiences negative acceleration as he goes into the slide that will ultimately bring him to rest in contact with the bag. (*Note:* At the end of his period of positive acceleration there will be an instant when he is no longer increasing his forward velocity nor has yet started to decrease it—that is, a moment of zero acceleration.)

Problems may arise, however, when the acceleration of a body that moves first in one direction and then in the opposite direction is being considered. Consider the volleyball blocker in Fig. 3-4. If the upward direction is taken as positive, the player's acceleration between positions (a) and (b) is positive

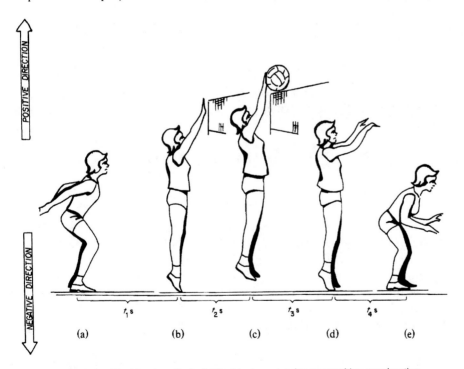

Figure 3-4. Blocking in volleyball. The blocker experiences positive acceleration each time she is in contact with the ground and negative acceleration while in the air.

because in position (b) she has a high velocity in the upward (positive) direction and in position (a) she has zero velocity:

$$\bar{a} = \frac{\text{large positive velocity} - 0}{t_1}$$

$$= \text{some positive value}$$

Her acceleration in the interval between positions (b) and (c) is negative:

$$\bar{a} = \frac{0 - \text{large positive velocity}}{t_2}$$

$$= \text{some negative value}$$

So far, all is consistent with what was said earlier about the base runner—when the athlete "speeds up," she experiences positive acceleration; conversely, when she "slows down," she experiences negative acceleration. Now, however, the difficulty arises. Between positions (c) and (d) the athlete's acceleration is again negative. In position (c) she has zero velocity and in position (d) she has a high velocity in a downward (or negative) direction. Hence:

$$\bar{a} = \frac{\text{large negative velocity} - 0}{t_3}$$

$$= \text{some negative value}$$

Between positions (d) and (e) the athlete's high negative velocity is reduced to zero, and in this process she once again experiences positive acceleration:

$$\bar{a} = \frac{0 - \text{large negative velocity}}{t_4}$$

$$= \text{some positive value}$$

In other words, during these last two intervals the pattern established earlier has been completely disrupted—the athlete has experienced negative acceleration while "speeding up" and positive acceleration while "slowing down."

It is thus important to recognize that when directions are designated as positive and negative, these adjectives can no longer be used in conjunction with acceleration to indicate, respectively, "speeding up" and "slowing down."

UNITS IN LINEAR KINEMATICS

With one exception, the units used in the measurement of the quantities described so far provide few problems. In the International System of Units—or S.I. System as it is called—measurements of length are made in meters (m) and measurements of time in seconds (s), minutes (min), or hours (h). The units of measurement for those quantities that are some combination of these basic quantities of length and time are derived in logical fashion. For example, because speed is determined by dividing a measurement of length by a measurement of time (average speed = distance/time), the unit for speed is one in which a unit of length is divided by a unit of time. Thus the meter per second (m/s) and the kilometer per hour (km/h) are units of speed.

With distance and displacement measured in units of length, and speed and velocity measured in m/s, km/h, etc., the only quantity so far unaccounted for—and the only one likely to create any difficulty—is acceleration. A glance at the right-hand side of the equation for average acceleration—Eq. (3-3)—reveals that the numerator is the difference between two velocities and is thus logically measured in a unit appropriate to velocities. The denominator is a measurement of time and is likewise measured in a unit appropriate to times. Thus, for example, if the velocity unit used is the meter per second and the time unit is the second, the unit for acceleration is the meter per second per second (m/s^2).

An example may help to clarify this. Consider a swimmer whose forward velocity is 1.8 m/s, 2 s after the start of a race (Fig. 3-5). Since his velocity was 0 m/s when the gun went off (he's an honest swimmer!), his change in forward velocity in the first 2 s is 1.8 m/s. If this change is averaged out over the 2-s time period, it can be seen that on average he changed his forward

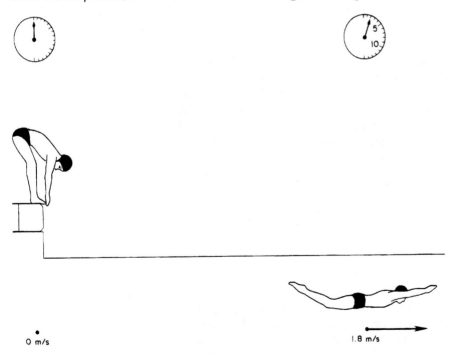

0 m/s   1.8 m/s

Figure 3-5. Acceleration is the rate at which the velocity changes with respect to time. This swimmer's forward velocity changed by 1.8 m/s in 2 s or, on average, 0.9 m/s each second. His average acceleration was thus 0.9 m/s².

Figure 3-6. Velocities of release represented in vector form.

velocity by 0.9 m/s for each of the 2 s. In other words, his average forward acceleration was 0.9 m/s².

ACCELERATION DUE TO GRAVITY

The downward acceleration that a body experiences while in the air is due to the influence of the earth on all bodies near to its surface, an influence known as *gravity*. The acceleration due to gravity is essentially constant—it varies slightly from place to place on the earth's surface—and, because it is of especial significance in so many situations, is generally designated by a separate letter *g*. The magnitude of the acceleration due to gravity (and it is important to remember that *g* represents simply an acceleration and nothing else) is approximately 9.81 m/s².

VECTORS AND SCALARS

Most of the kinematic (and kinetic) quantities considered in this text may be classified into two groups. Those, such as distance and speed, that can be completely described in terms of their magnitude are known as *scalars*; while those such as displacement, velocity, and acceleration, that require specification of both a magnitude and a direction are called *vectors*.*

Because arrows can also be considered to have both a magnitude (that is, a length) and a direction, it is often very useful to represent vectors by arrows. The instantaneous velocities of the bodies depicted in Fig. 3-6 are

---

* Not all quantities that can be described in terms of a magnitude and a direction are in fact vector quantities. A few, such as angular displacement (see pp. 47-48), have a magnitude and a direction but do not qualify as vectors (see the next section).

represented by the arrows shown. The length of each arrow represents the magnitude of the velocity to some chosen scale (in this case, 1 cm = 8 m/s) and the direction in which the arrow is drawn indicates the direction in which the vector is acting.

When the place-kicker in Fig. 3-7 imparts a velocity to the football in the direction of the middle of the goal posts, the ball travels in a straight line in that direction (Fig. 3-7[a]). If there is a crosswind blowing, this too imparts a velocity to the football. At the instant shown in Fig. 3-7(b), the football (at O) has a velocity (represented by the vector OK) imparted to it by the kicker, and a second velocity (represented by the vector OW) imparted to it by the wind. The net effect (or *resultant*) of these two velocity vectors can be found by completing the parallelograms of which OK and OW are adjacent sides and then constructing the diagonal through the

RESULTANT VECTOR

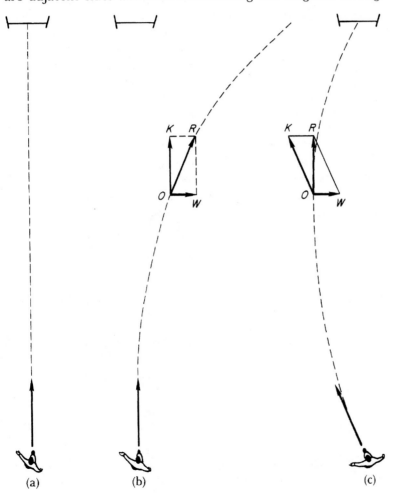

(a) (b) (c)

Figure 3-7. The parallelogram construction to find the summed effect of two vectors.

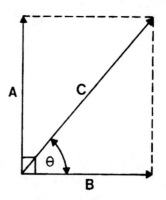

Figure 3-8. The resultant of two vectors at right angles to each other.

point O. This diagonal represents in magnitude and direction the resultant velocity of the ball. In other words, as a result of the combined effects of the kicker and the wind, the ball moves in the direction indicated by the diagonal OR and with a speed represented by the length of that diagonal. Of course, a good kicker knows all this from experience and thus makes due allowance for the wind in directing his kick (Fig. 3-7[c]).

A parallelogram such as the one obtained in the previous example is known as a *parallelogram of vectors*. Fortunately it is not necessary to go to the trouble of carefully measuring lines and angles and constructing such a parallelogram to determine the magnitude and direction of the resultant. Instead this can be found with relative ease by using an appropriate formula. When the angle between two vectors (A and B in Fig. 3-8) is a right angle, the magnitude of their resultant (C) can be found by using the theorem of Pythagoras:

$$C = \sqrt{A^2 + B^2}$$

$$(3\text{-}4)$$

and the direction in which this resultant acts can be found using simple trigonometry.* If the angle formed between vector B and the resultant is θ:

$$\tan \theta = \frac{A}{B}$$

and, therefore,

$$\theta = \arctan\left(\frac{A}{B}\right)$$

$$(3\text{-}5)$$

If these formulas are now applied to the example of Fig. 3-7(b), the magnitude of the resultant and the direction in which it acts are given by

* Readers without a background in elementary trigonometry should refer to Appendix A.

$$OR = \sqrt{OK^2 + OW^2}$$

and

$$\theta = \angle ROW$$

$$= \arctan\left(\frac{OK}{OW}\right)$$

If the angle (β) between the two vectors A and B is not a right angle, the process of arriving at the magnitude and direction of their resultant is a little more involved. The magnitude of the resultant, found using a trigonometrical identity known as the *cosine rule*, is given by

$$C = \sqrt{A^2 + B^2 + 2AB \cos \beta} \qquad (3\text{-}6)$$

and the direction in which the resultant acts is given by

$$\theta = \arctan\left(\frac{A \sin \beta}{B + A\cos \beta}\right) \qquad (3\text{-}7)$$

where θ is again the angle formed between vector B and the resultant C.

VECTOR COMPONENTS

In football the objective is to advance the ball down the field and across the opponent's goal line. In the course of doing this, however, the ball is generally moved both forward and sideways and only rarely in a straight line directly downfield. Consider, for example, the football play shown in Fig. 3-9. In this play the quarterback receives the ball from the center, drops back several yards, and then throws a pass to his halfback who has run down the right-hand side of the field. If the play starts with the ball at S in the hands of the center and ends with the ball at E in the hands of the halfback, it can be seen that the effect of this play (that is, the resultant displacement) can be represented by an arrow joining points S and E. Looked at in a slightly different way, it can also be seen that the effect of the play has been to give the ball a certain displacement (represented by the arrow SR) toward the right sideline and a certain displacement (represented by the arrow SD) down the field. These two separate displacements, which can be added by means of a parallelogram of vectors to arrive at the resultant, are said to be *components* of the resultant.

In many sports activities, one or both of a set of components are of greater concern than the resultant itself. In football, as can be readily appreciated, it is not the resultant displacement that determines the success of a given play, but rather the downfield component of this displacement.

The process of breaking down a resultant vector into two components is

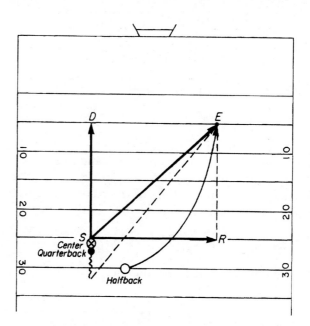

Figure 3-9. A pass play in football—an example in which a component of a vector is more important than the vector itself. In this play, the quarterback takes the ball from the center, drops back 5-6 yd, and then throws it (dashed line) to a halfback who has run (along the curved line) to receive it at *E*. The halfback is then tackled at *E*. The downfield component (*SD*) of the displacement of the ball (*SE*) is the gain made on the play and is much more important than the displacement itself. (*Note:* For the sake of simplicity, none of the other offensive or defensive players are shown.)

most commonly used in biomechanics in arriving at the horizontal and vertical components of displacements, velocities, accelerations, etc. These components can be determined graphically by following a procedure that essentially reverses the construction of a parallelogram of vectors, or by the use of elementary trigonometry. Suppose, for example, that it is desired to compare the horizontal and vertical velocities obtained by a champion high jumper with those obtained by a champion long jumper, at the instant of takeoff in their respective events. Suppose too that a velocity of 5.0 m/s at an angle of 60° to the horizontal is taken as representative of championship performance in the high jump, and that a velocity of 9.0 m/s at an angle of 25° to the horizontal is representative of championship performance in the long jump.*

To arrive at the horizontal and vertical components of the high jumper's takeoff velocity using the graphical method, the following steps would be necessary (Fig. 3-10):

- Choose a suitable linear scale (for example, 1 cm = 1 m/s).
- Using the chosen scale, draw an arrow to represent the jumper's takeoff velocity.

---

* Assuming appropriate values for the other factors that have a bearing on the outcome, the above would result in a high jump of 2.31 m and a long jump of 7.95 m.

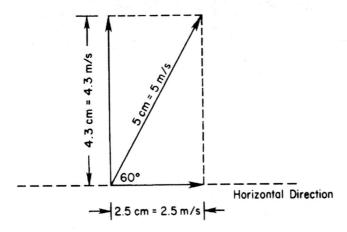

Figure 3-10. The graphical method for resolving a vector into components.

- Through each end of this arrow, draw straight lines to represent the horizontal and vertical directions. (*Note:* The acute angle between the horizontal lines and the line representing the takeoff velocity must be equal to the angle of takeoff, in this case 60°.)
- Measure carefully the lengths of two adjacent sides of the parallelogram thus formed and, using the linear scale originally chosen, convert these measurements to velocities. The velocity determined from the side of the parallelogram representing the horizontal direction is the horizontal component of the takeoff velocity (or, more simply, the horizontal velocity at takeoff). The other velocity determined is the vertical velocity at takeoff. It should be noted that the accuracy of the results obtained in using this method hinges very largely on the drafting skill of the person using it.

The trigonometrical method for determining the component velocities is less time consuming and more accurate and is therefore the better of the two methods. To find the horizontal and vertical components of the long jumper's takeoff velocity using this method, a rough sketch of the parallelogram constructed in using the graphical method is first drawn and the relevant information is attached (Fig. 3-11). Then, because:

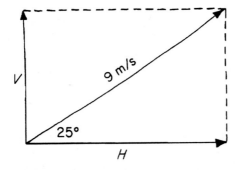

Figure 3-11. The trigonometrical method for resolving a vector into components.

$$\frac{H}{9} = \cos 25°$$

$$H = 9 \cos 25°$$
$$= 8.16 \text{ m/s}$$

and similarly:

$$V = 9 \sin 25°$$
$$= 3.80 \text{ m/s}$$

It is perhaps of interest to note that the ratio of horizontal velocity to vertical velocity for one event is approximately the reverse of that for the other. This fact has some important implications for the teaching and coaching of these events.

UNIFORMLY ACCELERATED MOTION

When a body experiences the same acceleration (in both magnitude and direction) throughout some interval of time, its acceleration is said to be *constant* (or *uniform*). Under such circumstances the average acceleration of the body is exactly the same as its acceleration at any instant during the period involved. This rather obvious fact permits three important equations—known as the equations of uniformly accelerated motion—to be obtained. These equations are:

$$v_f = v_i + at \qquad (3\text{-}8)$$
$$d = v_i t + \tfrac{1}{2}at^2 \qquad (3\text{-}9)$$
$$v_f^2 = v_i^2 + 2ad \qquad (3\text{-}10)$$

where, *for a given direction*, v_i = the initial velocity (that is, the instantaneous velocity at the start of the motion under consideration); v_f = the final velocity (the instantaneous velocity at the end of the motion); d = the displacement the body has undergone; t = the time involved; and a = the acceleration.

While in-the-air motion is of little concern in some activities (such as wrestling, fencing, bowling, and weight lifting), in others (such as diving, tumbling, ski-jumping, and all the field events) such motion is the very essence of the activity. It is in the analysis of in-the-air activities (where the uniform acceleration is that due to gravity) that the equations of uniformly accelerated motion have their most important applications. However, before considering some of the factors of importance in such cases, it may be useful to consider some simple examples and to develop a procedure for attacking problems of this kind.

Until quite recently, the motion-picture camera was widely used in the analysis of sports movements. It was used by coaches to record the action in games, meets, and workouts. It was also used by researchers who were concerned with obtaining precise measurements from the resulting films.

So that the speed at which bodies were moving could be accurately determined from such films, it was often necessary to find out how many frames of film were being exposed each second. One way of doing this was to film a shot being dropped to the ground from some known height. The time taken for the shot to fall this distance can be determined using the following general procedure:

1. Write the information that is required:

$$\text{The time taken: } t = ?$$

2. Write the information that is known:

$$\text{Initial velocity:} \quad v_i \quad = 0 \text{ m/s}$$
$$\text{Acceleration:} \quad a \quad = -9.81 \text{ m/s}^2$$
$$\text{Displacement:} \quad d \quad = -2 \text{ m, say}$$

3. Determine which of the three equations of uniformly accelerated motion contains all the variables recorded in steps 1 and 2:

$$d = v_i t + \tfrac{1}{2}at^2$$

4. Substitute the appropriate values in this equation, and determine the information required:

$$-2 \quad = (0 \times t) + (\tfrac{1}{2} \times -9.81 \times t^2)$$
$$-2 \quad = -4.91\, t^2$$
$$t \quad = \sqrt{\frac{-2}{-4.91}}$$
$$= 0.64 \text{ s}$$

A count of the number of frames of the film taken between the instant of release of the shot and the moment of it hitting the ground is then made. (The frame showing the shot at the instant of release is not included in arriving at this total, but all subsequent frames up to and including the one showing the shot at the instant it touches the ground are included). This figure (say, 42) can then be used together with the computed time to determine the number of frames per second at which the camera is filming and the average time interval between frames:

$$\text{Camera speed} \quad = \frac{42}{0.64}$$

$$= 65.63 \text{ frames per second}$$

$$\text{Average interval between frames} \quad = \frac{0.64}{42}$$

$$= 0.015 \text{ s}$$

Another application of these equations is found in the simple ruler-dropping test used to measure a person's response time (Fig. 3-12). In this test a ruler (or rod) is held by the tester between the outstretched index finger and thumb of the subject's dominant hand, so that the top of the subject's hand is level with the bottom of the ruler. The subject is instructed to catch the ruler just as soon as possible after it has been released by the tester. The distance between the bottom of the ruler and the top of the subject's hand when the ruler has been caught (that is, the distance the ruler fell) is used to determine the subject's response time.

So that a direct reading of the response time can be obtained, an appropriate scale is marked on the ruler. If it is desired to have the scale graduated in 0.1 s intervals, the distance of the first gradation from the bottom of the ruler can be determined as follows:

Displacement:	d	= ?
Time:	t	= 0.1 s
Acceleration:	a	= 9.81 m/s^2
Initial velocity:	v_t	= 0 m/s

Using Eq. (3-9),

$$d = v_t t + \tfrac{1}{2}at^2$$
$$d = (0 \times 0.1) + (\tfrac{1}{2} \times 9.81 \times 0.1 \times 0.1)$$
$$= 0.049 \text{ m}$$

The location of the other gradations on the scale can be determined in similar fashion.

While the equations discussed in this section are important in the analysis of many sports techniques (and this will become evident in the next section), considerable care must be exercised in using them. Consider a track coach

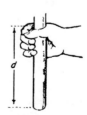

Figure 3-12. Handgrip response time—an example of the application of the equations of uniformly accelerated motion.

who is anxious to increase the horizontal velocity with which a long jumper leaves the takeoff board. Seeking some fairly precise measure of this velocity, the coach decides to time the athlete's approach run and use this time in computing the horizontal velocity at takeoff:

Final velocity:	v_f	=	?
Displacement (that is, the run-up length):	d	=	50 m, say
Initial velocity:	v_i	=	0 m/s
Time:	t	=	6s, say

Using Eq. (3-9), the coach first finds the acceleration because this is needed to determine the athlete's horizontal velocity:

$$d = v_i t + \tfrac{1}{2}at^2$$
$$50 = (0 \times 6) + (\tfrac{1}{2} \times a \times 6^2)$$
$$50 = 18a$$
$$a = \frac{50 \text{ m/s}^2}{18}$$

Then, using Eq. (3-8), the coach computes the final horizontal velocity:

$$v_f = v_i + at$$
$$= 0 + \frac{50}{18} \times 6$$
$$= 16.67 \text{ m/s}$$

Now on the surface this appears to be a singularly useful technique. It would enable the coach to abandon such subjective comments as "Yes, that looked a bit faster" and "I don't think you were quite so fast that time" in favor of quite objective observations like "That was 1 m/s faster than your last one." Unfortunately it has one limitation that renders the whole method utterly useless: *the equations of uniformly accelerated motion (as their name suggests) apply only in the case of a body whose velocity is changing at a constant rate*. Since a long jumper's acceleration is changing throughout the approach run (in fact, throughout each and every running stride), it is clear that these equations cannot be used in the manner outlined in the previous example. (Incidentally, such misuse would almost inevitably result in a much higher value for the horizontal velocity than was actually obtained. While the figures used in the previous example are reasonable enough, the resulting horizontal velocity is far in excess of that ever achieved by any sprinter!)

Many sports involve the projection of a body into the air. In shot-putting, baseball, soccer, and tennis, the body projected into the air (the *projectile*) is

PROJECTILES*

---

* For the sake of simplicity, the effects of air resistance will be ignored throughout the ensuing discussion of projectile motion. These effects will be considered in Chap. 7, Fluid Mechanics.

an inanimate one. In diving, gymnastics, and the jumping events (and occasionally in the other sports already mentioned), the projectile is an animate one—the performer. In all such sports, the quality of performance depends very largely on the performer's ability to control and/or predict the outcome of the projectile motion involved. The tennis player executing a delicate drop shot must stroke the ball in such a way as to ensure that it travels high enough and far enough to clear the net and yet not so far as to make it easy for the opponent to return. In short, the player must exert a very fine degree of control over the motion of the ball. A kick-return man on a football team has no control whatever over the flight of the ball but he must successfully predict its motion and position himself appropriately to receive it. To these people, and all others concerned with sports involving projectile motions, a practical understanding of the factors that govern the behavior of projectiles is of critical importance.

For purposes of analysis, the horizontal and vertical motions of a projectile may be considered separately. For example, when a stationary soccer ball is kicked upfield from a goal kick, the velocity imparted to the ball generally acts in a direction at some angle θ to the horizontal (Fig. 3-13[a]). If this velocity is resolved into its horizontal and vertical components, the effect of the kick can be studied by considering each of these components in turn.

Horizontal Motion. The horizontal velocity of the soccer ball in Fig. 3-13 at the instant it is released or projected into the air is $v \cos \theta$. Further, because there is nothing which tends to change the rate at which it is moving horizontally (ignoring air resistance), it maintains this same horizontal velocity throughout its flight. This means, of course, that its horizontal acceleration is zero during this period.

The horizontal distance the ball travels while it is in the air, a distance

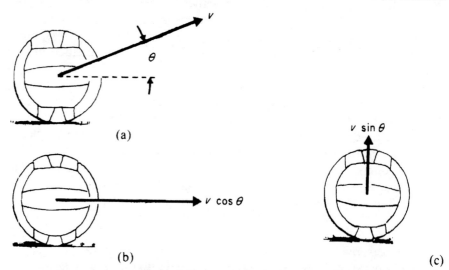

(a)

(b)

$v \sin \theta$

(c)

Figure 3-13. Resultant, horizontal, and vertical velocities of a soccer ball at the moment of "release" in a goal kick.

known as the *range* of the projectile, can be found using the procedure described on p. 29. If T = the time of flight of the projectile and $v \cos \theta$ = the horizontal velocity, as before, the range of the projectile, R, is given by:

Displacement	d	$= R = ?$
Time	t	$= T$
Initial velocity	v_i	$= v \cos \theta$
Acceleration	a	$= 0$

Using Eq. (3-9)

$$d = v_i t + \tfrac{1}{2} a t^2$$
$$R = v \cos \theta \times T \qquad\qquad (3\text{-}11)$$

From this equation it is apparent that if a soccer player making a goal-kick (or any other performer who projects a body into the air) wishes to alter the range of the projectile, he (or she) can do so only by altering the horizontal velocity of release and/or the time of flight.

Since the time of flight is obviously of great importance in sports that require controlling or predicting the range of a projectile, those involved with such sports must have an understanding of the factors that determine the time of flight. Such understanding is also needed in sports such as diving and trampolining, where, both the range and the time of flight are critical factors in determining the quality of performance.

Vertical Motion. The horizontal velocity of the soccer ball in Fig. 3-13 acts parallel to the ground and thus has no tendency to lift the ball into the air. The lifting of the ball is due entirely to the vertical velocity imparted to it prior to release. The time of flight of the ball is also largely determined by the vertical velocity at release.

The time of flight is equal to the time it takes the projectile to reach the peak of its flight (designated here as t_{up}) plus the time it takes to return from this peak to the point of landing (t_{down}):

$$T = t_{up} + t_{down}$$

The time to reach peak height, t_{up}, can be found using the procedure outlined on p. 29.

Time:	t	$= t_{up} = ?$
Initial velocity (that is, the vertical velocity at release):	v_i	$= v \sin \theta$
Final velocity (that is, the vertical velocity at peak):	v_f	$= 0$
Acceleration:	a	$= -g$

Using Eq. (3-9),

$$v_f = v_i + at$$
$$0 = v \sin \theta - gt_{up}$$
$$t_{up} = \frac{v \sin \theta}{g} \tag{3-12}$$

The time of descent, t_{down}, can be expressed as a function of the vertical displacement, d_{down}, that the projectile undergoes during the descent:

Time: $t = t_{down} = ?$

Initial velocity (that is, the vertical velocity at peak): $v_i = 0$

Acceleration: $a = -g$

Displacement: $d = -d_{down}$

Using Eq. (3-9),

$$d = v_i t + \frac{1}{2}at^2$$
$$-d_{down} = -\frac{1}{2}gt_{down}^2$$
$$t_{down} = \sqrt{\frac{2d_{down}}{g}} \tag{3-13}$$

Now, the vertical displacement, d_{down}, depends on the height at which the projectile lands. If it lands above the level from which it was released (as, for example, when the ball lands on the hoop during a free throw in basketball), d_{down} is less than d_{up}, the vertical displacement the projectile experiences in rising to its peak height. If it lands at the level from which it was released (as is frequently the case when a goal kick is taken in soccer), d_{down} is equal to d_{up}. Finally, if it lands below the level at which it was released (as in shot putting), d_{down} is greater than d_{up}.

When the projectile lands at the level from which it was released (the simplest of the three possibilities just referred to), d_{down} can readily be found by determining d_{up}:

Displacement: $d = d_{up} = ?$

Initial velocity: $v_i = v \sin \theta$

Final velocity: $v_f = 0$

Acceleration: $a = -g$

Using Eq. (3-10),

$$v_f^2 = v_i^2 + 2ad$$
$$0 = (v \sin \theta)^2 - 2gd_{up}$$
$$d_{up} = \frac{(v \sin \theta)^2}{2g} \tag{3-14}$$

Then, since $d_{down} = d_{up}$, substitution of this expression into Eq. (3-13) yields a new expression for t_{down}:

$$t_{down} = \sqrt{\frac{2}{g} \times \frac{(v \sin \theta)^2}{2g}}$$

$$= \frac{v \sin \theta}{g} \qquad (3\text{-}15)$$

Comparison of Eqs. (3-12) and (3-15) quickly reveals that, when release and landing are at the same level, it takes exactly the same time for a projectile to reach the peak of its flight as it does for it to return to its original level. This finding has important implications in a number of sports. For example, a gymnast who is attempting to do a double back somersault should have half the stunt (that is, the first somersault) completed by the time the peak of the flight is reached. Similarly, an outfielder racing to catch a high fly ball should be at least halfway to the required position by the time the ball reaches its peak height. (*Note:* In this latter example, any difference between the height of release and the height of "landing" can safely be ignored, since the distances involved are huge by comparison.)

With t_{up} and t_{down} known, the time of flight can easily be computed:

$$T = t_{up} + t_{down}$$

$$= \frac{v \sin \theta}{g} + \frac{v \sin \theta}{g}$$

$$= \frac{2v \sin \theta}{g} \qquad (3\text{-}16)$$

This result also has important implications. Since g is constant for any given location (see p. 22), the time of flight depends solely on $v \sin \theta$, the vertical velocity at release. Thus, any performer who wishes to alter the time of flight of a projectile that lands at the same height as that from which it was released can do so only by altering this parameter. The punter who wishes to increase the time of flight of a football so that his teammates can get down the field to "cover the punt" must somehow increase its vertical velocity at the instant it leaves his foot; the gymnast who needs more time in the air to complete a tumbling stunt must increase the vertical velocity with which he (or she) leaves the ground; and the basketball player who wishes to decrease the time the ball is in the air when making a long pass must correspondingly decrease the vertical velocity with which the ball leaves the hands.

If a projectile is released at a height above or below the level at which it lands, d_{down} is given by:

$$d_{down} = d_{up} + h$$
$$= \frac{(v \sin \theta)^2}{2g} + h \qquad (3\text{-}17)$$

where h = the height at which the projectile was released minus the height at which it landed—or, in other words, the height of release relative to the height of landing. From this definition, it can be seen that h is negative when the projectile lands above its point of release and positive when it lands below that point. (*Note:* For the sake of simplicity, h will be referred to here as the height of release. It is essential, however, that its complete definition—the height of release *relative to the height of landing*—be remembered throughout.)

Substituting Eq. (3-17) into (3-13) and combining the result with Eq. (3-12) yields the following somewhat lengthy expressions for the time of descent and the time of flight when the points of release and landing are not at the same level:*

$$t_{down} = \sqrt{\frac{(v \sin \theta)^2 + 2gh}{g}} \qquad (3\text{-}18)$$

$$T = \frac{v \sin \theta + \sqrt{(v \sin \theta)^2 + 2gh}}{g} \qquad (3\text{-}19)$$

This latter result indicates that where release and landing are not at the same level, the time of flight can be modified by altering the vertical velocity of release and/or the height of release. Thus shot-putters who want to increase the time of flight of the shot and thereby enable it to carry further (see Eq. [3-11]) have two means at their disposal—they can increase the vertical velocity of the shot at the instant of release or they can increase the height from which they release it. The relationship between height of release and time of flight is also well known to tumblers and divers, who frequently increase their heights of release during the initial stages of learning a new stunt or dive. Tumblers do this by using elevated takeoffs (the top of a vaulting box, a springboard, or a mini-tramp), while divers achieve the same effect by "taking the dive up" to a higher board than they ultimately plan to use.

Range of Projectile. The range of a projectile was shown earlier—Eq. (3-11)—to be equal to the product of the horizontal velocity at release and the time of flight:

$$R = v \cos \theta \times T$$

---

*It may be of interest to note here that when release and landing are at the same height—that is, $h = 0$—Eq. (3-19) reduces to Eq. (3-16), thus confirming what has already been demonstrated in such cases.

Substitution of the time of flight for a projectile that lands at the level from which it was released [Eq. (3-16)] yields an expanded expression for the range in such cases:

$$R = v \cos \theta \times \frac{2v \sin \theta}{g}$$

$$= \frac{v^2 \, 2 \sin \theta \cos \theta}{g}$$

This expression can be simplified by using the trigonometrical identity

$$\sin 2\theta = 2 \sin \theta \cos \theta$$

and obtaining

$$R = \frac{v^2 \sin 2\theta}{g} \qquad (3\text{-}20)$$

Thus, with g constant, the horizontal range depends on v and θ, the magnitude and direction of the initial velocity, respectively—or, to put it in even simpler terms, on the speed and angle of release. It is clear too that, in general, the greater the speed of release, the greater will be the horizontal range, and this, of course, is consistent with everyday experience. For example, the harder a ball is thrown or kicked, the farther it will go.

A quick look at a table of sine values (Appendix A) shows that they vary from 0.0000 (when the angle is 0°) to 1.0000 (when the angle is 90°). The maximum value that can be obtained if the sine of an angle is taken is therefore 1. Thus, for any given speed of release, the maximum value of the horizontal range will be obtained when:

$$\sin 2\theta = 1$$

This occurs when $\qquad 2\theta = 90°$

that is, when $\qquad \theta = 45°$

Hence, if all else is equal, the optimum angle at which to project a body in order to obtain the maximum horizontal range is 45°.

This applies, however, only to situations in which release and landing are at the same level. Where the level from which the body is projected is above the level at which it lands, the horizontal range is obtained by use of Eq. (3-11) and (3-19):

$$R = v \cos \theta \times \left(\frac{v \sin \theta + \sqrt{(v \sin \theta)^2 + 2\,gh}}{g} \right)$$

which reduces to

$$R = \frac{v^2 \sin \theta \cos \theta + v \cos \theta \sqrt{(v \sin \theta)^2 + 2gh}}{g} \qquad (3\text{-}21)$$

Close inspection of Eq. (3-21) shows that in this situation there are just three factors that have any influence on the horizontal range of a projectile—the speed, angle, and height of release. (Once again g is taken to be a constant.) Of these three it can readily be seen that the greater the speed and the height of release, the greater will be the resulting range. (Assuming θ is constant and less than 90°; if $\theta = 90°$, R will be zero irrespective of the speed or the height or release. The body will go straight up and straight down again!)

Regrettably the optimum angle of projection cannot be found as readily as in the case in which release and landing are at the same level. In the present case, the optimum angle depends on both the speed and the height of release. Table 3-1 shows how the optimum angle of release varies with these two factors in shot-putting. From this table it can be seen that:

- The optimum angle of release is always less than 45°.
- For any given height of release, the greater the speed of release, the more closely the optimum angle approaches 45°.
- For any given speed of release, the greater the height of release, the less is the optimum angle.
- Equal increases in either height of release or speed of release do not yield consistently equal changes in the optimum angle or the resulting distance.

(*Note:* These conclusions hold true in general and not just for those values included in Table 3-1.)

TABLE 3-1 Variation of Optimum Angle with Height and Speed of Release in Shot-Putting[a]

Height of Release (m)	Speed of Release (m/s)					
	9	10	11	12	13	14
1.8	39.9°	40.7°	41.4°	41.9°	42.3°	42.7°
	(9.90 m)	(11.87 m)	(14.03 m)	(16.40 m)	(18.96 m)	(21.73 m)
2.0	39.4°	40.3°	41.0°	41.6°	42.0°	42.4°
	(10.07 m)	(12.04 m)	(14.21 m)	(16.57 m)	(19.14 m)	(21.91 m)
2.2	39.0°	39.9°	40.7°	41.3°	41.8°	42.2°
	(10.23 m)	(12.21 m)	(14.38 m)	(16.75 m)	(19.32 m)	(22.09 m)
2.4	38.5°	39.5°	40.3°	41.0°	41.5°	41.9°
	(10.39 m)	(12.37 m)	(14.55 m)	(16.92 m)	(19.50 m)	(22.27 m)

[a] The distances obtained by the indicated combinations of speed of release, height of release, and optimum angle are shown in parentheses. These distances do not include extra distance (approximately 0.3 m) that the shot is in advance of the inside edge of the stop board at the instant of release.

Having determined that three factors influence the horizontal range of a projectile, it is now of some importance to consider just how much influence each of these factors has. The field events coach should know, for example, whether it is best for a shot-putter to concentrate his (or her) main efforts on obtaining (1) a greater speed; (2) a more nearly optimum angle; or (3) a greater height, at the instant of release. The graphs presented in Fig. 3-14 show the results obtained when a shot-putter, who records a distance of 12.03 m by releasing the shot at a height of 2.0 m, a speed of 10.0 m/s and an angle of 40°, increases each of these factors by a comparable amount.

Fig. 3-14(a) shows the changes in the distance of the throw that would result if the athlete changed the height of release while keeping the speed and angle of release unaltered. A 5 percent increase in the height of release—that is, an increase from 2.0 m to 2.10 m—would yield an increase of 0.085 m in the distance of the throw.

Fig. 3-14(b) shows the changes in the distance of the throw that would result if the athlete changed the speed of release while keeping the other two factors unaltered. A 5 percent increase in the speed of release—from 10.0 m/s to 10.5 m/s—would yield an increase of 1.057 m in the distance of the throw.

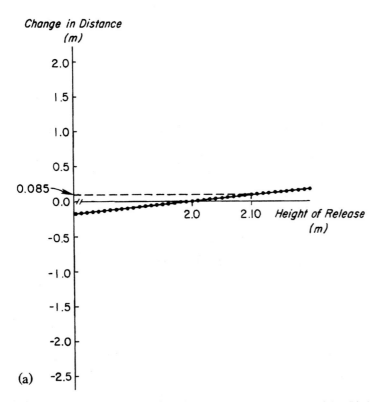

Figure 3-14. The effects produced by 5% changes in (a) the height; (b) the speed; and (c) the angle at which a shot is released.

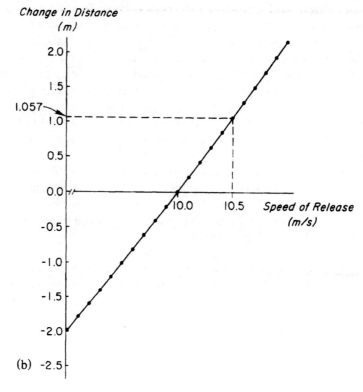

(b)

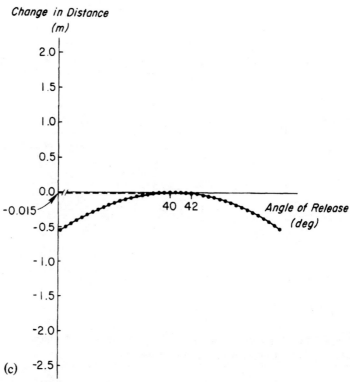

(c)

Figure 3-14. (continued)

Finally, Fig. 3-14(c) shows the effects of corresponding changes in the angle of release. Here, a 5 percent increase in the angle of release—from 40° to 42°—yields a decrease of 0.015 m in the distance of the throw.

These curves (which, incidentally, are typical of those that would be obtained for any normal combination of height, speed, and angle of release) show very clearly that an increase in release speed is much more effective in terms of increasing the horizontal range than comparable increases in either the angle or height of release. Thus, in general, shot-putters are best advised to concentrate their attention more on developing fast release speeds than on increasing the height of release or optimizing the angle of release.

Trajectory. The path that a projectile follows in its passage through the air (the *trajectory* of the projectile) is also of some interest. Consider again the soccer ball that is kicked upfield from a goalkick, and let it be supposed that a speed of 20 m/s is imparted to the ball at an angle of 30° to the horizontal. The horizontal and vertical displacements at the end of each successive 0.1 s of the flight can readily be obtained using Eq. (3-9). Values for these displacements are shown in Table 3-2.

If these displacements are represented graphically, the form of the graph is a smooth, symmetrical curve (Fig. 3-15). If, too, the same process

TABLE 3-2 Horizontal and Vertical Displacements at End of Each 0.1 s of Flight[a]

Time from Instant of Release (s)	Horizontal Displacement (m)	Vertical Displacement (m)
0.0	0.00	0.00
0.1	1.73	0.95
0.2	3.46	1.80
0.3	5.20	2.56
0.4	6.93	3.21
0.5	8.66	3.77
0.6	10.39	4.23
0.7	12.13	4.60
0.8	13.86	4.86
0.9	15.59	5.03
1.0	17.32	5.10
1.1	19.06	5.07
1.2	20.79	4.94
1.3	22.52	4.71
1.4	24.25	4.39
1.5	25.98	3.97
1.6	27.72	3.45
1.7	29.45	2.83
1.8	31.18	2.12
1.9	32.91	1.30
2.0	34.65	0.39
2.038	35.28	0.00

[a] Soccer ball kicked from ground level with a speed of 20 m/s at an angle of 30° to the horizontal.

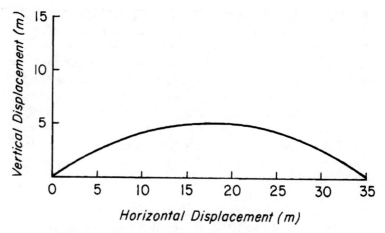

Figure 3-15. Trajectory of a soccer ball following a goal kick.

is followed for a series of release speeds and angles, the resulting curves are all of this same general form (Fig. 3-16). These curves are members of a special class of curves known in geometry as *parabolas*. And, since each curve is no more than a map or representation of the path followed by the body concerned, it can be seen that, in the absence of air resistance, the flight path of a projectile is parabolic in form.

Limitation. In any consideration of projectile motion in sports, it should be recognized that it may not be possible for the performer to obtain the

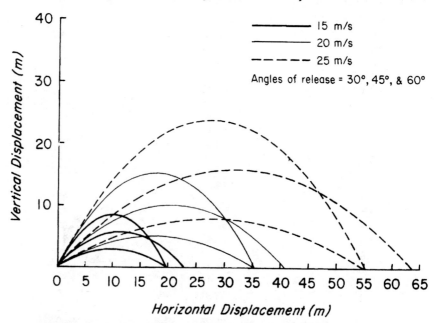

Figure 3-16. Parabolic paths followed by projectiles released at a variety of speeds and angles.

same release speeds over a wide range of release angles. If a shot-putter directs all his (or her) efforts in a horizontal direction, gravity has no tendency to reduce the release speed of the shot. However, as soon as the shot-putter begins to direct some effort vertically, gravity opposes this effort. The shot-putter pushes the shot upward at the same time as gravity tends to pull it downward. As a result of this opposition of gravity the release speed that the shot-putter is able to impart to the shot is reduced. Thus, while a particular shot-putter might seem well advised to try to obtain a greater angle of release, the advantage to be gained from this may be lost or more than lost by a concomitant reduction in the speed of release he (or she) is able to produce. To further complicate matters, the human body is so constructed that greater forces can be exerted, and higher velocities generated, in some directions than in others. Although there is little information in the literature on this aspect of projectile motion in sports, the initial indications are that in the case of the shot put, these several contributing factors result in top-class throwers releasing the shot at an angle of "about 36–37 degrees."[1]

1. Carefully measure and rule a large square on several sheets of unlined paper. These squares represent the border of the 12 m by 12 m floor exercise mat used in gymnastics. Attach these sheets to a clipboard or something similar, take 2 or 3 sharp pencils, and go off to a gymnastics meet. If you can't do this for any reason (gymnastics is out of season, there's no gymnastics in your area, etc.), watch a gymnastics meet on television or videotape.

   In the floor exercise, the gymnast performs tumbling "passes" (usually along the diagonals of the mat), runs, dance steps, and so forth, that take him (or her) all over the mat. Your task is to plot the path followed by several gymnasts as they move back and forth around the mat. Start by making a mark at the point where the exercise begins and another at each point where the gymnast turns to head off in another direction. Quickly sketch lines joining these points as you go. You'll probably need some practice before you develop a system that lets you accurately record the path followed by the gymnast. Try to get good records of at least 5 or 6 gymnasts. Make a note of the score that the judge gave each gymnast. If you are able to attend a meet, indicate due North with an arrow on the side of each page. If you watch a meet on television or on videotape, pretend you know where due North is and indicate it on each page.

   When you have finished, clean up your work by ruling straight lines (where the gymnast moved in a straight line) and by carefully sketching curves (where he or she moved along a curved path). Then, using the best method you can think of, measure the total length of the path followed by each gymnast. Also measure the distance between the points at which the gymnast started and finished his (or her) routine. Finally, convert your measurements to real-life lengths or distances and answer the following questions:
   (a) What was the distance covered by each of your gymnasts?
   (b) What was the displacement experienced by each of your gymnasts?
   (c) Was there any relationship between the distances covered and the scores awarded by the judges? (You could check this by drawing a graph with the

scores on the vertical axis and the distances on the horizontal axis. You might also compute a correlation coefficient, if you know how to do this. Or, you might simply compare the average score for the gymnasts who had the longer distances with the average score for the gymnasts who had the shorter distances.)

2. Use a similar procedure to analyse the performances of women gymnasts competing on the balance beam.

3. A triathlete swims 800 m South, rides 40 km East, and runs 30 km North, in that order. What distance did he travel? And what displacement did he experience?

4. Speed skiing is a relatively new and exciting winter sport, vividly described in the following paragraph:

Speed skiing takes human beings as fast as they can go without mechanical propulsion. Picture a skier at the top of a slope so steep it looks like the wall of an elevator shaft. When that skier pushes away and drops into a tuck position, he or she goes from zero to 60 mph in three seconds. In six seconds 100 mph. When the "speed trap" is reached, up to 1000 meters from the start, the skier has hit 130 mph. That's accelerating faster than a Ferrari. The men's world record is 139 mph.[2]

(a) Can you think of any other human activity in which a person might go faster than 139 mph "without mechanical propulsion"?

(b) Given the previous information, what would the speed skier's average acceleration be over the first 3 s of his (or her) descent? Over the first 6 s? Over the second 3 s (that is, between 3 s and 6 s)? Convert the speeds to km/h before working out your answers to these questions. (Assume that the skier moves in a straight line and doesn't drift to left or right.)

(c) The "speed trap" mentioned is a 100-m-long test section. The time the skier takes to traverse this section (which is easily converted to the average speed over the section) determines his (or her) place in the competition. How long did it take the man who set the world record of 139 mph to traverse the speed trap? (*HINT:* Watch the units you use here.)

5. A basketball player is doing depth jumps as part of a training program designed to increase her jumping ability. To do this, she steps off a 50-cm-high bench to land on both feet on the floor and then, with a minimum of delay, jumps upward as high as she can. Assuming that the upward vertical direction is positive, in what direction (positive or negative) is her vertical acceleration

(a) during the flight phase from the bench to the floor?

(b) during the first part of the support phase on the floor—that is, from the instant of touchdown until she is at her lowest point?

(c) at the instant she is at her lowest point?

(d) during the second part of the support phase on the floor—that is, from the instant she is at her lowest point until the instant of takeoff during the flight phase from the floor to the peak of her upward flight?

(e) at the instant she reaches her peak height?

In what direction would these same accelerations be if the upward vertical direction was negative?

What is the magnitude of the athlete's acceleration when she is at the peak of her flight?

6. In a strange foreign land, yet to be discovered, lengths are measured in oogols and times in hoohahs. Assuming the people there know their mechanics, in what units do they measure velocities and accelerations?

7. Complete the following table showing typical values for velocities at release and angle of release.

Component and Resultant Velocities at Release, and Angles of Release for Selected Motor Skills

Motor Skill	Horizontal Velocity (m/s)	Vertical Velocity (m/s)	Resultant Velocity (m/s)	Angle of Release (deg)
Hammer throw	____	____	30.4	38.5
Baseball fast ball	40.0	0.1	____	____
Basketball free throw	____	9.6	12.0	____
Basketball dunk	0.5	____	____	-86.0

8. A local gymnastic club is participating in a Fourth of July parade. For this event, they have placed a trampoline on the bed of a truck and the club's best gymnasts are performing stunts on the trampoline while the truck is being driven along the parade route. One of the gymnasts performs a back somersault with his body in a fully extended (or layout) position and lands in the center of the trampoline bed, the spot from which he took off.

   (a) Did he have any horizontal velocity at takeoff and, if so, in which direction was it?

   (b) In what direction did his resultant velocity at takeoff act? Use some combination of the words *upward, downward, forward,* and *backward* to describe the direction, where *forward* refers to the direction in which the truck is moving.

   (c) If he performed this stunt exactly as he would have if the trampoline had been resting on the ground instead of on the moving bed of a truck, why did he not land behind the point from which he took off? In other words, why did the truck not tend to "drive out from under him" while he was in the air?

9. A tower diver performs a handstand dive. The distance he falls vertically from takeoff until his hands first touch the water (entry) is 10 m. How long does it take him to fall that 10 m? And what is his vertical velocity at entry? Convert this latter velocity to m.p.h. to get a good idea of just how fast he's traveling. (Ignore air resistance when making your calculations.)

10. A baseball is thrown from second base to first base in a double play. If the ball is released with a vertical velocity of 3 m/s and is caught 18 m away at the same height as it had at the instant of release:

    (a) What is its vertical velocity at the end of its flight?

    (b) what is its vertical velocity at the peak of its flight?

    (c) What horizontal distance has it traveled by the time it reaches the peak of its flight?

    (d) How long does it take to get from second to first?

    (Ignore air resistance when making your calculations.)

11. A tennis ball lands in the service court and bounces towards the receiver who is standing 8 m away.

(a) If the ball leaves the ground with a horizontal velocity of 25 m/s, and does not hit the ground before reaching the receiver, how long will it take to reach her?

(b) If the ball has an upward vertical velocity of 6 m/s when it leaves the court, how high above the ground will it be 0.1 s later? 0.2 s late? When it reaches the receiver?

(c) How fast will the ball be traveling horizontally when it reaches the receiver?

(d) How fast will it be traveling vertically when it reaches the receiver?

(e) What will the magnitude and direction of its resultant velocity be when it reaches the receiver?

(Ignore air resistance when making the computations.)

12. A rugby player punts the ball and then races downfield to tackle the man who catches it. If the ball leaves his foot at a height of 1.0 m and with a speed of 20 m/s at an angle of 65°, how fast must he run—or, more precisely, what must his average speed be—if he is to reach the man at just the same moment he catches the ball 1.5 m above the ground?

(Ignore air resistance when making the computations.)

Why are the values for the speed and angle of release and the correct answer for this question inconsistent with what actually happens when a rugby ball is punted in real life?

13. A soccer goalkeeper takes a goal kick and the ball leaves his foot with a horizontal velocity of 22 m/s and a vertical veolcity of 12 m/s. How far will it travel before it lands on the ground? If instead of landing on the ground the ball is intercepted in flight by an opposing player who contacts the ball with his head 2.5 m above the ground, how far will the ball have traveled horizontally before contact is made? (*Hint:* Be careful here. There are two possible answers.)

Recommended Readings

BRANCAZIO, P. J. (1984). *Sport Science: Physical Laws and Optimum Performance.* New York: Simon & Schuster, pp. 25–55 (Man in motion); pp. 245–280 (Gravity); pp. 281–314 (What goes up must come down).

DYSON, G. H. G. (1977). *The Mechanics of Athletics.* New York; Holmes & Meier, pp. 14–27 (Motion).

ENOKA, R. M. (1988). *Neuromechanical Basis of Kinesiology.* Champaign, Ill.: Human Kinetics Books, pp. 3–23 (Motion).

HAY, J. G. and REID, J. G. (1988). *Anatomy, Mechanics, and Human Motion.* Englewood Cliffs, N.J.: Prentice Hall, pp. 114–132 (Describing linear motion [linear kinematics]).

RACKHAM, G. (1975). *Diving Complete.* London: Faber & Faber, pp. 151–164 (Time).

TRICKER, R. A. R., and TRICKER, B. J. K. (1966). *The Science of Movement.* London: Mills & Boon, pp. 1–12 (The problems of movement).

WATKINS, J. (1983). *An Introduction to Mechanics of Human Movement.* Boston: MTP Press Limited, pp. 4–20 (Linear motion).

Notes

1. Zatsiorsky, V. (1990). The biomechanics of shot putting techniques. In G-P. Bruggeman and J. K. Ruhl (Eds.), *Techniques in Athletics: Conference Proceedings* (pp. 118–25). Köln, Federal Republic of Germany: Deutsche Sporthochschule Köln.

2. Steinbreder, J. Faster than you can say schuss. *Sports Illustrated* 76(3): January 27, 1992 (page not numbered).

ANGULAR KINEMATICS

The basic concepts involved in the description of angular motion (that is, in angular kinematics) are very closely related to those encountered in the description of linear motion (that is, in linear kinematics).

When a rotating body moves from one position to another, the *angular distance* through which it moves is equal to the length of the "angular path" it follows—that is, the sum of all the angles through which it moves in passage from initial to final positions. Consider, for example, a child on a swing (Fig. 4-1). If the swing is released from a position 40° behind the vertical, and then swings forward and backward as shown before coming to rest, the angular distance (ϕ) through which the child travels is:

$$\phi = (70° + 50° + 30° + 10°)$$
$$= 160°$$

The *angular displacement* that a rotating body experiences is equal in magnitude to the angle between the initial and final position of the body. Thus, if the initial position of the child in Fig. 4-1 is considered to be 0°, and counterclockwise is taken as the positive direction (as is usually the case),

**ANGULAR
DISTANCE AND
ANGULAR
DISPLACEMENT**

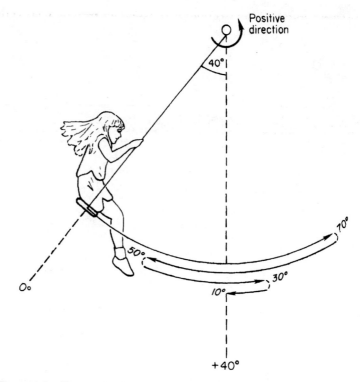

Figure 4-1. The angular distance through which the child moves before coming to rest is much greater than the magnitude of the angular displacement she experiences.

the final position of the child is + 40°. The angular displacement (θ) which the child experiences is:

$$\theta = \text{Final position} - \text{initial position}$$
$$= +40° - 0°$$
$$= +40°$$

(*Note:* The plus sign is normally omitted. It has been included here merely to emphasize that the direction of rotation is an important consideration in determining angular displacements.)

ANGULAR SPEED AND ANGULAR VELOCITY

The average angular speed of a body is obtained by dividing the angular distance through which the body moves by the time taken:

$$\bar{\sigma} = \frac{\phi}{t} \tag{4-1}$$

where $\bar{\sigma}$ = the average angular speed.

The average angular velocity is obtained in similar fashion by dividing the angular displacement by the time taken:

$$\bar{\omega} = \frac{\phi}{t} \qquad (4\text{-}2)$$

where $\bar{\omega}$ = the average angular velocity and θ = the angular displacement, and specifying the direction.

Both average and instantaneous values may be determined for angular speed, angular velocity, and angular acceleration (see next section); and, as is the case with their linear counterparts (speed, velocity, and acceleration), it is the instantaneous values that generally yield the most useful information.

Angular Acceleration

The average angular acceleration, $\bar{\alpha}$, is the rate at which the angular velocity of a body changes with respect to time. In algebraic form,

$$\bar{\alpha} = \frac{\omega_f - \omega_i}{t} \qquad (4\text{-}3)$$

where ω_i = the initial angular velocity, and ω_f = the final angular velocity. Taking the child in Fig. 4-1 as an example, if her angular velocity is 90°/s at the instant she passes through the vertical on her downward swing and 0°/s as she reaches the limit of her forward swing 0.3 s later, her average angular acceleration over that period is

$$\bar{\alpha} = \frac{0°/s - 90°/s}{0.3 \text{ s}}$$

$$= -300°/s^2$$

This chapter began with a reference to the close relationship between the quantities used in the description of linear motion and those used in the description of angular motion. Now that the latter have been defined (thus

LINEAR AND ANGULAR KINEMATICS

TABLE 4-1 Quantities Used in Linear and Angular Kinematics

Linear Kinematics	Angular Kinematics
Distance	Angular distance
Displacement	Angular displacement
Speed = $\dfrac{\text{distance}}{\text{time}}$	Angular speed = $\dfrac{\text{angular distance}}{\text{time}}$
Velocity = $\dfrac{\text{displacement}}{\text{time}}$	Angular velocity = $\dfrac{\text{angular displacement}}{\text{time}}$
Acceleration = $\dfrac{\text{final velocity} - \text{initial velocity}}{\text{time}}$	Angular acceleration = $\dfrac{\text{final angular velocity} - \text{initial angular velocity}}{\text{time}}$

permitting an appropriate comparison), an examination of Table 4-1 will readily reveal the truth of this statement.

UNITS IN ANGULAR KINEMATICS

Perhaps surprisingly, no less than three units are commonly used in the measurement of angular distance. Only two of these are used with any frequency in sports, but because the derivation and use of at least one important relationship hinges on a knowledge and understanding of the third unit, all three will be considered here.

In diving, it is customary to speak of "full-twisting one-and-a-half's," "inward two-and-a-half's" and other dives described in similar terms. Although direct reference is rarely made to the unit of angular distance used in such descriptions, this is universally understood to be one *revolution* (rev). Thus in a "double-twisting one-and-a-half" the diver executes two complete turns or revolutions about the long axis of his or her body (the double twist) and one and one-half revolutions about a horizontal axis parallel to the end of the diving board (the one-and-a-half somersault).

A much smaller unit, the *degree* (1/360 rev), is widely used in everyday life and in certain situations in sports.* The loft of a golf club, for example, is normally specified in terms of the number of degrees that the clubface is set back from the vertical.

The third unit, the *radian* (rad), is rarely used in connection with sports techniques but is widely used in engineering and other fields. The radian is probably best defined with reference to a figure. Consider the circle in Fig. 4-2. If the arc PQ is equal in length to the radius of the circle center O, then the angle POQ—formed by the radii joining the ends of the arc to the center of the circle—is equal to 1 rad.

Unfortunately, the radian can be a somewhat mystifying unit unless some basis for comparison with other units is available. A rough approximation of the number of degrees in a radian can be obtained if one considers that since $OP = OQ =$ the arc PQ, the figure OPQ closely approximates an equilateral triangle. And, because each of the angles within an equilateral triangle is equal to 60°, it can be surmised that 1 rad must be approximately equal to 60°—actually slightly less than 60° because PQ is a curved line rather than a straight one and this causes a reduction in the size of the angle POQ.

A much more precise figure for the number of degrees in a radian can be obtained by considering how many times an arc of a length equal to the radius can be divided into the circumference of a circle:

---

* While it is rarely, if ever, used in a practical teaching or coaching situation, an even smaller unit, the *minute* (1/60 of a degree) is sometimes used for research purposes when a highly precise measurement is required.

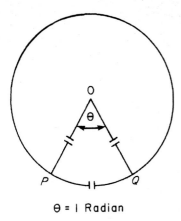

θ = 1 Radian

Figure 4-2. A radian is the angle subtended at the center of a circle by an arc equal in length to the radius.

$$\frac{\text{Circumference}}{\text{Radius}} = \frac{2\pi r}{r}$$

$$= 2\pi$$

From this it can be seen that 2π rad must be equal to 360°, or 1 rev. By simple division it can be determined that

$$1 \text{ rad} = 57.3°$$
$$= 0.16 \text{ rev}$$

And so, the diver who was earlier described as performing a "double-twisting one-and-a-half" might, with equal accuracy, have been said to execute a "720 twisting 540" or a "4π twisting 3π"!

The graphical representation of the vectors associated with angular motion is complicated by the fact that whereas the motion of the body is circular, the standard method of representing vectors is by means of a straight line (or, more precisely, an arrow). To overcome this difficulty, a convention known as the *right-hand thumb rule* is used. In accordance with this rule, an angular-motion vector is represented by an arrow drawn so that if the curled fingers of a person's right hand point in the direction of rotation, the direction of the arrow coincides with the direction indicated by the extended thumb (Fig. 4-3). The magnitude of the vector is represented by the length of the arrow in the usual way.

Any angular-motion vector (such as angular velocity or angular acceleration) can be represented in this way and can be either added to a corresponding vector to obtain a resultant or can be resolved into components, in precisely the same manner as outlined in the previous chapter (Fig. 4-4).

ANGULAR-MOTION VECTORS

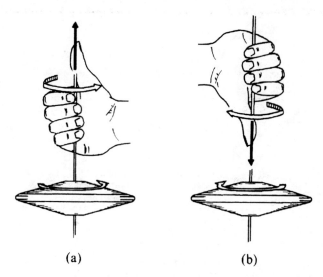

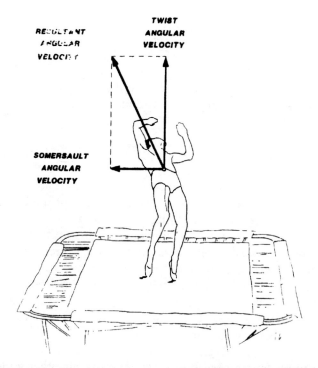

Figure 4-3. The right-hand thumb rule used to obtain a graphical representation of the angular velocity of a discus. (*Note:* the discus is shown rotating as it would if thrown away from the observer by [a] a left-handed thrower; and [b] a right-handed thrower.)

Figure 4-4. The parallelogram of vectors is used here to determine the resultant angular velocity of a gymnast about to perform a double-twisting back somersault on the trampoline.

(*Note:* Although angular displacement has both a magnitude and a direction and can therefore be represented by an arrow, it is not a vector, because angular displacements cannot be summed using the parallelogram of vectors. This can readily be demonstrated by taking a book and turning it through 180° about one edge and then through another 180° about a second edge (Fig. 4-5[a]). If these two angular displacements are appropriately represented by arrows and a parallelogram is constructed in the usual manner, the diagonal of that parallelogram (Fig. 4-5[b]) is in no way representative of the "resultant" or total angular displacement that has taken place. This is perhaps most clearly shown in Fig. 4-5(c), where the final position of the book as indicated by the parallelogram construction can be seen to be quite different from the actual final position (Fig. 4-5[a]).

VELOCITY AND ANGULAR VELOCITY

In many sports an athlete uses angular motion to increase the velocity of an implement. The hammer thrower whirls three or four times in the circle at an increasing rate with the object of having the hammer moving with as great a velocity as possible at the moment he releases it. The golfer does the same kind of thing when she swings her driver in an arc from the limit of her backswing around to the point of contact with the ball. A softball pitcher also seeks to have his fast ball moving at the maximum possible velocity as he releases it near the low point of the angular motion of his arm. In almost all projectile activities in sports, the performer relies on angular motion(s) preceding the release to obtain a specified (in the previous examples, a maximum) velocity of projection. It is therefore important that the relationship between velocity and angular velocity be clearly understood.

If the golfer of Fig. 4-6 moves the clubhead from P to Q in some time t, the average speed $\bar{s}$ of the clubhead is given by

$$\bar{s} = \frac{\text{distance}}{\text{time}}$$
$$= \frac{\text{arc } PQ}{t}$$

The average angular speed of the club during the same time is given by

$$\bar{\sigma} = \frac{\text{angular distance}}{\text{time}}$$
$$= \frac{(\text{arc } PQ/r)}{t}$$
$$= \frac{\text{arc } PQ}{rt}$$

(*Note:* The angular distance is measured in radians; and the number of radians involved is found by dividing the length of the arc PQ by the radius

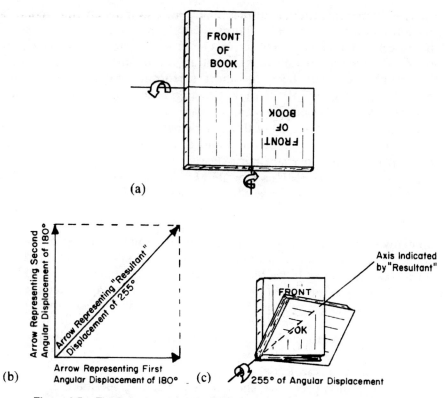

(a)

(b)

(c)

Figure 4-5. The summing of angular displacements does not proceed in accord with the parallelogram-of-vectors construction.

Figure 4-6. The velocity of the club head is equal to the product of its angular velocity and the radius of rotation.

r.) If the first of these equations is now substituted into the second, a relationship between the average speed and the average angular speed is obtained:

$$\bar{\sigma} = \frac{\bar{s}}{r}$$

or, rearranging,

$$\bar{s} = \bar{\sigma} r$$

If the distance (or time) over which the average speed and the average angular speed are computed is so small that these latter quantities have no opportunity to change, a similar equation relating the instantaneous speed and angular speed can be derived:

$$s = \omega r \qquad (4\text{-}4)$$

Finally, since the instantaneous speed and the instantaneous velocity of a body are equal in magnitude (p. 16) and the instantaneous angular speed and instantaneous angular velocity are similarly equal in magnitude, Eq. (4-4) can be rewritten as follows:

$$v_T = \omega r \qquad (4\text{-}5)$$

where v_T = the velocity of the clubhead tangential to its path. As already suggested, this relationship between velocity and angular velocity is of considerable importance in many sports activities. In hammer throwing, for example, it summarizes the athlete's whole credo—to obtain the maximum velocity of the hammer (that is, maximum v_T) by sweeping the hammer through the widest possible radius (maximum r), while turning as fast as can be controlled (maximum ω).

This equation also shows that for a constant angular velocity, the longer the radius, the greater the velocity—a fact that, again, has not been lost on the hammer throwers. Felton,[1] for example, has computed that "a six-inch [15 cm] increase in the hammer's effective radius can produce more than 30–40 feet [9–12 m] in distance thrown, provided turning speed and release angle remain constant."

ACCELERATION OF A BODY MOVING ON A CURVED PATH

The acceleration of a body moving on a curved path can be considered in terms of components acting along and at right angles to the path followed by the body—the *tangential component* and the *radial component*, respectively. Consider the example of the bowler in Fig. 4-7. During the delivery phase the ball moves vertically downward at one point near the start of the delivery, and then just before release it moves horizontally forward. In

Figure 4-7. Acceleration during the delivery in bowling.

between these two points it moves in a series of directions between downward and forward. Now, a change in the direction of motion of a body requires that it be accelerated, just as surely as does a change in its rate of motion. In the case of the bowling ball, the change in direction comes about because the restraining effect of the bowler's arm will not allow the ball to travel along the same line for any two consecutive instants. This restraining effect causes the ball to be accelerated toward the center of the circle along which it is moving (that is, toward an axis through the shoulder joint). This acceleration is called the *radial acceleration* (a_R), and its magnitude is found using the equation

$$a_R = \frac{v_T^2}{r} \qquad (4\text{-}6)$$

where v_T = the velocity of the ball tangential to its path and r = the length of the radius. Thus, if the tangential velocity of the ball at A (Fig. 4-7) is 6 m/s and the distance from the center of the ball to the shoulder joint (that is, the radius) is 0.75 m,

$$a_R = \frac{(6 \text{ m/s})^2}{0.75 \text{ m}}$$
$$= 48 \text{ m/s}^2$$

In the normal bowling action both the magnitude and direction of the ball's motion change continuously as the ball is swung downward and forward to the point of release. The rate at which the velocity of the ball changes as it moves along its curved path is the *tangential acceleration* and is given by

$$\bar{a}_T = \frac{v_{Tf} - v_{Ti}}{t} \qquad (4\text{-}7)$$

where a_T = the average tangential acceleration, v_{Ti} = the initial tangential velocity, v_{Tf} = the final tangential velocity, and t = the time during which this change in velocity occurs.

Thus, if the ball is moving with a tangential velocity of 6 m/s at A and with a tangential velocity of 6.3 m/s at B, 0.02 s later

$$\bar{a}_T = \frac{(6.3 - 6.0) \text{ m/s}}{0.02 \text{ s}}$$

$$= 15 \text{ m/s}^2$$

(*Note:* The tangential acceleration of the ball during its passage from A to B is accompanied by a substantial increase in the radial acceleration. Assuming that the length of the radius remains constant, the radial acceleration at B is $(6.3)^2/0.75 = 52.92$ m/s^2.)

ACCELERATION AND ANGULAR ACCELERATION

The relationship between the tangential acceleration and the angular acceleration of a body can be derived from Eq. (4-5) and written as follows:

$$a_T = \alpha r \qquad (4\text{-}8)$$

where a_T = the instantaneous tangential acceleration, and α = the instantaneous angular acceleration. Thus, if the ball in Fig. 4-7 is being angularly accelerated about the shoulder joint at 25 rad/s^2 at A, its tangential acceleration is:

$$a_T = (25 \times 0.75) \text{ m/s}^2$$

$$= 18.75 \text{ m/s}^2$$

Exercises

1. A right-handed tenpin bowler takes up his stance with his right (upper) arm 10° forward of a downward vertical line through his right shoulder. He then swings his arm clockwise (as viewed from his right-hand side) until it reaches a position 20° above a horizontal line through his shoulder. From this backward limit of his backswing, he then swings his arm counterclockwise and releases the ball. If his arm is 15° forward of a downward vertical line through the shoulder at release:
   (a) What angular distance has it traveled during the combined backswing and delivery action described here? Express your answer in three different ways: in degrees, in revolutions, and in radians.
   (b) If counterclockwise is the positive direction, what angular displacement has it experienced?
   (c) If the backswing and delivery took a total of 2.2 s, what was the average angular speed of his arm? How does this average angular speed compare with the instantaneous angular velocity of the arm at the peak of the backswing, and at the instant of release?
   (d) If the backswing and delivery took a total of 2.2 s, what was the average angular velocity of the arm?
   (e) If counterclockwise is the positive direction as before, what was the instantaneous angular acceleration of the arm at the peak of the backswing: positive, negative or zero?

2. A failed scientist from a bygone era proposed a new mechanical quantity called a gwizz (G). According to his definition, a gwizz is equal to the displacement of a body (d), multiplied by its average velocity (v) squared, divided by its average acceleration (a). That is

$$G = \frac{d\,\bar{v}^2}{\bar{a}}$$

In what metric units would a gwizz be expressed?
The gwizz is a linear kinematic quantity. How would be the angular equivalent of the gwizz be defined? (*Hint:* Substitute the angular equivalent for each of the quantities on the right hand side of the equation above.)

3. A right-handed softball player is pitching to a batter. In what direction should an arrow drawn to represent the angular velocity of her right arm be made to point? Upwards? Downwards? Horizontally to her right? Horizontally to her left? Some other direction?

4. A diver performs a back dive with a half twist from the 1-m board. This involves half of a backward somersault in a layout position (so that the diver can enter the water headfirst) and a simultaneous half rotation about the long axis of the body (so that the diver can enter the water as if he'd done a front dive). Imagine yourself standing behind the board (that is, at the opposite end of the board to the diver) watching him perform this dive. As he takes off, his left shoulder moves away from you and his right shoulder moves towards you. From directly above, he would appear to be rotating counterclockwise about his long axis.
   (a) In which direction would a vector representing the angular velocity of his somersaulting motion point—upwards, downwards, to your left, or to your right?
   (b) In what direction would a vector representing the angular velocity of his twisting motion point—upwards, downwards, to your left or to your right?
   (c) In what direction would a vector representing his resultant angular velocity point—upwards, downwards, to your left, to your right, or some combination of these directions? If a combination, what combination?

5. A marching band is participating in a street parade. In the center of an intersection the band performs a pinwheel (or gate turn) to the right, turning into a street that runs perpendicular to the one they have been marching along. In this maneuver, the person on the right-hand end of each rank marches on the spot, while those to his or her left march on a curved path. Consider the cases of three people in the front rank of the band—the one on the right-hand end, the one in the middle, and the one on the left-hand end. How do the angular displacements they experience about the long axes of their bodies compare? How do the angular velocities at which they make the turn compare? How do the lengths of the curved paths followed by the person in the middle of the line and the one on the left-hand end compare? How do the average speeds at which these two must march compare? Where would *you* prefer to be in the rank?!!

6. The cyclists in Figure 4-8 are rounding a turn at the bottom of a hill. The path they follow in doing this is a gentle curve that becomes progressively sharper as they near the corner. The radius of the path followed by one of these riders is 20 m at one point in the initial gentle part of the turn, and then decreases to a

Figure 4-8. Cyclists rounding a turn at the bottom of a hill.

minimum value of 17 m, 1.5 s later. His tangential velocity at these two instants are 12 m/s and 11.5 m/s, respectively. What is his radial acceleration at the two points? What is his average tangential acceleration between the two points?

Recommending Readings

Brancazio, P. J. (1984). *Sport Science: Physical Laws and Optimum Performance.* New York: Simon & Schuster, pp. 25–55 (Man in motion).

HAY, J. G., AND REID, J. G. (1988). *Anatomy, Mechanics, and Human Motion.* Englewood Cliffs, N.J.: Prentice Hall, pp. 137–41. (Describing angular motion [angular kinematics]).

Notes

1. Felton, S. (1970). The hammer throw. In F. Wilt and T. Ecker (Eds.), *International Track and Field Coaching Encyclopedia* (p. 345). West Nyack, N.Y.: Parker Publishing.

CHAPTER
5

LINEAR KINETICS

INERTIA

When a body is lying at rest, it is reluctant to do anything other than to remain at rest. A heavy barbell lying on the floor of a weight-training room shows this reluctance by the resistance it provides when attempts are made to move it. A body in motion is similarly reluctant to change what is it doing, as anyone who has thrust out a bare hand to stop a hard-driven baseball or cricket ball can testify. This characteristic of a body (its reluctance to change whatever it is doing) is known as its *inertia*.

MASS

The quantity of matter of which a body is composed is called its *mass* and is a direct measure of the inertia that the body possesses. Thus, a lightly laden (or less massive) barbell is easier to lift than a heavily laden (or more massive) one. Similarly, it is easier to alter the motion of a running back who has a relatively small mass than it is to effect the same alteration in the motion of a lineman who has a larger mass.

FORCE

A body's state of being "at rest" or "in motion" can be changed by the action of some other body. The pushing or pulling action that this other body has, and that causes the change, is termed a *force*. Thus, a body at rest can be made to move when another body exerts a force on it. Similarly, a body in motion can be slowed, speeded, or have the direction of its motion altered if another body exerts a force on it.

However, while the introduction of a force can produce or alter motion, not all forces are sufficiently large to have this effect. Consider again the heavy barbell lying on the floor of the weight-training room. Two weight lifters take turns at attempting to lift it. The less strong of the two struggles hard but ultimately fails to get the barbell off the floor. By his efforts, however, he does *tend* to move the barbell, for he gets it closer to that point where it would move upward than it would have been if he'd left it alone. The stronger weight lifter succeeds in lifting the barbell from the floor, thereby changing it from a state in which it is lying at rest to one in which it is in motion. Thus, although force was exerted on the barbell in an upward direction in both cases, the results obtained were somewhat different. These two different results provide a basis for a more formal and complete definition of force than that already given—force is that which alters or tends to alter a body's state of rest or of uniform motion in a straight line.

INTERNAL AND EXTERNAL FORCES

When a snooker player hits the cue ball into the tightly packed triangle of reds at the start of a game, the cue ball exerts a force on each of the balls with which it makes contact. In turn, these balls exert forces on those they contact. If it is said that the 16 bodies involved (the 15 red balls and the cue ball) comprise a system, it is normal to refer to the forces that they exert on one another as *internal forces*—that is, forces that are internal to the system. When the scattering balls make contact with the padded cushions surrounding the table and exert forces on them, these are termed *external forces*, because the bodies involved (the cushions and the snooker balls) are not all within the system. If one of the reds or the cue ball hit, say, the pink or the blue ball, the forces exerted would similarly be termed external forces.

It should be fairly obvious that whether forces are regarded as internal or external depends entirely on how the system is defined at the outset. If all 22 of the snooker balls are regarded as bodies within the system, the forces that they exert on one another are rightly classified as internal forces. If the scope of the system is further enlarged to include the whole snooker table as well, then the forces between the cushions and the snooker balls are also internal forces.

It can thus be seen that the classification of forces into internal and external is purely a matter of convenience. In biomechanics it is generally regarded as convenient to consider the constituent parts of the human body as "the system" and any force exerted by one part on another as an internal force. For example, whenever the contraction of a muscle causes forces to be exerted on the bones to which it is attached or on the cartilage within a joint or on the ligaments surrounding a joint, these forces are regarded as internal forces. Conversely, the forces due to air resistance, gravity, and contact with the ground or some other body are regarded as external forces.

NEWTON'S FIRST LAW OF MOTION

The ancient Greeks believed that a body moved when there was a force acting on it and that it ceased moving if the force was removed. This belief was rejected by the great Italian scientist Galileo Galilei (1564–1642) and subsequently replaced by a law formulated by Sir Isaac Newton (1642–1727). This law, now known as Newton's first law of motion, may be expressed as follows:

Every body continues in its state of rest or motion in a straight line unless compelled to change that state by external forces exerted upon it.

It is perhaps of interest to note that this law, which so succinctly summarizes many of the concepts outlined in the preceding sections, has not been proved directly. Since it is impossible to produce here on earth a situation in which there are no forces acting on a body, it has not been possible to arrive at those conditions necessary to test the theory. However, this is an academic rather than a practical limitation, for the law has never been shown to be inconsistent with experience.

NEWTON'S LAW OF GRAVITATION

In considering sports techniques it is common to think in terms of forces resulting from the contact between one body and another—the tennis racket makes contact with the ball and exerts a force upon it, a basketball strikes the backboard and exerts a force against it, and the wrestler takes a grip on his opponent and exerts forces on him.

In addition to forces that are the direct result of contact between two bodies, there are other forces that exist whether or not the bodies are in contact. These are forces that tend to make bodies gravitate toward each other. The nature of these forces was first described by Newton. According to the well-known story, Newton was hit on the head by an apple falling from a tree. After reflecting on this incident he formulated what is now known as *Newton's law of gravitation:*

Any two particles of matter attract one another with a force directly proportional to the product of their masses and inversely proportional to the square of the distance between them.

Expressed algebraically, the law reduces to

$$F \propto \frac{m_1 m_2}{l^2}$$

(5-1)

where F = the force acting on each particle, m_1 and m_2 = their respective masses, and l = the distance between them.

In sports, the total of all the attractive forces that the particles of one body exert on the particles of any other body is generally so small that its effect is imperceptible. Thus, although each of the balls on a billiards or snooker table exerts on each of the others a force "directly proportional to the product of their masses and inversely proportional to the square of the distance between them," these forces are so small that they can be disregarded.

The one body whose effect on others cannot be disregarded, and the one that makes a consideration of Newton's law of gravitation of some significance in the analysis of sports techniques, is the earth. The attraction that the earth has for all other bodies is known as *gravity* and, as indicated by Eq. (5-1), varies directly with the mass of the body involved and inversely with its distance from the earth (strictly speaking, with its distance from the center of the earth). Thus, if all else is equal, a massive heavyweight weight lifter experiences a much greater attractive (or gravitational) force than does a much less massive jockey. On the other hand, a skydiver leaping out of an aircraft at 3,000 m is subjected to a lesser gravitational attraction than if he (or she) merely leapt from a 3 m diving board. The difference in the forces in the latter case is fairly small, because even though values of l are squared in arriving at the magnitudes of the forces, the addition of 3,000 m to the radius of the earth—a radius of approximately 6,400,000 m—makes very little difference.

The effects that differences in l have on sports performances are nonetheless the subject of press comment before most Olympic Games. This interest on the part of the press stems from the fact that because the earth has the appearance of having been pushed in or flattened at the poles, some parts of the earth's surface are farther from the earth's center than others. Competitors in a shot put competition at the equator, for instance, are approximately 21 km farther from the earth's center than they would be if they competed at either of the poles. This means that the gravitational force that pulls the shot down to the ground is slightly less and thus more favorable at the equator than at the poles.

MOMENTUM

Every body in motion—from a track sprinter to a long-distance swimmer to a bowling ball rolling down a lane—has a certain mass and a certain velocity. The product of these two is known as the *momentum*, or quantity of motion, that the body possesses.

The momentum of a body is generally of little importance in sports unless that body becomes involved in a collision with another body. Then, the result of the collision hinges very largely on how much momentum each of the bodies had just before the collision took place. The greater the momentum of a body, the more pronounced the effect that it produces on other bodies in its path. If, for example, two bowlers use identical techniques and each releases the ball at precisely the same velocity, the bowler who is using the ball that has the greater mass (and therefore the greater momentum) is more likely to score well than the bowler with the less massive ball. This comes about because the ball with the greater momentum has the tendency to cause the pins to fly about more dramatically, knocking the other pins down and contributing to a better score than does the ball with less momentum.

A difference in momentum may also result from a difference in the velocity at which a body moves. In softball or baseball, for example, batters control the momentum the bat has at the instant of contact with the ball, by controlling its velocity. If they want to hit a home run, they try to have the bat moving at a very high velocity as it strikes the ball. Conversely, if they want to bunt, they try to have the bat moving at a very low velocity.

NEWTON'S SECOND LAW OF MOTION

A little experimentation with a putter and a golf ball quickly reveals that if the ball is lying on a flat, level green and is struck by the putter, it will move off in the direction in which it has been struck—or, to be more precise, in the direction of the force that has been applied to it. One does not have to be especially perceptive to note also that the harder the ball is hit (that is, the greater the force that is applied to it), the faster it will move off across the green. Equivalent observations might be made in many similar situations—for example, in passing in soccer or basketball; and in hitting in squash, hockey, or volleyball.

What may not be quite so obvious, but is true nonetheless, is that when the body to which a force is applied is already moving, the same two things occur—it moves, or tends to move, in the direction in which the force acts; and its change in speed in that direction is related to the size of the force. The truth of this statement is often not obvious because the body may also retain some motion in another direction. The defensive basketball player in Fig. 5-1 provides an example. Imagine that a pass is thrown in such a way that he can just get his outstretched hand to it. If he exerts a force on the ball in the direction *OA*, he will cause the ball to move in that direction. The ball will, however, retain some motion in the direction in which it was traveling originally—the direction *OB*. If the arrows *OX* and *OY* represent the velocity vectors due to the force exerted by the defensive man and to the original motion of the ball, respectively, the ball will be deflected in the direction of their resultant *OR*.

Newton summarized these various effects in precise scientific fashion when he formulated his *second law of motion*. This law may be stated as follows:

The rate of change of momentum of a body is proportional to the force causing it and the change takes place in the direction in which the force acts.

Expressed algebraically,

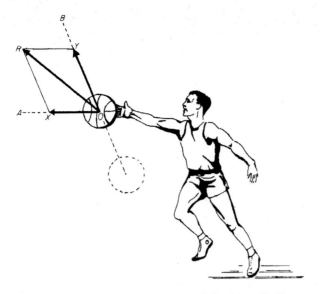

Figure 5-1. A deflected pass in basketball—the applied force accelerates the ball in the direction in which the force acts.

$$F \propto \frac{m_f v_f - m_i v_i}{t}$$

or, for a body of constant mass,

$$F \propto m \frac{v_f - v_i}{t}$$

$$\propto ma$$

Now in mathematics a statement of this kind can be changed from an "is proportional to" to an "is equal to" statement by multiplying one side by a constant. Thus, if k is the symbol used for the constant,

$$F = kma \tag{5-2}$$

Mass. The unit of mass in the S.I. system of measurement—the system used in this text—is the *kilogram* (kg).

UNITS IN LINEAR KINETICS

Force. The unit of force is the Newton (N) and is defined in terms of the acceleration it produces. A force of 1 N is the force that will produce an acceleration of 1 m/s^2 in a body of 1 kg mass.

It might also be noted that this last statement can be rearranged to provide a definition of the unit of mass—namely, a mass of 1 kg is the mass that, when acted upon by a force of 1 N, will have an acceleration of 1 m/s^2.

It is pertinent now to reconsider the statement of Newton's second law as it appears in Eq. (5-2). If the values discussed in the preceding paragraphs are substituted into this equation, one arrives at

$$F = kma$$
$$1 \text{ N} = k \times 1 \text{ kg} \times 1 \text{ m/s}^2$$

that is,

$$1 = k \times 1 \times 1$$

from which it can be seen that the value of k is 1 and that Eq. (5-2) can be reduced to the well-known form

$$F = ma \tag{5-3}$$

Other units. All the other units used in linear kinetics are defined in terms of those of length, time, and force or mass. For example, the unit of momentum is arrived at in the following manner:

$$\text{Momentum} = \text{mass} \times \text{velocity}$$
$$\text{Unit of momentum} = \text{unit of mass} \times \text{unit of velocity}$$
$$= \text{unit of mass} \times \text{unit of length/unit of time}$$
$$= \text{kilogram} \times \text{meter/second (or kg} \cdot \text{m/s)}$$

WEIGHT

The attractive (or gravitational) force that the earth exerts on a body is called the *weight* of the body. Thus a wrestler who experiences a gravitational force of 600 N is said to have a weight of 600 N. Weight, then, is merely the name given to a particular force and, just as g stands for a specific acceleration (the acceleration due to gravity, p. 22), W (the letter used to designate a body's weight) stands for a specific force.

Newton's law of gravitation (pp. 62-63) indicates that the force of attraction the earth exerts on a body, the force just now defined as the weight of the body, varies slightly depending on its location. For example, a wrestler who weights 1000 N in Nairobi, Kenya, would weigh 4.5 N more than this in Helsinki, Finland. The mass of a body, a quantity often misunderstood and confused with its weight, differs in this respect. Whereas the weight of a body changes according to where it is located, its mass remains constant irrespective of location. When it is recalled that the mass of a body was described (p. 60) as the quantity of matter of which it is composed, the truth of the last statement is perhaps easier to accept, for it would seem logical to expect that the amount of matter in a body would remain the same when the body was shifted from one place to another.

Although mass and weight differ in this way, the two quantities are closely related. Consider a trampolinist at the peak of her flight. The earth exerts a downward force W on her, and as a result she is accelerated back toward the bed with an acceleration g. The relationship between her weight, her mass, and the acceleration due to gravity is evident from Newton's second law. Substituting in Eq. (5-3),

$$F = ma$$
$$W = mg \qquad (5\text{-}4)$$

or, if this is rearranged,

$$m = \frac{w}{g}$$

Thus, a trampolinist who weighs 400 N can be seen to have a mass of 40.77 kg:

$$m = \frac{400}{9.81}$$
$$= 40.77 \text{ kg}$$

or one of mass 45 kg to weigh 441.45 N:

$$W = 45 \times 9.81$$
$$= 441.45 \text{ N}$$

NEWTON'S THIRD LAW

When an athlete runs, he pushes downward and backward against the ground, thereby exerting a force against it in that direction. The athlete himself goes upward and forward as a result of this driving action. It can easily be reasoned from Newton's first law that this upward-and-forward motion could only result from the athlete having had a force exerted on him in that direction (Fig. 5-2[a]). A weight lifter performing a bench press applies force to the barbell to lift it. The barbell in turn "pushes down' on the hands of the weight lifter (Fig. 5-2[b]). A basketball player dribbling the ball exerts force on it to push it down toward the floor. As he does so, the ball resists his action and exerts force against his hand. This he senses as an increase in the pressure against his fingers. When the ball strikes the floor, it exerts another force, this time against the floor. After first contacting the floor, the ball slows down and changes the direction in which it is moving. Again, from Newton's first law, it is clear that this could happen only if some body had exerted a force on the ball (Fig. 5-2[c]).

An endless number of examples could be cited, where one body exerts a force against another and receives in return a force exerted in the

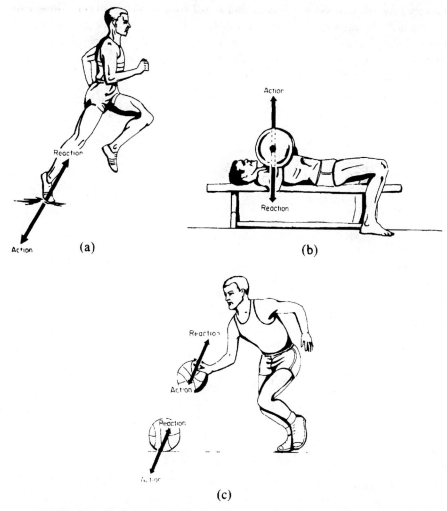

Figure 5-2. Examples of Newton's third law (a) in running; (b) in performing a bench press; and (c) in dribbling a basketball.

opposite direction. This characteristic action of two bodies exerting forces on each other forms the basis of Newton's third law of motion, which is generally stated in the form:

To every action there is an equal and opposite reaction.

However, because the terms *action* and *reaction* have no precise meanings in biomechanics, and their use can therefore lead to unnecessary confusion, this law is more usefully expressed as:

For every force that is exerted by one body on another there is an equal and opposite force exerted by the second body on the first.

Irrespective of which of the previous statements is used, it is customary to call one of the two forces involved the "action" and other the "reaction," although there are no universally accepted rules regarding which is which.

Newton's third law goes beyond the observations made concerning the examples depicted in Fig. 5-2; for not only does it refer to opposing forces but it also indicates that these are equal in magnitude. The truth of this latter condition is sometimes difficult for people to accept. The main reason appears to be that the effects that two bodies produce on each other are often quite different. The runner bounds forward and nothing much seems to happen to the earth—the other body involved; the barbell is moved upward and the body appears unaffected, and so on. These seeming contradictions can all be explained in terms of Newton's second law, which indicates that for a constant force the acceleration that a body experiences is inversely proportional to its mass:

$$F = ma$$

therefore

$$a = \frac{F}{m}$$

and

$$a \propto \frac{1}{m}$$

In other words, the larger the mass, the less the acceleration. Now if both the earth and the runner have a force of the same size exerted against them, it is reasonable to expect that the effect would be more obvious in the case of the runner than in the case of the earth. The earth in fact would seem to be unaffected—but only because its colossal mass, compared with that of the runner, would not make apparent the acceleration it experienced.

Exactly the same thing is true in the other cases mentioned. In the case of the weight lifter his body position is such that, at least with regard to vertical forces, he is firmly anchored or fixed to the earth. This means, in effect, that the two bodies interacting with each other are the barbell and the lifter-plus-earth, and again the effect on the first is more apparent than that on the second. This process of adding the mass of a large body to the mass of a smaller one is very important in many sports and probably none more so than rifle shooting. When a rifle is fired, equal and opposite forces are exerted against the bullet and the rifle. Because the mass of the bullet is small, it acquires a high velocity as a result of the force exerted against it. The rifle, on the other hand, acquires a lesser velocity in keeping with its greater mass. This lesser velocity is still sufficient to send the rifle traveling backward fast enough to deliver a painful blow to the shoulder of the marksman foolish, or inexperienced, enough to hold it incorrectly. To avoid having this happen, the good marksman effectively increases the mass of the rifle by holding it firmly into the shoulder, thus making the two bodies involved the bullet and the rifle-plus-marksman. If the marksman shoots from a prone-lying position, the mass is again increased to be rifle-plus-marksman-plus-earth, and the acceleration that this "body" experiences is small indeed.

Difficulties often arise in understanding how this third law of Newton's is applied in specific cases. Consider, for example, the athlete in Fig. 5-3(a). This man is doing some heavy resistance training aimed at strengthening his legs. The question frequently asked in such situations is, "If the rope pulls on the man with a force exactly equal and directly opposite to that with which the man pulls on the rope, how can he ever move forward?" This kind of question arises if due consideration has not been taken of all the forces that act on each body. The athlete has four external forces exerted upon him:

- the pulling force, P, along the line of the rope;
- his body weight, W;
- a ground-reaction force, R (See Fig. 5-3[a]), and
- an air-resistance force, A.

These forces are shown in Fig. 5-3(b). What happens to the athlete—whether he moves forward or struggles without avail—depends only on the resultant of these forces. If the horizontal components of A and P combine to be equal in magnitude to the horizontal component of R, the athlete is unable to move forward. (His weight, of course, has no horizontal component and thus has no direct influence on motion in a horizontal direction.) If, on the other hand, the combined horizontal components of A and P are less than the horizontal component of R, the athlete moves forward. The motion of the tray that the athlete is striving to pull along can be predicted in a similar fashion.

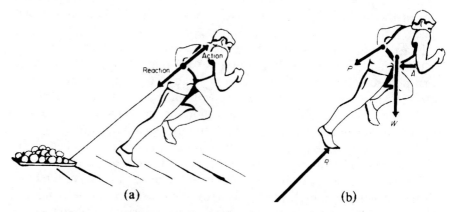

Figure 5-3. The action and the reaction act on different bodies and thus do not forestall motion by canceling each other out.

(*Note:* In deciding how a body will move under specific conditions, it is usually helpful to start by drawing what is known as a *free-body diagram.* This is a diagram like Fig. 5-3[b], in which the body of interest is depicted completely removed or free from its environment and in which *all* the external forces acting on the body are represented in appropriate vector form. The components of the external forces that act in a given direction are then examined carefully to determine how the body will move in that direction or, if the exact magnitude of the forces is not known, to determine what conditions are necessary to get the body moving as required.)

Statements such as "in long jumping, a forceful stamp of the takeoff foot accentuates the upward motion" and "in the high jump, stamp the takeoff foot hard, so that the push up will be as forceful as possible (Newton's third law)" appear from time to time in the literature. The statements also result from a misunderstanding of Newton's third law. The error stems from the fact that the ground reaction to a foot stamp (and the reaction to any other force that is ever applied) occurs at the same instant that the force is applied. Therefore, any such strong ground reaction would occur far too early in the sequence of movements at takeoff to be helpful to the jumper. (From a physiological standpoint, the wisdom of stamping the foot and jarring the leg in this way would also seem open to question.)

NORMAL REACTION

When a body lies or moves on the nonvertical surface of another, its weight (or a component of it) acts on this second body in a direction at right angles to the surface of contact. The second body exerts an equal force on the first body, in the opposite direction (the *normal* direction). This force is called the *normal reaction* (Fig. 5-4) External force may be used to add to or subtract from the weight component. If this is done, the normal reaction is similarly affected.

FRICTION

The force of attraction that the earth exerts on a body is called the body's weight. A number of other forces are similarly given special names. One of these is the force that arises whenever one body moves or tends to move across the surface of another. This force, which always opposes the motion or impending motion, is called *friction.*

Because there are distinct differences in the nature of the friction that arises under varying circumstances, two types of friction will be considered here: sliding friction and rolling friction. A third type, the friction that is present in fully-lubricated bearings, will not be considered because of its complexity and its very limited application to sports techniques.

Sliding Friction. Friction acts only when a body is in motion or has some tendency to start moving across the surface of another body. A barbell disc lying on the floor is acted upon by two forces: one, its weight *W*, and the other *R*, an upward supporting force exerted by the floor (Fig. 5-5[a]). Under the action of these two forces the disc has no tendency to slide across

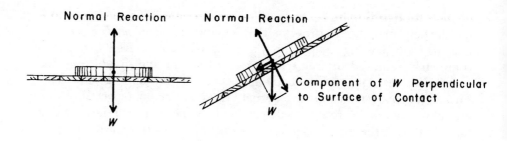

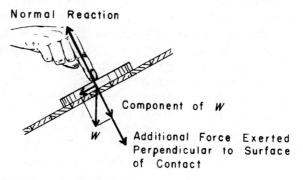

Figure 5-4. The normal reaction.

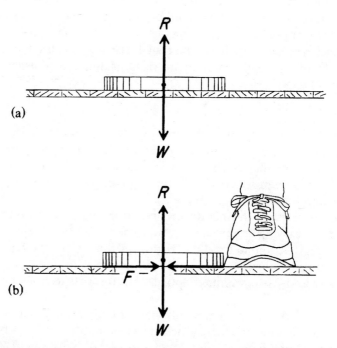

Figure 5-5. Friction acts to oppose forces that cause, or tend to cause, the sliding of one body over another.

the floor and thus there is no friction acting to oppose this tendency. If a weight lifter gives the disc a push with his foot, the disc will tend to slide. Only then will friction (F) act in opposition to this tendency (Fig. 5-5[b]).

Another important characteristic of friction is that, until sliding commences, the magnitude of the friction is equal to that of the force tending to cause the body to slide. In other words, until sliding commences, friction effectively cancels out the force tending to cause the body to slide, and no sliding takes place. Once the friction has reached its upper limit in magnitude (*limiting friction*), sliding is about to commence. A lineman pushing against a blocking sled (Fig. 5-6) can be used to illustrate this concept.

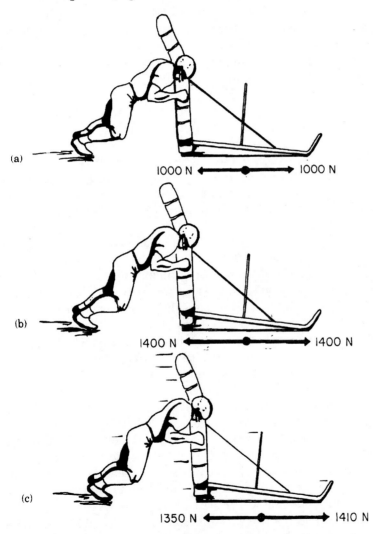

(a)

1000 N ← ● → 1000 N

(b)

1400 N ← ● → 1400 N

(c)

1350 N ← ● → 1410 N

Figure 5-6. Until sliding is imminent, friction increases as the force tending to cause the body to slide increases. Once the latter force exceeds the maximum friction (limiting friction), the body begins to slide. At this point, the opposing friction decreases in magnitude.

Suppose the magnitude of the limiting friction is 1400 N. If the lineman exerts a horizontal force of 1000 N against the sled, the magnitude of the friction will also be 1000 N and the sled will not move horizontally (Fig. 5-6[a]). If the lineman increases the horizontal force he exerts to 1400 N, the sled still will not move horizontally, although, with the magnitude of the friction stretched as it were "to the limit," it is on the point of doing so (Fig. 5-6[b]). Finally, if the lineman musters another few Newtons of horizontal force, the friction is no longer capable of completely neutralizing the effect of his efforts, and the sled starts to slide. In fact, once the sled starts to slide, the friction drops below its limiting value of 1400 N (Fig. 5-6[c]).

There are many situations in which athletes try to increase the friction (or "grip") between two surfaces to prevent sliding. Baseball pitchers use resin to improve their grip on the ball; gymnasts use magnesium chalk to improve their grip on the apparatus; and pole-vaulters use sticky adhesive tape and, probably too, a spray grip, resin, or Venice turpentine to achieve a similar result. Basketball boots have soles that have been specially designed to increase the "grip" between shoe and floor, and the pimpled rubber surfaces of table tennis bats ensure a better "grip" between bat and ball than smooth rubber surfaces alone would allow.

Occasionally one seeks not to increase the "grip" between two surfaces or objects but instead to reduce it. Ballroom dancing provides an example. Competitors in this activity normally wear fairly smooth leather-soled shoes, and the floor is specially treated to permit the optimum amount of sliding in the execution of various steps. Such people will testify that there is nothing as destructive of good technique as shoes or a floor that do not permit the feet to slide correctly.

In all these examples, performers attempt to increase or decrease the "grip" between two bodies by altering the nature of the two surfaces that bear upon each other. In some cases they modify one or both of the surfaces involved (for example, the soles of basketball boots); in others they interpose a substance that has a high limiting friction when in contact with each of the two surfaces and thus has the effect of binding them together (for example, resin and magnesium powder).

Another method often used to achieve the same kind of result is to alter the force that holds the two bodies in contact with each other. The climber in Fig. 5-7 uses this method to increase his grip on the rock face he is climbing down. He knows that the farther he leans away from the rock face, the more the line of the force exerted by the rope will tend to thrust his feet firmly against the surface of the rock (that is, the farther he leans away from the rock face, the greater will be the component of the force exerted by the rope that will be acting at right angles to the face). Thus the rope helps to hold the two surfaces (soles of boots and rock) together and thereby to reduce the tendency for the boots to slip. (Incidentally, as the climber leans progressively farther away from the rock face, the magnitude of the force exerted by the rope is enhanced in two ways—by changes in both the magnitude and the direction of the force exerted via the rope.)

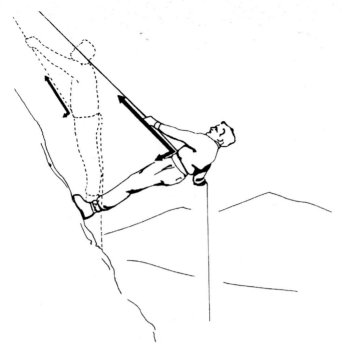

Figure 5-7. The rock climber increases the limiting friction between his feet and the rock by leaning well away from the rock face.

The friction that the lineman has to overcome to start the blocking sled moving (Fig. 5-6) can be increased or decreased in similar fashion. He can reduce the force holding the two surfaces (sled and ground) together by driving forward and upward instead of directly forward. This, he soon learns, reduces the friction he is fighting to overcome. His coach, however, has a simple answer to this. He stands on the sled, forces the sliding surfaces more firmly together, and thus increases the friction.

From these examples it is apparent that there are two ways in which the friction between bodies can be modified: (1) by altering the nature of the bearing surfaces; and (2) by changing the forces that hold these surfaces together. These conclusions are summarized in two very similar statements. The first, sometimes referred to as the *first law of friction*, states that

For two dry surfaces, the limiting friction is equal to the normal reaction multiplied by a constant, the value of this constant depending only on the nature of the surfaces.

That is,

$$F = \mu R \qquad (5\text{-}5)$$

where F = the limiting friction, R = the normal reaction, and μ = the constant known as the *coefficient of limiting friction*. Thus, in the case of the lineman and the sled, if the weight of the sled (and therefore the normal reaction) is, say, 2000 N, the coefficient of limiting friction is 0.7:

$$F = \mu R$$

$$\mu = \frac{F}{R}$$

$$= \frac{1400 \text{ N}}{2000 \text{ N}}$$

$$\doteq 0.7$$

By pushing in a forward and upward direction, the lineman can reduce the weight supported by the ground. If in doing this he reduces the normal reaction by 200 N, he also reduces the limiting friction—but only by 0.7 of that amount:

$$F = \mu R$$

$$= 0.7 \times 1800 \text{ N}$$

$$= 1260 \text{ N}$$

$$\text{Reduction in } F = (1400 - 1260) \text{ N}$$

$$= 140 \text{ N}$$

(Note: Use of this example assumes that it is reasonable to regard the base of the sled and the ground as "two dry surfaces.")

One important feature of Eq. (5-5) is that it shows the limiting friction is independent of the area of contact between the two bodies. Thus, if all else were equal, a person walking down a steep slope would have the same tendency to slip regardless of whether his (or her) shoe size was 5 or 15!

The second statement is practically identical to the first and concerns the magnitude of the friction when a body is actually sliding. This is given by the equation:

$$F_S = \mu_S R \tag{5-6}$$

where F_S = the sliding friction; R = the normal reaction, as before; and μ_S = the *coefficient of sliding friction*. In any given case, the value of this latter coefficient is less than the value for the coefficient of limiting friction. This is in accord with the everyday experience that it is easier to keep a body sliding than it is to start it sliding in the first place.

Rolling Friction. Experienced golfers carefully study the path that the ball will follow, before making a putt. They look closely at the length of the grass and the way it is lying (the so-called grain). They look, too, at whether the grass is wet or dry and how soft the ground is, for they know that all these things have a bearing on how easily the ball will roll across the green toward the hole. Field hockey and soccer players also study the condition of the playing surface carefully, for they realize that how well the ball rolls across this surface depends very much on how hard, smooth, and dry it is.

Whether they realize it or not, all these people (and others like them who are concerned in some way with a ball rolling across a surface), are actually considering the friction that will oppose the motion of the ball when it rolls across the playing surface. This kind of friction, called *rolling friction*, occurs because both the ball and the surface upon which it is rolling are slightly deformed in the process. Although in general these deformations are too small to be visible, they are sufficient to create some opposition to the motion of the ball.

Everyday experience suggests that this opposition, the rolling friction, is a good deal less in magnitude than is sliding friction, which (as has already been noted) is less again than limiting friction. While coefficients of limiting and sliding friction are normally within a range from 0.1 to 1.0, rolling friction is generally of a magnitude equivalent to a coefficient on the order of 0.001. (A coefficient of 0.0 would be indicative of perfectly smooth or frictionless surfaces.) In other words, rolling friction is approximately 100 to 1000 times less than sliding and limiting friction.

The magnitude of the rolling friction depends, among other factors, on the nature of the ball and the surface involved, the normal reaction, and the diameter of the ball. Of these, the only one commonly considered in sports is the first, the nature of the ball and the surface involved. In general, very little can be done directly about either of these things—the performers having little say in the type of ball to be used (this being largely fixed by the rules) or in the condition of the playing surface. What they can, and must, do if they wish to achieve the best of which they are capable, is to check the prevailing conditions and adjust their games accordingly. If the playing surface is heavily grassed and is soft and wet, the rolling friction will be relatively high and the players will have to exert more force than usual to offset the effect of this high rolling friction. For example, golfers should endeavor to stroke the ball more firmly when putting under such conditions. If, on the other hand, the surface is hard and fast, rolling friction will be relatively low and the forces required less than usual. An alternative to modifying the forces exerted is to change completely the technique that is used; for example, a field hockey player, involved in a match on a soft ground, may want to use aerial (or "flick") passes in preference to drives that might be stopped prematurely in the "holding" conditions.

IMPULSE

The shot-putter in Fig. 5-8 is performing a standing throw from a special platform that measures the forces he exerts against it. These forces are detected by sensitive strain gauges built into the platform and are then recorded and plotted against time. Figure 5-8 shows a record of the horizontal forces that are exerted in the line of the throw—positive forces are those exerted on the ground in the direction of the throw and negative

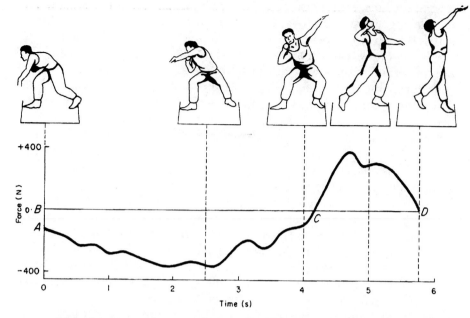

Figure 5-8. Horizontal forces exerted against the ground during the execution of a standing shot put. (Adapted from Payne, A. H., Slater, W. J., and Telford, T. [1968]). The use of a force platform in the study of athletic performance. *Ergonomics*, 11:123–44.)

forces are those exerted on the ground in the opposite direction. From this record it can be seen that the magnitude of the force is changing continually during the throw and that the direction of the force also changes. This continually changing horizontal force may be thought of as having a certain magnitude for a very small period of time, then a slightly different magnitude for the next small period of time, and so on. If one of these small time periods is considered, the product of the force (F) and the small time during which the force acts (t) is defined as the *impulse* of the force:

$$\text{Impulse} = F \times t \qquad (5\text{-}7)$$

This product of a constant force and the time during which it acts is also equal to the narrow rectangular area under the force-time curve for that time interval. The total impulse is the sum of all the infinite number of such smaller impulses and can be shown mathematically to be equal to the total area under the force-time curve. Thus in Fig. 5-8 the area bounded by the force-time curve and the lines CB and BA represents the total impulse (291 N · s) in the negative direction, and that bounded by the curve and the line CD represents the total impulse (107 N · s) in the positive direction. The algebraic sum of these two values is the total impulse:

$$\text{Total impulse} = (107 - 291) \text{ N} \cdot s$$
$$= -184 \text{ N} \cdot s$$

A useful relationship involving impulse can be obtained by rearranging the algebraic statement of Newton's second law:

$$\bar{F} = m\bar{a}$$

Since $\bar{a}$, the average acceleration, has previously been equated with $(v_f - v_i)/t$ [Eq. (3-3)], this expression can be substituted for $\bar{a}$ in the previous equation:

$$\bar{F} = \frac{m(v_f - v_i)}{t}$$

or

$$\bar{F} = \frac{mv_f - mv_i}{t}$$

Rearranging this expression yields

$$\bar{F}t = mv_f - mv_i \qquad (5\text{-}8)$$

In other words, the impulse of a force $(\bar{F}t)$ is equal to the change of momentum $(mv_f - mv_i)$ that it produces.

A knowledge of this *impulse-momentum relationship* is basic to an understanding of many sports techniques. Among these are the techniques used in starting in track, swimming, football, and a number of other sports.

The results obtained by Henry[1] in his study of sprint starting in track provide an example of how the impulse-momentum relationship applies in such cases. Henry studied the effects that different foot spacings had on the performance of a crouch start and found that use of a bunch start (with the feet 28 cm apart) got his subjects off the starting blocks faster than use of either a medium or an elongated start (feet 41 cm and 53 cm apart, respectively). He also found that use of the bunch start resulted in significantly slower times at 10 yd (9.14 m) and 50 yd (45.72 m) than did use of either of the other two starts. At first glance these two findings appear contradictory, for it would seem logical to expect the starting method that enabled runners to clear their blocks fastest would enable them to get to 10 yd, and probably to 50 yd, in the least time. This apparent contradiction is the result of differences in the horizontal impulses exerted against the blocks. When the subjects used the bunch start, the horizontal impulses they exerted against the blocks were limited by the relatively short time in which they were in contact with the blocks and thus in a position to exert horizontal forces against them. This in turn limited their horizontal velocities as they left the blocks. (*Note:* Because the initial horizontal momentum is zero and the mass of the subject is constant in any given case, the horizontal velocity on leaving the blocks is directly proportional to the horizontal impulse exerted against the blocks—see Eq. [5-8]). An explanation for Henry's seemingly odd results is now apparent—although the subjects cleared their blocks soonest when using the bunch start, the slight time advantage they had was soon offset because their horizontal velocities as they left the blocks were relatively small.

CONSERVATION OF MOMENTUM

When a bowling ball strikes a pin, the force exerted by the ball on the pin is exactly equal and directly opposite to that exerted by the pin on the ball (Newton's third law). The time during which these forces act is also exactly the same—either the two bodies are in contact or they're not, and each will exert force on the other only when they are in contact. (Noncontact gravitational forces that the two bodies exert on each other are trivial and can safely be ignored.) Because the impulse is the product of the force and the time, the impulse each body receives is exactly equal in magnitude and opposite in direction to that which the other body experiences. Furthermore, according to the impulse-momentum relationship, the respective changes in momentum of the two bodies must also be equal and opposite. Thus, because the momentum lost by the ball is equal and opposite to that gained by the pin, the total momentum of the system (ball-plus-pin) is unaltered by the impact. These ideas are summarized in an extension of Newton's first law known as the *principle of conservation of momentum*:

In any system of bodies that exert forces on each other, the total momentum in any direction remains constant unless some external force acts on the system in that direction.

In the example of the bowling ball and pin, as in most other examples in sports, the total momentum is only approximately constant, because the external forces of friction and air resistance are acting. However, because the magnitude of the external forces is so small, it would be reasonable to expect the approximation to be a fairly close one in this instance.

IMPACT

There is a large group of sports in which one body collides (or impacts) with another and in which the success of a participant depends very largely on his (or her) ability to predict the outcome of such impacts. In squash, handball, and racquetball, players are continually called upon to predict where the ball will go following an impact with a wall, the floor, and even the ceiling (in the latter two games) and to position themselves ready for their next shot in accord with this prediction. If they misjudge the outcome of the impact, they are very likely to find themselves in a position from which it is difficult, perhaps impossible, to make a suitable return shot. When players do position themselves correctly, their next task is to play the ball in such a manner as to obtain the best results. To do this, they must know how the ball will react to the various ways in which they might hit it and then choose the way that is most appropriate to the situation.

Tennis and table tennis players have very similar problems to those of their squash, handball, and racquetball counterparts, for, in addition to predicting the outcome of an impact between the ball and some part of the playing court, each of these people also faces the problem of what will happen to the ball once it strikes a racquet or bat. In a somewhat different way, golfers, hockey players, and batters in softball or baseball also face this kind of problem, as do athletes kicking in football, heading in soccer, or passing and spiking in volleyball. In view of the prominent role of the impact situation in so many sports, it is important to consider the factors that influence the outcome when two bodies collide.

Elasticity. When a ball hits a fixed surface, both the ball and the surface are compressed. Then, because most bodies tend to return to their original shape after they've been slightly deformed, the ball rebounds from the surface as both bodies strive to restore themselves to their former shape. The same sequence of compression and restitution takes place when two moving bodies (for example, a bat and a ball) impact with each other. The property of a body that causes it to endeavor to regain its original shape once it has been deformed is called its *elasticity*, a property possessed by most of the bodies involved in impacts in sport.

Coefficient of Restitution. Elasticity differs from one body to another. Some return very quickly to their original shape, while others do so much less quickly. Because there is no way of directly calculating the elasticity of a body, it is necessary to rely on the results of experiments to help predict the outcome of any given impact.

Sir Isaac Newton investigated the properties of elastic bodies and the results of impacts between them and formulated the following empirical law (*Newton's law of impact*):

If two bodies move toward each other along the same straight line, the difference between their velocities immediately after impact bears a constant relationship to the difference between their velocities at the moment of impact.[*]

In algebraic terms,

$$v_1 - v_2 = -e(u_1 - u_2)$$

or

$$\frac{v_1 - v_2}{u_1 - u_2} = -e \tag{5-9}$$

where v_1 and v_2 = the velocities immediately after impact of bodies 1 and 2, respectively; u_1 and u_2 = their respective velocities immediately before impact; and e = a constant known as the *coefficient of restitution*.[†]

* If the two bodies are not traveling along the same straight line before impact, their component velocities along a line perpendicular to the surface of contact obey this law.
† Newton's law of impact, like many empirical laws, is only approximately true. For instance, as the velocity of impact increases, the value for *e* for two given bodies changes to some extent.

Because this law indicates that how two bodies move after impact depends on how they were moving before impact and on a coefficient e, it is important to consider those factors on which the value of e depends. Probably the easiest way of doing this is to examine what happens in a very simple impact situation when various conditions are modified. Consider a ball that is dropped onto a fixed surface (for example, the floor). If the ball is called body 1 and the floor is body 2, the velocities of body 2 before and after the impact are both zero for all practical purposes. That is, $u_2 = v_2 = 0$. Equation (5-9) then reduces to:

$$\frac{v_1}{u_1} = -e \tag{5-10}$$

Because velocities are more difficult to measure than are distances, it is desirable to convert this form of the law into yet another form. This is done by considering the ball's motion before and after impact with the floor and by using the appropriate equation of uniformly accelerated motion (Eq. [3-10]) to arrive at expressions for v_1 and u_1. From Fig. 5-9 it can be seen that

$$u_1 = \sqrt{2gh_d} \tag{5-11}$$

and it can be shown similarly that

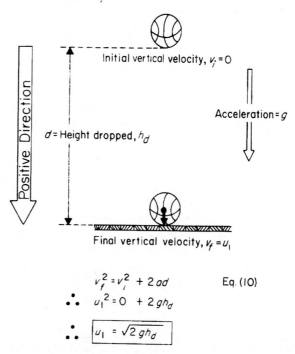

Figure 5-9 content:

Initial vertical velocity, $v_i = 0$

Acceleration $= g$

Positive Direction

$d =$ Height dropped, h_d

Final vertical velocity, $v_f = u_1$

$$v_f^2 = v_i^2 + 2ad \qquad \text{Eq. (10)}$$
$$\therefore \quad u_1^2 = 0 + 2gh_d$$
$$\therefore \quad \boxed{u_1 = \sqrt{2gh_d}}$$

Figure 5-9. Deriving an expression for the velocity at impact when a ball is dropped from a known height.

$$v_1 = \sqrt{2gh_b} \qquad\qquad (5\text{-}12)$$

where h_d and h_b are, respectively, the height from which the ball was dropped and the height to which it subsequently bounced. If these expressions are substituted in Eq. (5-10), this latter becomes

$$e = \sqrt{\frac{h_b}{h_d}} \qquad\qquad (5\text{-}13)$$

(*Note:* Because the velocity of the ball after impact is in the negative direction [Fig. 5-9], the negative value of the square root is taken in Eq. [5-12]).

Equation (5-13) suggests a way in which the factors that influence the value of e can be examined. If a ball is dropped from a known height and the height to which it bounces is noted, the value of e for that situation can easily be computed. If slight changes are made in the conditions (for example, using a different ball or a different landing surface), the effects that these changes have on the value of e can be noted. The results of two such experiments are shown in Tables 5-1 and 5-2. It is quite clear from these results that the nature of the two impacting bodies determines to a large extent what value e takes. It is also clear that it would be incorrect to refer to "the coefficient of restitution of a body," for this coefficient depends not just on one of the impacting bodies but on both of them.

Some years ago in major league baseball there was a brief flare-up between the Chicago White Sox and the Detroit Tigers over charges leveled by the Tigers that their opponents had been artificially cooling the balls used in a five-game series played in Chicago. The White Sox countercharged that the balls used the previous weekend in a four-game series in Detroit had been heated and dried out and that this had led to a 53-run scoring spree quite out of keeping with the total of 17 runs scored in

TABLE 5-1 The Coefficient of Restitution for Balls Dropped from a Height of 6 ft (1.83 m) onto a Hardwood Floor

Type of Ball	Height Bounced (m)	Coefficient of Restitution[a]
"Super ball"	1.44	0.89
Basketball	1.06	0.76
Soccer	1.05	0.76
Volleyball	1.01	0.74
Tennis—well worn	0.91	0.71
—new	0.81	0.67
Lacrosse	0.70	0.62
Field hockey	0.46	0.50
Softball	0.18	0.31
Cricket	0.18	0.31

[a] Values for the coefficient of restitution vary from 0.0 when the impact is said to be inelastic, because the bodies do not separate after the impact, to a never-attained limit of 1.0.

TABLE 5-2. The Coefficient of Restitution for a Volleyball Dropped from a Height of 6 ft (1.83 m) onto Various Surfaces

Type of Surface	Height Bounced (m)	Coefficient of Restitution
"Proturf"	1.05	0.76
Wood	1.03	0.75
"Uniturf"	1.03	0.75
Steel plating	1.02	0.75
Concrete	1.00	0.74
Tumbling mat (2.5 cm thick)	0.83	0.67
Gravel	0.67	0.61
Grass	0.34	0.43
Gymnastic landing mat (20 cm thick)	0.33	0.42

Chicago. Whether the temperature of the balls used in these matches was deliberately or accidentally changed may never be revealed. What is known, though, is that a ball will become more "lively" than usual if it is heated and less so if it is cooled. Baila,[2] a schoolboy who was especially interested in the White Sox–Tigers affair, has demonstrated these effects using the same simple ball-dropping experiment already described here (Table 5-3). The effect of changes in temperature is also well known to squash players, for whom the pregame warm-up serves to prepare the ball for the game (by getting it warm) as much as it does to prepare the players.

The extent to which this velocity before impact affects the value of e has been well demonstrated by Plagenhoef,[3] who reported values obtained when a number of balls were dropped from a height of 100 in. (2.54 m) onto a "firm, wood floor" and when the same balls were "kicked or thrown to obtain velocities between 50 and 60 mph" (22.4 and 26.8 m/s). In each case the value for e was less when the velocity before impact was between 50

TABLE 5-3. The Effect of Temperature Changes on the Coefficient of Restitution*

Type of Ball	Coefficients of Restitution (The height of the bounce when each ball was dropped from a height of 6 ft [1.83 m] is shown in parentheses)		
	Cooled (1 h in freezer)	Normal	Heated (15 min at 225°)
Baseball	0.50 (0.46 m)	0.53 (0.51 m)	0.55 (0.55 m)
Solid rubber ball	0.57 (0.59 m)	0.73 (0.98 m)	0.80 (1.17 m)
Golf ball	0.67 (0.82 m)	0.80 (1.17 m)	0.84 (1.29 m)
"Super ball"	0.91 (1.52 m)	0.91 (1.52 m)	0.95 (1.65 m)

* Adapted from data in D. L. Baila, (1966). "Project: Fast ball—Hot or cold?" *Science World*, September 16, pp. 10–11.

and 60 mph than when the ball was dropped from 100 in. (equivalent to a velocity before impact of approximately 0.3 mph [0.15 m/s]). The differences in the value of e ranged from 0.02 (0.6 to 0.58) for a golf ball to 0.3 (0.8 to 0.5) for a handball.

Direct and Oblique Impact. There are few examples in sports where two bodies collide with each other directly. That is, where they are either both moving along the same straight line immediately prior to impact or one of them is at rest and the other is moving along a line at right angles to the surface where contact occurs. Figure 5-10 shows a number of cases of this so-called *direct impact*.

Far more common in sport than direct impacts are those in which the two bodies do not collide directly or "head-on." This type of collision is called an *oblique impact*. A bounce pass in basketball is an example of an oblique impact, because before contacting the floor the ball travels at some

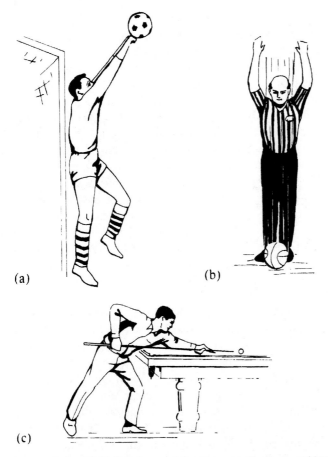

(a)

(b)

(c)

Figure 5-10. Examples of direct impact: (a) a soccer goalkeeper punching away a lobbed shot at goal; (b) a basketball official testing the bounce of the ball; and (c) the cue striking a ball in billiards or snooker.

angle to it other than a right angle. In short, the ball approaches the floor from an oblique angle. The same thing is true of a layup shot, because the ball is thrown or placed against the backboard at an oblique angle. Most of the shots played in racquet games (tennis, squash, etc.) also involve oblique impacts, for only rarely is the racquet moved to meet the ball along the same line the ball is traveling. This is partly because players of these games usually try to hit the ball away from their opponents and this means striking it obliquely so that it will not merely return in the same direction from which it came.

To analyze oblique impacts in some detail, it is convenient to consider them under two headings:

- oblique impact with a fixed surface (for example. a bounce pass in basketball);
- oblique impact with a moving body (for example, as in tennis when the racquet makes an oblique impact with the ball).

Oblique Impact with a Fixed Surface.   When a ball (or, any other body) strikes the floor (or any other fixed surface), it exerts forces on it. These forces can be resolved into components that act along the surface and components that act at right angles to the surface. If both the ball and the surface were smooth (that is, their coefficient of limiting friction was the impossible 0.0), the ball would not be able to exert force along the surface of the floor because it would not be able to "grip" the floor and "push" it in that direction. The floor, similarly, would not be able to exert any force against the ball in the opposite direction. There would be a total absence of friction between the two bodies. In this theoretical situation, the only forces that the ball could exert on the floor (and, of course, that the floor could exert on the ball in reaction) would be those that acted at right angles to the surface. In practice, and especially where a ball has had spin imparted to it, the effect of friction (that is, of the forces acting along the surface) can be quite pronounced indeed. These effects, which can be simply added to those produced by the forces acting at right angles to the surface, will be referred to later.

Figure 5-11 shows a squash ball bouncing on the floor in the course of a rally. The velocity it has at the instant it makes contact with the floor of the court is indicated by the vector u and its horizontal and vertical components by u_H and u_V, respectively. Now, because the ball and the floor are imagined to be perfectly smooth and there are thus no horizontal forces acting on either body, there are no forces that can alter the horizontal motion of the ball. The horizontal velocity after impact must therefore be the same as it was before impact, that is, $v_H = u_H$. The same is not true, however, of the vertical velocity, for both its direction and magnitude are changed as a result of the impact. In the first place, the force that the floor exerts on the ball causes the ball to reverse the direction of its vertical motion. Then, in addition, the elasticity of each of the bodies concerned (the ball and the

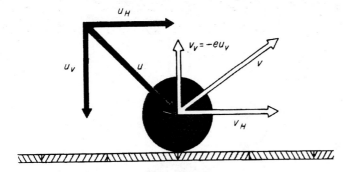

Figure 5-11. Velocity changes during an oblique impact.

floor) modifies the magnitude of the vertical velocity in accordance with Eq. (5-9):

$$\frac{v_V}{u_V} = -e$$

or
$$v_V = -eu_V$$

where v_V equals the vertical velocity of the ball immediately after impact.

The important thing about this relationship is that since e is always less than one, the right-hand side always has a value less than u_V. (*Note:* The negative sign on the right-hand side merely indicates that the direction of the motion has been reversed.) In other words, v_V, the vertical velocity after impact, is always less in magnitude than u_V, the vertical velocity before impact. How much less depends obviously on the value of e. In the case of squash balls the value of e, found by dropping a ball onto a wooden floor from a predetermined height, is about 0.6. Thus the vertical velocity after impact is approximately six-tenths of the vertical velocity before impact.

By combining the horizontal and vertical velocities, the resultant velocity after impact can be determined and its direction compared with that of the resultant velocity before impact. For this latter purpose, it is customary to define these two directions in terms of the angle that each makes with a line perpendicular to the surface at the point of contact (that is, the common normal). The angle that the direction of the velocity before impact makes with this perpendicular is called the *angle of incidence*, and the angle that the direction of the velocity after impact makes with it is called the *angle of reflection* (Fig. 5-12).

Because the horizontal velocities before and after impact are equal in magnitude, and the vertical velocity after impact is less in magnitude than that before impact, the angle of reflection is greater than the angle of incidence. It is important to note that this last statement applies only to oblique impact on a fixed surface, when the effects of friction are negligible or not considered. When frictional effects are taken into account, the relationship between the angles of incidence and reflection is modified in a

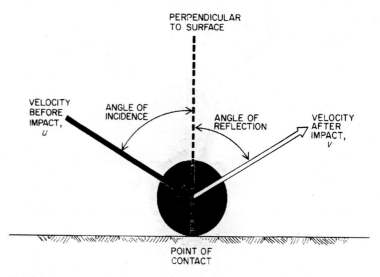

Figure 5-12. The angles of incidence and reflection in an oblique impact.

manner dependent entirely on the situation. Under such circumstances no blanket statement can be made concerning how these angles compare. Certainly the often-made statement that "the angle of incidence is equal to the angle of reflection," is utterly wrong except

- in that very rare situation where the effect of friction on the horizontal velocity exactly balances the effect of elasticity on the vertical velocity, and
- when there is a direct impact between two bodies and there is no friction involved.

In this latter case, which has limited practical significance, the angle of incidence (0°) exactly equals the angle of reflection (0°).

Possibly one of the best examples of how a knowledge of the relationship between angles of incidence and reflection influences success can be seen in the game of snooker. For instance, consider the situation represented in Fig. 5-13.

Here the player must hit the white cue ball W so that the first ball it hits is the red ball R. Directly in the path between these two is a ball C of some other color. To execute the shot successfully, the player clearly has to "bank" the cue ball off the cushion so that it passes around the ball C and hits the red. To do this, he must aim at a point on the cushion such that the angle of incidence so formed will lead to an angle of reflection consistent with the cue ball hitting the red. If he misjudges the point of contact, the cue ball will pass to either side of the red and he will incur a penalty. Fortunately for him, however, the width of the ball means that he can have the cue ball hit any of a number of points within a narrow range and still make subsequent contact with the red. He has, in short, some margin for error. But all this is quite negative, for by successfully executing the shot

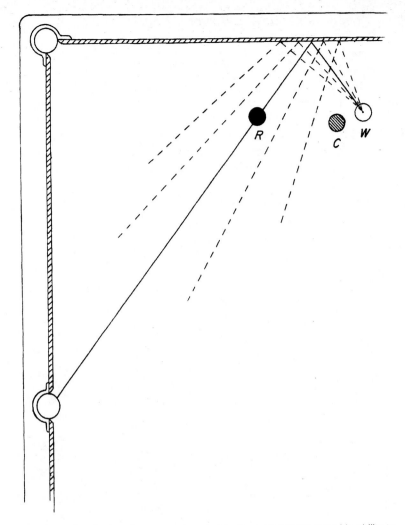

Figure 5-13. A player's success in snooker depends largely upon his ability to select an appropriate angle of incidence.

and having the cue ball hit the red, the player merely avoids being penalized. To make a more positive contribution to his total score he must endeavor to put the red into one of the six pockets around the table. If he decides to try to put the ball into the center pocket on the left-hand side in Fig. 5-12, the cue ball must contact the red in such a way that it will then follow the appropriate path. This means that the cue ball must strike the red at a precise point (or, at best, within a very narrow range of points), and this in turn reduces drastically the range of acceptable points of contact of the cue ball with the cushion. Clearly, then, the success of the snooker player hinges first on his ability to select the correct point of aim from his knowledge of the angles involved and then, of course, on his ability to execute the shot in a manner consistent with his intention.

Oblique Impact with Moving Bodies.   Undoubtedly the most involved cases of oblique impact between two bodies are those in which both bodies are moving or are free to move. All the cases of hitting, kicking, and heading fall within this category.

To determine what happens in these cases it is necessary to use the equation that defines the coefficient of restitution (Eq. [5-9]), another that expresses the conservation-of-momentum principle, and some basic trigonometry. The result is two rather involved equations for the speed and direction of a body after such impact. In Fig. 5-14, a baseball bat is shown at the moment it makes an oblique impact with a ball. The velocity vectors u_1 and u_2 represent the velocity of the ball and the bat, respectively. If the acute angle between these vectors is α, the respective masses of the two bodies are m_1 and m_2, and their mutual coefficient of restitution is e, the

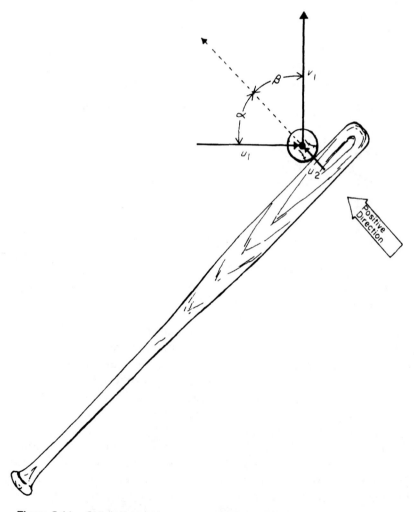

Figure 5-14.   Oblique impact between two bodies in motion.

speed and direction of the ball after impact are given by the following expressions:

$$v_1 = \sqrt{\left[\frac{m_2 u_2(1 + e) + u_1 \cos \alpha(em_2 - m_1)}{m_1 + m_2}\right]^2 + (u_1 \sin \alpha)^2} \quad (5\text{-}14)$$

$$\beta = \arctan\left[\frac{(u_1 \sin \alpha)(m_1 + m_2)}{m_2 u_2(1 + e) + u_1 \cos \alpha(em_2 - m_1)}\right] \quad (5\text{-}15)$$

(*Note:* For the sake of simplicity it has been assumed [1] that the bat behaves in the same manner as a sphere of equal mass and comparable elasticity; [2] that forces applied by the batter during the typically very short period of contact between the bat and ball have no effect on the outcome; [3] that there is no friction involved when the two bodies impact; and [4] that the velocity of that part of the bat that makes contact with the ball is in a direction at right angles to the surface of contact between bat and ball. The first two of these assumptions are the subject of ongoing research on such impacts in sports.[4,5,6])

Equations (5-14) and (5-15) are especially helpful if one is interested in analyzing what happens in a particular case. Suppose, for example, one wanted to analyze what happened in the case of the baseball bat striking a ball. First a set of values is chosen for each of six variables involved. Then five of the variables are kept constant while the value of the sixth is changed. The speed and direction of the ball after impact are calculated for each of a series of values of this sixth variable. This, in effect, amounts to saying, "If all else is equal, what happens to the speed and direction of the ball after impact, as such-and-such a value increases and decreases?" This process is repeated until each of the six variables has been varied while the other five remained constant. A summary of the sort of results that can be obtained from such an analysis is presented in Table 5-4. The initial values chosen in this example were

$$m_1 = 0.15 \text{ kg}$$
$$m_2 = 0.85 \text{ kg}$$
$$u_1 = 35 \text{ m/s}$$
$$u_2 = 15 \text{ m/s}$$
$$e = 0.5$$
$$\alpha = 30°$$

The results in Table 5-4 show what happens under these circumstances. For instance, they show that if all else is equal, the speed of the ball after impact can be increased by:

- increasing the mass of the bat,
- decreasing the mass of the ball,

TABLE 5-4 Speed and Angle of Reflection of a Baseball Following Oblique Impact with a Bat

Quantity Varied		Speed of Ball after Impact (m/s)	Angle of Reflection (deg)
Mass of bat (kg) (weight in ounces in parentheses)	0.57 (20)	34.6	36.7
	0.71(25)	35.7	34.2
	0.85 (30)	36.5	32.5
	0.99 (35)	37.1	31.4
	1.13 (40)	37.6	30.5
Mass of ball (kg) (weight in ounces in parentheses)	0.09 (3)	38.3	29.3
	0.12 (4)	37.3	30.9
	0.15 (5)	36.5	32.5
	0.18 (6)	35.7	34.2
	0.21 (7)	34.9	35.9
Velocity of bat (m/s)	5	26.0	50.0
	10	31.0	39.7
	15	36.5	32.5
	20	42.2	27.4
	25	48.1	23.5
Velocity of ball (m/s)	15	25.8	18.3
	25	31.0	26.5
	35	36.5	32.5
	45	42.2	37.0
	55	48.0	40.5
Angle of incidence (deg)	0	34.0	0.0
	10	34.3	12.0
	20	35.2	23.0
	30	36.5	32.5
	40	37.9	40.3
	50	39.3	46.7
	60	40.3	51.7
Coefficient of restitution	0.3	29.9	41.5
	0.4	33.1	36.6
	0.5	36.5	32.5
	0.6	39.9	29.2
	0.7	43.4	26.5

- increasing the initial velocity of the bat,
- increasing the initial velocity of the ball,
- increasing the angle of incidence, or
- increasing the value of the coefficient of restitution.

These results have clear-cut implications for hitters who wish to improve their ability to hit the ball "out of the park." They indicate that to achieve this objective a hitter should use a more massive bat, pick a ball that is moving at a high velocity, and swing the bat harder so that it has a greater velocity at the moment of impact. (*Note:* It is assumed that the mass of the ball and the coefficient of restitution are both effectively beyond the control of the batter and thus of little practical significance. In addition, the idea of increasing the speed of the ball after impact by delaying the swing and thus increasing the angle of incidence would appear to have relatively little to recommend it. If the bat were brought into contact with the ball early in the swing, it would almost certainly be at the expense of a considerable reduction in the velocity of the bat. This, of course, would tend to negate any advantage to be derived from increasing the angle of incidence. Furthermore, even in the unlikely event that the velocity were not reduced, an increase in the angle of reflection would also increase the possibility that the ball would end its flight in foul territory.)

Spin and Friction. The previous discussion of direct and oblique impact has assumed that no friction has been involved. In point of fact, however, friction plays an important part whenever two bodies collide with each other. Consider a table tennis ball bouncing on a table. When it strikes the table, it has a tendency to keep moving at the same speed and in the same direction as it was immediately before impact (Newton's first law). Because of this tendency the ball exerts a force on the table in that direction. In reaction the table exerts an equal and opposite force on the ball (Newton's third law). The effects produced by the vertical component of that reaction force were considered in a previous section. The horizontal, or frictional, component opposes the horizontal motion of the ball and causes a reduction in its horizontal velocity. In addition to this (and for reasons that will be discussed in the next chapter) the friction tends to impart some spin to the ball.

If the ball is spinning at the moment it makes contact with the table, the magnitude of the friction is modified according to the rate and direction of that spin. As a direct consequence, the speed and direction of the ball after impact are also modified. The table tennis player in Fig. 5-15 is driving the ball back into the opponent's court. To do this he swings his bat in a forward and upward direction across the line of flight of the ball so that when his bat makes contact with the ball, it not only sends it back toward the other end of the table but also imparts a large amount of spin to it. This spin, which results from the back of the ball (that is, the part in contact with the bat) being lifted upward and forward during the stroke, is known as *topspin*. Viewed from the same position as taken by the artist who drew Fig. 5-15, a ball with topspin appears to be rotating in a clockwise direction. (It is sometimes not realized that the direction in which a body appears to be rotating depends on the position of the observer. Had the artist taken up his position on the other side of the table, the same topspin drive would have appeared to lead to a counterclockwise rotation of the ball.) When the ball subsequently strikes the table, it has both linear and angular motions—a linear motion along its direction of travel and an angular motion about an axis through the center of the ball.

Consider the part of the ball that makes contact with the surface of the

Figure 5-15. A forehand topspin drive in table tennis. The application of topspin to the ball ensures that it will come off the table fast and at a low angle and thus be difficult to return.

table. As a result of its linear motion this part of the ball, like all its other parts, has a forward velocity in the horizontal direction. In addition it has a horizontal velocity in the backward direction, due to its angular motion. (With a ball that has had topspin imparted to it, the part of the ball that is lowermost at any instant is traveling directly backward, relative to the center of the ball. At the same time each of the other parts is momentarily traveling in some other direction—Fig. 5-16) It is the resultant of these two velocities that indicates what horizontal velocity that part of the ball has as

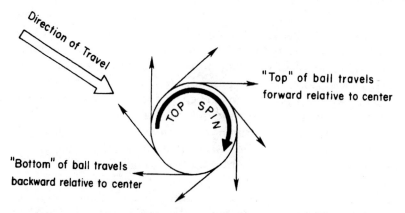

Figure 5-16. Points on the surface of a spinning ball move with different velocities relative to the center of the ball.

it strikes the table. This in turn determines the direction in which the friction that the table exerts on the ball will act and, to a large extent, how the ball will move after impact. If the backward horizontal velocity due to the ball's spin is greater than the forward horizontal velocity due to its linear motion, the friction acts in a forward direction. Under these conditions, friction acts not to decrease the horizontal velocity but rather to increase it. The ball, in fact, comes off the table with a greater horizontal velocity than it possessed when it hit the table. Because the horizontal velocity has been increased (and the vertical motion unaltered) by the spin, the angle of reflection is also greater than it would have been had no spin been imparted to the ball. These effects are well known to table tennis players, who deliberately apply heavy topspin with their offensive strokes so that the ball will come off the table fast and at a low angle and thus be difficult to return.

The previous analysis can be similarly applied when the spin of the ball is in other directions. A defensive chop in table tennis is executed by bringing the bat downward and forward across the path of the ball. This imparts a *backspin* (that is, a rotation in exactly the reverse direction to topspin) to the ball, which on landing tends to make the ball slow down (as increased friction opposes its horizontal motion) and to decrease the angle of reflection. Because a ball hit like this travels forward comparatively slowly after impact with the table, this type of backspin stroke is a very effective one from a defensive standpoint, for the ball cannot now be hit back with as great a speed as if it had been traveling faster. (See similar example of hitting in baseball, pp. 90-93.) In some sports (notably tennis, table tennis, and cricket) a *sidespin* is imparted to the ball and this, for the very same reasons just outlined, causes the ball to change its motion in a lateral direction as a result of impact with the playing surface. In such cases, the ball is said to "kick" or "break" to one side or the other.

PRESSURE

When the girl in Fig. 5-17 stands erect, her body weight of 600 N is supported on the soles of her feet, an area of some 0.02 m². If she lies down, her body weight is still 600 N, but the area over which this weight is supported is increased to 0.12 m². If the force exerted on a body (the ground-reaction force equal to the girl's weight, in this example) is divided by the area involved, the average *pressure* or force per unit area is obtained. Thus, when the girl is standing,

$$\text{Pressure} = \frac{\text{force}}{\text{area}} \qquad (5\text{-}16)$$

$$= \frac{600 \text{ N}}{0.02 \text{ m}^2}$$

$$= 30,000 \text{ N/m}^2 \text{ (or } Pascals\text{)}$$

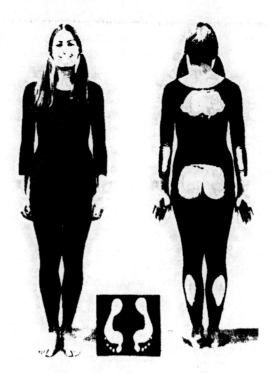

Figure 5-17. The average pressure on a supporting surface varies with the area of the surface involved. When the girl stands erect, the soles of her feet (see inset) support her weight and the average pressure is relatively large because the area involved is small. When she lies on her back, the area of the supporting surface (shown in white in the right-hand photograph) is markedly increased and the average pressure is correspondingly reduced.

and when she is lying,

$$= \frac{600 \text{ N}}{0.12 \text{ m}^2}$$

$$= 5000 \text{ Pa}$$

where Pa is the standard abbreviation for Pascals.

This concept of pressure is of particular importance with respect to safety measures in sports, and failure on the part of athletes to minimize the pressure that any one part of their bodies must withstand can lead to serious injuries. In parachuting, performers frequently find it necessary to spread the forces that their bodies must withstand over a large area by initiating a rolling action as soon as they contact the ground. Failure to execute this technique correctly has been known to result in fractures of one or both legs. High jumpers and pole vaulters similarly spread the forces involved when they land flat on their backs on a soft landing pad. In the days when dirt and sand pits were used for these events, the forces exerted on the jumper at landing were so great that if the weaker parts of the body had been called upon to withstand their share, serious injury would certainly have resulted. Landing on the back was thus rarely seen. Instead, athletes in these events generally tried to land on their feet and to cushion the shock as best they could by dropping onto other parts of the body as soon as they landed. Exponents of judo are another group for whom the concept of spreading force over a large area is of fundamental importance. This is readily apparent in the considerable emphasis placed on use of the correct techniques of falling in the early stages of learning the sport and, in fact, at all levels at which the sport is practiced. The same basic concept is used in most of those sports where athletes wear special protective clothing. Such clothing serves to spread the force over a large area in cases where athletes cannot do this effectively by moving their bodies. In baseball, for instance, a batter hit on the head by the ball has no way of effectively spreading the force by moving his body. However he can wear a helmet which transmits the force over a large area via the suspension system inside it. The same thing is the basis for the use of protective helmets in football and motorcycling; for the wearing of gloves in baseball, cricket, and boxing; and for other similar items of equipment in football (various joint pads), baseball (face masks, chest protectors, etc.), and other sports.

WORK

Many words used in everyday language take on much more precise meanings when used in science. One such word is *work*. In everyday usage, work is anything in which physical or mental effort is used to achieve some goal. In biomechanics, the term *work* has a much more limited meaning:

The work done on a body by a force is equal to the product of its magnitude and the distance that the body moves in the direction of the force, while the force is being applied to it.

Expressed in algebraic form,

$$W = Fd \qquad (5\text{-}17)$$

where W = the work done by the force, F = the magnitude of the force, and d = the appropriate distance.

Consider a weight lifter performing a two-hand snatch—a lift in which a barbell is raised overhead in one continuous movement. If he exerts a constant upward force of 1800 N against the barbell, while lifting it the first 0.5 m from the floor, the work done by the upward force during this portion of the lift is:

$$W = 1800 \text{ N} \times 0.5 \text{ m}$$
$$= 900 \text{ N} \cdot \text{m (or } \textit{Joules)}$$

If the force acts in the same direction as the body moves, the work done by the force is said to be *positive work*. If the force acts in the opposite direction to that in which the body moves, the work done by the force is *negative work*. Thus in the example of the weight lifter the work done by the upward force is positive and the work done by gravity (the weight of the barbell, say, 1400 N) is negative; that is,

$$W = -(1400 \times 0.5)$$
$$= -700 \text{ J}$$

where J is the standard abbreviation for Joules. The total work is the sum of these two (that is, 200 J) and is equal to the work done by the resultant of the two forces:

$$W = (1800 - 1400) \times 0.5$$
$$= 200 \text{ J}$$

When a person does a pull-up on a horizontal bar, the muscles of the arms and shoulders provide a vertical force that lifts the body. Because the direction in which the body moves is the same as that in which the resultant muscle force acts, these muscles are said to do positive work. When the person then lowers the body, these same muscles exert an upward force to help control the descent. (In the absence of this force, the body would plummet and the person would feel a very abrupt jerk when the arms became fully straight.) During the descent these muscles are said to do negative work.

POWER

In computing the work done by a force, no account is taken of the length of time that is involved in getting the work done. Thus, if a weight lifter does, say, 1500 J of work in raising a barbell overhead, the amount of work is in no way dependent on how long he (or she) took to perform the feat. Whether the lift took 0.5 s, 1 s, or even 2 s, the amount of work done is still 1500 J. What does change though is the *power*, or the rate at which the work is performed. To arrive at this value, the work done is divided by the time taken:

$$P = \frac{W}{t} \tag{5-18}$$

where P = the power developed, W = the work done, and t = the time taken. Thus, although the work done in the previous example is constant throughout, the power developed changes as follows:

Time (s)	Work (J)	Power (J/s or Watts)
0.5	1500	3000
1.0	1500	1500
2.0	1500	750

The term *energy* is another that is widely used outside technical discussions. This usage, though, is not as frequently at variance with the technical definition of the word as is the case with work. Energy formally defined is "the capacity to do work" and thus, when people say they have no energy or, alternatively, that they are bursting with energy, they could reasonably be interpreted as meaning they had either no capacity for work or a great capacity to do work.

It is customary to refer to the three types of energy that are of greatest interest in biomechanics as types of *mechanical energy*. These three types are those in which bodies have energy by virtue of their motion, their position, and their state of deformation.

Kinetic Energy. The energy that a body has because it is moving is known as its *kinetic energy*. The amount of kinetic energy that a body possesses is given by the equation:

$$E_k = \tfrac{1}{2}mv^2 \tag{5-19}$$

where E_k = the kinetic energy, m = the mass of the body, and v = the velocity at which it is moving.* Thus, a skier who has a mass of 70 kg and who is traveling at a velocity of 25 m/s has a kinetic energy of 21,875 $kg \cdot (m/s)^2$:

$$E_k = \tfrac{1}{2} \times 70 \text{ kg} \times 25 \text{ m/s} \times 25 \text{ m/s}$$
$$= 21{,}875 \text{ kg} \cdot (m/s)^2$$

The unit of kinetic energy given here derives logically from considering the units used to measure the various quantities on the right-hand side of Eq. (5-19). It is, however, a rather clumsily worded unit and for this reason is rarely, if ever, used. Instead, because energy is "the capacity to do work" and this latter quantity is measured in Joules, it is convenient to use the same unit in measuring all three kinds of mechanical energy. This change in the unit used is greatly helped by the fact that

$$1 \text{ kg} \cdot (m/s)^2 = 1 \text{ N} \cdot m$$
$$= 1 \text{ J}$$

Therefore, whenever the kinetic energy of a body is being computed, and the mass is expressed in kilograms and the velocity in meters per second, the answer can be taken to be in Joules.

---

* Strictly speaking, the kinetic energy defined by Eq. (5-19) is the *kinetic energy of translation*— that is, the kinetic energy that a body possesses because of its linear (or translatory) motion. Because the human body usually experiences linear and angular motions simultaneously, it is convenient to consider the mass of the body to be concentrated at a central point—the center of gravity, pp. 126–143—and to compute the kinetic energy of translation of the body with reference to this point.

The energy that a body possesses because of its angular (or rotary) motion is known as its *kinetic energy of rotation* and is computed using an equation very similar to Eq. (5-19). For the sake of simplicity, the kinetic energy of rotation is disregarded in the following discussion.

Potential Energy. A trampolinist at the peak of his flight has the capacity to do work because of his position relative to the surface of the earth. When he falls back toward the trampoline bed, his weight does work "equal to the product of its magnitude and the distance that the body moves in the direction of the force." The energy due to the position that a body occupies relative to the earth's surface is called *potential energy* and can be determined by multiplying the weight of the body (the force) by its height above the surface (the distance):

$$E_p = Wh \qquad (5\text{-}20)$$

where E_P = the potential energy, W = the weight of the body, and h = its height above the ground.

If the trampolinist is performing on a pit (or ground level) trampoline and is, say, 700 N in weight and 3 m above the bed at the peak of his flight, his potential energy at this time is

$$E_p = 700 \times 3$$
$$= 2100 \text{ J}$$

Unless he also has some horizontal velocity at this instant (and, in general, only poor trampolinists do!), his velocity and kinetic energy are both zero. As the trampolinist falls back toward the bed, the potential energy he possessed at the peak of his flight is gradually reduced. After he has fallen 0.5 m it is 1750 J (that is, 700×2.5 J); after 1 m, it is 1400 J (700×2 J); and so on until finally he reaches the bed of the trampoline with no potential energy at all. During this process, however, his body is being accelerated toward the bed by gravity and, as it gets progressively faster, it acquires more and more kinetic energy. If the appropriate equations are used (Eq. [3-10] and [5-19]), it can be computed that after he has fallen 0.5 m, his kinetic energy is 350 J; after 1 m, it is 700 J; and so on until, at the moment he reaches the bed, it is no less than 2100 J. Addition of the kinetic energy and potential energy at each of these heights in turn reveals that this sum is constant and equal to 2100 J:

At 3.0 m: E_k = 0 J E_p = 2100 J Sum = 2100 J
At 2.5 m: E_k = 350 J E_p = 1750 J Sum = 2100 J
At 2.0 m: E_k = 700 J E_p = 1400 J Sum = 2100 J

At 0.5 m: E_k = 1750 J E_p = 350 J Sum = 2100 J
At 0.0 m: E_k = 2100 J E_p = 0 J Sum = 2100 J

If the trampolinist's ascent, from takeoff to peak of flight, were similarly analyzed, exactly the reverse process could be observed. At takeoff his kinetic energy is 2100 J and his potential energy is zero and, as he rises, this kinetic energy is gradually transformed into potential energy until at the peak of his flight he has 2100 J of potential energy and no kinetic energy. Again, as in the case of the descent, the sum of the kinetic and potential energies throughout the ascent is a constant 2100 J.

These characteristic changes in kinetic and potential energies during the performance of a stunt on the trampoline have been well demonstrated in a study by Baker[7] (Fig. 5-18). The following points should be noted:

- In the airborne phases the kinetic energy decreases and the potential energy increases during the ascent, and the reverse process occurs during the descent.
- The sum of the kinetic and potential energies has some constant value during each of the airborne phases.
- The gymnast retains some potential energy on landing because he is performing on a trampoline bed that is some distance above ground level. Differences in the value of this potential energy as he makes each of his three landings depend on his body position.

A little thought on the matter suggests that the changes in kinetic and potential energies experienced by a trampolinist must also be experienced by any body that becomes airborne, and confirmation of this is contained in the *law of conservation of mechanical energy*, which, for present purposes, may be stated as

When gravity is the only external force acting on it, the mechanical energy of a body is constant.

Thus, when a body is in flight (and the effects of air resistance are small enough to be ignored), the sum of the body's kinetic and potential energies is constant.

Work-Energy Relationship. There is an important relationship among work, kinetic energy, and potential energy that has several useful applications in the analysis of sports techniques. Consider an arrow about to be fired horizontally from a bow and assume that a constant horizontal force is exerted on the arrow from the moment the archer releases it until it loses contact with the string. (This means, of course, that it experiences a constant horizontal acceleration during this period—Newton's second law.) Immediately before the bowstring is released, the arrow is at rest and therefore possesses no kinetic energy. Then, when the archer releases the bowstring, work is done on the arrow until it loses contact with the string, by which time it has come to possess a certain amount of kinetic energy. Looking at this process in some detail (Fig. 5-19) it can be seen that the constant horizontal acceleration of the arrow is $v_f^2/2d$. Substituting this term into the equation of Newton's second law [Eq. (5-3)] yields:

$$F = \frac{mv^2_f}{2d}$$

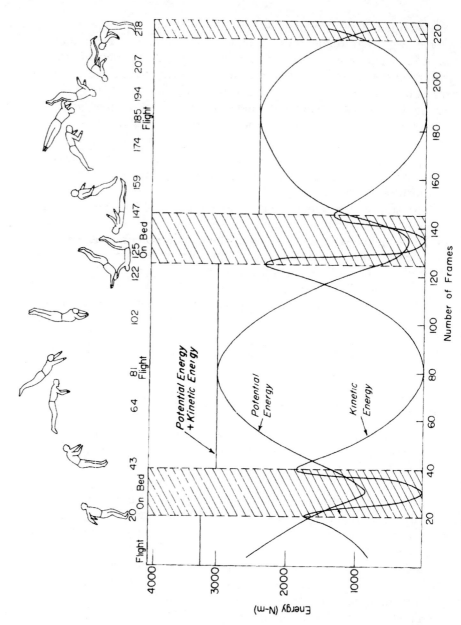

Figure 5-18. Mechanical energy changes during the execution of a trampoline stunt.

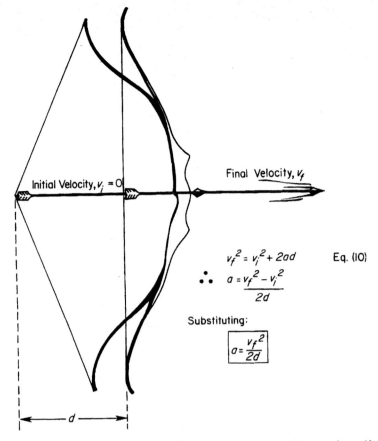

Initial Velocity, $v_i = 0$

Final Velocity, v_f

$$v_f^2 = v_i^2 + 2ad \qquad \text{Eq. (10)}$$

$$\therefore \quad a = \frac{v_f^2 - v_i^2}{2d}$$

Substituting:

$$a = \frac{v_f^2}{2d}$$

Figure 5-19. Deriving an expression for the average acceleration experienced by an arrow as it leaves the bow.

where F = the horizontal force exerted on the arrow. If this equation is rearranged:

$$Fd = \tfrac{1}{2}mv^2_f \qquad (5\text{-}21)$$

the left-hand side is equal to the work done on the arrow by the bowstring, and the right-hand side is the kinetic energy that the arrow possesses as it leaves the bow. In other words, as it leaves the bow, the arrow possesses kinetic energy equal to the amount of work that has been done on it.

The process outlined here is essentially reversed during the final stages of the arrow's motion, when the arrow hits the target and gives up all the kinetic energy that it possessed just before impact. A small amount of this energy is converted into nonmechanical forms such as sound energy (reflected in the noise made as the arrow hits the target) and heat energy (generated by the friction as the arrow and the material of the target rub against each other). The arrow gives up the remaining kinetic energy to do an equal amount of work on the target. This last fact has important implications in such activities as catching and landing.

When a ball is being caught, the kinetic energy of the ball is used to do work on the hands of the person who catches it. Now, the ball can do work equivalent to the kinetic energy either by exerting a large force against the hands as they move over a small distance or by exerting a smaller force as the hands move over a greater distance. For example, if a ball does 40 J of work against a person's hands, the force exerted is 400 N if the hands move 0.1 m:

$$W = Fd$$

$$F = \frac{W}{d}$$

$$= \frac{40}{0.1}$$

$$= 400N$$

and only 80 N if the hands move 0.5 m:

$$F = \frac{40}{0.5}$$

$$= 80 \text{ N}$$

It is for this reason that skilled catchers allow their hands to move (or "give") with the ball as they catch it, for they know that otherwise the force that the ball exerts on the hands may be sufficient to cause them to fumble the catch and perhaps even to injure their hands. (*Note*: The preceding discussion assumes, for the sake of simplicity, that the person catching the ball exerts a constant force on it until it has been brought to rest.)

The sport of boxing provides another example in the fighter with a so-called "glass jaw," a man who is especially vulnerable to a punch to this part of his anatomy. This condition probably stems from a lack of mobility in the boxer's neck, which does not allow his head to travel or "ride" with a punch so that the force of the blow can be reduced to a tolerable level. If such a lack of mobility does not allow him to do this effectively, the force of each of the blows he receives is correspondingly increased, and under such circumstances it is little wonder that he soon earns a reputation for being easy to knock out.

To date, this discussion has been confined to changes in the kinetic energy of a body as work is done on or by that body. However, changes in potential energy must also be taken into account, if the body experiences changes in its elevation as well as changes in its velocity.

Consider again the bow and arrow of Fig. 5-18, and imagine the arrow directed vertically upward rather than horizontally. Assume too that a constant vertical force is exerted on the arrow from the instant the archer releases it until the instant it leaves the bowstring. If the speed at which the arrow leaves the bowstring is v_f, the acceleration of the arrow during the period that the bowstring is applying force to it is $v^{2f}/2d$, as before. The force exerted on the arrow during the same period is equal to $F - W$, where F is the upward vertical force exerted via the bowstring and W is the weight of the arrow. (For simplicity, air resistance and the friction due to the passage of the arrow across the bow and the archer's hand are ignored.) If these values are now substituted into Eq. (5-3):

$$F - W = \frac{mv^2_f}{2d}$$

and rearranged,

$$(F - W)d = \tfrac{1}{2}mv^2_f \qquad\qquad (5\text{-}22)$$
$$Fd = \tfrac{1}{2}mv^2f + Wd$$

it can be seen that the work done by the bowstring is equal to the sum of the changes in kinetic and potential energy that result. (This is the so-called *work-energy relationship*.) Thus, for example, if a 600 N basketball player raised her body 30 cm and acquired a velocity of 3.5 m/s by the time she left the ground in a center jump, the work done by the muscles producing this motion could be computed as follows:

$$\text{Work} = (\tfrac{1}{2} \times \frac{600}{9.81} \times 3.5^2) + (600 \times 0.3)$$
$$= 374.6 + 180$$
$$= 554.6 \text{ J}$$

Similarly, the work done by a weight lifter in raising a 1000 N barbell a distance of 2 m to a stationary position overhead (that is, $v_f = 0$) can be computed using Eq. (5-22):

$$\text{Work done by lifter on barbell} = (\tfrac{1}{2} \times \frac{1000}{9.81} \times 0) + (1000 \times 2)$$
$$= 0 + 2000$$
$$= 2000 \text{ J}$$

If the athlete himself weighs 800 N and raises his body 0.7 m in the course of getting the barbell aloft, the total work done by the lifter is

$$\text{Work done on barbell} + \text{work done on lifter} = 2000 + 560$$
$$= 2560 \text{ J}$$

Strain Energy. Whenever a body has the capacity to do work because it has been deformed and has a tendency to return to its original shape, it is said to possess *strain energy*. A fully drawn bow has the capacity to do work by virtue of the deformation it has undergone. This capacity is clearly apparent when the bowstring is released and the bow does work on the arrow. At this point the strain energy (or at least a large part of it) possessed by the bow is used to give kinetic energy to the arrow. When a trampoline bed is depressed by a gymnast landing on it, it possesses a certain amount of strain energy as a result of the deformation that it undergoes. Then, as it returns to its normal state, it does work on the gymnast, causing him to gain both kinetic and potential energy. A vaulter using a fiberglass pole puts a deep bend in it as a result of the work he does in the early stages of the vault. The strain energy that the pole then possesses enables it to do work on the athlete as it straightens later in the vault. In a well-executed vault this work done by the pole is clearly evident in the marked upward surge that the vaulter experiences as the pole recoils.

Exercises

1. For the purpose of analyzing techniques used in a game of pool, the player's cue, the balls on the table, and the table itself are defined as the system of interest. Identify three internal and three external forces that you might expect to be exerted in the course of the player executing a shot. In doing this, make sure you identify both the body that exerts the force and the body upon which the force is exerted. For example, you might say "The force exerted by the _____ on the _____ "

2. (a) An adventurer who climbs high mountains and explores deep caves stands on a high mountain top in Mexico. Does he weigh more, the same as, or less than he would if he were standing at the South Pole?

   (b) Tired of the view for the mountain top, he travels to the South Pole where—believe it or not!—he discovers a cave that goes deep below the Earth's surface. When standing at the bottom of this cave, does he have more, the same, or less mass than he had when he was standing atop the mountain in Mexico?

   (c) While at the bottom of the cave, the dope drops his flashlight. Ignoring air resistance, will it fall with an acceleration of < 9.81 m/s^2, 9.81 m/s^2, or > 9.81 m/s^2?

3. (a) A two-man bobsled weighs 2000 N. At the start of a race, the two men push the sled as hard as they can. If the resultant horizontal force (that is, the forward horizontal force exerted by the men minus the backward horizontal force exerted by the track against the runners of the sled) at a given instant is 1500 N, what is the instantaneous acceleration of the sled? (Ignore any effect that gravity and air resistance might have when making your calculation.)

   (b) After the men have pushed the sled over a set number of strides, the driver jumps into the sled. This decreases the horizontal pushing force by about half, increases the mass of the system being pushed (now sled-plus-driver), and increases the friction between the track and the runners of the sled. Again ignoring any effect that gravity and air resistance might have, what would you expect to happen to the acceleration of the sled? What would you expect to happen to it when the second man (the brakeman) jumps into the sled a short time later?

(c) If the gradient of the track is 10 percent—that is, the track descends 1 m for every 10 m of horizontal travel—part of the weight of the sled and the men in it acts to accelerate the sled down the slope. If the men together weigh 1825 N, what would be the down-the-slope component of the weight of the sled-plus-men? What would be the acceleration down the slope if this were the only force acting on the sled?

4. Locate a set of needle-type (or analog) bathroom scales. Assume an erect-standing position on the platform of the scales and have a friend record the weight shown. With this friend kneeling beside the dial of the scales so that he (or she) can see clearly what happens, suddenly relax the muscles of your legs and let your body drop for a short distance. If you do this right, the needle will rapidly swing to a lower reading and then just as rapidly swing back in the opposite direction to a value well above the reading recorded initially. Then, finally, as you come to a complete stop with your legs partly flexed, the needle will oscillate back and forth—because you so violently set it vibrating—and eventually settle at the weight you recorded initially.

(a) What two vertical forces are acting on your body when you are initially standing on the scales?

(b) What is the magnitude of the resultant of these two forces when you are standing on the scales?

(c) What is your vertical acceleration when you are standing on the scales?

(d) In what direction is your vertical acceleration when you initiate the dropping action?

(e) In what direction does the resultant of the two forces act when you initiate the dropping motion—upward or downward?

(f) Do the changes in the reading on the scale indicate that your weight changes during the course of the exercise you were asked to perform? Do you lose weight as you descend and then get it back again later?

(g) How do you explain the down-up-down sequence in the readings on the scale when you perform a down-and-stop motion?

5. As a skier goes into a turn, he briefly relaxes the extensor muscles of his hip and knee joints and allows his body to accelerate vertically downward for an instant. What effect does this motion—known as *down-unweighting*—have on the force holding the skis against the snow? What effect does it have, therefore, on the friction forces that the snow exerts on the skis? What effect does it have, therefore, on the skier's ability to turn his skis?

6. There is another movement sequence used in making a turn in skiing known as *up-unweighting*. In this maneuver, the skier vigorously extends his hip and knee joints over a short distance. Explain what you would expect to happen if you did this maneuver on a set of bathroom scales and then explain why such a maneuver might be useful in executing a ski turn.

7. A girl performs a sit up on an inclined board. To do this without slipping down the board, she hooks her feet under a bar near the upper end of the board. This bar then lies across the instep of each foot. In what direction do the forces that her feet exert on the bar act? Use some combination of the terms *upward*, *downward* (for directions along the line of the board), and *into* and *out of* (for directions perpendicular to the surface of the board) to describe the direction of these forces. In what direction do the forces that the bar exerts on her feet act? (*Hint:* If you have doubts about the answer to these questions, you might like to find an inclined exercise board and try performing a situp on it.)

8. Figure 5-20 shows competitors in a sawing contest at the World Lumberjack Championships held annually in Hayward, Wisconsin. Make a sketch of the saw being used and superimpose on it vectors indicating all of the forces exerted upon it. In other words, make a free-body diagram of the saw. What purpose do you think is being served by the wedge pushed into the top of the cut and by the oil can being used by the man sitting on the log?

9. Cross-country and alpine skiers apply wax to the soles (or undersurfaces) of their skis. Why do they do this? Alpine skiers use skis with steel edges. Why? In the case of the alpine skiers, is the application of wax and the use of steel-edged skis consistent, or do these two things effectively contradict each other?

10. In the sport of curling, a heavy round "stone" with a gooseneck handle is slid along the ice towards a target 36.6 m away. In some cases, one or more of the players on the same team as the person who delivered the stone use hard whisk brooms to sweep vigorously across the path of the oncoming stone. Why do they do this?

11. A croquet player hits a ball with her mallet. The ball leaves the head of the mallet traveling at a speed of 2 m/s. It then rolls across the lawn towards the intended target. Name all of the external forces that act on it as it rolls across the lawn. If there were no horizontal forces acting on the ball as it rolled, what would its speed be 0.5 s later? 1.0 s later? 1.5 s later?

12. The game of lawn bowls is played on a large, flat, well-manicured grass green. The objective of the game is to roll your bowls down the green so that they are closer to a small white ball (called the jack) than are the bowls of your opponent. If your opponent manages to get his bowls tightly clustered around the jack, your only hope of saving the situation may be to send your last bowl down very

Figure 5-20. Competitors in a sawing contest.

hard and knock the jack off the green. This thoroughly legal tactic is called killing the end.

   (a) If a bowl weighing 15.6 N and traveling at 2.5 m/s strikes a jack weighing 2.3 N and transfers all of its momentum to the jack, which was stationary before the ball hit it, what speed will the jack have when it breaks contact with the bowl?

   (b) What momentum would the combined bowl-plus-jack have had when they were briefly moving together?

   (c) At what speed will the bowl be traveling immediately after the bowl and jack separate?

13. (a) The U.S. Tennis Association rules state that "the ball shall have a bound of more than 135 cm and less than 147 cm when dropped 254 cm upon a concrete base." What are the maximum and minimum acceptable values of the coefficient of restitution according to this rule?

   (b) Locate the rule book for some other ball game and see what limits are placed on the coefficient of restitution in that case.

   (c) Can you find any ball game for which there is no rule governing the elasticity of the ball?

14. Two billiard balls roll toward each other along the same straight line, collide, and separate. The velocities of the balls immediately before impact are 4 m/s and −8 m/s; and immediately after impact are −5 m/s and 4 m/s, respectively. What is the coefficient of restitution for the impact between the two balls?

15. A raquetball strikes the floor traveling at an angle of 50° to the vertical and leaves the floor traveling at an angle of 30° to the horizontal. What are the angles of incidence and reflection? And (much tougher question), if the floor is very smooth and the effects of friction are so small that they can be ignored, what is the coefficient of restitution for the ball-floor impact?

16. Can you name five factors that influence the speed and direction (angle of reflection) at which a football leaves a punter's foot, without looking back at the text?

17. A basketball player performs a layup shot in which he places the ball against the backboard using an underhand motion. In other word, he performs what is often called a finger roll. In the course of this, he imparts a certain amount of topspin to the ball. Is the vertical velocity that the ball has after impact with the board—that is, the velocity parallel to the surface of the board—more than, the same as, or less than it would have been if no spin had been imparted to the ball?

18. Two identical tennis balls are hit so that they leave their respective tennis rackets at the same heights, speeds, and angles of release. One is hit with topspin, and the other with no spin. They land on identical court surfaces. Which has the greater downward vertical velocity at impact with the court? Which has the greater horizontal velocity after impact with the court? Which ball has the greater angle of reflection? Which rises to the greater height during the bounce? Which attains its peak height farther from the point at which it bounced? (Ignore air resistance when answering these questions.)

19. (a) At the instant she lands on the end of the board following her hurdle step, a diver who weights 540 N has a downward vertical velocity of 3.2 m/s. At the instant of takeoff from the board, she has an upward vertical velocity of 4.4 m/s. Assuming that her body positions at touchdown and takeoff are

identical, and ignoring any horizontal velocity she may have, how much did her kinetic energy change while she was in contact with the board? How much did her potential energy change while she was on the board? What was the total change in her kinetic-plus-potential energy?: How much work did she do against the board during the takeoff? How much work did the board do against her? (*Note:* Work is not a vector quantity.)

(b) Assuming that there was no loss in mechanical energy to other forms of energy (heat, sound, etc.) during the takeoff, how much strain energy was invested in the board when the board and the diver were momentarily at rest, with the diver 1 m lower than she had been at touchdown on the board?

Recommended Readings

BRANCAZIO, P. J. (1984). *Sport Science: Physical Laws and Optimum Performance.* New York: Simon & Schuster, pp. 56–82 (What makes things move?); pp. 93–100 (More about forces); pp. 160–179 (Energy); pp. 202–244 (Collisions).

BRODY, H. (1987). *Tennis Science for Tennis Players.* Philadelphia: University of Pennsylvania Press, pp. 61–71 (Understanding the motion of the ball [the bounce]).

DAISH, C. B. (1972). *The Physics of Ball Games.* London: English Universities Press, pp. 4–12 (Impact); pp. 13–21 (More about impact): pp. 35–40 (Power); pp. 91–98 (Bouncing).

DYSON, G. H. C. (1977). *The Mechanics of Athletics.* New York: Holmes & Meier. pp. 28–33 (Forces 1: Newton's laws); pp. 34–73 (Forces 2).

ENOKA, R. M. (1988). *Neuromechanical Basis of Kinesiology.* Champaign. Ill.: Human Kinetics Books, pp. 31–53 (Force).

FARIA, I. E., and CAVANAGH, P. R. (1978). *The Physiology and Biomechanics of Cycling.* New York: John Wiley, pp. 51–56 (How powerful am I?); pp. 57–70 (What is slowing me down?, hills and tires).

HAY, J. G., and REID, J. G. (1988). *Anatomy, Mechanics and Human Motion.* Englewood Cliffs N.J.: Prentice Hall, pp. 143–74 (Explaining linear motion [linear kinetics]).

KELLEY, D. L. (1971). *Kinesiology Fundamentals of Motion.* Englewood Cliffs, N.J.: Prentice Hall. pp. 87–97 (An introduction to forces).

TRICKER, R. A. R., and TRICKER, B. J. K. (1966). *The Science of Movement.* London: Mills & Boon, pp. 13–27 (The role of friction in movement): pp. 83–99 (The conservation of momentum); pp. 100–106 (Force and mass).

WATKINS, J. (1983). *An Introduction to Mechanics of Human Movement.* Boston: MTP Press Limited, pp. 21–62 (Linear motion).

Notes

1. Henry, F. M. (1952). Force-time characteristics of the sprint start. *Research Quarterly,* 23:301–18.
2. Baila, D. L. (1966). Project: Fast ball—Hot or cold? *Science World,* September 16:10–11.
3. Plagenhoef, S. (1971). *Patterns of Human Motion: A Cinematographic Analysis* (pp. 82–83). Englewood Hall, N.J.: Prentice Hall.
4. Baker, J. A. W., and Putnam, C. A. (1979). Tennis racket and ball responses during impact under clamped and freestanding conditions. *Research Quarterly,* 50:164–170.
5. Watanabe, T., Ikegami, Y., and Miyashita, M. (1979). The effects of grip firmness on ball velocity after impact. *Medicine and Science in Sport,* 11:359–61.
6. Liu, Y. K. (1983). Mechanical analysis of racket and ball during impact. *Medicine and Science in Sports and Exercise,* 15:388–92.
7. Baker, J. (1969). Cinematographic analysis of a rebound tumbling event. Unpublished term paper, University of Otago, New Zealand.

ANGULAR
KINETICS

The terms or basic concepts involved in a discussion of the causes of angular motion—that is, in angular kinetics—are very closely related to those encountered in linear kinetics.

Suppose that a gymnast gives a landing mat a sharp kick to alter its position. What happens to the mat depends on the line of action of the force the gymnast exerts upon it—that is, on the straight line along which the force is directed. If the line of action passes through the center of the mat [Fig. 6-1[a]), the mat is translated some distance in the direction in which the force acts. If it doesn't pass through the center of the mat, the mat is translated and rotated simultaneously, with the direction of the rotation depending on which side of center the line of action passes (Fig. 6-1[b]) and [c]). Unless a body is fixed at some point, any rotation imparted to it occurs about an axis passing through the center of the body—strictly speaking, through the center of gravity of the body, a point whose precise location will be considered in some detail in a later section, p. 126.

A force whose line of action does not pass through the center of gravity of the body on which it acts (or through the point at which a body is fixed) is called an *eccentric force*

ECCENTRIC FORCE

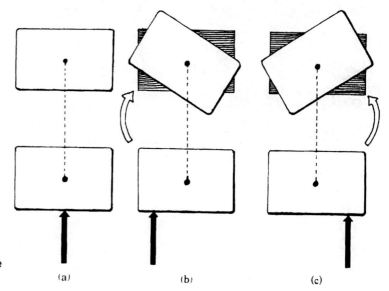

Figure 6-1
Eccentric forces cause translation and
rotation while those that act through the
center of a body cause only translation.

(a)   (b)   (c)

COUPLE

To continue with the movement of gymnastic equipment, suppose that two gymnasts are trying to turn a vaulting horse at right angles to its present position. To do this, they arrange themselves as shown in Fig. 6-2 and exert equal and opposite parallel forces (F_1 and F_2) against the apparatus. Considering each of these as a separate eccentric force, it can be seen that F_1 tends to translate the horse in a positive direction and to rotate it clockwise, while F_2 tends to translate the horse in a negative direction and rotate it clockwise. Because the two forces are equal in magnitude, their tendencies to translate the horse in opposite directions are also equal and thus effectively cancel each other out. The remaining tendency of each force, to rotate the apparatus clockwise, is in no way hindered (and, in fact, is enhanced) by the presence of the other, and the horse is simply rotated on the spot. An arrangement like this of two equal and opposite parallel forces is termed a *couple*.

To summarize, it has been shown in these last two sections that

- a force directed through the center of a body tends to cause translation,
- a couple tends to cause rotation, and
- an eccentric force tends to cause simultaneous translation and rotation.

These are the basic causes of the three forms of motion commonly observed (see Chap. 2).

MOMENT

When a couple is exerted on a body, it tends to cause the body to rotate. The extent of this tendency depends on two factors related to the nature of the couple. The first is the magnitude of the forces involved—the greater the

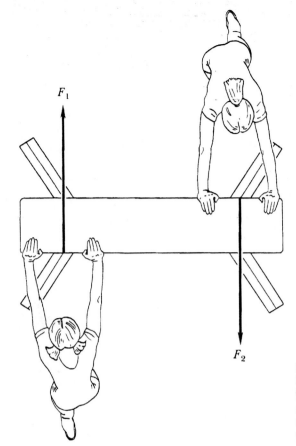

F_1

F_2

POSITIVE DIRECTION

Figure 6-2.
Equal, oppositely directed, and parallel forces constitute a couple. (*Note: F*₁ and *F*₂ are the resultant horizontal forces exerted by the respective gymnasts on the horse.)

forces, the greater their tendency to produce rotation. In the case of the two gymnasts, the harder they push, the more likely they are to cause the horse to rotate. The second is the distance between the lines of action of the two forces constituting the couple—the greater the distance, the greater the tendency to produce rotation. If the two gymnasts push against the horse along lines that pass close to the center of the horse, their tendency to cause the horse to rotate is less than if they exert the same forces nearer the ends of the apparatus. The product of these two factors is a measure of the turning effect that a couple possesses and is called the *moment* of the couple, or the *torque*. Thus:

$$M = Fx \qquad (6\text{-}1)$$

where M = the moment of the couple, F = the magnitude of one of the forces involved, and x = the shortest, or perpendicular, distance between the lines of action of the two forces (the so-called *moment arm*).

The words *moment* and *torque* are also used to describe the turning effect produced when a force is exerted on a body that pivots about some fixed point. Consider the case of an oarsman who, at the completion of the pull phase, lifts the blade of the oar out of the water preparatory to moving it back into position to begin the next stroke (Fig. 6-3[a]). To get the oar into this position, he pushes forward and sideward on the oar handle. The resultant force that he exerts on the oar handle (*F* in Fig. 6-3[a]) tends to rotate the oar counterclockwise and to translate it in the direction in which the force acts. Since the oar simply rotates about an axis through the swivel (the fixture that supports the oar partway along its length), it must be concluded that when the oarsman exerts force on the oar handle, the swivel exerts an equal, opposite, and parallel force (Fig. 6-3[a]) on the shaft of the oar. This latter force cancels out the translatory tendency of the force applied by the oarsman and, together with that force, makes up a couple

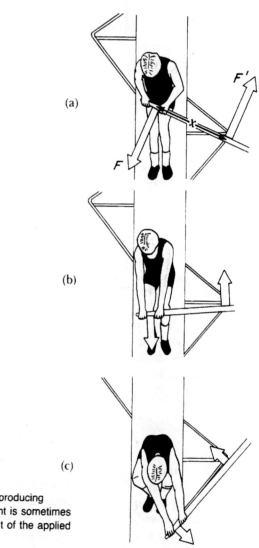

(a)

(b)

(c)

Figure 6-3.
The moment of a couple producing rotation about a fixed point is sometimes referred to as the moment of the applied force.

that produces the observed rotation of the oar. In cases such as this, it is customary to ignore the force exerted at the pivot and, when dealing with the magnitude and direction of the turning effect, to speak simply of the *moment of the force*. For example, the moment of the force exerted by the oarsman in Fig. 6-3 is Fx, where x is the distance from the pivot to the line of action of F. (*Note:* This custom or convention does not alter the magnitude of the moment—considered as the moment of F about the axis through the swivel or the moment of a couple FF', its magnitude is still Fx.)

In the case illustrated in Fig. 6-3(a) the oarsman exerted force on the oar handle in a direction at right angles to the midline of the oar. If the force he exerted was 100 N and the distance from its line of action to the swivel (that is, the moment arm) was 0.9 m, the moment of the force was 90 N·m.

If the oarsman were to apply a force of the same magnitude in a direction other than at right angles to the oar (say, at 65°), the resulting moment could be computed in two ways.

The first method involves determining the length of the moment arm and multiplying it by the magnitude of the force. In Fig. 6-4(a) the length of the moment arm x is given by:

$$\frac{x}{0.9 \text{ m}} = \sin 65°$$

$$x = 0.9 \text{ m} \times \sin 65°$$
$$= 0.9 \text{ m} \times 0.91$$
$$= 0.819 \text{ m}$$

and, using this result, the moment of the force is:

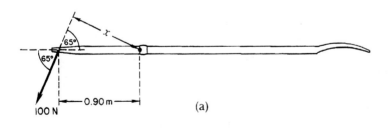

(a)

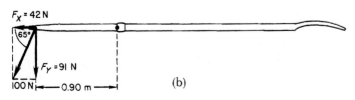

(b)

Figure 6-4.
The moment of a force may be computed in two different ways.

$$M = 100 \text{ N} \times 0.819 \text{ m}$$
$$= 81.9 \text{ N} \cdot \text{m}$$

The second method involves resolving the force into two components, one acting along the midline of the oar and the other at right angles to this midline. The moment of each of these components is then considered separately. For an oarsman exerting a force of 100 N at an angle of 65° (Fig. 6-4[b]), the component F_X acting along the midline is given by:

$$\frac{F_X}{100 \text{ N}} = \cos 65°$$

$$F_X = 100 \text{ N} \times \cos 65°$$
$$= 100 \text{ N} \times 0.42$$
$$= 42 \text{ N}$$

and the component F_Y acting at right angles is given by

$$\frac{F_Y}{100 \text{ N}} = \sin 65°$$

$$F_Y = 100 \text{ N} \times \sin 65°$$
$$= 100 \text{ N} \times 0.91$$
$$= 91 \text{ N}$$

Because its line of action passes through the axis at O, the component F_X has a zero moment arm and thus no tendency to cause the oar to rotate. The rotational effect must therefore be due to component F_Y:

$$M_Y = 91 \text{ N} \times 0.9 \text{ m}$$
$$= 81.9 \text{ N} \cdot \text{m}$$

At first glance it probably seems that the first method is considerably shorter than the second. However, if consideration of the component F_X were eliminated from the second method (and it was included here merely to show that such elimination was justified), it can be seen that the two methods are equivalent in both length and result.

From a practical standpoint, if the oarsman wants to modify the moment of the force that he applies to the oar, he has two basic alternatives—he can alter the magnitude of the force or he can adjust the length of its moment arm. With respect to this second alternative he has at least three ways in which he can make this adjustment:

- he can alter the point at which the force is applied by moving his hands along the oar handle,
- he can adjust the position of the button on the oar and thereby alter the distance from the end of the oar handle to the swivel, and
- he can modify the direction of the force that he exerts.

There are numerous other examples in sports where one part of a body is "fixed" and an applied force causes the body to rotate. In most of these examples, performers can alter either the magnitude of the force or the length of its moment arm to modify the turning effects that their actions produce. In some cases, though, there is only one option. The diver in Fig. 6-5 is a case in point. At the instant shown she is acted on by a moment about an axis through her toes equal to the product of her body weight and the moment arm x and, because her weight is constant, the only way in which she can modify this moment is to alter the length of the moment arm.

RESULTANT MOMENT

When a body is acted on by a number of forces each of which has a tendency to cause it to rotate about some point, the net effect of these various tendencies is obtained by summing the moments about the point in question. Consider the seesaw in Fig. 6-6(a). The boy on the left creates a moment equal to his weight W_L multiplied by the distance x and tends to rotate the seesaw in a counterclockwise direction. Similarly, the boy on the right creates a moment equal to the product of his weight W_R and the distance y and tends to rotate the seesaw in a clockwise direction. If x and y are equal, and they are approximately so in most cases, which moment is greater will depend only on the relative weights of the two boys. Suppose $x = y = 1.5$ m, the boy on the left-hand end of the seesaw weighs 400 N, and the boy on the other end weights 320 N. If counterclockwise is

RESULTANT MOMENT

W

Figure 6-5.
The diver is acted upon by a moment equal to the product of her weight and the horizontal distance from her line of gravity to the transverse axis about which she rotates.

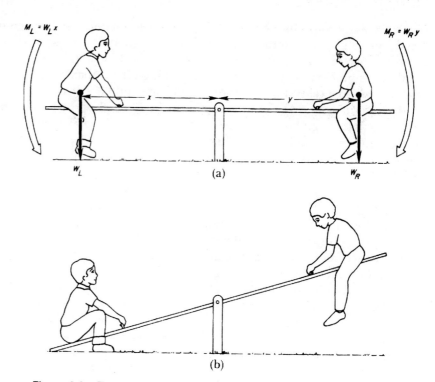

Figure 6-6. The resultant of the moments exerted by each boy determines which way the seesaw rotates.

regarded as the positive direction, the counterclockwise moment is 600 N·m and the clockwise moment is −480 N·m. The sum (or resultant) of these two moments is 120 N·m and, being positive, acts in a counterclockwise direction. The left-hand end of the seesaw thus moves downward and the right-hand end moves upward.

When the seesaw reaches the position shown in Fig. 6-6(b), it tends to remain there. Now this could not happen if there existed a resultant moment acting on the seesaw. The conclusion one must come to, therefore, is that the ground exerts a force on the seesaw and that this force has a moment exactly equal to the difference between the moments of the weight forces. Under these circumstances, and in the absence of any additional forces being introduced, the seesaw would remain in the same position indefinitely. This would be very dull sport indeed, and so as the seesaw approaches the position depicted, the boy on the left-hand end places his feet on the ground and drives hard with his legs. The ground reaction that this evokes is generally sufficient to produce a resultant moment that reverses the direction of the rotation and sends the right-hand end of the seesaw down to the ground.

EQUILIBRIUM

When all parts of a body are at rest or are moving with the same constant velocity, the body is said to be in a state of equilibrium. The gymnast performing a cross on the still rings (Fig. 6-7) provides a suitable example to illustrate some of the characteristics of a body in equilibrium. The body of the gymnast is acted upon by three external forces—F_R and F_L (the forces exerted on his right and left hands by the rings and acting at some angle θ to the horizontal) and W (his weight).

From the information contained in Fig. 6-7, the resultant force in any direction can be computed. For example:

$$\text{Resultant vertical force} = F_R \sin \theta + F_L \sin \theta - W$$
$$\text{Resultant horizontal force} = F_R \cos \theta - F_L \cos \theta$$

Suppose that the resultant vertical force works out to be some positive value. Then from Newton's second law (p. 64), it is apparent that the gymnast's body is being accelerated upward due to the resultant force acting in that direction. Alternatively, if the resultant force were some negative value, the acceleration would be in the reverse direction. Both of these alternatives are unacceptable, however, because they are at odds with the facts—the gymnast's body is not being accelerated at all. Therefore, if the resultant vertical force can be neither positive nor negative, the only possible conclusion is that it must be zero. The same reasoning leads to the conclusion that the resultant horizontal force (and, for that matter, the resultant force in any direction) must also be zero. Thus, one characteristic of a body in equilibrium is that the resultant of the components of force in any direction is zero.

The information of Fig. 6-7 also permits the resultant moment about any point in the plane of the figure to be computed. For example:

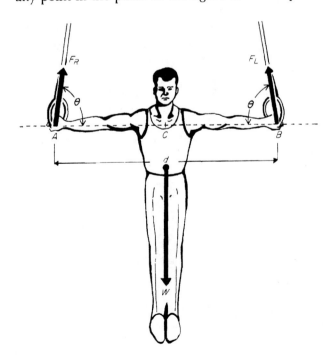

Figure 6-7.
A gymnast performing a cross on the rings is in equilibrium under the influence of the various forces that act upon him.

Resultant moment about $A = (F_L \sin \theta \times d) - \left(W \times \dfrac{d}{2}\right)$

Resultant moment about $B = \left(W \times \dfrac{d}{2}\right) - (F_R \sin \theta \times d)$

Resultant moment about $C = \left(F_L \sin \theta \times \dfrac{d}{2}\right) - \left(F_R \sin \theta \times \dfrac{d}{2}\right)$
(midpoint of the line AB)

If any of these resultant moments has either a positive or a negative value, the gymnast will rotate about an axis through the point in question. Since it is already known that the gymnast is not rotating at all, these resultant moments (like the resultant forces considered earlier) must all be equal to zero. Thus, a second characteristic of a body in equilibrium is that the resultant of the moments of force, about any point in the same plane as that in which the forces act, is zero. (*Note:* If a body is in equilibrium, the sum of the forces acting in any direction and the sum of the moments about any point in the plane are *necessarily* equal to zero. The reverse, however, it not true. The fact that the sum of the forces and the sum of the moments acting on a body are each equal to zero is not *sufficient* to guarantee that the body is in equilibrium. Consider, for example, the case of a record rotating on a turntable. Since the record is not being linearly accelerated, the sum of the forces acting on it in any direction must be equal to zero [Newton's second law]. Similarly, since the record is rotating at a constant rate and is thus not being angularly accelerated, the sum of the moments acting upon it must also be equal to zero [angular analogue of Newton's second law, p. 157]). However, because all parts of the record are not moving with the same constant velocity, the record is *not* in equilibrium. Readers interested in a more detailed discussion of the issues involved here are referred to an excellent paper by Andrews.[1])

When a body is in equilibrium, the characteristics just cited can often be used to work out the magnitudes of unknown forces. Suppose, for example, that the gymnast in Fig. 6-7 weighs 600 N, that $\theta = 75°$, and that $d = 1.8$ m. Then, by taking the moments about the point A:

$$(F_L \sin \theta \times d) - \left(W \times \frac{d}{2}\right) = 0$$

$$(F_L \sin 75 \times 1.8 \text{ m}) - (600 \text{ N} \times 0.9 \text{ m}) = 0$$

$$F_L = \frac{540 \text{ N} \cdot \text{m}}{1.8 \text{ m} \times 0.966}$$

$$= 310.6 \text{ N}$$

The magnitude of F_R, which by now should be obvious, could be confirmed by taking moments about B (or C) or by using one of the resultant force equations. For example:

$$F_R \cos \theta - F_L \cos \theta = 0$$

$$F_R = \frac{F_L \cos \theta}{\cos \theta}$$

$$= 310.6 \text{ N}$$

The inward and upward components of the forces exerted by the rings on the gymnast's hands are, respectively, $F \cos \theta = 80.4$ N and $F \sin \theta = 300$ N, the latter showing that the gymnast's weight is supported equally by each of the rings—a fact suggested by the symmetry of the gymnast's body position.

The conditions of equilibrium expressed here are often used in problems concerned with the amount of force necessary to upset a body's equilibrium—for example, in the construction of hurdles. The international rules relating to the construction of hurdles for track events state that a hurdle "shall be of such a design that a force . . . equal to the weight of 3.6 kilograms [35 N] applied to the centre of the top edge of the top bar is required to overturn it."* To prevent hurdles from overturning when forces of less than this are applied to the crossbar, counterweights are placed on the supporting legs of the hurdle. But how should these weights be arranged? Consider the 1.07 m (3 ft 6 in) hurdle in Fig. 6-8. When a force of 35 N is applied to the top of the hurdle, the counterclockwise moment about the axis AB is 35 N × 1.07 m = 37.5 N·m. If each supporting leg weighs 8 N and this weight acts downward at the midpoint of its 0.6 m length, the clockwise moment due to the two legs is: 8 N x 0.3 m × 2 = 4.8 N·m. It is now pertinent to consider how heavy the counterweights must be and where they should be placed. Because the maximum moment arm for each weight is 0.6 m and the clockwise moment each must produce is [(37.5 N·m − 4.8 N·m)/2] = 16.4 N·m, the lightest the weights can be is 16.4 N·m/0.6 m = 27.3 N. If the counterweights are heavier than this, the moment arm will have to be reduced. Similarly, if the height of the hurdle is lowered to 3 ft (0.91 m), the counter-weights must be brought closer to the axis, for now the "overturning moment" is reduced to 31.9 N·m and the opposing moment must be likewise reduced.

LEVERS

According to dictionary definitions, a lever is a "bar or some other rigid structure, hinged at one point, and to which forces are applied at two other points." The hinge or pivot point of a lever is known as the *fulcrum*. One of the forces that acts on the lever is known as the *weight* (or *resistance*) that

---

* Since the rule does not state in which direction this 35 N force is to be considered to act, it is quite meaningless if taken literally. For the remainder of this discussion, however, it will be assumed that the force should be considered to act in a forward horizontal direction. It is also assumed that the word *overturn* is used to mean the movement of the vertical parts of the hurdle beyond the vertical rather than the complete upsetting of the hurdle so that it cannot return to its original upright orientation.

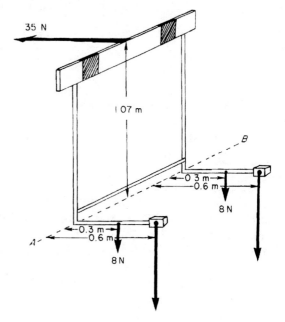

Figure 6-8.
To conform with the rules, a hurdle must be so constructed that the resultant moment will cause it to overturn when a given force is applied to the rail.

opposes movement and the other as the *force* that causes or tends to cause the lever to move.

Oars, vaulting poles, baseball bats, and ski poles are examples of levers used in sports. However, by far the most important levers in any analysis of human movements are those within the body itself—the bones. For whatever influence the body has on external levers such as those just mentioned, ultimately results from the action of these internal levers. At this stage it is important to note that levers are not necessarily long, straight, and thin (or "barlike") but can be any shape. Thus, despite their irregular shapes, the mandible and os innominatum can serve as levers just as readily as can, say, the humerus and femur, which are more akin to the popular conception of a lever (Fig. 6-9).

The functions of levers are basically twofold:

1. A lever can increase the effect produced when a force is exerted on a body. Unless some mechanical aid is used, it is generally necessary to exert a force at least as large as the weight of a body if one is to hold or lift it. With the assistance of a lever, however, a body can be lifted or held in position by exerting forces that may be considerably less than the weight of the body. For example. the football player in Fig. 6-10 maintains his head in the position shown by using his skull as a lever, with the base of the skull as the fulcrum about which the lever tends to turn. The weight of his head plus the helmet he wears (say, 72 N) is one of the two forces applied to the lever; the other is the force applied by the trapezius muscle to the back of the skull. If the forces and fulcrum are arranged as shown, the force *F* that the trapezius must exert to keep the lever in equilibrium is given by:

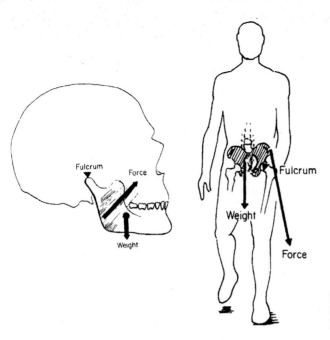

Figure 6-9.
Levers are not necessarily long, thin, and barlike.

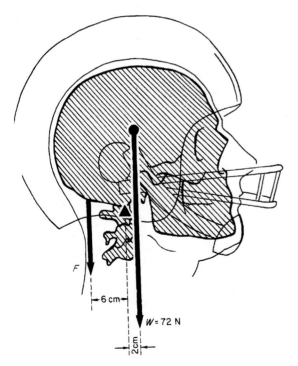

Figure 6-10.
A lever may be used to increase the effect that a small force is capable of producing.

$$F \times 6 \text{ cm} = 72 \text{ N} \times 2 \text{ cm}$$

$$F = \frac{72 \text{ N} \times 2 \text{ cm}}{6 \text{ cm}}$$

$$= 24 \text{ N}$$

Thus, because the skull acts as a lever, the muscular force that must be exerted to maintain a 72 N body in equilibrium is no more than 24 N. In other words, the lever has served to increase markedly the effect that a relatively small force can produce.

2. A lever can increase the distance through which a body can be moved in a given time or, expressed another way, to increase the speed with which a body can be moved. Fig. 6-11 shows the legs of a footballer in the process of punting. In this example, the lever under consideration is that formed by the part of his kicking leg below the knee. This lower leg lever rotates about a fulcrum at the knee joint as a result of the force exerted by the muscles that extend the knee and against the resistance of the force exerted by the ball on the foot.* If the lever moves through an angle of 30° during the time the ball is in contact with the foot, the point A to which the muscular force is applied moves through an arc of 2.6 cm (that is, assuming the dimensions shown in Fig. 6-11).

$$\text{Arc } AA' = \text{circumference} \times \frac{30}{360}$$

$$= \pi \times \text{diameter} \times \frac{30}{360}$$

$$= 3.14 \times \overset{5}{\cancel{10}} \text{ cm} \times \frac{\overset{1}{\cancel{30}}}{\underset{\underset{6}{\cancel{12}}}{\cancel{360}}}$$

$$= 2.6 \text{ cm}$$

During this same time the point B at which the ball makes contact with the foot moves through an arc of 26 cm, exactly 10 times as great. Because it takes exactly the same time for A to travel 2.6 cm as it does for B to travel 26 cm the average linear speeds of A and B are also in the ratio 1:10. Thus a lever can be used to effect an increase in speed at which a muscular force is capable of moving a body.

(*Note*: The lever in the previous example consisted not of one bone but rather of a series of bones "bound together" by ligaments and muscles. It was, in a sense, a momentary lever—a lever "assembled" for a specific task

---

* For the sake of simplifying the example, the additional resistance provided by the weight of the lower leg is disregarded here.

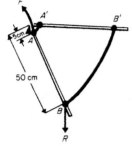

Figure 6-11.
An example of the use of a lever to increase the speed at which a body part is moved.

and then "disassembled" once the task had been completed. This kind of composite lever, although perhaps not described as such, appears with great regularity in analyses of sports techniques.)

For the sake of brevity, the two purposes that levers may serve and that have been described here will henceforth be referred to as (1) increasing the force, and (2) increasing the speed.

Which of the two functions a lever serves depends only on the distances from the lines of action of the force and the resistance to the fulcrum—the so-called force and resistance arms. If, as shown in the example of Fig. 6-10, the force arm is longer than the resistance arm, the function of the lever is to increase the force. On the other hand, if the force arm is shorter than the resistance arm (Fig. 6-11), the lever serves to increase the speed. Finally, if both arms are of equal length, no advantage is gained by using the lever—it serves to increase neither the force nor the speed. (*Note:* Because most of its bony levers have a force arm that is shorter than the resistance arm, the human body is generally considered to be much better equipped to make fast movements than to make forceful ones.)

Levers have been classified into three orders (or classes) according to the relative location of the points at which the force, fulcrum, and resistance act. A lever in which the fulcrum lies between the points at which the force and the resistance are applied is termed a *first-class lever*; that in which the fulcrum is at one end and the resistance applied closer to it than is the force is termed a *second-class lever*; and that in which the fulcrum is again at one end but the relative positions of the force and resistance are reversed is termed a *third-class lever*. However, since the significant thing about a lever is not its geometry but the function it serves (Fig. 6-12), this arbitrary, nonfunctional classification of lever types would seem to add nothing to warrant its further consideration here.

CENTER OF GRAVITY

When a body is acted upon by gravity, every particle of which it is composed experiences an attraction toward the earth (Newton's law of gravitation, p. 62). The resultant of all these attractive forces is the weight of the body, and the direction of the resultant is parallel to that of the lines of action of the individual forces. This much, at least, would seem to be fairly obvious. What is not generally so obvious is the answer to the question: Through what points does the line of action of this resultant force act? This section considers the answer to that question.

Consider a practice relay baton, consisting of a length of broomstick. The location of the line of action of its weight W can be found by attempting to balance the baton on a sharp edge (Fig. 6-13). Apart from the force applied at the edge (or fulcrum), the only other force acting on the baton is its weight. Therefore, if the baton rotates in a clockwise direction upon being released, it must be assumed that the line of action of the weight passes to the right of the fulcrum, for only in this way could the weight have a clockwise moment of force (Fig. 6-13[a]). Similarly, if the baton rotates in a counterclockwise direction, the line of action of the weight must pass to the left of the fulcrum (Fig. 6-13[b]). Finally, if the baton maintains its

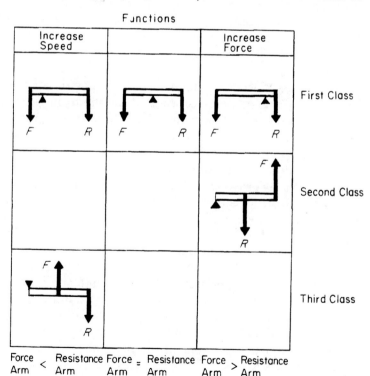

Figure 6-12.
Levers—functional and geometric classifications.

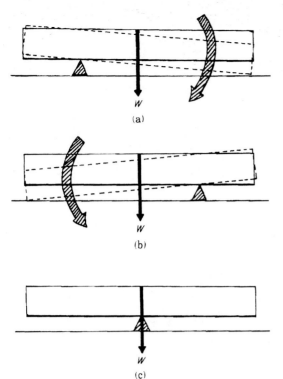

(a)

(b)

Figure 6-13.
Determining the gravity line.

(c)

position once it has been released, the moment of the weight about the fulcrum must be zero (Fig 6-13[c]). Because this could occur only if the length of the moment arm was zero, the line of action of the weight has thus been established. It is a vertical line (sometimes referred to as the *line of gravity* or *gravity line*) passing through the baton and through the point on the fulcrum upon which the baton is balanced.

When the baton is turned so that it stands on one end, the line of gravity runs down its length rather than across it as before. Suppose that the balancing procedure is followed with the baton in this position. When the baton is balanced on the fulcrum, there is not just one vertical line directly above the fulcrum but instead a whole plane (Fig. 6-14[a]). Which of the vertical lines in this plane is the line of gravity can be established by rotating the baton and then rebalancing it. In this way a second vertical plane containing the line of gravity is found (Fig. 6-14[b]). Since the line of gravity must lie in the second plane as well as in the first one, it must be the line formed where the two planes intersect (the only line that does lie in both planes). And so, once again, the position of the line of gravity has been established.

When the two lines of gravity found so far (that is, one when the baton lay on its side and one when it stood on end) are considered together, it is found that they intersect at a central point (Fig. 6-14[c]). This point is called the *center of gravity* of the body and will always be directly above the fulcrum if the baton is balanced.

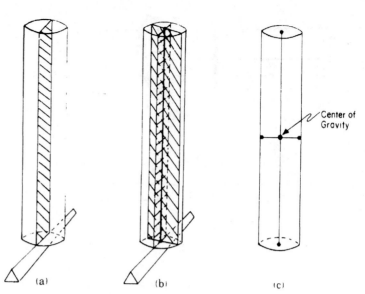

Figure 6-14.
Determining the center of gravity (balance method).

The center of gravity of a body can also be found by suspending it. In Fig. 6-15 a cardboard cutout of a volleyball player is suspended from a point *A*. If the cutout is moved so that its center of gravity lies to the right of the vertical line through *A* (that is, the line *AB*), a clockwise moment exists that causes the cutout to rotate in that direction. Then, when the center of gravity swings across the line *AB*, a moment in the opposite direction comes into effect and this soon causes the body to reverse the direction in which it is swinging. Eventually, after oscillating back and forth in this way, the cutout comes to rest. When this occurs, the moment of the weight about the pivot at *A* must be zero, and thus the center of gravity must lie on a line directly below this point. The direction of the line *AB* is marked on the cutout, which is then suspended from a second point (not on the line that has just been drawn) and made to oscillate anew. When the suspended cutout again comes to rest, a second vertical line is drawn through the point of suspension. The point at which the two drawn lines intersect is the center of gravity of the cutout (that is, assuming that the cutout is thin and that the third dimension can therefore be disregarded).

Two important facts concerning centers of gravity can be demonstrated using these methods. The first is that the center of gravity need not lie within the physical limits of a body. If each of the bodies in Fig. 6-16 (the Roman ring, basketball, football helmet, and boomerang) were systematically balanced or suspended and the center of gravity located, it would be found in every case that this point lay not within the material of the body but somewhere in the space within, or around it.

Occasionally the center of gravity is referred to as the point of balance of a body and it is either stated or implied that this is the point on which it is possible for it to be balanced or supported. However, the fact that the center of gravity can lie outside the body (that is, beyond its physical limits)

Figure 6-15. Determining the center of gravity (suspension method).

renders this interpretation quite meaningless, as attempts to balance a ring by providing support at its center of gravity will readily show.

The possibility of the center of gravity lying outside a body has aroused some interest with respect to high jumping and pole vaulting, where it has been contended that if an athlete assumed a position similar to that of the boomerang, he (or she) could conceivably pass over the bar while the center of gravity passed under or through it (Figs. 6-17 and 6-18). To date, however, there appear to have been few well-substantiated claims of athletes having succeeded in doing this.

A boomerang normally consists of a piece, or a number of laminated pieces, of wood cut or bent into a characteristic V shape. To illustrate the second important fact about centers of gravity, imagine a special boomer-

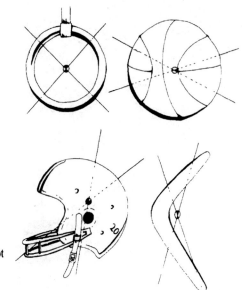

Figure 6-16.
The center of gravity of a body need not lie within the physical substance of the body.

ang in which the angle between the "arms" can be adjusted. If the center of gravity of this boomerang is found for a variety of arm positions (Fig. 6-19), it can be seen that its location changes as the positions of the arms are altered. Initially the center of gravity lies within the substance of the body, then, after moving outside it as the angle between the arms is increased, it returns to lie within the body as the angle approaches 180°.

This same phenomenon can be demonstrated using an athlete as a subject. The athlete in Fig. 6-20(a) is lying on a plank balanced on the edge of a piece of wood with a triangular cross-section. (The weight of the board is small compared with the weight of the athlete and, for the sake of

Figure 6-17. The Fosbury flop technique of high jumping affords the possibility of an athlete passing over the bar while his (or her) center of gravity passes through it or beneath it.

Figure 6-18. A pole vaulter might also have his center of gravity pass through or beneath the bar while he himself passes over it.

Figure 6-19. The center of gravity of a body moves as the parts of the body move.

simplicity, is ignored in what follows.) With both arms extended above her head, her center of gravity lies approximately 95.4 cm from the soles of her feet. (The alternate black and white stripes in Fig. 6-20—and, too, in Fig. 6-22—are each 10 cm in width.) If she lowers one arm and puts it by her side, and the system is once again balanced, it is found that her center of gravity has moved toward her feet. (In the case of the subject pictured in Fig. 6-20[b], the center of gravity was approximately 93.2 cm from the soles of her feet, in this second position.) Thus, as before, the location of the center of gravity of a body whose parts are free to move depends on the orientation of those parts. As the parts move, so too does the center of gravity.

Basketball players in a jump-ball situation, volleyball players leaping to spike, and line-out forwards in rugby all make good use of this fact. Take, for example, the basketball player. When he jumps for the ball, he swings both arms forward and upward to assist him in gaining height. Then, once he has left the floor, he allows one arm to drop down to his side while he

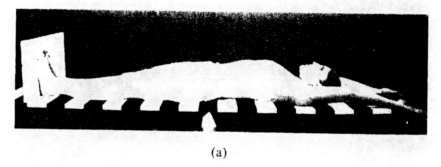

(a)

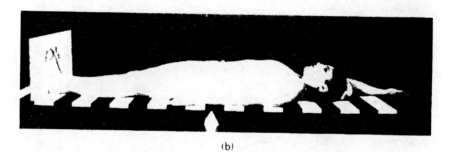

(b)

Figure 6-20. From a position in which both arms are extended overhead, the lowering of one arm to a position next to the side causes the athlete's center of gravity to move 2.2 cm closer to her feet. The distance to which the athlete can reach beyond her center of gravity is increased by the same amount.

strives to get maximum reach with the other. Apart from any other consideration, this dropping of one arm definitely acts to his advantage. With both arms extended overhead he can reach a certain distance beyond his center of gravity. With one arm lowered, this reach-beyond-center-of-gravity distance is increased by about 3 cm because his center of gravity is now lower in his body. In short, the maximum height to which an athlete's center of gravity rises is determined by the velocity and height of his take-off—he is simply a projectile and thus subject to the laws governing projectile motion (see pp. 31–43); and how much beyond this maximum height he is capable of reaching depends on how he orients his body (Fig. 6-21).

The location of the center of gravity of a human body, at rest and in motion, is of considerable significance in many analyses of sports techniques. Many methods have been devised to estimate the position of the center of gravity of a human body. (*Note:* The word *estimate* is used advisedly because the location of a human body's center of gravity changes with each beat of the heart, with each breath the person takes, with ingestion of food, and with changes in the disposition of the various body fluids. As a result, the accuracy with which its position can be determined at any one

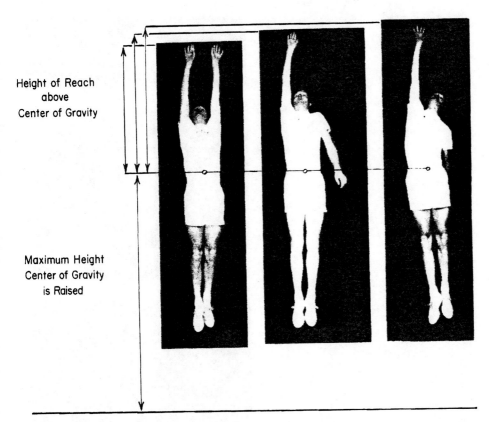

Height of Reach
above
Center of Gravity

Maximum Height
Center of Gravity
is Raised

Figure 6-21. Adjusting the body position to obtain the highest reach possible from a given jump.

instance is very much open to question. Duggar, the author of an excellent review of the literature in this area, has stated that "the most exacting measurements will not ensure pin-pointing the location of the CG of a particular man to within 1/3 cm"[2] Indeed, variations of the order of 1/2 to 2/3 cm have been reported as resulting from forced inspiration alone.[3])

Reaction-Board Methods. Possibly the simplest method used to find the center of gravity of a living human subject is that which involves the use of a so-called *reaction board*. This board is supported horizontally on two "knife edges," one of which rests on a block of wood while the other rests on the platform of a set of scales. After the initial reading on the scales (R_1) has been noted, the subject lies in a supine position on top of the board with the soles of the feet pressed against a vertical fitting placed so that the surface in contact with the feet lies directly above one of the knife edges (Fig 6-22[a]). The new reading on the scales (R_2) is then noted.

Now, because the board was in equilibrium before the subject lay upon it, and because the board-plus-subject is in equilibrium when the subject

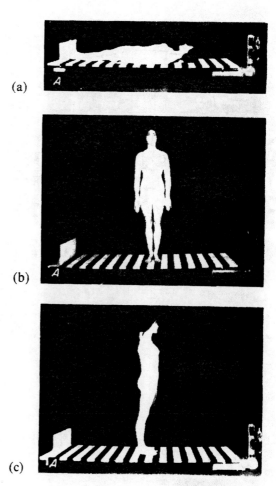

(a)

(b)

(c)

Figure 6-22.
Using a reaction board to determine the location of the center of gravity in one dimension.

does lie down, it must be concluded that whatever forces and moments are introduced by the presence of the subject are themselves in equilibrium. The forces introduced are (1) the reactions to the increases in weight borne by the platform of the scales and by the wooden block; and (2) the weight of the subject. Consider the moments of these newly introduced forces about the point A in Fig. 6-22(a). The moment of the force $R_2 - R_1$ applied by the platform of the scales to the knife-edge resting upon it is $1.8(R_2 - R_1)$ N·m and acts in a counterclockwise direction. (*Note:* The horizontal distance between the knife-edges of the reaction board is 1.8 m, in this case.) The moment of the weight force is Wx N·m, where x m is the unknown horizontal distance of the center of gravity from the point A. This moment acts in a clockwise direction. Because the body is in equilibrium, these moments must be equal in magnitude. That is:

$$Wx = 1.8(R_2 - R_1)$$

Therefore:

$$x = \frac{1.8\,(R_2 - R_1)}{W}\ \text{m} \qquad\qquad (6\text{-}2)$$

As an example, consider the data obtained for the subject in Fig. 6-22(a):

Weight: $W = 450$ N

Initial scale reading: $R_1 =\ \ 85$ N

Final scale reading: $R_2 = 300$ N

The horizontal distance of the subject's center of gravity from A is then computed, using these data:

$$x = \frac{1.8(R_2 - R_1)}{W}$$

$$x = \frac{1.8(300 - 85)}{450}$$

$$= 0.86\ \text{m}$$

This procedure determines the position of the center of gravity only in terms of distance from the soles of the feet. Its position laterally (that is, relative to the left- or right-hand side of the body) or frontally (that is, relative to the front or back of the body) can be obtained, using the same basic method, by having the subject assume an erect standing position on the reaction board (Fig. 6-22[b] and [c]). (*Note:* While it would seem reasonable to assume that changing from the position shown in Fig. 6-22[b] to that of Fig. 6-22[c] would not alter the location of the center of gravity relative to the body, it would hardly seem reasonable to expect the same result when the body position was changed from supine to erect standing.

Mainly because of shifts in the disposition of the body viscera and fluids, the distance of the center of gravity from the soles of the feet when the subject was standing would probably be slightly less than when she adopted a lying position.)

Another, similar method of locating the center of gravity of an individual involves the use of a large reaction board supported on scales at two or more points. In the example depicted in Fig. 6-23, the board has three metal spikes protruding from its under surface. The spikes at the points A and B each rest upon the platform of a set of scales, while the remaining spike (at C) rests on a solid block. After the initial readings R_{A1} and R_{B1} are noted, the subject adopts the required position on top of the board. The scale readings R_{A2} and R_{B2} are then taken and the location of the center of gravity is determined by taking moments about the lines AC and BC. The distance of the center of gravity from each of these lines (x and y, respectively) is given by the equations:

$$x = \frac{(R_{B2} - R_{B1})h}{W} \tag{6-3}$$

and:

$$y = \frac{(R_{A2} - R_{A1})h}{W} \tag{6-4}$$

Figure 6-23. Using a large reaction board to locate the center of gravity in two dimensions.

where h = the altitude of the equilateral triangle ABC, and W = the weight of the subject.

This method, or some modification of it, has been used in a number of studies of sports techniques.[4,5,6] The following procedure is generally followed in such instances:

1. The subject is filmed performing the required technique.
2. The film is viewed and the frames to be used in the analysis are selected.
3. The reaction board is used as a screen and a life-size image of the subject, as he (or she) appears in the frame to be analyzed, is projected onto the board.
4. A chalk line is drawn on the board around the projected image of the subject.
5. After the initial scale readings have been taken, the subject assumes the position represented by the chalk outline.
6. The position of the subject's center of gravity is then obtained using the method already described.
7. Steps 3 to 6 are repeated as required.

There are a number of practical limitations inherent in this method. Chief among these are the need to have the subject available throughout and the considerable time involved in locating the center of gravity for each position.

Mannikin Methods.   To overcome these limitations, a number of workers[7,8,9] have devised mannikins that can be posed in a variety of positions and whose center of gravity can quickly be determined using the methods of suspension or balance. Unfortunately, the use of a mannikin introduces new problems at the same time as it overcomes old ones. Among these is the problem that arises if the weight of the mannikin is not distributed in the same way as the weight of the human body that it represents. For example, Page[10] has reported that when a simple cardboard mannikin, posed in an erect standing position, has both arms moved to a fully extended position overhead, its center of gravity is raised the equivalent of some 12.7 cm. On the other hand, studies by Swearingen[11] and his co-workers[12] have yielded mean values of 5.7 cm and 6.1 cm, respectively, for the shift in the center of gravity when human subjects perform the same action.

While not a particularly easy undertaking, it is possible to overcome this problem by weighting the various parts of the mannikin so that its weight distribution closely approximates that of a human body.[13] Even when this is done, however, the usefulness of a mannikin is restricted by the fact that it can assume only a limited number of positions. As a result, other methods are needed to locate the center of gravity for body positions that are not part of the mannikin's "repertoire."

Segmentation Method. The most versatile method for finding the center of gravity of a human body is the *segmentation method*, which hinges upon a simple, yet important, relationship. Consider the barbell in Fig. 6-24(a). Each of the discs weighs 200 N, the bar itself weights 100 N, and the lines of action of these weight forces are as shown. If a line *AB* is drawn in a plane perpendicular to the weight forces and at a horizontal distance of, say, 0.3 m from the left-hand end of the bar,* and if the other dimensions are as shown in Fig. 6-24(b), the moments of the weights about this line are:

(a)

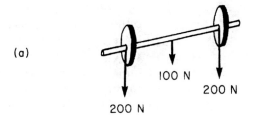

(b)

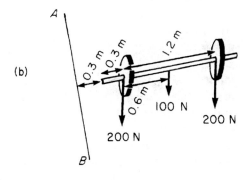

(c)

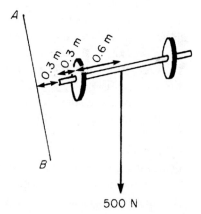

Figure 6-24.
A simple example to demonstrate that the sum of the moments of a number of forces about a given axis is equal to the moment of their resultant about the same axis. ("The sum of the moments is equal to the moment of the sum [resultant].")

$$200 \text{ N} \times 0.6 \text{ m} = 120 \text{ N·m}$$
$$100 \text{ N} \times 1.2 \text{ m} = 120 \text{ N·m}$$
$$200 \text{ N} \times 1.8 \text{ m} = 360 \text{ N·m}$$
$$\text{Sum of these moments} = 600 \text{ N·m}$$

The resultant weight of the discs and the bar is 500 N and acts through the center of gravity of the loaded barbell at the midpoint of the bar (Fig. 6-24(c)]. The moment of this resultant about *AB* is

$$500 \text{ N} \times 1.2 \text{ m} = 600 \text{ N·m}$$

which is exactly the same as the sum of the moments of the weights considered separately.

This computational process could be repeated any number of times for any combination of disc and bar weights and for any position of the line *AB* (in a plane perpendicular to the weight forces) and exactly the same relationship would be found in each case—the sum of the moments of the separate weight forces would be equal to the moment of their resultant. This relationship is of importance because it provides a means of locating the center of gravity of a body. Suppose, for example, that it were desired to find the center of gravity of a barbell loaded as shown in Fig. 6-25. Suppose, too, that a line *CD* (equivalent to *AB*) were drawn at a distance of 0.6 m from the left-hand end of the bar. The moment of the resultant weight (500 N) about this line is 500x N·m, where x m equals the horizontal distance between the center of gravity of the barbell and *CD*. The sum of the moments of the separate forces about *CD* is 864 N·m:

$$\text{Sum of moments} = (110 \text{ N} \times 0.9 \text{ m}) + (90 \text{ N} \times 1.5 \text{ m}) + (300 \text{ N} \times 2.1 \text{ m})$$
$$= (99 + 135 + 630) \text{N·m}$$
$$= 864 \text{ N·m}$$

The relationship between the moment of the resultant and the sum of the moments of the separate weights can now be used to determine x, the horizontal distance of the center of gravity from *CD*:

$$500x = 864 \text{ N·m}$$
$$x = \frac{864 \text{ N·m}}{500 \text{ N}}$$
$$= 1.73 \text{ m}$$

* In this example, the line *AB* has been drawn at right angles to the line of the bar to simplify the subsequent arithmetic (Fig. 6-24[b]). This, however, is purely a matter of convenience—there is no restriction on the orientation of the line except that it must lie "in a plane perpendicular to the weight forces."

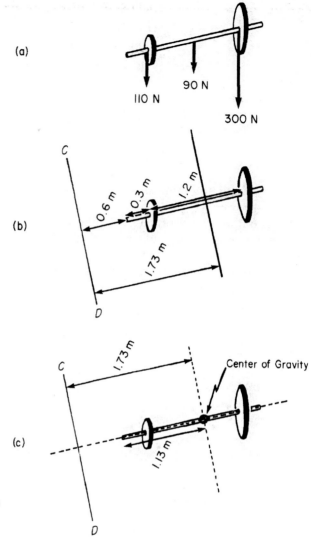

Figure 6-25.
Using the "sum of the moments is equal to the moment of the sum" to locate the center of gravity of a barbell.

A brief look at the arrangement of the discs and bar should be all that is necessary to establish that the center of gravity of the loaded barbell must also be on the line running lengthwise through the center of the bar. Combining these two results reveals that the center of gravity of the loaded barbell lies in the center of the bar at a distance of 1.73 m from *CD* or, more meaningfully, 1.13 m from the left-hand end of the bar.

The method used here to find the distance of the center of gravity of a body from some arbitrarily chosen line can be used to find the center of gravity of an athlete in action. This can be done from a photograph, provided information is available concerning (1) the weights of the various parts or segments of the athlete's body (arm, forearm, hand, thigh, etc.); and (2) the locations of the centers of gravity of these segments.

A number of studies have been conducted in which one of the objectives was to obtain average values for these quantities. Some investigators[14][15][16][17][18] have frozen cadavers, cut them into segments, weighed the segments, and balanced or suspended them to find their centers of gravity. Others[18][19] have had living subjects immerse selected segments and by noting either the volume of water displaced or the change in total body weight have computed the weight of these segments. Still others[20][21][22] have attempted to arrive at appropriate values by purely mathematical means.

Of all the data available on the weight of body segments and the locations of the centers of gravity of the segments, those obtained by Clauser et al.[16] (Tables 6-1 and 6-2) seem to be the most appropriate for use in analyses of sports techniques.

TABLE 6-1 Weights of Body Segments Relative to Total Body Weight

Segment	Relative Weight
Head	0.073
Trunk	0.507
Upper arm	0.026
Forearm	0.016
Hand	0.007
Thigh	0.103
Calf	0.043
Foot	0.015

Source: Adapted from data presented in Clauser, C. E. McConville, J. T., and Young, J. W. (1969). *Weight, Volume and Center of Mass of Segments of the Human Body* (p. 59). AMRL Technical Report 69–70. Wright-Patterson Air Force Base, Ohio: AMRL]

As an example in the use of the segmentation method, suppose one wanted to locate the center of gravity of the athlete in Fig. 6-26. The steps to be taken are as follows:

1. Mark on the photograph the position of those reference points (Table 6-2) associated with each segment. The positions of reference points obscured by other body parts should be estimated carefully.

2. Construct a stick-figure representation of the subject by ruling straight lines between appropriate reference points. (The trunk line is obtained by joining the midpoint of the line between the right and left hip joints to the midpoint of the trunk at the level of the suprasternal notch.

3. Measure the length of each segment line, and divide these various lengths in the appropriate ratio as indicated in Table 6-2. Mark the points of division (that, is the centers of gravity of the segments) on their respective lines.

4. Rule two arbitrary axes (*OY* and *OX*), one to the left and one below the stick figure.

5. Prepare a form like that shown in Table 6-3, and enter the weights of the segments in Column 1.

6. For each segment, measure the perpendicular distance from the center of gravity to the line *OY*, and enter this distance in the appropriate place on the form (Table 6-3, Column 2).

TABLE 6-2 Locations of Centers of Gravity of Body Segments

Segment	Center-of-Gravity Location Expressed as Percentage of Total Distance Between Reference Points
Head	46.4% to vertex; 53.6% to chin-neck intersect
Trunk	43.8% to suprasternal notch; 56.2% to hip axis
Upper arm	49.1% to shoulder axis; 50.9% to elbow axis
Forearm	41.8% to elbow axis; 58.2% to wrist axis
Hand	82.0% to wrist axis; 18.0% to knuckle III
Thigh	40.0% to hip axis; 60.0% to knee axis
Calf	41.8% to knee axis; 58.2% to ankle axis
Foot	44.9% to heel; 55.1% to tip of longest toe

Source: Adapted from data presented in Clauser, C. E., McConville, J. T., and Young, J. W. (1969). *Weight, Volume and Center of Mass of Segments of the Human Body* (pp. 46–55) AMRL Technical Report 69–70. Wright-Patterson Air Force Base, Ohio: AMRL. and in Hinrichs, R.N. (1990). Adjustments to the segment center of mass proportions of Clauser et al. (1969). *Journal of Biomechanics.* 23:949–951

7. To find the moments about *OY*, multiply the weight of each segment by the distance of its center of gravity from the line, and enter these values on the form (Table 6-3, Column 3.)

8. Find the sum of the moments about *OY* by adding the contents of Column 3 on the form.

Figure 6-26. The segmentation method for locating the center of gravity.

TABLE 6-3 Form for Computation of Center-of-Gravity Coordinates

Segment	Column 1 Segment Weight	Column 2 Distance to OY (cm)	Column 3 Moments about OY	Column 4 Distance to OX (cm)	Column 5 Moments about OX
Head	0.073	6.8	0.496	6.9	0.504
Trunk	0.507	6.8	3.448	4.7	2.383
Right upper arm	0.026	7.5	0.195	6.3	0.164
Right forearm	0.016	7.8	0.125	7.1	0.114
Right hand	0.007	8.2	0.057	8.2	0.057
Left upper arm	0.026	6.2	0.161	6.4	0.166
Left forearm	0.016	5.2	0.083	7.3	0.117
Left hand	0.007	4.2	0.029	8.3	0.058
Right thigh	0.103	5.3	0.546	3.2	0.330
Right calf	0.043	3.1	0.133	3.4	0.146
Right foot	0.015	1.2	0.018	3.8	0.057
Left thigh	0.103	6.9	0.711	2.2	0.227
Left calf	0.043	7.8	0.335	1.2	0.052
Left foot	0.015	9.4	0.141	2.2	0.033
	1.000		Sum of moments = 6.478		Sum of moments = 4.408

9. Add the contents of Column 1. If the procedure outlined here has been correctly followed, all parts of the body will have been taken into account and this total will be equal to 1 (that is, the sum of the weights of all the body parts, expressed in terms of the total body weight.)

Then, because the moment of the resultant weight about OY is equal to 1 multiplied by some unknown distance x, and because this is equal to the sum of the moments of the segments considered separately, x is equal to the sum found in step 8. (In the present example, $x = 6.478$ cm.)

10. Rule a line $O'Y'$ parallel to OY and at a distance x from it. The center of gravity of the subject lies on this line.

11. Repeat steps 5 to 10, taking moments about OX instead of OY. The center of gravity of the subject lies on the line $O''X'$ drawn parallel to OX and at the computed distance from it. And, finally, because the center of gravity lies on both $O'Y'$ and $O''X'$ and these two lines have only one point in common (the point where they intersect), it is here that the center of gravity is situated.

While the segmentation method outlined here is both accurate and versatile, the large amount of measuring and computational work involved makes it very time consuming. However, people conducting detailed analyses of sports techniques make use of computers to overcome this problem.

STABILITY

The punching bag in Fig. 6-27 is in a state of equilibrium, under the action of two forces—its weight W and an equal and opposite force R exerted by

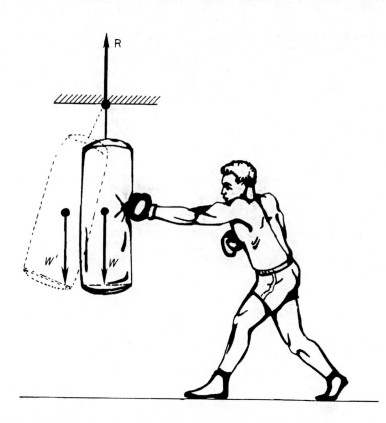

Figure 6-27.
Stable equilibrium.

the supporting rope. When a boxer punches the bag, it undergoes a slight displacement from its original position and its state of equilibrium is disrupted. In this process, the line of action of the weight moves to the left of the point at which the bag is attached to the ceiling and the counter clockwise moment of the weight thus created tends to return the bag to its original position. A body, like the punching bag, that tends to return to its equilibrium position after being displaced is said to be in *stable equilibrium*.

The gymnast performing a balance on the beam (Fig. 6-28) is also in equilibrium under the action of a pair of forces. In this case, however, the effect of a small displacement from this equilibrium position produces quite different results, for the moment of her weight tends to rotate her farther away from her original position rather than back toward it. A body like this, which tends to move away from its equilibrium position once it has been displaced, is said to be in *unstable equilibrium*.

Like the bodies in the two previous examples, the tennis ball of Fig. 6-29 is in a state of equilibrium. However, since it has no tendency either to return to its original position or to move still farther away from it, its response to a slight displacement is quite different from that of the other two bodies. This comes about because no matter in what position the ball is placed (that is, on a level surface), the weight and reaction forces are exactly equal and opposite. Such a body is in a state of *neutral equilibrium*.

The stability of a body in equilibrium (which is, of course, what the terms

Figure 6-28.
Unstable equilibrium.

stable, unstable, and *neutral* refer to) depends on a number of factors. These are:

- the position of the line of gravity relative to the limits of the base,
- the weight of the body, and
- the height of the center of gravity relative to the base.

The role of the first factor, the position of the gravity line relative to the limits of the base, may be considered in terms of the stance adopted by the

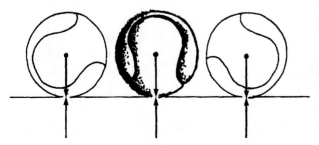

Figure 6-29.
Neutral equilibrium.

wrestler in Fig. 6-30(a). If the wrestler's feet are close together (Fig. 6-30(a)], and the line of gravity is therefore close to the limits of the base, a small angular displacement will set him rotating progressively farther from his initial equilibrium position. In short, the wrestler is in unstable equilibrium. Conversely, if the wrestler's feet are wide apart (Fig. 6-30 (b)], and the line of gravity is far from the limits of the base, a small angular displacement will be insufficient to overturn him and he will instead rotate back towards his initial equilibrium position. In short, the wrestler is in stable equilibrium.

In responding to an attack from a specific direction, a wrestler will usually shift his weight in the direction of this attack. In this process, the line of gravity is moved closer to the limit of the base in one direction and farther from it in the opposite direction. The wrestler might thus be said to be in stable equilibrium in one direction and in unstable equilibrium in the other.

Because the area of the base (the area enclosed by a line drawn around the outermost limits of those points upon which the body is supported) is inevitably increased in this process, it is frequently stated that the area of the base is a factor influencing the stability of a body. This is only true to the extent that an increase in the area of the base increases the distance of the gravity line from the limits of the base. (*Note:* Readers interested in pursuing this matter further are referred to a study by Londeree[23] in

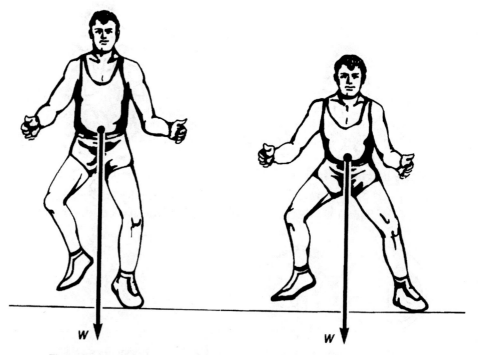

Figure 6-30. The stability of equilibrium is influenced by the distance of the line of gravity from the limits of the base.

which this and other issues related to the stability of equilibrium are considered at some length.)

Athletes in a variety of sports make use of the relationship between the location of the line of gravity and the stability of a body. A swimmer, poised for the start of a race, has the line of gravity passing close to the forward limit of the base so that when the gun is fired he (or she) will be able to disrupt the state of equilibrium and initiate forward motion with a minimum of effort. A track sprinter does something similar, and for exactly the same reason, when he (or she) rocks upward and forward into the "set" position. A defensive basketball player who expects the opponent to drive toward the basket will have the line of gravity passing somewhat closer to the backward limit of the base than it does to the forward limit. In this way the defensive player is a little less stable in a backward direction and therefore more ready to respond to a driving action on the part of the opponent.

That the weight of a body is also a factor governing its stability can be seen by once again considering the wrestler in Fig 6-30(b). Here the moment opposing attempts to upset his equilibrium is the product of his weight and some fixed distance. Obviously then, the greater his weight, the greater his stability. This factor is one of the obvious reasons for the division of athletes into weight classes in such sports as wrestling, judo, and boxing.

Finally, imagine a skittle that could be balanced on either end and whose base dimensions were identical in both cases (Fig. 6-31). The center of gravity of the skittle lies on its midline (or axis of symmetry) and nearer to the more massive end than to the other. If the skittle is balanced in its "normal" position (Fig. 6-31[a]) and then given an angular displacement θ as shown, its line of gravity still passes through the base and the skittle tends to return to its original equilibrium position. However, if the inverted skittle (Fig. 6-31[b]) is given the same angular displacement, its line of gravity passes outside the limits of the base and the skittle falls. The reason for the skittle being less stable in an inverted position than in a normal one can be deduced by considering the factors that have been shown to influence the stability of a body—the location of the line of gravity relative to the base limits and the weight of the body. Since these factors are identical, in both cases, the difference in stability must be due to some other factor. This factor, the most obvious difference between the two positions, is the height of the center of gravity above the base. If all else is equal, the lower the center of gravity, the more stable the equilibrium.

MOMENT OF INERTIA

The resistance of a body to changes in its motion is known as its inertia. In the case of linear motion, the inertia of a body is measured by its mass—the more massive a body, the greater its inertia and the more difficult it is to change its linear motion. With angular motion a similar state of affairs exists except that it is not only the mass of a body that determines its resistance to changes in its motion, but also how this mass is distributed

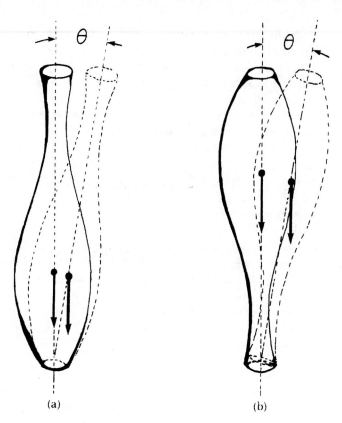

Figure 6-31.
If all else is equal—as it is in the case of
the skittles depicted here—the higher the
center of gravity of a body, the less its
stability.

(a)   (b)

relative to the axis about which the body is rotating or tends to rotate. If the
mass is concentrated close to the axis, it is much easier to alter the angular
motion of a body than if the same mass is farther from the axis. When a
child uses a full-sized baseball bat and "chokes up" on the handle, he (or
she) is instinctively acknowledging and making use of this fact. For, by this
action the child moves the axis of rotation of the bat closer to the major
mass of the bat and thereby makes the swing (angular motion) easier to
control. Small children do the same kind of thing when using adult-sized
eating utensils.

The angular-motion equivalent of mass as a measure of a body's resistance to a change in its motion is termed the *moment of inertia* and, as
indicated, takes into account both the mass of the body and how this mass
is distributed relative to the axis of rotation. Suppose the axis of rotation
for the bat in Fig. 6-32 is represented by the line *XY*. Suppose too that the
particle of matter located at the point *A* has a mass m_1 and is a distance r_1
from the axis *XY*. Then, according to formal definitions of the moment of
inertia, this particle's moment of inertia about the axis *XY* is

$$I_1 = m_1 r_1^2$$

Similarly, another particle (say the particle at *B*) has a moment of inertia

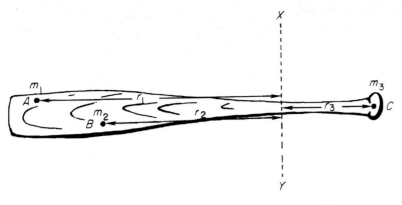

Figure 6-32. Defining the moment of inertia of a baseball bat.

$$I_2 = m_2 r_2$$

and yet another (that at C), even though on the opposite side of the axis, has a moment of inertia

$$I_3 = m_3 r_3^2$$

If the moments of inertia of all the particles comprising the bat are summed, the result is the moment of inertia of the bat about XY:

$$
\begin{aligned}
I &= I_1 + I_2 + I_3 + \ldots \\
&= m_1 r_1^2 + m_1 r_1^2 + m_2 r_2^2 \ldots \\
&= \Sigma\, mr^2
\end{aligned}
\tag{6-5}
$$

The moment of inertia of a body may be determined in a variety of ways. If the body is regular in shape (for example, square, rectangular, circular, or spherical) or is made up of parts that are themselves regular, its moment of inertia can be determined mathematically. If, like many of the bodies involved in sports, it is irregular in shape, its moment of inertia is probably best found using an experimental method. One of the methods often used for this purpose (the *compound pendulum method*) involves suspending the body and setting it to oscillate about an axis through the point of suspension. The time that it takes to complete one cycle of oscillation (the *period* of the swing) is then used to compute the moment of inertia of the body about that axis using the equation:

$$I_O = \frac{W h T^2}{4\pi^2} \tag{6-6}$$

where I_O = the moment of inertia about the axis through the point of suspension, O; W = the weight of the body; h = the distance from the center of gravity of the body to the point O; and T = the period of the swing.

Experimental methods have been used to obtain values for the moments of inertia of segments of the human body (Table 6-4), and these values can be used in determining the moment of inertia of a whole body. The procedure, somewhat akin to that of finding a body's center of gravity by the segmentation method, involves the use of a relationship known as the *parallel-axes theorem*. This theorem (which enables the moment of inertia of a body about any axis to be computed if its moment of inertia about a parallel axis through its center of gravity is known) is probably stated most simply in algebraic form:

$$I_A = I_{CG} + md^2 \qquad (6\text{-}7)$$

where I_A = the moment of inertia of the body about an axis through the point A; I_{CG} = the moment of inertia of the body about a parallel axis through its center of gravity; m = the mass of the body, and d = the distance between the parallel axes. The two terms on the right-hand side of Eq. (6-7) are know, respectively, as the *local term* and the *remote (or transfer) term*.

An example may help to clarify the meaning of this theorem. Suppose one wanted to compute the moment of inertia of a sprinter's leg as it rotated about an axis through the hip joint in the recovery phase of a running stride (Fig. 6-33). The moment of inertia of the thigh about a transverse axis through its center of gravity and parallel to the hip axis is given in Table 6-4 as 0.1052 kg·m². The mass of the thigh is given in Table 6-1 as 0.103 times the total body mass. If this latter is, say, 70 kg, the mass of the thigh is 7.21 kg. The distance between the thigh center of gravity axis and the hip is, say, 0.3 m. Then, according to the parallel-axes theorem, the moment of inertia of the thigh about the hip axis is

$$
\begin{aligned}
I'_{hip} &= I_{CG} + md^2 \\
&= (0.1052) + (7.21)(0.3)^2 \\
&= 0.7541 \ \text{kg·m}^2
\end{aligned}
$$

TABLE 6-4 Moments of Inertia of Selected Body Segments about Transverse Axes through Their Centers of Gravity

Segment	Moment of Inertia (kg·m²)
Head	0.0248
Trunk	1.2606
Upper arm	0.0213
Forearm	0.0076
Hand	0.0005
Thigh	0.1052
Calf	0.0504
Foot	0.0038

Source: Adapted from Whitsett, C. E. (1963). *Some Dynamic Response Characteristics of Weightless Man*, (p. 11). AMRL Technical Documentary Report 63–70. Wright-Patterson Air Force Base, Ohio: AMRL.

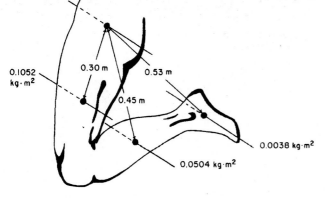

0.1052 kg·m²

0.30 m

0.53 m

0.45 m

0.0038 kg·m²

0.0504 kg·m²

Figure 6-33.
The moment of inertia of a sprinter's leg can readily be determined using the parallel-axes theorem.

Similar computations yield the moment of inertia of the calf about the hip axis:

$$I''_{hip} = I_{CG} + md^2$$
$$= (0.0504) + (3.01)(0.45)^2$$
$$= 0.6599 \text{ kg·m}^2$$

and the moment of inertia of the foot about the hip axis:

$$I'''_{hip} = I_{CG} + md^2$$
$$= (0.0038) + (1.05)(0.53)^2$$
$$= 0.2987 \text{ kg·m}^2$$

The moment of inertia of the whole lower limb about the hip axis is then found by simply adding the values for the three segments:

$$I_{hip} = I'_{hip} + I''_{hip} + I'''hip$$
$$= (0.7541 + 0.6599 + 0.2987)\text{kg·m}^2$$
$$= 1.7127 \text{ kg·m}^2$$

Obviously this procedure could be extended to include all the segments of a body. In this way, the moment of inertia of the whole body about an appropriate axis could be found. (Fig. 6-34 shows the moments of inertia of a human body in some common diving and gymnastic positions.)

PRINCIPAL AXES

The rotation of a body is commonly described with reference to three axes (known as *principal axes*), which pass through its center of gravity. These axes are perpendicular to each other and are so located that the body's moment of inertia about one of them is larger (and about another is

$$I_{CG} = 3.5 \text{ kg} \cdot \text{m}^2$$

$$I_{CG} = 6\,5 \text{ kg} \cdot \text{m}^2$$

$$I_{CG} = 15.0 \text{ kg} \cdot \text{m}^2$$

$$I_{HBAR} = 83.0 \text{ kg} \cdot \text{m}^2$$

Figure 6-34. Moments of inertia in some typical diving and gymnastic positions.

smaller) than it is about any other axis that passes through the center of gravity of the body.

For a human body in an erect standing position, the principal axes are closely approximated by lines drawn through the center of gravity and passing from the top of the head to the feet (the *longitudinal axis*), from left to right (the *transverse axis*), and from front to rear (the *frontal* or *antero-posterior axis*). For positions other than erect standing, the locations of the principal axes are not so obvious. They can nonetheless be determined using methods described by Hinrichs.[24]

The angular momentum H possessed by a rotating body is equal to the product of its moment of inertia and its angular velocity:

ANGULAR MOMENTUM

$$H = I\omega \qquad (6\text{-}8)$$

Thus, if the diver in Fig. 6-34(a) is rotating at 10 rad/s about the transverse axis through his center of gravity, his angular momentum is

$$3.5 \times 10 = 35 \text{ kg·m}^2/\text{s}$$

(Note again the parallel between corresponding quantities in linear and angular motion: momentum = mv; angular momentum = $I\omega$.)

The angular momentum of a human body about a given axis is determined in a manner similar to that used to determine its moment of inertia about a given axis. Consider the gymnast in Fig. 6-35. Here H_S, the angular momentum of a segment about the transverse axis through G, the center of gravity of the body, is given by:

$$H_S = I_S\omega_{S/G_S} + m_S r^2 \omega_{G_S/G} \qquad (6\text{-}9)$$

where I_S = the moment of inertia of the segment about the transverse axis through G_S, the center of gravity of the segment; $\omega_{S/G}$ = the angular velocity of the segment about the transverse axis through G_S; m_S = the mass of the segment; r = the distance G_SG; and $\omega_{G_S/G}$ = the angular velocity of G_S about the transverse axis through G. As in Eq. (6-7), the two terms on the right-hand side of Eq. (6-9) are known as the local term and remote term, respectively.

The total angular momentum (H) of the gymnast's body about the transverse axis through G is obtained by summing the angular momenta for all segments:

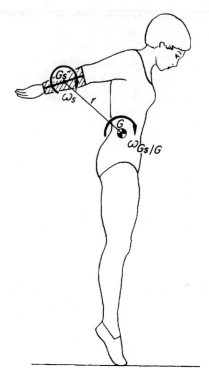

Figure 6-35.
Procedure for computing the angular momentum of a segment about the transverse axis through the center of gravity of a body.

$$H = \sum_{S=1}^{S=N} H_s$$

$$= \sum_{S=1}^{S=N} (I_S\omega_{S/G_S} + m_S r^2 \omega_{G_S/G})$$

(6-10)

where N = the number of segments into which the body is divided. Readers interested in obtaining further information concerning the computation of the angular momentum of a human body are referred to a study by Hay, Wilson, Dapena and Woodworth.[25] Angular momentum values for athletes performing various sports techniques can be found in Hay and Reid.[26])

ANALOGUES OF NEWTON'S LAWS OF MOTION

Just as most of the quantities of linear kinematics and linear kinetics have equivalent (or analogous) forms in angular motion, so too do Newton's laws of motion. Although perhaps not so widely known as the laws applying to linear motion, these analogous forms are nonetheless of considerable importance in obtaining an understanding of many sports techniques.

The First Law.   For present purposes, the angular analogue of Newton's first law can be stated as follows:

A rotating body will continue to turn about its axis of rotation with constant angular momentum, unless an external couple or eccentric force is exerted upon it.

This statement, perhaps better known as the *principle of conservation of angular momentum*, means that a spinning body will continue spinning indefinitely (and with the same angular momentum) unless some other body exerts a couple or an eccentric force on it that causes it to modify its angular motion.

This fact is of particular significance to divers, gymnasts, jumpers, and other athletes who leave the ground during the course of their events. Consider the example of a diver performing a tucked backward one-and-one-half somersault dive (Fig. 6-36). As he leaves the board, his extended body has certain amounts of linear and angular momentum—linear mo-

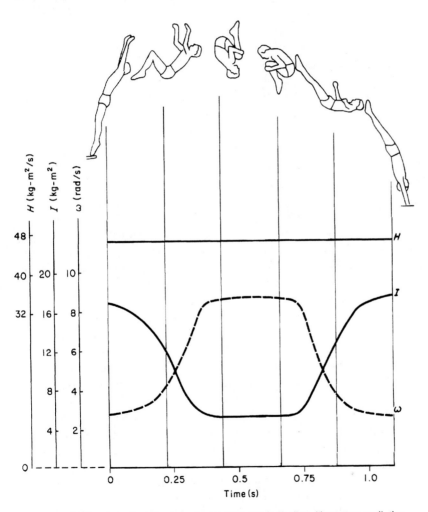

Figure 6-36. A tucked backward one-and-one-half dive illustrates well the interplay between angular momentum, moment of inertia, and angular velocity.

mentum to project him high into the air and to give him time to complete his mid-air actions, and angular momentum to rotate him through the required one-and-one-half somersaults. Shortly after takeoff the diver moves into a tucked position, thereby moving his body mass much closer to the axis of rotation and decreasing his moment of inertia. Because his angular momentum can be altered only by an external couple or eccentric force, the internal forces involved in this tucking process have no effect upon it—it is the same when he is in the tuck as it was when he left the board in an extended position. A quick glance at Eq. (6-8) shows that the only way a diver can decrease his moment of inertia and yet still retain the same angular momentum is to increase his angular velocity by a corresponding amount. This is exactly what happens. At takeoff he has a relatively large moment of inertia and a relatively small angular velocity. When he tucks, he decreases his moment of inertia and increases his angular velocity—and, of course, it is this latter effect that he is trying to produce. He wants to rotate quickly enough to complete his one-and-one-half somersaults in time to prepare himself for a controlled entry. As the diver comes out of his tucked position and extends his body in preparation for entry, this whole process is reversed—his angular velocity decreases as his body extension causes his moment of inertia to be increased.

A trampolinist performing the stunt known as "swivel hips" makes use of the same interdependence of angular velocity and moment of inertia as he brings his body mass close to the axis of rotation during the flight (Fig. 6-37). The beginner gymnast learning how to do a handspring also makes

Figure 6-37.
Swivel hips, another example of the
conservation-of-angular-momentum
principle.

use of the same principle when he tucks in preparation for landing (Fig.
6-38). Instinctively he knows that he has insufficient angular momentum to
enable him to complete the stunt in the approved manner, so he tucks and
increases his angular velocity so that he can at least avoid crashing on his
back.

The Second Law. The angular analogue of Newton's second law can be
stated as follows:

*The rate of change of angular momentum of a body is proportional to the torque
causing it and the change takes place in the direction in which the torque acts.*

or it can be expressed algebraically in the form

$$T \propto \frac{(I_f\omega_f - I_i\omega_i)}{t}$$

Figure 6-38. Good form in the handspring, contrasted with the poor form used
by a beginner to "salvage" the stunt.

where T = the applied torque, I_i and I_f = the initial and final moments of inertia, and ω_i and ω_f = the initial and final angular velocities. If $I_1 = I_2$, this relationship reduces to

$$T \propto I \frac{(\omega_f - \omega_i)}{t}$$

$$\propto I\alpha$$

where α = the angular acceleration. With the methods explained on p. 65, this equation can be converted to the form

$$T = I\alpha \qquad (6\text{-}11)$$

The diver in Fig. 6-36 provides a useful example of the application of Eq. (6-11). At the instant depicted, her body is being angularly accelerated about an axis through her feet. The torque causing this angular acceleration is equal to the product of the diver's weight and the horizontal distance x. If the diver is executing a dive requiring a large amount of rotation (say, a forward two-and-a-half), she will want this torque to be relatively large so that her body can leave the board with sufficient angular velocity to enable her to complete the dive. On the other hand, if she is executing a dive that involves very little rotation (say, a plain forward dive), she will have little need for angular acceleration during the takeoff and will want to keep the applied torque relatively small. Because her weight is constant, and the only other factor that influences the magnitude of the torque is the distance x, the only way in which she can control this torque is by making alterations in the magnitude of x. This is exactly what she does. By varying the amount of forward body lean that she has at takeoff, she controls the magnitude of x and hence also the magnitude of the torque applied at this time.

The Third Law.   The angular analogue of Newton's third law can be stated as follows:

For every torque that is exerted by one body on another there is an equal and opposite torque exerted by the second body on the first.

Sports offer countless examples to illustrate this angular equivalent of Newton's third law. Probably the most common is that in which an athlete applies a torque to one part of his (or her) body by contracting a muscle (or group of muscles), thereby causing that part to rotate. The equal and opposite reaction to this applied torque causes some other part of the body to rotate, or tend to rotate, in the opposite direction.

   When a long jumper swings his legs forward ready for landing, a torque equal and opposite to that exerted on his legs is applied to the remainder of his body. The net effect is that as the jumper swings his legs forward and upward, in say a clockwise direction, the remainder of his body moves forward and downward in a counterclockwise direction (Fig. 6-39).

It should be noted here that since the angular accelerations obtained when equal torques are applied to two different bodies depend on their respective moments of inertia [Eq. (6-11)], the effect on one body is rarely equal to that produced on the other—see the corresponding linear case, pp. 69–70. This is evident in a basketball jump shot, for example. When a player propels the ball toward the basket by extending the elbow and flexing the wrist, the remainder of the body is acted upon by torques equal in magnitude and opposite in direction to those causing these movements. Because the moment of inertia of the rest of the body is much greater than that of either the forearm or hand, the effects of these equal torques appear to be quite different. Whereas the forearm and hand sweep quickly through a relatively large angle, the remainder of the body exhibits only a slight tendency to rotate in the opposite direction.

Angular "action-reaction" effects are by no means limited to a forward-backward (or sagittal) plane. In an across-the-body (or frontal) plane these effects are very clearly seen in the instinctive responses of a gymnast who senses she is about to topple off a balance beam (Fig. 6-40). As soon as she feels she is starting to overbalance, she rotates her arms (and perhaps her nonsupporting leg) in the direction in which she is falling. The effect of these actions is to cause the rest of her body to rotate in the opposite direction. If this maneuver is successfully carried out, her tendency to overbalance is arrested.

Figure 6-39.
Angular action and reaction in a long-jump landing.

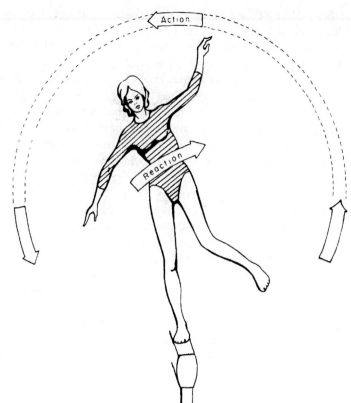

Figure 6-40.
The gymnast's instinctive actions create
an angular reaction tending to restore her
balance.

The tennis player in Fig. 6-41 exerts torques to produce the clockwise backhand stroke depicted. These torques are accompanied by equal and opposite torques, which tend to turn the rest of his body in a counterclockwise direction. However, because his feet are in firm contact with the

Figure 6-41.
The reaction to the tennis player's
backhand drive is "absorbed" by the
ground.

ground, this contrary tendency is transmitted to the ground. Now, the moment of inertia of the tennis player about the axis in question is relatively small and the angular acceleration he experiences is thus clearly apparent—one can readily see how he is affected by the torques produced by his muscles. In contrast, the moment of inertia of the earth is enormous, and the angular acceleration it experiences as a result of the torques transmitted via the player's feet is quite imperceptible. Players are often exhorted, therefore, to keep both feet in contact with the ground so that the reactions that accompany the strokes they make can be "absorbed" in this way.

TRANSFER OF MOMENTUM

When a body is in the air and the angular momentum of one part of the body is decreased, some part (or all) of the rest of the body must experience an increase in angular momentum if the total angular momentum is to he conserved (or held constant). For example, consider the case of a diver performing a piked front dive (Fig. 6-42). As he goes into his piked position, the angular momentum of his legs is reduced to near-zero—they appear to be stationary in the air—and the angular momentum of his arms and trunk is increased. Then, as he assumes his position for entry, this process is reversed. The angular momentum of the arms and trunk is reduced to near-zero—and they appear to remain stationary—while the legs swing upward and into line with the rest of the body. This process whereby momentum is redistributed within the body is commonly referred to as a *transfer of momentum*.

A similar process occurs in diving, gymnastics, and a few other activities where performers execute movements in flight that involve both somersaulting and twisting. Such movements generally involve a transfer (or "trading") of part of the somersaulting angular momentum, initiated during the takeoff, for the twisting angular momentum needed during the flight.

Consider the case of a diver who leaves the board to execute a front dive (Fig. 6-43[a]) and then, while in the air, swings one arm sideways to bring it down alongside his body. The reaction to this motion is a contrary rotation of the rest of his body about his frontal axis—a side-somersaulting rotation that tilts his body in the opposite direction (Fig. 6-43[b]). Although impossible in practice, suppose that the diver's arm is so massive that, in reaction to its downward movement, his body is brought into a horizontal position (Fig. 6-43[c]).

Now when the diver left the board he possessed a certain amount of angular momentum about a horizontal axis perpendicular to the line of the board (an axis sometimes referred to as the *axis of momentum*) and, because the transverse axis of his body coincided with this horizontal axis, he experienced a somersaulting rotation. When his body was subsequently rotated into a horizontal position, his longitudinal axis was brought into line with the axis of momentum. Thus, in keeping with the conservation-of-

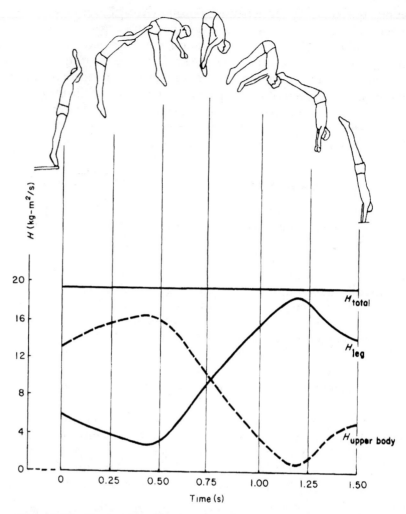

Figure 6-42. The angular momentum of a diver performing a piked front dive is first localized in his upper body and then in his legs.

angular-momentum principle, his body acquired the same mount of angular momentum about its longitudinal axis as it had previously possessed about its transverse axis. In other words, by readjusting the position of his body relative to the axis of momentum, the diver was able to "trade" all his somersaulting momentum for twisting momentum.

In practice, the actions used to make the body tilt—generally both arms moved in the same angular direction—are insufficient to produce more than a very limited amount of side-somersaulting rotation. As a result, only part of the diver's somersaulting angular momentum is "traded" for twisting angular momentum, and the dive is executed with both somersaulting and twisting proceeding simultaneously. Finally, because the trading of somersaulting for twisting angular momentum requires the diver to move

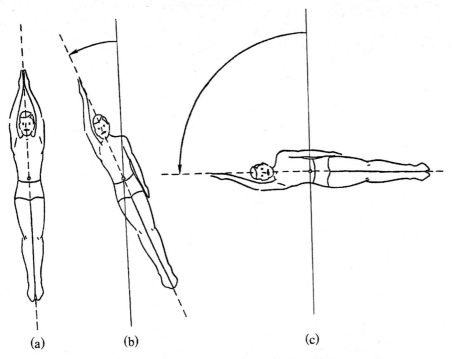

(a)   (b)   (c)

Figure 6-43. With appropriate actions to rotate him sideways, a diver can "trade" somersaulting angular momentum for twisting angular momentum.

his body out of alignment with the vertical plane of his flight path, his body is not correctly positioned for entry once he has completed the prescribed number of twists and somersaults. To correct for this, the good diver reverses the direction of his earlier arm action, thereby imparting sufficient side-somersaulting rotation to his body to bring it back into its original alignment for entry.

The concept of transferring momentum is most frequently used in explaining what takes place in situations other than those in which a body is in the air. For example, a diver performing a backward dive swings the arms upward and backward prior to leaving the board. Then, as the arms near the limit of their range of motion in this direction, they begin to slow down. The angular momentum that the arms lose at this time (or at least a large portion of it) is "matched" by a corresponding increase in the angular momentum of the rest of the body. Now, although the angular momentum of a body is not necessarily conserved in situations like this (since the body is subject to external torques that tend to alter its angular momentum), the effect is qualitatively very similar to cases in which the angular momentum is conserved— one part of the body loses (or "gives up") angular momentum at the same time as another part experiences a gain in angular momentum.

The concept of transferring momentum should not be used to explain what happens in cases like this. Because external forces and torques acting on the body can completely change the outcome, one might argue that the slowing of one part of the body causes a transfer of momentum to another when exactly the opposite is true. For example, Putnam[27,28] studied punt kicking and found that the slowing of the thigh of the kicking leg, as it approached the forward limit of the range of motion of the hip joint, did not produce a transferring of angular momentum to the lower leg and foot, as is commonly supposed. Instead, she found that the angular momentum of the lower leg and foot would have been greater if the thigh had not been forced to slow down.

INITIATING ROTATION IN THE AIR

Although the angular analogues of Newton's laws indicate quite clearly that a body cannot acquire angular momentum unless acted upon by an external torque, the possibility of initiating rotation in the air has been of considerable interest for some time. Sparking much of this interest has been the performance of cats, rabbits, guinea pigs, and other animals, which have the ability to right themselves when falling upside down. While initially some doubts were expressed that these animals initiated the turns in the air rather than at the time of takeoff, it is now widely accepted that this is the case.

How are these turns initiated in apparent defiance of Newton's laws? The answer most frequently put forward lies in the relationship between the moments of inertia of the body parts that interact when an angular action is initiated in the air. Consider the cat being dropped in Fig. 6-44. As the cat begins to fall, it bends (or pikes) in the middle (Fig. 6-44[a]), brings

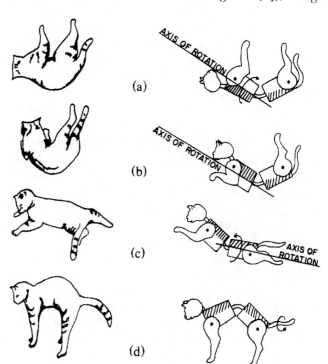

(a)

(b)

(c)

(d)

Figure 6-44.
A falling cat initiates rotation in the air in the absence of an external torque and in apparent defiance of the law of conservation of angular momentum. (The figures from which these diagrams were redrawn first appeared in *New Scientist,* the weekly international review of science and technology, 128 Long Acre, London WC2, and appear with the publisher's permission.)

its front legs in close to its head, and rotates its upper body through 180° (Fig. 6-44[b]). In reaction to this rotation, its lower trunk, hind legs, and tail, all of which are some considerable distance from the axis of rotation, rotate in the opposite direction. However, because the moment of inertia of these body parts is much greater than that of the upper body, the angular distance through which they move is correspondingly small ("about 5°" according to McDonald[29]). To complete the required 180° turn, the cat then brings its hind legs and tail into line with its lower trunk and rotates these body parts about an axis running longitudinally through its hind-quarters (Fig. 6-44[c]). The reaction is again very small, this time due to the disposition of the upper body relative to the axis. Finally, to make any minor adjustments necessary, the cat rotates its tail in a direction opposite to that in which it is desired to move the body. (Since Manx cats and cats completely without tails can right themselves if held upside down and dropped, these final movements of the tail are clearly *not* essential ingredients of the righting maneuver.)

It should be carefully noted that throughout this whole sequence of movements the angular momentum of one body part has always been "matched" with an equal and opposite angular momentum of some other part and that, as a consequence, the total angular momentum has been quite unaffected. In short, the cat has *not* defied Newton's laws but has merely appeared to do so.

Research by Smith and Kane[30] and Kane and Scher[31], has suggested an alternative explanation of the process by which the cat rights itself when dropped in an inverted position. The basic concepts involved here are perhaps most clearly demonstrated and explained with the aid of a simple experiment on a "frictionless" turntable (Fig. 6-45). If the girl in Fig. 6-45

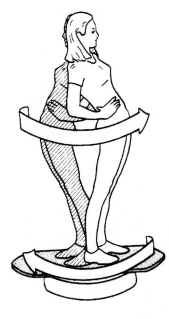

Figure 6-45.
Rotation of the hips in one direction produces a rotation of the whole body in the opposite direction. The body's angular momentum is conserved in this process, sometimes referred to as "hula-hooping."

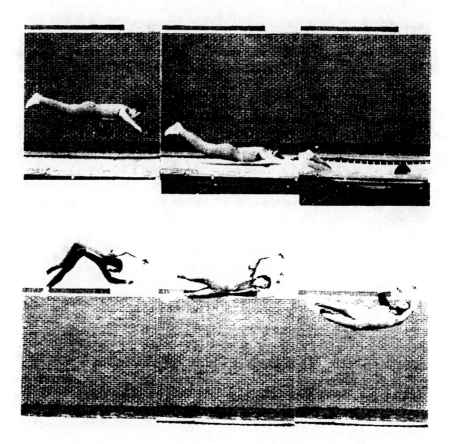

stands on the turntable and then moves her hips in a large, counter clockwise circling motion as shown, the turntable rotates in a clockwise direction, eventually carrying the girl through as many complete revolutions as she chooses.

As the girl performs the circling motion with her hips, both her upper and lower body acquire counterclockwise angular momentum about a vertical axis through her feet. Simultaneously, and because there are no external forces acting upon her to change the zero angular momentum she had initially, the turntable and her body as a whole rotate in a clockwise direction.

The angular momentum in the clockwise direction exactly matches the angular momentum in the counterclockwise direction and the sum of the two remains equal to zero. Assuming that the turntable is truly frictionless and that the girl is thus accurately simulating what would happen if she were in the air, the hip-circling motion—occasionally referred to as "hula-hooping"—permits the girl to initiate a twisting rotation "in-the-air" and in the absence of any prior angular momentum.

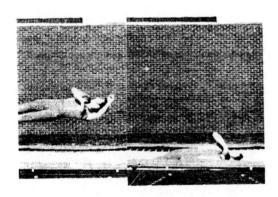

Figure 6-46.
A trampolinist can initate a rotation in the air, as in this front-drop, pike, half-twist, flat-back sequence.

With all the interest in this question of how a falling cat rights itself, some interesting side results have been reported:[32]

- If dropped upside down, a cat can turn over within its own standing height.
- The cat's eyes and the mechanisms of its inner ear both play a part in sensing the need to initiate a turn. Of these, the eyes seem to be the more important—a blindfolded cat dropped from as low as 90 cm lands clumsily, while a cat without an intact inner ear mechanism can still right itself efficiently. However, a cat deprived of both sensory organs made no attempt to right itself when dropped upside down.
- A blindfolded cat, rotated in a special apparatus to "confuse" the organs of its inner ear, was reported to have rotated over and landed on its back when it accidentally slipped feet first out of the apparatus!

The possibility of athletes' using similar techniques has been the source of some interest, and various writers have discussed the matter relative to diving,[33][34][35][36] gymnastics,[37][38] and track and field.[39][40] The question has also interested those engaged in research related to man's ability to maneuver in a weightless state.[41][42][43]

From all this research and speculation several conclusions have been reached:

- A person can initiate rotation while in the air. A simple demonstration of this can be given by a trained gymnast who does a series of consecutive, pike-to-front-drop movements on a trampoline and executes a half twist to land in a flat back position (instead of in a front drop) when called upon to do so (Fig. 6-46). A shouted command to the gymnast shortly after he leaves the bed—and at which time he has zero angular momentum because that is what is required to perform a series of consecutive front drops—enables him to demonstrate the point convincingly.

- A person's ability to initiate rotation in the air is a function of how much training or practice he (or she) has had—in a plain jump from a 1-m board, a trained diver can initiate a twist in the air and turn through as much as 450°, while an untrained person can rarely exceed 90°.

- The basic mechanism involved appears to be similar to that used by the cat, although there are variations from movement to movement and from one individual to another in performing the same movement.

- Starting positions in which the body is arched or piked facilitate the initiating of rotation. In addition, it appears that while a person can, with relative ease, initiate a twisting rotation while in the air, initiating rotations about either of the other two principal axes does not appear to be quite so easy.

The extent to which divers, trampolinists, and others involved in "aerial activities" actually use such techniques is anything but easy to determine. It is clear though that some of the movements in such activities are executed in a manner consistent with the initiation of catlike rotations in the air.

CENTRIPETAL AND CENTRIFUGAL FORCE

In a well-executed standing long jump, the pectorals, deltoids, and other muscles of the chest and shoulders exert forces on the arms of the performer. The resultant of these forces (F in Figure 6-47) can be resolved into two components: one that acts along the line of the arm and through the shoulder joint axis about which the arm rotates (the radial component F_R); and one that acts at right angles to this line (the tangential component F_T). F_R is responsible for the radial acceleration that changes the direction in which the arm is moving and F_T is responsible for the angular acceleration that increases the tangential velocity of the arm (see pp. 55–57). Because F_R acts toward the axis (the "center of rotation"), it is frequently referred to as the *centripetal* (or "center-seeking") *force*.

The magnitude of F_R is obtained by combining the equations for Newton's second law ($F = ma$) and for radial acceleration ($a_R = v_T{}^2/r$). Thus:

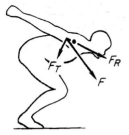

Figure 6-47.
The resultant force (F) can be resolved into radial and tangential components (F_R and F_T, respectively). The radial component is also known as the centripetal force.

$$F_R = m \frac{v_T^2}{r} \qquad (6\text{-}12)$$

Further, because $v_T = \omega r$ [Eq. (4-5)], it is sometimes useful to substitute $\omega^2 r^2$ for v_T^2 in Eq. (6-12). The right-hand side of this equation is then expressed in terms of angular rather than linear velocity.

$$F_R = mr\omega^2 \qquad (6\text{-}13)$$

Consider now the case of a badminton player performing a "wristy" backhand shot in which the forearm is held stationary while the wrist moves rapidly from full flexion to full extension. The racket has a mass of 0.10 kg and its center of gravity is 0.36 m from the axis through the wrist and is moving with a speed of 20 m/s (Fig. 6-48). Then using Eq. (6-12), the centripetal force applied to the racket must be:

$$\frac{0.10 \times 20^2}{0.36} = 111.1 \text{ N}$$

Further, since the player's hand is the only other body in contact with the racket, this 111.1 N force must be applied to the racket by the hand. Now

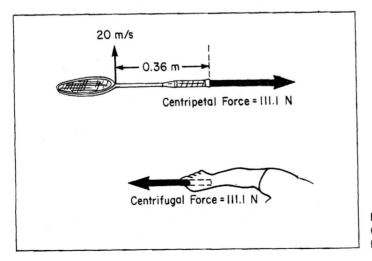

20 m/s

0.36 m

Centripetal Force = 111.1 N

Centrifugal Force = 111.1 N

Figure 6-48.
Centripetal and centrifugal forces in a backhand shot in badminton.

whenever one body exerts a force on another "there is an equal and opposite force exerted by the second body on the first" (Newton's third law). Thus, if the hand exerts a force of 111.1 N on the racket, the racket in turn exerts a force of 111.1 N in the opposite direction on the hand. This force, which always acts away from the center of rotation, is termed the *centrifugal* (or "center-fleeing") *force.* *Note:* The two words centripetal and centrifugal often cause problems because they look and sound so much alike. Their deliberate mispronunciation is one way to avoid some of these problems:

> These two words have opposite meanings, but their proper pronunciations sound somewhat alike: *centrip't'l* and *centrif'g'l*. To avoid dangerous confusion in discussions, it would be wise to mispronounce them: centri-*pet'l* and centri-*fewg'l*.[44]

The concept of a centrifugal force is frequently the source of confusion. The two principal reasons appear to be:

- A failure to recognize that centrifugal and centripetal forces do not both act on the same body. Apart from the fact that Newton's third law indicates that the "action" acts on one body and the "reaction" on another, it should be obvious that the resultant of two equal and opposite forces acting on a body is zero and that application of a zero force would not change the direction in which a body is moving.
- A failure to realize that "actions" and "reactions" occur simultaneously. Thus, if a tennis player released his (or her) grip on the racket partway through a stroke, both the centripetal force exerted by the hand on the racket and the centrifugal force exerted by the racket on the hand would cease to exist at the same time. Under such circumstances, and in accord with Newton's first law, the racket would tend to continue traveling in the same direction as it was at the moment of release (that is, tangent to the point on the arc at which it was located at that instant). (*Note:* Contrary to what is often supposed in such cases, the racket does not have a tendency to travel radially outward under the action of a centrifugal force because [a] the centrifugal force acts on the player's hand and not on the racket; and [b] even if it did act on the racket, it would cease to exist at the moment the corresponding centripetal force was removed.)

Centripetal and centrifugal forces are exerted whenever a body moves on a curved path. In sports, however, there are times when these forces seem more important than others because athletes must make conscious adjust-

---

* Some authorities on mechanics define the centrifugal force, acting on a body moving along a curved path, as an imaginary force that has a magnitude equal to the magnitude of the resultant force on the body, and that acts through the center of gravity of the body in a direction opposite to that of the resultant force. The definition of centrifugal force presented above is preferred because it is considered to be simpler in concept and more useful in practice than this alternative definition.

ments in technique to allow for their existence. Probably the most striking examples are seen when track sprinters and cyclists negotiate a bend in the track. Here the only body that can exert the required centripetal force on them is the ground, the only body with which they are in contact. If the ground exerts an inward horizontal force against the foot of the runner (or against the wheels of the bike), this eccentric force will have the required effect of changing the direction of motion. However, it will also have the undesirable effect of rotating the runner (or cyclist) outward. (Remember, an eccentric force causes both translation and rotation—see p. 111). To combat this rotary effect, the athlete leans inward so that the vertical component of the ground reaction will also act eccentrically and provide a moment in the opposite direction to that produced by the eccentric centripetal force. When the speed of athletes exceeds a certain limit (as it often does in cycling and motor sports) or the radius of the track is very small (as at many indoor track meets), the ground is no longer able to provide the necessary amount of centripetal force. This means that, unless some additional provision is made, the athletes will have to slow down going into the bends or risk failing to negotiate them safely. It is to avoid these problems that banked tracks are built for cycling velodromes and indoor track meets. In this way the component of the athlete's weight acting down the slope can contribute to the centripetal force required, and the need for an inward directed force exerted by the ground is at least reduced, and perhaps eliminated entirely.

Exercises

1. (a) A male ballet dancer performs a standing leap in which he rotates through 720° about his long axis and then lands on the spot from which he took off. To achieve the rotation he needed about his long axis he exerted a couple against the floor via his feet. How do we know this? Or, to state the same question another way, how do we know he didn't use an eccentric force to produce the rotation? If he turned towards his left, in what direction did he exert horizontal force against the floor with his left foot during the takeoff? And with his right foot?

   (b) Would it be easier for him to generate the needed moment about his long axis if he had his feet close together, or somewhat apart, or doesn't it make any difference? (Assume here that the longitudinal axis of the dancer is vertical at takeoff.)

2. When a golfer hits a long putt on a green, the ball first slides for some distance and then begins to roll. Why does it slide initially? What causes it to change from sliding to rolling?

3. (a) Turn to page 119 and trace the left arm of the gymnast in Figure 6-7 and the arrow representing the force F_L exerted by the ring on the gymnast's left hand. Sketch an arc to close off the shoulder end of the segment. Place a dot on the tracing to indicate the location of the left shoulder joint. Add an arrow and a label (W), to represent the weight of the arm segment acting down through its center of gravity; and another arrow and label (F) acting

upward and outward through the shoulder joint, to represent the force that trunk exerts on the shoulder. Finally, draw a curved arrow and attach a label (*M*) directed counterclockwise around the shoulder joint, to represent the moment exerted by the muscles and other tissues crossing the shoulder joint. With these things done, you now have a free-body diagram of the gymnast's left arm.

(b) Add thin arrows to represent the distances (*a* and *b*, respectively) from the center of gravity of the segment to the shoulder joint and from the hand to the shoulder joint.

(c) Taking moments about the shoulder joint (*S*), develop an algebraic equation for *M*, the moment due to the muscles and other tissues crossing the shoulder. Because this is primarily due to muscle action, this moment is a rough measure of the muscular effort that the gymnast must make to hold the cross position.

(d) Using your knowledge of where the center of gravity of the arm is located along the length of the arm, and making the best estimates you can of the weight and length of a gymnast's arm, develop a set of values that you can substitute in the equation you derived in 3(c). Then, calculate the magnitude of the moment at the shoulder.

(e) Finally, compute the moment at the shoulder for the case when the gymnast has his arms straight and at his side, and is supporting himself on the rings in this position. Why is it easier for the gymnast to maintain this position than it is to maintain the cross position.

4. The following statement appeared in a book on the use of mechanics to analyze sports techniques: "The weight of the mass on any one side of the center of gravity must be equal to the weight on the opposite side." Why is this statement incorrect?

5. Find a large, clear photograph of an athlete performing in his (or her) sport and paste it to a strong piece of cardboard. When the paste is dry, take a pair of scissors and cut carefully around the outline of the athlete's body. Get a thumbtack, a roughly 50 cm length of light string, and a small weight (a washer, or a nut or something similar). Tie the weight to one end of the string and the thumbtack to the other. Stick the thumbtack through the cardboard cutout near the edge of the cutout and into a vertical surface (a wall or bulletin board, for example). Make sure that the string and the weight are on the side of the cutout farther from the vertical surface and that the cutout can rotate freely from side to side. You'll probably have to wriggle it about a little to get the hole large enough to allow this. Hold the weight and string away from the surface of the cutout and set it swinging from side to side. When it comes to rest, lower the weight and allow it to come to rest in a vertical position. Take a pencil and a ruler and rule a line on the cutout along the line of the string. Pull the thumbtack out and push it through the cutout near the edge at some distance away from its previous position. Repeat the remaining steps just described. Why is the point where the two lines intersect *not* the center of gravity of the athlete?

6. A football lineman decided that he will be able to move forward and backward from his initial three-point stance with equal ease if he has his center of gravity an equal distance from the forward and backward limits of his base. In short, halfway between a line through his supporting hand and a line through the ball of his rear foot. To test how good he is in assuming such a position, he sets up a reaction board and takes an initial scale reading. He then takes up his three-point stance facing along the length of the board. A friend rules a line through his supporting hand and the ball of his rear foot, and takes a second reading from the scales. If the relevant data are as follows, how good is he at assuming the position he wants?

Weight of player = 1100 N

Distance between knife edges of reaction board = 180 cm

Distance from hand to knife edge on scales = 60 cm

Distance from foot to knife edge on scales = 160 cm

Initial reading on scales = 80 N

Final reading on scales = 460 N

Figure 6–49.

7. Use the segmentation method to determine the location of the center of gravity of the athlete in Figure 6-49.

8. Use the segmentation method to locate the centers of gravity of the segments, and of the whole body, of the athlete in Figure 6-50. Then use the data of Whitsett (Table 6-4), and the parallel axes theorem, to compute the moment of inertia of the whole body about the athlete's transverse axis.

Figure 6–50.

9. A skydiver is falling with his body in a prone position and his arms and legs straight and at angles of 45 degrees to the line of his trunk. If he adducts his legs so that they are straight and together, and brings his straight arms together over his head, what happens to his moment of inertia about his longitudinal axis? About his transverse axis? And about his frontal axis?

10. (a) In the hope of making things easier to understand, a leading sports bio-mechanist refers to the three principal axes of the human body as the somer-saulting, side-somersaulting, and twisting axes. In this book, they are referred to more traditionally as the longitudinal, transverse, and frontal (or antero-posterior) axes. Can you figure out which of the traditional terms coincides with each of the new terms he has suggested?

(b) A cheerleader performs three separate stunts—an aerial cartwheel (a cart-wheel in which the hands do not touch the ground), a back somersault, and a pirouette (a rapid turn while balanced on the ball of one foot). About which of her principal axes does she rotate in each case? Use whichever of the two sets of terms you prefer to describe the axes.

11. Figure 12-19 shows a gymnast performing a giant swing on a horizontal bar. If you were not told which way the gymnast was rotating (clockwise or counter-clockwise), how could you tell from the body positions he adopted during the course of the motion? (*Hint:* To complete the giant swing, the gymnast maxi-

mizes the moment of his weight during the descent and, without assuming an ugly body position, minimizes the moment of his weight during the ascent.)

12. A female gymnast performs a giant swing backward on the upper bar of a set of uneven parallel bars. As she swings downward, she abducts (or straddles) her legs to avoid striking her shins on the lower bar. What effect does this action have on (a) her moment of inertia about an axis running along the length of the upper bar; and (b) the moment due to her weight about that axis? Why is it very difficult to determine what effect this action has on her angular acceleration about that same axis?

13. A figure skater stands on her left skate, with arms extended sideways at shoulder level, and swings her right leg so that her right foot describes a wide-sweeping arc. A moment later, she brings her right leg in close to the left leg and crosses her arms in front of her chest. What happens to her moment of inertia about her longitudinal axis when she brings her limbs inward? What happens to her angular velocity about this axis? What happens to her angular momentum about this axis? (Be careful with this last question. Remember she is not up in the air when she performs these movements.)

14. A gymnast is performing a dismount on the horizontal bar. During the flight phase he vigorously rotates his arms in a counterclockwise direction about a transverse axis through his shoulder joints. This is a sign that the gymnast is off-balance and is trying to correct his body position. About what principal axis will this action of the arms tend to rotate him? In what direction (clockwise or counterclockwise) will it tend to rotate him? What can you say about his angular momentum about the principal axis involved, at the instant he released his grip on the bar?

15. A trampolinist sets out to perform a front somersault in which he takes off from his feet in an erect position and lands on his feet in an erect position. He misjudges badly and lands instead on his hands and knees after completing one-and-one-quarter revolutions—one-quarter more than intended. There are several things that he might do to improve his performance. List as many of these as you can and explain in biomechanical terms how each of them might serve to improve the performance.

16. At what point in the backswing and subsequent delivery action of a right-handed tenpin bowler would you expect the angular acceleration of her right arm to be the greatest? *Hint:* Draw a free-body diagram of the arm at selected stages in the sequence of arm movements. Then determine when the moment about a transverse axis through the right shoulder is likely to be the greatest. If you are familiar with the length-tension (or force-length) relationship in muscle, you might also wish to consider what influence this might have here.

17. You are standing on the side of a swimming pool opposite the end of a 1-m diving board. A diver moving from left to right across your field of view performs a standing back dive with a pike. In this dive, the diver takes off with his back toward the far end of the pool, leaps in the air and brings his legs high overhead so that his toes are pointing at the ceiling. At the peak of the flight, the diver's toes are met by his hands which have been high overhead since takeoff, seemingly awaiting the arrival of the toes. The diver then opens out of this piked position and enters the water hands first with his body fully extended in a vertical direction. In the course of all this, the diver's arms and trunk appear to remain stationary while the legs sweep up and around in a clockwise direction to meet them. Then, once the peak of the dive has been reached, the

roles are reversed. The legs appear to remain stationary while the arms and trunk are rotated in a clockwise direction in preparation for entry. Can you explain this alternation of zero and rapid angular motions of the segments of the body in terms of (a) a summation of their angular velocities; and (b) a transfer of angular momentum from one segment to another?

Recommended Readings

ALLMAN, W. F. (1984). In W. Schrier and W. F. Allman (Eds.). *Newton at the Bat: The Science in Sports*. New York: Scribner's, pp. 38–43 (Pool-hall science).

BRANCAZIO, P. J. (1984). *Sport Science: Physical Laws and Optimum Performance*. New York: Simon & Schuster, pp. 118–59. (Rotating bodies); pp. 83–93, 100–109 (More about forces).

COOKE, P. (1984). In W. Schrier and W. F. Allman (Eds.). *Newton at the Bat: The Science in Sports*. New York: Scribner's, pp. 145–49 (Physics on the high dive).

DYSON, G. H. C. (1977). *The Mechanics of Athletics*. New York: Holmes & Meier, pp. 74–132 (Angular motion).

ENOKA, R. M. (1988). *Neuromechanical Basis of Kinesiology*. Champaign, Ill.: Human Kinetics Books, pp. 65–94 (Types of movement analysis).

FARIA, I. E., AND CAVANAGH, P. R. (1978). *The Physiology and Biomechanics of Cycling*. New York: John Wiley, pp. 89–108 (How do I pedal?).

FROHLICH, C. (1980). The physics of somersaulting and twisting. *Scientific American*, 242:154–64.

HAY, J. G., AND REID, J. G. (1988). *Anatomy, Mechanics, and Human Motion*. Englewood Cliffs, N.J.: Prentice Hall, pp. 179–214 (Explaining angular motion [angular kinetics]); pp. 235–38 (Free body diagrams).

RACKHAM, G. (1975). *Diving Complete*. London: Faber & Faber, pp. 141–50 (Body movement and free fall).

TRICKER, R. A. R., AND TRICKER, B. J. K. (1966). *The Science of Movement*. London: Mills & Boon, pp. 28–47 (Simple problems of balance in physics).

WATKINS, J. (1983). *An Introduction to Mechanics of Human Movement*. Boston: MTP Press Limited, pp. 63–141 (Angular motion).

Notes

1. Andrews, J. G. (1981). Mechanical system equilibrium—An abused concept. *Proceedings of the 1981 Annual Meeting of the American Society of Engineering Education, Los Angeles*. 1:130–33.
2. Duggar, B. C. (1962). The center of gravity of the human body. *Human Factors*. 4:131
3. Mosso, A. (1984). Application de la balance a l'étude de la circulation du sang chez l'homme. *Archives Italiennes de Biologie*, 5:130–43.
4. Groves, W. H. (1950). Mechanical analysis of diving. *Research Quarterly*. 21:132–44.
5. McIntosh, P. C., and Hayley, H. W. B. (1952). An investigation into the running long jump. *Journal of Physical Education*. 44:105–8.
6. Payne, A. H., and Blader, F. (1970). A preliminary investigation into the mechanics of the sprint start. *Bulletin of Physical Education*, 8:21–30.
7. Abalakov, W. M. (1975). Cited by D. D. Donskoi in *Grundlagen der Biomechanik* (pp. 161–62). Berlin: Verlag Bartels & Wernitz KG.
8. Dempster, W. T. (1961). Free body diagrams as an approach to the mechanics of human posture and motion. In F. Gaynor Evans (Ed.), *Biomechanical Studies of the Musculo-Skeletal System* pp. 105–6). Springfield. Ill.. Chs. C Thomas.
9. Page, R. L. (1968). The movement of the center of gravity of the human body. *The Leaflet*, March: 18–19.
10. Ibid.
11. Swearingen, J. J. (1962). *Determination of Centers of Gravity of Men*. Oklahoma City: Civil Aeromedical Research Institute.
12. Santschi, W. R., DuBois, J., and Omoto, C. *Moments of Inertia and Centers of Gravity of the Living Human Body*. AMRL Technical Documentary Report 63–36. Wright-Patterson Air Force Base, Ohio: AMRL
13. Dempster. Free body diagrams as an approach to the mechanics of human posture and motion (pp. 105–6).
14. Braune, W., and Fischer, O. *The Center of Gravity of the Human Body as Related to the Equipment of the German Infantry*. Treatises of the Mathematical-Physical Class of the Royal

Academy of Sciences of Saxony, 7, Leipzig, 1889. USAF, Air Material Command Translation no. 379. Dayton, Ohio: USAF.

15. Dempster, W. T. (1955). *Space Requirements of the Seated Operator.* WADC Technical Report 55–159. Wright-Patterson Air Force Base, Ohio: WADC.

16. Clauser, C. E., McConville, J. T., and Young, J. W. (1969). *Weight, Volume and Center of Mass of Segments of the Human Body.* AMRL Technical Report 69–70. Wright-Patterson Air Force Base, Ohio: AMRL.

17. Chandler, R. F., and others (1975). *Investigation of Inertial Properties of the Human Body.* AMRL Technical Report 74–137. Wright-Patterson Air Force Base, Ohio: AMRL.

18. Cleveland, H. G. (1955). The Determination of the Center of Gravity of Segments of the Human Body. Ed.D. dissertation, University of California, Los Angeles, Calif.

19. Dempster. *Space Requirements of the Seated Operator.*

20. Hanavan, E. P. (1964). Mathematical Model of the Human Body. M.S. thesis, Air University, USAF.

21. Kulwicki, P. V., Schlei, E. J., and Vergamini, P. L. (1962). *Weightless Man: Self-Rotation Techniques. AMRL Technical Domentary Report 62–129. Wright-Patterson Air Force Base, Ohio: AMRL.*

22. Whitsett, C. E. (1963). *Some Dynamic Response Characteristics of Weightless Man.* AMRL Technical Documentary Report 63–10. Wright-Patterson Air force Base, Ohio: AMRL.

23. Londeree, B. R. (1969). Principles of stability: A re-examination. *Research Quarterly,* 40:419–22.

24. Hinrichs, R. N. (1978). Principal Axes and Moments of Inertia of the Human Body: An Investigation of the Stability of Rotary Motions. M.A. thesis, University of Iowa.

25. Hay, J. G., and others (1977). A computational technique to determine the angular momentum of a human body. *Journal of Biomechanics,* 10:269–77.

26. Hay, J. G., and Reid, J. G. (1982). *The Anatomical and Mechanical Bases of Human Motion* (p. 223). Englewood Cliffs, N.J.: Prentice Hall.

27. Putnam, C. A. (1980). Segment Interaction in Selected Two-Segment Motions. Ph.D. dissertation, University of Iowa.

28. Putnam, C. A. (1983). Interaction between segments during a kicking motion. In H. Matsui and K. Kobayashi (Eds.), *Biomechanics VIII-B* (pp. 688–694). Champaign, Ill.: Human Kinetics Publishers.

29. McDonald, D. (1960). How does a cat fall on its feet? *The New Scientist,* 7:1647.

30. Smith, P. G., and Kane, T. R. (1967). *The Reorientation of a Human Being in Free Fall.* Stanford University Division of Engineering Mechanics: Technical Report no. 171.

31. Kane, T. R., and Scher, M. P. (1969). A dynamical explanation of the falling cat phenomenon. *International Journal of Solids and Structures,* p. 5.

32. McDonald. How does a cat fall on its feet?, pp. 1647–48.

33. Dyson, G. H. G. (1977). *The Mechanics of Athletics* pp. 171–211. London: University of London Press.

34. Eaves, G. (1969). *The Mechanics of Springboard and Firmboard Techniques.* London: Kaye & Ward Ltd.

35. Lanoue, F. R. (1936). Mechanics of Fancy Diving. M. Ed. thesis, Springfield College.

36. McDonald, D. (1961). How does a man twist in the air? *New Scientist,* 10:501–3.

37. Horne, D. E. (1968). *Trampolining: A Complete Handbook* (p. 111). London: Faber & Faber, Ltd.

38. van Gheluwe, B., and Duquet, W. (1977). A cinematographic evaluation of two twisting theories in the backward somersault. *Journal of Human Movement Studies,* 3:5–20.

39. Chapman, H. A. L. (1957). Rotation—Its problems and effects. In D. Canham and P. Diamond (Eds.), *International Track and Field Digest* (p. 243). Ann Arbor, Mich.: Champions on Film.

40. Dyson. *The Mechanics of Athletics* (pp. 123–26).

41. Kane, T. R., and Scher, M. P. (1970). Human self-rotation by means of limb movements. *Journal of Biomechanics,* 3:39–49.

42. Kulwicki, Schlei, and Vergamini. *Weightless Man: Self-Rotation Techniques.*

43. Smith and Kane. *The Reorientation of a Human Being in Free Fall.*

44. Rogers, E. M. (1960). *Physics for the Inquiring Mind* (p. 302). Princeton, N.J.: Princeton University Press.

7

FLUID MECHANICS

All motion in sports is influenced by the fluid environment in which it takes place. Basketball players driving down the court are slowed a little by the need to push their way through the surrounding air. Skin divers are affected even more by the fluid environment in which they operate. Swimmers compete in two different fluid environments (the water and the air) simultaneously and their motion is influenced by the effects that each of these has on those parts of their bodies that move through them. Their motion is also influenced by the behavior of the interface between the water and the air and, in particular, by the formation of waves.

In a great many instances the effects produced by the fluid environment are so small that they can reasonably be disregarded in all but the most precise analysis. Garfoot,[1] for example, has computed that a 16 lb (71 N) shot, otherwise destined to be thrown approximately 17.07 m, would have this distance reduced by about 0.12 m as a result of air resistance. As this constitutes less than 1 percent of the total distance, the common practice of ignoring the effects of air resistance in shot-putting is clearly justified.

In other cases, the effects of fluid resistance may be very pronounced indeed. Among these are those (like swimming, rowing, canoeing, yachting, and water skiing) concerned with motion through water and those concerned with high-velocity motion through the air (either as projectiles in such sports as skydiving, ski-jumping, archery, baseball, and golf or as nonprojectiles in skiing, ice skating, and motor racing).

The ability of a body to float (that is, to maintain a stationary position at the surface of the water) is of some importance in most aquatic sports. In swimming, for instance, a person's floating ability can influence success at both beginner and championship levels. Logically, a person who is able to float with ease is likely to learn how to swim more readily than one who floats only with difficulty or not at all.[2] At the other end of the performance scale, a champion swimmer who floats high in the water is likely to encounter less resistance to forward motion than one who cannot float as well. If all else is equal, such a swimmer has an advantage over opponents who have less floating ability. (*Note:* While the ability to float is an advantage in swimming, its importance should not be overrated. Many people who cannot float have learned to swim without much difficulty and some of these have even broken world records and won Olympic titles in the sport).

Buoyant Force. The swimmer in Fig. 7-1(a) is floating horizontally on the surface of the water. Because she is in a state of equilibrium in this situation, the sum of the forces acting on her in any direction must be equal

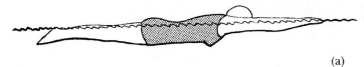

(a)

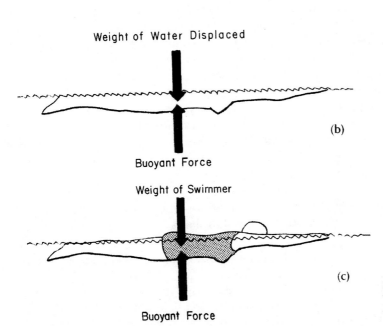

Weight of Water Displaced

(b)

Buoyant Force

Weight of Swimmer

(c)

Buoyant Force

Figure 7-1.
The buoyant force is equal to the weight of the water displaced.

to zero. In the vertical direction (and this is the important one in determining whether a body floats on the surface or sinks below it), the only forces acting are her weight and whatever vertical forces the water exerts on her. Clearly then, the resultant of these upward vertical forces (the so-called *buoyant force*) that the water exerts must be equal in magnitude to her body weight. This simple conclusion leads to the fundamental condition determining whether a given body will float. If the weight of the body is greater than the maximum buoyant force that the water can provide, the body will sink. If it is not, the body will float. Expressing this in mathematical terms, a body will float only if:

The weight of the body ≤ the maximum buoyant force

With the maximum buoyant force obviously of great importance in determining whether a body can float, it is relevant to examine the factors that govern the magnitude of this force.

When the swimmer lies on the surface, she pushes aside (or displaces) a certain amount of water. Before this happens, this displaced water lies in equilibrium under the forces acting upon it. In the vertical direction, these forces are its own weight and the vertical upthrust, or buoyant force, exerted on it by the water below. And, since the water is in equilibrium, the two forces are necessarily equal in magnitude (Fig. 7-1[b]). Now when the swimmer adopts her prone-lying position, she does nothing to alter the state of the water below the water that she displaces. Consequently, the force that this water exerts on her is exactly the same as that which it previously exerted on the displaced water (Fig. 7-1[c]). In other words, she experiences a buoyant force equal in magnitude to the weight of the water that she displaced. (This equality of the buoyant force and the weight of the displaced water was first discovered by Archimedes—while taking a bath! —and is widely known as *Archimedes' principle*.) The maximum volume of water that the swimmer could displace would be a volume equal to that of her own body—such a maximal displacement occurring only if she were totally immersed in the water. This limit on the volume of water that can be displaced sets the upper limit on the magnitude of the buoyant force that can be exerted on the swimmer. The maximum buoyant force has the same magnitude as the weight of a volume of water equal to the volume of the swimmer's body.

Specific Gravity. The fundamental condition determining whether a body can float can now be restated as follows. A body will float only if:

The weight of the body ≤ the weight of an equal volume of water

In dealing with mathematical expressions of this kind it is permissible to divide both sides of the expression by an equal amount. Suppose, therefore, that both sides of the previous expression were divided by "the weight of an equal volume of water." The resulting statement would then read: A body will float only if:

$$\frac{\text{The weight of the body}}{\text{The weight of an equal volume of water}} \leq 1$$

The fraction on the left-hand side is known as the *specific gravity* of a body and, as can be readily surmised, is a useful measure of its capacity to float.

The factors that determine the specific gravity of a human body shed a good deal of light on why some people can float with ease while others have no hope of doing so at all. The specific gravity of a human body (or, indeed, of any other body) is determined by its composition or physical makeup. Because a human body is made up of a variety of tissues (bone, muscle, fat, etc.) and because these themselves have different specific gravities, the amount of each that a person's body contains has a good deal to do with whether he (or she) can float. If the body contains a large amount of fat, which is relatively very light (specific gravity ≈ 0.8), the person is much more likely to be able to float than if he (or she) is lean and heavily muscled (specific gravity of muscle ≈ 1.00) or "heavy boned" (specific gravity of bone ≈ 1.5–2.0).

The importance of body composition in determining an individual's specific gravity, and thus the ability to float, is reflected in a number of ways:

- The volume of air in the lungs has a pronounced effect on an individual's ability to float. If a person inhales deeply, this adds considerably to the volume of air that is normally in the lungs (the residual air) and increases both the volume of the chest and the volume of the whole body. The increase in body weight that accompanies this increase in volume is negligible. (The specific gravity of air is about 0.0012, which is very small indeed.) With the numerator of the expression for specific gravity remaining virtually unaltered, and the denominator being markedly increased, the overall effect of this deep inhalation is to reduce the body's specific gravity substantially. The likelihood of the person being able to float is therefore enhanced. Conversely, if a person exhales forcefully, the specific gravity of the body is increased and floating ability is correspondingly decreased. The importance of this factor in terms of human flotation is clearly evident in the remarks of Whiting[3] who, after reviewing literature on this subject, stated that while most men and most women will float in water if they have taken a full inhalation, the majority of the men will sink unless they have more than just residual air in their lungs.

- As the relative proportions of the major body tissues change with age, so too does a person's specific gravity and ability to float. In general, the nearer a person is to the extremes in age (that is, the nearer the person is to being very young or very old) the more likely it is that the body's specific gravity will be low enough to permit him (or her) to float.

- Women, because of their greater proportions of fat, tend to have lower specific gravities than men and are thus more likely to be able to float.
- Black American children have been found to have a greater bone density and greater percentage of compact bone than their white counterparts.[4] In keeping with these differences in body composition, tests of floating ability have repeatedly shown a greater percentage of "nonfloaters" in groups of black Americans than in corresponding groups of whites.[5,6,7]
- Studies[8,9] on the physiques of champion swimmers have shown that, in general, these people have slightly higher proportions of fat in their physiques than do champion athletes in most other sports.

Center of Buoyancy. In Fig. 7-1(b), the water that is subsequently displaced by the swimmer is in equilibrium under the action of two vertical forces—its weight and the buoyant force. The fact that this water is in a state of equilibrium means that these two forces must not only be equal in magnitude but must also act along the same straight line. Thus the buoyant force, like the weight, must act through the center of gravity of the about-to-be-displaced water. When the swimmer assumes the position of Fig. 7-1(c), the magnitude and line of action of the buoyant force are exactly as before, and the point through which the buoyant force acts (previously the center of gravity of the displaced water) is called the *center of buoyancy*.

The location of the center of buoyancy is of particular significance in determining what happens to a swimmer's body once a prone-lying position is assumed on the surface. If the center of gravity of the swimmer and the center of buoyancy coincide, or lie vertically one above the other, the body will retain its horizontal position. This, though, is a relatively uncommon situation, especially for males. (In tests of back-floating ability conducted by Whiting,[10,11] only one in six female subjects was able to maintain a horizontal floating position, and his male subjects fared even worse. In fact, of the 291 male subjects aged 15 yr and over, not one could maintain the position!) If the center of buoyancy does not coincide with the center of gravity or lie with it on the same vertical line, it is almost invariably found to be nearer the head than is the center of gravity. This then means that the weight and the buoyant force act as a couple that tends to force the legs and feet downward (Fig. 7-2[a]).* In cases like this, the feet drop steadily until a point is reached at which the center of gravity and the center of buoyancy lie along the same vertical line. The body then floats in this position (Fig. 7-22[b]).

---

* In Fig. 7-2(a) the magnitude of the weight is slightly greater than that of the buoyant force. Thus, the couple that produces the observed angular acceleration is actually made up of the buoyant force and a part of the weight equal in magnitude to the buoyant force. The remaining part of the weight serves to accelerate the body downward.

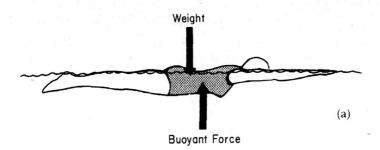

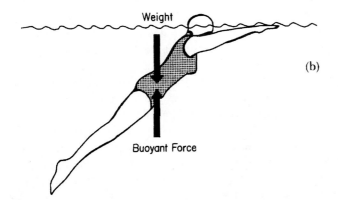

Figure 7-2.
Whether a body floats horizontally or
rotates to some inclined position is
governed by the relative positions of the
lines of action of the weight and the
buoyant force.

RELATIVE MOTION

When a water-skier skims across a lake in the wake of a speedboat, it appears to an observer on the shore as if the water is still and the skier is moving across it at some speed—say 15 m/s. However, if the skier looks down, he (or she) can very easily get the reverse impression—that the skier is stationary and that the water is rushing past at this same 15 m/s. No matter which of these two viewpoints is taken, the difference between the speeds of the water and the skis (that is, the motion of one relative to the other) is exactly the same, namely, 15 m/s.

Now it so happens that the effect that the water has on the skis depends on their relative motion rather than on the speed of either one. For this reason either of the viewpoints (that of the observer or that of the skier) can be taken in making an analysis of these effects.

In analyses of the influence of fluids on the motion of bodies involved in sports, it is generally more convenient to consider the body to be at rest and the fluid to be moving past it. Ganslen,[12 13] for example, has used this approach in his analyses of discus and javelin flight. To do this, he placed the implements in a wind tunnel and regulated the flow of air past them so that the relative motion of air and implement was the same as it would be if the implement were thrown in the normal way. [*Note:* It is perhaps of interest to note here that the resistance provided by air is fundamentally a "scaled" equivalent of the resistance provided by water. For this reason (provided due care is taken to get the scaling factors correct) it is possible to test how a supersonic aircraft, a glider, or even a discus will behave in flight, by noting its reaction to simulated flight in water.]

FLUID RESISTANCE

When a discus is placed in a wind tunnel and air is made to flow past it, two simultaneous effects are produced. First, the direction of motion of the air, especially that nearest the discus, is altered so that it can pass around the obstruction in its path. Second, the air near the surface of the discus is slowed down as a result of coming into contact with the discus. These changes in the speed and direction of the airflow are brought about because the discus exerts forces on the air. In reaction, the air exerts equal and opposite forces on the discus.

The component of these latter forces that acts in the original direction of the airflow (that is, in the direction the air was traveling before making a "detour" around the discus) is known as the *drag* (Fig. 7-3). When a body moves through a fluid, it is this drag, this component of the force exerted by the fluid against the body, that reduces the speed of the body along its path. When a swimmer pushes off at the completion of a turn, it is the drag that slows the forward motion of the glide and makes it necessary for the swimmer to resume kicking and stroking. It is the drag too that drastically reduces the speed of a badminton bird after it has been hit and that causes it to follow a flight path that does not even approximate a parabola.

The component of force acting at right angles to the drag component is known as the *lift* (Fig. 7-3). An example of the importance of this lift component can be drawn from the sport of water-skiing. Before starting a

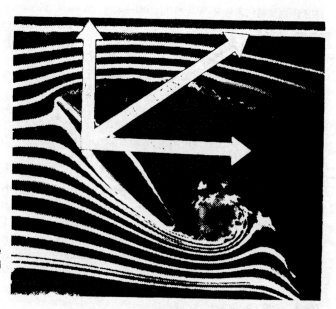

Figure 7-3.
Lift and drag forces acting on a discus mounted in a wind tunnel. The lines indicating the path followed by the air are obtained by injecting smoke through small jets positioned upstream. (Photograph courtesy of Richard V. Ganslen.)

run, a water-skier assumes a predetermined position in the water, with the skis slanted forward and upward and the tips just out of the water. Then, when the skier is drawn forward by the pull of the rope, the lift component of the force exerted by the water on the skis causes the skier to be lifted up onto the surface of the water. The need to have the correct amount of lift sets definite limits on the starting position the skier can adopt and still be successful in getting up. If the skis are near vertical, the drag will be very large and the lift practically nonexistent. A similar lack of lift will be evident if the skis are near horizontal when the skier starts moving forward. In both cases, the skier will almost certainly fail to obtain a successful start.

The magnitudes of the drag and lift forces acting on a body moving through a fluid (or immersed in a moving fluid) can be computed with the aid of two very similar equations:

$$F_D = C_D \, \rho \, A \, \frac{v^2}{2} \tag{7-1}$$

$$F_L = C_L \, \rho \, A \, \frac{v^2}{2} \tag{7-2}$$

where F_D and F_L = the drag and lift forces, respectively; C_D and C_L = the coefficients of drag and lift, respectively; ρ = the mass per unit volume or the density of the fluid involved; A = the frontal or cross-sectional area exposed to the flow; and v = the velocity of the body relative to the fluid.

The coefficients of drag and lift are numbers which characterize the "shape" of the body concerned and which also take into account (and thus vary with) changes in the pattern of flow around the body. In general, blunt, nonstreamlined bodies have large values for C_D and C_L while long, streamlined bodies have correspondingly smaller values. [*Note:* In the context of this discussion, the term *shape* includes the orientation of the body relative to the flow. Thus, for example, a long, slender body (like a javelin or a rowing shell) has small values for C_D and C_L if its long axis is parallel to the flow and larger values if its long axis is perpendicular to the flow. In this latter case, the otherwise slender, streamlined body behaves as if it were a blunt, nonstreamlined one.]

From Eqs. (7-1) and (7-2), it is apparent that there are four basic factors that govern the magnitude of the drag and lift forces that act on a body—the "shape" of the body and the pattern of flow around it (represented by C_D and C_L), the size of the body (represented by A), the nature of the fluid involved (represented by its density, ρ), and the velocity of the body relative to the fluid.

Surface Drag.   When air rushes past the discus in Fig. 7-4(a), the layer in contact with the discus is slowed down as a result of the forces that the discus exerts upon it. This layer of air tends to slow the layer next to it,

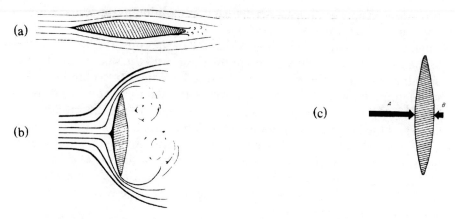

Figure 7-4. The form drag experienced by a discus is a function of its orientation to the oncoming flow.

which layer in turn tends to slow the next one, and so on. As a result of this progressive slowing of the air farther and farther away from the surface of the discus, the thickness of the air that is affected by this process gets progressively larger the farther the air travels along the body. After a certain distance, which varies according to the velocity and nature of the body, this layer of affected air (the so-called *boundary layer*) becomes unstable. Then, instead of neighboring portions of the flow traveling along parallel paths as they did at the outset, they suddenly become violently mixed up. This transition from flow in parallel layers (called *laminar flow*) to flow with violent intermixing of the air (*turbulent flow*) results in the boundary layer becoming even thicker still. The process of slowing and mixing the air in close proximity to the surface of the discus requires that the discus exert force on it and, in reaction, that the air exert force on the discus. This latter force is known as the *surface drag*.

The magnitude of the surface drag that a given body experiences depends on a number of factors, including (1) the velocity of the flow relative to that of the body; (2) the surface area of the body; (3) the smoothness of this surface; and (4) the fluid involved. [*Note:* Nos. (2) and (3) are embodied in the size and shape factors—A and C_D in Eq. 7-1]. It is unlikely however, that a coach or an athlete would consider making adjustments in more than one or two of these four in an effort to reduce surface drag.

A rowing coach might take the surface area into account in selecting the shell a crew should use. On this subject, Wellicome[14] provides some interesting figures relating the surface drag of an eight-oared shell to its wetted surface area (Table 7-1). The importance of the observed differences in surface drag is thrown into bold relief by Wellicome's statement that "Broadly speaking, a change of 1 lb [4.5 N] in resistance at 17 ft/sec [5.2 m/s] means a half length margin over 2,000 metres."[15] Thus, the difference in surface drag between a 18.5 m long hull with a 50-cm beam and the same length hull with a 70 cm beam is equivalent to 3½ lengths (or 64 m) over the normal racing distance!

TABLE 7-1 Rowing Shell Dimensions, Surface Area, and Surface Drag

Overall Length of Hull (m)	Beam Width (cm)	Wetted Surface Area[a] (sq m)	Surface Drag[a] (N)
17.0	50	8.5	276
	60	9.0	294
	70	9.6	307
18.5	50	9.0	289
	60	9.6	302
	70	10.0	320
20.0	50	9.7	302
	60	10.1	316
	70	10.6	329

[a] The wetted surface area and surface drag were computed for a shell and crew weighing a total of 8450 N and moving at a speed of 5.2 m/s.

Adapted from data in Wellicome, J. F. (1967). Some hydrodynamic aspects of rowing. In J. G. P. Williams and A. C. Scott (Eds.), *Rowing: A Scientific* Approach (pp. 32–33). London. Kaye & Ward, Ltd.

The second factor that an athlete or a coach might consider in an effort to reduce surface drag is the smoothness of the surface of the body. The hulls of rowing shells are usually highly polished with this in mind, and Wellicome has suggested that a hull that was very rough might cost a crew as much as three lengths in the course of a 2000-m race.[16] The rough surfaces presented by the large metal latches (or buckles) on a pair of ski boots have been shown to increase the drag on a downhill racer to such an extent that it adds about 0.3 to each minute of a race.[17] In an event that normally lasts about 2 min and in which the difference between winning and losing is often a mere few hundredths of a second, this factor of surface smoothness is obviously a very important one. Some interest in the relationship between surface smoothness and surface drag has also been shown in swimming. For instance, Karpovich,[18] in an early study of water resistance in swimming, found that the use of a woolen swimsuit produced an increase in the resistance of a swimmer performing a glide compared with that found when the same swimmer used a silk suit, or no suit at all.

Form Drag. Because of its position, the discus in Fig. 7-4(a) has only a very small effect on the air flowing past it. However, if the discus is rotated through 90°, its effect on the airflow is appreciably increased (Fig. 7-4(b)].

As the oncoming air strikes the front face of the discus in Fig. 7-4(b), it is deflected outward from the center. When it reaches the rim, it is unable to make the sharp change in direction necessary to allow it to continue inward along the rear surface of the discus. (To actually achieve this would require that the air be acted upon by some large force that would accelerate it in the required direction. Since the only force even tending to produce such an effect is that provided by the neighboring layers of air, there is little prospect of this happening.) Instead the flow breaks away (or separates) from the boundary formed by the discus. Later, and farther downstream, the pressure of the neighboring air forces the two diverging parts of the flow back together again.

In the course of this separation of the flow from the boundary, and the subsequent reuniting of the diverging parts, a "pocket" is formed behind the discus. In the state of turbulence that exists in this pocket, whirling currents of air (*eddy currents*) are formed. These currents ultimately detach themselves from behind the discus and flow downstream, where they eventually disintegrate.

An important characteristic of this turbulent pocket is the low pressure that prevails within it. This, together with the high pressure resulting from the oncoming airflow striking the front of the discus and being abruptly redirected outward, leads to a resultant pressure in the original direction of the flow. This is shown diagrammatically in Fig. 7-4(c), where the vector A represents the resultant force (in the direction of the flow) on the front face of the discus and B the corresponding force on the rear face. The difference between these two vectors is the *form drag*.

Like surface drag, the magnitude of the form drag depends on a number of factors. Among these, and particularly relevant in a variety of sports, are (1) the cross-sectional area of the body perpendicular to the flow; (2) the shape of the body; and (3) the smoothness of its surface. [Strictly speaking, (3) is included in (2) and represented in Eq. (7-1) by the C_D. They are considered separately here in the interests of clarity.]

In speed skating, competitors adopt a position in which their trunks are horizontal and their arms are held behind the body so that the cross-sectional (or frontal) area, and with it the form drag, can be reduced (Fig. 7-5). Racing cyclists crouch forward over the handlebars and jockeys huddle behind the necks of their mounts with the same objective in mind. The descent of a skydiver is largely controlled by the frontal area. If the skydiver descends feet (or head!) first, the frontal area and form drag are both relatively small and, since the latter will not therefore slow the descent very greatly, the skydiver falls at a comparatively rapid rate. To avoid this, competent skydivers assume a position in which their frontal areas are as large as they can make them, thus slowing their rate of descent and prolonging their time of free fall. Then, when they finally resort to using their

Figure 7-5.
The speed skater adopts a near-horizontal trunk position in order to reduce his form drag and to put his hip extensors in a position where they can be most effective in driving him forward.

chutes, they further decrease their rate of descent by again increasing the frontal area.

The influence that the shape of a body has on the magnitude of the form drag depends on the extent to which the body is streamlined. If the front of a body is shaped so that the direction of the flow is changed only gradually as it comes into contact with the body, the pressure on the front is markedly less than if the flow direction is abruptly altered. If, in addition, the rear of the body is tapered so that the flow is not required to make any sharp turns to remain in contact with it, the separation of the flow from the boundaries of the body, the low-pressure turbulent pocket, and the accompanying eddy currents are all greatly reduced. Thus, if all else is equal, a body with a gently rounded front and a tapered back (that is, a streamlined body) will have less form drag than one that is not streamlined.

The relationship between streamlining and form drag is used in several sports. In yachting, canoeing, and rowing, consistent with other factors that must be taken into account, every effort is made to have the hull streamlined so that it will encounter as little form drag as possible. The positions adopted by speed skaters, speed skiers and downhill skiers (Fig. 7-6) are aimed not only at reducing the frontal area but also at making the athlete as streamlined as possible under the circumstances.

In some sports there is a need to make the form drag as great as possible and therefore bodies that are not streamlined are used. In sailing downwind it is mainly the form drag of the sails that propels the boat forward and so the less streamlined these are, the greater is the force pushing the boat through the water. A somewhat similar situation exists in rowing, where the firmer the purchase that the blade of the oar makes on the water, the greater the force that goes into propelling the boat forward. For this reason the blades of oars are designed to create a large amount of form drag when they are moved through the water.

The smoothness of a body's surface influences its form drag because of the effect it has on the boundary layer. Consider a ball moving through the air. When air strikes the ball and is directed outward to pass around it, a

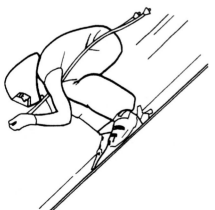

Figure 7-6.
The speed skier adopts the so-called egg position to keep form drag to a minimum.

boundary layer is formed close to the surface of the ball (see Surface Drag, pp. 185–187). Then, as the flow continues around the ball, it separates from the boundary and creates the turbulent pocket already described. Now the point at which the flow separates from the ball very largely governs the magnitude of the form drag. If this separation point is near the front of the ball, a large turbulent pocket is created and the form drag is relatively high. If it is near the back of the ball, the reverse is true. The point at which the flow separates depends largely on the nature of the boundary layer around the front of the ball. If the boundary layer is laminar (that is, adjoining layers of air flowing parallel to one another), the separation point will be farther toward the front of the ball than if it is turbulent.

The two principal factors that determine whether the boundary layer is laminar or turbulent—at least from a sports point of view—are the velocity of the flow and the smoothness of the surface of the ball. With respect to the first of these, once the flow reaches a certain critical speed, the boundary layer becomes turbulent and the form drag is drastically reduced. Lyttelton,[19] for example, reported that the drag on a cricket ball was reduced to approximately one-fourth of its previous value once this critical speed had been attained. The second of these factors, the smoothness of the surface of the ball, is important because it partly determines the magnitude of the critical speed—a magnitude that is greater if the surface of the ball is smooth than it would be if it were rough. The importance of this fact in the game of golf is reputed to have been first discovered by Scottish caddies who found that a well-worn or cut ball could be driven farther than a new one of the smooth type then in use. This finding ultimately led manufacturers of golf balls to dimple the surface of their product so that it would perform better. Incidentally, Bade[20] cites some interesting figures relating the depth of the dimple to the length of the carry, the flight phase of the drive, and to the total length of the drive:

Depth of Dimple (mm)	Carry (m)	Total Length of Drive (m)
0.05	107	134
0.10	171	194
0.15	194	212
0.20	204	218
0.25	218	239
0.30	206	219

Bade, E. (1952). *The Mechanics of Sport* (p. 54). Kingswood, Surrey, England: Andrew George Elliot.

Wave Drag.   When a swimmer does a racing dive he flings himself forward off the starting block in a near-horizontal direction. During the first part of the dive he is totally "immersed" in the air through which he is moving. Then, once he has entered the water (and before he returns to the surface), he is again totally "immersed," this time in the water through which he is gliding. During each of these successive immersions the swimmer's forward progress is opposed by the drag exerted on him by the surrounding fluid. When he is in the air, he is acted upon by the form and surface drags exerted by the air as he passes through it. Similarly, when he is underwater, he is subjected to the form and surface drags attributable to the water around him. In these respects he is no different from any other body that moves through a fluid in which it is totally immersed, for all such bodies experience form and surface drags.

The swimmer is different when he comes to the surface and settles into his normal stroking and kicking pattern, for now he is no longer completely immersed in one fluid but is instead operating at the interface between two fluids—the water and the air. In cases like this—and there are a number of them in sports—the body involved is subjected to yet another kind of drag. And this arises because in its movement along the interface, the body exerts forces that create waves. The reaction to these forces, called the *wave drag*, is a resistance force additional to those of the form and surface drags.

The events that led to the adoption of one of the present rules governing breaststroke swimming provide an example of the importance of wave drag. Up until the mid-1950s, most breaststroke swimmers swam on the surface of the water in the usual way. Around this time, however, some of the world's leading exponents of the stroke realized that they could swim faster underwater than they could on the surface. This had a pronounced effect on the way breaststroke events were swum. For example, in the men's 200-m breaststroke at the 1956 Olympic Games, several of the leading competitors swam almost the whole first length underwater and then came to the surface during the remainder of the race only when forced to by their need for air. What these swimmers had apparently discovered was that, although one could expect an increase in both surface and form drags when the body was completely submerged, the concomitant decrease in wave drag was sufficient to more than offset these increases. The rules for breaststroke events were promptly changed, and now the number of strokes that can be executed underwater is limited to one per length.

Lift. Many participants in sports are concerned with improving their performances by controlling the drag acting on a body. In addition, some of these people are also concerned with exerting a measure of control over the lift (the component of the air resistance force at right angles to the drag). Discus and javelin throwers, for example, try to throw the implements so that they will encounter a minimum amount of drag (and thus be slowed down as little as possible) and at the same time experience a maximum amount of lift (so that they can be "held up" in the air and their time of flight extended). Ski-jumpers aim to achieve exactly the same kind of result during their flight through the air, and water-skiers, as suggested earlier, seek the same effects at the start of a run.

At any given velocity of flow, the magnitudes of the lift and drag depend in part on how the body is oriented. If it is inclined perpendicular to the direction of the oncoming flow (as, for example, in the case of the discus in Fig. 7-4[b]), it will have a relatively large drag and little, if any, lift. On the other hand, if it is parallel with the flow (as in Fig. 7-4[a]), it will have the smallest amount of drag possible but again little, if any, lift. It seems obvious therefore that if the body is to experience any marked lifting effect, the angle between the flow and the plane of the body (the so-called *angle of attack*) must be other than 0° or 90°—neither of which produce this effect. This in turn means that the drag must be somewhat greater than the minimum value that can be obtained. In short, a compromise is necessary between the conflicting objectives of maximum lift and minimum drag, since it is clearly impossible to obtain both at the same time.

For a few sports, efforts have been made to work out scientifically which angle of attack affords the best compromise between lift and drag. As an illustration of how this is done, consider the data in Table 7-2, which have been taken from Ganslen's study of the aerodynamics of discus flight. These data show how the lift and drag forces on a discus vary with changes in the angle of attack. The lift increases from 0 N (at 0°) to 13.8 N (at 27° and 28°) and then decreases to 0 N again (at 90°). Concomitantly, the drag increases steadily from 1.17 N (at 0°) to 17.73 N (at 90°). The problem of working out which angle of attack provides the most appropriate compromise between the two components is overcome by expressing them as a ratio (lift/drag) and taking that angle for which the value of the ratio is the greatest. The final column of Table 7-2 contains the lift/drag ratios and reveals that, in this instance, the best angle of attack of those measured is 10°.

TABLE 7-2 Lift and Drag Forces on a Discus (Wind velocity 24 m/s)

Angle of Attack (degrees)	Lift (N)	Drag (N)	Lift/Drag Ratio
0	0.00	1.17	0.00
10	4.33	1.50	2.89
20	10.64	4.13	2.58
25	12.83	5.79	2.22
27	13.80	6.88	2.01
28	13.80	7.41	1.86
29	11.01	7.94	1.39
30	11.21	8.18	1.37
35	10.12	8.74	1.16
40	8.50	9.55	0.89
45	8.90	11.13	0.80
50	8.62	12.22	0.71
60	6.88	14.98	0.46
70	4.77	16.43	0.29
80	2.55	16.88	0.15
90	0.00	17.73	0.00

Adapted from data in Ganslen, R. V. (1958). Aerodynamic factors which influence discus flight. Research report, University of Arkansas.

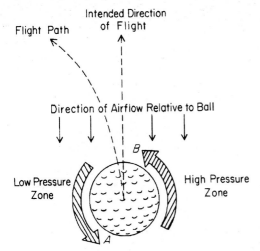

Figure 7-7.
The spin imparted to a golf ball causes an imbalance in the pressures exerted on it and a corresponding deviation from a straight-line path (Magnus effect).

The use of streamlined "wings" (or *airfoils*) mounted on Grand Prix racing cars provides an interesting application of the principles of fluid resistance. The idea is to increase the friction between the track and the tires as the car goes into a turn. This is done by mounting the airfoil upside down so that instead of being lifted—as an airplane is lifted by its wings as it roars down the runway—the car is forced down hard against the track. In other words, the lift component of the air resistance acts downward rather than upward. With the normal reaction increased in this manner, the objective of increasing the friction between the car and the track is thus achieved.

The Magnus Effect.   The graceful (and maddening!) curved flight of a ball that has been sliced or hooked is well known to golfers. In tennis, baseball, soccer, volleyball, and many other sports it is also well known that a ball can be made to curve in flight if sufficient spin is applied to it before it is projected into the air.

This effect (known as the *Magnus effect*, after the German scientist who is wrongly credited with first noting it) can be explained in the following manner. When a body rotates, it tends to carry around with it the fluid that is in direct contact with its surface. This fluid, in turn, tends to similarly influence the neighboring fluid. In this manner, the body acquires a boundary layer that rotates with it. For the golf ball in Fig. 7-7, the arrows A and B indicate the direction in which the ball and its boundary layer are rotating. Because of this rotation, the air in the boundary layer on the left-hand side of the ball (that is, at the instant shown in Fig. 7-7) is moving backwards *relative to the center of the ball*.* It therefore meets the oncoming airflow at a speed which is smaller than would be the case if the ball were

---

* Unless the ball is moving forward very slowly or has an enormous amount of spin imparted to it, this left-hand side of the ball will still be traveling forward *relative to the ground*.

not rotating. Conversely, the air in the boundary layer on the right-hand side of the ball is moving forwards relative to the center of the ball and thus meets the oncoming flow at a speed which is greater than it would be if the ball were not rotating. A zone of high pressure develops where the boundary layer and the oncoming flow meet at an increased speed on the right-hand side of the ball; and a zone of low pressure develops where they meet at a decreased speed on the left-hand side. The net result of this discrepancy in the pressures on either side of the ball is a resultant force acting on the ball from right to left. This resultant force causes the ball to deviate from a straight-line path.

While the Magnus effect produces embarrassing results in some sports, it can often be used to the performer's advantage. Even in golf, where slicing and hooking are very common faults, the Magnus effect is used to advantage in other ways. For example, when a golf ball is driven correctly, a certain amount of backspin is imparted to it. This backspin causes a high-pressure zone to develop beneath the ball, and this results in the ball experiencing a force that lifts it and prolongs its time of flight. Cochran and Stobbs[21] give an interesting illustration of just how important this is when they compare the results obtained from two otherwise identical drives —one in which backspin is applied to the ball in the normal way and the other in which the ball leaves the club without spin of any kind. In the first case, the ball rises about 21 m in the air, remains airborne for 5.5 s, and carries horizontally a distance of some 183 m. In very sharp contrast, the nonspinning ball rises less than 6 m, is airborne for only 2.1 s, and carries little more than 102 m.

Tennis and table tennis players produce exactly the reverse effect when they execute a topspin drive. In their cases, the resultant pressure force acts downward, the time of flight is reduced, and the time an opponent has in which to make a satisfactory return is similarly reduced. Because this very often forces the opponent into rushing the shot and committing errors, topspin drives are widely used as offensive strokes.

The Magnus effect can also be helpful when a corner kick is taken in soccer. If the ball is kicked slightly off-center so that it acquires a rotation about a vertical axis, the resultant pressure can result in the ball being sufficiently deflected from its straight-line path that a goal can be scored directly from the kick (Fig. 7-8).

Exercises

1. The amount of air that people have in their lungs has a bearing on whether they can float. In any given test of floating, fewer people float after breathing out completely than float after taking a deep breath. Can you explain exactly why the amount of air you have in your lungs has a bearing on how likely you are to be able to float?

2. The water in the Dead Sea (in Israel) and the Great Salt Lake (in Utah) has a much higher salt content than the water in other lakes. It also has a greater salt content than the water in the oceans of the world. From your knowledge of Archimedes' Principle, can you explain precisely why this greater salt content

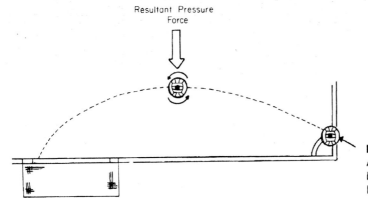

Resultant Pressure Force

Figure 7-8.
A soccer player can score from a corner by imparting the appropriate spin to the ball as he kicks it.

makes it easier for people to float in the Dead Sea and the Great Salt Lake than elsewhere?

3. How does the specific gravity of the water in the Great Salt Lake compare with that of the water in a normal lake?

4. A swimmer lies on her back in a fully extended position (arms straight and stretched overhead, legs straight and together) on the surface of the water. Moments after taking up this position, her feet begin to sink and they keep sinking until her body has rotated into a vertical position. What can you say about the positions of her center of gravity and center of buoyancy relative to one another when she initially took up her position? What can you say about them when she came to rest in the vertical position?

5. The same swimmer takes up an identical position at the surface of the water, except that this time she flexes her knees so that both lower legs hang vertically downward. In this position, she is able to remain floating at the surface of the water. What happened to the location of her center of gravity when she flexed her knees? What happened to the location of her center of buoyancy? How did the locations of these two points compare after she had flexed her knees?

6. A sprinter, who lives in the Chicago area, thinks he will be able to improve his running speed if he can find a way to train at speeds greater than he is normally capable of reaching. To test his idea, he goes to Chicago's O'Hare Airport late at night and practices running as fast as he can on one of the moving sidewalks. If the sidewalk is moving forward at 3 m/s and the athlete can normally run at up to 10 m/s, what is the maximum speed he might hope to reach on the walkway? (Incidentally, what is the maximum speed he might hope to reach if he turned around and ran in the opposite direction to that in which the walk-way was moving?) Can you see why this type of training is unlikely to have a beneficial effect?

7. If the sprinter of the previous question ran at 10 m/s on a walkway which was traveling in the same direction at 3 m/s, how would the air resistance he encountered compare with the air resistance he encountered when running at 10 m/s on a normal track? (Assume that the air is still in both cases.)

8. Speed skiers attach tapered lightweight "fins" (called *farings*) behind their lower legs; and skiers, cyclists, and lugers wear helmets that taper to a point behind their heads. Can you explain how these tapered shapes reduce the air resistance the athlete encounters despite increasing the surface area of the athlete and his (or her) equipment?

9. Alpine and speed skiers wear very smooth-surfaced suits to reduce the air resistance they encounter as they plunge down the mountainside. Golf balls have specifically roughened (dimpled) surfaces to reduce the air resistance they encounter as they fly through the air. How do you explain these contradictory solutions to the same problem? Or, to put it another way, why don't skiers wear dimpled suits and golfers use smooth golf balls?

10. A canoeist, sitting in the stern of his canoe, pulls the blade of his paddle backward through the water. Then, near the end of the stroke, he turns the blade so that it faces backward and outward. Correctly performed, this action keeps the canoe moving straight ahead. Can you explain why the canoe would deviate from its straight-line path if the canoeist did not make this change near the end of the stroke? And, can you explain how this change serves to keep the canoe on a straight course?

11. The long axis of a javelin is 35° to the horizontal at the instant of release. If its horizontal and vertical velocities at that instant are 22 m/s and 17 m/s, respectively:
    (a) What is the magnitude and direction of its resultant velocity at release?
    (b) Assuming that it has been thrown in still air, what is its angle of attack? (Be sure to indicate whether the angle of attack is positive or negative.)
    (c) How does this angle of attack compare with those used by top male javelin throwers?
    (d) Would this angle of attack be changed (and, if so, how would it be changed) if the javelin were being thrown with a tail wind instead of in still air?

12. When a ball is thrown with an overarm action, the thrower's hand passes downward and forward beneath the ball during the release. This action of the hand relative to the ball serves to impart a backspin to the ball. What happens to the ball during its subsequent flight—does it fall faster, at the same rate, or slower than it would without the backspin?

13. When a ball is thrown with a sidearm action by a right-handed thrower, the thrower's hand passes forward and to the left behind the ball during the release. This action of the hand relative to the ball serves to impart a sidespin to the ball. What happens to the ball during its subsequent flight—does it deviate more to the thrower's left, no more to left or right, or more to the thrower's right, than it would without the sidespin?

Recommended Readings

BRANCAZIO. P. J. (1984). *Sports Science: Physical Laws and Optimum Performance.* New York: Simon & Schuster, pp. 315–46 (Moving through fluids); pp. 347–79 (Living with resistance).

COOKE. P. (1984). In W. Schrier and W. F. Allman (Eds.), *Newton at the Bat: The Science in Sports.* New York: Scribner's, pp. 83–86 (Indv's wings of victory).

DAISH, C. B. (1972). *The Physics of Ball Games.* London: English Universities Press, pp. 41–56 (The flight of balls through the air); pp. 57–72. (The swerve of balls in flight).

EPSTEIN HOOVER. S. (1984). In W. Schrier and W. F. Allman (Eds.), *Newton at the Bat: The Science in Sports.* New York: Scribner's, pp. 134–39 (Skiing on air).

FARIA, I. E., AND CAVANAGH, P. R. (1978). *The Physiology and Biomechanics of Cycling.* New York: John Wiley, pp. 71–88 (What is still slowing me down?, drag and friction.)

HAY, J. G., AND REID, J. G. (1988). *Anatomy, Mechanics, and Human Motion.* Englewood Cliffs, N.J.: Prentice Hall. pp. 220–32 (Fluid mechanics).

PERLMAN, E. (1984). In W. Schrier and W. F. Allman (Eds.), *Newton at the Bat: The Science in Sports.* New York: Scribner's, pp. 91–93 (Hang gliding: Science in the clouds); pp. 131–33 (Ballistics of speed skiing).

Tricker, R. A. R., and Tricker, B. J. K. (1966). *The Science of Movement.* London: Mills & Boon, pp. 131–40 (Hydrodynamics).

Whidden, T., and Levitt, M. (1990). *The Art and Science of Sails: A Guide to Modern Materials, Construction, Aerodynamics, Upkeep and Use.* New York: St. Martin's Press.

Whiting, H. T. A. (1963). Variations in floating ability with age in the male. *Research Quarterly,* 34:84–90.

Whiting, H. T. A. (1965). Variations in floating ability with age in the female. *Research Quarterly,* 36:216–18.

Notes

1. Garfoot, B. P. (1968). Analysis of the trajectory of the shot. *Track Technique,* 32:1006.
2. Cadman, J. R. (1975). An investigation into the correlation between buoyancy and the time taken for prepubescent children to learn to swim. St. Paul's College, Cheltenham, England.
3. Whiting, H. T. A. (1970). *Teaching the Persistent Non-Swimmer* (p. 6). London: G. Bell & Sons, Ltd.
4. Malina, R. M. (1969). Growth and physical performance of American negro and white children. *Clinical Pediatrics,* 8:476–83.
5. Lane, E. C., and Mitchem, I.C. (1968). Buoyancy as predicted by certain anthropometric measurements. *Research Quarterly,* 35:21–28.
6. Mitchem, J. C., and Lane, E. C. (1968). Buoyancy of college women as predicted by certain anthropometric measures. *Research Quarterly,* 39:1032–36.
7. Stallman, R. K. (1971). The relationship of body density and selected anthropometric measures to the acquisition of beginning swimming skills. Ph.D. dissertation, University of Illinois.
8. Carter, J. E. L. (1966). The somatotypes of swimmers. *Swimming Technique,* 3:76–79.
9. Cureton, T. K. (1951). *Physical Fitness of Champion Athletes.* Urbana, Ill.: University of Illinois Press.
10. Whiting, H. T. A. (1963). Variations in floating ability with age in the male. *Research Quarterly,* 34:84–90.
11. Whiting, H. T. A. (1965). Variations in floating ability with age in the female. *Research Quarterly,* 36:216–18.
12. Ganslen, R. V. (1958). Aerodynamic factors which influence discus flight. Research report, University of Arkansas.
13. Ganslen, R. V., and Hall, K. G. (1960). *Aerodynamics of javelin flight.* Fayetteville; AK.: University of Arkansas.
14. Wellicome, J. F. (1967). Some hydrodynamic aspects of rowing. In J. G. P. Williams and A. C. Scott (Eds.), *Rowing: A Scientific Approach.* London: Kaye & Ward, Ltd.
15. Ibid., p. 34.
16. Ibid., p. 28.
17. Raine, A. E. (1970). Aerodynamics of Skiing. *Science Journal,* 6 (p. 29).
18. Karpovich, P. V. (1933). Water resistance in swimming. *Research Quarterly,* 4:26.
19. Lyttleton, R. A. (1957). The swing of a cricket ball. *Discovery,* 18:188.
20. Bade, E. (1952). *The Mechanics of Sport* (p. 54). Kingswood, Surrey, England: Andrew George Elliot.
21. Cochran, A., and Stobbs, J. (1968). *The Search for the Perfect Swing* (p. 162). London: Heinemann Education Books, Ltd.

8

Derived from the English children's game of rounders, baseball is today the national game of the United States and the principal summer game of Canada, Japan, and several Latin-American countries.

BASIC CONSIDERATIONS

The four basic skills of greatest importance in baseball are throwing (which includes pitching), catching, batting, and base running.

Throwing

The objective in throwing is to move the ball from one point to some other specified point in the shortest possible time (in fielding) or with the optimum linear and angular velocities (in pitching).

Fielding. The time taken in moving the ball from one point to another is the sum of the time taken to execute the throwing movement (that is, from initiation of the movement until the ball is released) and the time of flight. The first of these depends on the average speed of the ball during the throwing movement and by the distance through which the ball moves (Eq. [3-1]). The average speed of the ball is governed, in turn, by the magnitude and direction of the forces exerted upon the ball and the times for which they act. The second is governed by the velocity and height of release and, to some extent, by air resistance. These relationships are summarized in Fig. 8-1.

Pitching. With the ball initially at rest in the pitcher's glove, the linear velocity that it possesses as it leaves his hand on its way to the batter is directly related to the forces applied to it during the act of pitching, and to the distances over which these forces are applied (Work-energy relationship [101–105]). The pertinence of this latter parameter is reflected, for example, in the long (1.35–1.5 m) stride that pitchers use to ensure that the distances over which forces are applied are as large as they can be, consistent with other requirements and limitations.

The magnitude and direction of the angular velocity of the ball largely determines the extent to which the Magnus effect (see pp. 193–194) operates and hence the amount to which the ball can be made to deviate from its normal parabolic flight path. The successful pitching of curves, sliders, and so on is thus very dependent on the optimum angular velocity being obtained at the moment of release.

The angular velocity with which the ball leaves the pitcher's hand depends on the torque applied to it during the release. The magnitude of this torque is directly related to the magnitudes and directions of the forces exerted on the ball via the pitcher's fingers. In practice, these forces are a function of the grip employed and the actions of the pitcher's wrist and fingers during the release.

The relationships among the biomechanical factors that influence success in pitching are summarized in Fig. 8-2.

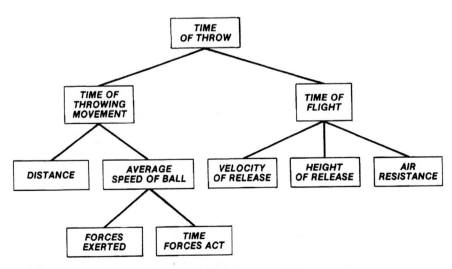

Figure 8-1. Basic factors in fielding.

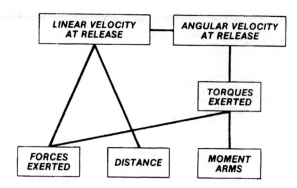

Figure 8-2.
Basic factors in pitching.

Catching

The objective here is to take hold of a ball flying through the air and to reduce its velocity to zero or near-zero. To achieve this objective a player must exert forces on the ball in a direction opposite to that in which it is traveling. In the process of exerting these forces, the player's hand, the means by which the forces are transmitted, is subjected to a certain amount of pressure. The magnitude of this pressure on the hand largely determines the player's ability to "hold" the ball. If he attempts to catch the ball in such a manner that the pressure becomes intolerably large, the player suffers acute discomfort and perhaps even an injury to his hand. In addition, he is very likely to drop the ball, thereby completely negating his efforts. The pressure exerted on any part of the player's hand is dependent on the magnitude of the force being exerted on the hand and by the area over which this force is distributed. Thus, to avoid the undesirable consequences of having too great a pressure on the hand, players strive to decrease the force exerted and to increase the area over which this force is spread.

Batting

The objectives in batting are to hit the ball at will and to impart to it that velocity necessary to displace it to some specific point within (or outside!) the ballpark.

The displacement experienced by a batted ball may be thought of as the sum of two displacements, one resulting from its flight through the air and the other from the bouncing and rolling that it does once it strikes the ground. The first of these is governed by the velocity and height at which the ball leaves the bat and by the air resistance that it encounters in flight.

The velocity of "release" is governed by the respective masses of the bat and ball, their respective velocities before impact, and their mutual coefficient of restitution. In practice, however, the batter has a measure of control over only three of these factors: the velocities of bat and ball before impact and the mass of the bat (pp. 90–93).

For all practical purposes, the height of "release"—which is governed by the height of the ball as it enters or approaches the strike zone and by the height of pitch at which the batter prefers to swing—is of relatively minor importance.

Apart from the drag force, the principal effect that air resistance has on the flight of the ball is that due to the Magnus effect (pp. 193–194). Since this effect is due solely to the fact that the ball is spinning, the generally unwelcome deviations that result from it must be attributed to the factors that produce such spin.

The spin (or angular velocity) with which a ball leaves the bat can be regarded as the summed effect of the spin imparted to the ball by the pitcher (and over which the batter has no real control) and the spin imparted by the bat during its period of contact with the ball. This latter spin is the result of a frictional force that is created whenever the impact between bat and ball is an oblique one.

The bouncing-and-rolling displacement experienced by the ball depends on the velocity at which it strikes the ground (which, in turn, depends on the same factors that govern the flight displacement) and on the forces to which it is subsequently subjected.

The factors that determine the displacement experienced by a batted ball are summarized in Fig. 8-3.

Base Running

A base runner's purpose is to traverse the distance from one base to the next without being tagged or thrown out. Apart from making the correct decision concerning whether he should run, the most important facet of his performance is the time he takes to cover the required distance. This time depends on the distance involved and on the average speed of the runner.

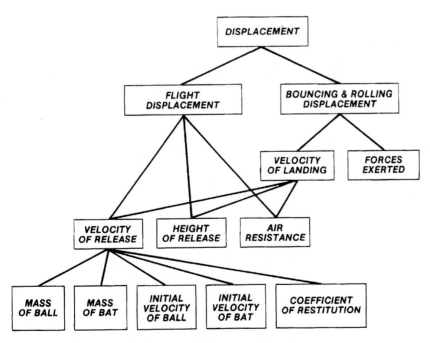

Figure 8-3. Basic factors in batting.

A base runner's average speed is a function of his speed at all points on his run—his speed in starting, in running, and in sliding or stopping. His speed in starting, running, and stopping (like that of a runner on a track, football field, or basketball court) is equal to the product of stride length and stride frequency (see pp. 396–402). These in turn are determined very largely by the reaction to the forces that the runner exerts against the ground. A runner's speed in sliding is similarly governed by the reaction to the forces that he exerts against the ground.

TECHNIQUES
Throwing

Throwing is involved in two major aspects of the game of baseball—pitching (the more highly specialized aspect) and fielding. Since the techniques used in each of these have much in common, and to discuss them both in detail would be needlessly repetitive, the discussion that follows is largely restricted to a consideration of pitching. However, a number of the factors of specific importance in the throwing used in fielding the ball are also considered.

Pitching (Fig. 8-4). Having received the signal from the catcher, the pitcher takes up a position preparatory to beginning the sequence of movements that will culminate in the release of the ball in the direction of the strike zone. If the time involved in delivering the pitch is unimportant, some pitchers adopt a stance in which the back (or pivot) foot is placed across the rubber and the front (or striding) foot is somewhat behind and

Figure 8-4.
An example of good technique in pitching from a windup stance.

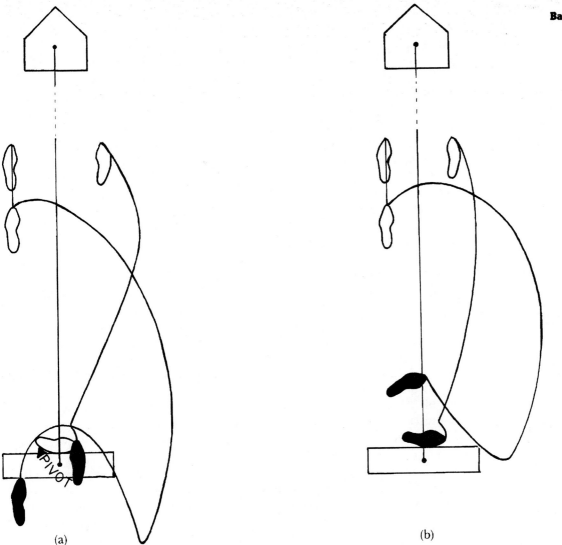

(a)

(b)

Figure 8-5. Paths followed by the feet in pitching from (a) a windup stance; and (b) a set stance. (The paths depicted here were obtained from overhead, time-exposure photographs of small lights placed on a pitcher's feet.)

to the side (the wind up stance, Fig. 8-5[a]).* However if there are men on base and, in particular, if there is a man on either first or second, the time taken to deliver the pitch becomes important. To reduce this time, and with it the chance of a runner stealing a base, pitchers often adopt a stance in which the first 90° or more of the angular motion involved in pitching from a wind up stance is eliminated (the set stance, Fig. 8-5[b]).

* The terms *front* and *back* are used here with reference to the position of the feet as the ball is released; the front foot is the one nearer the batter and the back foot is the one farther from the batter at that instant.

From a wind up stance* with his hands at waist height in front of his body and with the ball concealed in his glove, the pitcher initiates his pitching action by swinging his hands upward to a position overhead. This movement, accompanied by an approximately 90° turn of the pivot foot and by a shifting of weight from the striding foot to the pivot foot, is employed primarily to initiate the motion in a rhythmic manner, in the hope that this will relieve tension and assist in obtaining a correct timing of the movements that follow.

The winding-up actions (and pitchers vary considerably in the number and range of these that they employ) are followed by a coordinated series of movements involving a backward push with the striding foot as it leaves the ground to pass forward over the rubber; a swing of the striding leg, bent at the knee, forward and across the body; an approximately 90° rotation of the hips and upper body; a lowering downward and backward of the pitching hand; and a backward inclination of the trunk.

The first of these movements (the backward push of the striding foot) has the effect of moving the pitcher's center of gravity forward of his pivot foot. Thus when the pivot leg is forcefully extended moments later, the center of gravity is already moving forward and, more important, is in a position to be driven forward rather than upward. The other four movements listed serve to increase the distance through which the pitcher can apply force to the ball. Thus they contribute to an increase in the amount of work that can be done on the ball and to the magnitude of the velocity with which it can leave the pitcher's hand. The inclination of the trunk also enables the pitcher to bring additional muscular forces—those due to the contraction of the lateral muscles of his trunk—into effect.

Just as he is about to move forward into his delivery, the pitcher lowers his center of gravity by bending the knee of his pivot leg. Then, with his center of gravity some distance forward of his pivot foot, he vigorously extends this leg to drive himself forward into his stride. This movement is assisted by a simultaneous forward sweeping movement of the striding leg, which carries the striding foot across in front of his body to land to one side of an imaginary line joining the midpoint of home plate to the midpoint of the pitching rubber. (For a right-handed pitcher, the striding foot lands to the left of this line.) This off-line placement of the striding foot permits the hips to be more completely rotated to the front than if the foot were placed on line.

As the striding foot strikes the ground, the force involved in decreasing the body's vertical motion is reduced by allowing the knee to bend and increase the distance over which work is done on the body.

While the striding foot is being moved forward the some 1.5–1.7 m of the average stride, the pitcher's hips and trunk are turned toward the front, his elbow is brought forward and upward, and his upper arm is externally rotated. Then, once the striding foot has been grounded, the hip

---

* Because the actions in pitching from a set stance are basically an abbreviated form of those used in pitching from a wind up stance, only the latter are discussed here.

and trunk rotations are completed and the pitching arm is whipped forward to complete the throw.

Because the resultant force exerted by the horizontal adductor muscles initiating this final action of the arm passes below the center of gravity of the flexed throwing arm—Fig. 8-6(a)—it serves not only to pull the upper arm forward but also to externally rotate it.[1] A short time later—Fig. 8-6(b)—the resultant force exerted by the shoulder abductor muscles begins to act in a similar fashion to supplement the external-rotating effect of the horizontal adductors. Finally, once the arm has reached a position with the forearm and hand nearly horizontal—Fig. 8-6(c)—it is immediately, and very rapidly, rotated internally and simultaneously extended at the elbow. To avoid injury to the elbow, this extension of the elbow is usually halted just prior to release.

(*Note*: It is perhaps of interest to observe here that, because of the sheer speed of the movements at this stage, the pitcher's arm assumes positions that are quite impossible for him to reproduce when he is stationary—Fig. 8-7.)

The angle between the pitcher's forearm and the horizontal as viewed from the front or rear at the instant the ball is released, varies from one pitcher to another. Some use an action involving an angle of approximately 90° (an overhand or overarm pitch); others, of approximately 0° (a sidearm pitch); and still others, probably the majority, an angle somewhere between these two extremes (a three-quarter pitch).

As one might expect, the height at which the ball is released also varies

(a)   (b)   (c)

Figure 8-6. (a) The horizontal adductors pull the arm forward and externally rotate it. (b) The shoulder abductors act to supplement the external rotating effect of the horizontal adductors. (c) From this position, the arm is internally rotated and the elbow extended. (Based on Feltner, M., and Dapena, J. [1986]. Dynamics of the shoulder and elbow joints of the throwing arm during a baseball pitch. *International Journal of Sport Biomechanics*, 2:235–59.

Figure 8-7.
The initial movements of the pitcher's
delivery place his throwing arm in an
extreme position. (Photograph courtesy of
Alan Goldis.)

from pitcher to pitcher and, with some pitchers, from one type of pitch to another. Atwater[2,3] studied the pitching techniques of four Major League pitchers and one college varsity pitcher. She found that all of her subjects released the ball within 30–45 cm above head level and that the curve ball was released from 5-25 cm higher than the other pitches thrown by each subject. She also found that this increased height of release was associated with an increased lateral trunk lean away from the pitching arm.

Since the ball will fly at a tangent to the arc it is following immediately prior to release, the angle at which the ball should be released, and thus the point on the arc at which this should occur, is clearly of considerable importance. This angle is governed by a number of factors:

- The height at which the ball is released;
- The amount the ball will drop under the influence of gravity before it reaches the plate;
- The amount the ball will deviate upward or downward as a result of air resistance (and specifically, the Magnus effect) before it reaches the plate; and

• The height at which it is desired to place the ball within the strike zone.

The height at which the ball is released is a function of the physique of the pitcher and the length of stride and the type of arm action (that is, overhand, three-quarter, or sidearm) that he uses. The amount the ball drops due to gravity is governed by the length of time it takes to traverse the roughly 17 m from the point of release to the plate. This, in turn, is governed by the horizontal velocity of the ball at the instant it is released— the smaller this velocity, the longer it will take the ball to reach the plate and the farther it will drop under the influence of gravity. The amount the ball deviates upward or downward as a result of air resistance has been studied by Selin[4] and been found to depend primarily on the direction in which the ball is spinning and the orientation of the axis about which it is spinning.

The data presented in Selin's study provide a basis for examining the extent to which each of the factors involved influences the angle at which the ball must be released. If each of the six types of pitch Selin studied were to be thrown horizontally at the maximum speed he recorded for them, the downward deviations due to gravity, while the ball traversed the 17 m from the point of release to the plate, would be as shown in Table 8-1. The maximum values recorded by Selin for the upward deviations due to air resistance are also shown in Table 8-1. The summed effect of gravity and air resistance in this situation is obtained by adding algebraically the vertical deviations due to these two influences. (*Note:* For each type of pitch, the figure in the right-hand column of Table 8-1 represents the least downward deviation that could have been obtained—and then only if all the factors of maximum speed, horizontal direction of release, and maximum upward deviation had been combined in one throw.)

Now, if the pitcher releases the ball at a height of 2.15 m (that is, a height of 1.77 m above the 0.38-m-high mound) and if the batter's armpits are 1.50 m above the ground, the total downward deviation must be in the

TABLE 8-1 Vertical Deviations of a Pitched Baseball Due to the Effects of Gravity and Air Resistance

Type of Pitch	Maximum Speed Recorded (m/s)	Vertical Deviation Due to Gravity[a] (m)	Vertical Deviation Due to Air Resistance[a] (m)	Total Vertical Deviation[a] (m)
Fast ball	36.88	−1.05	0.82	−0.23
Change-up	27.43	−1.90	0.73	−1.17
Knuckle ball	27.74	−1.86	0.69	−1.17
Curve ball	33.83	−1.25	0.00	−1.25
Slider	31.09	−1.48	0.00	−1.48
Sidearm-curve ball	28.04	−1.82	0.00	−1.82

[a] Positive values indicate upward deviations, and negative values indicate downward deviations.

Based upon data in Selin, C. (1959). An analysis of the aerodynamics of pitched baseballs. *Research Quarterly*, 30:232–40.

vicinity of 0.65 m if the ball is to be placed near the upper limit of the strike zone. Except for the fast ball, the computed total deviations in Table 8-1 far exceed this value. It is clear, therefore, that pitchers of the caliber of Selin's subjects (pitchers in the Big 10 Conference) cannot throw other than their fast ball to the top of the strike zone by releasing it in a horizontal direction. Instead, they must release the ball at some angle above the horizontal.

If the batter's knees are 0.65 m above the ground and the ball is released by the pitcher at a height of 2.15 m, the maximum downward deviation that will permit the ball to pass above the lower limit of the strike zone is 1.50 m. Remembering that the final values in Table 8-1 represent the minimum downward deviations that Selin's subjects might have obtained, it appears that unless close to maximum speed and maximum upward deviation can be obtained, pitchers of a comparable standard must throw all but their fast ball at angles above the horizontal to get them into the strike zone.

The distance from the front edge of the pitching rubber to the heel of the front (or stride) foot—the stride length—has been studied by Atwater[5] and Schutzler.[6] Atwater found that none of her five subjects had the back foot in contact with the rubber at release, that their stride lengths ranged from 1.28–1.65 m, and that most were "quite consistent in their stride length, both between windup and stretch [set] deliveries of the same pitch, and among the various pitches thrown."

Schutzler studied 58 major league, triple-A minor league, and college varsity pitchers in game situations and concluded that *among* pitchers, there was a tendency for longer strides to be taken by faster pitchers. However, *within* pitchers, stride length was not longer for a subject's fastest pitches compared to his slowest pitches or for pitches delivered from the windup versus the stretch position. (*Note:* To allow comparison to be made among pitchers of different heights, stride lengths were expressed as percentages of the pitcher's height and leg length in this study.) The following ranges were suggested as guides in identifying overstriding and understriding in pitchers who, like Schutzler's subjects, throw fast balls at more than 80 mi/h (35.8 m/s):

"Stringent Range"   81.6–90.0% height
"Lenient Range"   77.4–94.2% height

Because adjustments in the length of stride and in the position of the pivot foot on the rubber have frequently been cited as means to correct consistent errors in a pitcher's placement of the ball over the plate, Edwards[7] conducted a study to examine carefully just what effect such changes produced. Using 47 pitchers from five midwestern universities he found that:

- changing the length of the stride will not necessarily correct the fault of consistently pitching a fast ball high or low in relation to the strike zone, and

• changing the position of the pivot foot on the pitching rubber will not necessarily correct the fault of consistently pitching a fast ball inside or outside home plate.

Once the ball has left the pitcher's hand, the angular motions of his arm and upper body are gradually reduced to zero as he "follows through." Although nothing that the pitcher does once the ball has been released can have any effect upon it, the follow-through is an important part of the pitcher's action. First, by allowing him to bring his various angular motions to a halt over a relatively large distance, the follow-through ensures that the internal muscular and ligamentous forces involved are much less than they would be if his body (and, most important, his pitching arm) were brought to a halt more abruptly. In this way, follow-through helps the pitcher avoid the risk of injury commonly associated with high internal forces. Second, if the angular motions of the pitcher's body were brought to a halt prior to, or during, the release, the forces responsible would almost certainly impair the application of appropriate forces to the ball. In this sense, therefore, the pitcher's follow-through is important not so much because of what it achieves but because of the undesirable effects that would almost certainly be produced if it were absent.

Immediately after his follow-through is completed, the pitcher must prepare to serve in his role of fielder. Since this requires that he assume a position with his weight supported evenly on both feet (so that he can move with equal facility in either lateral direction) and since his follow-through will probably have been completed with one foot in the air and all his weight supported on the other, he must quickly readjust his position by thrusting against the ground with his supporting (striding) foot.

A listing of the fastest speeds of release ever recorded is presented in Table 8-2. A number of authors have reported results of studies in which the speeds of release for various types of pitch, and for various subjects, have been determined. A summary of a selection of these is presented in Table 8-3. It is interesting to note, and a cause for some confidence, that the tabulated speeds reported by the various authors are in excellent agreement.

The use of a windup stance is generally regarded as permitting the pitcher to impart a greater velocity to the ball than he could if he used a set stance.

To examine this premise, Atwater compared the release velocities obtained when pitches were thrown from windup and set stances and found that:

> . . . *as the ball velocity data on the five pitchers in this study indicate, eight of the 17 pitches were fastest from the windup, seven of the 17 pitches were fastest from the stretch, and two of the 17 were identical in speed. Thus, 47 percent or less than half of the windup pitches were faster than pitches thrown from the stretch position. Also, none of these five pitchers consistently threw all their pitches faster from a windup than from a stretch position.*[8]

TABLE 8-2 The Fastest Speeds of Release Recorded for Pitched Baseballs

Pitcher (Club)	Year	Speed km/h	(m/s)
Nolan Ryan (Angels)	1974	162.2	(45.1)
J. R. Richard	1978	160.9	(44.7)
Jim Maloney	1965	160.1	(44.5)
Rich Gossage	1980	159.9	(44.5)
Lee Smith	1984	159.3	(44.3)
Bob Feller (Indians)	1946	158.7	(44.1)
Steve Barber (Orioles)	1960	153.7	(42.7)
Don Drysdale (Dodgers)	1960	153.4	(42.6)
Atley Donald (Yankees)	1939	152.4	(42.3)
Joe Wood	1914	152.1	(42.3)
Steve Dalkowski (Minors)	1958	150.5	(41.8)
Sandy Koufax (Dodgers)	1960	150.0	(41.7)
Joe Black (Dodgers)	1953	150.0	(41.7)
Dee Miles (Phila. A's)	1939	149.2	(41.4)
Johnny Podres (Dodgers)	1953	148.2	(41.2)
Christy Mathewson (Giants)	1914	146.9	(40.8)
Ryne Duren (Yankees)	1960	146.6	(40.7)
Herb Score (Indians)	1960	146.4	(40.7)
Mickey Lolich (Tigers)	1974	146.3	(40.6)
Bob Turley (Yankees)	1960	146.0	(40.6)
Walter Johnson (Senators)	1914	139.4	(38.7)

Based on data in Merry, D. (1975). Baseball's fastest pitchers. *Street and Smith's Baseball Yearbook* (p. 64). New York: Condé Nast Publications; and in Thorn, J., and Holway, J. (1987). *The Pitcher* (p. 148). New York: Prentice Hall Press.

TABLE 8-3 The Speeds of Pitched Baseballs (m/s)

	Kenny[a] (High school, college, amateur, and professional pitchers)			Slater-Hammel and Andres[b] (College pitchers)			Selin[c] (High school, college, amateur, and professional pitchers)			Atwater[d] (College and major league pitchers)		
	Min.	Mean	Max.	Min.	Mean	Max.	Min.	Mean	Max.	Min.	Mean	Max.
Fast ball	25.9	29.3	33.8	26.2	29.0–36.3	38.7	26.7	31.7	36.9	32.6	35.9	38.4
Slider							28.0	29.9	31.1	32.6	35.0	36.6
Curve ball	24.1	26.2	29.9	22.9	24.4–31.7	32.9	22.6	27.7	33.8	26.2	29.1	32.3
Sidearm-curve ball	23.5	25.9	30.2				27.4	27.7	28.0			
Knuckle ball							22.9	25.6	27.7	31.1	31.1	31.1
Change-up							19.1	24.1	27.4	29.0	30.7	32.6
Screw ball										29.9	30.5	31.1

[a] Adapted from data contained in Kenny, J. D. (1938). A study of relative speeds of different types of pitched balls. M.A. thesis, State University of Iowa.

[b] Slater-Hammel, A. T., and Andres, E. H. (1952). Velocity measurement of fast balls and curve balls. *Research Quarterly*. 23:96.

[c] Selin, C. (1959). An analysis of the aerodynamics of pitched baseballs. *Research Quarterly*, 30:235.

[d] Atwater, A. E. (1977). Biomechanical analysis of different pitches delivered from the windup and stretch positions. Paper presented at the 24th Annual Meeting of the American College of Sports Medicine, Chicago, Ill.

In view of this rather surprising result, Atwater suggested that the values of a windup delivery should be reexamined. More recently, Elliott, Groves, and Gibson[9] found no difference in the release velocities recorded when eight "international pitchers" pitched from a windup stance and when they pitched from a set stance; and Wolff reported that the "traditional two-hands-over-the-head motion is rapidly being phased out of the game."[10]

The behavior of the ball in flight—a source of considerable controversy over the years—has also been a subject of study.[11][12][13] In what has probably been the most exhaustive study of this question to date, Selin[14] filmed over 200 pitches made by 14 pitchers from the Big 10 Conference and conducted a detailed analysis on a selected 30 of these pitches. For each pitch this detailed analysis included a determination of the velocity of the ball, the rate and direction of its rotation, the axis of rotation, and the amounts it deviated in horizontal and vertical directions from the parabolic path it would have followed in the absence of air resistance. Among the conclusions reached as a result of this analysis were:

1. Every pitch showed either or both a vertical deviation or a horizontal deviation from the path it would have followed in the absence of air resistance. (The ranges of the deviations recorded are shown here in Table 8-4.)
2. Within the ranges for the rates of rotation and velocities recorded in the study, the amount of deviation was determined primarily by the vertical angle—the obtuse angle between a vertical line drawn through the center of the ball and the axis of rotation, as viewed from the pitching rubber. In general, as the vertical angle approached 90°, the vertical deviation increased and the horizontal deviation decreased; and as the vertical angle approached 180°, the vertical deviation decreased and the horizontal deviation increased. (The mean vertical angle, and the direction of rotation for those types of pitch in which the ball rotated in a consistent direction, are shown in Fig. 8-8.)

TABLE 8-4 Ranges of Horizontal and Vertical Deviations of 30 Selected Pitches

Type of Pitch	Range of Horizontal Deviations[a] (cm)	Range of Vertical Deviations[b] (cm)
Fast ball	9 to 64	9 to 82
Curve ball	−37 to − 3	−55 to 0
Slider	−24 to −12	−61 to 0
Sidearm-curve ball	−24 to −15	−49 to 0
Change-up[c]	−46 to 18	−61 to 73
Knuckle ball[c]	−76 to 24	−61 to 69

[a] Deviation to the right (as a pitch is viewed by the pitcher) is regarded as positive, deviation to the left as negative.

[b] Upward deviation is regarded as positive, downward as negative.

[c] Some pitches rotated in a clockwise direction, others in a counterclockwise direction.

Adapted from Selin, C. (1959). An analysis of the aerodynamics of pitched baseballs. *Research Quarterly*, 30:232–40.

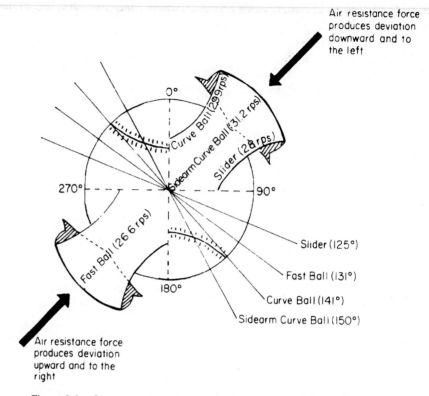

Air resistance force produces deviation downward and to the left

Air resistance force produces deviation upward and to the right

Figure 8-8. Speeds (in revolutions per second), axes, and directions of rotation for various types of pitch thrown by right-handed pitcher and as viewed from the pitching rubber.

3. The direction of deviation of the knuckle ball was apparently not related to the direction of rotation of the ball. With such low speeds of rotation (a mean of 5.3 rps compared with a range of means from 24.5–31.2 rps for the other types of pitch) the orientation of the seams relative to the axis of rotation and relative to the airflow may have determined the direction of the deviation.

A study by Watts and Sawyer[15] supports the contention that the orientation of the seams plays a major role in determining the flight path of a knuckle ball. After conducting a series of experiments in a wind tunnel, these investigators concluded that "the nonsymmetrical location of the roughness elements (strings) gives rise to a nonsymmetrical lift (lateral) force. A very slowly spinning knuckleball will have imposed upon it a lateral force that changes as the positions of the strings change."

It is of some interest to note that although Watts and Sawyer and Selin are in general accord on the role of the seams in producing lateral motion, their findings are at variance on the matter of speeds of rotation. While Selin[16] reports horizontal deviations of as much as 76 cm with speeds of rotation as high as 4.3 rps (equivalent to three complete revolutions between release and arrival over the plate), Watts and Sawyer conclude that, to be effective, a knuckle ball should be thrown so that it rotates substantially less than once on its path to home plate.

4. The fast balls consistently displayed positive (upward) vertical deviation and this apparently created an illusion in which, although the ball fell toward the ground during the flight, its failure to fall as rapidly as expected made it appear to the batter to rise or hop as it approached the plate.

Fielding. As suggested earlier, when a fielder throws the ball, the objective is to complete its displacement from one point to another specified point in the shortest possible time. The time involved is the sum of the time spent in applying force to the ball and the time the ball spends in flight. The impulse-momentum relationship (p. 00) suggests that, if all else is equal, the velocity at which a ball is released is directly proportional to the time taken to make the throw. Thus, because the time of flight depends on the velocity of the ball at release, the time of flight depends also on the time taken to execute the throwing movement. It is well to realize, however, that a reduction in the time of flight brought about by an increased velocity of release may not be greater than the increase in time that was needed to bring about this alteration in velocity. In other words, the total time involved may not have been decreased. For this reason an infielder may quite frequently use a short flick throw to, say, second base rather than a throw with a more complete body and arm action that involves a shorter time of flight but a longer overall duration. On the other hand, an outfielder making a long throw to one of the bases or to home plate will almost certainly be most effective (that is, will complete the throw in the least time) if he puts his body in such a position that he can apply maximum force to the ball.

If the height at which the ball is released and the height at which it lands, or is caught, are considered to be constant, the time of flight depends on the vertical velocity of the ball at the moment it is released. The greater the vertical velocity at release, the longer the time of flight. Therefore, in all throws, the ball should be released with as little vertical velocity as possible consistent with the successful completion of the throw. Since the vertical velocity at release also determines the extent to which the ball rises in flight, this is tantamount to saying that all throws should be as low as possible.

The equations presented in Chap. 3 to describe the motion of projectiles can be used to estimate the minimum amounts that a ball must be made to rise in order for a throw to be completed successfully. If it is assumed that the ball is released and caught at the same height, and that it is thrown at a speed of 30 m/s (approximately equal to the mean speed for fast ball pitches), it must rise roughly 1 m in a 27.4 m throw from base to base and almost 5.5 m in a 90 m throw from the outfield. (*Note:* Because the equations used here do not take into account the effects of air resistance, these figures can be regarded only as rough estimates of the true figures.

Whether they are underestimates or overestimates depends on the unknown effects of drag, which would tend to require that the height be increased, and of the Magnus effect, which would influence the flight of the ball in accord with the magnitude and direction of the spin imparted to it.)

Catching

In most sports the act of catching is performed by using both hands in an equal symmetrical fashion. Baseball and softball are unusual, because in these sports one hand plays a major role in catching while the other serves in a supporting capacity. Even more unusual is the fact that the major role is played by the nondominant hand. However, since this frees the dominant hand and arm for the throw that invariably follows a catch, the reason for this use of the nondominant hand is not hard to find.

In the process of being caught, a ball gives up a certain amount of the kinetic energy that it possesses, to do work on the hands of the person making the catch. The amount of work done is equal to the loss in kinetic energy incurred in the process—that is, assuming that the losses to nonmechanical forms of energy and the work done by gravity as the ball gives up potential energy are both sufficiently small that they can be disregarded. Thus, if the ball is brought to rest, the work done is equal to the kinetic energy it possessed immediately before it made contact with the player's glove. If the ball is merely slowed down, in preparation for a throw, the work done is equal to the difference between its kinetic energy at contact with the glove and the lowest value it attains.

Since the amount of work done is thus fixed by the circumstances in a particular case, the product of the force that the ball exerts on the hands and the distance through which the hands move is similarly fixed (work = force × distance). Thus, if a player making a catch is to reduce the magnitude of the force exerted against his hands, he has just one way of achieving this—he must increase the distance through which this force acts. For this reason—and, in some cases, to reduce the time of flight of the ball—a player making a catch will generally extend his arms so that the glove meets the ball at some distance from his body. Then, once the ball has struck his glove, his nongloved hand quickly smothers any possibility of it rebounding out of the glove, and his arms bend to allow the distance over which the ball is slowed down to be increased. (*Note:* This latter action also assists in putting the player in a position to execute a throw, once the catch has been completed.)

If a small amount of flexion is retained at the elbow as the player reaches his hands to meet the ball, the force it exerts as it strikes the glove initiates the further elbow flexion needed to cushion the impact. This effect is largely lost if the elbows are completely extended as the ball strikes the glove, for then the force exerted by the ball tends to act along the line of the extended arm and thus has little tendency to cause the arm to bend. As a result, there is every likelihood that the catch will be dropped, unless the player's conscious timing of the required elbow flexion is quite precise.

Because it thus introduces an unnecessary problem in timing, the practice of fully extending the arms to meet the ball is to be avoided.

In addition to providing a thick protective layer and increasing the actual area that his extended hand can cover, a player's glove also serves the very important function of distributing the forces involved in catching the ball over a wider area than would be feasible with just the bare hand. In this way, the pressure on any one part of the hand can generally be kept within tolerable limits.

In preparing to catch the ball, a player should adopt a body position that takes into account that the force exerted on him by the ball will generally have a tendency to rotate him about some axis through his feet. Thus, if the moment of this force is relatively large, it may be necessary for him to lean forward slightly in the direction of the oncoming ball so that his weight can effectively counter the rotary effect attributable to the ball.

Batting

Whether one agrees with the authority on batting who claims that "hitting a baseball is the single most difficult thing to do in sport,"[17] there can be no denying that, as the principal offensive weapon in baseball, batting is one of the most important skills in the game.

For the purpose of the analysis contained in this section, batting is divided into four phases or parts: (1) stance; (2) stride; (3) swing; and (4) follow-through (Fig. 8-9).

Stance. The body position adopted by a batter as he waits for the pitcher to release the ball has a marked influence on the batter's subsequent actions.

One of the most important considerations is the placement of the bat-

Figure 8-9. An example of good batting technique.

ter's feet relative to the plate. The position of his feet in a forward and backward sense* is a compromise between two conflicting factors. First, the farther the batter is away from the pitcher (that is, the nearer he is to the back of the batter's box), the longer it will take for any given pitch to reach him and thus the more time he will have to decide if and how he will hit it. On the other hand, the farther back he is, the greater is the chance that a ball could be pitched to the outside of the strike zone and move away beyond the reach of his swinging bat. Thus the batter is obliged to place his feet in a position that will allow him the longest possible time to evaluate the pitch and yet still permit him to meet all legal pitches with the so-called fat part of the bat.

The position of the feet, relative to a midline through the plate, is also fixed to a large extent by the batter's ability to bring this part of the bat to meet the ball at any point across the 43 cm width of the plate. If he stands close to the plate, he is likely to be troubled by an inside pitch, while if he stands far away, he is likely to experience a similar difficulty with an outside pitch.

The alignment of the batter's feet relative to one another is also a matter of some importance. In this case, the batter has essentially three choices. He can place his feet in a line parallel to that linking the midpoints of home plate and the pitching rubber (that is, in a so-called *square* or *parallel* stance); or he can place them in a line directed toward either right or left field. For a right-handed batter, the latter alternatives are known, respectively, as *closed* and *open* stances.

The choice between these stances depends among other things on two interrelated factors: (1) the distance through which the batter must move his various body parts in making his swing; and (2) the time from the moment the swing is initiated until the bat is in a suitable position to make contact with the ball—a time often erroneously referred to as the batter's reaction time.

In using an open stance, the batter's hips, shoulders, and arms are rotated somewhat more to the front than they would be if he used either a square or closed stance. As a direct consequence, he has less distance to move them in order to bring the bat into position to meet the ball and, if all else is equal, requires less time in which to execute his swing. Thus, an open stance is likely to be particularly suitable for a batter who (through lack of strength) consistently has difficulty in getting his bat around early enough to make appropriate contact with the ball. In addition, a batter who does not have this problem but who needs a split second longer to evaluate the pitch before initiating his swing might also benefit from adopting an open stance rather than a square or closed one.

The use of a closed stance enables a batter to exert the muscular forces responsible for rotating his hips, shoulders, and arms to the front, over a

---

* The terms *front* (and *forward*) and *back* (or *backward*) are used here with reference to the positions of the feet of the batter relative to the pitcher. The front foot is the one nearer the pitcher and the back foot is the one farther from the pitcher.

longer distance than is possible with either of the other two stances. Because the batter is thus able to do more work and to apply more force to the ball at impact, this type of stance is suitable for those who can execute their swings with sufficient speed that getting the bat around to a suitable position to meet the ball is not a problem.

The square stance, involving a position of the feet in between that of the other two stances, affords batters a compromise between the slower swing possible with an open stance and the more forceful hit possible with a closed one.

Another factor that may influence the batter's choice of stance is whether his dominant hand and his dominant eye are both on the same side. If they are, there is some evidence to suggest that he is likely to perform better with an open stance than with a closed one. Adams[18] compared the batting performances of six right-handed, right-eyed batters who used an open stance with those of six others of similar dominances who used a closed stance and found that the ones who used an open stance performed significantly better. In the course of a season, the batters who used an open stance struck out 91 times in 713 times at bat (12.8%) while those who used a closed stance struck out 105 times in 576 (18.2%).

The distance between the batter's feet (the width of his stance) is logically dependent to a certain degree on his stature—a tall batter tending to place his feet a greater distance apart than a short one. However, irrespective of their heights, highly skilled batters generally adopt a stance in which the feet are slightly more than shoulder width apart.

The question of how the batter's weight should be distributed when he takes his stance is one of many on which there seems to be a lack of scientific evidence. Two factors that bear on this question are the ease with which the striding foot can be lifted and moved forward (the more weight there is on this foot, the more difficult is this action); and the position of the batter's center of gravity as he prepares to rotate his hips to the front at the beginning of his swing (the farther forward his center of gravity, the more completely extended his rear leg is likely to be and thus the less forceful the hip rotation he can expect to produce.) These two factors alone would seem to support the contention that a greater proportion of the batter's weight should be borne by his back leg than by his front one.

Mason[19] found that, in practice, most batters placed more weight on the front foot than on the back foot, while waiting for the ball to be delivered. On average, 65% of the bodyweight was placed on the front foot and 35% on the back foot. At the end of this "waiting phase," and in preparation for the striding motion to follow, the batters then transferred their weight onto the back foot.

Like several other aspects of his stance, the position in which the batter holds the bat is something of a compromise. If he holds it in a vertical position (that is, with its center of gravity directly above his hands), he does not have to apply a torque to the bat to maintain it in position. Holding the bat in this way, therefore, involves less muscular work than holding it in any other position and, as such, affords the batter as easy and relaxed a carriage of the bat as is possible under the circumstances. While this is clearly one of the advantages of holding the bat in a vertical position, the need for the batter to rotate the bat downward through approximately 90° in order to make contact with the ball is something of a disadvantage, for this additional rotation (compared with what is necessary when the bat is held horizontally) provides additional sources of possible error. If the batter holds the bat in a horizontal position, the situation is essentially reversed—he avoids the possibility of making errors due to increasing the range of his motion but increases the likelihood of becoming unnecessarily tense because of the additional muscular work he must perform. Which of these two extreme positions (or which intermediate position) a batter uses is likely to depend on his own judgment of the relative importance of the advantage and disadvantage associated with each. If he considers the additional rotation the more serious drawback, he is likely to hold the bat in a horizontal or near horizontal position. Conversely, if he regards the increased muscular work involved and the associated risk of unnecessary tension in the arms and shoulders as the more important consideration, he will likely hold the bat in or near a vertical position.

Stride.   The purpose of the stride is to start the forward movement of the batter's weight in preparation for the swing that follows a split second later (approximately 0.04 s after the striding foot is planted firmly, according to Hubbard and Seng[20]).

To execute the stride, the batter lifts his front foot, advances it a short distance in the general direction of the pitcher, and then plants it firmly on the ground.

The height to which the batter lifts his striding foot as he brings it forward should be no greater than that necessary to ensure that his cleats clear the ground. If he lifts his foot higher than this, he increases the time necessary to perform the stride and introduces additional room for error by increasing the range of the movement.

The direction in which the stride should be taken has been the subject of considerable discussion. Some authors[21,22,23] suggest that skilled batters should modify the direction of their stride according to whether the ball is pitched inside or outside. Others, like Williams,[24] contend that because the stride is initiated as the ball is released by the pitcher (a point verified by Hubbard and Seng[25]) and because the batter cannot know exactly where it is going at this time, the direction of the stride should be consistent for all pitches. This latter contention is supported by the work of Breen,[26] who after "studying hundreds of major league batters and thousands of feet of motion picture film" concluded that one of the five "mechanical attributes" outstanding hitters have in common is consistency in the length and direction of their stride. Regardless of the type of pitch, the better hitters (and major league players Aaron, Banks, Mantle, Mays, Musial, and Williams were among those studied) planted their striding foot in the same spot. The poorer hitters were not consistent in the placement of the foot.

It is generally recommended by batters and batting coaches that the length of the stride should be relatively short (of the order of 10–30 cm). The principal advantages in a stride length of this order, as compared to a longer one, would seem to be:

- The batter's center of gravity remains sufficiently close to his back foot to allow a forceful hip rotation during the swing.
- The smaller range of motion leaves less scope for error and thus improves the batter's chance of obtaining a consistent action.
- The forward and downward movement of the batter's head is reduced and with it the possibility that his sighting of the ball may be impaired by this movement.

Swing. From the instant the ball is released by the pitcher, the batter has roughly half a second in which to hit it before it passes behind him into the catcher's mitt. During this time, his first task is to evaluate the pitch and make his decision as to whether he will swing at the ball. In this part of the process, the longer the batter can study the flight of the ball before making his decision (that is, the longer his *decision time*), the more likely it is that he will make the correct choice. And, since consistently making the correct choice is an important prerequisite for success in batting, the longer the decision time a batter can allow himself, the better his performance is likely to be.

Having made a decision to swing, the batter's second task is to bring his bat around to meet the ball. The time he needs to do this (referred to here as his *swing time*) is also related to the standard of his batting performance, for if all else is equal, the shorter a batter's swing time, the longer his decision time and thus the higher the level of performance that he can produce.

The findings of Breen,[27] who reported the swing times of some proven Major League hitters and compared them with that of a Major League hitter with a batting average below .300, serve to illustrate this point. The respective lengths of the decision and swing times for a pitch traveling at 31.7 m/s (the mean speed for fast balls as reported by Selin[28]) and the position of the ball at the latest moment the batter can still successfully commit himself to swinging at it are shown in Fig. 8-10. The advantage enjoyed by a top-class hitter, by virtue of his short swing time, is clearly evident.

The movements involved in a successfully executed swing proceed in a sequential fashion, with the hips, shoulders, arms, and finally the wrists and bat being driven forcefully around to the front.

The hip action, preceded by a "cocking" (or movement in the opposite direction) during the stride, is the result of the reaction to forces exerted against the ground by the batter's rear (nonstriding) leg and is accompanied by an inward rotation of this leg. Once the hip rotation is well ad-

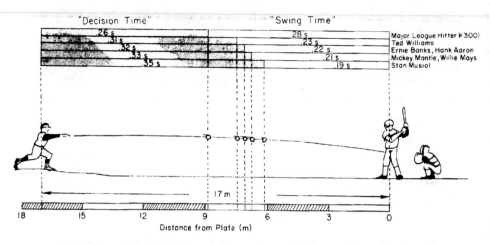

Figure 8-10. Decision and swing times in batting. (Based on data in Breen, J. L. [1967]. What makes a good hitter? *Journal of Health, Physical Education, Recreation*, 38:36, 39.)

vanced, the rotation of the shoulders begins. Then, when the shoulders have been brought around roughly parallel with the hips, the arm swing is initiated.

Because the linear velocity of the point on the bat at which the ball makes contact is of such critical importance in determining what subsequently happens to the ball (see pp. 90–93), good batters hold their leading arm straight, or nearly straight, during the swing. In this way the radius of the arc along which the "contact point" moves and the linear velocity of this point are kept as large as possible.

So that the bat can be appropriately aligned when it is brought forward to meet the ball and so that the forces exerted on the bat impart to it a velocity in the desired direction, the rotation of the hips, shoulders, and arms should each take place in an approximately horizontal plane. With respect to this, Breen[29] found that the center of gravity of outstanding hitters "follows a fairly level plane throughout the swing," while that of lesser hitters showed a definite downward trend indicative of a "dipping of the shoulders."

The final contribution to the swing is made by the batter's wrists, just before the bat meets the ball. Some controversy surrounds the action of the wrists at this time, for while apparently no one questions that the wrists should be "uncocked" or straightened out (a movement known to anatomists as ulnar or medial deviation), some authorities contend that the wrists should be rolled (that is, the wrist of the upper hand on the bat should be rolled over the wrist of the lower hand) and that this action should be initiated as the bat makes contact with the ball. However, since any additional muscular force that might be applied to the bat and thence to the ball as a result of such an action would likely be very small and possibly in an undesirable direction, and since an examination of motion pictures and still photographs of top-class batters fails to reveal any such action while the ball is in contact with the bat, the desirability of rolling the wrists in this way seems very much open to question. Because it is quite evident in a batter's follow-through that he has rolled his wrists, it could well be hypothesized that the controversy surrounding this question stems from an incorrect interpretation of the timing of the wrist-rolling action and the purpose that it serves. Instead of a protective movement initiated after the ball leaves the bat (and which it seems most likely to be), the action appears to have been looked upon as an additional source of muscular force to be used during the period of contact between bat and ball.

Follow-through. As in the case of pitching, the follow-through in batting serves the dual purpose of reducing the risk of injury and preventing interference with the application of force to the ball.

Base Running

Running to First Base. Because there can be no question of whether a man should run, and because he is not required to stop as soon as he reaches the base, running to first base is generally simpler than running between bases.

As in running between any pair of bases, the time taken to reach first base depends on the distance covered by the runner and on his average speed over that distance. In regard to this, Garner's[30] study of the time taken by right-handed and left-handed batters to reach first base produced some interesting results. When his 35 subjects batted left-handed, the mean distance they had to run to reach first base (27.04 m) was less than the corresponding mean distance (28.14 m) when they batted right-handed. However, this advantage was reversed when average speeds were considered, for the subjects' average speed when they batted right-handed (6.48 m/s) was slightly faster than when they batted left-handed (6.46 m/s). When both of these factors were considered together, it was found that the advantage of batting left-handed (that is, a shorter distance to run) outweighed that of batting right-handed (that is, a greater average speed). Thus, the subjects reached first base in a significantly shorter time when batting left-handed than they did when batting right-handed:

$$\frac{\text{Mean time to reach first base}}{\text{when batting left-handed}} = \frac{27.04 \text{ m}}{6.46 \text{ m/s}}$$

$$= 4.18 \text{ s}$$

$$\frac{\text{Mean time to reach first base}}{\text{when batting right-handed}} = \frac{28.14 \text{ m}}{6.48 \text{ m/s}}$$

$$= 4.34 \text{ s}$$

Running between Bases. Because the techniques used during the middle part of the run differ so little from those employed in sprinting on a track, the main interest here centers on methods of starting and stopping.

In taking a lead off the base there are two methods in common use—the standing (or stationary) lead and the walking lead. Each has its advantage. With a stationary lead the runner generally has his weight supported evenly on both feet and thus is in a position to move toward either base with equal facility. With a walking lead, on the other hand, the runner is able to get a faster start because he is already in motion at the time he makes his decision to run.

The advantage that the walking lead has over the stationary lead, in terms of starting speed, is clearly evident in the results of Kasso,[31] who tested the time taken by 10 high school players to reach a line 25 ft (7.62 m) from first base using four different leads. From fastest to slowest, the mean times recorded were ranked as follows:

1.   6 ft (1.83 m) walking lead.

2. $= \begin{cases} 4 \text{ ft } (1.22 \text{ m}) \text{ walking lead.} \\ 8 \text{ ft } (2.44 \text{ m}) \text{ stationary lead.} \end{cases}$

4.   6 ft stationary lead.

All the differences between two means with different rankings were found to be statistically significant. (*Note:* To some extent the question of a walking lead versus a stationary lead is an academic one, for a good pitcher will prevent a runner from obtaining a walking lead by making the runner stop before he pitches the ball.[32])

To come to a stop at the end of his run, a runner must be subjected to forces in the opposite horizontal direction to that in which he is moving. If the runner simply runs onto the base, he evokes such forces from the ground by overstriding during the last few steps of his run (see p. 399–400). If he slides, the frictional forces exerted on him by the ground as he slides across its surface supplement whatever forces are exerted backward against his feet during the latter stages of his run.

For a runner to slide, it is necessary for him to move his body from its sprinting position to a horizontal or near-horizontal position. This can be done in basically two ways: (1) by rotating the body forward some 70-90° into a prone position (a head-first slide); or (2) by rotating it backward 90-110° into a supine position (a feet-first slide). Although, at the time of writing, there appears to have been no published research concerning the relative merits of these two methods, and specifically how they compare in terms of speed, it would seem reasonable to expect that the head-first slide would be the faster of the two, for, as the runner's body is rotating forward, his legs are in position to drive strongly backward against the ground. Thus it is possible that the transition from a running position to a sliding position might well be effected with little if any loss of forward speed. The reverse of this argument applies in the case of the feet-first slide, for as the runner's body rotates into position, his legs move into a progressively less favorable position for the exerting of force backward against the ground. On other criteria, such as comfort, ease of learning, and safety, there can be little doubt that the advantages favor the feet-first method.

The techniques employed in changing direction to round one base and head for the next vary in the distance that the runner covers and in his average speed over that distance. If he runs straight to the base, makes a 90° turn to his left, and heads directly to the next base, he covers the least possible distance. His average speed, however, is likely to be less than if he followed a curved path as he made the change in direction. On the other hand, if he follows a curved path, the distance he runs is greater than it would be if he followed a straight path. (*Note:* This difference in distance obviously depends on how soon the runner begins to "round out" the turn. If he begins his curving run, say, 20 m from the base, he will clearly run farther than if he began it at, say, 5 m from the base.) Thus it can be seen that, in comparing any two methods, each one is likely to have an advantage over the other. The question is—which one has the greater advantage? Although it seems most unlikely that all the methods in common use are exactly equal in terms of effectiveness, there is as yet little scientific evidence to support any one method in preference to another.

Recommended Readings

ADAIR, R. K. (1990). *The Physics of Baseball.* New York: Harper & Row Pub.
ALLMAN, W. F. (1984). In W. Schrier and W. F. Allman (Eds.), *Newton at the Bat: The Science in Sports.* New York: Scribner's, pp. 3–13 (Pitching rainbows: The untold physics of the curve ball); pp. 14–19 (What makes a knuckle ball dance?).
FELTNER, M., AND DAPENA, J. (1986). Dynamics of the shoulder and elbow joints of the throwing arm during a baseball pitch. *International Journal of Sport Biomechanics,* 2:235–59.
QUIGLEY, M. (1984). *The Crooked Pitch: The Curveball in American Baseball History.* Chapel Hill, N.C.: Algonquin Books.

Notes

1. Feltner, M., and Dapena, J. (1986). Dynamics of the shoulder and elbow joints of the throwing arm during a baseball pitch. *International Journal of Sport Biomechanics,* 2:253–59.
2. Atwater, A. E. (1977). Biomechanical analysis of different pitches delivered from the windup and stretch positions. Paper presented at the 24th Annual Meeting of the American College of Sports Medicine, Chicago, Ill.
3. Atwater, A. E. (1982). Basic biomechanics applications for the coach. In J. Terauds (Ed.), *Biomechanics of Sports* (pp. 21–30). Del Mar, Calif.: Academic Publishers.
4. Selin, C. (1959). An analysis of the aerodynamics of pitched baseballs. *Research Quarterly,* 30:232–40.
5. Atwater. Biomechanical analysis of different pitches delivered from the windup and stretch positions.
6. Schutzler, L. L. (1980). A cinematographic analysis of stride length in highly skilled baseball pitchers. M.S. thesis, University of Arizona.
7. Edwards, D. K. (1963). Effects of stride and position on the pitching rubber on control in baseball pitching. *Research Quarterly,* 34:9–14.
8. Atwater. Biomechanical analysis of different pitches delivered from the windup and stretch positions.
9. Elliott, B. C., Groves, J. R., and Gibson, B. (1988). Timing of the lower limb drive and throwing limb movements in baseball pitching. *International Journal of Sport Biomechanics,* 4:59–67.

10. Wolff, R. (1989). Baseball's old windup is winding down. *Sports Illustrated*. 70, April 10, [no page numbers].

11. Briggs, L. L. (1959). Effect of spin and speed on the lateral deflection (curve) of a baseball; and the Magnus effect for smooth spheres. *American Journal of Physics*. 27:589–96.

12. Selin. An analysis of the aerodynamics of pitched baseballs. pp. 232–40.

13. Verwiebe, F. L. (1942). Does a baseball curve? *American Journal of Physics*, 10:119–20.

14. Selin. An analysis of the aerodynamics of pitched baseballs.

15. Watts, R. G., and Sawyer, E. (1975). Aerodynamics of a knuckleball. *American Journal of Physics*, 43:960–63.

16. Selin. An analysis of the aerodynamics of pitched baseballs, pp. 232–40, 96.

17. Williams, T., and Underwood, J. (1968). Hitting was my life: Part V—science of batting. *Sports Illustrated*, 29:41

18. Adams, G. L. (1965). Effect of eye dominance on baseball batting. *Research Quarterly*. 36:3–9.

19. Mason, B. R. (1987). Ground reaction forces of elite Australian baseball batters. In B. Jonsson, ed., *Biomechanics X-B* (pp. 749–52). Champaign, Ill.; Human Kinetics Publishers.

20. Hubbard, A. W., and Seng, C. N. (1954). Visual movements of batters. *Research Quarterly*, 25:57.

21. McCord, B. (1969). The physics in hitting. *Athletic Journal*, 50:46.

22. Watts, L. (1966). Classroom approach to batting. *Scholastic Coach*, 35:20.

23. Weiskopf, D. (1969). Be a .300 hitter! *Athletic Journal*, 49:118.

24. Williams and Underwood. Hitting was my life: Part V—science of batting. pp. 43–44.

25. Hubbard and Seng. Visual movements of batters, p. 48.

26. Breen, J. L. (1967). What makes a good hitter? *Journal of Health. Physical Education. Recreation*, 38:36, 39.

27. *Ibid.*, 39.

28. Selin. An analysis of the aerodynamics of pitched baseballs, p. 235.

29. Breen. What makes a good hitter?, pp. 36–39.

30. Garner, C. W. (1937). Difference in time taken to reach first base in right and left hand batting. M.A. thesis, State University of Iowa.

31. Kasso, R. A. (1963). A comparison of two methods of leading off first base. M.S. thesis, Springfield College.

32. Square, R. (1964). *How to Develop a Successful Pitcher* (p. 173). Englewood Cliffs. N.J.: Prentice Hall.

CHAPTER

9

BASKETBALL

Unlike baseball, which was first played somewhat earlier, basketball has developed to such an extent (since its invention by James Naismith in December, 1891) that it is now played in almost every country in the world.

BASIC CONSIDERATIONS

The analysis in this chapter is divided into five sections involving three offensive techniques (passing, dribbling, and shooting) and two used on both offense and defense (footwork and jumping).

Passing

A player's objective in making a pass is to complete the displacement of the ball from his (or her) hand or hands to those of a predetermined teammate. Except in rare instances (for example, in the case of some handoffs that a center might use or in the even rarer case of a pass rolled along the floor), this task involves motion of the ball through the air.

The flight of the ball, like that of all such projectiles, is governed by its velocity and its height at release and by the air resistance it encounters in flight. The passer seeks, therefore, to use the combination of these three factors that will produce the optimum result.

Velocity at Release. The velocity with which the ball leaves the passer's hand or hands is determined by (a) its velocity before the passing action is initiated; (b) the forces that are subsequently exerted upon it; (c) the time for which these forces act; and (d) the mass of the ball.

In general a player has available a large number of muscular forces that may be used to ensure that the ball obtains a release velocity of the desired magnitude and direction. However, because success depends on completing the actions involved before the defense can react and intercept the pass, it is important that those muscular forces that can be exerted most quickly be given priority. Thus the muscular forces producing flexion of the fingers, flexion of the wrist, and extension of the elbow should be the first to be called upon. Only when these forces are insufficient (as, for example, when a long pass is needed to initiate a fast break) should the less readily-available forces of the trunk and legs be used.

For a pass to be completed successfully, the horizontal direction in which the ball is projected must allow for any displacement that the receiver undergoes while the ball is in flight. Thus, the ball must be thrown a sufficient distance forward of a moving receiver to allow the hands and the ball to arrive at the same point at the same time.

Height at Release. For any given case, the height at which the ball is released depends on the type of pass used.

Air Resistance. While the cross-sectional area of a basketball is large compared to that of similar projectiles used in sports, the velocity at which it moves through the air is relatively small. Further, since the velocity is a more potent factor in determining the magnitude of the drag force than is the cross-sectional area, the drag on a basketball is also relatively small—so small, in fact, as to be of little practical significance.

When a player throws a pass, he (or she) almost invariably imparts spin to the ball. With the majority of passes this is a backspin that tends to slow the rate at which the ball falls under the influence of gravity (see Magnus effect, pp. 193–194). Provided the amount of backspin is not so great as to cause the receiver to have difficulty catching the ball, its existence can only be regarded as desirable, for it enables the ball to follow a slightly more direct path than would otherwise be possible. On the other hand, if sidespin is imparted to the ball at release, the lateral deviation of the ball during flight will at least disconcert the receiver and at worst may cause him (or her) to miss the ball completely. In general, therefore, the application of sidespin to the ball should be avoided. The one exception to this is in bounce passing where spins other than a backspin may occasionally be imparted to obtain a particular result once the ball strikes the floor.

To complete a pass, the ball must be caught by the receiver. The basic factors governing catching in basketball are essentially the same as those already discussed in connection with baseball except that no glove is used and the catch is generally made with both hands playing virtually identical roles.

Although not always clearly understood by players of the game—if their actions can be taken as any indication—the objective in dribbling is to advance the ball when passing is impossible or less desirable.

The act of dribbling consists of a number of repetitions of the following series of actions:

- The dribbler applies forces to the ball and propels it (generally in a forward and downward direction) toward the floor. The forces applied by the dribbler, together with the force exerted on the ball by gravity and the distance over which these forces act, determine the velocity with which the ball leaves the hand. Ignoring the presumably negligible effect of air resistance, this velocity and the height of release determine the subsequent flight path of the ball.
- The ball follows a curved flight path until it makes contact with the floor.
- The floor exerts forces on the ball, altering both the magnitude and direction of its velocity. As in the many similar cases of impact in sports, the velocity of the ball as it leaves the floor depends principally on its velocity immediately before impact (assuming, as seems reasonable, that the other factors involved are essentially constant in any given situation).
- The ball follows a curved path as it ascends from the floor to again make contact with the dribbler's hand. (*Note:* To ensure that the hand is in position to receive the ball as it rebounds from the floor, the dribbler must be moving with an average horizontal velocity approximately equal to that of the ball.)
- The dribbler applies force to the ball to reduce its upward velocity to zero preparatory to propelling it back toward the floor. The amount of force the dribbler must exert to bring about this change in the velocity of the ball depends on the distance over which the force is applied and the velocity at which the ball is moving when the hand makes contact with it.

The objective in shooting is very similar to that in passing, for it involves completing the displacement of the ball from one position (the hand or hands of the shooter) to another (the inside of the hoop). As Wooden puts it—a shot is "a pass to the basket."[1]

Aside from the question of applying force to the ball (in which process the factors of importance are identical with those already discussed in connection with passing), the principal factors governing the outcome of a shot are those that determine the flight path of any projectile—its height, speed and angle of release, and the air resistance encountered in flight.

Height of Release. The height of release is determined by the position of the player's body at the instant of release. This is determined, in turn, by the type of shot used. A dunk shot, for example, must be released with the center of gravity of the ball at least 3.17 m above the floor (that is, the height of the rim plus the radius of the ball), while a jump shot is often released from heights as low as 2.5 m, and a set shot from even lower heights. Finally, the type of shot used is generally influenced by the shooter's position on the court, by his (or her) preference for one type of shot over others that might be equally suitable, and by the need to get the shot away without having it blocked by an opponent.

Speed and Angle of Release. Assuming a height of release that is fixed in some manner by these various factors, the combination of speed and angle of release that is most likely to result in a successful shot depends on the distance of the shot, the position and caliber of the player guarding the shooter, and the angle to the horizontal at which the ball approaches the basket (the *angle of entry*).

Distance of the Shot. The distance of the shot directly influences the speed of release required—a tip-in or layup requiring markedly less speed than, say, a 6-m shot. Further, since the speed and angle of release required for a successful shot are interdependent, the distance of the shot indirectly influences the angle of release.

Because the effects of small deviations from the optimum speed and angle of projection become more pronounced the longer the ball is in the air, shooting accuracy also varies with the distance of the shot. While this in itself is little more than common knowledge, a study by Bunn[2] of the actual relationship between shooting accuracy and the distance of shots during competitive play has provided some interesting information (Fig. 9-1). His data suggest, for example, that on the average, a shot from 9 ft (2.74 m) is better than one from 24 ft (7.32 m) despite the fact that successful shots from the latter distance are worth 3 pts. Conversely, one shot from 24 ft is better than one from 5 ft (4.57 m). In this case, the success rate is lower (19.5% vs. 28%), but the reward (3 pts vs. 2 pts) is more than correspondingly greater. Incidentally, Bunn's 28 percent figure for shots from 15 ft compared with free-throw percentages that generally average in the neighborhood of 60–70 percent vividly demonstrates the effect that an active defense has in reducing shooting accuracy.

Position and Caliber of Defensive Player. The position, physique, and jumping ability of the player guarding the shooter all have a bearing on the speed and angle of release that can be successfully employed. The closer the defensive player is to the shooter, the taller and longer armed the player is, and the higher the player can jump, the more likely it is that he (or she) will be able to reach high enough to block the shot. Thus, the speed and angle at which the ball is released must be such as to allow it to pass beyond the reach of the defensive player.

Angle of Entry. The role of the angle of entry is a rather complex one and as such warrants detailed consideration.

If the ball approaches the hoop from directly above (that is, its angle of

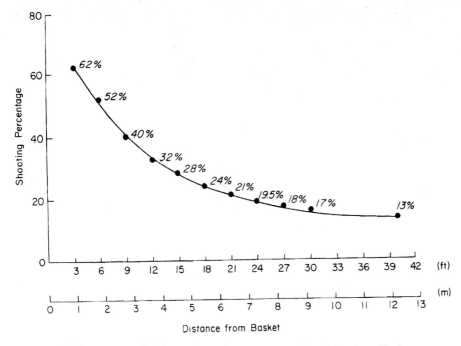

Figure 9-1. Shooting accuracy varies with the distance of the shot. (Redrawn with permission from Bunn. *Scientific Principles of Coaching.*)

entry is 90°), it is presented with an 18-in.(45.7 cm)-diameter circular opening through which it can pass [Fig. 9-2(a)]. If it approaches from a lesser angle [Fig. 9-2 (b), (c), and (d)], the opening at right angles to its path is elliptical with one diameter 45.7 cm in length and the other—the one that ultimately determines whether the ball can pass through the hoop without touching the rim—less than 45.7 cm. The actual length of this second diameter can be computed using the equation:

$$d = (45.7 \sin \alpha) \text{ cm}$$

where d = the length of the diameter in question and α = the angle of entry.

When the angle of entry is such that d is equal to the diameter of the ball, the lower limit of possible angles of entry has been reached, for with any lesser angle the ball will inevitably strike the rim of the hoop.* With a ball of diameter 24.7 cm (the midpoint in the range of diameters permissible within the rules) this lower limit can be found by letting d = 24.7 cm and by solving for α:

* Generalizations concerning the outcome when the ball hits the rim of the basket are very difficult to make because of the large number of variables involved. The discussion here, therefore, is confined to angles of entry that permit the ball to pass through the hoop without touching the rim.

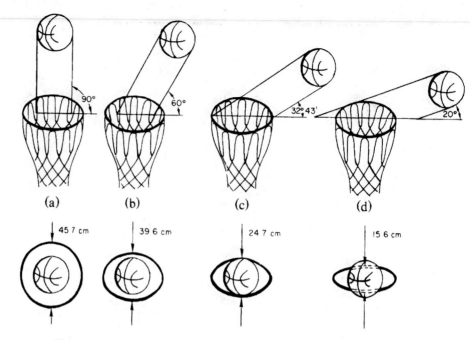

Figure 9-2. The scope for error in the range of a basketball shot varies with the angle at which the ball approaches the hoop; that is, with the angle of entry. (*Note:* The top half of the figure shows a series of oblique side views of the basket while the bottom half shows a corresponding series of oblique front views.)

$$24.7 = 45.7 \sin \alpha$$

$$\sin \alpha = \frac{24.7}{45.7}$$

$$= 0.5405$$

$$\alpha = 32°43'$$

The maximum angle of entry is obviously 90°, which angle is obtained if the ball is released from a point directly above the basket.

Because d increases as the angle of entry increases, the margin for errors in the range or distance of the shot is also related to the angle of entry. The nearer the angle of entry is to 90°, the greater is this margin. The horizontal distance that the center of the ball can be away from the center of the hoop and still pass "cleanly" through the hoop (that is, the margin for error) can be closely approximated using the equation:

$$E = \pm(22.9 \sin \alpha - r) \text{ cm}$$

where E = the margin for error, α = the angle of entry, and r = the radius of the ball. Using this equation, and $r = 24.7/2$ cm, the relationship between E and α can readily be shown:

Angle of Entry, α	Margin for Error, E (cm)
90°	± 10.5
80°	± 10.2
70°	± 9.1
60°	± 7.4
50°	± 5.1
40°	± 2.3
32° 43′	0.0

Therefore, from this standpoint alone, it would seem that the optimum angle of entry is one that is as close to 90° as possible. Several other aspects of the matter must be considered, however. One of these is the fact that for any given shot, the higher the angle of entry, the higher must be both the speed and angle at which the ball is released. In the case of a 15-ft (4.57 m) shot (for example, a free throw) released from a height of 7 ft (2.13 m) above the floor, the relationships between the angle of entry and the speed and angle of release, respectively, are shown in Fig. 9-3.

A careful consideration of Fig. 9-3 reveals that in this case, at least, angles of entry close to 90° are a practical impossibility. For example, an 87° angle of entry requires that the ball be released with a speed of approximately 20 m/s (or 72 km/h)—a speed well beyond the capabilities of an athlete using any orthodox shot. Even if an athlete could readily project the ball at such a speed, few indoor arenas would have ceilings high enough to "accommodate" the shot, for the ball would rise to a height of approximately 22 m above the level of the court—a height roughly equal to that of a six-storied building!

Another factor that should be taken into account is the effect that small errors in the angle of projection have on the distance of the shot. In this respect, Mortimer has demonstrated that if all else is equal, "the seriousness

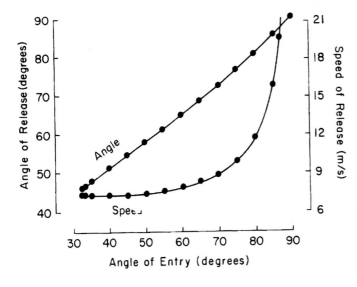

Figure 9-3.
For a given height of release and distance of shot (7 ft [2.13 m] and 15 ft [4.57 m], respectively, in the present example) only one combination of speed and angle of release will yield a given angle of entry.

of a 1° error increases with the angle of projection. As the angle increases, the same 1° error . . . causes the ball to deviate farther and farther from the center of the basket."[3] Thus, while a high angle of projection is desirable in that it leads to a high angle of entry, it is less desirable than lower angles in the demands it puts on accuracy as the ball is released.

From all of this it can be seen that the question of the optimum angle of entry for a given shot is not a simple one. Probably the most difficult aspect of the whole question is how each of the various factors combine to determine the optimum angle of entry. In the case of a 4.57-m shot released at a height of 2.13 m, the extent to which each of the factors considered here influences the optimum angle of entry can be gauged from the data contained in Table 9-1. This table shows a range of angles of entry between 32°43' (the theoretical minimum) and 89°59'; the angle of release necessary to attain each of these angles; the margin for error in the length of each shot; and the errors in the length of the shot resulting from deviations of 1° from the required angle of release. Where the error resulting from a 1° deviation in release angle exceeds the margin for error that is available, the release angle concerned clearly requires a higher degree of accuracy from

TABLE 9-1 Optimum Angles of Entry and Release for a 15-ft (4.57-m) Shot

Angle of Entry (degrees)	Angle of Release (degrees)	Margin for Error (cm)	Error Due to 1° Error in Angles of Release[a] (cm)	
			+ 1°	− 1°
32.72	46.1	0.0	3.6	− 4.7
33	46.4	0.1	3.4	− 4.4
34	47.1	0.5	2.8	− 3.8
35	47.7	0.8	2.1	− 3.1
36	48.4	1.1	1.5	− 2.5
37	49.1	1.4	0.9	−· 1.9
38	49.8	1.8	0.4	− 1.2
39	50.4	2.1	− 0.2	− 0.6
40	51.1	2.4	− 0.8	− 0.1
41	51.8	2.7	− 1.4	0.5
42	52.4	3.0	− 1.9	1.1
43	53.1	3.3	− 2.5	1.7
44	53.8	3.6	− 3.0	2.2
45	54.5	3.8	− 3.6	2.8
46	55.1	4.1	− 4.1	3.4
47	55.8	4.4	− 4.7	3.9
48	56.5	4.6	− 5.2	4.5
49	57.2	4.9	− 5.8	5.1
50	57.9	5.2	− 6.4	5.6
60	64.9	7.5	− 12.7	12.1
70	72.4	9.1	− 22.5	21.9
80	80.7	10.2	− 47.3	46.7
89.98	89.98	10.5	− 27,034.9	27,035.8

[a] A positive number indicates that the center of the ball passes beyond the center of the basket by the stated amount, while a negative number indicates that it falls short of the center of the basket by the stated amount.

the shooter than do the release angles for which this is not the case. The data in the latter cases (that is, those that exhibit the greater "tolerance" of small errors on the part of the shooter) are shaded in Table 9-1. From these figures it seems reasonable to suggest that an angle of release between 49° and 55° will provide the shooter with a greater likelihood of success than any angle outside this range.

Figure 9-4 shows the trajectories for shots with release angles within the range mentioned compared with those for shots with release angles of 46° (the minimum possible for a successful shot) and 65°. (The latter value has been chosen as roughly representative of the maximum angle of release that might conceivably be used in a game situation.) From the figure it is clear that the optimum angles of release yield trajectories with a "low arch" rather than the "medium arch" or "high arch" advocated by most writers on the subject.

Shibukawa[4] extended the preceding analysis to include a consideration

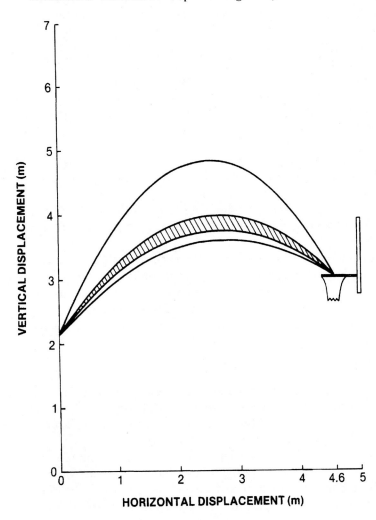

Figure 9-4.
Free-shooting: The paths followed by a ball released from a height of 7 ft (2.13 m) at angles of 46°, 49°, 55°, and 65°. The optimum angles of release yield paths within the shaded area.

of the effects of errors in both the angle of release and the speed of release. He concluded that (1) "considering only the angle of release, this region [49–55°] certainly appears to be . . . optimal"; (2) "if the speed of the ball is also taken into account, . . . angles of release greater than 52 or 53 degrees would probably be preferable." In short, it appears that an angle of release of 52–55° affords the greatest likelihood of success under the conditions described here.

When the ball strikes the rim or the backboard, instead of passing "cleanly" through the hoop, what happens to it next depends on the combined effect of the many factors that influence any elastic impact (see pp. 80–89). Assuming that the masses of the two bodies concerned and their coefficient of restitution are constant, the most important factors in determining the outcome are likely to be the point at which the ball makes contact with the rim or backboard, its velocity at that instant, and the extent to which it is spinning. Although it is very difficult to generalize in cases of such complexity, it would probably be true to say that contact nearer the back of the hoop than the front; a soft shot (that is, a relatively low speed at contact); and the presence of some backspin on the ball would all be likely to improve the odds on the ball rebounding through the hoop.

Brancazio performed an analysis of shooting mechanics that was similar in some respects to the one presented here and very different from it in others. His main conclusion, however, was consistent with the one reached here. He concluded that:

> . . . the [optimum] launching angle for a basketball shot will be between 45° and 52°, depending on the distance and height of the point of release.[5]

(*Note:* His computations were for shots made from distances of 10-25 ft [3.0-7.6 m] from the basket and released from heights of 7.5-10 ft [2.3-3.0 m].)

Shibukawa studied the case in which the ball strikes the backboard and then passes "cleanly" through the hoop and concluded that this leads "to a somewhat higher rate of success than . . . shooting the ball directly for the basket."[6] His results also supported the notion, presented earlier, that backspin improves the likelihood of the ball rebounding through the hoop after first striking the backboard.

Body Position and Footwork

To be effective on offense, a player must be able to outmaneuver a defensive opponent with rapid changes in speed and direction of movement. Conversely, to be effective on defense a player must be able to react readily to an opponent's attempts to outmaneuver him (or her).

In attempting to achieve these objectives—whether starting from a stationary position, coming to a stop, or merely changing the speed or direction of movement—an athlete must exert forces to accelerate (or decelerate) the body. The magnitude and direction of these forces determine the nature of the acceleration that results (Newton's second law). It is, therefore, important that the player assume a position from which he (or she) can readily apply forces that are consistent with the demands of the situation. Because these forces result mainly from the action of muscles of the legs and are transmitted to the floor via the feet, the positions of the legs and feet are especially important in this regard.

Where starting from a stationary position is concerned, the greater the ease with which the player can disrupt the equilibrium state (that is, the less the stability of equilibrium), the more rapidly the player can begin moving in a given direction—and thus the more likely that the player will be effective in eluding an opponent or in preventing an opponent eluding him (or her). Therefore, when considering the optimum position to adopt to start quickly, a player should take into account the factors that influence the stability of equilibrium in addition to those that govern the ability to apply the necessary forces.

Jumping

In basketball, a player's purpose in jumping is to increase the height to which he (or she) can reach. The maximum height to which a player can reach is the sum of (1) the maximum height to which the center of gravity can be lifted; and (2) the distance to which the player can reach beyond this height. As in the case of other projectiles, the first of these is governed by the height of the player's center of gravity and by the vertical velocity, at the instant of takeoff. The second is a function of the body position in the air. (See pp. 132–133 for a detailed consideration of the effects of variations in body position.)

In some instances the actual height to which a player reaches is less important than obtaining an advantage over the opponent in terms of time. For example, in executing a jump shot it is more important that a player get the shooting hand to a height of, say 2.5 m, before the opponent is able to reach to that height than it is to get the hand up to some greater height. In these cases, where speed in initiating a jump is more important than the maximum height to which the athlete can reach, the muscle actions (similar to those already discussed in connection with passing and shooting) must be such as require the least possible time consistent with the completion of the task.

TECHNIQUES
Passing

Of the two main methods of advancing the ball down the court (passing and dribbling), passing is generally the most effective and widely used. Although there exists a large variety of passes that might be used, in practice only a few of these are commonly employed. The others generally have inherent limitations that restrict their use to special situations and/or to specially gifted players.

The frequency and effectiveness with which the more common types of pass are used in competition have been studied by Allsen and Ruffner.[7] After analyzing the charts of 72 selected games (24 each at college, high school varsity, and college intramural level) they found that the two-hand chest pass was more frequently used than any other type of pass—38.6 percent of all passes recorded were of this type. Next most frequent were the one-hand baseball pass (18.9 percent); the two-hand overhead pass (16.6 percent); and the one- and two-hand bounce passes (7.3 and 7.2 percent, respectively). The one-hand baseball pass resulted in a lower percentage of completions than any other type of pass. On 9.3 percent of all baseball passes attempted, the ball was lost to the opposition. The next least successful were the one-hand bounce pass (9.1 percent), the two-hand shoulder pass (7.7 percent), and the two-hand bounce pass (7.3 percent). The best results were obtained with the two-hand chest pass and the little-used two-hand shovel pass, both of which resulted in the ball being lost only 2.5 percent of the time.

Chest pass. As indicated by the results of Allsen and Ruffner, the two-hand chest pass is both the most frequently used and most reliable of the various passes in basketball.

To execute the pass, the ball is held at approximately chest height with the thumbs pointed toward each other and the fingers comfortably spread behind the ball. From this position the ball is drawn backward a little as the wrists are "cocked" before applying force to the ball in the direction of the pass. This cocking action places the wrists in such a position that the muscles that flex the wrist can exert force over a longer distance and thus do more work on the ball than would otherwise be possible. The cocking of the wrists is immediately followed by a coordinated series of actions in which the elbows are extended and the wrists and fingers are rapidly flexed (or "snapped") to apply force to the ball. These actions are frequently accompanied by a step and a shifting of the body weight in the direction of the throw. Because the pass should normally be directed so that the ball can be caught by the receiver at some point between the waist and the shoulders, it must usually be released at an angle slightly above the horizontal in order to allow for the effects that gravity has on it during its flight. (*Note:* While it may be very effective in producing the kind of passing action required, it is as well to recognize that the common admonition of teachers and coaches to "throw the ball in a straight line parallel to the floor" is actually asking the impossible.)

For relatively short passes of less than 3-4 m, all the force that needs to be applied to the ball can usually be provided by the muscles controlling the wrists and fingers, with those extending the elbow perhaps also making a small contribution. For longer passes, a greater involvement of the elbow extensors and the muscles of the legs and trunk is normally required. The extent to which the various body parts contribute is reflected in the follow-through once the ball has been released—a short follow-through of wrists and fingers characterizing short passes and a complete follow-through with both arms characterizing longer ones.

Overhead Pass.   Although most widely used as a pass to a post or pivot player, and as a pass to a cutter, the two-hand overhead pass can be particularly useful in other situations. Tall players often find it easy to protect the ball by holding it overhead. Thus, they are naturally in the ideal position from which to make an overhead pass. Similarly, a player receiving the ball overhead is probably in a better position for this kind of pass than for any other.

The two-hand overhead pass is made from a position in which the ball is held above and slightly forward of the head. (Apart from affording greater protection of the ball from defensive players behind, this forward position makes it a little easier for the player to direct the pass forward and downward than would be the case if the ball were held directly overhead.) The ball is held in the hands with fingers spread and pointing upward and with the thumbs directed inward toward each other. To make it difficult for the defense to get to the ball, the elbows are kept partially flexed and pointing outward.

The passing movement consists of a quick forceful flexion of the wrists and fingers, often accompanied by a forward step and a lifting of the body up onto the toes. Provided these latter movements are performed quickly enough not to reveal the passer's intention prematurely, they slightly increase the odds on successfully completing the pass by increasing the speed and height at which the ball is released.

Except for those passes that are deliberately lofted beyond the reach of a defensive player, overhead passes are almost invariably directed forward and downward toward the chest of the receiver. The angle at which the ball is directed below the horizontal is governed by the distance of the pass and the speed of the ball at release—the longer the pass, or the less the speed of release, the nearer the angle of release must approach the horizontal.

Since most of the force applied to the ball derives from the action of the wrists and fingers, the follow-through after the ball has been released is naturally limited.

Bounce Pass.   As a means of passing the ball through congested areas, or past a tall long-limbed opponent, the bounce pass has few, if any, equals.

The two-hand bounce pass is executed in a manner identical to that of the two-hand chest pass except for the point at which the pass is aimed. Instead of being directed at the receiver's chest, a bounce pass is released in the direction of a point on the floor partway between the passer and where the receiver will be when he (or she) catches the ball. While to date there appear to have been no published reports of research which touch upon this aspect of the bounce pass, practical experience suggests that the ball should be bounced at a point about two-thirds of the distance between passer and receiver.

As in other similar cases, the result of the impact between the ball and the floor is influenced by whatever spin has previously been imparted to the ball. Topspin is frequently applied to increase the distance of a bounce pass and backspin to make the ball "come up" softly into the hands of a cutter. Sidespins are also used on occasion.

Because the distance that the ball must travel is greater for a bounce pass than for a direct one and because impact with the floor generally reduces the speed of the ball, a bounce pass will take a greater time to complete unless the force applied to the ball by the passer is correspondingly increased. For this reason, a bounce pass frequently requires a greater contribution of force from the muscles of the legs and trunk than is necessary for an equivalent chest pass. The increase in either the time to complete the pass or the force applied to the ball (which necessarily accompany the use of a bounce pass) increases the scope for error in the execution of the pass.

Baseball Pass.   The baseball pass is used most as a means of initiating a fast break following a rebound or the scoring of a goal.

Consistent with the name, the passing action is similar to that used in a baseball throw. For a right-handed throw the ball is raised over and behind the right shoulder with the right hand behind the ball (fingers spread and pointing upward) and the left one guiding the ball back into position. The feet are comfortably spread and positioned so that a line joining the heel of the back foot to the toes of the front foot closely approximates the intended direction of the pass. (Such a position of the feet enables the hips to be fully rotated to the front during the throw and thus allows the muscles that produce this motion to add their contribution to the speed of the ball, should this be necessary.) From this initial side-facing position the throw is made with a rotation of the hips and trunk to the front followed by a coordinated action of the throwing shoulder, elbow, wrist, and fingers.

Dribbling

Although the height and speed of a dribble vary according to the situation, the technique used is basically the same in all cases.

The dribbling action is initiated by placing one hand on top of the ball and, by extending the elbow and flexing the wrist and fingers, pushing it down toward the floor. Then, as the ball rises, one hand (generally the same hand as pushed it down) is placed on top of the ball and the procedure reversed. The wrist and elbow "give" as the hand accompanies the ball up to the high point of its bounce.

When a child first attempts to dribble a basketball, he (or she) invariably keeps the hand fairly rigid and hits the ball instead of pushing it. Because the time during which force is applied is much less than it would be if the child were to use the proper pushing technique, a much greater force must be applied to the ball to obtain the same result (impulse-momentum relationship, pp. 79–80).

Further, because the hand is in contact with the ball for only a very short time, the child is less able to sense deviations from the required speed and path of the ball and to apply the forces necessary to correct them. The beginner's first attempts at dribbling are generally characterized, therefore, by a sharp stinging sensation in the hand (due to the relatively high force involved) and by an all-too-evident lack of control (due to the small period of contact between the hand and the ball).

The time during which a skilled dribbler's hand is in contact with the ball is probably a good deal longer than is commonly supposed. In a high dribble, the hand is normally placed on the ball when it is approximately 60 cm from the floor, accompanies the ball upward another 30–60 cm, and then pushes the ball down again through roughly the same distance. Thus, the hand may be in contact with the ball for as much as half of its journey. However, since the ball is moving relatively slowly as it nears the end of its upward motion—the farther it is from the floor, the smaller is its speed—the half of its journey in which the ball and hand are in contact is of longer duration than the other half. (*Note:* In the stroboscopic photograph of a basketball player performing a high dribble [Fig. 9-5] the player's hand is in contact with the ball in six out of eight [or 75%] of the exposures recording the dribbling cycle.) Because the main reason for a player electing to use a low dribble is to obtain a greater control over the ball and thus to reduce the chances of an opponent knocking it away, the proportion of time during which the player is in contact with the ball is even greater for a low dribble than it is for a high one.

Shooting

Shooting, the only means by which it is possible to score points, is probably the most important skill in the game of basketball. In light of this, it is little wonder that the techniques of shooting have received concentrated attention from coaches and players.

There are a wide variety of shots that a player might use in attempting

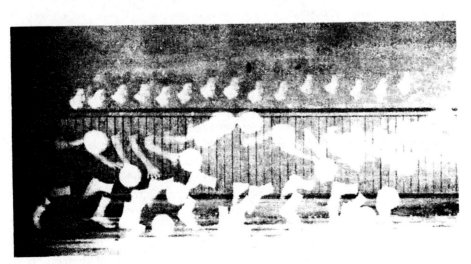

Figure 9-5. Stroboscopic photograph of good technique in the execution of a high dribble. Note the length of time that the hand is in contact with the ball—consecutive photographs have been taken at equal intervals of time.

to put the ball in the basket. Of these, some have been found by experience to offer better chances of success than others. Logically enough, these shots are used with greater frequency in games than those less likely to be successful. In a study of rebounding, Allsen[8] reported the frequency with which various types of shots were used in 39 selected games. His analysis, which unfortunately did not include layups or tip-ins, showed that the one-hand jump shot was by far the most commonly used. This type of shot was used in 67.2 percent of the 3180 field-goal attempts recorded. Next in order were the one-hand set shot (21.0 percent), the right-hand hook shot (8.0 percent), and the left-hand hook shot (2.3 percent).

Set Shot. The similarity of the actions involved to those used in both layups and jump shots has resulted in the set shot being frequently regarded as the foundation upon which these other shooting techniques are developed. Were this not enough reason in itself, the relative ease with which it can be learned has provided added support for the suggestion that the set shot is the logical one to be learned first.

For the execution of a set shot, the foot on the same side as the shooting hand is placed a short distance forward of the other foot and pointed in the direction of the basket. The back foot is positioned slightly to the side and pointing forward and outward at approximately a 45° angle. This placement of the feet is the reverse of that used in almost all other sports techniques in which a ball is projected into the air, in that the forward foot is the one on the same side as the dominant hand. The main reason for this is that in set shooting, unlike projection techniques in many other sports, the need for accuracy far outweighs the need to develop high velocities at release. Thus, the opportunity to develop such velocities by incorporating large hip, trunk, and shoulder rotations is declined in favor of a position that permits the forces exerted on the ball to act almost exclusively in the direction of the basket. From this standpoint alone it would be appropriate if the back foot were also pointed at the basket, so that whatever forces were exerted by the back leg would be more likely to act in that direction. However, the desirability of increasing the shooter's stability by increasing the area of his base probably outweighs this consideration. Certainly most good shooters rotate the back foot outward to some extent.

For a right-handed shot, the ball is held at chest height with the left hand underneath, in a position to support and guide it during the initial stages in the act of shooting. The right hand is directly behind and somewhat below with palm forward and fingers pointing upward. The left hand then lifts the ball up past the face and into a position from which the shot is completed with an extension of the right elbow and a flexion of the right wrist and fingers. This whole sequence of actions is coordinated with an extension of the shooter's legs and a forward movement of the center of gravity.

So that the forces exerted on the ball as a result of these latter actions might more readily act in the direction of the basket, the shoulders are rotated a little to the left during the final stages leading up to the moment of release. This puts the shooter's eyes, right shoulder, elbow, and wrist and the ball in a direct line to the basket.

The extent to which the legs contribute to the force applied to the ball varies with the strength of the player and the distance of the shot. With youngsters who lack the strength to project the ball very far, the range and force of the leg action used is necessarily a good deal more than that required by stronger players for a shot of the same distance. Similarly, the farther the shot is from the basket, the more likely it is that the legs will have to contribute force to support that available from the arms and shoulders.

Hudson[9] studied the techniques used by three groups of college women when shooting free throws and found:

- The high-skill group (members of the United States team at the World University Games) released the ball with the shoulder more flexed and the ball at a greater height than the low-skill group (members of an instructional class). For the purposes of this comparison, differences in the heights of the subjects were taken into account by dividing the height of release by the standing height of the subject.
- The high-skill group had the center of gravity almost directly over the midpoint of the base (as viewed from the side) at release. The low-skill group had it approximately 17 percent of the base length farther forward at this time.
- There were no significant differences among the groups in the mean angles of release. These mean values ranged from 52.4° to 52.9° and thus fell within the 49–55° limits found earlier (p. 233) to be likely to yield the best results. They also fell within the 52–55° limits suggested by Shibukawa.

Jump Shot.   A jump shot can be made at the end of a dribble, after moving to receive a pass, or from a stationary position. Whatever the case, the techniques involved are essentially the same.

The position of the shooter's feet at the start of the jump varies from player to player. Some prefer to have their feet in a position akin to that described for set shooting, while others—probably the majority—show preference for a position in which the feet are parallel to each other and equidistant from the basket.

The upward jump preceding the shot is obtained by a quick forceful extension of hip, knee, and ankle joints. The amount to which these joints are flexed prior to the jump should be just sufficient to allow the shooter to obtain a "lead" over the defensive player (see p. 235). While additional bending might well result in a higher jump, the extra time involved in the takeoff provides the opponent with a better chance of being ready to block the shot. The truth of this is especially evident when a shooter increases the bend in the knees prior to starting upward into the jump. With the shooter's intention so clearly "telegraphed" in this way, it is little wonder that an alert defensive player can often block the resulting shot.

As the shooter extends the legs and pushes down against the floor with the feet, the ball (held in the same manner as for a set shot) is raised to a position just forward of the head. This lifting of the ball continues until just prior to the release when the ball, still held by both hands, is high overhead. From this position the left hand is lowered as the right arm directs the ball into the air with an action similar to that used in a set shot.

Because, in general, the shoulders are not rotated in quite the same way as previously described for the set shot, it is usually necessary for the shooter to turn the palm of the shooting hand outward slightly (that is, to pronate it), to ensure that the ball does not deviate from the straight-line path to the basket.

Techniques used in the execution of a jump shot have been subjected to close scrutiny by Penrose and Blanksby,[10] and Yates and Holt.[11]

Penrose and Blanksby analyzed the performances of eight "top-level" and eight "average-level" basketball players executing jump shots from a distance of 5.5 m. Each subject approached the basket from a distance of 10 m, performed a one-count (jump) or two-count stop, as instructed, and executed the jump shot. The results obtained from a detailed analysis of films taken with cameras placed in line with, and at right angles to, the subjects' line of approach formed the basis for the following conclusions:

> The top-level group differed from average players in that they demonstrated (1) more height but less horizontal distance during the hurdle step, (2) greater ball motion prior to takeoff [that is, a lower position of the ball at landing from the hurdle step and a greater vertical velocity of the ball at takeoff], (3) a more vertical trunk at takeoff and release, (4) the ball to be further behind the shoulder in the ready position, (5) the elbow to be closer to the ball-basket line (while in the ready position), (6) the nonshooting hand to be removed from the ball much later, (7) the shot to be released with less velocity and later in the jump, (8) less horizontal displacement (float-forward and lateral), (9) greater consistency in execution, (10) smoother patterns of motion.
>
> The one-count method of landing differed from the two-count in that during the one-count method: (1) more height but less horizontal distance was achieved during the hurdle step, (2) foot spacing was closer to the parallel position, (3) the trunk was more vertical in the stop position and at release, (4) greater height was attained during the jump, (5) the shot release angle was higher, (6) there was less horizontal displacement (float-forward and lateral), (7) differences between "top and average level" players were reduced, (8) smoother patterns of motion resulted.

Yates and Holt analyzed the performances of 15 subjects who ranged in shooting ability from "inaccurate" (5 percent success) to "high percentage" (82 percent success) when shooting jump shots from 10 ft (3.05 m) and 20 ft (6.10 m). They concluded that:

- More successful shooters demonstrated a greater angle at the shoulder at the point of releasing the basketball (lateral view). (*Note:* The data of Yates and Holt thus supported the similar finding of Hudson [p. 241].)

- More successful shooters used a much smaller elbow angle at the start of the shot than the poorer performers.
- A greater backspin during flight was associated with the high performance shooters. (*Note:* For shots that rebound from the backboard into the basket, this finding is consistent with the similar finding of Shibukawa [p. 234].)
- The successful shooters demonstrated a closer alignment of the upper arm with the vertical at release, than the lower percentage shooters.

The instant at which the ball should be released relative to the instant at which the peak of the shooter's jump is reached is a topic on which there has been some disagreement. While Szymanski's study[12] of films of four NBA guards executing the jump shot revealed that in all cases the ball was released "before the peak of the jump was reached," leading coaches (for example, Auerbach,[13] Cousy,[14] and Sharman[15]) are almost unanimous in agreeing that the ball should be released at the peak of the jump.

This question of the timing of the release can be resolved by considering the forces that must be exerted on the ball if the shooter is to achieve his (or her) objective. To project the ball in the direction of the basket requires that both horizontal and vertical velocities be imparted to it before it is released. Regardless of when the ball is released, its vertical velocity at that instant is equal to the sum of the vertical velocity of the shooter and the vertical velocity of the ball relative to the shooter—the former resulting primarily from the forces exerted by the legs at takeoff and the latter from vertical forces exerted by the arms and shoulders. Now, because only a certain amount of vertical velocity is necessary in any given case, the amount obtained from each of these sources can be adjusted to meet the needs of the occasion. If the shooter has strong arms and shoulders, or if the shot is a relatively short one, the ball may be released at the peak of the jump. In such cases, the vertical velocity of the shooter (and thus the contribution of the legs to the vertical velocity of the ball) is zero. For shots requiring more force than can reasonably be generated by the arms and shoulders alone, it is imperative that some of the force from the legs be used. Or, in other words, that the ball be released before the peak of the jump is reached, at which time the shooter still retains some vertical velocity. (*Note:* On the basis of the results obtained by Szymanski, it would appear that even highly skilled performers must use some of the force generated by their legs to impart the necessary velocity to the ball when shooting from a distance of 25 ft [7.62 m] from the basket—the shooting distance used in the study.)

Penrose and Blanksby[16] determined the time of release, relative to the time at which the shooter's center of gravity reached its peak height, and found that, in shots taken from a distance of 5.5 m, average players released the ball 0.02 s and top players 0.08 s, after the peak of the jump was reached. While this result demonstrates that when shooting from this distance, the required vertical velocity can be generated by the arms and shoulders alone and in spite of the contrary influence of the rest of the body, there seems to be little virtue in releasing the ball so late in a game situation—unless of course, the presence of a defensive player affords no better option.

Layup Shot. A layup shot is one in which a player catches the ball on the move (either from a pass or at the end of a dribble), takes the one step permitted by the rules, leaps high into the air, and lays the ball up against the backboard so that it will rebound into the basket (Fig. 9-6).

To perform this movement legally and effectively, a player making a right-handed shot must gather the ball while in midair and about to land on the right foot or at the instant when the right foot contacts the ground. If the ball is taken earlier (that is, when the left foot is in contact with the ground), the player will either violate the rules governing "traveling" or make an unbalanced shot off the wrong foot. If the ball is taken later than described, the player is likely to have to rush the final phases of the complete movement and make a hurried and inaccurate shot. Immediately following the grounding of the right foot, a normal running stride is taken onto the left foot from which the final jump and shot is made. During the transition from right to left foot, the ball is held close to the body at about waist height. The takeoff for the final leap—directed in a vertical rather than a horizontal direction so that the shooter can gain the maximum height from which to release the ball—is made by extending the left leg vigorously in conjunction with a high lift of the right knee. During this movement the ball is being shifted from its waist-high position, past the face, to a position where at the maximum height of the jump it is as high as possible and about to be released.

The ball is normally released at the peak of the jump where it is most

Figure 9-6. The layup shot.

likely to be beyond the reach of the defensive player and from where it has the least distance to travel before hitting the backboard. (The less this latter distance, the less room there is for error in the displacement of the ball.) One of the most common faults in layup shooting—releasing the ball with too great a velocity—can also be guarded against to some extent if the ball is released at the peak of the jump. At this instant, the vertical velocity of the body is zero and thus the contribution of the body velocity to the ball velocity is lower than at any other time.

Two different positions of the shooting hand (and hence the arm) are in common use. In one, the hand is placed behind and below the ball with palm forward and fingers pointing upward. From this position, force is applied to the ball as the elbow extends and the wrist and fingers flex. In the other position, the shooting hand is under the ball, palm upward and fingers pointing forward. The release is effected with a lifting action of the arm followed by a flexion of the wrist just as the ball is about to leave the hand.

Because the first of these positions enables the shot to be made in a forward and upward direction (the direction in which the arm forces must be applied if the ball is released at the peak of the jump following a vertical takeoff) and because the arm action involved is similar (though of a much lesser range) to those used in jump and set shots, this method would appear to be the most appropriate for the majority of situations. However, where for one reason or another the velocity of takeoff for the final jump has a substantial horizontal component, it may well be best to use the hand-under-the-ball technique. For, assuming the ball is not moving backward relative to the shooter, it will have a horizontal velocity at least equal to that of the shooter as it is about to be released. If this velocity is in excess of what is needed—a situation that frequently arises—it becomes necessary for the shooter to apply a backward horizontal force to the ball. To do this when the hand is directly behind and below the ball is at best very difficult, and perhaps even impossible. However, when the hand is under the ball, as already described, the final wrist-flexing action can provide the required backward force (Fig. 9-7).

A prerequisite to success in executing most offensive and defensive skills is an ability to move quickly from one position on the court to another.

Body Position and Footwork

Starting. In starting from a stationary position, the stance of the athlete has a direct bearing on the speed with which he (or she) can carry out a movement. With respect to this, an examination of those factors that govern the stability of equilibrium of a body—one of the two main considerations in starting—might suggest that the optimum starting position was one in which the athlete had the legs straight and the feet together and was balanced on the toes, for in this position the center of gravity would be high and near the limits of a very small base. All of this, of course, is consistent

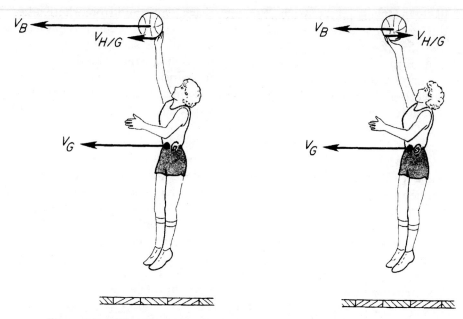

Figure 9-7. Different positions of the hand produce different results in the execution of a layup shot: (a) with the hand behind the ball, the horizontal velocity of the ball (V_B) is equal to the sum of the horizontal velocity of the player's center of gravity (V_G) plus the horizontal velocity of her hand relative to her center of gravity ($V_{H/G}$)—that is, $V_B = V_G + V_{H/G}$; (b) with the hand in front of the ball, $V_B = V_G - V_{H/G}$.

with the requirements for moving quickly in any direction—*except in one major respect*. Because the athlete's legs are straight, they are not in a position to apply the force necessary to produce a rapid acceleration. Thus a compromise must be reached between the conflicting demands of a near-minimum of stability and an optimum production of force. To achieve this compromise, the player adopts a stance in which the feet are spread, the heels are on the floor, the hip and knee joints are partially flexed (all of which contribute to the optimum production of force), and the center of gravity is over the midpoint of the base (overall the least stable position left open to it).

Slater-Hammel[17] studied the effect of four initial body positions upon the time that a player takes to move the whole body diagonally forward (to left or right) in response to a signal or stimulus. The four positions studied were:

- knees straight with weight distributed over feet,
- knees straight with weight on balls of feet,
- knees bent with weight distributed over feet, and
- knees bent with weight on balls of feet.

In each case the feet were parallel and approximately hip width apart, the body was bent forward, and the hands were placed in front of the body.

Slater-Hammel found that the times for the starting positions with the body weight distributed over the feet were significantly shorter than those for the positions with the weight over the balls of the feet. (A subsequent analysis of changes in weight distribution revealed that most subjects consistently rocked back on their heels in getting started. Slater-Hammel therefore suggested that starting from positions with the weight on the balls of the feet took longer than when the weight was distributed over the feet because of the additional time spent in lowering the heels to the floor.) While times tended to be shorter for positions in which the knees were bent than for those with knees straight, the differences were not statistically significant and it was concluded that "the position of the knees had no marked effect upon the time taken."

The findings in a study by Cotten and Denning[18] are strongly supportive of those obtained by Slater-Hammel. In this study, the four starting positions used in the Slater-Hammel study were again used and the times taken to travel a short distance in each of three directions (left, right, and straight ahead) were recorded. The results revealed that the knees-bent and feet-flat positions were generally superior to the knees-straight and weight-on-balls-of-feet positions. The authors concluded that

> [From] the information provided by both studies, it appears that a knees bent, feet flat stance is the best choice for optimum reaction-movement time. Hence, it would seem coaches and physical educators should consider abandoning the traditional "weight on balls of feet" stance in favor of the feet flat stance.[19]

Stopping. To stop, a player must exert horizontal forces against the floor in the direction in which he (or she) is traveling. If this is done correctly, the reaction to these forces reduces the motion of the center of gravity to zero before it can pass beyond the limits of the base formed by the feet. This reaction also causes the player to rotate in the direction in which he (or she) is moving. This rotational effect can be combated, however, if the player so positions the body that the vertical component of the reaction from the floor creates a moment in the opposite direction. (The sequence of an athlete performing a stride stop in Fig. 9-8 illustrates the application of these concepts in a specific situation.)

Jumping The height to which a person can jump depends in part on whether the jump is made from a stationary position or at the end of an approach run. If all else is equal, jumps using an approach run result in higher heights being attained than jumps from a stationary position. The truth of this contention has been demonstrated by Enoka[20] in his study of the jump-and-reach scores obtained by volleyball spikers with jumps from a standing position and jumps following one-, three-, and five-stride run-ups. The means for all three of the latter (respectively, 58 cm, 64 cm, and 65 cm) were significantly greater than the mean for standing jumps (57 cm). Therefore, in situations where maximum height is required, and

Figure 9-8. Stroboscopic photograph of a player executing a stride stop.

where time and other factors permit, a player should use a run-up preceding a jump. In rebounding and in jump-ball situations, for example, a player should endeavor to step into the position for takeoff rather than execute the jump from a stationary position.

While using some form of run-up preceding the takeoff can increase the height to which a player is able to reach, it can also create problems. Because the player is moving horizontally as the feet are placed in preparation for the jump, the player's body has a tendency to continue moving in this direction. If left unchecked, this tendency causes the player to take off in other than a vertical direction, thereby increasing the possibility of committing a foul. With respect to this latter possibility, it is important to recognize that the horizontal distance that a player travels in reaching the peak of a jump is only about half the total horizontal distance the player will travel before landing. Thus, jumping to maximum height without committing a foul is only half the battle, for the player must still return to the floor without infringing—and this is a point that is sometimes overlooked. To eliminate these problems, the player must reduce the horizontal velocity to zero by placing the feet forward of the center of gravity and exerting appropriate horizontal forces against the floor.

The actual jump itself results from a powerful extension of hip, knee, and ankle joints, supplemented by a forward and upward swing of the arms. The range and speed of the motion at each of the joints involved depends on a number of factors. Chief among these are the situation in the game and the proximity of opponents who may be disputing possession with the player concerned. Where possible, however, the position adopted by the jumper prior to beginning the upward movement should be such as to permit a range and speed of joint motion consistent with obtaining the maximum vertical velocity at the instant of takeoff.

Recommended Readings

Bishop, R. D., and Hay, J. G. (1979). Basketball: The mechanics of hanging in the air. *Medicine and Science in Sport,* 11:274–77.

Brancazio, P. J. (1981). Physics of basketball. *American Journal of Physiology,* 49: 356–65.

MAUGH II, T. H. (1984). In W. Schrier and W. F. Allman (Eds.), *The Science in Sports*. New York: Scribner's, pp. 25–28 (In search of the perfect jump shot).

Notes

1. Wooden, J. R. (1966). *Practical Modern Basketball*, p. 71. New York: The Ronald Press Co.
2. Bunn, J. W. (1972). *The Scientific Principles of Coaching* (p. 256). Englewood Cliffs, N.J.: Prentice Hall.
3. Mortimer, E. M. (1951). Basketball shooting. *Research Quarterly*, 22:238.
4. Shibukawa, K. (1975). Velocity conditions of basketball shooting. *Bulletin of Institute of Sport Science* (pp. 59–64). Tokyo University of Education: The Faculty of Physical Education.
5. Brancazio, P. J. (1984). *Sport Science: Physical Laws and Optimal Performance* (pp. 306–14). New York: Simon & Schuster.
6. Shibukawa. Velocity conditions of basketball shooting, p. 64.
7. Allsen, P. E., and Ruffner, W. (1969). Relationship between the type of pass and the loss of the ball in basketball. *Athletic Journal*, 50:94, 105–7.
8. Allsen, P. E. (1967). The rebound area. *Athletic Journal*, 48:97–98.
9. Hudson, J. L. (1982). A biomechanical analysis by skill level of free throw shooting in basketball. In J. Terauds (Ed.), *Biomechanics of Sports* (pp. 95–102). Del Mar, Calif.: Academic Publishers.
10. Penrose, T., and Blanksby, B. (1976). Film analysis: Two methods of basketball jump shooting techniques by two groups of different ability levels. *The Australian Journal for Health, Physical Education and Recreation*, 71:14–23.
11. Yates, G., and Holt, L. E. (1982). The development of multiple linear regression equations to predict accuracy in basketball jump shooting. In J. Terauds (Ed.), *Biomechanics in Sports* (pp. 103–9). Del Mar, Calif.: Academic Publishers.
12. Szymanski, F. (1967). A clinical analysis of the jump shot. *Scholastic Coach*, 37:8–9, 59–61.
13. Auerbach, A. (1953). *Basketball for the Player, the Fan, and the Coach* (p. 20). New York: Pocket Books.
14. Cousy, B., and Power, F. G. (1970). *Basketball Concepts and Techniques* (pp. 47, 56). Boston: Allyn & Bacon.
15. Sharman, B. (1967). *Sharman on Basketball*. Englewood Cliffs, N.J.: Prentice Hall.
16. Penrose and Blanksby. Film analysis: Two methods of basketball jump shooting techniques by two groups of different ability levels, p. 20.
17. Slater-Hammel, A. T. (1953). Initial body position and total body reaction time. *Research Quarterly*, 24:91–96.
18. Cotton, D. J., and Denning, D. (1970). Comparison of reaction movement times from four variations of the upright stance. *Research Quarterly*, 41:196–99.
19. Ibid.
20. Enoka, R. (1971). The effect of different lengths of run-up on the height to which a spiker in volleyball can reach. *New Zealand Journal of Health, Physical Education and Recreation*, 4:5–15.

10

Historically the result of a progressive series of developments from the English game of rugby, the present-day game of football with its blocking, forward pass, platoon system, and so forth, is now so distinctly American that similarities between the two games are sometimes difficult to discern. The overwhelming popularity of football, however, is there for all to see. For such is the vast spectator appeal of the game that it now dominates the American sporting scene.

BASIC CONSIDERATIONS

The six basic skills of greatest importance in football are passing, catching, running, blocking, tackling, and kicking.

Passing

The term *pass*, defined as the transfer of possession from one player to another of the same team, includes the "snapping" of the ball from the center to the quarterback, the punter, or the holder for a place-kick; the handoff from one player to another; and the forward and lateral passes.

A player's objective in making a pass in football is exactly the same as that of a player executing a pass in basketball—to complete the displacement of the ball from his hand (or hands) to those of a predetermined teammate (p. 255).

Basically there are two types of pass: those that involve motion of the ball through the air—the forward and lateral passes, and the center snap to the punter or to the holder for a field goal or point-after-touchdown attempt; and those that do not involve motion of the ball through the air—the center snap to the quarterback and the handoff from one player to another.

For passes in the first category, the basic factors are those that influence the outcome of any projectile motion—namely, the speed, angle, and height of release and the air resistance encountered in flight.

The speed of release is determined by the magnitude and direction of the muscular forces exerted and the distance over which they act. Thus, a player executing a pass attempts to position his body so that he can apply appropriate muscular forces over such distance that the ball acquires the desired speed of release. For passes requiring a large speed of release (for example, long forward passes) this means positioning himself so that the muscular forces of his legs and trunk may be used (in addition to the forces of his arms and shoulders) and so that these latter forces can be applied over a near-maximum range. For passes requiring less speed at the instant of release (for example, most lateral passes) forces exerted by the muscles of the arms and shoulders over a relatively short range will generally suffice.

The optimum direction in which to release the ball is governed by a number of factors. First, the ball should be directed toward that position in which the receiver's hands will be located when it arrives. (In practical terms, this means that the ball should be directed toward a point some distance ahead of the intended receiver.) Second, the angle to the horizontal at which the ball is released must allow it to arrive in the required position at the appropriate time. Finally, the angle at which the ball is released must allow it to pass safely beyond the reach of any opposing players positioned between the passer and the receiver.

The height of release is fixed by the type of pass involved (an orthodox forward pass usually being released at a greater height than a lateral pass, which in turn is almost always released at a greater height than a center snap to the punter); the physical characteristics of the player executing the pass; and the body position adopted for the purpose.

While no reliable experimental data appear to be available concerning the effects of air resistance on a thrown football in flight, it seems likely that these effects are fairly pronounced and thus of considerable practical significance. This conclusion is supported by the computations of Brancazio, who stated that "The available data point to a top launching speed of about 100 ft/sec [30.5 m/s] . . . for a forward pass" and computed that "a football thrown with an initial speed of 100 ft/sec and launched at the optimum angle of 43° should travel 231.9 feet [70.7 m] in the air."[1] Using an appropriate height of release, and ignoring the effects of air resistance, this is equivalent to a range of 96.7 m (see Eq. 3-21). Thus the computations of

Brancazio suggest that air resistance reduces the distance of a forward pass by up to 26 m (or 27%).

The relationships among the factors that determine the outcome of a pass in which the ball is projected into the air are summarized in Fig. 10-1.

The principal task of players involved in executing a snap or handoff pass is to ensure that the ball is always acted upon by an upward vertical force of a magnitude at least equal to the weight of the ball. For if it is not—and this is unquestionably the reason for most of the fumbles that occur in such situations—the ball experiences a downward acceleration that, unless countered, will ultimately result in it striking the ground.

Catching

Although there are differences in the magnitude of the forces exerted on the receiver's (or catcher's) hands, and consequently in the techniques employed, the basic factors of importance in catching a football are the same as those involved in catching a baseball (p. 200) or a basketball (p. 226).

Running

Because the techniques that yield the greatest speed differ from those that afford the best chance of avoiding an opposing player, the running done by a football player (who generally has both objectives in mind) is necessarily something of a compromise.

The speed at which a player runs is governed by the length of his stride and the number of strides he takes in a given time (speed = stride length × stride frequency, pp. 396–402). Thus, if a player is running without any immediate danger of being obstructed or interfered with by a member of the opposing team, he is likely to attain the best results in exactly the same manner as does a sprinter—by using the combination of stride length and stride frequency that yields the greatest speed.

A player's ability to avoid an opponent by changing his speed and the direction in which he is moving depends on the nature of the forces he can exert against the ground via his feet, and on the rapidity with which he can bring these forces into play. Thus, from the standpoint of being able to

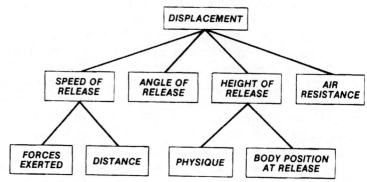

Figure 10-1.
Basic factors in passing.

avoid an opponent, the optimum running technique is one that permits the athlete to exert large forces against the ground, in any given direction, and at the instant it first becomes apparent that such action is desirable.

Blocking

When one player throws a block on another, the outcome of the resulting impact is governed in large measure by the same factors that determine the outcome when any two bodies collide—namely, the masses and initial velocities* of the bodies involved and their mutual coefficient of restitution (pp. 80–95). Of these five factors, it is mass and initial velocity over which a player has the greatest control.

If a man executes a block in which both his feet are off the ground at the instant he makes contact with his opponent, the mass involved in the impact is simply that of the man himself. However, if he executes a block with his feet firmly braced against the ground, the mass with which his opponent interacts is effectively much greater than before due to the contribution exacted from the ground. In short, it might be said that his opponent is now interacting with the man-plus-the-earth rather than with the man alone.

The velocity at which a player is moving as he makes contact with his opponent is also of considerable importance in determining the outcome when a block is thrown—in general, the greater the speed of a blocker in the direction in which he desires to force his opponent, the greater the likelihood that he will achieve his objective.

Because he has little if any control over the mass and initial velocity of his opponent, a player preparing to throw a block must attempt to take these variables into account in the movements he makes. Thus, because of the difference in the speed at which the opponent is moving (and perhaps, too, because of a difference in mass), the body movements needed to effectively block a hard-running defensive man pursuing a punt will almost certainly be different from those used by an offensive lineman offering protection to the passer.

While the role of the coefficient of restitution must be acknowledged, it seems almost certain that the other variables already referred to are more important in determining the outcome when a block is thrown.

Tackling

Tackling may be regarded as a specialized form of blocking in which the objective is to reduce the ball carrier's motion to zero in the shortest possible time. Except for a few relatively minor differences, the basic factors involved in this process are the same as those just discussed with relation to blocking.

Kicking

There are four types of kick in common use. In three of these (the kickoff, the field-goal attempt, and the try for a point-after-touchdown), the ball is

* The term *initial velocity* is used here to mean the velocity immediately prior to impact.

placed on a kicking tee appropriately positioned on the ground. In the fourth (the punt) the kicker releases the ball at near-waist height and then strikes it with his foot after it has fallen some distance toward the ground. In each case the ultimate success of the kick depends on the speed, height, and angle at which the ball leaves the kicker's foot and on the air resistance it encounters in flight.

The speed and angle at which the ball leaves the foot is governed by the same factors that determine the result of any elastic impact—the masses and initial velocities of the bodies involved and their coefficient of restitution. Because it may be assumed that the mass of the ball and the coefficient of restitution are essentially constant, and because the initial velocity of the ball is zero in three of the four cases and very small in the fourth, it can readily be seen that the factors of greatest importance in fixing the speed and angle at which the ball is projected into the air are the effective mass and initial velocity of the kicker's foot. The former may be determined by the extent to which muscular actions are used to bind the various body segments together as a unit and by the contribution exacted from the ground via the nonkicking foot (see Blocking, p. 253). The latter, the initial velocity of the kicker's foot, is determined by the forces exerted upon it and by the distance over which they act.

Except in the case of the punt, the height of the ball (or, more precisely, the height of the center of gravity of the ball) at the instant of release is subject to relatively little variation. (A ball kicked from a tee generally leaves the kicker's foot at about 25-30 cm above the ground—a height of approximately 12-15 cm higher than it had before impact.) The height of the ball as it leaves the punter's foot can vary from as little as 25 cm to as much as 75 cm, depending on the requirements of the situation. For example, if a long, low kick is required, the ball is contacted close to the ground. Conversely, if a high and somewhat shorter kick is required, the ball is contacted well above the ground. The reason for this relationship lies in the fact that, as the height of release is altered, the angle at which the kicking foot is inclined at impact and, thus, the angle of release are also altered (Fig. 10-2).

The behavior of a ball in flight is governed by the lift and drag forces which act upon it. These, in turn, are governed by the relevant coefficients of lift and drag, the density of the air, the cross-sectional area presented to the flow and the velocity of the ball (Eq. 7-1 and 7-2, p. 185). The effects that these forces have on the distance traveled by a football following a kick have been the subject of studies by Cunningham and Dowell,[2] Brancazio,[3] and Dowell and Colfer.[4] In the first of these studies, the authors compared the distances actually achieved by two highly skilled punters with the distances predicted using Eq. 3-20 (p. 37) and measures, taken from motion-picture films, of the speed and angle of release. (*Note:* Since Eq. 3-20 defines the range of a projectile in the absence of air resistance, the difference between predicted and actual ranges can be taken as a measure of the influence that air resistance has on the flight of the projectile). They concluded that " . . . in general, air resistance cuts the distance a football

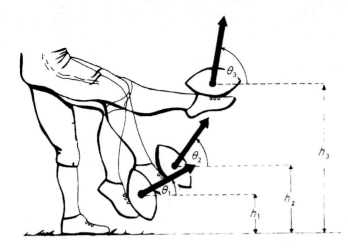

Figure 10-2.
In punting, the height of release (*h*) and the angle of release (Θ) are interdependent.

travels in half." Brancazio[5] computed the effect that air resistance has on the distance of punts kicked so that the ball travels "nose-first" and "end-over-end." His results for the "nose-first" case—the only one that could be usefully compared with the findings of Cunningham and Dowell—indicated that air resistance reduced the distance of the punt by just 18%. Without more information than is currently available on the methods used in each of these studies, or without further research on the subject, it is impossible to determine which of these widely different results is correct. In the meantime, one can only conclude that air resistance probably reduces the distance of a nose-first punt by something like 20-50%

Dowell and Colfer used a similar approach to that of Cunningham and Dowell to determine the effect that air resistance had on the "angle of projection and range of a football kicked from placement." In this instance the authors concluded that:

> The angle that a skilled place kicker kicks the football in relation to the horizontal is approximately 30 degrees, some 15 degrees below the theoretical 45 degrees for gaining maximum distance while in flight.
>
> The distance that a place-kicked football will travel in air is approximately one-fourth as far as it would travel in a vacuum. Therefore, it may be concluded that air resistance drastically affects the trajectory of a place-kicked football.[6]

Although no explanation was offered as to why the effects of air resistance on the range of a place-kick should be so much greater than those observed previously in the case of a punt, the marked differences in the speeds of release suggest an answer. The average speeds of release for three different types of punt ranged from 36 m/s to 38 m/s; the average speed for the place kicks was 49 m/s.

TECHNIQUES

For all the stress that football coaches seem to place on the importance of their players acquiring a mastery of the basic techniques of the game, these same techniques (with only one or two exceptions) have been virtually untouched by scientific analysis.

Passing*

Center Snap. The first pass in each play is that made by the center to either the quarterback, the punter, or the holder for a field-goal or point-after-touchdown attempt.

Center Snap to Quarterback. The center takes up his initial position with both hands on the ball, his head directly above the ball and inclined backward slightly so that he can see his defensive opponent, his back parallel with the ground, his knees well flexed, and his feet spread laterally at slightly more than shoulder width apart.

The positions of the feet relative to one another are subject to some variation—some centers taking a stance with one foot a few centimeters forward of the other (a so-called staggered stance), while others assume a position in which their feet are level with each other (a parallel stance).

The snap is made with a rapid backward and upward sweeping motion of the right hand. During the first part of this motion, the left hand is also brought backward and upward, guiding the ball toward the quarterback's hands. While coaches differ considerably in their opinions concerning the way in which the ball should be moved as it is brought upward, the method most widely advocated involves a turning of the ball through 90° to the left so that it can be presented to the quarterback with its long axis parallel to the line of scrimmage.[7]

As the center sweeps the ball from the ground, he takes a short, quick step forward. This slightly reduces the distance that the ball must travel to reach the quarterback's hands and, much more important, gives the center more momentum than he would otherwise have. This latter is of importance if he is to complete his blocking assignment effectively.

Center Snap to Punter (Fig. 10-3). The snap to the punter differs from the snap to the quarterback in several respects. The need to get the ball into the hands of the punter as soon as possible after it is taken from the ground requires that the center impart a considerable speed to it in the short time at his disposal (the release speeds recorded in a study conducted by Henrici[8] ranged from 13.25–14.23 m/s). To acquire this speed, the center usually takes up his position slightly farther behind the ball than for a snap to the quarterback—thereby increasing the distance over which he may exert force on the ball. In addition, some centers position their hands on the ball so that both can contribute to the speed at which the ball is swept backward. (This is in contrast with the snap to the quarterback in which one hand propels the ball and the other serves in a guiding role.) Although there appear to have been no studies conducted in which these two meth-

---

* Throughout the ensuing discussion it is assumed that the passer is right-handed.

Figure 10-3. The two-handed technique for executing a center snap to the punter.

ods have been compared, it seems likely that the two-handed method is slightly faster than the one-handed—the increase in the torque available when two hands are used to accelerate the ball about the axis through the shoulders almost certainly being greater than the increase in the moment of inertia of the rotating system (arms-plus-ball) that tends to offset it ($T = I\alpha$, Eq. 6-11).

While the center invariably has his head inclined slightly upward and his eyes focused on the man in front of him when snapping the ball to the quarterback, a head-down position that enables the center to see back between his legs is frequently used when snapping the ball to the punter. The relative merits of these two methods (the visual and the nonvisual) have been studied by Slebos,[9] who found that the visual method was superior to the nonvisual in terms of accuracy but no different in terms of flight time (that is, the time from the ball being lifted from the ground until it struck a target 11 m behind the center).

Center Snap to Holder.   Apart from the fact that the ball must be passed a lesser distance (6.5 m as compared to 12-14 m) and must be directed to a point closer to the ground (since the receiver is in a semikneeling position rather than standing erect), the snap to the holder for a place-kick is essentially the same as the snap to the punter.

Handoff.   The basic techniques involved in the execution of a handoff are depicted in Fig. 10-4. The following points should be noted:

(a)   (b)   (c)

Figure 10-4.
The handoff to a runner.

a. * The quarterback's hand is wrapped around the ball with the fingers underneath supporting its weight; his eyes are focused on the abdomen of the player to whom he is giving the ball; and his shoulders are rotated in order to increase the length of his reach. (*Note:* A two-handed grip is generally preferred for handoffs between players who are in close proximity to each other because of the greater security of possession that it entails. In the situation depicted, however, a two-handed grip would restrict the quarterback's reach and make it difficult for him to place the ball in the required position.)

The player receiving the ball has his right ("inside") elbow high—to provide an unobstructed path for the ball and his left arm moving into position to provide support and protection. To observe the action taking place ahead of him, and for purposes of deception, the runner keeps his head up throughout the exchange.

b. The ball has been pressed into the runner's abdomen, his arms have closed around it—the left below the ball providing the necessary upward force to prevent the ball from falling—and the exchange is complete.

c. A little more than one step later, the arm positions have been adjusted to conceal the ball and to place the hands over the ends of the ball, where they can act to prevent it from being dislodged sideways when the runner is hit.

Forward Pass. The techniques involved in executing a forward pass vary slightly according to the situation in the game and the type of forward pass (drop-back, roll-out, or jump) that is used. Since the similarities in the techniques far outweigh the differences, however, only the drop-back forward pass is considered here.

Once the ball has been received from the center, the quarterback's first task is to retreat to the position from which he intends to make the pass. For this purpose there are three basic techniques in common use:

- The crossover, in which the quarterback has his body positioned at right angles to the line of scrimmage and retreats with a sideways running action. (*Note:* The distinctive crossing of one leg in front of the other, which is inherent in this action, gives this method its name.)
- The sprint-back, in which the quarterback turns his back and sprints directly away from the line of scrimmage.
- The backpedal, in which the quarterback faces the line of scrimmage and retreats by running backward.

While there are unquestionably numerous other factors that must be considered before deciding which of these methods is best employed by a given quarterback or in a given situation, it is of interest to note that a study by Pannes[10] revealed no significant differences in the length of time that it took quarterbacks to drop back to a specific distance using the three methods.

The technique used in the crossover method is shown in Fig. 10-5 (b)—

* The letters in parentheses refer to the corresponding positions in Fig. 10-4.

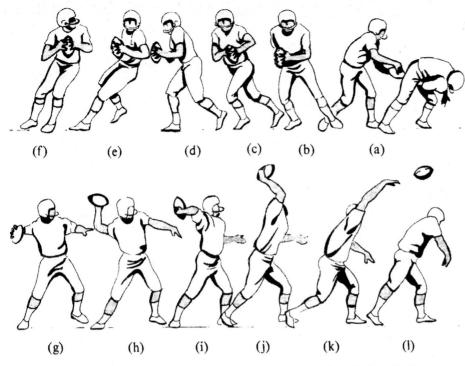

Figure 10-5. An example of good technique in retreating from the line of scrimmage using the crossover method and throwing a forward pass.

(g). After receiving the ball from the center, the quarterback (a) shifts his weight to his left slightly (thereby facilitating the lifting of the right foot), pivots on the ball of the left foot; and (b) drives vigorously against the ground by extending the hip, knee, and ankle joints of the left leg. His body is inclined at a near-60° angle to the horizontal at this latter instant—an orientation similar to that adopted in many sports when runners experience marked accelerations. As he completes his third retreating step (d), the quarterback grounds his right foot some distance ahead of his center of gravity (relative to the direction in which he is moving). This action is accompanied by a reaction from the ground that serves to brake his forward motion (pp. 399–400). The process of deceleration continues (e)–(f) as the left and then the right foot are grounded at the end of the fourth and fifth steps, respectively. Note that the quarterback's body leans in one direction as he strives to build up speed (b)–(c) and then in the other as he slows to a halt (e). A detailed consideration of the factors influencing the way in which the body leans as it is being accelerated, and decelerated, is presented in Chap. 15, pp. 411–412.

Once the quarterback has completed his fifth step and brought his horizontal motion momentarily to zero (f), his next task is to readjust his body position, or "set" himself, in preparation for the throw. To do this he pushes downward against the ground with his left foot, evoking a reaction that causes his center of gravity to be lifted and shifted toward his right. With his weight over his right foot and the right knee slightly bent, the quarterback is now in a position to step forward into the throw. The step of the left foot in the intended direction of the throw is accompanied by a raising of the ball to a position above the right shoulder and behind the head (g)–(h).

In the throw itself the hips are brought around to the front, as the right leg extends and drives the right hip forward (h)–(j): the muscles responsible for trunk rotation contract and draw the right shoulder around to the front—a movement aided by the left arm being pulled backward at the same time (h)–(j); and the upper arm is rotated first about a near-vertical axis (horizontal adduction) and then about a near-horizontal axis (medial rotation) to bring the ball to the point at which it is released (k).

The follow-through of the right arm across the body (l) completes the throwing action and provides some protection to the player in the event of his being hit by an oncoming defensive man.

Although there are some differences in the range and speed of the movements involved, the overall pattern of movement used in making a forward pass in football is very similar to that employed in baseball (for pitching and other overarm throws); in basketball (for a one-handed baseball pass); and in javelin throwing (pp. 202, 238, and 495, respectively).

Lateral. Basically there are two types of lateral pass—the one-handed and the two-handed. In the one-handed pass, the ball is released about midway between knee and hip height and near the end of a forward and upward swing of the right arm. The forward and upward motion of the hand as the ball is being released imparts a spin to it that tends to prevent it wobbling in flight. Unfortunately this spin also tends to make the ball a little harder to catch than would otherwise be the case. The two-handed pass is very similar to the one-handed except that the tendency of one hand to impart a spin to the ball in one direction is balanced by the tendency of the other hand to produce the reverse effect. As a result the ball generally leaves the passer's hands with no spin about its long axis. However, unless the wrists are "cocked" so that the ball is kept in a near-vertical position as it is swung forward and upward—an orientation that it then tends to retain once it has been released—the forward and upward swing of the arms tends to impart an end-over-end type of rotation about a transverse axis through the ball's center of gravity. This "tumbling rotation," like the "spiral rotation" of the one-handed pass, tends to make it more difficult to catch the ball than would otherwise be the case.

Catching

Although variations in the speed and direction at which the ball is traveling relative to the receiver necessitate variations in the techniques used to catch the ball, all such techniques have certain characteristics in common. Regardless of how the ball is moving as he attempts to make the catch, the receiver's first responsibility is to position his hands and body so that, as he makes contact with the ball, he is able to begin exerting the forces necessary to reduce its motion to zero (strictly speaking, to reduce the motion of the ball relative to the receiver to zero). In general this means moving so that the hands are positioned, palms toward the oncoming ball, across the flight path that it is following (Fig. 10-6[a] and [b]). Then, as contact is made, the hands give slightly to reduce the force of the impact and therewith the possibility of the ball rebounding from the hands, and the fingers close around the ball providing both the couple necessary to reduce its angular motion to zero and the upward force to prevent it from falling toward the ground (Fig. 10-6[c]). In those cases where the catch is made at some distance from the body the arms are flexed once the ball has been brought under control and the ball is thus drawn in close to the body (Fig. 10-6[d]). The positions of the hands and arms are then adjusted quickly in an effort to reduce the possibility of the ball being dislodged if the receiver is hit.

Running

Any discussion of the techniques used in running must consider the techniques used to get the body moving initially as well as those used once the player is in "full stride."

Starting.   The question of the best body position (or stance) to adopt to get away quickly once the starting signal has been given is a complicated one. Among the factors that must be taken into account are:

- The direction in which the athlete is required to move may vary considerably from one play to the next, and the initial stance that affords the best start on one occasion may be much less than satisfactory on another.

(a)   (b)   (c)   (d)

Figure 10-6. Catching the football.

- The need to conceal the direction in which the player intends to move—in order to avoid "tipping off" the opposition—makes it unwise to vary the stance adopted in an attempt to use the optimum one for each occasion.

- The stance adopted must be consistent with the task that the player is expected to perform once he is in motion. For example, if a halfback is to take a handoff from the quarterback after he has taken three strides, the stance he uses must permit him to be in a suitable position to receive the ball at that time.

In view of these various limiting conditions, it is clear that the optimum stance for any given player must necessarily be something of a compromise. It must give him the best all-round results in terms of speed (that is, taking into account the various directions in which he might be called upon to move during the course of a game) and permit him to complete the specific task assigned to him.

Stances are generally classified according to the number of limbs in contact with the ground (thus, the two-, three-, and four-point stances) and according to whether the feet are equal or unequal distances from the line of scrimmage (parallel and staggered stances, respectively).

Which of the various combinations of foot position and points of contact affords the fastest start is a question that has attracted a considerable (and perhaps disproportionate) amount of attention from researchers.

The relative merits of the two- and three-point stances used by backfield players have been studied by several investigators.

Holtz[11] compared times taken to run 7 yd (6.4 m) obliquely forward to the right, obliquely forward to the left, and straight ahead when using a two-point staggered stance with those obtained using a three-point staggered stance. He found that, for each of the three directions, the times obtained when the three-point stance was used were significantly faster than those obtained when the two-point stance was used.

Warshawsky[12] compared times to run 8 yd (7.3 m) to the right, to the left, and straight ahead when using two- and three-point staggered stances and found that the two-point stance was significantly faster than the three-point when running to left and right. However, the three-point stance was significantly faster than the two-point when running straight ahead.

Robinson[13] compared times taken to run 10 ft (3.0 m) in five different directions (90° to the right, 45° to the right, straight ahead, 45° to the left, and 90° to the left) using each of three different stances (a two-point parallel stance, a two-point staggered stance, and a three-point staggered stance). His results indicated that there were no significant differences in the times recorded when running 90° to the right, 45° to the right, or 45° to the left; the two-point stances were significantly faster than the three-point stance when running 90° to the left; and the two-point staggered stance was significantly faster than each of the other two stances when running straight ahead. On the basis of these results, Robinson contended that the best stance for all-around starting ability was the two-point staggered stance.

The obvious lack of agreement among the results obtained by Holtz, Warshawsky, and Robinson is almost certainly due to differences in the experimental procedures used. For example, two of the investigators found that use of the three-point staggered stance yielded significantly better results than did use of the two-point staggered stance when the subjects ran straight ahead. The third investigator found exactly the opposite. This difference in result could have been due to differences in the distance over which times were recorded—7 yd and 8 yd on the one hand and 3.3 yd on the other. In other words, the two-point staggered stance may be faster than the three-point staggered stance over 3.3 yd and yet slower over 7 yd and 8 yd. (*Note:* A comparable situation exists in track where use of the bunch [or bullet] start has been shown to yield faster times off the blocks but slower times to 10 yd [9.1 m] than those obtained when a medium start is used [pp. 000-000].) Another possibility is that differences in the weight distribution of the subjects while in the three-point stance may have led to the markedly different results. A study by Kadatz[14] is of particular interest in this respect. Kadatz studied the effect of variations in the amount of weight supported on the hand in a three-point stance and found that the time between the starting signal and the first movement of the subject (the reaction time) was decreased significantly with each successive increase in the amount of weight on the hand. He also found that the time from the first movement of the subject until he had traveled forward 7 yd (0.9 m)—the movement time—was significantly less when 35% of the weight was supported on the hand than when only 5% was thus supported. In short, it may be that the three-point staggered stance is superior to the two-point staggered stance only if sufficient weight is placed on the supporting hand. Another possible explanation—and one which is related to the matter of weight distribution—is that in some cases the actions used by the subjects were not typical of those that a running back would use in an actual game situation. Holtz, for example, states, "Most of the subjects when running from a three-point stance stayed as close to the ground as possible and hence would have had difficulty in getting the ball from the quarterback."[15] It is conceivable, therefore, that the superiority of the three-point stance found in the studies of Holtz and Warshawsky was due to the use of positions and actions atypical of the game situation.

Differences in the results obtained when the subjects ran in directions other than straight ahead may similarly be accounted for by differences in the procedures used by the several investigators.

It should be obvious from the preceding discussion that, despite extensive research efforts—of which the studies cited are only a sample—the relative merits of the two- and three-point stances have yet to be clearly and convincingly demonstrated.

The relative merits of the three- and four-point stances used by linemen have also been subjected to examination.

Fitch[16] compared the "starting speeds" (movement times over a distance of 1.5 m) of linemen using various combinations of initial stance and weight distribution and concluded:

- The three stances used in the study—the three-point staggered stance, the three-point parallel stance, and the four-point parallel stance—were equally effective in terms of starting speed in each of the six directions for which times were taken. (These six directions were 90° to the right, 45° to the right, straight ahead. 45° to the left, 90° to the left, and straight back.)
- For moving straight ahead and at an angle of 45° to the right, the times recorded when the subjects had their weight forward were significantly less than those recorded when they had their weight back. There were no significant differences associated with differences in weight distribution when the subjects moved in any of the other four directions.

(*Note:* Fitch's findings that a position in which the weight is forward decreases the time when charging forward—compared with that obtained when the weight is back—is in close agreement with the findings of Kadatz referred to previously.)

Bolt[17] conducted a cinematographical study in which he compared the times taken by 10 experienced linemen to (1) pull out and run 8 ft (2.4 m) to the left; (2) pull out and run 8 ft to the right; and (3) charge forward 2 ft (0.61 m), using three- and four-point staggered stances. The results obtained from this study are tabulated next.

Direction	Result
Moving to the right	Eight of the subjects were faster using the three- point stance. Two of the subjects were faster using the four-point stance.
Moving to the left	Four of the subjects were faster using the three-point stance. Five of the subjects were faster using the four-point stance.
Moving straight ahead	One of the subjects was faster using the three-point stance. Seven of the subjects were faster using the four-point stance.

On the basis of these results Bolt concluded that there "seemed to [be] a definite advantage gained by the use of the four-point stance for the line charge"; the three-point stance was superior for pulling out to the right: and neither stance was superior for pulling out to the left. He also made an interesting point concerning the relationship between which hand is on the ground in the three-point stance and the ability of a lineman to move to left or right:

> *It should be mentioned here that all the men participating in the experiment used the three-point stance with the right hand down. This method seems to help them pull to the right but to hinder them in pulling to the left. If it can be assumed that placing the left hand on the ground would help the individual to pull out to the left, but hinder him in pulling to the right, there is a logical basis for the practice of some coaches who have their men on the right side of the line assume a stance with their right hand down and pull only to the right and the men on the left side of the line assume a stance with the left hand down and pull only to the left.*[18]

Numerous other characteristics of the stance and of the initial movements involved in starting have been the subject of study.

Miles and Graves[19] examined the effects of variations in the way the starting signal was called on the "speed of charge" (actually the time from the starting signal until a recording device was triggered as the subject began to move forward); the "unison of charge" (the extent to which the times for the seven subjects tested together varied); and the number of offsides charged against the subjects. Anticipatory (for example, charging on the fourth number called) and nonanticipatory (charging when a specified digit is called) signal systems were compared. The signals were called at 40, 60, 100, and 120 digits per minute or, in other words, with 1.5, 1.0, 0.6, and 0.5 s, respectively, between digits.

The results indicated that

- Reaction to anticipatory signals is . . . much more prompt than to non-anticipatory . . .
- Offsides are rather more numerous with anticipatory signals.
- Unison of play is somewhat better with anticipatory signals . . .
- The rate at which the signals are called makes a very great difference. The favorable rate for anticipatory signals is 100 single digits per minute, while for non-anticipatory signals the best rate appears to be about 60 single digits per minute.
- The best position for a starting signal within a series of digits appears to be from about two seconds to five seconds after the men have set. This ordinarily falls on the fourth or fifth digit called. Offsides are considerably less when charging occurs early in the series of digits. This applies to both kinds of signals.
- Calling digits in non-rhythm converts the ordinary anticipatory series into one producing much slower speed. . . . Non-rhythm does not appear to increase offsides. . . . However, it does produce poorer unison of charge.
- In anticipatory signals the players tend to start the charge at the same moment when the ball starts in action; whereas in non-anticipatory signals they get away almost one-tenth of a second after the ball has moved. This fact gives their opponents a real advantage, and counts strongly against non-anticipatory signals in general.[20]

Thompson, Nagle, and Dobias[21] also studied the response of football players to various types of starting signals. They found that rhythmic-digit starting signals resulted in significantly faster times (to react and take an 18-in. [46-cm] step forward with the back foot) than did either nonrhythmic word-digit or nonrhythmic color signals.

The force with which a charging lineman makes contact with his opponent is another topic that has interested researchers.

Owens[22] examined the effects of variations in the front-to-rear and lateral spacings of the feet and in the hand-to-toe anterior-posterior spacing on (1) movement time; and (2) force of shoulder impact at the end of movement through a 36-in (91-cm) horizontal distance. Among his findings were the following:

- No one of the 40 different stances used in the study was significantly superior to another in terms of the force exerted at impact.

- The force exerted at impact appeared to be closely related to the movement time and to the weight of the individual.

(Note: Rosenfield[23] and Elbel, Wilson, and French[24] also studied factors that influenced the force at impact and in both cases found a significant relationship between body weight and the force exerted at impact—findings in keeping with that of Owens. In the studies of Rosenfield and Elbel, Wilson, and French no significant relationship was found between the *response time*—that is, the time from the instant the starting signal was given until the instant the subject's shoulder struck a dummy and triggered a recording device—and the force exerted at impact. Unfortunately the authors of each of these studies referred to the response time as the "speed of charge" and, since this might well convey the totally false impression that the speed of a player at the instant of impact is not a factor in determining the force exerted, it should be carefully noted that *the speed at which subjects were traveling at the instant of impact was not measured in either of these studies.)*

Owens[25] also studied the effects of rhythmical and nonrhythmical preparatory and starting signals on the force of impact but found no significant differences. He did find, however, that the response time was shortest and the number of offsides was greatest when a rhythmical count was used in giving the preparatory and starting signals.

Running. Were it not for the need to change speed and direction in an attempt to avoid would-be tacklers and blockers, the basic running techniques used in football would be practically identical to those used by track athletes (pp. 406–412). However, when a good player is in imminent danger of being tackled or blocked, he changes quickly from the normal running action of a sprinter to one that affords him a better chance of avoiding his opponent. This process generally involves a marked reduction in his stride length and a concomitant increase in his rate of striding—the combined effect of which is to increase the time during which he is in contact with the ground and thus to minimize the delay in initiating evasive action once the opponent "commits himself" (that is, makes his intentions apparent). The evasive action itself generally takes the form of applying force in a lateral direction by thrusting downward and sideways against the ground and/or against the opponent. Successfully executed, such action carries the runner beyond the grasp of his opponent and into position to continue on his way.

Blocking

Although writers on the subject commonly list as many as 10 to 15 types of blocking maneuver, the majority of these are simply variants of the two basic blocks—the shoulder block and the cross-body block.

Shoulder Block. In executing a shoulder block the blocker drives his head directly forward toward his opponent's abdomen. Then, having concealed his intention until the very last moment, he slides his head to one side or the other so that hard contact is made with the shoulder. To increase the area in contact and thus his ability to control his opponent, the blocker holds his upper arm in a position so that it forms an almost straight-line extension of the blocking shoulder. The hand on the same side is held close to the chest (perhaps even gripping the jersey) to reduce any tendency to use it illegally.

In driving forward into his opponent and once contact has been made, the blocker takes short, fast steps that permit him to remain in almost continuous contact with the ground—a situation that permits an almost uninterrupted application of large forces against the opponent. In addition, these short driving steps are made with the feet spread well apart to reduce the possibility of the blocker being knocked off-balance by the force of the impact or by his opponent's subsequent attempts to break clear.

Cross-Body Block. The initial movements in a well-executed cross-body block look very much like those used in executing a shoulder block—the blocker drives forward with short, fast steps, his feet well apart and his head directed at his opponent's abdomen. Then, just before contact is made, he quickly turns his arms and head to one side and swings his body around so that he contacts his opponent at waist level with his hip and side.

The results of a study by Klumpar[26] suggest that delaying the sideways turning of the body until the last moment before contact is made is a factor of considerable importance in determining the effectiveness of a cross-body block. In 92 percent of the successful cross-body blocks that he analyzed, the blocker turned his head and shoulders when he was approximately 30 cm away from his opponent. In only 46 percent of the unsuccessful cross-body blocks analyzed did the blocker get that close to his opponent before beginning to turn sideways. Thus it would seem that on many occasions a blocker becomes so concerned with the body position required that he overlooks or underestimates the importance of timing.

The results obtained in another study of blocking techniques might very well be attributable to this same failing. Nordman[27] conducted a study to determine the relative effectiveness of the shoulder block and the cross-body block used against defensive backfield players (that is, linebackers, defensive halfbacks, and safety men). After analyzing 26 game films (11 high school games and 15 college games), he concluded that for both high school and college teams the shoulder block is superior to the cross-body block in downfield blocking situations—225 (or 77 percent) of the 293 shoulder blocks observed were effective in preventing the defensive man from tackling the ball carrier compared to 104 (or 56 percent) of the 185 cross-body blocks that were similarly effective.

Head-on Tackle (Fig. 10-7). The tackler's approach toward the ball carrier is almost identical to the approach he would use if he were going to **Tackling**

Figure 10-7. Executing a head-on tackle.

execute a shoulder block. The one major exception is the low and wide-spread position of his arms—a position adopted to thwart any last-minute evasive action on the part of the ball carrier and to enable the tackler to get a firm grasp of his opponent at the earliest possible moment. Once contact has been made, the tackler wraps his arms tightly around his opponent's thighs, vigorously extends his hip, knee, and ankle joints, and lifts his opponent clear of the ground—the latter action depriving the ball carrier of the opportunity to exert the forces necessary to sustain his forward motion. The tackle is completed with both players falling to the ground under the influence of gravity. (*Note:* The continued driving action of the tackler's legs acts to hasten the completion of the tackle by moving the center of gravity of the combined ball-carrier-plus-tackler system farther away from the transverse axis through the feet about which the system tends to rotate.)

Side-on Tackle (*Fig. 10-8*). Except that the angle at which the tackler approaches the ball carrier is different, the technique used in making a side-on tackle is practically identical to that employed in executing a head-on tackle.

Kicking*

Although they have a great deal in common, it is convenient to consider the techniques of place-kicking and punting under separate headings.

Place-Kicking. A place kick may be considered to consist of four consecutive phases or parts: (1) the initial stance; (2) the approach; (3) the swing and kick; and (4) the follow-through.

Initial stance. The kicker takes up his initial position at some predetermined distance behind the kicking tee—in general, approximately 2 m behind the tee for field-goal and point-after-touchdown attempts and some 5–10 m for kickoffs. (To minimize the undesirable effects of variations in the length of his approach, the good kicker takes care to see that this distance is always exactly the same for kicks of the same type.) The position

---

* Throughout the ensuing discussion it is assumed that the athlete kicks with the right foot.

Figure 10-8. Executing a side-on tackle.

adopted is one in which the athlete stands with his right foot slightly in advance of his left; his knees bent a little in readiness for the extension of the legs that will drive him forward into his approach; his trunk erect or inclined slightly forward—the latter requiring slightly more muscular effort than the former but putting the body in a slightly better position from which to move forward; his arms hanging in a relaxed, comfortable position; and his head inclined forward with eyes focused on the spot where the ball will be at the instant he kicks it.

Approach. The approach in field-goal and point-after-touchdown attempts begins with a short step of the right foot. This is followed by a much longer step that brings the left foot into the position it will occupy as the right foot is swung downward, forward, and upward into the ball.

The opinions of writers on the subject are in general agreement as to the optimum position of the left foot relative to a line through the ball in the intended direction of the kick—most recommend a position some 5 cm to 10 cm to the left of this imaginary line, a position consistent with the normal lateral spacing of the feet as a person brings one foot past the other in such activities as walking and running. Opinions differ markedly, however, when it comes to the position of the left foot in a forward-and-backward direction. Bahr,[28] states that the left foot should be "neither behind nor in front of the ball," while Dodd[29] recommended a distance of "about two and a half inches [6 cm]," behind and Bunn,[30] to cite just one of the many other opinions available, suggested that "the non-kicking foot should be placed about 6 inches [15 cm] back of the point of the ball." The only quantitative data available at the time of writing do little to resolve the question. In a study of the place-kicking technique of professional Jim Bakken, Becker[31] found that the left foot was placed behind the ball at distances ranging from 26–28 cm—distances considerably in excess of those normally recommended. Since it is very likely that the position of the left foot has a considerable bearing on the results obtained by a place kicker, the conflicting opinions of experts and the current lack of quantitative data suggest that this is a topic worthy of further investigation.

There has been a good deal of interest in recent years in the so-called soccer-style place-kick. In this style the kicker takes up his position some distance to the left of the intended line of the kick and then moves in an arc as he takes his two approach steps to bring him up to the ball.

The various claims made in favor of the soccer-style kick have attracted the attention of a number of researchers. Plagenhoef[32] conducted an analysis of the techniques employed by a former professional soccer and football player and found that the side-approach (soccer-style) kick produced a much greater ball velocity than did the straight approach:

Type of Kick	Ball Velocity (Average of five kicks)
Side approach (instep kick)	29.11 m/s
Straight approach (instep kick)	24.99 m/s
Straight approach (toe kick)	24.99 m/s

He then examined the two factors of greatest importance in determining the velocity with which the ball leaves a kicker's foot—the effective mass of the foot and its velocity immediately before impact—and concluded that since the side approach was no better than the straight approach for obtaining "maximum foot velocity," the effective mass of the foot was the more important factor. Manzi[33] compared the soccer-style approach and the straight approach in terms of the distance and accuracy of the resulting place-kicks and concluded that

- The soccer-style approach leads to greater accuracy at each of the three distances (20, 26, and 32 yd [18.3, 23.8, and 29.3 m] from the goal post) at which trials were conducted.
- Either method of approaching the ball, where the number of steps is limited to two, will produce the same or similar distance kicked.

(*Note:* The length of the approach run used by the subject in Plagenhoef's study was not reported.)

Swing and Kick.   As his left foot is grounded, the kicker begins the vigorous forward swing of his right leg that will ultimately bring the right foot into contact with the ball. The swing begins with the right knee bent at a near 90° angle and the right foot at about hip height and well behind the line of the body. (The extent to which the foot is behind the body—probably a function of the length of the last stride of the approach—influences the distances through which forces may be exerted upon it.) From this position the flexors of the right hip contract forcefully to swing the thigh forward and downward about a transverse axis. During this initial part of the swing the thigh, lower leg, and foot maintain an essentially constant relationship to one another and rotate as a unit. Then, as the thigh nears that point at which it will pass vertically beneath the hip, its angular velocity begins to decrease; the lower leg and foot experience a marked angular acceleration; the knee extends rapidly—probably aided by a contraction of the knee extensor muscles of the thigh; and the foot swings at ever-increasing speed downward, forward, and finally upward into the ball.

The position of the kicker at the instant his foot strikes the ball and his actions during that brief interval in which his foot is in contact with the ball—approximately 0.015 s according to Roberts and Metcalfe[34]—are obviously of critical importance in determining the final outcome. The following points deserve mention:

- The foot is moving in an upward and forward direction at the instant contact is made with the ball.
- The knee is still slightly flexed as the foot strikes the ball and the last few degrees of extension take place while the foot is in contact with the ball. According to Roberts and Metcalfe, "The rate of knee extension, 15 msec [0.015 s], before contact is of the order of 1500 to 2000 degrees per sec, and it is faster or nearly the same throughout contact."[35]
- The right hip is flexed to approximately 140° as contact is made and throughout the period of contact, indicating that the angular motion of the thigh has been reduced to zero.
- The head is forward and the back is somewhat rounded to allow the eyes to be focused on the ball.
- The arms (the left forward and the right to the side and slightly backward) act to "balance" the action of the legs.

Marshall[36] constructed a mechanical kicking machine to examine the effect of various factors on the distance achieved in place-kicking and, on the basis of an extensive series of tests, concluded that:

- The optimum point of contact for the toe on the ball was approximately 14 cm up on the seam when the ball was tilted 15° toward the kicker and the tee was set 38 cm in front of the point directly below the axle (a point roughly equivalent to the knee joint of the kicking leg). When the ball was placed in this position, the angle between the kicking leg and the vertical was approximately 10°. If the ball was moved away from the kicker and the tilt increased, it was possible to locate other positions from which the ball could be kicked almost as far.
- There were no significant differences in distances obtained in kicking a leather football compared with those obtained in kicking a rubber football.
- The use of a detachable rubber kicking toe produced no significant changes in the distance that the ball could be kicked.
- The position of the laces made very little difference in the direction of the flight or the distance that the ball traveled when kicked under the optimum conditions (that is, those specified in the first item in this list).
- A medium-high, slowly revolving, end-over-end kick results from kicking the ball at the optimum height and with the optimum tilt.
- Height may be obtained either by tilting the ball toward the kicker or by striking it lower with the toe.

Bona[37] trained two groups of beginning kickers for a period of 6 weeks (one group using a toe kick and the other an instep kick) and then tested them for accuracy in point-after-touchdown and field-goal kicks and for distance when kicking off. He found that

- The group that used the toe kick was significantly more accurate than the group that used the instep kick when attempting points-after-touchdown.
- There was no significant difference between the two groups in terms of accuracy in kicking field goals or in distance achieved in kicking off.
- There were no significant differences between the groups in terms of either accuracy or distance when kicks with rubber and leather footballs were compared.

Follow-through. The follow-through in place-kicking serves to protect the body from injury and to ensure that the forces necessary to stop the leg swing do not interfere with the act of projecting the ball into the air.

Although the discussion thus far has been concerned primarily with the place-kicks used when field goals and extra points are attempted, much of what has been said applies equally well to the place-kick used to start the game after touchdowns and at the beginning of each half. However, there are also some differences between the two types of kick—a man taking a kickoff having some distinct advantages over one attempting a field goal or a point-after-touchdown. In the first place, he has a virtually unlimited amount of time in which to make his kick. This places him at an advantage compared with a man attempting to kick a field goal or an extra point, for the accuracy and/or distance that the latter can obtain is almost certainly limited by a need to get the ball into the air quickly. Second, the path that the ball must follow in order to pass beyond the reach of the oncoming defensive men increases the demand for accuracy on the part of a kicker attempting field goals and points-after-touchdown. The man taking the kickoff has considerable latitude in this respect and the possibility of the ball's being deflected early in its flight is a relatively remote one. The possibility that it may have to be kicked so high as to cause a reduction in the total distance of the kick is even more remote.

Punting (Fig. 10-9). The basic techniques used in punting are very similar to those used in kicking field goals and extra points. The principal differences between the two arise as a result of the punter having first to

Figure 10-9. Punting.

catch the ball and then, as he is moving forward onto his left foot, to release it in a downward and forward direction where it will eventually be hit as the right foot swings through. (*Note:* Although the punter imparts no forward velocity to the ball at the time he releases it—he simply lets it drop or guides it downward with his hands—the ball retains the forward velocity it had as a result of the kicker's forward motion. Fortunately for the kicker who would otherwise overrun it, the ball thus falls in a forward and downward direction once it has been released.)

The importance that various factors have in determining the success of a punt have been investigated by Smith.[38] From a cinematographic analysis of three punters (an expert, an average punter, and a beginner), he arrived at the figures shown in Table 10-1.

Since there was very little difference between the three subjects on each of the other measurements taken, Smith concluded that the five parameters listed "made up the difference between good and poor punters, and that these points should be stressed in coaching the punting of a football."[39]

The factors influencing success in punting were also the subject of a study by Alexander and Holt.[40] These two researchers filmed a series of punts executed by "two exceptional Canadian punters" and selected for analysis an average and an exceptional punt by each subject. The results obtained (Table 10-2) shed considerable light on several long-standing questions concerned with punting techniques. It was found, for example, that there was virtually no difference (less than 3 percent) in the speeds of the kicking foot immediately prior to contact for average and exceptional punts. This finding, which "contradicted the generally accepted theory that the speed of the foot . . . is the critical factor in punting performance,"[41] led Alexander and Holt to suggest that the critical factor in punting was not the speed of the kicking foot itself but the force that this foot imparted to the ball—the latter a function of both the speed of the foot and the manner in which contact was made between foot and ball. With respect to the nature of the contact between foot and ball, Alexander and Holt observed that "Whenever the ball is met on the instep across the laces—as is commonly advocated—the metatarsals are brought into play" and "the foot 'gives' and causes a loss of energy in the same way that a boxer 'gives' with a blow. When, however, the ball is contacted higher on the ankle and more across the foot, the foot does not 'give.' "[42] They concluded, therefore, that

TABLE 10-1 Characteristics of the Technique Used by Punters of Different Ability

	Expert	Average	Beginner
Distance ball dropped	16 cm	46 cm	76 cm
Velocity of ball at release	28 m/s	27 m/s	23 m/s
Angle of release	47.5°	31.5°	32°
Distance kicked	56 m	52 m	42 m
Time per kick (catch to release from foot)	1.385 s	1.548 s	1.697 s

Based on data presented in Smith, H. (1949). "A cinematographical analysis of football punting." M.S. thesis, University of Illinois.

TABLE 10-2 Characteristics of the Techniques Used to Produce Average and Exceptional Punts

	Distance (m)	Speed of Foot Before Contact (m/s)	Speed of Ball After Contact (m/s)	Angle of Ball Across Foot (deg)	Body C.G. Lift in Follow-Through (cm)
Subject K. C.					
Average	41	23.7	30.1	10	15
Exceptional	61	24.4	33.0	24	6
Subject D. D.					
Average	37	20.7	26.3	15	21
Exceptional	55	20.9	27.6	25	15

Source: Based on data presented in Alexander A., and Holt, L. E. (1974). Punting, a cinema-computer analysis. *Scholastic Coach*, 43:14–16, 44.

the most efficient application of force is obtained if the ball is contacted high on the ankle and with its long axis across the line of the foot. They also noted that the extent to which the punter is lifted in the follow-through is an indication of the efficiency of the ball-foot contact. "Good contact produces a slower moving leg in the follow-through; hence, less or no lift of the body."[43]

Recommended Readings

BRANCAZIO, P. J. (1984). *Sport Science: Physical Laws and Optimum Performance*. New York: Simon & Schuster. pp. 343–46 (Moving through fluids).

Notes

1. Brancazio, P. J. (1984). *Sport Science: Physical Laws and Optimal Performance* (pp. 345–46). New York: Simon & Schuster.
2. Cunningham, J., and Dowell, L. (1976). The effect of air resistance on three types of football trajectories. *Research Quarterly*, 47:852–54.
3. Brancazio, P. J. *Sport Science: Physical Laws and Optimal Performance* (pp. 345–46).
4. Dowell, L. J., and Colfer, G. R. (1980). Effect of air resistance on the angle of projection and range of a place kicked football. *TAHPER Journal*, Winter, pp. 12, 45.
5. Brancazio. *Sport Science: Physical Laws and Optimal Performance* (p. 344).
6. Dowell and Colfer. Effect of air resistance on the angle of projection.
7. McKain, H. L. (1963). Techniques of executing fundamental skills of football. M.A. thesis, State University of Iowa (pp. 73–74).
8. Henrici, R. C. (1967). A cinemagraphical [sic] analysis of the center snap in the punt formation. M.S. thesis, University of Wisconsin.
9. Slebos, W. G. (1968). A comparison of the visual and the non-visual methods of the spiral center pass. M.S. thesis, The University of Iowa.
10. Pannes, N. (1967). A comparison of the lengths of time for three techniques of quarterback dropback passing to three different depths. M.S. thesis, Springfield College.
11. Holtz, L. (1962). Speed of starting from selected stances used in football. M.A. thesis, State University of Iowa.
12. Warshawsky, L. (1963). A comparative time study of two backfield stances in football. M.S. thesis, University of Illinois.
13. Robinson, F. H. (1949). A comparison of starting times from three different backfield stances. M.Ed. theses, Springfield College.
14. Kadatz, D. M. (1965). The relationship of weight distribution and charging time for football lineman. M.A. thesis, University of Alberta.

15. Holtz. Speed of starting from selected stances used in football, p. 10.
16. Fitch, R. E. (1956). A study of linemen stances and body alignments and their relation to starting speed in football. P.E.D. dissertation, Indiana University.
17. Bolt, D. (1949). Four-point stance in football. *Athletic Journal*, 29:68–69.
18. Ibid., p. 69.
19. Miles, W. R., and Graves, B. C. (1931). Studies in physical exertion: III. Effect of signal variation on football charging. *Research Quarterly*, 2:14–31.
20. Ibid., p. 31.
21. Thompson, C. W., Nagle, F. J., and Dobias, R. (1958). Starting signals and movement times of high school and college football players. *Research Quarterly*, 29:222–30.
22. Owens, A. (1960). Effect of variations in hand and foot spacing on movement time and on force of charge. *Research Quarterly*, 31:66–76.
23. Rosenfield, R. J. (1950). Measuring reaction time and force extended by football players. M.A. thesis, University of Kansas.
24. Elbel, E. R., Wilson, D., and French, C. (1952). Measuring speed and force of charge of football players. *Research Quarterly*, 3:295–300.
25. Owens. Effect of variations in hand and foot spacing on movement time and on force of charge, pp. 66–76.
26. Klumpar, E. (1959). An analysis of blocking in football. M.A. thesis, State University of Iowa.
27. Nordman, G. R. (1959). A comparison of the effectiveness of the shoulder block and the body block in football. M.A. thesis, State University of Iowa.
28. Bahr, M. (1985). Matt Bahr on soccer-style place-kicking. In D. Herbst (Ed.), *The Art of Place-Kicking and Punting* (p. 93). New York: Linden Press/S & S.
29. Dodd, R. L. (1954). *Bobby Dodd on Football* (p. 274). Englewood Cliffs, N.J.: Prentice Hall.
30. Bunn, J. W. (1972). *Scientific Principles of Coaching* (p. 191). Englewood Cliffs, N.J.: Prentice Hall.
31. Becker, J. W. (1963). The mechanical analysis of a football place kick. M.A. thesis, University of Wisconsin.
32. Plagenhoef, S. (1971). *Patterns of Human Motion: A Cinematographic Analysis* (pp. 98–103). Englewood Cliffs, N.J.: Prentice Hall.
33. Manzi, R. (1967). A comparison of two methods of place kicking a football for distance and accuracy. M.S. thesis, Springfield College.
34. Roberts, E. M., and Metcalf, A. (1968). Mechanical analysis of kicking in biomechanics. In J. Wartenweiler, E. Jokl, and M. Hebbelinck (Eds.), *Biomechanics* (p. 317). Basel, Switzerland: S. Karger.
35. Ibid., p. 317.
36. Marshall, S. (1958). Factors affecting place-kicking in football. *Research Quarterly*, 3:202–8.
37. Bona, R. C. (1963). A comparison of the instep kick to the toe kick in football. M.S. thesis, Washington State University.
38. Smith, H. (1949). A cinematographic analysis of football punting. M.S. thesis, University of Illinois.
39. Ibid.
40. Alexander, A., and Holt, L. E. (1974). Punting, a cinema-computer analysis. *Scholastic Coach*, 43:14–16, 44.
41. Ibid.
42. Ibid.
43. Ibid.

CHAPTER

11

The basic techniques of golf have probably been subject to more wide-spread examination than those of any other sport. One manifestation of this interest in the techniques of the game is the large number of instructional books and articles written on the subject by players, coaches, teachers, and others. Unfortunately, within this considerable volume of material there exist numerous areas of disagreement as to what constitutes the optimum technique for making each of the various shots. In addition, most of the arguments presented in favor of one technique over another are based upon nothing more secure than personal opinion and experience. The outstanding exception to this is a book by Cochran and Stobbs.[1] This book, the end product of a 6-year research project sponsored by the Golf Society of Great Britain (G.S.G.B.), examines objectively some of the basic techniques in the game of golf. It provides scientifically established answers to many of the questions about which there has been so much discussion and disagreement hitherto. Many of the results obtained in the G.S.G.B. project are referred to in this chapter.

BASIC CONSIDERATIONS

The objective in golf is to displace the ball from one position to another with the least number of shots possible. The initial position of the ball is on the tee, and the desired final position is within the hole some prescribed distance away.

The displacement of the ball is usually effected by a shot, or sequence of shots, in which the ball travels some distance through the air and then bounces and rolls a farther distance. With the exception of putting, the initial passage of the ball through the air (the carry) is generally responsible for a greater proportion of the displacement achieved than is the bouncing and rolling (the run) that follows. The contributions of the carry and the run in a series of typical drives are shown in Table 11-1. (The figures in this table have been obtained using equations derived by the G.S.G.B. research team.[2])

The Carry

For any given case, the length of carry obtained depends on (1) the speed and (2) the direction at which the ball leaves the face of the club; (3) the height of the ball at that instant; and (4) the air resistance that it encounters in flight.

Speed of Release. The speed of a body immediately following an elastic impact is governed by the masses and initial velocities of the bodies involved in the impact and by their mutual coefficient of restitution (pp. 80–95). In the case of a golf ball struck by a club, three of these five factors are either fixed by the rules or are subject to such little variation that they may safely be regarded as constant. These are the mass of the ball (4.4 g); the initial velocity of the ball (0 m/s); and the coefficient of restitution which, although it varies for differing speeds of impact, is primarily a function of the materials of which the clubhead and ball are constructed.

Variations in the mass of the clubhead, the second body involved in the impact, effect the ease with which the club can be swung and thus the speed of the clubhead at impact—increasing the mass of the clubhead reduces its impact speed, while decreasing the mass increases its impact speed. A

TABLE 11-1 The Relative Contributions of the Carry and the Run to the Total Length of a Drive

Total Length of Drive (m)	Carry (m)	Percentage of Total Length	Run (m)	Percentage of Total Length
160	127	80	33	20
180	151	84	29	16
200	175	88	25	12
220	199	91	21	9
240	223	93	17	7
260	247	95	13	5
280	271	97	9	3

Note: (1) These results are for "squarely struck *drives*" with a British 4.1-cm diameter ball. Differences between these figures and the equivalent figures for an American 4.3-cm diameter ball are almost certainly negligible. (2) The computation of the total length of drive assumes "some sort of average ground conditions."

change in impact speed tends to have a corresponding effect on the speed of the ball at release. Thus, for example, increasing clubhead mass decreases the impact speed and tends to decrease the speed of the ball at release. However, if there were no difference in impact speed, an increase in clubhead mass would tend to increase the speed of the ball at release. With an increase in clubhead mass tending therefore to both decrease and increase the speed of the ball, it is of some importance to establish which of these two tendencies dominates.

The effects that changes in the mass of the clubhead have on the initial velocity of the ball, and thus on the length of a shot, have been reported by Daish.[34] Following an analysis in which four golfers of "varying ages . . . and a fair range of golfing ability" swung a club whose weight was varied from 1.0 N to 3.4 N, Daish concluded that "varying the mass of the clubhead over the wide range from 5 to 11 oz [1.4 N to 3.1 N] has little or no significant effect on the initial velocity imparted to the ball" and "should produce no difference of any consequence in the length of shot obtained." In short, it appears that these two contrary tendencies effectively cancel each other and the speed of the ball at release is unaltered.

While it might well be thought that the "body" interacting with the ball during impact is a combined unit of club-plus-golfer-plus-earth, experiments have shown that this is not the case. In fact, at impact the clubhead behaves essentially as if it were not directly connected to the golfer. The truth of this has been dramatically demonstrated by the G.S.G.B. research team,[5] who found that the length of drives hit with a No. 2 wood with a freely moving hinge between the clubhead and the clubshaft varied little from those hit with a normal club—30 drives with each club yielded averages of 197 and 201 m, respectively. Even then, it was considered likely that this small difference was probably due to factors other than those operating at impact.

Because each of the factors so far considered has been shown to allow little effective variation, it is apparent that observed differences in the speed at which the ball leaves the club must be mainly due to differences in the one remaining factor—the speed of the clubhead at impact. Now, because the clubhead is momentarily at rest at the peak of the backswing, its speed at the instant of impact must be determined by the forces exerted on the club during the downswing and the times over which these forces act (impulse-momentum relationship). Of these forces (gravity, air resistance, and the muscular forces applied to the grip), it is clearly the last that is capable of the widest variation. Differences in the speed at which the ball leaves the club are therefore more likely to be due to differences in the muscular forces applied to the grip than to differences in any other single factor.

Direction of Release. The direction in which the ball is moving at release must be considered in terms of both the angle that the vector representing the velocity of the ball makes with the horizontal (the angle of release) and the angle it makes with the intended line of the shot. These angles are measured in vertical and horizontal planes, respectively.

The angle of release is governed primarily by the inclination of the clubface (that is, its loft). Consider the velocity of the clubhead immediately before impact to be resolved into two components—one acting perpendicular (or normal) to the clubface and the other acting parallel with the clubface (Fig. 11-1[a]). At impact the natural tendency of the clubhead to keep moving as it was an instant earlier (Newton's first law) results in the ball experiencing forces in the same direction as these components (Fig. 11-1[b]). The normal force causes the ball to be accelerated in that direction. The end product of this acceleration (the normal component of the velocity of the ball as it leaves the club) is influenced by the elasticity of both bodies—the less the elasticity, the less the magnitude of this component. The effect of the force along the clubface is governed by the limiting friction between the surfaces in contact—those of the clubface and the ball. If the force exerted exceeds that of the limiting friction, some slippage occurs and the component velocity of the ball in this direction following impact is reduced. In fact, if the surfaces were perfectly smooth, the release velocity of the ball would have a zero component along the clubface and the ball would fly off in a direction perpendicular to this surface. However, because the surfaces of the clubface and the ball are both "rough," this situation is unlikely to apply in practice. Instead, the ball is generally acted upon by a friction force that not only causes it to be released in a direction slightly below the perpendicular to the clubface, but also causes it to acquire a certain amount of backspin.

With respect to motion in the horizontal plane—strictly, a horizontal plane upon which the path of the ball is considered to be projected—the success of any given shot depends on bringing the clubhead to meet the ball so that the horizontal directions in which the clubhead is moving and the

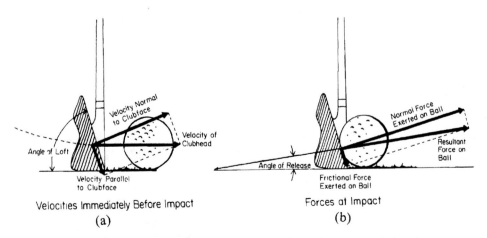

Figure 11-1. (a) Components of clubhead velocity immediately before impact. (b) Components of the force exerted on the ball at impact.

clubface is "pointing" both coincide with the direction in which it is intended the ball should go (Fig. 11-2[a]). Failure to achieve this consistency in directions causes the path of the ball to deviate laterally from that intended (Fig. 11-2[b]).

Height of Release.   While the height of the ball at release, relative to the height of the point at which it will land, is a significant factor in determining the length of the carry, it is one over which the golfer has very limited control.

Air Resistance.   A golf ball in flight is subject to forces exerted upon it by the air through which it passes. These forces may be regarded as the summed effects of a resistance to the linear motion of the ball through the air (drag) and a resistance to the angular motion of the ball as it spins about an axis through its center of gravity. Of these two it is only the latter over which the golfer could be said to exert any real measure of control.

The resistance to the angular motion of the ball serves to modify the drag and also causes the ball to deviate vertically and/or laterally from the path it would otherwise travel. There are basically four types of angular motion that may be imparted to a ball—topspin, backspin, "slicing" sidespin, and "hooking" sidespin.

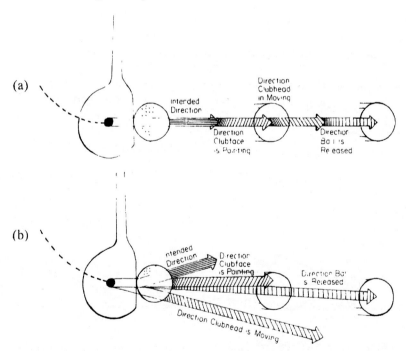

Figure 11-2.   (a) To obtain the intended direction of release, the directions in which the clubhead is moving and "pointing" must both coincide with that intended direction. (b) Failure to obtain the required coincidence of the three directions results in the ball deviating laterally from the desired direction.

Topspin, which markedly reduces the lift component and therewith the time of flight and the distance of the carry, is normally applied only in error. This most frequently occurs when the ball is "topped" (that is, the clubhead hits only the top part of the ball).

Backspin, on the other hand, is directly attributable to the "down-the-clubface" (or frictional) component of force that a lofted club normally applies to the ball. As already indicated (p. 194), this backspin provides the lift that the ball experiences and thereby lengthens the time it is in the air and the distance it carries. The magnitude of the lift obtained is closely related to the speed at which the ball rotates. In an experiment in which the effects of air resistance were measured by dropping a ball into the moving airstream within a wind tunnel (see relative motion, pp. 183–184), Davies[6] found that at an airspeed equivalent to what might normally be obtained with a high-iron shot the lift varied from 0 N (no spin) to 0.24 N (at 8000 rpm). Thus, at this latter rate of rotation (again, roughly that to be expected from a high-iron shot) the lift force was more than half the weight of the ball (0.45 N).

It is perhaps of interest to note that the shape of the grooves on the clubface has an influence on the amount of backspin applied to the ball. Neal and Hubinger[7] analyzed 160 shots by a low-handicap golfer, half hit with a 5-iron with U-shaped grooves and half with a 5-iron with V-shaped grooves. The mean angular velocity of the ball as it left the club was 107.9 rev/s (in the first case) and 73.6 rev/s (in the second).

Sidespin generally results from bringing the clubface across the intended line of the shot, during the period in which it is in contact with the ball. If the clubface moves across the intended direction line and toward the golfer (a movement known as bringing it from "outside-in"), a "slicing sidespin" is imparted to the ball. For a right-handed golfer this type of sidespin causes the ball to curve to the right of the intended line. A "hooking sidespin" is produced when the clubface is moved across the intended direction line in the opposite direction (that is, from "inside-out") and for a right-handed golfer causes the ball to curve to the left during its flight.

The Run

Of all those factors that have a part in determining what happens once the ball hits the ground, the only one that is capable of much variation and is not essentially fixed by the initial impact between club and ball is the co-efficient of restitution. If the coefficient of restitution is zero (that is, the impact is an inelastic one), the ball simply imbeds itself in the ground at the point at which it lands. However, if the coefficient of restitution is greater than zero, as is normally the case, the ball bounces following impact with the ground. In such instances, the distance covered during the bounce (and during each successive bounce) depends very largely on the magnitude of the coefficient. For example, if the ground is hard and the coefficient is therefore high, the ball is likely to cover greater distances with each bounce and to bounce more often than it would if the ground were soft. (According to Diaz,[8] the record for the longest drive stands at 632 yd [578 m]. This drive was made by an Irish professional golfer [Liam Higgins] during a long-driving contest held at Casement Aerodrome in Baldonnel, Ireland—a site chosen expressly for the purpose of ensuring high coefficients of restitution and long runs.)

After a number of bounces, the vertical velocity with which the ball strikes the ground decreases to the point where the ground-reaction force is insufficient to carry it once more into the air. At this point the ball begins to roll, the distance it rolls being governed by its horizontal velocity at the time and by the forces (for example, gravity and rolling friction) that subsequently act upon it.

The relationships between the displacement that a golf ball experiences and the factors that determine that displacement are summarized in Fig. 11-3.

Putting

In putting, the golfer has three distinct tasks to perform:

- Determine the direction to hit the ball in order to have it fall into the hole. If a straight line joining the ball and the hole runs directly uphill or downhill or goes across a part of the green that is smooth and flat,

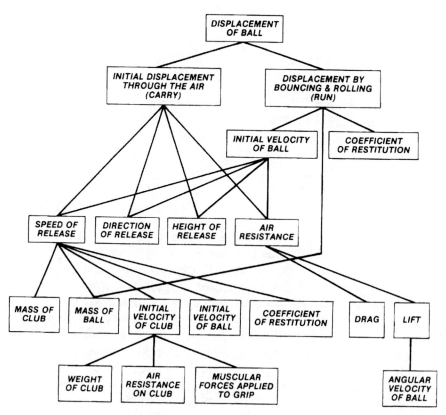

Figure 11-3. Basic factors in a golf drive.

choosing the best direction to hit the ball is a simple matter—it should be hit directly along this line. More common, though, are cases in which the surface between ball and hole slopes to one side or perhaps slopes in different directions at different points. In such instances, the golfer must take heed of the effect that gravity will have on the path the ball will take. For example, if the green slopes down to the right of the straight line between the ball and the hole, and the golfer directs the ball along this line, that component of the ball's weight that acts downhill will accelerate it in that direction. As a result, the ball will follow a curved path below the direct line between ball and hole and, unless the distance of the putt is very short or the slope of the green very small, this downward deviation will cause the ball to pass some distance below the hole. An experienced golfer therefore chooses to direct the putt above the line between ball and hole, knowing that gravity will tend to bring it down and around toward the hole.

- Determine how hard the ball must be hit to impart to it the speed necessary for it to cover the required distance. In this assessing of the "strength" of the putt, the experienced golfer takes particular note of the distance of the putt; the extent to which it is an uphill or downhill shot; whether the green is soft or hard, or dry or wet; and the length of the grass and the direction in which it lies.

- Finally, having thus determined the velocity that he (or she) intends to impart to the ball, the golfer's task is to execute the putting stroke in a manner consistent with this intention. Basically, this means that the golfer must have the face of the putter at right angles to the chosen line throughout the short period of impact and moving at a speed that will result in the desired speed being imparted to the ball.

TECHNIQUES
Grip

There are three principal methods of gripping the club for driving strokes—the overlapping (or Vardon) grip, the interlocking grip, and the baseball (or two-handed) grip. With respect to the relative merits of these three, the results of an experiment by Walker[9] are of interest. After comparing the performances of 24 male golfers who used each of the three grips in turn, Walker found that no one of the grips was statistically superior to either of the others, in terms of greater distance or accuracy.

Stance

The placement of the feet relative to one another and relative to the intended direction of the shot are of some importance in determining the velocity with which the clubhead meets the ball.

If the feet are placed together, the narrowness of the base inevitably makes the golfer conscious of the need to maintain balance and thus precludes a maximum contribution of force from the muscles of the legs and hips. A stance with the feet wide apart also hampers the production of force by these muscles. Logically, therefore, most skilled players use a spread of their feet somewhere intermediate between these two extremes—slightly more than shoulder width apart for shots requiring maximum or near-maximum effort, and closer together for shorter shots requiring only a limited contribution from the legs and hips.

The placement of the feet relative to the intended direction of the shot (as in baseball, the terms *open*, *square*, and *closed* are used to describe the basic variations) also depends to some extent on the length of shot required. For shots requiring maximum or near-maximum effort, there appears to be very little evidence to suggest that one option is superior to any other. However, for those shots (and particularly short pitches, etc.) where accuracy rather than maximum distance is the prime consideration, a somewhat open stance tends to restrict the range of the backswing, thereby decreasing the scope for errors in the execution of the swing, without preventing the required force from being obtained.

The Swing*

The swing, that succession of movements that culminates in the clubhead striking the ball, may be regarded as the central element about which the whole game of golf is built.

Although all actions of the golfer's body and the club from the first movement following the address (the position adopted by the player before beginning the swing) must be coordinated into one smooth sequence, it is convenient for the purposes of analysis to consider the full swing as consisting of four major parts—*backswing (or upswing)*, *downswing*, *impact*, and *follow-through*.

In both backswing and downswing the motion is essentially rotary and for simplicity may be considered in terms of two levers rotated about their respective axes. These levers are the club itself, rotating about an axis passing through the golfer's hands, and a combined shoulders-arms-hands lever, rotating about an axis inclined to the horizontal and passing through the golfer's chest (Fig. 11-4).

Backswing. The purpose of the backswing is to put the golfer and the club into the optimum position from which to start the downswing.

The backswing begins with a simultaneous backward movement of the clubhead and the hands and a rotation of the trunk to the right. These first movements are sometimes preceded by a "pressing" or "cocking" action in which the golfer gently pushes the right knee in toward the left one and then, as the knee returns to its original position, begins the withdrawal of hands and club. This movement (evident in the results of Carlsöö's study[10] of forces and muscular actions in the golf swing, and occasionally referred to by golf writers[11][12][13]) may serve to help the golfer initiate the backswing

---

* In the analysis of the swing that follows, it is assumed that the golfer is right-handed and executing a drive for maximum distance. The terms *forward* and *backward* are used with reference to the direction in which the golfer intends to hit the ball: *forward* is in that direction, and *backward* is the opposite direction.

Figure 11-4.
The golf swing may be analyzed in terms
of a shoulder-arms-hands lever
rotating about an axis through the upper
chest and a club lever rotating about
an axis through the hands.

in a systematic and relaxed manner, but apart from this would appear to have no particular merit, for it merely adds to an already wide range of possible sources of error.

As the combined backward movement of the hands and club and the rotation of the trunk continue, the left arm is raised and swung across the trunk, the wrists are cocked (or bent sideways toward the thumbs), and the left forearm is rolled so that the back of the left hand lies in an approximately vertical plane.

The end of the backswing is reached with the hands at or slightly above head height, the trunk rotated approximately 90° from its original position, and the wrists cocked so that the club shaft lies over and behind the head at some 45° above the horizontal.

According to Williams,[14] an objective examination of the paths followed by the hands and the clubhead during the upswings of top-class players reveals that the path of the hands varies hardly at all from player to player while the path of the clubhead varies considerably. He therefore concluded "that the path followed by the clubhead in the upswing has little significance and is a matter of personal preference."

Carlsöö[15] also reached some interesting conclusions regarding the backswing. He concluded, for example, that the backswing could be divided into two consecutive parts—an accelerating movement backward and upward lasting about 0.3 s and a retarding or braking movement lasting until the top of the swing about 0.35 s later. This retardation was characterized by a change in the direction of the horizontal couple that the feet exerted against the ground and by marked changes in muscular activity; the activity of those muscles that had initiated the backswing diminished and that of their antagonists (that is, those muscles that perform the opposite function) increased. Furthermore, the muscles that produced this retarding or braking effect on the backswing continued to be active in the downswing during which they acted as "very essential movement-promoting muscles."

Downswing. The objective of the downswing is to have the clubhead arrive at the point of impact moving at maximum speed in the required direction and with the face of the club "pointing" in that same direction.

The downswing begins with a forward movement of the hips that, with good golfers, actually begins approximately 0.1 s before the clubhead reaches the limit of its backswing.[16] This moving forward of the hips rotates the whole upper body (Fig. 11-5) and moves both levers through the first part of the downswing. The forces responsible for this forward movement of the hips and the lesser forces exerted by the same hip and leg muscles later in the downswing have been estimated to account for 2½ hp (1864 W) of the total 3-4 hp (2337–2983 W) generated in a good drive. Thus it can readily be seen that "the muscles of the hips and legs constitute the main source of power in long driving."[17]

The positions of the shoulders, arms, hands, and club relative to one another are unchanged as the hips are driven forward. Then, when the left arm reaches an approximately horizontal position, this first stage (the "one-piece stage" as Williams[18] calls it) comes to an end and the included angle between clubshaft and left arm, previously about 70°–80°, becomes progressively larger. From this point onward, the hands continue to move along their circular arc at a fairly constant speed while the clubhead's speed increases dramatically as the angle between the left arm and the clubshaft straightens out.

These relationships are summarized in Fig. 11-6. In this figure, ø is the angle between the shoulders-arms-hands lever and a downward vertical

Figure 11-5.
A forward movement of the hips initiates the downswing.

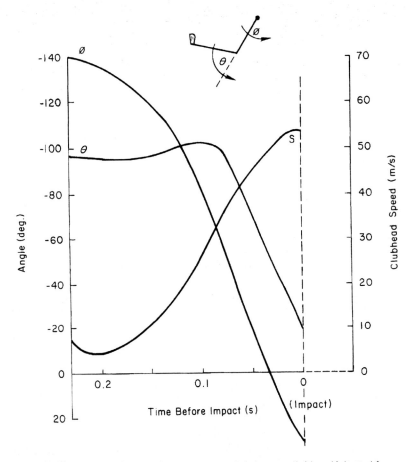

Figure 11-6. Changes in position and speed during a golf drive. (Adapted from Budney, D. R., and Bellow, D. G. [1979]. Kinetic analysis of a golf swing. *Research Quarterly*, 50:171–79.)

through the axis about which it rotates, θ is angle between the line of this lever and the shaft of the club, and S is the speed of the clubhead. (*Note:* The data on which this figure is based[19] were gathered on a professional golfer who exerted a "wrist-cocking" torque just before impact and thus slightly reduced his clubhead speed at impact).

To understand what happens during this second stage of the down-swing, it is necessary to consider the forces that the golfer's hands apply to the grip of the club (Fig. 11-7). The resultant of these forces may be resolved into two components:

1. A *radial component* (or centripetal force) acting toward the axis about which the shoulders-arms-hands lever rotates. This component serves to constrain the motion of the handgrip of the club to a circular arc and, because its line of action does not pass through the center of gravity of the club, also tends to cause the club to be

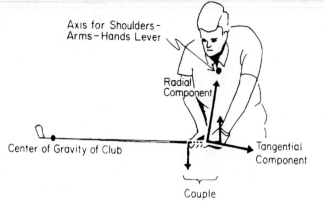

Figure 11-7.
The forces applied to the handgrip of the club, considered relative to the axis through the chest.

rotated (or, more precisely, to be angularly accelerated) relative to an axis through this point. The direction of this rotation is consistent with an "uncocking" of the wrists or, to put it another way, with a decrease in the angle formed by the lines of the club shaft and the left arm.

2. A *tangential component* acting, as the name suggests, in a direction tangential to the path followed by the handgrip of the club. This component serves to accelerate the handgrip, and the club as a whole, in the direction in which it acts. When its line of action does not pass through the center of gravity of the club, this component also tends to angularly accelerate the club in a direction opposite to that of the radial component. The net effect of these two components is to accelerate the club along a circular path and to cause it to rotate relative to an axis through its center of gravity. The direction of this rotation is governed by how the opposing tendencies of the two components compare.

In addition to the resultant force that the hands exert on the grip, there exists the possibility that the combined actions of the hands also result in a couple being applied to the grip. For, if the right hand is pressed down forcefully against a resistance of equal magnitude provided by the left hand, a couple that tends to uncock the wrists comes into existence. The question of whether such a couple exists is a source of some disagreement in the literature. Following an analysis of the swing of Bobby Jones, Williams[20] concluded emphatically that "The mathematics . . . proves beyond any argument that hand (or wrist-uncocking) leverage has nothing to do with accelerating the clubhead in what is usually referred to as the 'hitting area'." This view is supported by Milburn[21] who, after analyzing the drives of four "right-handed collegiate-level golfers and one right-handed low-handicap golfer from the community," concluded that the left wrist behaved as a "free hinge" during the latter stages of the downswing.

Cochran and Stobbs,[22] on the other hand, profess the more widely held view. Without presenting any evidence in support of their contention—their book is intended for the lay reader and therefore does not include all the detailed scientific evidence upon which it is based—they state that "The obvious way to add speed to the clubhead is by applying some effort at the hinge [the hands]. . . . To do this, the right arm has simply . . . to *push*: that is to try to straighten out at the elbow."

Until this question is satisfactorily resolved, any analysis of the second stage of the downswing should probably consider both possibilities. If the golfer does not apply a couple that contributes to the uncocking action of the wrists, this action must result solely because the torque due to the radial component exceeds that due to the tangential component. Alternatively, if a couple is applied via the hands, this couple, together with the radial component of the resultant force, must produce the characteristic "uncocking" action despite the contrary tendency of the tangential component.

The "uncocking" of the wrists during the second part of the downswing is often attributed to a centrifugal force acting on the clubhead to pull it outward, away from the axis about which it is rotating. While this explanation might have some superficial appeal, it is inconsistent with the facts of the matter, as a consideration of the forces acting on the club reveals.

Apart from gravity and air resistance (both of which can be instantly dismissed as having no direct bearing on the question), the only external forces acting on the club are those applied at the grip. Now, for the purposes of examining this particular question, consider the resultant of these forces to be resolved into a radial (or centripetal) component that acts *inward* along the line of the clubshaft and *toward the axis through the hands*, and a tangential component acting perpendicular to the line of the clubshaft. (*Note:* These are not the same radial and tangential components referred to earlier, *relative to the axis through the golfers chest*—compare Fig. 11-7 and 11-8). The reaction to the centripetal force exerted by the hands *on the club* is a centrifugal force that the club exerts on the hands. Thus, since the only centrifugal force involved, in the rotation of the club about an axis through the hands, acts not on the club but on the hands, it cannot possibly be responsible for pulling the clubhead outward.

As the downswing is executed, the right elbow is brought down and close to the right side of the body, in the process transmitting to the grip the force produced by the contraction of muscles on the right side of the body. During the final few centimeters that the hands travel in the downswing, the wrists are "rolled" through approximately 90° so that the back of the left hand and the clubface (until this time in a near-vertical plane parallel to the intended direction of the shot) are brought around perpendicular to that direction.

Impact.   The critical features of the swing at the instant of impact are the orientation of the clubface, the position of the clubhead, and the velocity at which it is moving. Theoretically—provided the clubface is at right angles to the required direction, the center of gravity of the clubhead is directly behind the center of the ball, and the clubhead is moving forward with the maximum speed possible, under the circumstances—the position of the

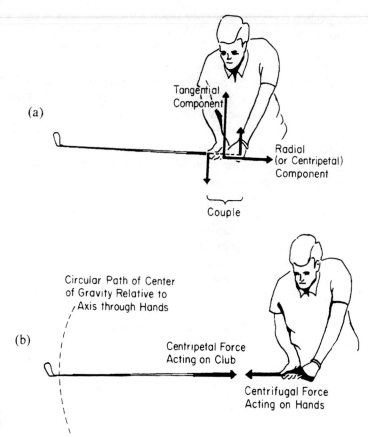

Figure 11-8.
Forces applied to the handgrip of the club, considered relative to the axis through the hands.

golfer is of little consequence. Experience suggests, however, that the need to satisfy these three conditions allows only minor variations in the position of the golfer at impact and that the optimum position has the following characteristics (Fig. 11-9).

- The clubhead is level with or just behind the hands. (Computer studies and observations of good golfers, referred to by Cochran and Stobbs,[23] suggest that the clubhead is moving fastest at, or possibly just before, the point where it catches up with the hands.)
- The back of the left wrist and hand is in a vertical (or near-vertical) plane perpendicular to the intended direction of the shot.
- The golfer's center of gravity is forward of a midline between the feet, thus placing a greater proportion of the body weight on the left foot than on the right one. In his study of a Swedish champion, Carlsöö[24] found that at impact the left foot transmitted a vertical force of 726 N to the ground, while the corresponding figure for the right foot, 235 N, was less than one-third of this. (*Note:* While some of this vertical force resulted from the actions taking place at impact—the golfer himself weighed only 823 N—it is clear that by far the

Figure 11-9.
The position at impact.

greater proportion of the golfer's weight was supported on his left foot.)

- The axis of the shoulders-arms-hands lever, passing through the golfer's chest, is in the same position it has been in throughout the downswing. The golfer brings this about by inclining the trunk, the lower end of which has been driven forward earlier by leg and hip action, slightly backward and by inclining the head forward with the eyes firmly focused on the ball. This latter serves to ensure that the axis is not lifted and thus tends to eliminate any risk of the ball being "topped."

Follow-through. The follow-through, which serves the same purposes as it does in other similar activities, consists of a gradual slowing down of the body and club movements that led up to the moment of impact.

Putting

Unlike driving, in which the need for maximum clubhead speed at impact largely determines the body actions that can be successfully employed, success in putting can be achieved using a wide variety of techniques (Fig. 11-10). For, aside from the obvious need to meet each of the three requirements mentioned earlier (pp. 282–283), present knowledge of putting techniques sheds very little light on what methods are most suitable. The truth of this statement was well borne out by the results of a cinematographical analysis of 16 "first-class" professionals in which it was found that "The only features where the professionals showed a measure of constancy were the ball position and the head position. Most of them had the ball placed opposite the left foot and their eyes almost directly above the ball."[25]

A study by Mann, Griffin, and Rodger has subsequently confirmed the first of these findings and raised doubt about the second. They found that

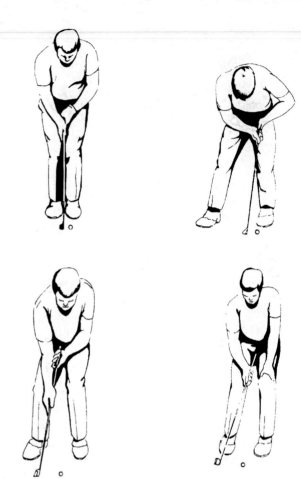

Figure 11-10.
Success in putting has been achieved using a wide variety of techniques.

the ball was consistently "played off the left heel"[26] and that "not one of the elite putters investigated positioned the eyes over the ball".[27]

They also found[28] that the 19 touring professionals, who were the subjects of their study, placed the left foot in virtually the same position, relative to the ball and the intended direction line, irrespective of the length of the putt. In this position, the ball was located "off the left heel" with both feet turned slightly towards the target. The position of the right foot was similar for all subjects but not as consistent as the left foot—a finding that Mann and his colleagues attributed to differences in physiques.

The time from the beginning of the backswing to contact with the ball (the completion time) ranged from 0.65 s (Paul Azinger) to 1.27 s (Don Pooley). For each subject, the completion time was virtually the same regardless of the length of the putt—from 4 ft (1.2 m) to 32 ft (9.8 m). This consistency in the completion times is illustrated in Table 11-2, which shows the results for Greg Norman (Australia) and Tom Kite (U.S.A.), two of the subjects. On the basis of these findings, Mann and his colleagues concluded that a near-constant completion time was a critical feature of a successful putting technique.

TABLE 11-2 Putting Times for Different Lengths of Putt

Length of Putt (m)	Backswing (s)	Downswing (s)	Completion Time (s)	Follow-through Time (s)
Greg Norman (Australia)				
1.2	0.62	0.30	0.92	0.70
2.4	0.63	0.29	0.92	0.75
4.9	0.63	0.30	0.93	0.74
9.8	0.63	0.30	0.93	0.73
Average	0.63	0.30	0.93	0.73
Tom Kite (U.S.A.)				
1.2	0.62	0.29	0.91	0.53
2.4	0.62	0.28	0.90	0.52
4.9	0.65	0.27	0.92	0.49
9.8	0.62	0.29	0.91	0.49
Average	0.63	0.28	0.91	0.51

Adapted from Mann, R., Griffin, F., and Rodger, P. (1991). Putting. *Golf Illustrated*, 7:43–46.

The average backswing distances increased from 17 cm (for a 1.2-m putt) to 39 cm (for a 9.8-m putt) and the average follow-through distances (that is, the distances traveled by the clubhead after impact with the ball) from 26 cm (for a 1.2-m putt) to 60 cm (for a 9.8-m putt). For each putting distance, the length of the average follow-through was thus about one and one-half times the length of the backswing.

With differing backswing times for different lengths of putt and near-constant completion times, the speed with which the clubhead was moved obviously varied accordingly. In short, the speed of both backswing and downswing increased as the length of the putt increased.

Cochran and Stobbs[29] also reported the results of a number of valuable experiments on putting. Among their many findings were the following:

- For all practical purposes it is impossible with a normal putter to put any useful spin on the ball.
- If the ball is hit off-center, the clubhead tends to rotate and the length and direction of the putt are affected. For example, an otherwise 20-ft (6.10-m) putt stops 4–6 ft (1.22–1.83 m) short and about 7 in (18 cm) to one side if it is hit 1 in. (2.5 cm) off-center. (If the reaction that the ball exerts on the club at impact does not pass through the center of gravity of the clubhead, it will tend to rotate the clubhead relative to an axis through the point—see eccentric force, p. 111–112. In this event the direction in which the ball is hit deviates laterally from that in which it would otherwise have moved. And, because the part of the clubface with which the ball is in contact is moving at a lesser speed than it would have been if the impact had not been off-center, the speed imparted to the ball is also reduced.)
- Distances lost and lateral deviations from the desired direction due to the balls being hit off-center could be reduced if some of the weight

of the clubhead could be shifted to the heel and some to the toe, still leaving the center of gravity in the middle. (An eccentric force exerted by the ball at impact causes the clubhead to be angularly accelerated. For any given case, the magnitude of this angular acceleration, and consequently the effect produced on the ball's subsequent motion, is inversely proportional to the moment of inertia of the clubhead—see angular analogue of Newton's second law, pp. 000-000. Thus, since the suggested redistribution of the weight of the clubhead increases its moment of inertia, the effects of an off-center hit will be less marked with such a putter than with one in which the weight is not so distributed.)

- The direction in which the ball sets off is governed more by where the face of the putter is pointing than by the direction in which the head of the putter is moving. Having the blade "square" at impact is therefore the most important single point to concentrate on in holing out.

- Random irregularities in the green ensure that putts hit in precisely the same manner will not necessarily yield the same results. An experiment designed to determine the importance of such irregularities on success in putting revealed that 2 percent of the missed putts from 6 ft (1.83 m), 50 percent of those from 20 ft (6.10 m), and 80 percent of those from 60 ft (18.29 m) could be attributed solely to this factor.

  (Incidentally, Diaz[30] has reported that the success rates of touring professional golfers is not as high as commonly supposed. Following a study in which data were gathered at 15 tournaments on the PGA tour—and in which at least 118 putts were hit at each 1 ft [0.3 m] interval from 2 ft [0.6 m] to 25 ft [7.6 m] from the hole—it was reported that the subjects made 83.1 percent of their putts from 3 ft [0.9 m], 54.8 percent from 6 ft [1.8 m], 33.5 percent from 10 ft [3 m], 16.8 percent from 15 ft [4.6 m] and 10.2 percent from 25 ft [7.6 m].)

- Comparison of the performances of professionals using blade, center-shafted, and mallet-style putters during tournament play revealed that no one type was significantly better than another.

- A scratch golfer would save something like six shots per round if the regulation diameter of the hole 4½ in. (11.43 cm) were doubled.

Recommended Readings

CHASE, A. (1984). In W. Schrier and W. F. Allman (Eds.), *Newton at the Bat: The Science in Sports.* New York: Scribner's, pp. 29–32 (A slice of golf).

COCHRAN, A., AND STOBBS, J. (1968). *The Search for the Perfect Swing.* London: Morrison & Gibb Ltd.

Notes

1. Cochran. A. C., and Stobbs, J. (1968). *The Search for the Perfect Swing.* London: Heinemann Educational Books.
2. Ibid., p. 229.
3. Daish, C. B. (1965). The influence of clubhead mass on the effectiveness of a golf club. *Institute of Physics and the Physical Society, Bulletin 16,* September, pp. 347–49.
4. Daish. C. B. (1972). *The Physics of Ball Games* (pp. 14–15, 102–9). London: The English Universities Press Ltd.
5. Cochran and Stobbs. *The Search for the Perfect Swing* (pp. 145–47).
6. Davies, J. M. (1949). The aerodynamics of golf balls. *Journal of Applied Physics,* 20:821–28.

7. Neal, R. J., and Hubinger, L. M. (1989). The effect of club-face groove on spin of a golf ball. In R. J. Gregor, R. F. Zernicke, and W. C. Whiting (Eds.), *Congress Proceedings: XII International Congress of Biomechanics* (No. 303). Los Angeles: University of California.

8. Diza, J. (1985). Set for takeoff? Well uh . . . *Sports Illustrated, 62*, January 14, pp. 86–87.

9. Walker, A. (1964). The relationship of distance and accuracy to three golf grips. M.S. thesis, Springfield College.

10. Carlsöö, S. (1967). A kinetic analysis of the golf swing. *The Journal of Sports Medicine and Physical Fitness, 7*:80–81.

11. Boros, J. (1968). *Swing Easy, Hit Hard* (p. 68). New York: Cornerstone Library.

12. McGurn, R., and Williams, S. A. (1969). *Golf Power in Motion* (p. 29). New York: Cornerstone Library.

13. Snead, S. (1965). *The Driver Book* (p. 57). New York: Cornerstone Library.

14. Williams, D. (1969). *The Science of the Golf Swing* (pp. 46–55). London: Pelham Books Ltd.

15. Carlsöö. A kinetic analysis of the golf swing, pp. 81–82.

16. Cochran and Stobbs. *The Search for the Perfect Swing* (p. 82).

17. Ibid., p. 81.

18. Williams. *The Science of the Golf Swing*, pp. 17–20.

19. Budney, D. R., and Bellow, D. G. (1979). Kinetic analysis of a golf swing. *Research Quarterly, 50*:171–79.

20. Williams. *The Science of the Golf Swing* (p. 23).

21. Milburn, P. D. (1982). Summation of segmental velocities in the golf swing. *Medicine and Science in Sports and Exercise, 14*:60–64.

22. Cochran and Stobbs. *The Search for the Perfect Swing* (p. 66).

23. Ibid., p. 58.

24. Carlsöö. A kinetic analysis of the golf swing, pp. 79, 81.

25. Cochran and Stobbs. *The Search for the Perfect Swing* (p. 136).

26. Mann, R., Griffin, F., and Rodger, P. (1991). Putting. *Golf Illustrated, 7*:43–46.

27. Mann, R., Griffin, F., and Rodger, P. (1991). Model putting: The mechanics. Personal communication.

28. Mann, Griffin, and Rodger. Putting.

29. Cochran and Stobbs. *The Search for the Perfect Swing* (pp. 128–42).

30. Diaz, J. (1989). Perils of putting. *Sports Illustrated, 70*, April 3, pp. 76–79.

CHAPTER 12

GYMNASTICS

The sport of gymnastics encompasses a broad field of activity. It includes the ten Olympic events (floor exercise, long horse vault, rings, horizontal bar, parallel bars, and side horse for men; and floor exercise, cross horse vault, beam, and uneven bars for women), rhythmic gymnastics and acrobatics.

Because the field is so broad, and the amount of space that can be devoted to it here is limited, this chapter is confined to a consideration of just three of the Olympic events—floor exercise, long horse vault, and horizontal bar.*

The discussion of each of these includes (1) a consideration of the basic concepts underlying the techniques used in the event; and (2) a series of brief analyses of selected techniques to show how these concepts apply in specific cases. With respect to the latter, elementary techniques are given preference over more advanced ones, although these too receive some attention.

---

* The basic concepts underlying techniques in most of the other Olympic events are similar to those for the events considered here. The biomechanical bases for the various techniques in the beam event, for instance, are almost identical to those described in connection with the floor exercise. Similar close relationships exist between the long horse and cross horse vault; and the horizontal bar on the one hand and the parallel bars, rings, and uneven bars on the other.

The movements used in floor exercises are widely regarded as forming the foundation upon which the rest of gymnastics is built. For this reason, the basic concepts underlying these movements deserve careful consideration.

Floor exercises are generally composed of leaps; springing and tumbling movements (including necksprings, headsprings, rolls, cartwheels, somersaults, etc.); and held positions exhibiting balance, suppleness, and strength.

In leaps (and in those springing and tumbling movements in which the gymnast is projected into the air), success depends on the ability

- to acquire lift and rotation at takeoff,
- to control rotation while in the air,
- to control both translation and rotation on landing, and
- to do these three things in an aesthetically-pleasing way.

The flight path of a gymnast who has left the ground (like that of all other projectiles) is determined by the velocity and height of the center of gravity at the instant of takeoff. Thus any attempt to improve the gymnast's performance by acquiring more lift must involve modifying either or both of these quantities if it is to have the desired effect. The rotation that a gymnast acquires at takeoff derives from two sources—a couple and/or an eccentric force.

Once the gymnast has left the ground, the only way in which he (or she) can control rotation is by adjusting the moment of inertia of the body. By bringing the masses of the various body parts closer to the axis of rotation through the center of gravity, the gymnast can increase the angular velocity of the body; conversely, by moving them farther away, the gymnast can decrease the angular velocity (conservation of angular momentum). The extent to which the gymnast can make such adjustments is generally limited, however, by the nature of the aesthetic and technical requirements of the activity. For example, a gymnast could tuck toward the end of a neckspring and thereby increase angular velocity, but this would be much less aesthetically pleasing than if the body was kept fully extended throughout the flight. Furthermore, it fails to meet the technical demands of the movement, which require that such springs be completed in an essentially straight position. Thus, although a gymnast can exert some control over rotation when in the air, it is *not* what the gymnast does in the air that is most important but what he (or she) does on the ground during the takeoff. For it is here that it is decided what angular momentum the gymnast will have during the flight and how long this angular momentum will have to take its effect (that is, how long the gymnast will be in the air).

At the instant the gymnast lands, his (or her) body is rotating about an axis through its center of gravity, which is itself translating. If the gymnast wishes to come to a stop (rather than to move off immediately into another movement), he (or she) must evoke such forces from the landing surface as will cancel this translation and rotation. The logical (and most used) method of doing this is for the gymnast to land so that the reaction forces evoked act eccentrically. These eccentric forces provide a rotating effect of such magnitude and direction as to reduce the angular velocity to zero. Their translatory effect similarly reduces the linear motion of the center of gravity to zero. If the gymnast wishes to move straight into another stunt, he (or she) tries to evoke a reaction consistent with the needs of this stunt. If these include a continuing rotation in the same direction (as in, say, a flip-flop followed by a back somersault), the gymnast endeavors to obtain a reaction that, rather than canceling the rotation, at least permits some of it to be retained, and perhaps even enhances it. On the other hand, if the gymnast wants to follow with a movement involving a rotation in the opposite direction (and this, it might be said, is much less likely), he (or she) tries to more than cancel the existing rotation and thus acquire some angular momentum in the desired direction.

Another important consideration is the distance over which the body moves while being brought to rest or while having its motion redirected. Whichever of these two is involved, a certain amount of work is done on the body, and the magnitude of the forces that act on it and that it must be able to withstand depends on the distance involved (work-energy relationship). In gymnastics, the need to reduce the magnitude of the force by increasing the distance is recognized, and all landings are accompanied by some flexion at the joints supporting the body—for example, the hip, knee, and ankle joints, for landings on the feet. Good form in floor exercises requires that the distance involved be kept within fairly narrow limits, however, and anything approaching maximum flexion at the joints involved renders the gymnast liable to be penalized.

McNitt-Gray[1] studied the effect that variations in the vertical velocity of impact had on the landing techniques of skilled male gymnasts and found that, as the velocity increased, the gymnasts progressively increased the flexion of their hip and knee joints during the landing. The maximum dorsi-flexion of the ankle was essentially the same for all velocities, suggesting that the limit of the range of motion in this direction may have been reached at even the lowest velocity. The changes in joint flexion from the lowest to the highest impact velocity were relatively small—the mean values were 32° (hip), 22.4° (knee), and -0.5° (ankle).

The basic concepts involved in rolling movements (forward and backward rolls, cartwheels, etc.) are exactly the same as those just described in connection with the springs and the other tumbling movements, except that here the gymnast does not leave the ground and is therefore not concerned with those factors that create lift.

For held or static positions, the gymnast endeavors to assume as stable an equilibrium position as is possible and consistent with aesthetic and technical demands. The gymnast thus seeks to have

- the gravity line passing through the midpoint of the base—or, to express it another way, to have the distance from the gravity line to the limits of the base as large as possible; and
- the center of gravity as low as possible.

In practice, however, it is only rarely that the requirements of the position permit the gymnast to exercise any substantial control over stability, except via the first of these.

TECHNIQUES
Front Scale,*
Standing Scale Frontways (F.I.G.),
Front Single Leg Lever,
Arabesque

This held position, like most others, can be moved into in a number of different ways. For the purpose of this analysis it is assumed that the gymnast moves into it in what is probably the simplest possible manner—from an erect standing position. From this position, the gymnast first shifts the center of gravity slightly to one side so that it is directly over the midpoint of the base provided by what will be the supporting leg. The gymnast then lowers the head and trunk forward, raises the arms, and—keeping both legs straight—simultaneously raises the free (or nonsupporting) leg behind.

In executing these movements the gymnast's task is to assume the desired final position without moving the gravity line relative to the base or, in other words, to keep the body as stable as possible, consistent with the requirements of the position. However, because the movement of the free leg does not tend to shift the center of gravity backward as far as it tends to be moved forward by the movement of the upper body, these actions have the effect of shifting the gravity line away from its central position. To prevent this, the gymnast moves the hips backward slightly as the upper body is lowered and the free leg is raised. This action serves to reduce the forward shift of the center of gravity due to the upper body, add to the backward shift due to the free leg, and add still farther to the backward shift by moving the supporting leg in that direction. The net result is that the gymnast's center of gravity retains its position directly over the midpoint of the base (Fig. 12-1).

Headstand

To perform a headstand from a crouch position, the gymnast places both hands on the floor about shoulder width apart and with the fingers comfortably spread. The gymnast then places the forehead in position well forward of a line joining the hands—it is generally considered that lines joining the three "points" of contact, head and hands, should form an approximately equal-sided triangle. Then, having ensured that the area of

---

* The terms used here to describe the various gymnastic positions and movements are those believed to be most widely used in the United States. However, since gymnastics terminology is anything but standardized, a number of synonymous terms are also listed. In each case where the first term given is different from that of the International Gymnastics Federation (F.I.G.), the term used by that body is indicated.

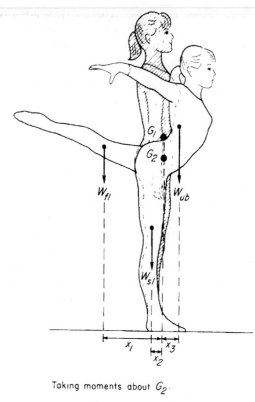

Taking moments about G_2.

$$(W_{fl} \cdot x_1) + (W_{sl} \cdot x_2) = (W_{ub} \cdot x_3)$$

where W_{fl} = weight of free leg

W_{sl} = weight of supporting leg

W_{ub} = weight of upper body

Figure 12-1.
Front scale.

the base will be as large as is practicable (by spreading the fingers and by putting the head well forward of the hands), the gymnast pushes off both feet and moves the hips upward and forward over the base. Having thus reached an angled headstand position (hips high, legs straight, and feet low), all that remains is for the gymnast to rotate the legs about an axis through the hip joints until they reach the vertical. In the course of this final upward motion of the legs, the gymnast's upper body rotates in the opposite direction thereby ensuring that the gymnast's center of gravity is kept over the midpoint of the base—in this case, the centroid of the triangle formed by the "points" of support.

To overcome any tendency of the center of gravity to move away from this position of maximum stability, the gymnast applies additional forces to the floor via the hands and head. If the center of gravity tends to move toward the forward limit of the base, the gymnast contracts the muscles that flex the neck and this increases the force that the head exerts against the floor. The resulting increase in the eccentric force, which the floor exerts in reaction to this, tends to overcome the body's tendency to rotate forward. Movement of the gymnast's center of gravity toward the backward limit of the base is similarly countered by contracting the wrist flexor muscles and increasing the force exerted by the hands against the floor.

Handstand

Although very similar in many respects, the handstand is considerably more difficult than the headstand because the higher center of gravity and the smaller base that the gymnast has in this position make it inherently less stable.

From a standing position, the gymnast steps forward, places the hands on the floor shoulder-width apart and with fingers spread, and then swings the rear leg upward and backward. As this leg approaches the limit of its swing, the forward leg is extended at the hip, knee, and ankle joints thereby exerting a force downward and backward against the floor. The reaction to this force has a relatively large moment about a horizontal axis through the gymnast's wrists and causes the body to rotate about that axis in the desired direction.

Once the gymnast's feet leave the floor, the body weight, acting through the center of gravity at some distance from the axis of rotation, serves to reduce the angular momentum acquired earlier. Recognizing that this will inevitably happen, the gymnast tries to acquire just as much angular momentum as the weight can effectively cancel by the time the body arrives in a position vertically above the hands. If the gymnast pushes off too hard and acquires more angular momentum than the weight can effectively overcome, he (or she) risks overbalancing because the body is moving too fast as it reaches the vertical position. Similarly, too little angular momentum reduces the chances of getting the body to the vertical.

Fortunately, the situation does not require quite the degree of precision that it might seem, for the gymnast can make adjustments that help achieve the desired equilibrium position despite *small* errors in the amount of angular momentum imparted to the body at the outset. If too much angular momentum has been acquired, the gymnast can contract the wrist flexors, increase the pressure exerted against the floor by the fingers, and thus increase the moment of the reaction opposing the angular motion. If too little angular momentum has been acquired, the gymnast can increase the angular velocity of the body by bending the arms or legs or by arching the back slightly (that is, by decreasing the moment of inertia). It should be pointed out here that while each of these latter adjustments may allow the gymnast to "save" the situation, they are all regarded as bad form in gymnastics and could incur some penalty in a competitive situation.

Once in a balance position, the gymnast works to maintain this in much the same way as in a headstand. To prevent overbalancing forward, the gymnast contracts the wrist flexors and increases the pressure exerted against the floor by the fingers; to prevent overbalancing in the opposite

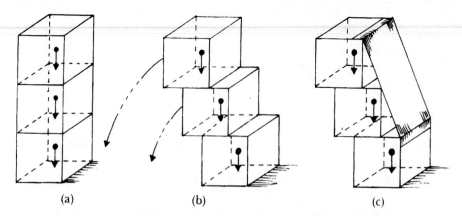

(a)   (b)   (c)

Figure 12-2. The resultant weight of the top two blocks in (a) falls within the limits of the base provided by the third block, and the structure is in equilibrium. In (b), although the line of gravity of each of the top two blocks passes within the limits of the base provided by the block below, the line of action of their resultant weight is such as to cause the structure to topple. If a strap is attached to the blocks as shown in (c), the forces exerted by the strap serve to maintain the structure in equilibrium.

direction, the gymnast increases the pressure exerted by the heels of the hands by contracting the wrist extensor muscles.

The gymnast's body should be in a straight rather than arched handstand position. For, apart from aesthetic considerations, it requires less effort on the part of the gymnast to maintain such a position. Consider the simple wooden blocks in Fig. 12-2. In (a), each of the two top blocks rests squarely upon the one below it and no forces other than their weights (and the reactions they elicit) are necessary to maintain them in position. In (b), the addition of the third block causes the superstructure to topple because, although the line of gravity of each block passes within the limits of its base, the resultant weight of the top two blocks falls outside the base supplied by the bottom one. These three blocks can be maintained in equilibrium, however, by the addition of an external force. If a strap or tape is fastened to them along the side indicated (Fig. 12-2[c]), the forces it exerts are sufficient to keep the system in equilibrium. Put in very simple terms, this is the essential difference between the straight and arched handstands. In the straight handstand, each "block" (or body part) rests upon the one below and the effort required of the gymnast to maintain this position is relatively small (Fig. 12-3[a]). In an arched handstand, the gymnast's muscles and ligaments must be additionally active to "tie" the precariously balanced body parts together (Fig. 12-3[b]). In short, it requires more effort to maintain such a position.

Forward Roll, Roll Forward (F.I.G.), Front Roll

The forward roll (Fig. 12-4) is one of the most basic of gymnastic movements and, as such, is one of the first stunts attempted by most beginning gymnasts.

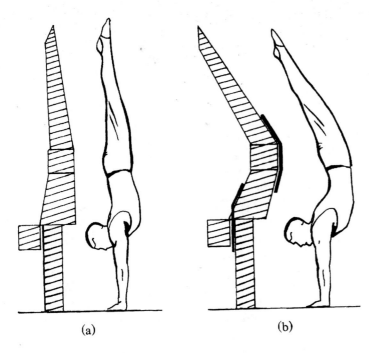

Figure 12-3.
Straight and arched handstands.

(a)   (b)

Possibly the most interesting thing about the biomechanics of the forward roll is the fundamental difference that seems to exist between the way in which beginners are often taught this movement and the way in which advanced gymnasts perform it. The beginner is commonly exhorted to "tuck up tight" or to "roll up into a ball" once the feet have left the floor. The rolling rotation is thus mainly controlled by the forces that are exerted while the feet are on the floor and only a very little by subsequent adjustments of body position (and thus, of course, of the moment of inertia). In this respect, this type of forward roll is very like those springs and tumbling movements in which the gymnast becomes a projectile—once the feet leave

Figure 12-4.
Forward roll.

the floor, the gymnast's control over the angular motion is relatively limited. The advanced gymnast (Fig. 12-4), on the other hand, initiates the roll and then, with the legs straight and the back only slightly rounded, controls the rotation with the legs. In this process, the gymnast extends the legs, reaches high with the feet, and brings them down and forward relatively fast. The angular motion of the legs is then slowed by the contraction of the hip flexor muscles—normally when the heels are about 60-90 cm from the floor—and, in reaction, the upper body is accelerated to bring it upward and over the feet. The additional angular momentum generated in this way supplements that which the body possesses as a result of forces exerted before the gymnast's feet left the floor.

Whichever of the two techniques of controlling the roll is used (and the latter would certainly appear to have the greater merit), the rolls are initiated in basically the same manner (see the first two positions, Fig. 12-4). From a position in which both feet are on the floor, the gymnast extends the legs and evokes a reaction from the floor that imparts angular momentum to the body. The gymnast then places the hands on the floor or mat (if they are not already there), bends the arms, tucks the head, and lowers the shoulders to the floor to initiate the rolling action.

The completion of the roll is also basically the same with both techniques. The advanced gymnast flexes at the hips and knees, thereby bringing the heels close to the buttocks and adopting a position similar to that used by the beginner. When the feet make contact with the floor and the buttocks start to lift off it, the moment of the weight tends to reduce the angular momentum (see also, kicking up into a handstand in previous section). If the gymnast is in any danger of having insufficient angular momentum to carry forward over the feet, he (or she) stays as tightly tucked as possible, thereby reducing the moment of inertia, increasing the angular velocity, and improving the chances of completing the movement satisfactorily.

Backward Roll, Roll Backward (F.I.G.)

Although most beginning gymnasts find it a little harder to learn, a backward roll (Fig. 12-5) is, in essence, merely the reverse of a forward roll. Starting from a crouch position, the gymnast pushes off so that the line of gravity passes outside the backward limit of the base. This movement, which results in backward angular momentum being imparted to the body, initiates the backward roll. In the middle part of the roll, the gymnast can use the same two alternatives described in conjunction with the forward roll—adopt a tightly tucked position and roll "like a ball" or roll in a more open position. If the gymnast chooses to do the latter, the parts played by the legs and upper body are the reverse of those they have in the forward roll, for when the gymnast's buttocks reach the floor, the upper body is thrust backward. When this backward angular motion of the upper body is slowed, the legs are accelerated and lifted up and over the head. Finally, by ensuring that the body has a small moment of inertia (that is, is piked if the

Figure 12-5.
Backward roll.

legs are straight or tightly tucked if they are not), the gymnast speeds the passage of the center of gravity over the hands. Once the center of gravity has passed beyond the hands, the gymnast extends the arms and lifts the head to arrive in the required finishing position.

The cartwheel (Fig. 12-6) is another elementary movement, generally taught fairly early in any sequence of gymnastic instruction. From a standing position with arms stretched upward and body facing the direction of travel, the gymnast takes a step forward and shifts the weight forward over the front foot. The gymnast then rotates the body sideways, swings the rear leg upward, and lowers the trunk until the hand on the same side as the front foot has been brought to floor level. Then, with this hand turned and placed on the floor, the gymnast pushes off strongly with the front foot. The reaction to this push substantially increases the angular momentum of the body and assists in lifting it into and beyond the vertical side-handstand

Cartwheel

Figure 12-6.
Cartwheel.

position. During the descent from this position, the gymnast supplements the angular momentum already developed by pushing against the ground with each hand as it passes below and behind the center of gravity. The movement is completed with the gymnast in a side-facing astride position.

Roundoff, Arab Spring

A roundoff is a cartwheel in which the gymnast brings both legs together in the side-handstand position and then, with the moment of inertia reduced to a near-minimum, executes a quarter turn about the long axis of the body before snapping the legs down toward the floor. The quarter turn made as the hands are placed on the floor together with the quarter turn executed as the feet pass overhead result in a landing facing in the direction from which the gymnast came. And herein lies the importance of this movement—it is a simple and yet effective way for the gymnast to change from forward-rotating to backward-rotating movements while moving in one direction along a straight line.

Neckspring, Neck Kip (F.I.G.), Backspring, Mat Kip, Snap Up

The neckspring is one of a whole family of gymnastic movements known as *kips* or *upstarts*. These movements are used to lift the gymnast's body and to rotate it forward from a horizontal position to a vertical (or near-vertical) one. To execute a neckspring, the gymnast moves into a back-lying position, with legs straight and raised overhead so that the feet point backwards. The body weight is supported on the shoulders, with palms placed on the floor behind them. From this position the gymnast whips the legs strongly in a forward and upward direction. Shortly after the legs have passed beyond the vertical position, their angular motion is abruptly decelerated by the contraction of the hip flexor muscles. The reaction to the forces exerted on the thighs by these muscles causes the upper body to be lifted and rotated in a forward and upward direction. As the gymnast's upper body is thus lifted from the floor, the neck and arms are forcefully extended to drive the body forward and upward into the air. If the reaction of the floor to these forces passes behind the center of gravity, it will not only lift the gymnast forward and upward but will also tend to increase his (or her) forward angular momentum at the same time. Once in the air, the gymnast maintains an arched-body position that keeps the moment of inertia about the transverse axis through the center of gravity as small as possible, without violating the tenets of good form. Then, when the feet touch the floor and if sufficient lift and angular momentum have been acquired at the instant of takeoff, the body rotates upward and over the feet into an erect standing position.

The angle of the legs to the horizontal at the moment their angular motion is arrested has been shown by Spencer[2] to be a critical factor in determining success in performing a neckspring. In successful trials he found that the mean angle of "leg thrust" was 52° to the horizontal and that this was significantly different from the mean angle of 64° for unsuccessful trials (that is, those in which the gymnast was unable to complete the movement by coming forward to a position "on or beyond a balance on the feet"). Thus it would appear that those who fail to complete this movement successfully tend to stop (or slow) the angular motion of their legs prematurely.

The fairly common practice of teaching the whipping action of the legs—by having the gymnast place the palms of the hands on the thighs to push them through the desired movement—is deserving of comment. To perform a neckspring a gymnast needs an appropriate blending of lift and angular momentum. If one is sacrificed to improve the other, the prospects of achieving this appropriate blending are likely to be reduced. In the present instance, the pushing of the palms against the thighs may lead to an increase in the angular momentum acquired by the legs. However, because this means that the muscles of the neck must now supply virtually all the force to project the gymnast forward and upward, this gain in angular momentum is obtained only at the expense of a marked decrease in lift. As a result, necksprings performed in this way almost invariably fail to carry the gymnast forward over the feet unless a tucked position is assumed during the latter stages of the flight. In effect, therefore, the gymnast merely exchanges one problem for another.

Handspring, Handspring Forward (F.I.G.)

Following a short run and a hop, which brings him (or her) into the appropriate position, the gymnast performs a handspring by rotating through a handstand into the air and over to land in a standing position. The hopping movement that leads into the handspring is made with the body inclined forward and the nonhopping leg extended behind. Then, when the hopping foot lands slightly behind the gymnast's center of gravity, the body is in a position to enable it to rotate forward without delay. As the body begins this forward rotation, the gymnast brings the nonhopping foot forward and places it on the floor in front of the other one. A simultaneous lowering of the arms and trunk, together with a thrust from the rear leg, moves the center of gravity forward, over, and beyond the front foot. The angular momentum that has already developed is added to by the strong upward swing of the rear leg and by the moment of the weight about a horizontal axis through the ankle of the front leg. As the gymnast reaches forward and places the hands on the floor, a forceful extension of the front leg substantially increases the angular momentum of the body and carries it upward toward the handstand position. Assuming that the gymnast has now acquired all the angular momentum needed, the next task is to develop the necessary lift to project him (or her) upward into the flight phase of the handspring. To do this, the gymnast contracts the appropriate muscles of the arms and shoulders and thrusts forcefully downward against the floor, as the center of gravity passes forward and over the hands. (A study[3] of the muscular action of a skilled performer has verified that a number of muscles that produce this kind of effect are particularly active at this time.) The factors governing the final phases of the movement (that is, from the moment the gymnast leaves the floor until the completion of the hand-spring) are identical to those outlined relative to the neckspring.

Forward Somersault, Salto Forward (F.I.G.)

The forward somersault, a tightly tucked forward roll performed while the gymnast is in the air, is normally preceded by a short run and a hurdle step (that is, a low jump to bring both feet together ready for takeoff). When the feet contact the floor at the end of this hurdle step, the gymnast cushions the shock of their landing by bending slightly at hip, knee, and ankle joints. This action also places these joints in positions from which, moments later, they can be extended to drive the body upward into the air. The reaction to this extension of the legs acts in an upward and backward direction and passes behind the gymnast's center of gravity. Thus, the reaction accounts not only for the lift that the gymnast obtains but also for the greater proportion of the subsequent angular momentum. The latter may be added to by a forward and downward movement of the arms from a position overhead or by an upward and backward swing of the elbows from a position in front of the body. Once off the floor, the gymnast quickly moves into a tucked position, thereby decreasing the moment of inertia and speeding the rotation. Then, toward the end of the flight (and in accord with the visual cues obtained by looking down in front of the body for the floor), the gymnast comes out of the tuck, slows the rotation, and prepares to land in an erect standing position.

Knight, Wilson, and Hay[4] and Nissinen[5] have conducted biomechanical analyses of the running front somersault executed with an upward and backward swing of the arms—the so-called Russian front somersault. Knight and his co-workers analyzed the performances of six male college gymnasts and concluded that, with this limited sample, high point scores were obtained when the somersaults had the following characteristics:

- A large horizontal displacement of the center of gravity during the preflight (or hurdle) phase.
- A touchdown position (following the preflight phase) in which the trunk was near-vertical, the upper arms were beside or behind the trunk, and the ankles were slightly plantar-flexed.
- A low-point position (that is, the position where the center of gravity has reached its lowest point) in which the upper arms were behind the trunk, the knees were minimally flexed, and the lower legs were slightly forward of the vertical.
- A takeoff position in which the upper arms were up to 60–70 degrees behind the trunk.
- A high flight path.
- A landing with the center of gravity high above the floor at the instant of touchdown.

Nissinen analyzed the performance of ten highly skilled gymnasts, all but one of whom used "the reverse arm lift or 'Russian' technique." He concluded:

- In the running forward somersault, although the hurdle step should be low and fast, there must be sufficient time for the gymnast to achieve an optimal position with the trunk nearly vertical and the legs together before the support phase.
- Although the braking component of the horizontal ground reaction force accounts for the majority of the angular impulse in the direction of the forward somersault, the gymnast's line of gravity should pass in front of the point of application of the ground reaction force before take-off. This permits the vertical ground reaction component to contribute positively to the angular momentum needed for the somersault.
- The reverse lift technique is superior to the front lift because it increases the vertical ground reaction force and provides local angular momentum in the direction of the somersault.[6]

Basically a backward handspring from a two-footed takeoff, a flip-flop can be performed either from a standing position or following a roundoff.

For a standing flip-flop, the gymnast adopts an erect position with the arms at the sides (or extended behind) and the feet slightly apart. Then, with the trunk still kept fairly erect, the gymnast bends at hip and knee joints and lowers the buttocks downward and backward (Fig. 12-7[a] to [b]). This places the center of gravity beyond the backward limit of the base. With the body thus beginning to rotate backward, the gymnast swings the arms vigorously in a downward, forward, and upward direction (Fig. 12-7[a] to [f]) and drives hard against the floor by extending first the hip, and then the knee and ankle joints (Fig. 12-7[d] to [g]). The reaction to the swing of the arms and to the drive of the legs projects the gymnast upward and backward into the air and, since its line of action passes behind the center of gravity (relative to the direction in which the body is moving), imparts the required backward angular momentum. Once off the ground, the gymnast maintains the body in as straight a position as possible consistent with its angular momentum and the length of time it will be in the air. In this respect, a markedly arched back is generally regarded as an indication that the takeoff was deficient and that as a result the gymnast is having to compensate (by decreasing the moment of inertia) to successfully complete the movement. When the hands reach the floor, the gymnast's angular momentum should be sufficiently large to allow the body to pass through a handstand position and (aided by the same kind of upthrust used in a handspring) continue into the air to an erect standing position. If the body does not have sufficient angular momentum at this time, the gymnast will almost instinctively bend the arms and legs (decreasing the moment of inertia about an axis through the wrists) in an attempt to rotate safely over the hands to land on the feet. Since this is an unattractive way to complete the movement, such last-minute adjustments can incur penalties in competition.

In a roundoff flip-flop, the gymnast already possesses a certain amount of backward angular momentum when the feet land at the end of the

Flip-Flop, Handspring Backward (F.I.G.), Flic-Flac, Back Handspring, Backflip, Flip-Flap

(a)   (b)   (c)   (d)   (e)

(f)   (g)   (h)

Figure 12-7. Flip-flop. The ground reaction forces exerted on the gymnast are indicated by the superimposed vectors. (Based on data in Payne, A. H., and Barker, P. [1976]. Comparison of the take-off forces in the flic-flac and the back somersault in gymnastics. In P V. Komi [Ed]., *Biomechanics V-B* [pp. 314–21]. Baltimore: University Park Press. Photographs courtesy of Howard Payne.)

roundoff and the need for angular momentum to be generated during the takeoff is generally not so great as it is for a standing flip-flop. As a consequence, a gymnast normally uses a much less vigorous and extensive arm swing in a roundoff flip-flop than in a standing one.

Backward Somersault, Salto Backward (F.I.G.)

This movement requires actions at takeoff that are somewhat similar to those required for a flip-flop and actions in the air that are akin to those for a forward somersault.

The actions at takeoff in a well-executed standing backward somersault and the ground-reaction forces associated with them are shown in Fig. 12-8.

Aside from the obvious difference in direction, the in-the-air actions required for a backward somersault differ from those used in a forward somersault in one major respect, the position of the head during the flight. Because of its position relative to the rest of the body, the gymnast performing a backward somersault can see the floor much earlier in the flight than when performing a forward somersault. (In the latter, the body obscures the view of the floor until relatively late in the flight). As a direct result of this difference between the two movements, it is much easier for the gymnast to achieve the correct timing of the movements in preparation for landing from a backward somersault than from a forward one.

Figure 12-8. Backward somersault. The ground reaction forces exerted on the gymnast are indicated by the superimposed vectors. (Based on data in Payne, A. H., and Barker, P. [1976]. Comparison of the take-off forces in the flic flac and the back somersault in gymnastics. In P. V. Komi [Ed.], *Biomechanics V-B* [pp. 314–21]. Baltimore: University Park Press. Photographs courtesy of Howard Payne.)

Some confusion exists concerning the role of the head in acquiring the backward angular momentum required to complete the somersault. Some coaches tell the gymnast to drive vertically upward at takeoff and then, on reaching the peak of the flight, to throw the head back to start the backward somersaulting action. While this advice often produces the desired results, it is quite incorrect from a mechanical standpoint. If the gymnast was projected vertically into the air with zero angular momentum (as implied in such instructions), the action of throwing the head back would produce a contrary reaction in the rest of the body. In other words, the rest of the body would start a forward somersaulting motion—albeit a very small one, considering the moments of inertia of the bodies involved.

The reasons why this advice often produces the required results are not difficult to find. First, if the head is kept in an erect position throughout the takeoff the gymnast is likely to obtain a greater vertical velocity than if it is allowed to start dropping back in anticipation of the somersault to follow. This greater vertical velocity at takeoff ensures that the gymnast has correspondingly more time in the air and thus more time to complete the desired rotation. Second, the sharp throwing-back of the head at the peak of the flight coincides with a quick tucking action in which the knees are brought to the chest and the hands are brought down to meet them. These actions simultaneously decrease the gymnast's moment of inertia and increase the angular velocity, relative to the transverse axis through the center of gravity. Since the throwing-back of the head and the sharp increase in the body's angular velocity occur at the same time, it has generally been assumed that the former is the cause of the latter. This is incorrect. The head is thrown back so that the gymnast can see where he (or she) is going; the angular velocity increases because the moment of inertia has been decreased; and the fact that these two actions occur simultaneously has little, if any, significance. Coaches who wish to give advice that is both helpful and correct should therefore omit any reference to the head action causing or initiating the required backward rotation.

In teaching the flip-flop and the backward somersault, coaches generally give quite different instructions for the two movements—for example, "Fall backward, leaving the feet behind while reaching and looking for the floor" and "Strive for height, jumping forward and upward before throwing the head back and tucking," respectively. The differences in takeoff actions were the subject of a study by Payne and Barker.[7] In this study, four skilled gymnasts performed each of the two movements from a force-platform—a device that recorded the forces exerted against it by the feet of the gymnasts. After examining force-time records and motion-picture films for the best trials by each subject, Payne and Barker concluded that the backward lean of the body is much more pronounced in the flip-flop (about 48° to the horizontal as the feet lose contact) than in the backward somersault (70°); that the more upright body position in the somersault and the "harder drive" associated with it yield additional vertical force; and that the time of flight for the somersault is almost twice that for the flip-flop. On the basis of these several findings they suggested that "the usual instructions from the coach in teaching these movements have a sound mechanical basis."

Bruggeman[8] has reported the results of a series of studies in which the techniques used in performing a roundoff or a flic-flac followed by a back somersault were analyzed. The techniques used by the 40 male gymnasts who were the subjects of these studies had several distinguishing characteristics:

- The average duration of the flight phase of the roundoff or flic-flac immediately preceding the touchdown for the back somersault was short, lasting barely 0.1 s.
- The average horizontal velocity of the center of gravity at touchdown was 4 m/s; and the average vertical velocity at the same instant was -0.4 m/s.
- The subjects had a large amount of backward angular momentum about their transverse axes at the instant of touchdown (the average value was 128 kg m^2/s); and lost more than 50 percent of this during the takeoff for the back somersault (the average value at the instant of takeoff was 56 kg m^2/s).
- The legs and trunk were responsible for the majority of the impulse exerted against the ground during the takeoff.
- At touchdown, when the extensor muscles of the legs were contracting eccentrically, the arms were accelerated to increase the load placed on the legs; during the subsequent "takeoff drive," when the extensors were contracting concentrically, the arms were decelerated to decrease the load on the legs.

Bruggeman concluded that a high linear velocity and a high angular momentum at touchdown are essential to ensure that the gymnast is in an optimal position to generate the impulse needed for a good back somersault. He also noted that "The movements of the arms, so often stressed by coaches, are clearly much less important from a mechanical point of view, and the pattern of their contribution is quite different from that commonly described in standard coaching textbooks."

LONG HORSE VAULT

The long horse vault differs somewhat from the other Olympic gymnastic events in that it consists of one short-duration movement (about 1¼ s from takeoff to landing) rather than a linked series of movements executed over a comparatively extended period (for example, 50–70 s for the floor exercises).

BASIC CONSIDERATIONS

The vault, performed over a horse 1.60 m long and 1.35 m high, is judged on five basic criteria—difficulty; the flight onto and off the horse (*preflight* and *flight*, respectively); body position during the execution of the vault; and "originality and/or virtuosity."

For the purpose of analysis, it is convenient to consider a vault as being composed of seven consecutive parts or phases: (1) run-up; (2) hurdle step; (3) takeoff; (4) preflight; (5) support; (6) flight; and (7) landing.

Run-Up

The purpose of the run-up is to get the gymnast to the optimum point for the takeoff into the hurdle step, with as much horizontal velocity as is possible consistent with the movements to follow. There are, therefore, two quite distinct requirements—speed and accuracy.

With respect to the first of these, the factors to be considered are those that govern the speed of any runner, regardless of the sport involved—the stride length and the stride frequency. Any improvements in this facet of a gymnast's performance can come about only by virtue of an improvement in one or both of these factors. The gymnast must either cover a greater distance with each stride or take more strides per second. (For a more complete discussion of the factors governing speed in running, refer to Chap. 15.)

Accuracy is primarily a function of intelligent practice. The wise gymnast makes use of the same methods for standardizing the run-up as do competitors in the jumping events on track and field programs. Paramount among these is the careful measurement of the length of the run-up—a practice by no means as widespread as it should be. It might be noted by way of comparison that because of the restriction that the rules impose on the length of the gymnast's run-up ("it may not exceed 25 meters, measured from the vertical line of the near end of the horse"), it should be possible for gymnasts to strike the correct spot for their takeoff into the hurdle step with more consistency than, say, long jumpers or pole-vaulters can strike their optimum takeoff spot, for these latter customarily use run-ups about 1½ times as long as the gymnast is permitted.

Hurdle Step

The hurdle step is the transitional phase between the run-up and the takeoff. Its purpose is to enable the gymnast to adjust the body position used in the run-up to one which is appropriate for the takeoff with as little loss in speed as possible.

To execute the hurdle step, the gymnast lowers both arms during the last step before the hurdle. Then, as the center of gravity moves over the foot from which the spring will be made into the hurdle step, the arms and free leg are swung in a forward and upward direction. Coordinated with the reaction to the drive from the other leg, these movements lift the gymnast into the air and impart backward angular momentum to the body. This angular momentum rotates the body into the backward inclined position needed at the instant of landing on the board.

During the flight phase of the hurdle step, the gymnast brings both feet together and the hands down behind the body, in preparation for the landing on the board and the subsequent upward drive into the takeoff.

Takeoff

In this, the most critical phase of the vault, the gymnast's objective is to obtain the velocity and height of takeoff and the amount of angular momentum that is optimum for the vault in question. Of these three quantities, the first and last are the most important. The second, the height of the gymnast's center of gravity at the instant of takeoff, is not amenable to very pronounced change. Provided the arms are extended forward and upward and the hip, knee, and ankle joints are extended at the moment the gymnast leaves the board, there is little else that can reasonably be done to improve the performance from this standpoint.

The magnitude of a gymnast's velocity at the instant of takeoff is governed by the velocity of the run and the changes in this velocity produced during the takeoff phase. These latter generally take the form of a sharp increase in the vertical velocity and a decrease in both horizontal and resultant velocities. The following average figures obtained in an analysis of 40 male competitors performing a handspring vault in the Pan American Games,[9] are fairly typical.

TABLE 12-1 Mean Values for Male Gymnasts Performing Handspring Vaults.

	At Takeoff for Hurdle Step	At Touchdown on Board	At Takeoff from Board
Horizontal velocity (m/s)	7.5	7.5	5.2
Vertical velocity (m/s)	1.3	−1.0	3.7
Resultant velocity (m/s)	7.6	7.6	7.1
Angle of takeoff or touchdown (deg.)	10	−8	35

Takei, Y. (1989). Techniques used by elite male gymnasts performing a handspring vault at the 1987 Pan American Games. *International Journal of Sport Biomechanics.*

Of particular importance in these changes is the pronounced increase in the vertical velocity. This is brought about in part by the reaction to the force of the impact between the feet and the board and in part by the reaction of the board to the forceful extension of the gymnast's hip, knee, and ankle joints and the vigorous forward and upward swing of the arms.

While there may be a few cases in which a backward angular momentum is imparted to the body during the takeoff, for the vast majority of vaults the gymnast needs angular momentum in the opposite direction. For example, 58 of the 60 long horse vaults listed in the F.I.G. *Code of Points*[10] require the gymnast to take off with a certain amount of forward angular momentum. To acquire this forward angular momentum, the gymnast ensures that the reaction forces exerted by the board in the latter stages of the takeoff pass at some distance behind the center of gravity. To ensure that this happens, the gymnast will often flex at the hips so that the center of gravity moves forward of the line of action of the reaction force—a line approximating that of the extended legs.

Preflight

The motion of the gymnast during this phase of the vault is governed by the velocity, height, and angular momentum at the instant of takeoff and by the body position in the air. Since the tenets of good form set fairly narrow limits on what this latter should be, those factors associated with the takeoff afford the only means of effecting substantial changes in the preflight.

Support

During the support phase, the gymnast modifies the body's angular motion and acquires lift for the flight off the horse. The modifications in the angular motion are dictated by the requirements of the particular vault. If the gymnast is required to continue rotating forward once the hands leave the horse, attention is directed towards ensuring that at least some of the forward angular momentum of the preflight is retained for the flight. On the other hand, if the gymnast is required to rotate backward during the flight, attention is focused on reversing the direction of the body's angular momentum.

In the first case, where the direction of rotation is the same throughout the vault, the inertia of the gymnast's body tends to carry the center of gravity forward over the hands, once these land on the horse. This forward rotation is enhanced if the reaction from the horse passes behind the gymnast's center of gravity and reduced if it passes forward of the center of gravity. As the center of gravity passes forward, over, and beyond the hands, a similar muscular action to that used in a handspring on the floor evokes from the horse a reaction that both lifts the gymnast forward and upward into the air, and if it acts eccentrically, alters the body's forward angular momentum. The changes in angular momentum that take place while the gymnast is in contact with the horse are exemplified in the following mean values for male gymnasts performing a handspring vault[11] and a handspring vault with tucked forward somersault.[12] (These data were gathered on 40 competitors at the Pan American Games, and 51 competitors at the Olympic Games, respectively.)

In those cases where the direction of rotation must be reversed during the support phase, the gymnast contracts the extensors of the shoulder joints and thrusts against the horse via the hands. The resultant of the reaction to this backward thrust and the vertical reaction from the horse passes forward of the gymnast's center of gravity. Acting in this way, it first causes the body's angular momentum to be reduced to zero and then to be increased in the opposite direction. Just before the hands leave the horse and while the center of gravity is still some distance behind them, the gymnast thrusts down hard against the horse. As in the previous, similar case, the reaction to this thrust projects the gymnast upward and forward into the air and provides additional angular momentum.

TABLE 12-2 Mean Angular Momentum Values for Male Gymnasts Performing Handspring and Handspring-Forward Somersault Vaults

	Handspring	Handspring-Forward Somersault
Forward angular momentum in pre-flight (kg·m²/s)	95	93
Change in forward angular momentum during horse contact (kg·m²/s)	−50	−29
Forward angular momentum in flight (kg·m²/s)	45	64

Taken. Techniques used by elite male gymnasts performing a handspring vault at the 1987 Pan American Games.

Flight

This phase of the vault is very similar to the preflight phase in that the same factors of velocity, height, and angular momentum at takeoff and body position in the air govern what happens to the gymnast. The only major difference lies in the fact that many vaults involve substantial changes in the gymnast's body position during the flight, while relatively few require comparable changes during the preflight. Consequently, adjustments in the body position of the gymnast can be used to control the flight to a much greater extent than is normally possible during the preflight.

Landing

Aside from the greater velocities that are involved, and the fact that there is no question of preparing for subsequent movements, the important factors in the landing phase of a vault are exactly the same as those involved in landing in floor exercises.

**TECHNIQUES
Straddle, Long
Astride Vault,
Long Fly**

Generally the first vault that a gymnast learns to perform over the long horse, the straddle (Fig. 12-9), is one of a small group of so-called counterrotation vaults (including squat, stoop, and hecht vaults) requiring forward rotation during the preflight and backward rotation during the flight.

After rotating forward to place the hands on the horse, the gymnast pushes forcefully downward and backward, to project the body into the air and to give it the required backward rotation. As the legs begin their rotation downward, the gymnast separates (or straddles) them so that the feet pass on either side of (and, hopefully, above) the horse. Then nearing the end of the flight, the gymnast brings the legs together in preparation for the landing. Because these abducting and adducting actions of the legs are symmetrical ones, the angular action of one leg is effectively canceled

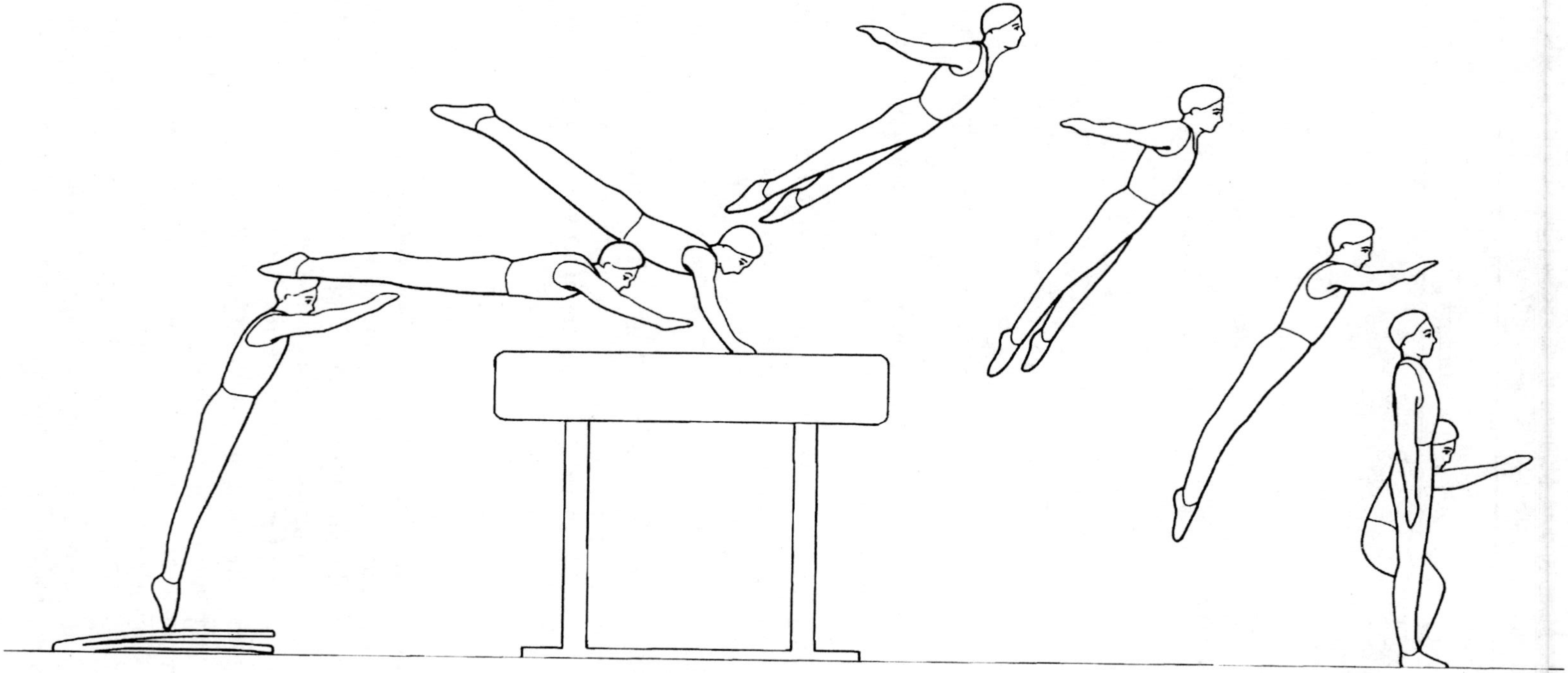

Figure 12-9. Straddle.

by the equal and opposite action of the other, and the motion of the rest of the body is unaffected.

The squat (Fig. 12-10) is very similar in many respects to the straddle. It differs mainly in that once the legs begin their rotation downward and forward after the hands touch the horse, the gymnast flexes the hip and knee joints so that the legs can pass forward and, seemingly, between the arms. Because the moment of inertia of the body about its transverse axis is less at this time than during the corresponding part of a straddle vault, the gymnast needs to impart less angular momentum to the body in a squat vault than in a straddle—that is, to obtain the same angular displacement prior to landing on the mat. Once the feet have passed forward over the end of the horse (by which time the hands have thrust downward and backward and then broken contact with the horse), the gymnast fully extends the body. The gymnast then retains this extended position until the feet have rotated underneath the body to a position somewhat forward of the center of gravity. The gymnast is then ready to land.

Squat, Through Vault

A logical development from the squat and stoop vaults, the hecht (Fig. 12-11) is the most difficult of the three. In the performance of a hecht vault, the downward and forward swing of the legs, which begins during the support phase, is executed with the whole body extended. Because the moment of inertia of the body about its transverse axis is thus much greater than in a squat (where the body is tucked) or a stoop (in which it is piked), the gymnast needs either to acquire more angular momentum or, by increasing the time of flight, to give the same amount more time to bring about the desired rotation. If the gymnast does acquire a relatively large angular momentum during the support phase, there is some danger of having the feet rotate downward into the horse and ruin the vault. In practice, therefore, the second alternative receives the greater attention. In order to increase the time of flight, the gymnast adjusts the angle of takeoff from the board so that the preflight is relatively low and the center of gravity has a greater upward velocity at the moment the hands touch the horse than is usually the case in squat and stoop vaults. This greater vertical velocity coupled with the change in vertical velocity produced by the forceful downward thrust that the gymnast then applies to the horse leads to an increase in the time of the flight as compared with that in squat or stoop vaults.

Hecht

The handspring (Fig. 12-12) is one of two basic vaults which form the foundation for most elite-level performances in gymnastic vaulting.[13] The other is the Tsukahara vault (or "Handspring sideways with ¼ turn and salto backward tucked"[14]).

Handspring, Handspring Forward (F.I.G.)

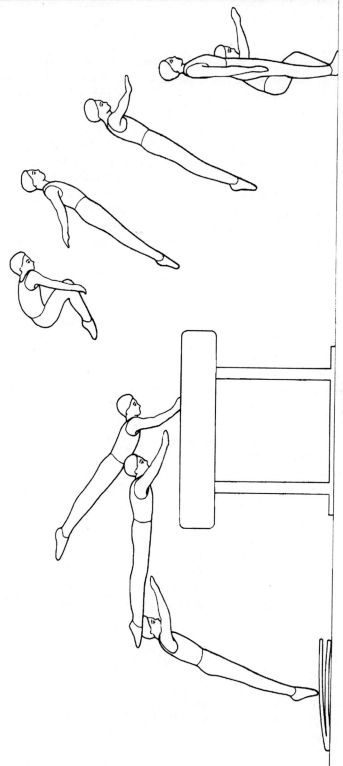

Figure 12-10. Squat.

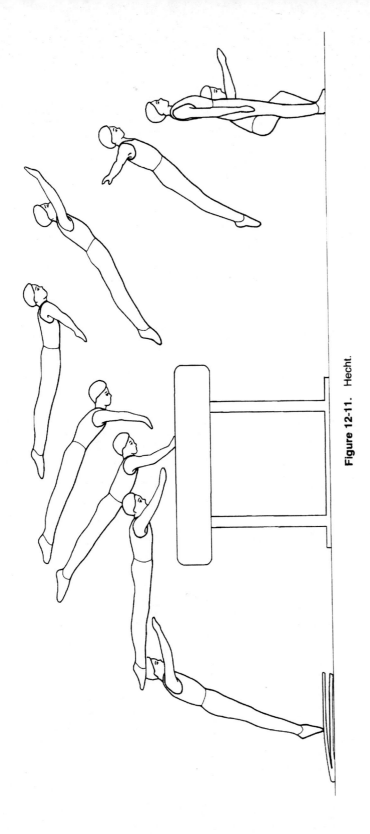

Figure 12-11. Hecht.

Figure 12-12. Handspring.

Because of its central importance in advanced vaulting. the handspring vault has been the subject of numerous biomechanical investigations. These investigations have served to identify those characteristics of vaulting technique that are associated with high levels of success in the performance of a handspring vault. For example, Takei[15] has found that the greater the gymnast's horizontal velocity at takeoff from the floor and from the board, the greater the score that he receives from the judges. He has also found that the less the angle of the gymnast's body to the horizontal (and thus the lower his center of gravity) at the instant of touchdown on the horse, the greater the score. Finally, he has shown that the greater the vertical forces exerted during the period the gymnast's hands are in contact with the horse, the greater is the change in vertical velocity that he experiences. Furthermore, the greater these measures of his performance, the greater is the vertical velocity he has at takeoff from the horse, and the greater the score.

In light of these findings, and the generally similar findings of other investigators, it is clear that the gymnast should emphasize a fast approach run; a fast, low takeoff from the board; a low preflight and a low position at touchdown on the horse; a "blocking" action in which the arms and shoulders remain firm during hand contact with the horse; and a strong upward thrust from the shoulders prior to takeoff from the horse.

Among the many variations of the handspring vault is one in which the gymnast is required to pass through a piked position during the flight off the horse—the so-called Yamashita vault. In effect, this vault requires that instead of executing the final "half somersault" (from the handstand on the horse to erect standing on the mat) in a straight body position, the gymnast does so passing into and out of a position in which the body has a much smaller moment of inertia. Because the body rotates faster in such a position than it does when fully extended, and because the required angular displacement is approximately the same, the gymnast needs less angular momentum to perform a Yamashita than to perform a handspring. While in itself this suggests that the Yamashita is less difficult than the handspring, empirical evidence indicates that the reverse is true. Apparently, the difficulties involved in correctly timing the changes in body position are of such magnitude as to more than offset the effects of differences in the amount of angular momentum required. Another variation used widely in competition at the elite level is the handspring with a tucked forward one-and-one-half somersault during the flight. Analyses of the techniques used in performing this vault have revealed that success depends very much on the same factors already mentioned with respect to the basic handspring vault.[16]

The Tsukahara (Fig. 12-13)—a vault named for the Japanese gymnast who first performed it in a major competition—consists of a takeoff from the board, a quarter turn about the longitudinal axis of the body during the preflight, a further quarter turn about the same axis, and a one-and-one-half backward somersault in the tucked position during the flight. (*Note:* A somersault performed between a takeoff from the hands and a landing on

Tsukahara, Handspring Sideways with ¼ Turn, and Salto Backward Tucked (F.I.G.)

Figure 12-13. Tsukahara.

the feet involves a rotation of approximately one-and-one-half revolutions. For reasons unknown, this is frequently referred to as a single somersault in gymnastics rather than the seemingly more logical one-and-one-half somersault.)

In a Tsukahara vault, the hands are placed on the middle one-third of the horse and, due to the cartwheeling (or roundoff) character of the preflight and hand-support phases, with one hand making contact about 0.1 s before the other.[17]

The inclination of the gymnast to the horizontal at the instant he first makes contact with the horse is much lower in the Tsukahara than it is in the handspring. Dillman, Cheetham, and Smith[18] reported average values for eight finalists in the Olympic Games of 10° and 33°, respectively.

HORIZONTAL BAR

Apart from the vaulting horse, the horizontal (or high) bar is generally the first piece of apparatus to which beginning gymnasts are introduced. It is on this that they learn the basic swinging movements that are of such importance not only on the horizontal bar, but on the rings and parallel bars as well.

BASIC CONSIDERATIONS

The rules governing competitive work on the horizontal bar state "The exercise consists without exception of elements of swing, which must be executed without interruption."[19] Thus, any considerations of the basic factors underlying horizontal bar exercises must be concerned with those factors applicable to swinging movements.

A gymnast swinging on a horizontal bar is acted upon by three forces and a couple (Fig. 12-14):

W, the body's weight acting vertically downward through the center of gravity.

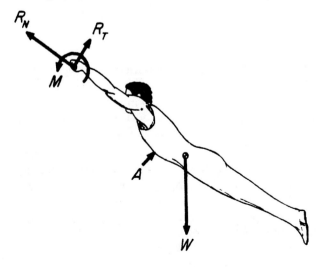

Figure 12-14.
A gymnast performing a horizontal bar exercise is acted upon by three forces (*W*, *R*, and *A*) and a couple (*M*).

R, a reaction force exerted by the bar against the hands. This force is here considered to consist of two components—a normal (or centripetal) component (R_N) which acts along a line from the center of gravity of the gymnast to the center of the bar; and a tangential component (R_T).

A, a small, and generally insignificant, air-resistance force.

M, the resultant moment of all the small frictional forces (or couples) exerted on the hands as they slide over the surface of the bar.

Weight

While the magnitude and direction of this force are constant, its line of action changes continually as the gymnast swings. These changes are reflected in the moment of the gymnast's weight about an axis through the bar. When the line of action passes through the bar (that is, the gymnast's center of gravity is directly above or below the axis), the moment is zero. Alternatively, when the line of action is displaced horizontally away from the bar as far as it can be without releasing the grip, the moment of the weight is as large as the gymnast can make it. This latter condition is obtained when the gymnast's body is fully extended in a horizontal position (for example, as in the downswing for a forward or backward giant swing). For other positions of the center of gravity, the moment of the weight is intermediate between these maximum and minimum values.

The direction of the moment of the weight also changes during the swing. When the gymnast's body is swinging downward, the moment of the weight is in the same direction as that in which he is moving. Then, as the gymnast swings beneath the bar and up the other side, the moment decreases to zero and then increases in the opposite direction. If the swing continues so that the center of gravity passes over the bar, the direction of the moment of the weight is again reversed. In the course of all this, the gymnast's weight serves to accelerate the downward motion and to retard the upward motion.

Centripetal Component

The principal function of the centripetal component is to repeatedly change the direction of the gymnast's motion so that the center of gravity moves along a curved path. The centripetal component varies in magnitude from zero (when a swing changes direction or when a component of the weight provides all the centripetal force needed) to some very large values indeed. Kunzle[20] has stated that the centripetal force is equivalent to 4 times the gymnast's body weight as he swings under the bar in a giant swing; Cureton[21] has reported obtaining a higher value (equal to 5 times the gymnast's weight) during the same movement; and Sale and Judd[22] and Nissinen[23] have reported still higher values (in the range of 4.8–5.4 and 6.5–9.2 times body weight, respectively) for similar exercises on the rings.

The tangential component of the bar reaction force is an eccentric force that serves to accelerate the body in the direction in which it acts and to angularly accelerate the body about an axis (most frequently a transverse axis) through its center of gravity. The magnitude of the tangential component is especially important during the final phases of circling and kipping movements that end with the gymnast on or above the bar.

Tangential Component

Moment

When a gymnast swings on a horizontal bar, the hands tend to rotate about it in accord with the rest of the body. This tendency is opposed by frictional forces that the bar exerts on the gymnast's hands. If the gymnast is swinging forward with what is commonly referred to as an *overgrasp* of the bar (forearms pronated, thumbs between the hands), these frictional forces are exerted along the curved length of the fingers toward the fingertips (Fig. 12-15[a]). Thus, they have the effect of elongating the fingers slightly and of wrapping them around the bar. For this reason, such a grip is generally regarded as a fairly secure one when the gymnast is swinging forward. When the direction of the swing is reversed, however, the effects are similarly reversed and the frictional forces tend to loosen or break the grip. Swinging "against the grip" in this way thus calls for considerable caution.

To overcome this problem, the gymnast adjusts the grip at carefully chosen moments during the course of the exercise. The optimum moments are those at which the bar reaction force and the gymnast's weight act so that the pressure on the hands is minimal. As a specific example, consider a gymnast who reaches the peak of a backward swing with the body horizontal. Because the angular velocity is zero at this instant, the centripetal force applied via the hands is also zero (see Eq. 6-9). In addition, since the weight is acting downward at right angles to the line of the arms, little (or none) of this force is transmitted via the hands to the bar. Thus there is a

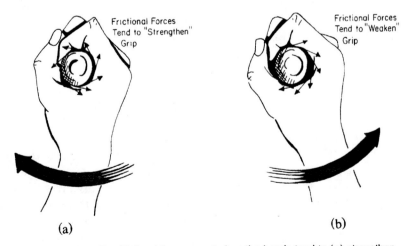

Frictional Forces Tend to "Strengthen" Grip

Frictional Forces Tend to "Weaken" Grip

(a)

(b)

Figure 12-15. The frictional forces exerted on the hands tend to (a) strengthen the grip when the gymnast swings forward; and (b) weaken it when the gymnast swings backward.

relative absence of pressure on the hands at this instant, which is, therefore, an opportune moment to adjust their position to obtain a more secure grip.

The body position just described is a desirable starting point in the discussion of another important concept in horizontal-bar exercises. At the instant mentioned (that is, the moment the peak of a backswing is reached) the gymnast's body has a certain amount of potential energy. Then, as it swings down, some of this potential energy is transformed into kinetic energy. However, because of the friction between the hands and the bar (and, to a much lesser extent, because of the air resistance), not all the potential energy that is lost is converted into kinetic form. Some of it is converted into other nonmechanical forms, of which the most important is probably the heat generated as the hands move about the bar. (Incidentally, this conversion of mechanical energy to heat energy is reflected in the high incidence of blisters—"blisters are friction burns"[24]—among horizontal-bar exponents.) The net result of this process is that the gymnast's body passes through the low point of the swing with less mechanical energy than it had at the outset. Then, as it moves upward in the forward part of the swing, the conversion from kinetic energy back to potential energy is accompanied by similar losses. As a direct consequence of these losses, the gymnast's center of gravity does not rise as far on the forward swing as it did on the preceding backward one—the vertical difference between the two positions reflecting the losses to other (nonmechanical) forms of energy.

The only way in which these energy losses can be offset—and of course, they must if the swing is not to be "damped out" entirely—is for the gymnast to do muscular work. In this way, the losses in mechanical energy due to friction and air resistance can be balanced, or more than balanced, by the gains from the conversion of chemical energy (involved in muscular contraction) to mechanical form. Therefore, as the gymnast swings forward beneath the bar, the body is arched slightly. This puts the appropriate muscles of the hips and shoulders in position so that they can be forcefully contracted to raise the legs and to press forward and slightly downward with the arms, as the gymnast starts to swing upward. These actions have two effects. First, they produce an increase in the body's potential energy by lifting it a little higher; second, they increase its kinetic energy (and its angular velocity) by decreasing the moment of inertia. Correctly executed, these movements therefore serve to maintain (or increase) the body's mechanical energy. And this is, of course, reflected in the range and speed of the swing.

These two characteristics of the swing are also influenced by the gymnast's body position during the downswing. Apart from losses due to friction and air resistance, the kinetic energy possessed by a gymnast's body as it passes beneath the bar is equal to the work done on it by gravity during the downswing.* The work done by gravity depends on the moment of the gymnast's weight and the angle through which the body is moved (that is,

---

* The angular analogue of the work-energy relationship can be expressed in algebraic form as $T\theta = \Delta(\frac{1}{2}I\omega^2 + mgh)$ where T = torque, θ = the angle through which this torque is applied, I = the moment of inertia, ω = the angular velocity, m = the mass, and h = the height of the center of gravity of the body involved.

the left-hand side of the equation in the footnote). Because the angle is usually determined by other factors (and, in particular, the height of the previous swing), the only way in which the gymnast can exert any measure of control over the kinetic energy obtained is by adjusting the body position and thereby altering the moment of the weight. Therefore, if the gymnast's body is to have a large amount of kinetic energy as it passes beneath the bar—and, in general, this is desirable—the gymnast must keep the center of gravity as far from the bar as possible during the downswing.

Air Resistance

The magnitude of this force is probably so small that its effects can be ignored.

TECHNIQUES
Underswing, Cast

An underswing (Fig. 12-16) is the usual method of initiating a large swing at the start of an exercise. From a standing position slightly behind the line of the bar, the gymnast springs forward and upward to grip the bar. Because the center of gravity is behind the bar as the gymnast takes hold of it, the body swings gently forward. Then, as the body approaches the end of the subsequent backward swing, the gymnast pulls up on the arms, brings the chest close to the bar, and simultaneously forces the body into an arched position. These adjustments in body position increase the extent of the backward swing and put the hip and trunk flexor muscles into position for the next phase of the movement. As the body starts to move forward from this position, the gymnast swings the legs forward and upward to bring them close to the hands, at the same time allowing the arms to straighten and the chest to fall away from the bar. Then, as the body approaches the forward limit of its swing, the gymnast extends the hip joints and thrusts the legs upward and outward. This action, accompanied by a forceful flexion of the shoulder joints, lifts the center of gravity up and away from the bar, giving the body a large amount of potential energy and putting it in such a position that the moment of the weight will be near-maximum as the gymnast begins the return swing.

Single Leg Upstart
(Leg Acting),
Single Leg Rise

The single leg upstart is probably the simplest way for a beginning gymnast to get on top of the bar. The movement begins with the gymnast swinging upward and forward with the body in an arched position. Then, near the forward limit of the swing, the gymnast pikes sharply at the hips and brings the legs close to the bar, with one leg passing beneath it and between the arms. This action produces a marked reduction in the moment of inertia of the gymnast's body and causes it to swing back faster than it would otherwise. As the body nears the limit of its backward swing, the gymnast presses down with the arms and extends the hips. This serves to raise the height of the center of gravity and to bring the hips in closer to the bar, thereby decreasing the moment of inertia even further. Correctly timed, these movements lead the gymnast to a straddle-sitting position atop the bar.

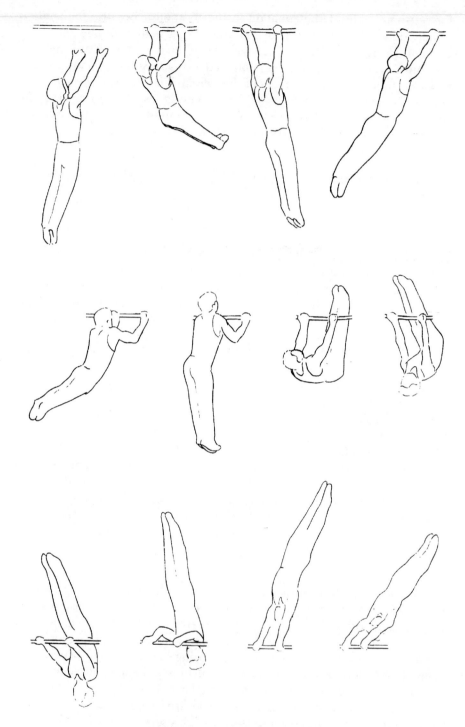

Figure 12-16. Underswing (or cast).

The forward kip (Fig. 12-17) is an important element in horizontal bar exercises at practically all levels of competition. It starts with a backward swing in which the hips are allowed to extend; reaches a position in which the hips are in a neutral (trunk and thighs aligned), or a slightly extended, position; and continues with a forward swing and a sharp piking at the hips.

Bober and colleagues[25] have suggested that the initial lengthening of the hip flexor muscles (as the hips extend during the backswing), and their subsequent shortening (as the hips flex during the forward swing) serves "to optimize the effect of [the] swinging movement." They also suggest that this sequence of lengthening and shortening the hip flexors is characteristic of skilled performance of the "kip-up." Bevan and Corser[26] suggested that "the timing of [the] piking movement is probably a crucial element in the skill." While coaching manuals frequently refer to the piking movement being executed at the start of the backward swing, Bevan and Corser found that all three of their subjects invariably began to pike much earlier than this—approximately 65–67 percent of the piking movement being completed before the end of the forward swing.

The piking movement brings the gymnast's ankles close to the bar and once again decreases the moment of inertia and increases the angular

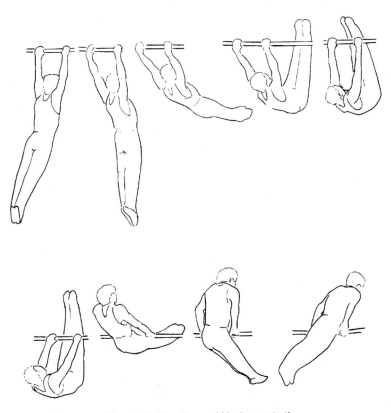

Figure 12-17. Forward kip (or upstart).

velocity. Then, as the center of gravity is about to pass under the bar in the course of the backward swing, the gymnast presses down hard with the arms and extends the hips. Correctly executed, these movements lift the center of gravity close to the bar and decrease the moment of inertia still further. The net result is that the gymnast continues to rotate upward and backward into a front support position.

Reverse Kip, Back Kip Backward (F.I.G.), Reverse or Back Upstart, Back Kip

Another in the family of kipping (or upstart) movements, the reverse kip (Fig. 12-18) starts as did the other two already discussed. When the hips are piked and the legs are brought back toward the bar, however, both feet pass between the arms, and the thighs are held in close to the body. This tightly piked position ensures that the moment of the weight is as large as it can be during the downward part of the swing and also places the hip extensors in position for a forceful contraction near the end of the backswing. At this point the gymnast drives the legs vertically upward (by extending the hips) and presses down hard with the arms. These movements lift the center of gravity above the bar, thereby putting the gymnast in a position to acquire the angular momentum necessary to complete the three-quarter backward seat circle that follows. As the body begins to swing downward from the peak of the backswing, the gymnast returns to the tightly piked position with a vigorous downward motion of the hips and legs. The angular reaction to this markedly increases the downward force acting on the bar and causes it to be deflected downward. As the body passes beneath the bar and the shoulders begin to rise, the gymnast extends at the hips, once again lifting the center of gravity and decreasing the moment of inertia. Correctly timed, this lifting action is facilitated by the recoil of the bar that thus gives up its strain energy to do work on the gymnast. With the center of gravity thus held in close to the bar, the gymnast rotates around and up to arrive in a back support position atop the bar.

During the final hip extension it appears as if the gymnast's legs remain stationary (or nearly so) while the upper body is lifted up and around into line with them. This occasionally leads coaches and observers into drawing the wrong conclusions concerning the nature of the movement. What actually happens is this: as the gymnast swings under the bar rotating in, say, a counterclockwise direction, both the trunk and the legs are rotating in that same direction. Then, as the gymnast extends at the hips, the rate at which the trunk is rotating counterclockwise increases. This additional counterclockwise action of the trunk produces a clockwise reaction of the legs. At this point these latter have two contrary tendencies: (1) to move counterclockwise due to the rotation of the whole body about the bar; and (2) to move clockwise in reaction to the trunk movement. The result is that these two effectively cancel each other and the gymnast's legs appear to remain stationary (or almost stationary).

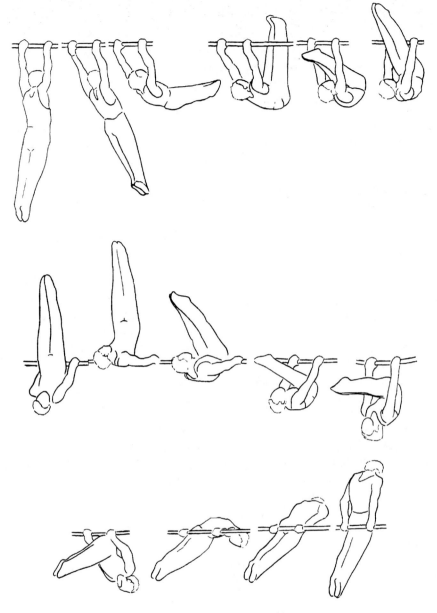

Figure 12-18. Reverse kip.

The back hip circle, one of the most elementary of all horizontal bar movements, starts with the gymnast in a front support position on top of the bar. From this position with the center of gravity vertically above the bar, the gymnast swings the legs backward and upward. This movement shifts the center of gravity in the same direction, increases the body's mechanical energy, and moves the line of action of the weight behind the bar. The moment thus created initiates the backward circling motion. As the legs

**Back Hip Circle,
Hip Circle
Backward (F.I.G.),
Backward Circle**

make their forward and downward swing, the gymnast brings the hips in close to the bar. Then, by piking at the hips as the upward movement begins, the gymnast decreases the moment of inertia sufficiently to allow a return to the front support position.

Front Hip Circle, Hip Circle Forward (F.I.G.), Forward Circle

Although basically very similar to the back hip circle, the front hip circle is somewhat more difficult to perform well. From a front support position, the gymnast presses downward and backward to move the center of gravity forward of the bar and initiate the rotation. Then rotating downward and with the head passing under the bar, the gymnast flexes forcefully at the hips, driving the head and shoulders around in the direction of the turn. This strong hip action serves to increase the angular velocity and to carry the gymnast around once again toward the front support position. Then, finally, to complete the full circle, the gymnast pushes the head and shoulders forward and over the bar while pressing downward and backward with the arms.

Back Uprise, Back Up

This movement is very commonly performed in sequence with two of the other movements analyzed here—the underswing and the back hip circle. As the gymnast swings backward under the bar following a high forward swing (or an underswing), he presses down strongly with the arms. This action increases the mechanical energy of the gymnast's body and causes it to move higher on the backswing than it would otherwise. In addition, the forward and downward movement of the arms (relative to the body) produces a forward and upward reaction of the legs. This latter slows their backward swing and keeps them some distance below the gymnast's shoulders throughout the remainder of the backswing. At the peak of the backswing the gymnast presses backward and downward with the arms. The angular reaction to this pressing movement pulls the hips into close proximity to the bar in preparation for the next movement—generally some form of backward circle. The movement of the hips into the bar is facilitated by the restrained backward swing of the legs that places the center of gravity closer to the bar than it would have been had a normal backswing been made.

Giant Swing Backward,* Backward Grand Circle

The giant swings form the basis of most advanced work on the horizontal bar. From a momentary handstand position on top of the bar, the gymnast presses with the arms to move the center of gravity backward and away from the bar. This movement is accompanied by a conscious stretching of

---

* Gymnastics terminology is often confusing when it comes to describing the direction of a rotation. For swinging movements beneath the bar the words *forward* and *backward* have their usual meaning. Thus, in forward swinging, the front of the body precedes the back, and in backward swinging the back of the body precedes the front. For movements in which the gymnast completely circles the bar, however, these directions are reversed. Thus, in a giant swing backward, the front of the body leads the back as the gymnast rotates around the bar.

the body aimed at moving the center of gravity as far as possible from the bar. Because it ensures that the moment of the weight is as great as it can be (and, consequently, that the kinetic energy at the bottom of the swing will also be as large as possible), the gymnast maintains this fully extended position throughout the downward swing. Then, about to pass under the bar, the gymnast arches the back slightly in preparation for the movements to follow. As the upward swing begins, the gymnast flexes sharply at the hips and presses downward and forward with the arms. These movements increase the potential and kinetic energies and offset the effects of friction and air resistance that would otherwise make it impossible for the gymnast to complete the full giant swing in good form (and, in particular, with straight arms). Passing through the horizontal once again and into the fourth quadrant of the circle, the gymnast arches the back and does further work against gravity by pressing downward with the arms. This downward pressing movement is generally preceded by a shift in the grip to place the hands more nearly on top of the bar than they were before—a shift that makes it easier to press downward a moment later. Ideally this hand shift takes place at a time when the centripetal force required to maintain the angular motion is equal to the component of the gymnast's weight acting along a line joining the center of gravity to the axis. Under such circumstances, the pressure between the gymnast's hands and the bar is at a minimum, and movements of the hands around the bar are relatively easy to make. The gymnast completes the circle by rotating upward into a momentary handstand on top of the bar. If all the preceding movements have been carried out effectively, the gymnast arrives in this position with the body in a straight line.

Giant Swing Forward, Grand Circle

The basic factors influencing the performance of a forward giant swing (Fig. 12-19) are similar to those for the backward giant. From a momentary handstand position the gymnast stretches upward, tucks the head, and allows the center of gravity to fall forward of the bar. During the downswing the gymnast retains this fully extended position. Approaching the bottom of the downswing, the gymnast flexes the hips slightly and then, as the upward swing begins, reverses this action, extending the hips and pressing downward and forward against the bar. As before, this increases both potential and kinetic energies and enables the gymnast to continue upward to finish atop the bar in a handstand position.

Bauer[27] found that the muscular torques needed to first flex and then extend the hips in a giant swing forward were smaller than those needed to perform the reverse sequence of actions in a giant swing backward, and suggested that "a giant swing beginner . . . start with a giant swing forward."

Kopp and Reid[28] measured the forces and torques exerted on the bar when members of the Canadian national team performed giant swings forward and backward. The maximum forces recorded were equal to approximately 3.5 times the gymnast's weight in each case. They concluded,

Figure 12-19. Giant swing forward.

therefore, that one type of giant swing does not require more grip strength than the other. The maximum torques recorded for the giant swing forward were, on average, 1.8 times greater than those recorded for the giant swing backward. They suggested that this could have been due to the difference in grips used in the two cases—the undergrip used in a giant swing forward "results in a severe supination of the wrists and forearms . . . which may increase the friction against the bar."

To finish a forward giant with a dismount over the bar, as is frequently done, the gymnast increases the range and force of the hip extension and arm-pressing movements in the third quadrant of the circle. The additional work done in this way is reflected in the potential energy (and height) of the gymnast at the high point of the flight.

Dismounts

The final phase of a horizontal bar exercise, the dismount, can be subdivided for the purpose of analysis into three parts—(1) the release; (2) the flight; and (3) the landing. The basic factors governing performance in all three of these are the same as those already described in the preceding sections, for corresponding parts of vaulting and floor exercises.

Recommended Readings

BRUGGEMANN, G-P. (1987). *Current Research in Sports Biomechanics*. Basel, Switzerland: S. Karger, pp. 142–76 (Biomechanics in gymnastics).

CHEETMAN. P. J., SREDEN, H. I., AND MIZOGUCHI, H. (1987). The gymnast on rings—A study of forces. *Soma; Engineering for the Human Body.* 2:3–35.

KANEKO. A. (1977). *Olympic Gymnastics.* New York: Sterling Pub. Co.

Notes

1. McNitt-Gray, J. L. (1991). Kinematic and impulse characteristics of drop landings from three heights. *International Journal of Sport Biomechanics,* 7:201–24.
2. Spencer, R. R. (1963). Ballistics in the mat kip. *Research Quarterly,* 34:213–18.
3. Hebbelinck, M., and Borms, J. (1968). Cinematographic and electromyographic study of the front handspring. In J. Wartenweiler, E. Jokl, and M. Hebbelinck (Eds.), *Biomechanics: Technique of Drawings of Movement and Movement Analysis.* Basel, Switzerland: S. Karger.
4. Knight, S. A., Wilson, B. D., and Hay, J. G. (1978). Biomechanical determinants of success in performing a front somersault. *International Gymnast,* 20:54–56.
5. Nissinen, M. A. (1978). Kinematic and kinetic analysis of the hurdle and support phases of a running forward somersault. M.S. thesis, University of Washington.
6. Ibid.
7. Payne, A. H., and Barker, P. (1976). Comparison of the take-off forces in the flic flac and the back somersault in gymnastics. In P. V. Komi (Ed.), *Biomechanics V-B* (pp. 314–21). Baltimore: University Park Press.
8. Bruggeman, G.-P. (1987). Biomechanics in gymnastics. In B. Van Gheluwe and J. Atha (Eds.), *Current Research in Sports Biomechanics* (pp. 142–76). Basel, Switzerland: S. Karger.
9. Takei, Y. (1989). Techniques used by elite male gymnasts performing a handspring vault at the 1987 Pan American Games. *International Journal of Sport Biomechanics,* 5:1–25.
10. International Gymnastics Federation (F.I.G.) (1989). *Code of Points* (pp. 152–67).
11. Takei. Techniques used by elite male gymnasts performing a handspring vault at the 1987 Pan American Games.
12. Takei, Y., and Kim, E. J. (1990). Techniques used in performing the handspring and salto forward tucked vault at the 1988 Olympic Games. *International Journal of Sport Biomechanics,* 6:111–38.
13. Bruggemann. Biomechanics in gymnastics, p. 155.
14. *Code of Points,* p. 160.
15. Takei. Techniques used by elite male gymnasts performing a handspring vault at the 1987 Pan American Games, pp. 1–25.
16. Takei and Kim. Techniques used in performing the handspring and salto forward tucked vault at the 1988 Olympic Games, pp. 111–38.
17. Dillman, C. J., Cheetham, P. J., and Smith, S. L. (1985). A kinematic analysis of men's Olympic long horse vaulting. *International Journal of Sport Biomechanics,* 1:96–110.
18. Ibid., p. 108.
19. *Code of Points,* p. 217.
20. Kunzle, G. C. (1957). *Olympic Gymnastics: Horizontal Bar* (p. 142). London: James Barrie Books, Ltd.
21. Cureton, T. K. (1939). Elementary principles and techniques of cinematographic analysis. *Research Quarterly,* 10:15–17.
22. Sale, D. G., and Judd, R. L. (1974). Dynamometric instrumentation of the rings for analysis of gymnastic movements. *Medicine and Science in Sports,* 6:209–16.
23. Nissinen, M. A. (1983). Kinematic and kinetic analysis of the giant swing on the rings. In H. Matsui and K. Kobayashi (Eds.), *Biomechanics VII-B* (pp. 781–786). Champaign, Ill.: Human Kinetics Publishers.
24. Brown, J., and Childers, P. (1966). Blister prevention: An experimental method. *Research Quarterly,* 27:187.
25. Bober, T., and others (1989). Influence of eccentric-concentric muscular contraction upon the kip-up maneuver in skilled and unskilled gymnasts. *Congress Proceedings: XII International Congress of Biomechanics* (Abstract no. 366).
26. Bevan, R., and Corser, T. (1969). Biomechanical study of gymnastic movements. *The Gymnast,* March, p. 30.
27. Bauer, W. L. (1980). Mathematical modeling and optimization and their influence on sports movements: possibilities and limitations. Paper presented at International Symposium on Biomechanics of Sport, Cologne, West Germany.
28. Kopp, P. M., and Reid, J. G. (1980). A force and torque analysis of giant swings on the horizontal bar. *Canadian Journal of Applied Sport Sciences,* 2:98–102.

Developed from baseball via the indoor version of that game, softball is a comparatively young sport that, perhaps surprisingly, enjoys an even greater international following than its parent.

While the rules of the two games differ considerably, the only major difference in techniques lies in the method of pitching. Unlike baseball, where the ball is usually pitched with something between an overarm and a sidearm action, in softball the rules require that the ball must be delivered with an underarm action.

Since the other techniques used in softball have already been analyzed in the chapter on baseball (Chap. 8), the discussion in this present chapter is confined to an analysis of pitching.

BASIC CONSIDERATIONS

The basic factors governing pitching in softball are identical with those already discussed relative to pitching in baseball.

Stance. In taking the initial position on the rubber, the pitcher places the feet approximately shoulder width apart with the heel of the right shoe in contact with the front half of the rubber and the toe of the left shoe in contact with the back half.* This position of the feet provides a relatively broad base and therefore reasonable stability; it affords the opportunity to obtain the maximum distance through which to exert force on the ball; and last, but not least, it conforms with the rules.

Having carefully placed the feet in the required position, the pitcher assumes an erect stance with the center of gravity directly over the left foot. Both hands are held in front at, or slightly below, waist height with the ball concealed in the glove (Fig. 13-1[a]).

Delivery. The two main methods of delivery are:

- the *windmill* (Fig. 13-1), in which the pitcher's arm rotates through approximately 360° in a vertical or near-vertical plane before the ball is released.
- the *slingshot* (Fig. 13-2), in which the pitcher's arm is moved backward and somewhat towards first base, until it is "above the head and nearly perpendicular to the ground"[1] before being brought forward again to the point where the ball is released.

While only the former is considered in this chapter, it should be noted that many of the points made apply equally well to both methods of delivery.

The windup preceding the release of the ball begins with the pitcher moving both hands downward and forward to a position near the knees. This movement draws the shoulders forward and, aided by a slight flexing of the knees, serves to set the center of gravity moving in a forward and downward direction. Once the hands have reached the low point of their downward motion, the pitcher pushes against the rubber with the left foot and then brings the left leg forward and upward in unison with a forward and upward swing of the arms (Fig. 13-1[c]). As a result of these actions the pitcher's center of gravity moves forward of the right foot and into a position from which, moments later, a forceful extension of the right leg drives it still farther in a forward and upward direction—Fig. 13-1(d) and (e). (*Note:* The flexing of the knees during the earlier downward swing of the hands not only decreases the body's moment of inertia and therefore facilitates the passage of the center of gravity over the right foot, but also puts the right leg into a position from which it can later drive strongly downward and backward against the ground.)

During the course of these striding movements, the arms continue forward and upward until they are roughly horizontal (Fig. 13-1[c]), at which stage the right arm continues its backward rotation while the left one remains where it is and assists in maintaining the required balance. As the right arm swings overhead and begins to descend (Fig. 13-1[d] and [e]), the

---

* For the sake of simplicity it is assumed throughout this analysis that the pitcher is right-handed.

(a)   (b)

(e)   (f)

Figure 13-1. The windmill pitch. (*Note:* The subject of this photo sequence— a pitcher who represented his country in international competition on several occasions—shows two minor deviations from the "ideal" form described in the text: [1] his right foot is farther back on the pitching rubber than it needs to be, and this slightly reduces the range of his pitching action; [2] his left foot lands slightly to the right of a direction line to the plate, thereby limiting the contribution that hip rotation can make to the speed of the ball.)

(c)

(d)

(g)

(h)

(i)

Figure 13-2. The slingshot pitch.

pitcher's body turns so that the hips and trunk face sideways. This action serves two main purposes:

- It places the body in a position where the muscles responsible for hip and trunk rotation can make a contribution to the speed of the ball at release.
- It increases the distance through which the ball may be accelerated.

The stride is completed when the heel of the left foot strikes the ground some 1.5–1.8 m from the rubber and slightly to the left of the intended line of the pitch. This off-line placement of the foot permits the hips to be fully rotated to the front and thus make a maximal contribution to the speed of the ball at release. After the left heel has landed, the rest of the foot is quickly grounded and the hip, knee, and ankle joints of the left leg flex to reduce the force of the impact.

Once the left foot has been grounded, the pitcher's body rotates to the front, partly due to the eccentric ground reaction evoked and partly as a result of the internal muscular forces exerted at that time. This rotation of the body brings the right shoulder forward and causes the path followed by the ball to be "flattened out" as it approaches the point of release. (*Note:* The path followed by the ball is determined by summing the effects produced by [1] the rotation of the right arm about an axis through the right shoulder; and [2] any displacement which that axis undergoes. With respect to the latter, if the axis is moved horizontally, the path followed by the ball is flattened or elongated in a horizontal direction. Similarly, if the axis is moved vertically—as it is earlier in the pitching sequence [Fig. 13-3]—the elongation occurs in a vertical direction.)

Release. Once the point of release has been reached, the centripetal force exerted on the ball by the pitcher's hand (and which has hitherto kept the ball moving along a curved path) is removed. Then, no longer restrained in this manner, the ball flies off in the direction it was moving at the instant of release (that is, in a direction tangential to its path at the point of release).

Because the direction in which the ball is moving as it leaves the pitcher's hand largely determines the ultimate success of a pitch, the point at which the ball is released is obviously of critical importance. If it is released before it reaches the correct (or optimum) point, it is likely to be lower than intended as it passes over the plate. Similarly, if the release takes place at some point beyond the optimum, the ball is likely to be higher than intended.

The flattening of the path followed by the ball during the latter stages of the delivery affords the pitcher some room for error in the point of release. For, with such a flattened path, a point of release that deviates slightly from the optimum produces a less marked difference in the direction in which the ball is released than would be the case if the ball's path were a true circular arc. Thus, the flattening of the path followed by the ball is not only an indication that the hip and trunk rotations have been correctly executed but, because it permits some latitude in the point of release, is also of value in itself.

The height at which the ball should be released, relative to the pitcher's body, depends on a number of factors, including the speed of the ball as it

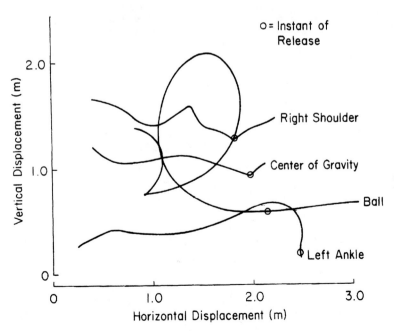

Figure 13-3.
The paths followed by the ball, the pitcher's center of gravity, right shoulder, and left ankle during the execution of a windmill pitch. [Adapted from data in East, D. J. [1969]. A cinematographical analysis of a softball pitch. Unpublished term paper, University of Otago, New Zealand. The pitcher in Fig. 13-1 was the subject in the cinematographic analysis conducted by East.)

is released and that point in the strike zone (high or low) at which it is desired to place it. In general, however, the optimum point of release lies somewhere between knee and hip height.

The speed of the ball at release has received attention from a number of investigators. Lieber[2] reported that Bill Massey "ace of the world champion Clearwater, Fla., team" attained a speed of 159 km/h (or 44.2 m/s)—a speed, incidentally, that is almost equal to the fastest ever recorded for a pitched baseball (Table 8-2). Other reported values (the 32.9 m/s and 33.2 m/s of the two male pitchers reported by Cooper and Glassow[3] and the mean of 26.8 m/s for the nine pitchers tested by Miller and Shay[4]) were probably obtained using less talented subjects than Massey and are therefore understandably somewhat lower.

Follow-through.   The follow-through after the release of the ball serves exactly the same purposes in softball as it does in baseball—namely, to reduce the speed of the various body parts (and in particular, the pitching arm) without risk of injury and without impairing the application of forces to the ball.

Once the follow-through is completed, the pitcher moves quickly into position to field the ball should it be hit in his (or her) direction. This need to move quickly into a fielding position is heightened by the fact that the pitching rubber is only 14.02 m from the plate (compared with 18.44 m in baseball) and the pitcher thus has even less time before the ball can be returned than does his (or her) baseball counterpart.

Notes

1. Kirby, R. F. (1975). Softball pitching styles. *Athletic Journal*, 55:36.
2. Lieber, L. (1961). The big hardball vs. softball duel. *This Week Magazine*, May 14.
3. Cooper, J. M., and Glassow, R. B. (1963). *Kinesiology* (p. 66). St. Louis: C. V. Mosby.
4. Miller, R. G., and Shay, C. T. (1964) Relationship of reaction time to the speed of a softball. *Research Quarterly*, 35:436.

SWIMMING

The techniques of swimming have undergone profound changes over the years. Chief among these have been the evolution of the front crawl, back crawl, and butterfly strokes and the concomitant relegation of breaststroke from its role as the premier stroke—a role it played in the early days of modern competitive swimming.

A competitive swimmer's objective is to swim the full distance of his (or her) race in the prescribed manner (that is, in accord with the rules governing starting, turning, finishing, and the execution of the stroke) and in the least time possible.

BASIC CONSIDERATIONS

The time taken from the instant the starting signal is given until a swimmer completes a race is equal to the time spent starting, plus the time spent stroking during the first length, plus the time spent turning, plus the time spent stroking during the second length, and so on:

$$t_{Total} = \underbrace{t_{Starting} + t_{Stroking} + t_{Turning}}_{(Length\ 1)} + \underbrace{t_{Stroking} \cdots}_{(Length\ 2)}$$

However, because there are obvious similarities between the stroking and turning techniques used during each lap, it is appropriate to consider the total time for the race to be simply the sum of the times spent starting, stroking, and turning:

$$t_{Total} = t_{Starting} + t_{Stroking} + t_{Turning}$$

Starting Time.   The time that a swimmer spends starting is equal to the time from the starting signal being given until the feet leave the block (the block time), *plus* the time from the feet leaving the block until first contact is made with the water (the flight time), *plus* the time from first contact with the water until the swimmer begins kicking and/or stroking (the glide time). Of these three times, the glide time has been found to be not only the longest in duration, but also the most closely related to the total starting time. In a study of the hands-between-the-feet grab starting technique, Guimaraes[1] found that the average times for three trials by each of 24 male high school swimmers were:

Block time	0.84 s
Flight time	0.35 s
Glide time	3.55 s
Total starting time	4.74 s

Furthermore, when the data for the three part times were correlated with the total starting time and the heights and weights of the subjects were held constant, it was found that the glide time was by far the most important of the three in determining the total starting time.[2]

The glide time depends on just two factors—the horizontal distance that the swimmer travels from first contact with the water (entry) until he or she begins kicking and/or stroking (the glide distance); and the swimmer's average horizontal speed over this distance (the glide speed).

Finally, the swimmer's average horizontal speed during the glide depends on his (or her) horizontal speed at the start of the glide—that is, at entry—and by changes in horizontal speed that occur during the glide. These latter, in turn, are determined by the impulses of the horizontal forces exerted by the water on the swimmer—forces which oppose the swimmer's forward motion—and by the mass of the swimmer (impulse-momentum relationship).

The relationships between the starting time and the factors that determine that time are summarized in Fig. 14-1.

Stroking Time.   The time that a swimmer spends stroking is completely determined by two factors—the distance involved and the average speed of the swimmer over that distance.

Assuming that the swimmer follows an essentially straight course, the

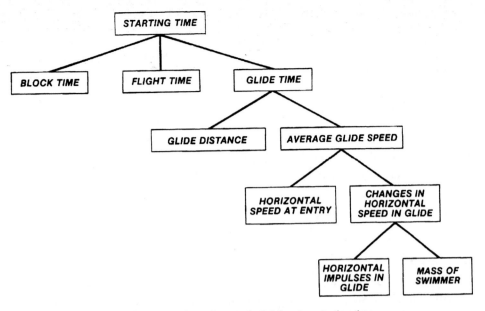

Figure 14-1. Basic factors that determine starting time.

distance involved is primarily dictated by the distance of the race. It is also influenced to some small extent by the location of the point at which the swimmer begins stroking at the start of the race, the points at which stroking ceases before the execution of the turns, and the points at which stroking resumes following the turns.

The average speed of the swimmer is equal to the product of two factors:

- The *average stroke length*—that is, the average horizontal distance traveled during the completion of one complete cycle of the swimmer's arms. Thus,

$$\text{Average stroke length, } \overline{SL} = \frac{\text{distance stroked}}{\text{number of complete arm cycles}}$$

- The *average stroke frequency*—that is, the average number of complete arm cycles executed in a given time. Thus,

$$\text{Average stroke frequency, } \overline{SF} = \frac{\text{number of complete arm cycles}}{\text{time spent stroking}}$$

(*Note:* The terms *distance per stroke* and *stroke rate* are often used by coaches in preference to the terms *stroke length* and *stroke frequency,* respectively.)

As an example, consider the butterfly swimmer who takes 10 strokes (or complete arm cycles) to cover 20 m in 12 s. The swimmer's average stroke length is

$$\overline{SL} = \frac{20 \text{ m}}{10 \text{ strokes}} = 2 \text{ m/stroke}$$

and his (or her) average stroke frequency is

$$\overline{SF} = \frac{10 \text{ strokes}}{12 \text{ s}} = 0.83 \text{ stroke/s}$$

The swimmer's average speed $\overline{S}$, the thing he (or she) is most concerned about, is equal to the product of these two factors:

$$\overline{S} = \overline{SL} \times \overline{SF}$$
$$= 2 \text{ m/stroke} \times 0.83 \text{ stroke/s}$$
$$= 1.66 \text{ m/s}$$

Because the speed at which swimmers move through the water (at least while they are stroking) is wholly dependent on their stroke length and stroke frequency, it is appropriate that the factors that determine the magnitude of each of these parameters should be considered next.

Stroke Length. The stroke length is governed by the forces exerted on the swimmer—the *propulsive forces*, which drive the swimmer forward through the water in reaction to the movements the swimmer makes, and the *resistive forces*, which the water exerts on the swimmer to oppose that motion.

Propulsive Forces. While the forces exerted on the swimmer in reaction to the movements of the arms are generally regarded as the prime source of forward propulsion, opinions differ concerning the magnitude of the contribution from the arms. Karpovich,[3] for example, determined the speeds that front crawl swimmers could develop using the arms alone, the legs alone, and the arms and legs together and concluded that good crawl swimmers derived about 70 percent of their forward speed from their arms and 30 percent from their legs. Armbruster, Allen, and Billingsley[4] accorded the arms even greater credit when they stated that "the arms provide about 85% of the total power of the sprint crawl stroke," and Counsilman[5] went still further with his statement that "the arm stroke in the crawl is the main source of propulsion and, in the case of most swimmers, the only source of propulsion."

Two studies in which swimmers were tethered to devices that recorded the forces they exerted while swimming "on the spot" shed some light on the relative contribution of the arms in strokes other than the front crawl. In the first of these, Mosterd and Jongbloed[6] found that the forces exerted by the arms and legs in the butterfly stroke were of approximately the same magnitude, while in the breaststroke "the work of the legs dominates a bit."

Magel[7] reached essentially the same conclusions: "In butterfly swimming, the propelling forces delivered by the arms and legs appear to be approximately the same. . . . The work of the legs makes a much larger contribution to the total propulsive force in this stroke [breaststroke] than in the front and back crawl, where the arms provide the major portion of the propulsive force." (*Note:* Although the extent to which the results of studies like these can be considered to apply in the case of a swimmer free to move forward in the water is unknown, it would seem likely that they provide a reasonable indication of what takes place under such conditions.)

While the importance of the arms as a source of propulsion has long been recognized, it is only over the last 20 years that the manner in which this propulsive force is obtained has become reasonably well understood. Prior to this time, it had generally been considered that the drag force exerted against the swimmer's arms, in reaction to efforts to move them directly backward, were responsible for the swimmer being propelled forward (Fig. 14-2[a]). Thus articles and texts on swimming routinely emphasized the importance of the arms being pushed horizontally backward through the greatest distance possible. However, in two classic papers published in 1971, Counsilman[8] and Brown and Counsilman[9] suggested that lift rather than drag may be the principal source of the propulsion generated by the arms.

An examination of the path followed by a swimmer's hands during one arm cycle of breaststroke provides a basis for considering the concepts involved here. In the course of such an arm cycle, the swimmer's hands move forward, outward, inward, and forward again (Fig. 14-3). They do not, as is generally supposed, move backward to any appreciable extent. (*Note:* While the hands move backward *relative to the shoulders*, the shoulders themselves are moving forward at approximately the same rate. The general impression, that the hands move backward through the water, is thus more apparent than real.) Now, if the swimmer's palms face outward and backward as the hands move outward in the pulling phase of the stroke, the resultant force exerted by the water on each hand will be in an inward and forward direction (Fig. 14-3). Further, if the hands are moving in a direction at a right angle to the direction of the swimmer's motion, the lift component of this resultant force acts in the direction in which the swimmer is moving and thus serves to propel the swimmer forward. The drag component acts at right angles to the direction in which the swimmer is moving and thus has no effect on the forward motion. During the so-called recovery phase of the stroke, the palms of the hands are directed inward and backward and the lift component of the resultant force on each hand once again acts to propel the swimmer forward. Under the circumstances described—and similar circumstances can be shown to exist to some extent in all four competitive strokes—it seems evident that lift plays a prominent role in propelling the swimmer through the water.

Since these general ideas were first put forward, several researchers

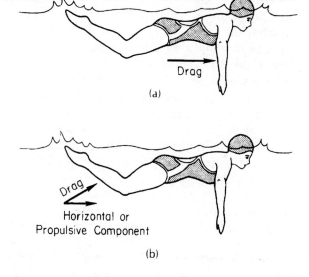

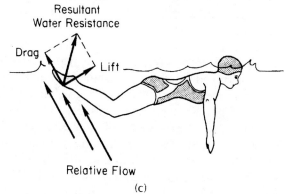

Figure 14-2.
(a) Propulsive drag due to arm action.
(b) Propulsive drag due to leg action.
(c) The relative flow of water past the foot during the downbeat of the leg in a flutter or dolphin kick. (Adapted from Kreighbaum, E., and Barthels, K. M. [1981]. *Biomechanics: A Qualitative Approach for Studying Human Movement* [p. 441]. Minneapolis: Burgess.)

have conducted studies aimed at examining the premise that lift is an important source of propulsion in swimming.[10][11][12][13][14][15][16] As a result of these and other studies, it is now well established that lift forces make an important contribution to the propulsion from the arms in all the competitive strokes, and are the major source of such propulsion in the breaststroke and butterfly stroke. In keeping with these developments, there has been a considerable shift in the emphasis that swimmers and their coaches place on the various aspects of the arm pull and, in particular, on the orientation (or "pitch") of the hand and arm relative to the direction in which these parts are moving.

Schleihauf[17] conducted a series of experiments in which plaster resin models of the human hand were immersed in an open-water channel and the lift and drag forces exerted under different flow conditions were measured. He found, among other things, that

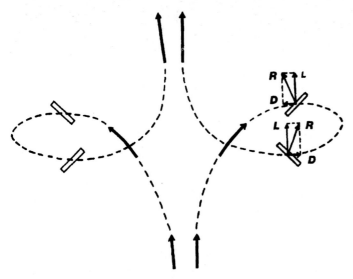

Figure 14-3.
With appropriate positioning of the hands relative to the direction in which they are moving (that is, with an appropriate angle of attack), lift may be the dominant propulsive influence.

- the coefficient of lift (and, by implication, the lift force) increased as the angle of attack increased up to about 40°, and then decreased;
- the coefficient of drag (and the drag force) increased as the angle of attack increased up to 90°;
- having the fingers together, rather than 0.64 cm or 1.27 cm apart, was "a distinct advantage . . . for lift-producing motions.";[18]
- having the fingers together or 0.32 cm apart was superior to having them 0.64 cm apart for maximizing the coefficient of drag (and the drag force);
- for situations requiring a high lift–drag ratio—as, for example, during the lateral motions of the hands in the breaststroke—a hand position with the thumb fully abducted is preferable to partially abducted thumb positions.

Wood[19] conducted a similar, but less comprehensive, series of experiments in which hand-plus-forearm models were placed in a wind tunnel and the lift and drag forces determined under different conditions. His findings concerning the coefficients of lift and drag were in general agreement with those of Schleihauf (the first two in the preceding list), although the angles of attack that yielded the maximum values for the coefficient of lift tended to be a little higher—50–60°, in the majority of cases. Finally, Thayer[20] determined the coefficient of lift and drag as a function of the angle of attack for a forearm-plus-hand model immersed in a flume. These coefficients were observed to increase steadily from minimum values at a 0° angle of attack to peak values at 45° and 75°, respectively.

There are three useful functions that the kicking actions of the legs may serve:

- They may aid in the production of propulsive forces—a function they serve in breaststroke, and probably, too, in the butterfly stroke.[21]

- They may serve to decrease the resistive forces that oppose the motion of the body through the water—a role now generally accepted as that which the kick serves in the front and back crawl.[22]
- They may serve to increase the propulsive forces and decrease the resistive forces simultaneously.

The propulsive function of the legs (where they serve such a function) has generally been accounted for in terms of drag. Thus, for example, when the swimmer in Fig. 14-2(b) thrusts her legs downward and backward as she executes the first beat of a dolphin kick, the resulting propulsive effect has been assumed to derive from the horizontal component of the drag force acting on her legs.

This view has been challenged by Kreighbaum and Barthels, who contend that

> *This assumption is the result of examining the movements of the legs in relation to the body of the swimmer rather than to the water through which the swimmer is moving. . . . If the actual resultant flow of water past the anterior surface of the moving foot and leg is examined during the downbeat, it can be seen that the flow is directed backward and upward along this surface; the backward component of flow results from the leg being towed forward by the moving body, while the upward component results from the downward motion of the foot and leg. The resultant flow direction creates a small angle of attack with the foot surface, and the conditions for generating lift force are present. The forward component of the lift force (thrust) is useful for body propulsion, while the upward component is felt as a resistance against the downward motion of the foot.[23]*

The situation described here is summarized in Fig. 14-2(c).

Although the account presented by Kreighbaum and Barthels has some appeal, its validity ultimately depends on whether the flow of the water (relative to the foot surface with which it interacts) is in the direction they have indicated. This depends, in turn, on the validity of their estimates of the relative magnitudes and the directions of the velocities of the center of gravity of the swimmer and of the feet relative to the center of gravity. Unfortunately, there is little if any research evidence available on the magnitudes and directions of these velocities. Until such evidence becomes available, the source of the propulsion generated by the legs in swimming must remain an open question.

Resistive Forces. Three types of resistive force act on a swimmer to decrease his (or her) stroke length—form drag, surface drag, and wave drag (pp. 185–191).

Form Drag. The magnitude of the resistive form drag encountered is governed by the speed at which the swimmer is traveling forward through the water and by the cross-sectional area that he (or she) presents to the "oncoming flow." Since any attempt to reduce a swimmer's form drag is aimed at increasing forward speed, any reduction gained by decreasing the forward speed clearly defeats the whole purpose of the exercise. Thus a decrease in cross-sectional area offers the most likely means by which a reduction in form drag can lead to an increase in a swimmer's forward speed. In practical terms this generally means an adjustment in the body position in the water and/or in the range of the stroking or kicking actions.

The effect that variations in body position and limb movements have on the resistance that a swimmer encounters has been studied by a number of researchers.

Counsilman[24] reported the results of a study in which a swimmer was towed in a prone position with his head held in a "normal" position with the water at hairline level, and in a high position with the water at eyebrow level. These results suggested that when the head is held in the higher position there is a significant increase in the drag. This is almost certainly attributable to an increase in the cross-sectional area that the swimmer presents to the flow—an increase due to the legs and feet dropping as the head is raised.

Alley[25] noted differences in the drag force associated with differences in the type of front crawl (or "flutter") kick used by a swimmer as he was towed through water at various speeds. When his subject was towed at speeds less than 1.3 m/s, yet greater than he could normally attain with his leg kick alone, the drag recorded was less with a "normal kick" (feet approximately 30 cm apart at maximum spread) than it was with a "short kick" (feet approximately 15 cm apart at maximum spread). In addition, the drag recorded when the subject kicked was considerably less than that recorded when his legs were idle. All of this suggests that, within the range of speeds involved, the leg kick is capable of decreasing resistance and that a "normal kick" is more effective than a "short kick" in this regard. Although the means by which the leg kick reduces resistance has not been established, it seems likely that the summed effect of the various vertical reactions to the movements of the legs and feet causes them to be raised higher in the water than they would otherwise be and that the associated reduction in cross-sectional area results in a corresponding decrease in the form drag encountered by the swimmer.

Kruchoski[26] obtained similar results in a study of the back crawl kick. He concluded that although the kick acted as a retarding force when a swimmer was towed at speeds greater than he could attain using his legs alone, the continuation of the kick resulted in less resistance being encountered than when the legs were not kicking.

Surface Drag. It has long been known that swimmers who shave their arms, legs, and trunk (and, in some cases, their heads) before major meets often perform at a higher level than they have previously. It has thus been assumed that shaving reduces the surface drag and permits the swimmer to swim faster. A number of alternative explanations have also been advanced. Counsilman, for example, has stated:

It is possible . . . that shaving the hair from the arms and legs may increase the swimmer's sensitivity to the "feel" or pressure of the water and, consequently, improve his coordination. It is more likely, however, that any improvement in performance that appears to result from shaving is either a normal improvement resulting from training or from the psychological effect that shaving might induce in the swimmer.[27]

Studies which have addressed the issue have yielded contradictory results. Clarys,[28] for example, has concluded that even when the body is in its most streamlined position, the form and wave drags it generates are so large that any surface drag that it might also generate would be negligible in comparison.

Sharp and colleagues[29] have concluded exactly the opposite. They recorded the blood lactate concentrations of four male and two female swimmers following 200-yd (183-m) swims on one day and then (after the swimmers had shaved all the hair from their "arms, legs and exposed torso") on the next day. They found that shaving substantially reduced the accumulation of blood lactate at both submaximal and maximal freestyle swimming speeds; and noted that a decrease in the blood lactate accumulation when swimming at set speeds is generally taken as evidence of (a) improved aerobic fitness, (b) improved mechanical efficiency, or (c) muscle glycogen depletion as a result of heavy training. They dismissed the first and third of these (because the decrease took place over a one-day period and their subjects were not engaged in swimming training at the time of the experiment) and concluded that the decreased lactate accumulation observed was due to a decreased physiological cost. They further noted that the decrease in blood lactate concentration with shaving was nearly as great as the decrease observed over an entire season of training; and that the average time recorded by their subjects for maximal-effort 200-yd swims improved with shaving by 6.1 s (from 2 min 21.6 s, to 2 min 15.5 s).

Given the contradictory findings of the studies by Clarys and by Sharp and colleagues, and the very substantial improvements reported in the latter, it is clear that the role of surface drag in swimming is deserving of more attention from researchers than it has so far received.

Wave Drag. The wave drag depends, among other things, on the swimmer's speed, body shape, and movements in proximity to the water surface.

The effect of the swimmer's speed on the magnitude of the wave drag has been suggested by the results of Alley[30] and Counsilman,[31] both of whom reported the formation of a pronounced bow wave as the speed at which they towed their subjects increased, and a corresponding sharp increase in the rate at which the drag increased relative to the speed.

Among those movements that are particularly effective in creating waves—and thus are particularly undesirable because of the increased drag that they produce—are large up-and-down movements of the swimmer's body. For this reason the practice of pressing vertically with the arms (downward near entry and upward near "release") should be avoided, since it serves merely to produce the kind of up-and-down motion mentioned.

Active and Passive Drag. The resistive forces to which a swimmer is exposed while stroking are often referred to as the *active drag*. This term is used to distinguish between the drag experienced when a swimmer is stroking and that experienced when a swimmer is being towed in some fixed position. The latter is referred to as the *passive drag*. Studies of the passive drag exerted on a swimmer have yielded results that are remarkably consistent. When a body is towed in a prone position, the passive drag varies approximately with the square of the velocity at which the body moves, ranging from about 30 N (at 1 m/s) to about 120 N (at 2 m/s).[32][33][34]

Studies of active drag have been confined almost exclusively to the front crawl stroke and have yielded remarkably inconsistent results. Some have yielded values for the active drag that were up to 3.1 times greater than those recorded for passive drag at the same velocity of the swimmer.[35][36][37][38][39] One has yielded values that were about the same as for passive drag.[40] And others have yielded values that were less than for passive drag.[41][42] These differences in the values for active drag are no doubt due in the main to differences in the methods used to obtain them, all of which have major limitations.

Stroke Frequency. The stroke frequency that a swimmer attains depends on the time spent in executing each of the two recognized phases of the arm stroke—the pull and the recovery. In the three strokes in which the arms are recovered out of the water, the recovery phase tends to be considerably shorter than the pull phase—presumably because of the decreased resistance encountered when the arm(s) move through air rather than water. (For example, Ringer and Adrian[43] found that the pull phase of a group of Yale Varsity swimmers averaged 0.758–0.759s [or 65–66% of the total time taken to execute one front crawl stroke] and the recovery phase, 0.391–0.400s [or 34–35%].) In the breaststroke there tends to be rather less difference between the times spent in executing each phase—however, the duration of the recovery (or inward-sculling) phase is still somewhat less than that of the pull (or pressing) phase.

The durations of the pull and recovery phases are functions of the following:

- The positions of the hand, forearm, and arm relative to an axis through the shoulder(s). If all else is equal, the less the moment of inertia of the arm, the less the time necessary to move it through a given range.
- The range of motion through which the limb moves. If all else is equal, the greater the range of motion, the greater the duration of the phase in question.
- The torque applied about the axis through the shoulder(s). Again if all else is equal, the greater the torque applied, the shorter the duration of the phase.

Thus a swimmer has at least three ways in which to modify the duration of the pull and recovery phases to obtain the optimum stroke frequency—the swimmer can modify the "shape" of the arm actions, adjust the range of these actions, or alter the muscular torques applied to produce them.

Interrelationship of Stroke Length and Stroke Frequency.

Stroke length and stroke frequency are to a very large extent interdependent. As swimmers increase their stroke length, they generally find it necessary to increase the time over which they apply forces during the pull phase of the stroke. Thus, while their stroke length increases, their stroke frequency tends to decrease. Similarly, to increase stroke frequency they generally tend to reduce the time they spend pulling, and this usually leads to a reduction in stroke length. Thus when swimmers increase one of these two factors, they must ensure that the other does not suffer a comparable (or more than comparable) decrease if they are to gain any advantage in terms of speed.

Several studies have been conducted to determine the effect that various factors have on stroke length and stroke frequency and thus on the resulting stroking speed. These may be classified according to the factors studied:

- *Stroke.* The average stroke frequencies for freestyle, butterfly, and breaststroke are very similar, and differences in stroke length determine the differences in the stroking speed attained.[44 45 46 47] For some reason, the average stroke frequency in the backstroke is considerably less, and the stroke length somewhat greater, than in the other strokes.

- *Distance of the Race.* As the distance of the race increases, the stroke length increases (except in the case of the butterfly stroke); the stroke frequency decreases; and the stroking speed decreases.[48 49 50]

- *Distance Traveled.* Except for finishing bursts in the final 1 or 2 laps of distance events, stroke length and stroking speed generally decrease throughout the course of a race. No similarly consistent pattern has been found with respect to stroke frequency. In some instances it decreases, in others it remains essentially constant, and in yet others it actually increases, as the race progresses.[51 52 53]

- *Sex.* The greater stroking speeds attained by male swimmers compared to females are primarily due to correspondingly greater stroke lengths. The stroke frequencies attained are generally very similar.[54 55 56 57]

- *Ability.* A comparison of the stroke lengths, stroke frequencies, and stroking speeds of elite swimmers with those of swimmers of slightly lesser ability generally show that the differences in stroking speed are due primarily to differences in stroke length. As a group, fast swimmers have greater stroke lengths than less-fast swimmers.[58 59 60]

- *Physique.* The stroking speeds of male freestyle swimmers has been found to be little influenced by the physique of the swimmer; however, the combination of stroke length and stroke frequency used to attain the stroking speed is apparently very much a function of the swimmer's physique.[61] The axilla cross-section area—that is, the area of the trunk exposed by a transverse section at the level of the axilla—

appears to be closely related with both the stroke length and stroke frequency. The greater this cross-sectional area, the greater the stroke length and the less the stroke frequency.[62]

- *Training.* Significant, positive relationships have been found between the average stroke lengths and stroking speeds in 200-yd (183-m) freestyle, butterfly and breaststroke events over the course of a season.[63] No significant relationships were found between the average stroke frequencies and stroking speeds.

Studies of stroke length and stroke frequency are often very confusing because the results obtained in one appear to be exactly the opposite of those obtained in another. Thus, if one notes how swimmers increase speed when moving down from 200 m to 100 m—usually by increasing stroke frequency and decreasing stroke length—one might conclude that the emphasis in training should be on increasing stroke frequency and decreasing stroke length. Then, if one examines the difference between a group of fast swimmers and a group of not-so-fast swimmers and notes that the faster swimmers have longer stroke lengths, one might conclude that the emphasis in training should be on increasing stroke length. Some exceptions aside, the truth of the matter appears to be that:

- to increase stroking speed in the short term (for example, on a given day), one should strive to increase stroke frequency; and
- to increase stroking speed in the long term (for example, over the course of a season), one should strive to increase stroke length.

Summary. The relationships between the stroking time and the factors that determine that time are summarized in Fig. 14-4.

Turning Time. The time spent executing each turn is equal to the time from the swimmer beginning to adjust his (or her) stroking actions in preparation for the turn (or in the process of initiating the turn) until first contact is made with the wall, *plus* the time from first contact to last contact with the wall, *plus* the time from last contact with the wall until the resumption of kicking and/or stroking.

The first of these three times (referred to here as the *time in*, for the sake of brevity) is determined by the distance from the wall at which the swimmer begins to adjust his (or her) stroking actions and by the swimmer's average speed over this distance—the distance in and average speed in, respectively. The *distance in* is determined primarily by the swimmer's perceptions of his (or her) approach speed and the remaining distance to the wall. The *average speed in* is determined by the swimmer's speed of approach and by the changes in that speed that occur prior to contact with the wall. (*Note:* In those cases where the swimmer makes contact with the wall without making any prior change in stroking technique, the time in, distance in, and average speed in are all equal to zero.)

The time from first contact to last contact with the wall—the *time of contact*, for short—is equal to the sum of the time of contact with the

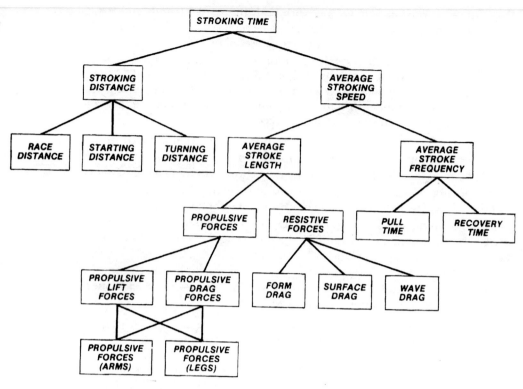

Figure 14-4. Basic factors that determine stroking time.

hand(s), the time from the loss of contact with the hand(s) to first contact with the feet, and the time of contact with the feet. Although there appears to be no research evidence on the matter, it seems likely that the time of contact with the feet is the most important of these three times. In a freestyle flip turn, the first two times are both equal to zero and the third is thus, by default, the most important. In the case of the turns used with the other three competitive strokes, the fact that the time of contact with the feet is directly involved in determining the speed at which the swimmer leaves the wall (impulse-momentum relationship) suggests that it is probably the most important. Finally, the time of contact with the feet is determined by the distance over which the swimmer's center of gravity moves during feet contact and his (or her) average speed over this distance. (*Note:* Although convenient because of its brevity, the expression *time of contact* is not completely suited to the purpose. In some cases it includes a period during which there is no contact between the swimmer and wall.)

The time from last contact with the wall until the resumption of kicking and/or stroking—the *time out*—is governed by the distance from the wall at which the swimmer decides to resume kicking and/or stroking and by the swimmer's average speed over that distance—the *distance out* and *average speed out*, respectively. The first of these depends on the swimmer's per-

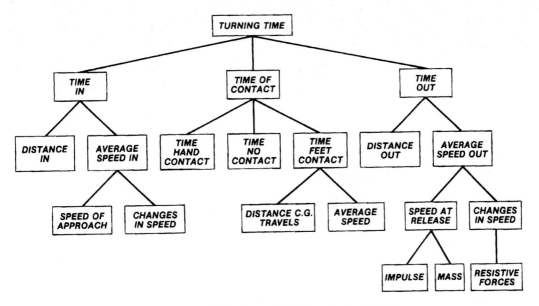

Figure 14-5. Basic factors that determine turning time.

ception of how his (or her) gliding and average stroking speeds compare. The second depends on the swimmer's speed at the moment contact was lost with the wall—the *speed at release*—and on the changes in speed that occur during the glide. These factors depend in turn on the impulse applied by the wall to the swimmer in reaction primarily to the driving extension of the legs, on the swimmer's mass (impulse-momentum relationship), and on the resistive forces.

Summary. The relationships between the turning time and the factors that determine that time are summarized in Fig. 14-5.

TECHNIQUES

The techniques of each of the competitive swimming strokes are considered here under four headings—body position, leg action, arm action, and breathing.

FRONT CRAWL
Body Position

The ideal body position for the front crawl (Fig. 14-6) would allow the swimmer to maximize the propulsive forces exerted and minimize the resistive forces encountered.

In attempting to satisfy these requirements, the good crawl swimmer assumes a prone position with the head relatively low in the water (waterline at or above the hairline), the hips slightly lower than the shoulders, and the legs relaxed and extended to the rear.

The elevation of the body relative to the waterline depends on the swim-

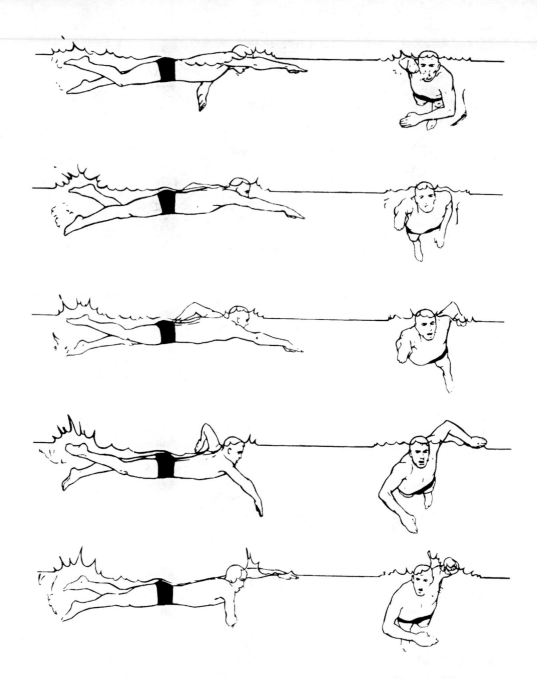

mer's buoyancy (a swimmer with a favorable specific gravity will "ride higher" than one who has a less favorable specific gravity) and on the speed at
which the swimmer moves through the water (the greater the speed, the
higher the swimmer will "ride" in the water). While a high body position in
the water serves to reduce resistive drag, the swimmer has little real control
over the factors that produce such a high position. The swimmer's buoyancy is fixed—barring drastic changes in body composition—and the speed

Figure 14-6. Front crawl. (Reproduced with permission from Counsilman, *The Science of Swimming.*)

of swimming should already be the fastest that can be managed. One thing that will certainly not produce a high body position and a concomitant reduction in drag is a conscious effort to achieve it. Where a favorable specific gravity is not the explanation, a high body position in the water is the result of a swimmer's speed and not the cause of it. To consciously attempt to get "on top of the water" by lifting the head or by pressing vertically downward with the arms in the early part of the stroke will inevitably more than offset any advantage normally associated with a high position. Either the legs will tend to drop as the head is raised (thereby increasing the swimmer's cross-sectional area and the form drag encountered) or the body, lifted by one arm and then dropped before the next arm can lift it again, will begin to oscillate vertically (increasing both form and wave drags).

Another aspect of body position that is often overlooked, and yet is definitely worthy of attention, is lateral alignment. If the head, trunk, or legs—those parts of the body that are generally immersed in the water—are allowed to deviate laterally from the straight-line direction in which the swimmer should be moving, the cross-sectional area of the body and the form drag are almost certain to be increased. Such deviations—generally caused by faulty breathing or arm actions—are therefore to be avoided.

Leg Action

Although the precise function of the leg action—to increase propulsion and/or to decrease resistance—has yet to be conclusively resolved, there appears to be fairly substantial agreement concerning which form of leg action produces the best results in practice. Most leading swimmers use an action (the so-called flutter kick) in which the legs alternate in a vertical, or near-vertical, up-and-down motion, first thrusting upward and backward as the leg is brought toward the surface and then downward and backward as it descends to complete the cycle. With the knee extended and the ankle plantar flexed, the upward action is primarily one of hip extension—the complete upward action being executed with the leg straight. The downward action, on the other hand, incorporates hip flexion, together with knee flexion and extension, in that order.

Several studies have been conducted in an attempt to resolve various questions that have been raised concerning the optimum leg action.

One of the earliest and probably the most comprehensive of these was a study by Cureton.[64] Among the many conclusions reached in this study were the following:

- The propulsive effects produced by the flutter kick do not derive "from the action of the two legs acting as a wedge on the V-shaped patch of water enclosed" but rather from an action akin to that used by fish.
- "A conservative statement would say that the up-kick is certainly as valuable, if not more so, for propulsion than the down-kick, although the evidence given indicates that it is *more* effective."
- Swimmers with the best kicks get a much greater percentage of their leg power from the hips (a mean of 51 percent was obtained for "four good sprinters of varsity caliber") than do swimmers with relatively poor kicks. One of Cureton's subjects in this latter category recorded 20.5 percent, while three others could not progress at all when they had to rely on hip action. (The figures were obtained by comparing times recorded when [1] knees, [2] ankles, and (3) knees-and-ankles were immobilized in turn, with those obtained when the subject used his normal flutter kick.)
- Expert swimmers with better kicks have greater flexibility in the ankles than average swimmers with poorer kicks. (Robertson[65] has since found significant relationships between ankle flexibility and propulsive force.)

- For the majority of the subjects, the best performances were recorded when the knees were allowed to bend to approximately 15°.
- For best results, a person should kick as wide a kick as physique and strength will permit, up to a maximum of 24 in. (61 cm). (A number of other investigators[66 67] have also endeavored to determine the optimum width of kick. However since their conclusions, like those of Cureton, are based upon tests in which the subjects were not using their arms, and thus were traveling at much lesser speeds than they would when swimming the full stroke, the applicability of their results to this latter situation is open to question.)
- The width and rate of kick are intimately related, a wide kick usually calling for a slower rate, and vice versa.

The effects produced by variations in the width of kick have also been studied by Alley,[68] who found that a normal kick (approximately 30 cm between feet at maximum spread) was superior to a short kick (approximately 15 cm between feet at maximum spread) on practically all the tests conducted. When his subject swam using only his legs, he produced greater propulsive forces with the normal kick than with the short one. When he was towed at speeds greater than he could normally attain with his legs alone, use of the normal kick resulted in less drag being created than did use of the short kick. Finally, when he swam using both arms and legs, a given arm action combined with a normal kick almost invariably produced greater propulsive forces than the same arm action combined with a short kick.

Attempts have also been made to determine the optimum number of kicks per complete arm cycle. Thrall,[69] for example, compared the performances of three varsity swimmers when they used a "normal" six-beat kick and when they used a "feathered" or two-beat kick. (*Note:* The actions of the legs are commonly referred to in terms of the number of downward beats that are made during a complete arm cycle.) He found that the average speed of his three subjects increased by 0.18 m/s, 0.24 m/s, and 0.21 m/s when they used a six-beat kick as compared to when they swam using their arms only. When they used a two-beat kick, the corresponding changes in speed were 0.03 m/s, 0.03m/s, and 0 m/s. He therefore concluded that, at least for the stroke frequency used in the study (1 cycle/s), the six-beat kick makes a greater contribution to forward speed than does the two-beat kick.

Eaves[70] has suggested that the widespread popularity of the six-beat crawl—most good sprint swimmers use a leg action of this kind—can be accounted for in terms of the swimmer's need to conserve angular momentum about his (or her) long axis. Thus he contends that as the swimmer's right arm and shoulder go down and the left arm and shoulder come up (near the beginning of the pull with the right arm), the left leg and hip must go down and the right leg and hip come up, to provide the necessary conservation of angular momentum. When the left arm and shoulder go down near the beginning of the next pull (with the left arm) the reaction from the lower body must be in the opposite direction—the right leg and hip going down and the left leg and hip coming up. This, he maintains, can only occur if the number of leg beats per half arm cycle (or per pull) is an odd number—that is, of the form $(2n + 1)$ where $n = 0, 1, 2, \ldots$ and so on. The number of beats per complete arm cycle must therefore be of the form $2(2n + 1)$ where $n = 0, 1, 2, \ldots$ and so on.

Of the various alternatives this theory permits, only the first three—2-beat, 6-beat, and 10-beat—are at all feasible. With respect to these, he concludes that "... the 2-beat crawl is too slow [see Thrall's conclusion] and the 10-beat crawl is too fast a leg-beat for most swimmers, leaving the 6-beat crawl as the only crawl-stroke comfortable as regards the speed of the leg-beat and the conservation of angular momentum."[71]

Arm Action

For the sake of analysis the arm action is generally considered to be divided into two parts:

- a *pull phase* that begins as the hand enters the water and ends as it leaves; and
- a *recovery phase* during which it is moved forward above the water in preparation for the next pull phase.

Pull Phase. The pull phase has three clearly identifiable parts (Fig. 14-7):

- The *initial press* (or *downsweep*) during which the motion of the hand is predominantly in a downward and forward direction. In this part of the pull phase, the resultant force exerted by the water on the hands is in an upward and forward direction (Fig. 14-8) and the lift component of this force acts to propel the swimmer in a forward, or near-forward direction.
- The *inward scull* (or *insweep*) during which the motion of the hand is predominantly in a medial (towards the midline of the body) and somewhat backward direction. In this part of the pull phase, the resultant force on the hands acts in a forward, or near-forward direction (Fig. 14-8) and both the lift and drag components of the resultant force make substantial contributions to the swimmer's forward propulsion.
- The *outward scull* (or *upsweep*) during which the motion of the hand is predominantly in a lateral (away from the midline of the body), backward, and upward direction. In this part, the resultant force on the hands acts in a forward, downward, and frequently medial direction (Fig. 14-8). Both the lift and drag components can make substantial contributions to the forward propulsion during this phase but, in general, the contribution of the lift component tends to dominate.

The propulsion that a swimmer derives from the motion of the hand through the water depends upon the path followed by the hand, the orientation of the hand to the flow (the angle of attack or pitch of the hand), and the speed of the hand.

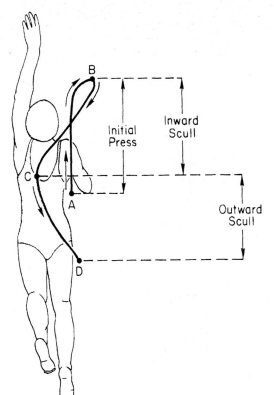

Figure 14-7.
The pull phase in the front crawl stroke is made up of an initial press, an inward scull, and an outward scull.

Hand path. World-class swimmers differ in the emphasis they place on each of the three parts of the pull. In this regard, Schleihauf[72] identified three different techniques. The first, which he calls the classic technique, is exemplified in the hand paths and force vectors shown in Fig. 14-8 and 14-9 (a).

The second technique involves a deep initial press, limited "in and out diagonal sculling motions," and an emphasis on "the upward and backward sweeping motions of the finish." An overhead view of the swimmer's hand path shows "much less midstroke crossover than that of the classic free-styler." In this technique, the elbow flexion of the inward scull and the subsequent elbow extension of the outward scull are deemphasized—perhaps because the swimmer lacks strength in the corresponding muscle groups. Instead emphasis is placed on shoulder extension and thus on the latissimus dorsi muscles which are primarily responsible for producing this motion. A relatively high stroke frequency is normally associated with the use of this technique—presumably because the length of the hand path and the ranges of the joint motion involved are less than in the other techniques.

The third technique involves an initial press and a finishing motion that are similar to those of the classic technique. The middle of the pull differs, however, in that the transition from the inward scull to the outward scull is

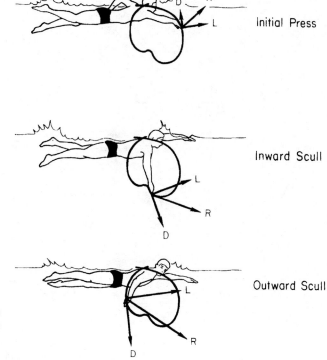

Initial Press

Inward Scull

Outward Scull

Figure 14-8.
Lift (*L*), drag (*D*), and resultant (*R*) forces exerted by the water on the hand during the three parts of the pull phase in the front crawl.

much more gradual than in the classic technique. The backward pushing motion of the hand during the transition from the inward to the outward scull is what distinguishes this technique from the other two.

Side views of the paths followed by the right hand in these three techniques are shown for purposes of comparison in Fig. 14-9.

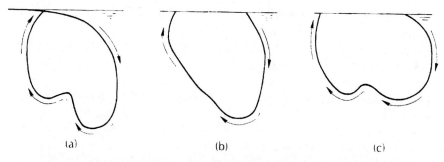

(a) (b) (c)

Figure 14-9. Side views of the paths followed by the right hand during one pull phase in swimming the front crawl: (a) the first, or classic, technique; (b) the second technique, commonly associated with a high stroke frequency; and (c) the third technique, characterized by the backward motion of the hand in the middle of the pull. (Adapted from Schleihauf, R. E. (1979). A hydrodynamic analysis of swimming propulsion.) In J. Terauds and E. W. Bedingfield (Eds.), *Swimming III* (pp. 70–109). Baltimore: University Park Press.

On the basis of his findings concerning the different techniques used by top-class swimmers, Schleihauf concluded that

> . . . *effective technique in freestyle can be generated for a broad range of swimming styles. Swimmers who exhibit skillful hand manipulation in sculling motions may be guided toward the so-called classic style. Others, who show a tendency toward a high rate of turnover and a deep press may choose to develop the qualities of the second technique. Finally, those best adapted to direct pushing motions may follow [the third] style.*[73]

Although medio-lateral motions are now an accepted feature of the hand paths of skilled freestyle swimmers, instruction on how to achieve such motions is conspicuously absent from most published accounts of freestyle technique. The hand can be moved towards and then away from the midline of the body

- by adduction and abduction of the shoulder joint (coupled, perhaps, with some flexion and extension at the elbow)—that is, by medio-lateral motions of the arm (and, perhaps, the forearm) relative to the trunk;
- by pulling the hand straight backward, while rolling the body about its longitudinal axis; and
- by some combination of these two.

A computer simulation study conducted by Hay, Liu and Andrews[74] suggested that it is the third of these mechanisms that is most commonly used in elite swimming. A subsequent analysis of 10 male college swimmers by Liu[75] concluded that the medio-lateral motions evident in the hand paths of his subjects were due approximately equally to body roll and to the medio-lateral motions of the upper limb relative to the trunk. However, because the amount of roll was much greater than needed to bring the hand across the body, the relative motions observed at the shoulder were exactly the reverse of what might have been expected. Instead of the arm being moved towards, and then away from, the midline of the body, it was moved away from and then towards the midline.

Angle of attack. Whichever of the three techniques of Figs. 14-8 and 14-9 is used, the propulsion that a swimmer derives from the hand depends in large measure on the hand's angle of attack—that is, on the angle between the plane of the hand and the direction in which the water is moving relative to the hand.

During the initial press, the wrist should be flexed partially to put the hand at an angle that will cause the lift component of the resultant force acting upon it to be directed forward. The lift component thus serves a useful, propulsive function. If the hand is held in line with the forearm during the press, the lift component of the resultant force on the hand—and the forward propulsion generated—will be small. (The drag component acts tangential to the path of the hand and is necessarily in an upward, or near-upward, direction during the press. It thus has little influence on forward propulsion, irrespective of how the wrist is held.)

During the inward scull the hand moves through the water with the thumb side leading; during the transition from inward to outward scull, the forearm is pronated and the hand rotated about its long axis; then, during the first part of the outward scull, the hand moves through the water with the little-finger side of the hand leading. In the course of this sequence of events, the swimmer's task is to maximize the force acting on the hand in the direction of swimming. This involves a continual adjustment in the pitch (or orientation) of the hand—an adjustment produced by supinating and pronating the forearm. Since the detailed, three-dimensional cinematographic analysis that reduces this process to an exact science is available to only a very few swimmers, this task is generally best accomplished by regular and systematic experimentation in practice.

The final part of the outward scull consists of an upward and backward sweeping motion. At the start of this sweeping motion, the hand is moving upward and backward, and both lift and drag forces make substantial contributions to the swimmer's forward propulsion. Later, when the hand is moving in a predominantly upward direction, the drag force acts in a downward, or near-downward, direction and it is only the lift force than can contribute significantly to propelling the swimmer forward. The magnitude of the lift force generated at this time depends, once again, on the angle of attack. If the hand is held in line with the forearm—or, worse yet, if the wrist is flexed—the angle of attack will be large and the lift component of the resultant force acting on the hand will be relatively small. If the wrist is extended, however, an angle of attack which is highly favorable to the production of lift can be obtained. For this reason, skilled swimmers extend the wrist, or allow the pressure of the water to extend it for them, during the final sweeping motion of the outward scull.

Hand speed. The forces exerted on a body moving through a fluid are proportional to the square of the velocity of that body (p. 185). The propulsive lift and drag forces exerted on a swimmer's hand are thus very much influenced by the speed—that is, the magnitude of the velocity—at which the hand is moved through the water.

As one might expect, the hand speed recorded for a good swimmer changes continually during the pull.[76][77] Although the hand-speed-versus-time pattern also varies from swimmer to swimmer, there is one consistent feature of the patterns exhibited by good swimmers—the maximum hand speed is attained during the final sweeping motion. This final sweeping motion is thus considered "the critical range of motion."[78]

Counsilman[79] conducted a number of informal studies in which college varsity, competitive masters, and poor swimmers were instructed to gradually increase their hand speed until they were 65–80 percent through the pull phase. He found, after very limited practice, that most (10 of 16) of the varsity swimmers and all of the masters and poor swimmers were able to reduce the number of strokes they took per 25-yd (22.9-m) length while maintaining or increasing their swimming speed. He concluded that "the evidence . . . appears to justify a greater emphasis in teaching the hand speed and acceleration pattern as a method of improving performance."

Maglischo and her colleagues[80] estimated the propulsive forces generated by the hands of distance freestyle swimmers on the 1984 U.S. Olympic team. For this purpose they divided the pull phase of the stroke into four parts—a downsweep and an insweep (as described earlier), and an outsweep and upsweep (the upsweep described earlier divided into two parts in which the motion of the hand was primarily out and up, respectively). They found that each of the five subjects of the study was able to generate large propulsive forces during only one or two of the four parts of the pull; and that those who gained most of their propulsion when their hands were moving in primarily vertical directions were not very effective when they were sweeping their hands in medial or lateral directions. The reverse was also true. Those who gained most of their propulsion when their hands were moving in a medial and/or lateral direction were much less effective when they swept their hands vertically.

Recovery Phase. At the completion of the pull, the swimmer lifts the hand from the water preparatory to swinging it forward for entry and the start of its next pull phase. The act of withdrawing the hand from the water is effected with a high lifting action of the arm (elbow high), coordinated with a rolling of the trunk, which elevates the shoulder and thus contributes to the lifting action of the arm. Once the hand is clear of the water, the arm is swung forward as those muscles that abduct and rotate the shoulder and flex the elbow come into play. To minimize the lateral angular reaction of the legs to the recovery action of the arm, the arm is brought forward in as near a vertical plane as the swimmer's body position will permit.

Breathing

In addition to being of obvious importance physiologically, the manner in which the swimmer breathes is of some consequence from a biomechanical standpoint. Unless the swimmer incorporates his (or her) respiratory movements into the whole stroke so that they neither interfere with the ability to produce propulsive force nor add to the resistance encountered, the resulting performance will be materially effected. To ensure that this does not occur or, if it must, to minimize the effects produced, the good swimmer generally tries to take the least number of breaths consistent with physiological needs and to take them in such a manner that the body position is changed as little as possible in the process. Thus when a breath is needed, the swimmer rotates the head about its long axis until the mouth, deep in the trough of the bow wave created by the head, is just clear of the water. The swimmer then inhales and returns the head, rotating once again about its long axis, to its original position.

Time trials conducted by Cureton[81] have shown "conclusively that swimmers can swim faster for short distances without breathing regularly and that they become slower in direct proportion to the number of breaths taken." The explanation for this might very well be accounted for in terms of resistance measures reported by Karpovich.[82] He found that ordinary turning of the head for breathing increased the resistance about 2.2 N at a speed of 0.9 m/s and about 6.7 N at a speed of 1.5 m/s.

Opinions differ with respect to the exhalation of air. Counsilman[83] has suggested that the air should be exhaled continuously during the period the face is in the water. Keskinen and Komi[84] have concluded otherwise. They measured the time during which ten male freestyle swimmers inhaled, held their breath, and exhaled during a set of five to six 400-m swims at progressively faster speeds (from fastest time for a training set plus 120 s to fastest time). They reported that all of their subjects chose to hold their breaths during the early part of the underwater stroke—instead of using the method of continuous exhalation—and stated that:

> One might suggest that breath-holding would support . . . the "breathing arm" during the catch and the first part of the pull phase. . . . The forcible violent exhalation especially in the middle of the underwater phase of the stroke cycle may add to the propulsive force component during stroking. . . . [The subjects] could then produce more force in the latter part of the pull, and during the push phase of the stroke cycle. . . . It is suggested that [breath-holding] may be a part of [an] efficient stroke pattern.[85]

BUTTERFLY STROKE

The dolphin butterfly stroke evolved from the orthodox breaststroke during the early 1930s. The first stage in this evolutionary process was the discovery that an out-of-the-water recovery action not only conformed with the then-existing rules governing breaststroke swimming but also markedly increased a swimmer's speed by decreasing the resistance encountered. This development was closely followed by the appearance of the so-called dolphin kick in which both legs move simultaneously in a vertical plane instead of in the roughly horizontal plane of the then-orthodox breaststroke kick. While this type of kick has since been shown to be vastly superior to previous types of breaststroke kick in terms of speed, it was many years before its use gained official sanction—it was 1955 before the

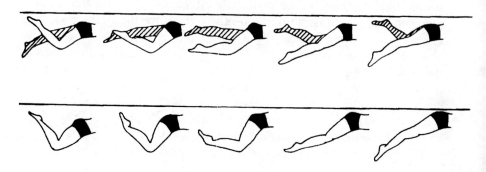

dolphin kick was officially accepted for intercollegiate competition and 1956 before it made its debut in an Olympic Games event.

Body Position

In some respects the body position adopted by a good butterfly stroke swimmer is similar to that adopted in a front crawl event. The swimmer assumes a prone position in the water; endeavors to minimize the drag opposing forward motion by keeping the head relatively low, the legs relatively high, and the up-and-down movements of the body to a minimum; and endeavors to optimize the propulsive forces exerted. In other respects there are differences. Because both arms pull and then recover together, the use of a body roll to facilitate either or both of these actions is not feasible. The swimmer's body therefore retains its prone position throughout each stroke. The simultaneous action of the arms also acts to the swimmer's advantage during the recovery, for since the action of one arm effectively balances (or reacts with) the opposite action of the other arm, the swimmer need have no concern that the legs will become misaligned and increase the resistance encountered.

Leg Action

Although perhaps not apparent to the casual observer, the leg action in the dolphin butterfly stroke is practically identical with that used in the front crawl except that both legs move together rather than in opposition and the number of beats per arm cycle is generally less. This is well illustrated by the sequences of Fig. 14-10. The top sequence depicts one complete cycle of the action of the right leg of a front crawl swimmer. (The actions of the left leg can be seen in the background.) The bottom sequence shows the actions of both legs during one cycle of a dolphin kick. Now, while there are *slight* differences in the inclination of the trunk and in the extent to which the hip, knee, and ankle joints are flexed during the downbeat, the similarity between the two sequences is obvious. (*Note:* These sequences have been taken from photographs of a swimmer kicking on a kickboard and

Figure 14-10. The leg action in the dolphin kick (lower sequence) is very similar to that in the front crawl (upper sequence).

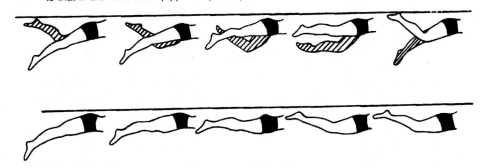

thus do not exactly replicate the actions used when the whole stroke is employed. Instead, since the legs are the sole source of propulsion in this case, the range and force of the kicks in Fig. 14-10 are somewhat greater than they would be in a whole stroke.)

In front crawl events, the number of downward beats of the legs per complete arm cycle usually varies with the length of the race—a six-beat crawl generally being used for sprint events and some lesser number for longer events. In butterfly events the swimmer normally executes two leg beats per arm cycle: the first, and generally the more forceful, starting as the hands enter the water; the second starting as the hands pass beneath the line of the shoulders and ending shortly before they leave the water.

Various aspects of the dolphin kick have been the subject of study. Barthels and Adrian[86] studied the muscular activity, the ranges of motion at various joints, and the timing of the kick of four intercollegiate swimmers and found the following:

- When only the legs were used for propulsion, no major-minor kick pattern was observed. For each subject, each kick in a sequence was identical in character to the others. When a full stroke was used, alternating major and minor kicks—that is, major and minor in terms of time and/or range of joint motion—were noted in all cases. On the basis of these findings Barthels and Adrian questioned the value of practicing series of identical kicks using the legs alone if refinement of the timing of the leg action is the desired objective.

- Coordinated contractions of the rectus abdominis and erector spinae muscles revealed their roles in producing, respectively, flexion and extension of the spine. When these two muscles contracted together, they served to stabilize the trunk. Barthels and Adrian concluded that "The activity of these muscles indicated an active participation by the trunk as an inherent part of the total kicking movement and would suggest the need for the study of spinal movement during the kick in future research."

- The muscles of the lower leg apparently became stretched due to the pressure of the water on the foot, and contracted reflexly to prevent further stretching. Barthels and Adrian concluded that "the development of flexibility for greater plantar-flexion of the foot would be more worthwhile than concentration on strength development in the lower leg."

- Some interrelationships between the ranges of motion at hip and knee joints were noted—a large range of motion at the hips being associated with a small range at the knees, and vice versa.

Kersten[87] examined the effects of two types of dolphin kick—kick A (a maximum knee action–minimum hip action kick) and kick B (a maximum hip action–minimum knee action kick)—on the time taken to swim 10 yd (9.1 m). He found that kick A was significantly faster than kick B when only the legs were used and that the whole stroke using kick A was significantly faster than the whole stroke using kick B. (In the latter case the difference between the mean times was 0.3 s for 26 highly trained competitive swimmers and 0.8 s for 8 less experienced swimmers.) He suggested therefore that his findings "appear to warrant the conclusion that the Dolphin leg drive when the subject utilizes maximum knee action and minimum hip action is more effective than the Dolphin leg drive when the subject utilizes maximum hip action and minimum knee action."

The arm action used in the butterfly stroke (like the body position and leg action) bears a strong resemblance to the corresponding action in the front crawl. Since both arms pull and then recover simultaneously, however, some modifications of the basic crawl stroke action are necessary.

Arm Action

Pull Phase. The hands enter the water (palms downward and slightly outward) in front of the shoulders and a little more than shoulder width apart. The arms are relaxed and almost straight and the elbows are a little higher than the hands. Then, as the hands move forward, downward, and backward to the catch position, they are brought slightly wider apart thereby tracing out the first part of the so-called double-S pull (also known as the hourglass or keyhole pull) currently used by virtually all good butterfly swimmers. From this position the hands are pulled backward and inward toward the midline of the body, pass beneath the shoulders, and finally go outward and upward to finish at (or near) the upper thighs.

The propulsive forces generated as the hands are brought towards the midline of the body are generally small and lift-dominated—that is, the lift components of the resultant forces exerted on the hands generally contribute more to the swimmer's forward propulsion than do the drag components. The propulsive forces generated during the essentially backward, pushing motion that follows are generally large and drag-dominated. Finally, the propulsive forces generated during the outward and upward sweeping motion that concludes the pull phase are generally large and dominated by either lift or drag depending on the angle of attack of the hands. If the wrists are allowed to extend during this final sweeping motion, the angle of attack is usually small and the propulsive forces lift-dominated. Conversely, if the wrists are flexed or held in a midrange position, the angle of attack is usually large and the propulsive forces drag-dominated. Both of these variations in technique have been observed in top-class swimmers.[88]

Recovery Phase. As the pull phase ends, the arms are well-nigh straight and the palms of the hands are facing inward. From this position the swimmer rotates the arms outward and then swings them forward and around, close to the surface of the water, and toward the point at which the next entry will be made. (*Note:* The bent-arm, high-elbow action characteristic of the recovery phase in the front crawl is not used in the butterfly stroke for at least two reasons: [1] the anatomical structure of the shoulder joint makes it a virtual impossibility to perform such an action unless the body rolls; and [2] the balancing of one arm by the other eliminates the need for such an arm action.)

Breathing

While raising the head to take a breath almost inevitably increases the resistance and thus adversely effects a swimmer's speed, a good swimmer minimizes this effect by appropriate timing of the breathing pattern. In the first place the swimmer breathes only as often as necessary to meet physiological needs—perhaps once every two to three arm cycles in sprint events and once every one to two arm cycles in the longer events. Second, the swimmer times the movements involved so that the head is lifted when it has the least distance to move to achieve the desired result. This occurs in the latter half of the pull phase when the shoulders have been elevated by the action of the arms and by the second beat of the leg action taking place at that time. Once the head has been lifted until the mouth is just clear of the water—any unnecessary elevating of the head will tend to force the legs lower and create added resistance—the swimmer inhales and lowers the face back between the arms, which by this time are swinging past the line of the shoulders on their way forward to the entry.

Originally a form of inverted breaststroke, the back crawl (Fig. 14-11) has since evolved into what might more aptly be described as an inverted front crawl—the simultaneous action of the arms and the so-called frog kick of the early technique having given way to the alternating arm action and the "flutter" kick of the modern stroke.

Figure 14-11. Back Crawl. (Reproduced with permission from Counsilman, *The Science of Swimming.*)

Body Position

The back crawl is the only competitive stroke in which the swimmer adopts other than a prone position in the water. In the back crawl the swimmer assumes a near-horizontal position on the back with the chin close to the chest (yet far enough away to allow the bow wave to break across the top of the head), the trunk and legs loosely extended, and the hips just low enough in the water to ensure that the kick will be beneath the surface. The relationship between the positions of the head and hips is of particular importance. If the swimmer has the head so far back that he (or she) is unable to see the water being disturbed by the kick, this is likely to cause the hips to rise to the point where the kick becomes ineffective. Thus, although the resistance encountered will almost certainly be less with the body in a horizontal position, the loss in the effectiveness of the kick might well outweigh any gains from that source. Conversely, if the head is brought too far forward, the hips are likely to be lowered more than is necessary to obtain an effective kick. The added resistance evoked in this manner and the lack of any offsetting advantage to such an alignment make it an unnecessary liability.

Leg Action

The leg action in the back crawl is essentially the same as that in the front crawl except for the obvious differences due to the change in the swimmer's position.

Arm Action

Good back-crawl swimmers use an arm action (Fig. 14-11) that consists of a pull phase (which begins with the arm nearly straight, continues with the arm bending to a near 90° angle, and finishes with the arm nearly straight) and a recovery phase (which proceeds in an essentially vertical plane, with entry being made at near-full reach, above and only slightly to the side of the shoulder).

The propulsive phase of the arm action currently used by good back-crawl swimmers consists of three consecutive parts:

- an initial downward and outward motion of the hand;
- an upward, and continuing outward, sweep of the hand during which the body attains its greatest forward velocity;
- a final downward and backward pushing motion of the hand.

During the first two of these phases, both the lift and drag components of the resultant force exerted on the hand contribute to the swimmer's forward propulsion—the lift component tending to dominate when the down-up-down motion of the hand is pronounced and the drag component tending to dominate when the hand path is flatter. During the final phase, the drag component is clearly the dominant source of the swimmer's propulsion.[89]

As well as providing propulsion, the final downward thrust also provides the impetus to roll the body about its long axis and facilitates the recovery of the arm by elevating the shoulder on the same side. In addition, the lowering of the opposite shoulder puts the arm on that side in a stronger anatomical position for the pull that is just beginning.[90] The recovery is executed with the arm, straight and relaxed, being lifted from the water and swung overhead in a vertical or near-vertical plane. The recovering of the arm in this manner eliminates the possibility that the feet may move laterally in reaction to the recovery—a very real possibility if a lateral recovery action is used.

Breathing

Since the swimmer's head is held in a constant position and the mouth and nose are clear of the water at all times other than during starts and turns, the optimum pattern of breathing is a physiological question rather than a biomechanical one.

BREASTSTROKE

Probably the first swimming stroke to be developed, the breaststroke is ill-suited to propel a person through water at speed—a fact attested to by its secure rating as the slowest of the four competitive strokes. The breaststroke does have some distinct advantages over the other competitive strokes outside the realm of competition. It may be used for long periods with a minimal output of energy, it allows the swimmer a clear view ahead, and it makes use of a very simple breathing technique—features that account at least in part for the important role the stroke plays in lifesaving and survival swimming.

Body Position

There are two styles of breaststroke in common use by competitive swimmers—the *flat style* and the *dolphin, undulating, or wave style* (to mention only some of the names by which it is known). In the former, the swimmer's trunk is kept in a near-horizontal position near the surface of the water throughout the stroke cycle; and in the latter, it oscillates between the horizontal and a position in which the hips are some 30-60 cm lower than the shoulders.

In the flat style, the recovery of the legs is effected by a flexion of the hips and knees. In the dolphin style, the recovery is effected by a lowering of the hips in the water and a flexion of the knees. These latter actions ensure that the trunk and thighs are in a more or less straight line throughout the stroke. This reduces the cross-sectional area of the body and thus the resistive forces encountered during the recovery of the legs. The lowering of the hips permits the feet to remain in the water when the knees are flexed, and thus ensures that the propulsive forces of the kick are not seriously compromised (if compromised at all) in the quest for a decrease in resistive forces.

Persyn, de Maeyer, and Vervaecke[91] reported that one swimmer who used a "jumping" (or dolphin) style in the 1972 Olympic Games had the least fluctuation in the forward velocity of the hip—a point often taken to represent the center of gravity in studies of swimming. In a later study, Van Tilborgh, Willems, and Persyn[92] reported that one of the 23 breaststroke swimmers whose techniques they studied used the "new-look, undulating breaststroke," and that this subject showed the least fluctuation in the forward velocity of his center of gravity of all the subjects in the sample. He also had the highest forward velocity of the center of gravity, and the least negative or resistive impulse, during the recovery phase. These findings, sparse though they are, support the claims often made in favor of the dolphin style over the flat style in breaststroke.

In breaststroke, the changes in the positions of the swimmer's limbs probably have a greater influence on the resistance encountered than do the corresponding changes in any other stroke. A study of the flat style by Kent and Atha[93] provided some interesting results concerning the magnitude of the resistance encountered at different stages in the breaststroke action (Fig. 14-12). When they towed their subjects through the water at velocities up to 1.5 m/s (equivalent to the average speed for a 2-min 13.3s, 200-m), they found that the resistance increased in the following order: glide, postthrust, breathing, prethrust, and recovered. When they towed their subjects at a velocity of 1.5 m/s, the resistance increased (relative to that recorded for the glide position) by a multiple of 1.91 for breathing, 2.01 for postthrust, 2.28 for prethrust, and 2.37 for recovered. (For example, with one subject who encountered resistance of 95 N when gliding at 1.5 m/s, the resistance values for the other four positions were 181 N for breathing, 191 N for postthrust, 217 N for prethrust, and 225 N for recovered. These results are depicted in Fig. 14-12. Similar results were recorded for the other two subjects.)

Two aspects of these results stand out. First, the resistance increased tremendously from that recorded for the glide to that recorded for the breathing position—an increase that almost doubled the resistance! Second, although the towing speed of 1.5 m/s is admittedly very fast the magnitudes of the resistive forces acting on the swimmer are almost certainly much larger than is commonly supposed.

It is surely no wonder that the lowest velocity during the stroke occurs when the hips and knees are flexed during the recovery phase (Fig. 14-12, middle position). Craig, Boomer, and Skehan[94] found that at this instant the velocity of some swimmers was zero, and the average for their 12 male subjects was 0.2 m/s. (*Note:* No mention was made of the style used by the subjects of this study, but the fact that they were "competent but not particularly skilled in swimming the breaststroke" suggests that they almost certainly used the flat style.)

Leg Action

For many years the so-called wedge kick was believed to be the optimum breaststroke leg action. In this type of kick, the recovery phase of the leg action began with the legs together and extended. The legs were then

Glide (95 N)

Breathing (181 N)

Recovered (226 N)

Pre-thrust (217 N)

Post-thrust (191 N)

Figure 14-12. Resistance encountered by a breast-stroke swimmer at selected instants in his stroke. Based on data in Kent M. R., and Atha, J. (1971). Selected critical transient body positions in breast-stroke and their influence upon water resistance. In L. Lewillie and J. P. Clarys (Eds.), *First International Symposium on Biomechanics in Swimming, Waterpolo and Diving Proceedings.* Université Libre de Bruxelles Laboratoire de L'effort.

drawn up with the heels held together and the knees moving outward away from each other. At the completion of the recovery phase, the ankles were dorsi-flexed, the heels were together, the knees were spread well apart, and the legs as a whole bounded a near-horizontal diamond-shaped area. The propulsive or driving phase began with the feet being thrust outward and backward to form a wide V or wedge between the legs. The final movement consisted of a vigorous slamming together of the legs, which, it was wrongly thought, produced a forceful backward expulsion of the wedge of water lying between them, and the propulsion that the swimmer experienced.

The wedge kick has been superseded by a kick (or kicks) in which the width of the leg action is less than in the wedge kick—and thus produces less resistance—and in which the emphasis is on either a forceful backward push (primarily with the soles of the feet) or an outward, downward and inward, propeller-like action of the feet that, so its proponents contend, uses lift forces to drive the body forward.[95][96][97] (*Note:* The reason for the apparent uncertainty as to just how many different kicks have come to supplant the wedge kick lies in the fact that the terms used to describe the different leg actions vary considerably from one authority to the next. Thus one person will refer to an action as if it were simply a variant of another, while a second will give each action a different name.)

For the purposes of further discussion two kicks will be defined here. These will be referred to as the *frog kick* and the *whip kick*, respectively.

Frog kick.

The recovery starts from the streamlined glide position. The legs are drawn up with the knees dropped slightly, turned outward, and separated more than the feet. As the legs are drawn up, the feet are turned out and the ankles dorsiflexed in preparation for the propulsive action.

In one continuous propulsive movement the knees are rotated inward as the soles of the feet thrust outward, backward and together. As the legs are brought together and extended the feet are also extended.[98]

Whip kick.

The whip kick (Fig. 14-13) is a kick in which relaxed knees drop toward the bottom and separate slightly as the heels are drawn toward the buttocks. The ankles are dorsiflexed and the feet turned outward to grip the water as the legs are whipped out, back, and together. As the legs are brought together and extended the feet are also extended.

In this kick the knees separate but remain closer together than the feet during the recovery and there is little or no rotation of the femur.

The basic criterion for differentiating a frog kick from a whip kick is the position of the knees in relation to the feet during the recovery . . . In the frog kick the knees separate beyond lines drawn between the heels and the hips while in the whip kick the knees stay within such lines.[99]

The relative merits of the wedge, frog, and whip kicks have been examined experimentally.

Cake[100] compared the performances of 11 experienced swimmers and 2 college classes of inexperienced swimmers, using the wedge kick and the frog kick (or what she termed the "semicircular arc whipping" action kick). She concluded (1) that for experienced swimmers, the frog kick developed a significantly greater amount of force, propelled the body through the water more rapidly, and used fewer kicks to cover a given distance than did the wedge kick; and (2) that her results provided no

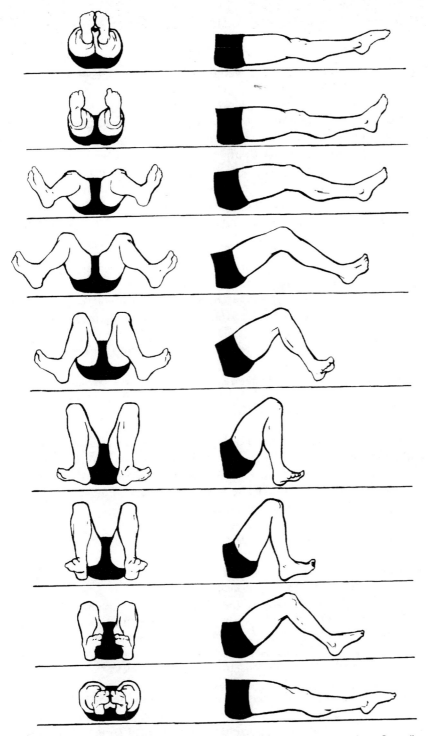

Figure 14-13. Breaststroke whip kick. (Reproduced with permission from Counsilman, *The Science of Swimming.*)

evidence to suggest that the frog kick was more difficult to learn than the wedge kick.

Counsilman[101] compared the wedge and whip kicks and found that the whip kick was superior to the wedge kick in every respect—speed, propulsive force, and economy of movement. In addition it could be used at a faster tempo than the wedge kick.

Deciding that the limitations of the wedge kick had already been adequately demonstrated, Over[102] confined her attention to comparing the frog and the whip kicks. With an experienced swimmer as the subject, she determined the propulsive force he could exert against a line being unreeled at approximately 0.72 m/s, the resistive force he encountered when being towed at 1.11 m/s, and the "free velocity" he could attain when using the frog and whip kick leg actions. Among her conclusions were the following:

- When speeds are comparable, the number of whip kicks taken to cover a given distance will be greater than the number of frog kicks necessary to cover the same distance. This, she said, suggests that the per-kick efficiency of the frog kick is greater than that of the whip kick.
- The frog kick is more powerful than the whip kick when executed against resistance.
- When measured at a speed similar to the whole stroke speed, use of the frog kick incurred more resistance to the swimmer's forward motion than did use of the whip kick.

Nimz and colleagues[103] compared anthropometric measures of the lower limb, and ranges of motion at the hip, knee, and ankle joints, for 24 male and female swimmers who used different types of breaststroke kick. Of the 24 subjects, 9 used a whip kick, 8 a wedge kick, and 7 a "kick with plantar flexed feet." The authors concluded that:

- Outstanding flexibility of the lower limbs is not a prerequisite to using the whip kick.
- Swimmers who use the whip kick do not need better flexibility than those who use the wedge kick.
- Use of the ineffective wedge kick cannot be explained by a lack of flexibility. Other explanations, such as the "manner and the development of the learning process," must be sought.
- The swimmers who used the kick with plantar flexed feet were less flexible than those who used the other two kicks.

Several other questions relating to the leg action used in the breaststroke have been the subject of study. For example, Soviet researchers Belokovsky and Ivanchenko[104] have reported the results of a series of studies concerned with the amplitude and force of the leg actions employed in breaststroke swimming. In the first of these studies, they determined the

> . . . the average angle of flexion in the hip joint [at the end of the recovery or pre-
> paratory phase of the leg cycle] was 137.4 ± 8.5°. The angle . . . for male swimmers
> ranged from 130 to 148° and that of female swimmers from 124 to 131°. These can
> be compared to the swimming technique of 1950s–1960s in which this angle was only
> 107.0 ± 15.6°. While the angle of flexion for the knee joint of male swimmers
> reached a right angle, that of female swimmers was 100–124°. In the last 5 years
> angular changes in the hip joints have tended to decrease by one-half and at present
> these angles are 34.0 ± 8.5°. Working amplitudes of female swimmers are 44–48°
> and those of male swimmers are less, 24–32°. At present, the mean knee joint angle
> in the preparatory phase is 40.1 ± 5.1° compared to 30.2 ± 2.8° in 1950–
> 1960.[105]

They next investigated the forces exerted by the swimmers as they executed simulated breaststroke kicks in which the initial flexion at the hips
and knees was made to vary from 90° to 180° and 40° to 90°, respectively.
Then, having arrived at what appeared to be the best combination (140°
and 50° to 60° of hip and knee flexion, respectively), they trained a group
of swimmers for one and a half months using a device that limited their hip
and knee flexion, at the end of the preparatory phase, to these amounts.
This procedure resulted in significant improvements in their "swimming
time over competitive distances" presumably, as compared to other swimmers who underwent similar training without the aid of the special device.
Finally, recognizing that the amplitudes of swimming movements are inversely related to the stroke rate, Belokovsky and Ivanchenko determined
the range of stroke rates that would permit the use of the recommended
pattern of leg movements and found that "the optimal rate is about 65
cycles per min [1.08 cycles/s]. Exceeding the optimal rate by 10 cycles per
min [0.17 cycles/s] results in substantial changes in swimming technique
and a decrease in the swimming speed."[106]

Arm Action

The arm action in the breaststroke consists of two phases:

- An *outward press*, during which the hands are moved forward and
  outward with the palms facing outward and backward (Fig. 14-14).
  The propulsive forces acting on the hands during this phase are
  lift-dominated.
- An *inward scull*, during which the hands are moved inward and forward with the palms facing inward and backward (Fig. 14-14). The
  propulsive forces acting on the hands are again lift-dominated.

The speed of the hands reaches a peak value near the end of the outward press, declines somewhat as the direction of motion changes from
outward to inward, and then increases to a second peak value near the

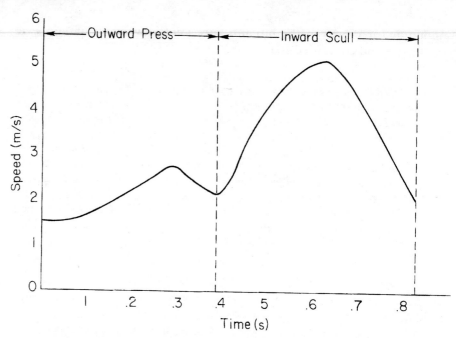

Figure 14-14. Hand speed during breaststroke. (Adapted from Schleihauf, B. [1976]. A hydrodynamic analysis of breaststroke pulling proficiency. *Swimming Technique*, 12:101.)

middle of the inward scull (Fig. 14-14). With good breaststroke swimmers, the peak hand speed attained during the inward scull is approximately twice that attained during the outward press. This has important, and perhaps surprising, implications. Because the forces acting on the hand are proportional to the square of the speed at which the hand moves (p. 185), the forces exerted during the inward scull—and, of most interest here, the lift-dominated propulsive forces—are much greater than those exerted during the outward press. In short, the inward scull is the dominant propulsive phase of a well-executed breaststroke arm action. It is not simply a recovery phase as has often been suggested.

Breathing

The head is lifted continuously through the latter part of the press and inward scull, and the breath is taken towards the end of the inward scull when the arms are approximately in line with the shoulders and the shoulders themselves are relatively high.

Kinnear[107] has pointed out that this taking of the breath late in the pull phase of the arm stroke "conforms to the Russian idea of performing all breathing movements outside a propulsive phase of the arm action in all strokes (in relation to the fixing of the rib cage for generating maximum power)." He also refers to the question of minimizing the number of breaths taken during a race—a question already mentioned several times in this chapter:

All swimmers favor breathing every arm stroke although some breath holding can be seen occasionally in the shorter distance races over 100 metres—but in no set pattern. This, I must admit, does surprise me because breath holding with no need to raise the head must result in a more stable stroke—it is done in butterfly and sprint crawl; why not in breaststroke?[108]

STARTS

When the gun is fired, the swimmer endeavors to get away from the block quickly and with as much forward speed as possible. Unfortunately, these two objectives (quickness off the block and maximum forward speed) are somewhat incompatible, for if the swimmer leaves the block as quickly as possible, the horizontal impulse developed is such that forward speed is less than it could be. Conversely, if the time necessary to develop a maximum horizontal impulse (and thus maximum horizontal speed) is taken, the swimmer will leave the block later than might otherwise be the case. The swimmer's task therefore is to arrive at that blending of quickness off the block and forward speed that affords the best results overall.

Front Crawl, Butterfly, and Breaststroke

The starting technique used up to the point of entry is essentially the same for front crawl, butterfly, and breaststroke events. At the command "Take your marks," the swimmer moves from an erect-standing preparatory position atop the block and assumes his (or her) starting position. In this position, the swimmer generally has the feet 15-30 cm apart, the toes curled over the forward edge of the block, the knees bent slightly, the hips well flexed, the arms extended near-vertically downwards with the hands gripping either the front edge of the starting block (between or outside the feet) or the side edges of the block and the head, neck, and trunk inclined in a forward and downward direction. The gripping of the block with the hands distinguishes this type of start—known as the *grab start*—from those that preceded it historically. In these earlier starts, the arms were allowed to hang vertically downward or were held back in line with the trunk when the swimmer adopted his (or her) starting position.

The factors that influence success in the performance of a hands-between-the-feet grab start have been studied by Guimaraes,[109 110] who analyzed a total of 72 starts performed by 24 experienced, high school swimmers. Each start was followed by a glide until the subject's fingers made contact with a touchpad mounted on a bulkhead 9 m from the start. The subjects were not permitted to kick or stroke. To eliminate whatever influence differences in the heights and weights of his subjects might have on the results, Guimaraes analyzed his data using a statistical procedure (partial correlation) which allowed him to hold these factors constant. He found that:

- The glide time (the time from first contact with the water until first contact with the touchpad) accounted for 95 percent of the variance in the start time (the time from the starting signal until first contact with the touchpad). The time the swimmers spent gliding was thus overwhelmingly more important than the time they spent on the block or in the air.

- The distance of the glide varied little from subject to subject and trial to trial and was not significantly related to the start time. The average horizontal velocity of the glide was thus the more important of the two factors (distance and average horizontal velocity) that determined the glide time.

- The drag forces exerted on the swimmer during the glide were almost certainly the most important factors in determining the average horizontal velocity during the glide and, thus, the start time. (*Note:* This conclusion was arrived at by deduction from other results. These forces were not actually measured in the study.)

- The horizontal velocity of the swimmer's center of gravity at entry (the instant of first contact with the water) was not significantly related to the start time.

- The forces exerted on the front edge of the block via the subject's hands were, almost without exception, in a forward and upward direction. They thus elicited a reaction from the block that tended to pull the swimmer downward and retard forward motion. Furthermore, the larger these forces were, the greater was the resultant horizontal impulse exerted on the swimmer and the shorter the start time. This seemingly contradictory result was explained in part by the finding of significant relationships between (1) the horizontal and vertical impulses exerted via the hands; and (2) the horizontal impulse exerted via the feet. This finding indicated that the greater the upward and forward impulses that the swimmer applied via his hands to the front edge of the block, the greater the backward horizontal impulse he could apply to the block via his feet. In short, it was concluded that the role of the arms and hands in a well-executed grab start is to facilitate the drive of the legs. (*Note:* Cavanagh, Palmgren, and Kerr[111] reached a similar, tentative conclusion following a preliminary study in which they determined the forces exerted via the hands during the performance of a grab start by an experienced, competitive swimmer.)

The position at which the hands grip the block have been examined in at least one study. Lewis[112] compared the times taken for the head to reach a line 8 m from the front edge of the block when five different starting techniques were used. The hands-between-the-feet and the hands-on-the-side-of-the-block grab starts were two of these five. The subjects—10 male college students with no prior training in racing starts—were trained over a period of 10 days during which they performed each start a total of 42 times under close supervision. The results obtained in the tests administered at the conclusion of the training period revealed no significant differences in the times taken to reach the 8-m mark.

A variation of the grab start in which one of the feet is placed some distance behind the front edge of the block—the so-called *track start*—has been the subject of several investigations.[113][114][115][116] The results of these investigations have been inconclusive; two[113][114] suggesting that the track start is inferior to the orthodox grab start and other starts, one[115] suggesting that the track start and the orthodox grab start yield similar results, and one[116] suggesting that the track start with a flat flight trajectory is superior to the orthodox grab start and other starts. These differences in results appear to have been due primarily to differences in the subjects (trained vs. untrained) and in the amount of prior training they had had in the use of each start.

Counsilman and colleagues[117] conducted two experiments—one with 37 male college swimmers and the other with 121 male and female swimmers between the ages of 10 and 17—to compare three starting techniques. These were the orthodox grab start with a low flight trajectory (also known as the *flat start*); a grab start with a high trajectory and a piking at the hips near the peak of the flight (variously known, according to the authors, as the *scoop start*, the *hole-in-the-water start*, the *sailor dive*, the *spoon start*, the *no-resistance start*—surely a misnomer!—and the *pike start*); and the track start.

In the first experiment, the subjects practiced each start 100 times over a period of 4 months and then performed "three 12.5-yd freestyle trials of each type of start." The average times were:

Flat start	4.16 s
Track start	4.25 s
Scoop start	4.37 s

Acknowledging that these results were biased because the subjects had been using the flat start for years, and had probably practised this type of start thousands of times, the authors took another approach. In this second experiment, the subjects received instruction in the three starts and then practiced each of them three times a day for four days. On the fifth day, they were tested and their performances recorded on videotape for later analysis. The main results are summarized in Table 14-1.

The acknowledged bias in the first experiment was less intrusive in the second. When asked to name the type of start they were accustomed to using, 40% of the males and 32% of the females named the flat start; 38% and 54% named the scoop start; and 12% and 14 percent named the track start. Thus, differences in the amount that each start had been practiced probably did not have much effect on the comparison of the flat and scoop starts, but may well have had an effect on comparisons involving the track start.

The authors concluded that the scoop start was not faster than the other starts, which are characterized by shallower entries; that the scoop start should not be used in pools of a depth less than 4 ft (1.22 m); and that coaches and swimmers should be urged to "eliminate this potentially dangerous technique."

TABLE 14-1 Mean Values for Measures of Three Starting Techniques

Variable	Sex	Starting Technique		
		Flat	Track	Scoop
Time for 10 yd (9.1 m) (s)	M & F	4.16	4.25	4.37
Angle of takeoff[a] (deg)	M	5.1	7.4	17.6
	F	0.6	0.8	3.4
Angle of entry[a] (deg)	M	31.0	34.5	47.4
	F	36.3	35.8	47.1
Distance of entry (m)	M	3.14	2.96	3.05
	F	2.74	2.62	2.74
Distance of head emerging (m)	M	6.46	6.00	6.86
	F	6.22	6.16	6.55
Depth (m)	M	0.73	0.70	1.22
	F	0.67	0.70	0.98

[a] Angles of takeoff and entry refer to the angle of a line representing the head, neck and trunk with the horizontal.

* Adapted from data in Counsilman, and others (1988). Three types of grab starts for competitive swimming. In B. E. Ungerechts, K. Wilke, and K. Reischle (Eds.), *Swimming Science V.* Champaign, Ill.: Human Kinetics Books.

Back Crawl

In the orthodox back crawl start, the swimmer starts in the water with the hands on the grip provided for the purpose and the feet on the end wall of the pool. On the command "Take your marks," the swimmer flexes the arms and pulls himself (or herself) upward and toward the starting block, getting as much of the body above the water as possible. Then, once the gun has been fired, the swimmer releases the grip, drops the head back, swings the arms sideways to a position overhead, and drives vigorously against the wall with the feet. These actions result in the swimmer being projected out above the surface of the water and ultimately into a streamlined gliding position.

TURNS
Freestyle and Backstroke Turns

Freestyle swimmers have used the so-called flip turn for many years. Backstroke swimmers have adopted the flip turn much more recently—following a rule change that made it permissible for them to roll from a back-lying position to a front-lying position in the last stroke before executing the turn. The adoption of the flip turn is expected to reduce turning time in backstroke events by 0.18 s per turn.[118]

The turn begins with a strong pulling motion that brings both arms alongside the swimmer's body. To bring the arms to this position (a position that facilitates the rotation to follow) the swimmer either stops one arm as it reaches the end of its pull and pulls the other one through to join it, or stops one arm at entry and allows the other to catch up with it before executing a two-handed pull back to the hips. In either case, the pulling action is accompanied by a flexion of the neck and spine, which drives the head and shoulders forward and downward below the surface of the water, and by a bringing together of both legs. The increased resistance experienced by the head and shoulders as they move out of alignment with the rest of the body, together with the moments evoked by a dolphin-like kick of both legs and a pressing downward and forward with the hands, cause the swimmer to somersault forward (Fig. 14-15). Near the end of this somersaulting movement, the feet strike the wall some 30–40 cm below the surface of the water and pointing almost directly upward. The swimmer then drives forcefully away from the wall while twisting about the long axis of the body. These movements culminate in the swimmer assuming a prone, extended, streamlined position for the glide to follow. When the speed of this glide has slowed to normal swimming speed, the swimmer settles once more into the normal cycle of stroking and kicking actions.

There are two major variants of the front crawl flip turn—the *pike turn*, in which the body is flexed at the hips and the legs are kept extended during the somersault; and the *tuck turn*, in which the somersault is performed with the body flexed at hips and knees. To determine which of these alternative techniques afforded the faster turn, Ward[119] conducted a study in which 14 members of a college life-saving class were matched and then divided into two groups. Each group was given instruction (10, 15-min sessions) in one of the two techniques. Each subject then performed 10 trials using the technique in which he had received instruction. These trials were recorded on film, and the time from the head reaching a given vertical plane until the feet contacted the wall (the *in time*) and the time from wall contact until the head again reached the vertical plane (the *out time*) were determined. The subsequent statistical analysis revealed that the tuck turn was significantly faster than the pike turn with respect to in time, out time, and total time (in time plus out time). Ward concluded, therefore, that "the tuck [turn] is the superior turn for most beginners."

The characteristics of the flip turn, and the contributions of the turn to the total time for an event, vary subtly as the distance of the race increases. Chow and colleagues[120] analyzed the performances of the finalists in the men's and women's freestyle events at a major international meet and found that as the distance of the race increased, the swimmers initiated their turns closer to the wall, executed their turns with a slower turning motion, and decreased the distance of the glide following the turn. They also noted that the correlation between the total turn time and the time for the event increased systematically as the distance of the event increased, suggesting that "a swimmer's turning technique assumes a progressively

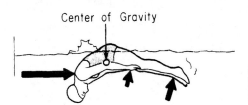

Figure 14-15.
Forces producing somersaulting rotation in the front crawl flip turn.

greater importance as the distance of the event increases." This latter finding is consistent with an earlier report that the percentage of the total time for the event that is spent turning ranged from 20.5 percent for 50-yd (45.7-m) freestyle events to 36.5 percent for 1000-yd (915-m) freestyle events, in a 25-yd (22.9-m) pool.[121]

Butterfly and Breaststroke Turns

Whereas the flip turn involves rotation about the swimmer's transverse and longitudinal axes, the turn most commonly used in butterfly and breaststroke events involves rotation that is primarily about the swimmer's frontal axis.

To execute an orthodox butterfly or breaststroke turn, the swimmer touches the end wall with both hands, bends the arms a little as forward speed is reduced to zero, and simultaneously begins to draw the knees up underneath the body. This rotation of the lower body toward the wall continues as the swimmer releases one hand and turns the head and trunk in the direction of the turn. The rotation of the swimmer about the frontal axis—most obvious at this time—is accelerated as the remaining hand pushes off from the wall. Then, once the feet have been placed against the wall, the forceful extension of the hip, knee, and ankle joints begins. The reaction to the forces thus exerted drives the swimmer away from the wall and eventually into the streamlined, prone-gliding position from which the normal swimming action is resumed.

Huellhorst, Ungerechts, and Willimczik[122] have suggested that (a) the time taken between first hand contact with the wall and the beginning of the push-off and (b) the velocity of the center of gravity of the swimmer at the end of the push-off, are important measures of how well a breaststroke turn is performed.

Recommended Readings

CLARYS, J. P., AND LEWILLIE, L. (Eds.) *Swimming II*. Baltimore: University Park Press.

COUNSILMAN, J. E. (1968). *The Science of Swimming*. London: Pelham Books.

COUNSILMAN, J. E. (1977). *Competitive Swimming Manual for Coaches and Swimmers*. Bloomington, Ind.: Counsilman Co.

HOLLANDER, A. P., AND DE GROOT, G. (Eds.) (1983). *Biomechanics and Medicine in Swimming*. Champaign, Ill.: Human Kinetics Publishers.

LEWILLIE, L., AND CLARYS, J. P. (Eds.) (1971). *First International Symposium on Biomechanics in Swimming, Waterpolo and Diving Proceedings*. Université Libre de Bruxelles Laboratoire de L'effort.

MAGLISCHO, E. W. (1982). *Swimming Faster: A Comprehensive Guide to the Science of Swimming*. Palto Alto, Calif.: Mayfield Publishing Company.

MAGLISCHO, C. W., AND OTHERS. (1987). The swimmer: A study of propulsion and drag. *Soma: Engineering for the Human Body*. 2:40–44.

MARTIN, R. B. (1989). *Biomechanics of Sport*. Boca Raton, Fla.: CRC Press, Inc., pp. 35–52 (Swimming: Forces on aquatic animals and humans).

TERAUDS, J., AND BEDINGIELD, E. W. (Eds.) (1979). *Swimming III*. Baltimore: University Park Press.

UNGERECHTS, B. E., WILKE, K., AND REISCHLE, K. (Eds.) (1988). *Swimming Science V*. Champaign, Ill.: Human Kinetics Books.

1. Guimaraes, A. C. S. (1982). A mechanical analysis of the grab starting technique in swimming. M.A. thesis, University of Iowa.

2. Hay, J. G., Guimaraes, A. C. S., and Grimston, S. K. (1983). A quantitative look at swimming biomechanics. *Swimming Technique,* August–October, pp. 11–17.

3. Karpovich, P. V. (1936). Analysis of the propelling force in the crawl stroke. *Research Quarterly,* 6:49–58.

4. Armbruster, D. A., Allen, R. H., and Billingsley, H. S. (1970). *Swimming and Diving* (p. 71). London: Kaye & Ward, Ltd.

5. Counsilman, J. E. (1968). *The Science of Swimming* (p. 25). Englewood Cliffs, N.J.: Prentice Hall.

6. Mosterd, W. L., and Jongbloed, J. (1963). Analysis of the stroke of highly trained swimmers. *Arbeitsphysiologie,* 20:291.

7. Magel, J. R. (1970). Propelling force measured during tethered swimming in the four competitive swimming styles. *Research Quarterly,* 41:72.

8. Counsilman, J. E. (1971). The application of Bernoulli's principle to human propulsion in water. In L. Lewillie and J. P. Clarys (Eds.), *Proceedings of the First International Symposium on Biomechanics in Swimming, Waterpolo, and Diving.* Université Libre de Bruxelles Laboratoire de L'effort.

9. Brown, R. M., and Counsilman, J. E. (1971). The role of lift in propelling the swimmer. In J. M. Cooper (Ed.), *Selected Topics on Biomechanics: Proceedings of the C.I.C. Symposium on Biomechanics* (pp. 179–88). Chicago, Ill.: The Athletic Institute.

10. Barthels, K. M., and Adrian, M. J. (1975). Three-dimensional spatial hand patterns of skilled butterfly swimmers. In L. Lewillie and J. P. Clarys (Eds.), *Swimming II* (pp. 154–60). Baltimore: University Park Press.

11. Rackham, G. W. (1975). An analysis of arm propulsion in swimming. In L. Lewillie and J. P. Clarys (Eds.), *Swimming II* (pp. 174–79). Baltimore: University Park Press.

12. Schleihauf, R. E. (1974). A biomechanical analysis of freestyle. *Swimming Technique,* 40:89–96.

13. Schleihauf, B. (1976). A hydrodynamic analysis of breaststroke pulling proficiency. *Swimming Technique,* 12:100–105.

14. Schleihauf, R. E. (1979). A hydrodynamic analysis of swimming propulsion. In J. Terauds and E. W. Bedingfield (Eds.), *Swimming III* (pp. 70–109). Baltimore: University Park Press.

15. Wood, T. C. (1979). A fluid dynamic analysis of the propulsive potential of the hand and forearm in swimming. In J. Terauds and E. W. Bedingfield (Eds.), *Swimming III* (pp. 62–69). Baltimore: University Park Press.

16. Schleihauf, R., Gray, L., and DeRose J. (1983). Three dimensional analysis of hand propulsion in sprint front crawlstroke. In A. P. Hollander, P. A. Huijing, and G. de Groot (Eds.), *Biomechanics and Medicine in Swimming* (pp. 173–83). Champaign, Ill.: Human Kinetics Publishers.

17. Schleihauf. A hydrodynamic analysis of swimming propulsion, pp. 71–83.

18. Ibid., p. 76.

19. Wood. A fluid dynamic analysis of the propulsive potential of the hand and forearm in swimming, pp. 62–65.

20. Thayer, A. M. (1990). Hand pressure forces as a predictor of resultant and propulsive hand forces in swimming. Ph.D. dissertation, University of Iowa.

21. Counsilman. *The Science of Swimming* (p. 69).

22. Ibid., pp. 25–30.

23. Kreighbaum, E., and Barthels, K. M. (1981). *Biomechanics: A Qualitative Approach for Studying Human Movement* (pp. 483–540). Minneapolis: Burgess.

24. Counsilman. *The Science of Swimming* (pp. 20–21).

25. Alley, L. E. (1952). An analysis of water resistance and propulsion in swimming the crawl stroke. *Research Quarterly,* 23:269.

26. Kruchoski, E. P. (1954). A performance analysis of drag and propulsion in swimming three selected forms of the back crawl stroke. Ph.D. dissertation, State University of Iowa.

27. Counsilman. *The Science of Swimming,* pp. 3, 5.

28. Clarys, J. P. (1979). Human morphology and hydrodynamics. In J. Terauds and E. W. Bedingfield (Eds.), *Swimming III* (p. 31). Baltimore: University Park Press.

29. Sharp, R. L., and others (1988). The effect of shaving body hair on the physiological cost of freestyle swimming. *Journal of Swimming Research,* 4:9–13.

30. Alley. An analysis of water resistance and propulsion in swimming the crawl stroke, p. 261.

31. Counsilman, J. E. (1955). Forces in swimming two types of crawl stroke. *Research Quarterly*, 26:133.

32. Clarys, J. P. (1976). Onderzoek naar de hydrodynamische en morfologische aspekten van het menselijk lichaam. Unpublished doctoral dissertation, Instituut voor Morfologie, Brussels.

33. Clarys. Human morphology and hydrodynamics, pp. 3–41.

34. Miller, D. I. (1975). Biomechanics of swimming. In J. H. Wilmore and J. F. Keogh (Eds.), *Exercise and Sport Sciences Reviews* (pp. 219–48). New York: Academic Press.

35. Clarys. Unpublished doctoral dissertation.

36. Clarys. Human morphology and hydrodynamics, pp. 3–41.

37. di Prampero, P. E., and others (1974). Energetics of swimming in man. *Journal of Applied Physiology*, 37:1–5.

38. Rennie, D. W., Pendergast, D. R., and di Prampero, P. E. (1975). Energetics of swimming. In L. Lewillie and J. P. Clarys (Eds.), *Swimming II* (pp. 97–104). Baltimore: University Park Press.

39. Schleihauf, R. E. (1984). The biomechanical analysis of swimming propulsion in the sprint front crawlstroke. Unpublished doctoral dissertation, Columbia University Teachers College.

40. Hollander, A. P., de Groot, G., and Ingen Schenau van, G. J. (1987). Active drag of female swimmers. In B. Jonsson (Ed.) *Biomechanics X-B* (pp. 717–24). Champaign, Ill.: Human Kinetics Publishers.

41. Hollander, A. P., and others (1985). Measurement of effective hand propulsive force during front crawl swimming. *Abstract Book, 10th International Congress of Biomechanics, Arbete och Halsa*, 14:111.

42. Vaart, A. J. M., and others (1987). An estimation of drag in front crawl swimming. *Journal of Biomechanics*, 20:543–46.

43. Ringer, L. B., and Adrian, M. J. (1969). An electrogoniometric study of the wrist and elbow in the crawl arm stroke. *Research Quarterly*, 40:361.

44. East, D. E. (1970). Swimming: An analysis of stroke frequency, stroke length and performance. *New Zealand Journal of Health, Physical Education and Recreation*, 3:16–27.

45. Craig, A. B., and Pendergast, D. R. (1979). Relationships of stroke rate, distance per stroke, and velocity in competitive swimming. *Medicine and Science in Sport*, 11:278–83.

46. Pai, Y-C., Hay, J. G., and Wilson, B. D. (1985). Stroking techniques of elite swimmers. *Journal of Sport Sciences*, 2:225–39.

47. Kennedy, P., and others (1990). Analysis of male and female Olympic swimmers in the 100-meter events. *International Journal of Sport Biomechanics*, 6:187–97.

48. Craig and Pendergast. Relationships of stroke rate, distance per stroke, and velocity in competitive swimming, pp. 278–83.

49. Craig, A. B., and others (1985). Velocity, stroke rate, and distance per stoke during elite swimming competition. *Medicine and Science in Sports and Exercise*, 17:625–34.

50. Pai, Hay, and Wilson. Stroking techniques of elite swimmers, pp. 225–39.

51. Hay, Guimaraes, and Grimston. A quantitative look at swimming biomechanics, pp. 11–17.

52. Craig and others. Velocity, stroke rate, and distance per stroke during elite swimming competition, pp. 625–34.

53. Pai, Hay, and Wilson. Stroking techniques of elite swimmers, pp. 225–39.

54. East. Swimming: An analysis of stroke frequency, stroke length and performance, pp. 16–27.

55. Craig, and others. Velocity, stroke rate, and distance per stroke during elite swimming competition, pp. 625–34.

56. Pai, Hay, and Wilson. Stroking techniques of elite swimmers, pp. 225–39.

57. Kennedy and others. Analysis of male and female Olympic swimmers in the 100-meter events, pp. 187–97.

58. Craig and others. Velocity, stroke rate, and distance per stroke during elite swimming competition, pp. 625–34.

59. Pai, Hay, and Wilson. Stroking techniques of elite swimmers, pp. 225–39.

60. Kennedy and others. Analysis of male and female Olympic swimmers in the 100-meter events, pp. 187–97.

61. Grimston, S. K., and Hay, J. G. (1986). The relationships among anthropometric and

stroking characteristics of college swimmers. *Medicine and Science in Sports and Exercise,* 18:60–68.

62. Ibid., pp. 60–68.
63. Hay, Guimaraes, and Grimston. A quantitative look at swimming biomechanics, pp. 11–17.
64. Cureton, T. K. (1930). Mechanics and kinesiology of swimming the crawl flutter kick. *Research Quarterly,* 1:87–121.
65. Robertson, D. F. (1960). Relationship of strength of selected muscle groups and ankle flexibility to the flutter kick in swimming. M.A. thesis, State University of Iowa.
66. Allen, R. H. (1948). A study of the leg stroke in swimming the crawl stroke. M.A. thesis, State University of Iowa.
67. Poulos, G. L. (1949). An analysis of the propulsion factors in the American crawl stroke. M.A. thesis, State University of Iowa.
68. Alley. An analysis of water resistance and propulsion in swimming and crawl stroke, pp. 253–70.
69. Thrall, W. R. (1960). A performance analysis of the propulsive force of the flutter kick. Ph.D. dissertation, State University of Iowa.
70. Eaves, G. (1971). Angular momentum and the popularity of the six-beat crawl. In L. Lewillie and J. P. Clarys (Eds.), *First International Symposium on Biomechanics in Swimming, Waterpolo and Diving Proceedings* (p. 143). Université Libre de Bruxelles Laboratoire de L'effort.
71. Ibid.
72. Schleihauf. A hydrodynamic analysis of swimming propulsion, pp. 104–8.
73. Ibid., p. 108.
74. Hay, J. G., Liu, Q., and Andrews, J. G. (1989). The influence of body roll on handpath in freestyle swimming. *Proceedings First I.O.C. World Congress on Sport Sciences* (pp. 285–86).
75. Liu, Q. (1990). The relationship of body roll and handpath during the pull phase in freestyle swimming. M.A. thesis, University of Iowa.
76. Schleihauf, R. E. (1981). Swimming propulsion: A hydrodynamic analysis. *The Third Sino-American Symposium on Physical Education and Sports Research Reports* (pp. 47–95, 183–98). Taichung, Taiwan: Tunghai University.
77. Schleihauf, Gray, and DeRose. Three dimensional analysis of hand propulsion in sprint front crawlstroke.
78. Schleihauf. Specificity of strength training in swimming: A biomechanical viewpoint.
79. Counsilman, J. E. (1981). The importance of hand speed and acceleration in swimming the crawl stroke. In J. M. Cooper and B. Haven (Eds.), *Proceedings of the Biomechanics Symposium, Indiana University, October 26–28, 1980* (pp. 226–38). Ind.: The Indiana State Board of Health.
80. Maglischo, C. W., and others (1986). A biomechanical analysis of the 1984 U.S. Olympic swimming team. *Journal of Swimming Research,* 2:12–16.
81. Cureton, T. K. (1930). Relationship of respiration to speed efficiency in swimming. *Research Quarterly,* 1:66.
82. Karpovich, P. V. (1933). Water resistance in swimming. *Research Quarterly,* 4:26.
83. Counsilman, J. E. (1986). *Competitive Swimming Manual for Coaches and Swimmers* (pp. 159–60).
84. Keskinen, K. L., and Komi, P. V. (1991). Breathing pattern of elite swimmers in aerobic/anaerobic loading. *Book of Abstracts: XIIIth International Congress on Biomechanics* (pp. 87–88).
85. Ibid.
86. Barthels, K. M., and Adrian, M. J. (1971). Variability in the dolphin kick under four conditions. In L. Lewillie and J. P. Clarys (Eds.), *First International Symposium on Biomechanics in Swimming, Waterpolo and Diving Proceedings* (pp. 105–18). Université Libre de Bruxelles Laboratoire de L'effort.
87. Kersten, O. A. (1960). Propulsion factors in swimming the dolphin butterfly. M.A. thesis, State University of Iowa.
88. Schleihauf. A hydrodynamic analysis of swimming propulsion, pp. 97–100.
89. Ibid., pp. 100–104.
90. Kruchoski. A performance analysis of drag and propulsion in swimming three selected forms of the back crawl stroke, pp. 47–48.
91. Persyn, U., de Maeyer, J., and Vervaecke, H. (1975). Investigation of hydrodynamic

determinants of competitive swimming strokes. In L. Lewillie and J. P. Clarys (Eds.), *Swimming II* (pp. 214–22). Baltimore: University Park Press.

92. Van Tilborgh, L., Willems, E. J., and Persyn, U. (1988). Estimation of breaststroke propulsion and resistance-resultant impulses from film analyses. In B. E. Ungerechts, K. Wilke, and K. Reischle (Eds.), *Swimming Science V* (pp. 67–71). Champaign, Ill.: Human Kinetics Publishers.

93. Kent, M. R., and Atha, J. (1971). Selected critical transient body position in breaststroke and their influence upon water resistance. In L. Lewillie and J. P. Clarys (Eds.), *First International Symposium on Biomechanics in Swimming, Waterpolo and Diving Proceedings* (pp. 119–25). Université Libre de Bruxelles Laboratoire de L'effort.

94. Craig, A. B., Boomer, W. L., and Skehan, P. L. (1988). Patterns of velocity in competitive breaststroke swimming. In B. Ungerechts, K. Wilke, and K. Reischle (Eds.), *Swimming Science V* (pp. 73–77). Champaign, Ill.: Human Kinetics Publishers.

95. Firby, H. (1975). *Howard Firby on Swimming* (pp. 69–73). London: Pelham Books.

96. Kreighbaum and Barthels. *Biomechanics: A Qualitative Approach for Studying Human Movement* (pp. 438–42).

97. Maglischo, E. (1982). *Swimming Faster: A Comprehensive Guide to the Science of Swimming* (pp. 146–55). Palto Alto, Mayfield Publishing Co.

98. Over, M. E. (1963). A comparison of the force and resistance of the frog kick and whip kick used in swimming the orthodox breast stroke. M.A. thesis, Long Beach State College (p. 5).

99. Ibid., pp. 7–9.

100. Cake, F. (1942). The relative effectiveness of two types of frog kick used in swimming the breast stroke. *Research Quarterly*, 13:201–4.

101. Counsilman, J. E. (1948). A cinematographic analysis of the butterfly breaststroke. M.S. thesis, University of Illinois. (Cited in Counsilman. *The Science of Swimming* [pp. 117–18]).

102. Over. A comparison of the force and resistance of the frog kick and the whip kick used in swimming the orthodox breaststroke.

103. Nimz, R., and others (1988). The relationship of anthropometric measures to different types of breaststroke kick. In B. E. Ungerechts, K. Wilke, and K. Reischle (Eds.), *Swimming Science V* (pp. 115–19). Champaign, Ill: Human Kinetics Books.

104. Belokovsky, V., and Ivanchenko, E. (1975). A hydrokinetic apparatus for the study and improvement of leg movements in the breaststroke. In L. Lewillie and J. P. Clarys (Eds.), *Swimming II* (pp. 64–69). Baltimore: University Park Press.

105. Ibid., p. 67.

106. Ibid., p. 69.

107. Kinnear, A. D. (1968). Breaststroke today. *Swimming Technique*, 4:112.

108. Ibid.

109. Guimaraes. A mechanical analysis of the grab starting techniques in swimming.

110. Hay, Guimaraes, and Grimston. A quantitative look at swimming biomechanics.

111. Cavanagh, P. R., Palmgren, J. V., and Kerr, B. A. (1975). A device to measure forces at the hands during the grab start. In L. Lewillie and J. P. Clarys (Eds.), *Swimming II* (pp. 43–50). Baltimore: University Park Press.

112. Lewis, S. (1980). Comparison of five swimming starting techniques. *Swimming Technique*, 16:124–28.

113. Ayalon, A., van Gheluwe, B., and Kanitz, M. (1975). A comparison of four styles of racing start in swimming. In J. P. Clarys and L. Lewillie (Eds.), *Swimming II* (pp. 233–40). Baltimore: University Park Press.

114. Counsilman, J. E., and others (1988). Three types of grab starts for competitive swimming. In B. E. Ungerechts, K. Wilke and K. Reischle (Eds.), *Swimming Science V* (pp. 81–91). Champaign, Ill.: Human Kinetics Books.

115. Zatsiorsky, V. M., Bulgakova, N. Z., and Chaplinsky, N. M. (1979). Biomechanical analysis of starting techniques in swimming. In J. Terauds and E. W. Bedingfield (Eds.), *Swimming III* (pp. 199–206). Baltimore: University Park Press.

116. Kirner, K. E., Bock, M. A., Welch, J. H. (1989). A comparison of four different start combinations. *Journal of Swimming Research*, 4:5–11.

117. Counsilman and others. Three types of grab starts for competitive swimming.

118. Hanley, R. D. (1992). The roll over turn. *Swimming Technique*, 28:29–31.

119. Ward, T. W. (1976). A cinematographical comparison of two turns. *Swimming Technique*, 13:4–6, 9.

120. Chow, J. W-C. and others (1984). Turning techniques of elite swimmers. *Journal of Sports Sciences*, 2:241–55.
121. Thayer, A. L. and Hay, J. G. (1984). Motivating start and turn improvement. *Swimming Technique*, 20:17–20.
122. Huellhorst, U., Ungerechts, B. E., and Willimczik, K. (1988). In B. E. Ungerechts, K. Wilke, and K. Reischle (Eds.), *Swimming Science V* (pp. 93–98). Champaign, Ill.: Human Kinetics Books.

15

TRACK AND FIELD: RUNNING

BASIC CONSIDERATIONS

In running events, an athlete's objective is to cover a given distance (either on the flat or over obstacles) in the least possible time. The time actually recorded by the athlete is determined by the distance of the event and by the athlete's average speed over that distance (Eq. [3-1]). The speed at which the athlete runs is equal to the product of two factors:

- the distance covered with each stride* taken—the *stride length*; and
- the number of strides taken in a given time—the *stride frequency* (also referred to as *stride cadence* or *rate of striding*).

Thus, a distance runner who has a 2-m stride and takes three strides per second runs at a speed of 6 m/s:

$$\text{Speed} = \text{Stride length} \times \text{Stride frequency}$$
$$= 2.0 \text{ m/stride} \times 3 \text{ strides/second}$$
$$= 6 \text{ m/s}$$

---

* In track and field, one-half cycle of running (for example, from touchdown on the left foot to the next touchdown on the right foot) is called a *stride*. In studies of human walking, one complete cycle of walking (for example, from left heel strike to the next left heel strike) is called a *stride* and one-half cycle is called a *step*.

Now if the distance runner were somehow able to increase the stride frequency to four strides per second while maintaining the same stride length as before, the speed would be markedly increased:

	STRIDE LENGTH		STRIDE FREQUENCY	

Original speed = 2 m/stride × 3 strides/second = 6 m/s

New speed = 2 m/stride × 4 strides/second = 8 m/s

However, if this increase in stride frequency were accompanied by a decrease in stride length to 1.5 m, the effort made to bring this change about would have been to no avail:

	STRIDE LENGTH		STRIDE FREQUENCY	

Original speed = 2.0 m/stride × 3 strides/second = 6 m/s

New speed = 1.5 m/stride × 4 strides/second = 6 m/s

In other words, the increase in stride frequency would be matched by a comparable decrease in stride length, and the running speed would be unaltered. An increase in one parameter accompanied by a decrease in the other may result in an improvement in speed if the decrease is less than comparable to the increase; for example:

	STRIDE LENGTH		STRIDE FREQUENCY	

Original speed = 2.0 m/stride × 3 strides/second = 6 m/s

New speed = 1.8 m/stride × 4 strides/second = 7.2 m/s

From all this, it is apparent that to increase speed, a runner must bring about an increase in one parameter without causing the other to be reduced a comparable (or, worse yet, a more than comparable) amount.

Because running speed is completely dependent on the magnitudes of the stride length and the stride frequency, it is important to consider the factors that determine these magnitudes.

Stride Length

The length of each stride taken by a runner may be considered as the sum of three separate distances (Fig. 15-1):

- the *takeoff distance*—the horizontal distance that the center of gravity is forward of the toe of the takeoff foot at the instant the latter leaves the ground;
- the *flight distance*—the horizontal distance that the center of gravity travels while the runner is in the air; and
- the *landing distance*—the horizontal distance that the toe of the lead-

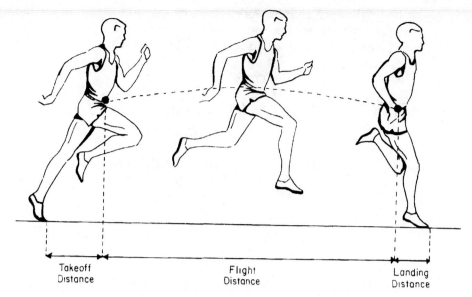

Figure 15-1. Contributions to the total length of a runner's stride.

ing foot is forward of the center of gravity at the instant the runner lands.

The contribution that each of these distances makes to the total length of the stride is indicated by the data in Table 15-1. These data are for 12 male sprinters with best 100-m times of 9.9-10.4 s, running at or near maximum speed.

The first of these three contributions depends on the position of the athlete's body at the instant of takeoff. The extent to which the runner extends the support leg before the foot leaves the ground, and the angle that the leg makes with the horizontal at this time, are of some importance with respect to the position of the body. The angle that the leg makes with the horizontal at the instant the foot breaks contact with the ground is subject to considerable variation. For example, in the case of the sprinter in Fig. 15-2, the angle varies from approximately 30° as he leaves the blocks to approximately 60° as he approaches full stride. Correspondingly, the horizontal distance from toe to center of gravity decreases from 90 cm to 40 cm.

TABLE 15-1 Relative Contributions to Stride Length (Distances expressed in percentages of total stride length).

	Minimum	Average	Maximum
Takeoff distance	22	26	30
Flight distance	50	57	64
Landing distance	12	17	20

Based on data in Atwater, A. E. (1981). Kinematic analysis of sprinting. In J. M. Cooper and B. Haven (Eds.), *Proceedings of the Biomechanics Symposium, Indiana University, October 26–28, 1980* (pp. 309–10). The Indiana State Board of Health.

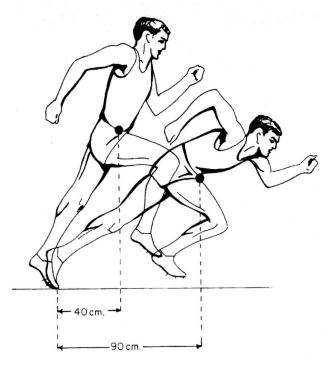

Figure 15-2.
The distance that a runner's center of gravity is forward of his foot at the instant the foot leaves the ground varies with the inclination of his body at that time.

40 cm.

90 cm.

During that part of the running stride in which the athlete is not in contact with the ground, the horizontal distance that he (or she) travels is determined by the factors that govern the flight of all such projectiles, namely, the speed, angle, and height of release and the air resistance encountered in flight. By far the most important of these is the speed of release, a quantity primarily determined by the ground-reaction forces exerted on the athlete. These in turn are a result of the forces, mainly from the extension of hip, knee, and ankle joints, that the runner exerts against the ground. While the influence of air resistance on running speed is certainly not confined to the flight phase of the stride, it is in causing variations in the horizontal distance that the runner travels during this phase that air resistance probably has its greatest effect.

The horizontal distance from the toe of the leading foot to the line of gravity at the instant the athlete lands is invariably the smallest of the three contributions to the total length of the stride. Its magnitude is limited by the need to ensure that the ground reaction forces evoked as the foot lands are as favorable as possible. Thus, while swinging the lower leg forward just before the foot lands might seem a logical way for a runner to increase stride length, the forward motion of the foot as it hits the ground evokes a backward reaction (a kind of "propping" or "braking" reaction) that reduces the runner's forward speed. In other words, the small gain in stride length is likely to be achieved only at the expense of a more-than-comparable reduction in the length and/or frequency of the strides that follow. (*Note:* This swinging forward of the lower leg, or "overstriding," is precisely the technique that runners use to slow down once they have passed the finish line—Fig. 15-3).

Stride Frequency

The number of strides an athlete takes in a given time is determined by how long it takes to complete one stride—the longer this takes, the less strides the athlete can take in a given time, and vice versa. The time taken to complete one stride may be regarded as the sum of the times during which the athlete is (1) in contact with the ground; and (2) in the air. The ratio of these two times in top-class sprinting varies from approximately 2:1 during the start to between 1:1.3 and 1:1.5 when the athlete is running at maximum or near-maximum speed.[1] Thus, while a sprinter spends approximately 67 percent of the time of each stride in contact with the ground during the first few strides, this figure decreases to 40-45 percent as top speed is approached.[2]

The time that the athlete is in contact with the ground is governed primarily by the speed with which the muscles of the supporting leg can drive the body forward and then forward and upward into the next flight phase.

Like other parameters associated with the motion of a projectile, the time the athlete spends in the air is determined by the velocity and the height of the center of gravity at takeoff and by the air resistance encountered in flight.

Studies on Stride Length and Stride Frequency

The stride length and stride frequency of sprinters of varying abilities have been the subject of a number of research papers. Notable among these are two in which the stride characteristics of some of the world's best male and female sprinters were investigated.

Figure 15-3.
Slowing down at the finish of a race.
(Photograph courtesy of Mike Conway.)

In the first of these two papers, Hoffman[3] examined the performance of 56 male sprinters with best times for 100 m ranging from 10.0 s to 11.4 s. This study revealed:

- A very close relationship existed between an athlete's standing height and his average stride length during a 100-m race. A similarly close relationship existed between the athlete's leg length—measured from the greater trochanter on the femur to the sole of the foot—and the average stride length. (*Note:* The average stride length was computed by dividing the distance from the start line to the end of the stride immediately before the finish line was reached, by the total number of strides taken. Thus, if the athlete's foot landed 1 m from the finish line at the end of the penultimate stride in the race, and he had taken 50 strides up to that point, his average stride length was 99/50 = 1.98 m.) On the average, the average stride length was equal to 1.14 times the athlete's height or 2.11 times his leg length.

- A very close relationship existed between each of these same two measurements (height and leg length) and the average stride frequency, although in this case the relationships were inverse ones. In other words, the average stride frequency decreased as the height and leg length of the athletes increased.

- The maximum stride length (defined by Hoffman as the average length of four strides taken between 50 m and 60 m in a 100-m race) could be fairly accurately estimated by adding 18 cm to the average stride length. The largest values of the maximum stride length actually measured were the 2.37-m distances of an Olympic triple-jump champion and a Soviet sprinter. However, estimated values of the maximum stride length for several of the sprinters for whom it was not possible to obtain actual measurements exceeded this figure. The highest estimate was 2.46 m.

- On the average, the maximum stride length was equal to 1.24 times the height of the athlete. If only the best 12 sprinters (100-m times of 10.7 s or better) were considered, this value increased to 1.265 times the athlete's height.

From data gathered on 20 male students at the University of Helsinki and on 12 of the "best male runners at Stanford University," Rompotti[4] concluded that "the normal full speed running stride length is 1.17 × Height ± 4 in. [10 cm]." Considering the obvious differences in the abilities of their respective samples, the results of Hoffman and Rompotti seem to be in very good agreement.

The results obtained by Atwater[5] in studies of 23 sprinters with best 100-m times of 9.9-10.4 s differed substantially from those reported by either Hoffman or Rompotti. For two groups of 12 subjects, the average stride lengths recorded were 2.5 m (recorded for one group at the 50-m mark) and 2.34 m (recorded for the other group at 60-m). These values were, respectively equivalent to 1.41 and 1.31 times the average height of the subjects and 2.65 and 2.47 times their average leg length. The differences between these results and those of the previous investigators are probably due to two interrelated factors—differences in the track surfaces (cinders versus synthetic surfaces) and in the caliber of the athletes involved.

In the second study conducted by Hoffman,[6] the subjects were 23 female sprinters with best 100-m times between 11.0 s and 12.4 s. As in the study of male sprinters, this group contained many outstanding performers. In general, the results obtained were very similar to those obtained in the earlier study (for example, on the average, the average stride length was equal to 1.15 times the athlete's height and 2.16 times the leg length).

Summary

The relationships between the time taken to run a given distance and the factors that determine that time are summarized in Fig. 15-4.

TECHNIQUES
Sprint Start

Of all the sports techniques that have been subjected to biomechanical analysis, few have been more thoroughly examined than the sprint start.

At the starter's command "On your marks," the athlete moves forward and adopts a position with the hands just behind the starting line, the feet on the starting blocks, and the knee of the back leg resting on the ground (Fig. 15-5[a]). On the command "Set," the athlete lifts the knee of the back leg off the ground, thereby elevating the hips and shifting the center of gravity forward (Fig. 15-5[b]). Finally, when the gun is fired, the athlete lifts the hands from the track, swings the arms vigorously (one forward, one backward), and with a forceful extension of both legs drives the body forward away from the blocks and into the first running strides (Fig. 15-5[c] to [e]).

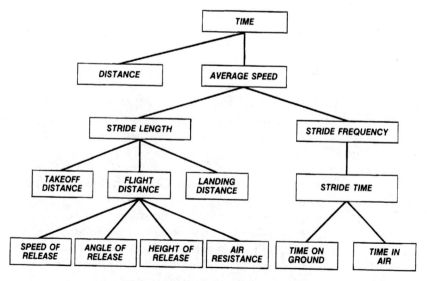

Figure 15-4. Basic factors in running.

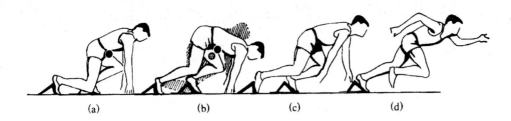

Figure 15-5. An example of good technique in the crouch sprint start.

There are three main types of crouch start—the bunch or bullet, the medium, and the elongated. The principal difference among these three types lies in the longitudinal distance between the feet (that is, in the distance from the toes of one foot to the toes of the other, as measured in the running direction). In the bunch start, the toes of the back foot are placed approximately level with the heel of the front foot. The toe-to-toe distance is therefore of the order of 25–30 cm. In the medium start, the knee of the back leg is placed so that it is opposite a point in the front half of the front foot when the athlete is in the "On your marks" position. Such a placement yields a toe-to-toe distance of somewhere between 40 cm and 55 cm. Finally, in the little-used elongated start, the knee of the back leg is placed level with or slightly behind the heel of the front foot, in the "On your marks" position. The resulting toe-to-toe distances are of the order of 60–70 cm.

A number of attempts have been made to determine which of these three types of start yields the best results in terms of sprinting performances. Henry[7] obtained force-time graphs of the leg thrust during the starts of 18 male sprinters who made runs using block spacings of 11, 16, 21, and 26 in. (28, 41, 53, and 66 cm). The time that elapsed from the firing of the gun until the athlete made his first movement and until he reached markers at 5, 10, and 50 yd (4.6, 9.1, and 45.7 m) from the starting line were recorded. On the basis of the results obtained, Henry concluded that

- Use of the 11-in. bunch start results in clearing the blocks sooner but with less velocity than secured from medium stances, resulting in significantly slower times at 10 yd and 50 yd—Table 15-2. (*Note:* This finding has been discussed in some detail on pp. 79–80.)
- The highest proportion of best runs and the smallest proportion of poorest runs result from starting with a 16-in. stance. A 21-in. stance is nearly as good.

TABLE 15-2 Time and Velocity Characteristics of Crouch Starts Using Various Block Spacings (Mean Values)

	Block Spacing			
	11 in. (28 cm)	16 in. (41 cm)	21 in. (53 cm)	26 in. (66 cm)
Time on Blocks (that is, time from gun to front foot leaving)	0.345 s	0.374 s	0.397 s	0.426 s
Block Velocity (that is, horizontal velocity as athlete leaves blocks)	6.63 ft/s (2.02 m/s)	7.41 ft/s (2.26 m/s)	7.50 ft/s (2.29 m/s)	7.62 ft/s (2.32 m/s)
Time to 10 yd (9.1 m)	2.070 s	2.054 s	2.041 s	2.049 s
Time to 50 yd (45.7 m)	6.561 s	6.479 s	6.497 s	6.540 s

Adapted from data in Henry, F. M. (1952). Force-time characteristics of the sprint start. *Research Quarterly*, 23:306.

- An elongated stance of 26 in. results in greater velocity leaving the blocks but the advantage is lost within the first 10 yd.

Henry's conclusion favoring the use of the medium starts has subsequently been supported by the results of studies by Sigerseth and Grinaker[8] and Hogberg.[9]

Numerous other aspects of crouch starting have been investigated. Bresnahan[10] studied the movements of trained sprinters as they left their marks and found that the order in which a right-handed sprinter broke his contacts with the track was left hand ($\overline{X} = 0.172$ s); right hand ($\overline{X} = 0.219$ s); right foot ($\overline{X} = 0.286$ s); and left foot ($\overline{X} = 0.443$ s). He also expressed the view that this sequence is "the only correct form" and all others are "to the detriment of a sprinter in starting."

Payne and Blader[11] studied the forces exerted against the starting blocks in over 150 starts made by 17 international-class sprinters and found:

- The pattern of forces evoked was characteristic of the particular athlete.
- In general, both rear and front feet started to exert forces on the blocks at the same instant, rarely being separated by more than 0.01 s.
- A strong rear leg action was characteristic of the better starts.
- The resultant force evoked by the athlete while on the blocks acted first in front of the center of gravity and then behind.

Baumann[12] determined selected characteristics of the sprint starts of 30 experienced sprinters grouped on the basis of recent performances over 100 m—Group 1 (10.2–10.6 s), Group 2 (10.9–11.4 s); and Group 3 (11.6–12.4 s)—and found that:

- The horizontal displacement-time, velocity-time, and acceleration-time curves for the start and first few strides "are characteristic for the individual subject like a fingerprint." (*Note:* Payne and Blader[13] reported a similar finding concerning the pattern of forces exerted against the blocks.)

- There was a significant difference between the reaction time of the rear foot and that of the front foot—the mean differences were 0.016 s, 0.019 s, and 0.027 s for groups 1, 2, and 3, respectively. (*Note:* These results are in general agreement with those of Henry[14] and Payne and Blader[15] except that the latter reported a difference in reaction times substantially less than that reported by Baumann for a comparable group—the top sprinters in Britain and Germany, respectively.)

- The good sprinters had a greater proportion of their body weight supported on the hands when they were in the "Set" position than did the sprinters of lesser ability. The proportions for each group (expressed as percentages of body weight) were: Group 1, 73–82 percent; Group 2, 62–75 percent; and Group 3, 52–67 percent.

Jackson and Cooper[16] used 12 male subjects with no specialized training in sprinting to investigate the effects of varying the distance between the hands, and the angle of the knee joint of the back leg, in the "Set" position. Their results supported the use of a narrow hand position—8 in. (20 cm) between the thumbs as opposed to 20 in. (51 cm)—and indicated that use of a back knee angle of 180° resulted in significantly slower times to 10 yd (9.1 m) and to 30 yd (27.4 m) than did back knee angles of 90° and 135°. There was no significant difference in the times to either distance when trials with angles of 90° and 135° were compared.

Numerous investigators have reported values for the time and distance required for a sprinter to reach top speed. Volkov and Lapin[17] reported that "maximal speed in sprint running is attained 4–5 sec after the start;" Mehrikadze and Tabatschnik[18] stated that "as a rule all athletes reach their maximum speed in 5 to 6 sec;" and Henry[19] stated that top speed is attained approximately 6 s after the gun is fired.

The distance traveled in the course of reaching top speed varies with the ability of the sprinter, with good sprinters covering greater distances than poor ones. According to Hill,[20] a sprinter reaches top speed between 30 yd and 50 yd (27.4 m and 45.7 m) from the start. Other investigators have reported higher values for the distances involved—Gundlach[21] reported 30–50 m and Mehrikadze and Tabatschnik[22] reported 50–70 m.

Although making no specific reference to the point at which top speed is reached, Henry and Trafton[23] have given a clear indication that a sprinter's gain in speed after the first 15–20 yd (13.7–18.3 m) is relatively small. Their experimental testing of a theoretical sprint velocity curve revealed that "90 percent of the maximum velocity is reached by 15 yards and 95 percent by 22 yards [20.1 m]." Mehrikadze and Tabatschnik[24] have presented similar findings expressed in terms of the times involved. According to these investigators, "running speed reaches 76% of the maximum in two seconds, 91% in three seconds and 95% in four seconds."

Despite a considerable volume of research into the biomechanics of the crouch start, many basic questions remain unanswered. For example: Do the results obtained from studies of male sprinters also hold true in the case of female sprinters, or do the acknowledged differences in strength, anatomical structure, and so on, cause the optimum block spacings and body position for female sprinters to be different from those of their male counterparts? What is the optimum angle for each starting block? What is the optimum design for starting blocks? (Should the faces of the blocks be curved or flat? What materials should be used on the face of the blocks? Should the tips of the spikes or the soles of the shoes bear on the face of the blocks? Should the block be large enough to support the heel as well as the forward part of the foot? Or do all of these factors have so little effect on the final outcome that they can be considered irrelevant?) These, and many other questions, await the attention of those interested enough to seek the answers.

Sprinting

The basic sprinting action is of considerable importance not only in track and field but in many other sports as well. Although success in sprinting obviously depends on an athlete's ability to combine the actions of the legs, arms, trunk, and so on, into a smoothly coordinated whole, for the purpose of the analysis that follows, the position and movements of each body part are considered separately.

Legs. The action of the legs in running is cyclic. Each foot in turn lands on the ground, passes beneath and behind the body, and then leaves the ground to move forward again ready for the next landing. This cycle can be conveniently subdivided into the following:

- a *supporting phase* that begins when the foot lands and ends when the athlete's center of gravity passes forward of it,
- a *driving phase* that begins as the supporting phase ends and ends as the foot leaves the ground, and
- a *recovery phase* during which the foot is off the ground and is being brought forward preparatory to the next landing.

Supporting phase. The function of the supporting phase is to arrest the athlete's downward motion—a downward motion imparted by gravity during the time the athlete is in the air—and to allow him (or her) to move into position to drive the body forward and upward into the next stride with the minimum loss of momentum.

To ensure that the forces involved in reducing the downward motion to zero are within limits that can readily be tolerated, the athlete instinctively sees to it that the distances through which they act are appropriately large (work-energy relationship, pp. 101–105). Thus when the foot makes contact with the track, the flexion of the hip, knee, and ankle joints is allowed to increase to cushion the shock of the impact. In the course of this process (and despite the views occasionally expressed by coaches that this does not or should not occur), the heel of the foot is almost invariably lowered to the track.

The manner in which a sprinter's foot makes contact with the track has been studied by Nett. Following an analysis of top-class athletes, he reported:

> In the 100 meter and 200 meter runs, the ground is contacted first on the outside edge of the sole, high on the ball (joints of the little toe) . . . In the 400 meter run, which is run at a somewhat slower pace, the contact point lies a bit further back toward the heel; the foot plant is now somewhat flatter . . . In the further course of the motion . . . even in the case of sprinters . . . the heel contacts the ground.[25]

Payne[26] also studied the nature of the contact between the foot and the track in running and found that in a group of 18 international sprinters competing in events up to 200 m, only one remained on the ball of the foot throughout ground contact—or, in other words, did not lower the heel to the track. In a group of 41 international runners competing over 400-1500 m, 6 used this same technique. Apart from the few notable exceptions mentioned, the results obtained by Payne were in excellent agreement with those obtained earlier by Nett.

Whether the athlete's forward momentum is reduced during the supporting phase depends on the nature of the horizontal forces the foot exerts on the ground or, more precisely, on the equal and opposite forces the ground exerts on the foot during this time.

The magnitude and direction of the horizontal force that the foot exerts as it lands are governed by the velocity of the foot *relative to the ground* at that instant. If the foot is traveling forward at the instant it strikes the ground, it will tend to continue to do so (Newton's first law) and will thus exert a forward horizontal force against the ground. In reaction the ground will exert a backward horizontal force that will retard the athlete's forward motion. If the athlete's foot is traveling neither forward nor backward at the instant it strikes the ground, the ground reaction is entirely vertical and the athlete's horizontal motion is unaffected. Finally, if the athlete's foot is moving backward at the instant it lands, a forward horizontal reaction is evoked and the athlete's forward momentum is increased.

Now it should be apparent from the foregoing discussion that for the second function of a supporting phase to be served effectively, the athlete's foot must not be moving forward at the instant it lands. To understand how a sprinter prevents this from occurring, or at least endeavors to prevent it from occurring, it is necessary to examine in some detail those factors that determine the velocity of the foot at the instant it strikes the track. When the athlete is in the air prior to the foot touching down, his (or her) center of gravity is moving forward with a horizontal velocity determined at the moment the athlete left the ground (ignoring the effects of air resistance). Those parts of the body that are not moving forward or backward relative to the center of gravity have this same horizontal velocity. The other parts of the body have horizontal velocities larger or smaller than that of the center of gravity depending on the direction (forward or backward) in which they move. Thus, for example, if an athlete's center of gravity is moving forward at 10 m/s and one foot is moving backward with a horizontal velocity of 2 m/s relative to the center of gravity and the other moving forward with a horizontal velocity of the same magnitude relative to the center of gravity, the actual horizontal velocities of the feet are, respectively, 8 m/s and 12 m/s. In other words, the horizontal velocity of a body part is equal to the horizontal velocity of the center of gravity of the body, plus the horizontal velocity of the part relative to the center of gravity.

It is obvious therefore that the only way in which the athlete can ensure that the foot is not moving forward at the instant it strikes the track (and thus that there are no retarding horizontal forces evoked at this instant) is to have it moving backward relative to the center of gravity with a horizontal velocity at least equal to that at which the center of gravity is moving forward. For example, if the center of gravity is moving forward at 10 m/s, the foot must be moving backward relative to the center of gravity at no less than 10 m/s to achieve the desired result.

Although it must be stressed that the horizontal velocity of the foot is the sole determinant of whether there is a braking or retarding effect when the foot lands, it has frequently been observed that such an effect is produced if the foot is more than a few centimeters forward of a vertical line through the athlete's center of gravity at this time. For example, Deshon and Nelson[27] found a significant positive correlation between (1) the angle the leg made with the ground at the instant the foot landed; and (2) the speed of running. They concluded, therefore, that "efficient running is characterized by . . . placement of the foot as closely as possible beneath the center of gravity of the runner."

There is some evidence to suggest that even if the foot is placed below or almost below the center of gravity, its backward velocity relative to that point is still insufficient to completely eliminate any retarding effect.[28,29] Futhermore, efforts to eliminate this retarding effect by employing a deliberate "pawing" action as the foot is brought down to the track may increase the risk of the athlete sustaining a hamstring injury.[30]

Driving phase. The athlete's task during the driving phase is to drive or thrust downward and backward against the ground. This drive, brought about by the forceful extension of the hip, knee, and ankle joints, causes the body to be projected forward and upward into the next stride.

The athlete's velocity as the foot leaves the ground (and thus the length of the stride to follow) is a function of the work done by the extensor muscles of the hip, knee, and ankle joints during the driving phase (work-energy relationship). Because the distance through which each of these muscle groups exerts force is thus important in determining the athlete's stride length, authorities on sprint running have often contended that the hip, knee, and ankle joints should be fully extended by the time the foot leaves the ground in full-speed running[31 32 33]. Recently, however, it has been reported that elite sprinters do not obtain complete extension of the hip and knee joints[34 35]. For example, Mann and Herman[36] have reported that the medalists in the men's 200 m at the 1984 Olympic Games had hip and knee angles at the instant of takeoff as shown in Table 15-3. (The top figure shown in each case is for a stride 125 m into the race—that is, about 10 m into the final straight; and the other for a stride 180 m into the race, when the athlete might be expected to be feeling the effects of fatigue.)

Although a definitive study has yet to be conducted on the subject, the recent evidence suggest that any additional forces exerted against the ground by completing the extension of the hip and knee joints are less important than the additional time it takes to generate these forces. In short, any increase in stride length produced by these additional forces may be more than offset by an accompanying decrease in stride frequency.

Recovery phase. During the recovery phase the athlete's foot is brought forward from behind the body to that point at which it next makes contact with the track.

As soon as the foot breaks contact with the track, the thigh of the same leg rotates backward a few degrees[37] and then rotates forward, about an axis through the hip joint. This latter, deliberate action (possibly supplemented by an involuntary physiological reaction to the stretching that the flexor muscles of the leg experience during the driving phase) results in the leg bending sharply at the knee and the foot being lifted to a position close to the buttocks. Once seen as an unnecessary and therefore wasteful motion, this high kickup of the foot is now recognized as an inevitable consequence of other important actions. In addition, it is seen to be of value in its own right, for it reduces the moment of inertia of the whole limb to a minimum (relative to a transverse axis through the hip joint) and thus enables it to be rotated forward about the hip joint rather more quickly than would otherwise be the case.

When the athlete's thigh reaches a horizontal or near-horizontal position, the lower leg swings forward about an axis through the knee and the whole limb begins its descent to the track.

TABLE 15-3 Hip and Knee Extension Angles at Takeoff in Elite Sprinting

	Carl Lewis (U.S.A.)	Kirk Baptiste (U.S.A.)	Thomas Jefferson (U.S.A.)
Hip Extension	167	170	167
	167	164	160
Knee Extension	157	156	158
	157	156	156

Adapted from Mann, R., and Herman, J. (1985). Kinematic analysis of Olympic sprint performance: Men's 200 meters. *International Journal of Sports Biomechanics, 1:159.*

The height to which the athlete brings the knee during the forward and upward swing of the thigh has been remarked upon by a number of researchers. Fenn[38] observed that proficient runners tend to raise the knee high as the free-swinging leg is thrust forward; Deshon and Nelson[39] concluded that a high knee lift was one of a number of factors characteristic of efficient running; and Sinning and Forsyth[40] found a "more acute angulation between the trunk and the thigh as running velocity increased."

Arms. Throughout the various phases of an athlete's leg action, the hips are rotated back and forth in a roughly horizontal plane. When the left knee is brought forward and upward in the recovery phase of the left leg cycle, the hips (viewed from above) rotate in a clockwise direction. The limit of this clockwise rotation is reached when the knee reaches its highest point in front of the body. Then, as the left foot is lowered toward the track and the right leg begins its forward and upward movement, the hips begin to rotate in a counterclockwise direction. The limit of this counterclockwise hip rotation is reached as the right knee reaches its highest point in front of the body. At this point the cycle is complete.

These rotary actions of the hips evoke contrary reactions in the athlete's upper body, for, as the athlete's left knee is swung forward and upward, the right arm is swung forward and upward and the left arm backward and upward, to balance this leg action. Then, as the left foot is lowered and the right leg starts to move forward, the actions of the arms are reversed.

Although the shoulders might also be rotated to balance the hip action, such rotation would of necessity be relatively slow. Thus, to avoid the complications that this slowness might introduce, good sprinters use an arm action of such range and vigor that there is no need for a contribution from the shoulders to achieve the required equality between hip action and upper body reaction.

In this arm action, the arms are flexed to about a right angle at the elbow and swung backward, forward, and slightly inward about an axis through the shoulders. At the forward limit of the swing the hands (generally held in a lightly clenched fashion) are at about shoulder height and at the backward limit are level with, or slightly behind, the hip.

The arm actions of sprinters have received very little attention from researchers in biomechanics. The arm actions used when running at middle- and long-distance pace have been studied by Hinrichs,[41] and his results have provided valuable information concerning the role of the arms in running. Hinrichs studied the arm actions of 10 "recreational runners" running on a treadmill at 5-min, 6-min, and 7-min mile pace (5.4 m/s, 4.5 m/s, and 3.8 m/s, respectively) and concluded that the main functions of the arms were:

- to make "... a small but meaningful contribution to lift (generally less than 10 percent of the total). As running speed gets faster and the total amount of lift becomes less (the vertical range of motion of the body generally decreases with running speed), the arms should become increasingly more important to lift."

- to generate an alternating positive and negative angular momentum about a vertical axis through the runner's center of gravity. This tends to cancel out the contrary alternating angular momentum of the legs. "The trunk was found to be an active participant in this balance of angular momentum with the upper trunk rotating back and forth with the arms and the lower trunk with the legs." The result was a relatively small total angular momentum about the vertical axis throughout the running cycle.

Trunk. During the support and driving phases, the athlete exerts vertical and horizontal forces against the ground. The equal and opposite reactions that these evoke tend to accelerate the athlete in the direction in which they act and, if they do not act through the center of gravity, to angularly accelerate him (or her). Thus at the instant depicted in Fig. 15-6, the athlete is acted upon by a vertical reaction R_V, which tends to accelerate him upward and rotate him forward about his transverse axis; and a horizontal reaction R_H, which tends to accelerate him forward and rotate him backward about the same axis. In addition, the athlete is acted upon by an air resistance force A, which in general opposes his motion and tends to rotate him backward. The moment tending to rotate the athlete backward is equal to

$$R_H y_H + A y_A$$

while that tending to rotate him in the opposite direction is equal to

$$R_V x_V$$

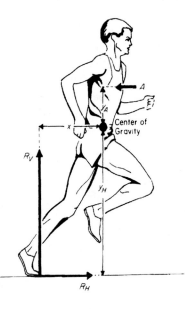

Figure 15-6.
The optimum inclination of the trunk is determined by the moments of the eccentric forces that act on the runner.

where y_H, y_A and x_V are the lengths of the respective moment arms. What happens to the athlete as a result of these opposing tendencies obviously depends on which of the two is the greater. And it is here that the inclination of the trunk comes into the reckoning, for it very largely determines the position of the center of gravity and thus, too, the lengths of the moment arms. For example, if the athlete in Fig. 15-6 were to increase the forward inclination of his trunk, his center of gravity would move forward and downward, decreasing y_H and increasing x_V. (*Note:* The magnitude of y_A would almost certainly change also, although the exact nature of this change would be difficult to predict.)

By making appropriate adjustments in the inclination of the trunk and thus modifying the moments involved, the good sprinter controls the rotation of the body about its transverse axis. When the sprinter drives downward and backward against the starting blocks, the horizontal component of the ground-reaction force is very large. Therefore, to prevent the backward-rotating effect of this force becoming overwhelmingly dominant, the sprinter leans well forward, keeping the moment arm of the horizontal reaction small and that of the vertical reaction large. In succeeding steps the sprinter's progressively greater forward speed makes it increasingly difficult to exert horizontal forces of the same magnitude as at the outset. Thus to prevent the forward-rotating tendency of the vertical reaction becoming dominant and perhaps causing a stumble, the athlete steadily raises the trunk as the horizontal forces decrease in magnitude. By the time the sprinter has reached top speed, the horizontal forces exerted against the ground have been reduced to the point where their resultant accelerating effect is just sufficient to balance the retarding effect of air resistance.* The backward-rotating tendencies of these two forces have been similarly reduced and the need for a pronounced forward lean of the trunk no longer exists. There is still, however, a need to combat the small backward-rotating tendencies of air resistance and the horizontal reaction. If this is not done, the body will eventually rotate into a position from which the athlete cannot apply the horizontal forces against the ground necessary to maintain top speed. Under such circumstances, commonly seen in the concluding stages of 400-m races, the athlete may lose speed to such an extent that he (or she) appears to be running on the spot. For these reasons most good sprinters retain a slight forward lean of the trunk even when running at top speed.

Middle- and Long-Distance Running

As the length of the race increases beyond 400 m—normally regarded as the longest sprint event—the athlete's stride length and stride frequency are both substantially reduced; so too are the range and vigor of most of his

---

* If the effects of air resistance were greater than those of the horizontal reaction, the athlete would lose speed. Conversely, if the effects of air resistance were less than those of the horizontal reaction, the athlete would gain speed. Thus, for the athlete to run "at top speed" these contrary effects must be equal in magnitude.

(or her) actions. The forcefulness of the extension of the hip, knee, and ankle joints during the driving phase is reduced. The extent to which the foot rises toward the buttocks and the height the knee is raised in front during the recovery phase are both reduced. The arms swing through a lesser range than they would if the athlete were sprinting, and part of their function of balancing the leg action may be assumed by the shoulders rotating in opposition to the hips. Finally, with reduction in both air resistance and horizontal ground reaction, the forward inclination of the trunk when running at a constant speed is generally less than it would be if the athlete were sprinting.

Hurdling

Expressed simply, hurdling is a specialized form of running in which, for most of a race, 1 stride in 4 (in the 110-m high hurdles and the 100-m low hurdles) and 1 stride in somewhere between 13 and 20 (in the 400-m intermediate hurdles) is exaggerated to allow the athlete to negotiate the hurdles safely.

High Hurdles

In the 110-m high hurdles, the distance from the start line to the first hurdle is 13.72 m; the distance between the 1.067-m-high hurdles is 9.14 m; and the distance from the last hurdle to the finish line is 14.02 m.

Although differences exist among athletes (and among meets for the same athlete), measures for the segments of a race generally indicate that the athlete's average speed reaches an initial maximum between the third and fourth hurdles, declines steadily until the last hurdle is cleared, and then increases dramatically to a final (and overall) maximum in the sprint to the finish line (Fig. 15-7).

Approach. While essentially the same as that of a sprinter, the starting technique employed by a high hurdler differs in two important respects:

- The foot that the hurdler has forward in the starting position must allow him to take the appropriate number of strides to the first hurdle and to arrive for the takeoff on the correct foot. For example, if the hurdler takes eight strides to the first hurdle (as do most good high hurdlers) and takes off from the left foot, this foot must be the forward one when he is in the starting position.
- The need for the athlete to be in a suitable position for takeoff at the first hurdle requires that the trunk be brought to an upright, or near-upright, position earlier than if he were competing in a flat sprint event.

Takeoff. The first part of the high hurdler's action at takeoff is almost identical to that of a normal sprinting stride. Once the takeoff foot has landed at the end of the last stride before the hurdle, the other foot (the lead foot) is brought up high under the buttocks. (Fig. 15-8[a]). Then with

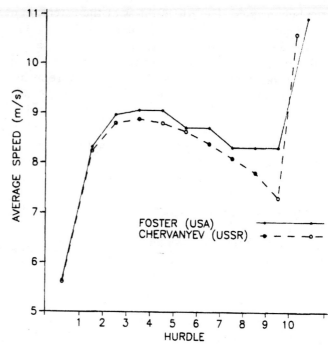

Figure 15-7.
Average speeds for segments of 110-m
high hurdles race. (Adapted from
Brejzer, W. and Kaverin W. [1982]. 110
hurdles: Analysis of competitive
activity. *Legkaya Atletika*, 8:14–15.)

the lead leg well flexed—to reduce its moment of inertia and facilitate its
rotation about an axis through the corresponding hip joint—the lead knee
is swung forward and upward (Fig. 15-8[b]). When the thigh of the leading
leg nears the limit of its forward and upward movement, the lower leg is
angularly accelerated in a forward, downward, and then upward direction.
This acceleration, probably aided by a contraction of the muscles that extend the knee joint, ultimately brings the leading leg into a near-straight
position (Fig. 15-8[c] and [d]). These actions of the leading leg tend to shift
the hurdler's center of gravity in a forward and upward direction and to
rotate the body backward. However, partly in reaction to the movements of
the lead leg and partly as a result of additional muscular forces, the hurdler's trunk is brought forward and downward at the same time as the lead
leg is being swung forward and upward (Fig. 15-8[a] to [d]). This action of
the trunk serves as a counter to the lifting and backward-rotating tendencies of the lead leg.

While the lead leg and trunk are being brought toward each other, the
takeoff leg first supports the athlete and then drives him forward and
upward toward the hurdle. As with the first part of the lead leg action,
these actions of the takeoff leg are very like those used at the equivalent
stages in sprinting.

The distance at which the hurdler takes off in front of the hurdle (that
is, the distance from the toe of the takeoff foot to the line of the hurdle)
depends on his height, leg length, speed, and technique. Of these factors,
the last two—the only two over which the hurdler has any control—are of

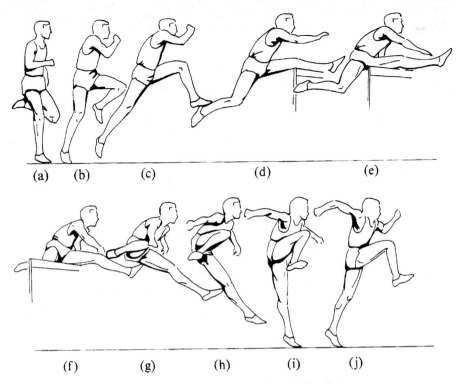

Figure 15-8. Technique in the high hurdles.

greatest practical importance. For a given takeoff distance, the greater the hurdler's horizontal velocity, the less the time he has in which to get the lead foot high enough to clear the hurdle. Thus, to allow himself sufficient time for this purpose (and to avoid disaster!), a good hurdler instinctively modifies the takeoff distance in keeping with changes in his horizontal velocity (that is, the hurdler increases takeoff distance as he increases his horizontal velocity and vice versa). The normal pattern of changes in take-off distances during a high hurdles event is thus one in which the distances increase steadily over the first few hurdles (as the hurdler gradually attains top speed) and decrease over the final few hurdles (as fatigue begins to reduce his speed). The hurdler's technique, and particularly the speed with which he can bring his lead foot up to the height of the hurdle, is also important in determining the takeoff distance. For, if all else is equal, the faster the lead leg action, the closer to the hurdle the hurdler can afford to be at the instant of takeoff. While takeoff distances clearly vary from one athlete to another, and from one hurdle to another for the same athlete, a distance of about 2.13 m is generally regarded as average for most athletes. Takeoff distances reported by Doherty[42] for six top-class hurdlers ranged from 1.75 m to 2.44 m and averaged 2.10 m. Takeoff distances to the first and second hurdles recorded for Guy Drut (France) when he won the 1976 Olympic Games final, were 2.20 m and 2.31 m, respectively.[43]

Flight. Once the hurdler leaves the ground, the only forces acting on him (assuming he doesn't hit the hurdle!) are gravity and air resistance. The former has no effect on his forward velocity but acts simply to bring him back to the ground. The time taken for this to be effected, and thus the time before the hurdler can next drive against the ground, is governed mainly by vertical velocity at takeoff—the greater the vertical velocity at this instant, the greater the time during which he is in the air. And, since the height that the hurdler's center of gravity rises in flight is directly related to his vertical velocity at takeoff, this means that the hurdler should skim across the hurdle with his center of gravity as low as safety and a balanced landing will permit if he is to get back to the ground and start driving again as quickly as possible. The air resistance encountered while airborne acts to reduce the hurdler's forward velocity. Although the magnitude of this force is probably fairly small—especially where the hurdler's forward "dip" is pronounced and his frontal area is therefore very small—the longer it acts, the greater is the reduction it effects in the hurdler's forward velocity. This is a further reason for him to seek to get back on the ground as soon as he can.

During the initial part of the flight, the hurdler's lead leg and trunk continue to move toward each other (Fig. 15-8[c] to [e]). These actions bring his center of gravity close to the lower limits of his body and thus reduce the height to which the athlete must raise his center of gravity to clear the hurdle. This effect is further enhanced by the forward and downward motion of the leading arm (Fig. 15-8[c] to [e]), and with some hurdlers by a dropping forward of the head so that the face is roughly parallel with the track.

Once the knee of the leading leg has crossed the hurdle, the motions of the trunk and lead leg are reversed, with the downward and backward action of the lead leg producing an upward and backward reaction of the trunk.

Although it may look very different, the action of the trailing leg during the flight phase is in reality very similar to the action during the recovery phase in normal sprinting. The one major difference is that as the trailing leg is brought forward, the thigh is lifted outward so that instead of passing vertically beneath the body (as in sprinting) it passes horizontally out to the side. This action permits the athlete to keep much lower than would otherwise be possible as he passes over the hurdle.

The upper-body reaction to the movements of the hurdler's trail leg generally takes the form of a contrary motion of the athlete's leading arm (Fig. 15-8[d] to [j]). However, if the athlete has an insufficient forward "dip" of the trunk, the moment of inertia of the leading arm may be so small that the arm must sweep back very fast indeed if it is to provide the needed reaction. And, since a fast-sweeping arm action like this tends to drag the athlete's shoulders and trunk away from their straight-to-the-front alignment and thus to interfere with the maintenance of balance and forward speed, such a situation is clearly to be avoided.

Landing. The hurdler lands with his body nearly erect (Fig. 15-8[i]) at a distance of approximately 1.35 m from the hurdle. (Landing distances reported by Doherty[14] ranged from 1.22 m to 1.52 m and averaged 1.38 m, while Drut's landing distance beyond the first hurdle was reported to be 1.31 m.[45]) The hurdler then drives vigorously forward into his next running stride (Fig. 15-8[j]). This forward drive is greatly facilitated by a strong forward and upward action of the trail leg, for such an action not only puts the trail leg in an ideal position to swing forward into the next stride (Fig. 15-8[i] and [j]) but it also tends to arrest the backward rotation of the trunk evoked by the movement of the lead leg—a rotation that, if unrestrained, would place the hurdler in such a position that he could not drive off effectively into the next stride. (*Note:* Failure to obtain a high, forward, and upward recovery of the trail leg is probably the most common cause of a shortened first stride and a consequent difficulty in covering the distance between hurdles in the required three strides.)

The speed of the leading foot relative to the ground determines whether the body experiences a momentary braking (or deceleration) at the instant of landing—if the foot is not moving backward at a speed at least equal to that at which the body is moving forward, braking must inevitably occur. Since this situation most frequently occurs when the athlete's foot lands well forward of his line of gravity, a placement of the foot below the center of gravity is generally regarded as a characteristic of good hurdling technique.

Between Hurdles. The distance from the point of landing to the point of takeoff for the next hurdle is negotiated in three running strides. Of these, the first is invariably the shortest and the second is usually the longest. The third, shortened by a few centimeters in preparation for takeoff, is usually somewhere between the other two. A striding pattern suggested by Mitchell[46] illustrates these differences:

Landing	1.37 m from the hurdle
Length of stride	1.68 m
Length of stride	2.06 m
Length of stride	1.91 m
Takeoff	2.13 m from the hurdle

Intermediate Hurdles

In the 400-m intermediate hurdles, the distance from the start line to the first hurdle is 45 m, the distance between the 0.914-m high hurdles is 35 m, and the distance from the last hurdle to the finish line is 40 m.

Just as the actions of middle- and long-distance runners might be regarded as less pronounced versions of the actions employed by sprinters, so too might the actions of men competing in the intermediate hurdles be regarded vis-à-vis their high-hurdling counterparts. With the height of the hurdle reduced by 15 cm, the intermediate hurdler can maintain his speed over the obstacles without resorting to the same vigorous, exaggerated action that the high hurdler must use to achieve the same end. The height of the hurdle for the women's intermediate hurdles is only 8 cm less than it is for the 100 m hurdles. The differences in technique between the two events are thus less pronounced than they are for the men.

The greatest technique problem facing the intermediate hurdler (aside from the actual hurdling action) is unquestionably that of how many strides to take between hurdles. Here there are a number of important considerations. First, the choice of the number of strides to use must be reasonably consistent with the length of the normal running stride, for any marked understriding or overstriding will undoubtedly reduce speed. (*Note:* Taking typical values for takeoff and landing distances and for the first stride after clearing the hurdle, Le Masurier[47] computed the average stride length necessary to cover the distance between hurdles in a given number of strides:

Number of Strides between Hurdles	Average Stride Length
13	2.49 m
14	2.31 m
15	2.13 m
16	1.98 m
17	1.85 m

He contends, though, "that for a hurdler to be able to flow economically between hurdles his natural stride must exceed the above figures by several inches.") Second, unless the athlete can hurdle reasonably well from either foot, it will be necessary to use an odd number of strides between hurdles. Third, due allowance must be made for the fact that as fatigue sets in, the athlete's stride length will tend to decrease.

While these often conflicting requirements have been met in a variety of ways over the years, a general trend toward (1) the use of fewer strides between the hurdles; and (2) the use of an even number of strides between hurdles at some point in the race is apparent. For example, whereas 17 strides between hurdles, or 15 strides between the first few hurdles and 17 strides between the remainder, were common patterns in the early days of the event, the first six finishers in the men's event at the 1988 Olympic Games used the following:

Andre Phillips (U.S.A.)
    13 strides throughout   47.19 s

Amadou Dia Ba (Senegal)
    13 strides to the 6th hurdle
    14 strides thereafter   47.23 s

Edwin Moses (U.S.A.)
    13 strides throughout   47.56 s

Kevin Young (U.S.A.)
    12 strides to the 5th hurdle
    13 strides to the 9th hurdle
    14 strides to the 10th hurdle   47.94 s

Winthrop Graham (Jamaica)
    14 strides to the 2nd hurdle
    13 strides to the 3rd hurdle
    14 strides to the 4th hurdle
    13 strides to the 5th hurdle
    14 strides to the 10th hurdle   48.04 s

Kriss Akabusi (Great Britain)
    13 strides to the 5th hurdle
    14 strides to the 9th hurdle
    15 strides to the 10h hurdle   48.69 s

Low Hurdles

In the 100-m low hurdles for women, the distance from the start line to the first hurdle is 13 m; the distance between the 0.84-m hurdles is 8.5 m; and the distance from the last hurdle to the finish line is 10.5 m.

Measures of the average speed for the segments of a race[48][49] differ considerably from those for the 110-m high hurdles (Fig. 15-9). Once the athlete's average speed reaches a maximum (usually between the second and third or the third and fourth hurdles), the rate at which it declines is markedly less than is the case in the high hurdles. Further, the increase to

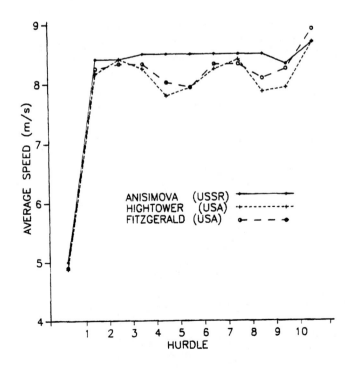

Figure 15-9.
Average speeds for segments of 100-m high hurdles race. (Adapted from Brejzer, W. and Kaverin W. [1982]. 110 hurdles: Analysis of competitive activity. *Legkaya Atletika*, 8:14–15.)

a final maximum is much less dramatic than in the high hurdles—presumably because the speed has not decreased to the same extent and because the distance from the last hurdle to the finish line is less.

The techniques used in this event are a blend of those used in the high hurdles (where the striding pattern of seven to eight strides to the first hurdle and three strides between hurdles is the same) and those used in the intermediate hurdles (where the height of the barrier is similar).

Steeplechase

In the 3000-m steeplechase, an athlete must negotiate a solidly constructed 0.914-m hurdle a total of 28 times and a water jump—consisting of a 0.914-m hurdle fixed in place in front of a 3.66-m square of water—a total of 7 times.

The orthodox technique for clearing the hurdles is essentially the same as that used by athletes in the intermediate hurdles, that is, a simplified form of the high-hurdling technique previously described. As in the intermediate hurdles, the ability to hurdle off either foot—although relatively rare among steeplechasers—is a distinct advantage, for it reduces the extent of the adjustment that the athlete may be called on to make to get into an appropriate position for takeoff. (It should be noted here that, unlike high and intermediate hurdlers, steeplechasers do not normally strive to cover the distances between obstacles in a set number of strides.)

The technique used in negotiating the water jump is shown in Fig. 15-10. As the athlete approaches the barrier, he adjusts his speed and his striding—the latter with the aid, perhaps, of a checkmark—so that he will arrive at the optimum point for takeoff with sufficient speed to allow him to complete the jump efficiently. Once his takeoff foot is grounded, he brings his leading leg forward, with knee well bent, in preparation for the spring onto the 12.7-cm wide rail (Fig. 15-10). With his eyes focused on the rail to minimize the risk of a faulty foot placement, he leaps into the air and places the arch of his foot against the near upper edge of the rail (Fig. 15-10). Then follows a period

Figure 15-10. An example of the techniques used in clearing the water jump in the 3000-m steeplechase.

of support during which the athlete maintains a compact body position as he rotates forward over and beyond the line of the rail. This compact position, with the supporting leg well bent and the trunk hunched forward over it, minimizes the athlete's moment of inertia about a transverse axis through his supporting foot and thereby enables him to rotate quickly forward into position for the next stage in the sequence. Once his center of gravity has passed some distance forward of the rail, and the sole of his foot has rotated so that his spikes are digging into its forward vertical face, the athlete drives backward and downward against the rail by vigorously extending the hip, knee, and ankle joints of his supporting leg. The reaction to this leg drive projects the athlete out over the water to a landing on the opposite foot some 30–45 cm from the water's edge—a "long jump" of some 3.2–3.4 m. (*Note:* While a few top-class athletes have made a practice of jumping completely over the water to land on the track beyond, the enormous amount of energy expended in performing such a feat raises grave doubts as to its efficiency.) The whole action is completed by the athlete stepping forward out of the water and onto his free leg.

Running

CAVANAGH, P. R. (1980). *The Running Shoe Book.* Mountain View, Calif.: Anderson World, Inc.
DYSON, G. H. G. (1977). *The Mechanics of Athletics.* New York: Holmes & Meier, pp. 133–50 (Running).
MACH, G. (1985). In *Athletes in Action*, Payne, H. (Ed.) London: Pelham Books, pp. 11–34 (Sprints).
NIGG, B. M. (1986). *Biomechanics of Running Shoes.* Champaign, Ill.: Human Kinetics Publishers, Inc.
PUTNAM, C. A. AND KOZEY, J. W. (1989). *Biomechanics of Sport.* Boca Raton, Fla.: CRC Press, Inc., pp. 1–34 (Substantive issues in running).
SUSANKA, P., AND OTHERS (1990). *International Amateur Athletic Foundation Scientific Research Project at the Games of the XXXIV Olympiad—Seoul 1988 Final Report.* London: International Athletic Foundation, pp. 11–90 (Time analysis of the sprint events).
VAUGHAN, C. L. (1984). *C.R.C. Critical Reviews in Biomedical Engineering,* 12:1–48 (Biomechanics of running gait).
WILLIAMS, K. R. (1985). *Exercise and Sport Sciences Reviews.* New York: Macmillan, pp. 389–441 (Biomechanics of running).
WILSON, H. (1985). In H. Payne (Ed.), *Athletes in Action.* London: Pelham Books, pp. 35–48 (Middle distance).
WILT, F. (1985). In H. Payne (Ed.), *Athletes in Action.* London: Pelham Books, pp. 49–58 (Long distance).

Hurdling and Steeplechasing

DYSON, G. H. G. (1977). *The Mechanics of Athletics.* New York: Holmes & Meier, pp. 151–61 (Hurdling and steeplechasing).
EWEN, A. (1985). In H. Payne (Ed.), *Athletes in Action.* London: Pelham Books, pp. 78–100 (Hurdles).
KERSSENBROCK, K., AND JURECKA, J. (1985). In H. Payne (Ed.), *Athletes in Action.* London: Pelham Books, pp. 101–14 (Steeplechase).
McDONALD, C., AND DAPENA, J. (1991). Linear kinematics of the men's 110-m and women's 100-m hurdle races. *Medicine and Science in Sports and Exercise,* 23:1382–91.
McDONALD, C., AND DAPENA, J. (1991). Angular momentum in the men's 110-m and women's 100-m hurdles races. *Medicine and Science in Sports and Exercise,* 23:1392–1402.
SUSANKA, P., AND OTHERS (1990). *International Amateur Athletic Foundation Scientific Research*

Project at the Games of the XXXIV Olympiad—Seoul 1988 Final Report. London: International Athletic Foundation, pp. 91–131 (Time analysis of the 110 meter and 100 meter hurdles).

Susanka, P., and others (1990). *International Amateur Athletic Foundation Scientific Research Project at the Games of the XXXIV Olympiad—Seoul 1988 Final Report.* London: International Athletic Foundation, pp. 133–75 (Time analysis of the 400 meter hurdling events).

Notes

1. Housden, F. (1964). Mechanical analysis of the running movement. In F. Wilt (Ed.), *Run, Run, Run* (pp. 240–41). Los Altos, Calif.: Track and Field News, Inc.
2. Atwater, A. E. (1981). Kinematic analysis of sprinting. In J. M. Cooper and B. Haven (Eds.), *Proceedings of the Biomechanics Symposium, Indiana University, October 26–28, 1980* (p. 309). Ind.: The Indiana State Board of Health.
3. Hoffman, K. (1971). Stature, leg length, and stride frequency. *Track Technique*, 46: 1463–69.
4. Rompotti, K. (1975). A study of stride length in running. In D. Canham and P. Diamond (Eds.), *International Track and Field Digest* (pp. 249–56). Ann Arbor, Mich.: Champions on Film.
5. Atwater. Kinematic analysis of sprinting, p. 308.
6. Hoffman, K. (1972). Stride length and frequency of female sprinters. *Track Technique*, 48:1522–24.
7. Henry, F. M. (1952). Force-time characteristics of the sprint start. *Research Quarterly*, 23:301–18.
8. Sigerseth, P. O., and Grinaker, V. F. (1962). Effect of foot spacing on velocity in sprints. *Research Quarterly*, 33:599–606.
9. Hogberg, P. (1964). The effect of the starting position on the straight speed short distance races. *Svensk Idrott*, XXV, no. 20. (Cited in *Index and Abstracts of Foreign Physical Education Literature*. Indianapolis, Ind.: Phi Epsilon Kappa Fraternity, IX.)
10. Bresnahan, G. T. (1934). A study of the movement pattern in starting the race from the crouch position. *Research Quarterly*, 5:5–11.
11. Payne, A. H., and Blader, F. B. (1970). A preliminary investigation into the mechanics of the sprint start. *Bulletin of Physical Education*, 8:21–30.
12. Baumann, W. (1976). Kinematic and dynamic characteristics of the sprint start. In P. V. Komi (Ed.), *Biomechanics V-B* (pp. 194–99). Baltimore: University Park Press.
13. Payne and Blader. A preliminary investigation into the mechanics of the sprint start, p. 27.
14. Henry. Force-time characteristics of the sprint start, p. 306.
15. Payne and Blader. A preliminary investigation into the mechanics of the sprint start, p. 27.
16. Jackson, A. S., and Cooper, J. M. (1970). Effect of hand spacing and rear knee angle on the sprinter's start. *Research Quarterly*, 41:378–82.
17. Volkov, N. I., and Lapin, V. I. (1979). Analysis of the velocity curve in sprint running. *Medicine and Science in Sports*, 11:332–37.
18. Mehrikadze, V., and Tabatschnik, B. (1982). An analysis of sprinting. *Legkaja Atletika*, 3. (Translated, condensed and reported in *Modern Athlete and Coach*, 21, April 1983, p. 8.)
19. Henry, F. M. (1952). Research on sprint running. *Athletic Journal*, 32:32.
20. Hill, A. V. (1927). *Muscular Movement in Man* (p. 51). New York: McGraw-Hill.
21. Gundlach, H. (1963). "Untersuchungen über den Zusammenhang zwischen Schrittgestaltung und Laufgeschwindigkeit bei 100-m-Läufern und -Läuferinnen unterschiedlicher Qualifikation," In *Theorie und Praxis der Körperkultur III and IV* (Cited in G. Schmolinsky, [Ed.], [1977] *Leichtathletik* [pp. 154–58]. Berlin: Sportverlag.)
22. Mehrikadze and Tabatschnik. An analysis of sprinting, pp. 8–10.
23. Henry, F. M., and Trafton, I. R. (1951). The velocity curve of sprint running. *Research Quarterly;* 22:412.
24. Mehrikadze and Tabatschnik. An analysis of sprinting, p. 8.
25. Nett, T. (1964). Foot plant in running. *Track Technique*, 15:462–63.
26. Payne, A. H. (1983). Foot to ground contact forces of elite runners. In H. Matsui and K. Kobayashi (Eds.), *Biomechanics VII-B* pp. 746–53. Champaign, Ill.: Human Kinetics Publishers.
27. Deshon, D. E., and Nelson, R. C. (1964). A cinematographical analysis of sprint running. *Research Quarterly*, 35:453–54.

28. Payne, A. H., Slater, W. J., and Telford, T. (1968). The use of a force platform in the study of athletic activities. *Ergonomics*, 11:123–43.

29. Tsujino, A. (1966). The kick in sprint running. *Kobe Journal of Medical Science*, 12:1–26.

30. Mann, R., and Sprague, P. (1980). A kinetic analysis of the ground leg during sprint running. *Research Quarterly for Exercise and Sport*, 60:334–38.

31. Mach, G. (1985). Spints. In H. Payne (Ed.), *Athletes in Action* (p. 19). London: Pelham Books.

32. Schmolinsky, G. (1978). (Ed.), *Track and Field* (p. 134). Berlin: Sportverlag.

33. Alford, J. (1970). The sprint races. In F. Wilt and T. Ecker (Eds.), *International Track and Field Coaching Encyclopedia* (p. 13). West Nyack, N.Y.: Parker Publishing.

34. Kunz, H., and Kauffman, D. A. (1981). Biomechanical analysis of sprinting: Decathletes versus champions. *British Journal of Sports Medicine*, 15:177–81.

35. Mann, R., and Herman, J. (1985). Kinematic analysis of Olympic sprint performances: Men's 200 meters. *International Journal of Sports Biomechanics*, 1:151–62.

36. Ibid., p. 159.

37. Dillman, C. J. (1971). A kinetic analysis of the recovery leg during sprint running. In J. M. Cooper (Ed.), *Selected Topics on Biomechanics: Proceedings of the C.I.C. Symposium on Biomechanics* (pp. 137–65). Chicago, Ill.: The Athletic Institute.

38. Fenn, W. O. (1930). Work against gravity and work due to velocity changes in running. *American Journal of Physiology*, 93:433–62.

39. Deshon and Nelson. A cinematographical analysis of sprint running, pp. 451–55.

40. Sinning, W.E., and Forsyth, H. L. (1970). Lower-limb actions while running at different velocities. *Medicine and Science in Sports*, 2:31.

41. Hinrichs, R. N. (1982). Upper extremity function in running. Ph.D. dissertation, Pennsylvania State University.

42. Doherty, J. K. (1963). *Modern Track and Field* (pp. 135–36). Englewood Cliffs, N.J.: Prentice Hall.

43. Ewen, S. (1978). An evaluation of the 1976 Olympic 110 m hurdles (men). *Track and Field Quarterly Review*, 78:3–4.

44. Doherty. *Modern Track and Field* (pp. 135–36).

45. Ewen. An evaluation of the 1976 Olympic 110 m hurdles (men), pp. 3–4.

46. Mitchell, L. (1969). Some observations on the high hurdles. *Track Technique*, 37:1187.

47. Le Masurier, J. (1969). Some factors of performance in the 400 meters hurdles. *Athletics Weekly*, 23, September 13, p. 14.

48. Schwirtz, A., and others (1986). Biomechanik des Hurdenlaufs. In R. Ballreich and A. Kuhlow (Eds.), *Biomechanik der Sportarten: Biomechanik der Leichtathletik* (pp. 16–27). Stuttgart: Ferdinand Enke Verlag.

49. Brejzer, W. and Kaverin, W. (1982). 110 hurdles: Analysis of competitive activity. *Legkaya Atletika*, 8:14–15.

16

TRACK AND FIELD: JUMPING

The standard jumping events in track and field are the long jump, the triple jump (formerly known as the hop, step, and jump), the high jump, and the pole vault.

In each of these events, the athlete's objective is to obtain a maximum displacement of the center of gravity in a given direction—in the long and triple jumps, in a horizontal direction; in the high jump and the pole vault, in a vertical direction—and then, in keeping with the rules governing the event, to extract as much credit as possible for having achieved this displacement. In the horizontal jumps this latter means that the athlete endeavors to get the feet as far forward as possible without falling back on landing. In the vertical jumps it means that the athlete strives to have the body pass over a bar set close to, or perhaps even above (p. 129), the maximum height that the center of gravity attains.

The distance with which an athlete is credited in the long jump may be considered to be the sum of three lesser distances:

- The horizontal distance between the front edge of the takeoff board and the athlete's center of gravity at the instant of takeoff (the takeoff distance, L_1 in Fig. 16-1).
- The horizontal distance that the center of gravity travels while the athlete is in the air (the flight distance, L_2 in Fig. 16-1).
- The horizontal distance between the center of gravity at the instant the heels hit the sand and the mark in the sand from which the distance of the jump is ultimately measured (the landing distance, L_3 in Fig. 16-1).

LONG JUMP
Basic
Considerations

The contribution that each of these distances makes to the total distance jumped is indicated by the data in Table 16-1.

The takeoff distance is a function of the accuracy with which the athlete places the foot on the takeoff board and the body position at the instant of takeoff.

The flight distance is governed by the same four variables that determine the motion of all projectiles—the speed, angle, and height of takeoff and the air resistance encountered in flight.

The athlete's speed at the instant of takeoff—by far the most important of these variables—depends on the speed developed in the run to the board and on the changes in speed associated with the adjustments made in preparation for takeoff. The ideal combination is one of maximum (controlled) speed in the run-up together with a minimum loss of speed in preparing for takeoff.

A combination of the horizontal speed developed in the run-up (and maintained through the takeoff) and the vertical speed (or lift) acquired at takeoff determines the athlete's angle of takeoff:

$$\text{Angle of takeoff} = \arctan \frac{\text{vertical speed at instant of takeoff}}{\text{horizontal speed at instant of takeoff}}$$

Figure 16-1. Contributions to the length of a hang-style long jump.

TABLE 16-1 Contributions to Distance in the Long Jump

	Distance	Percentage of Total
Takeoff distance	0.41 m	5.1
Flight distance	7.22 m	90.0
Landing distance	0.39 m	4.9
Total distance	8.02 m	

Hay, J. G., Miller, J. A., and Canterna, R.W (1986). The techniques of elite male long jumpers. *Journal of Biomechanics,* 19:855-66.

The lift that the athlete develops at takeoff is very much influenced by the speed of the run-up. The faster the run, the less time the foot spends on the ground at takeoff and the less vertical speed the athlete is capable of developing. Thus, because the horizontal speeds attained by the end of the run-up are so great and the times of takeoff are so small (O.08-0.14 s),[1] the angles of takeoff used by top-class jumpers are rather less than the near-45° angles that might otherwise be expected (Table 16-2).

The height of takeoff (that is, the difference between the height of the athlete's center of gravity at the instant of takeoff and at the instant of touchdown in the pit) depends on the athlete's body position at both instants. The athlete can exercise control over the height of takeoff in the first instance by driving the arms, leading leg, head, and trunk high at takeoff and, in the second, by delaying the landing for as long as feasible.

TABLE 16-2 Speeds and Angles of Takeoff for Top-Class Long Jumpers

Athlete	Distance of Jump Analyzed (m)	Speed of Takeoff (m/s)	Angle of Takeoff (deg)	Optimum Angle of Takeoff for Given Speed[1] (deg)
Mike Powell (U.S.A.)[a]	8.95	9.8	23.2	43.3
Bob Beamon (U.S.A.)[a]	8.90	9.6	24.0	43.3
Carl Lewis (U.S.A.)[b]	8.79	10.0	18.7	43.4
Ralph Boston (U.S.A.)[c]	8.28	9.5	19.8	43.2
Igor Ter-Ovanesian (USSR)[c]	8.19	9.3	21.2	43.2
Jesse Owens (U.S.A.)[c]	8.13	9.2	22.0	43.1
Elena Belevskaya (USSR)[d]	7.14	8.9	19.6	43.0
Heike Drechsler (GDR)[d]	7.13	9.4	15.6	43.2
Jackie Joyner-Kersee (U.S.A.)[d]	7.12	8.5	22.1	42.8
Anisoara Stanciu (Romania)[e]	6.96	8.6	20.6	42.9
Vali Ionescu (Romania[e]	6.81	8.9	18.9	43.0
Sue Hearnshaw (GB)[e]	6.75	8.6	18.9	42.9

[a] Data courtesy Senshi Fukashiro, Institute of Sports Medicine & Science, Agui, Japan.

[b] Hay, J. G., Miller, J A., and Canterna, R. W. (1986). The technique of elite male long jumpers. *Journal of Biomechanics,* 19:855–66.

[c] Popov, V. (1969). In M. Okamoto, (Trans.), *Training for the Long Jump* (p. 38). Tokyo: Baseball Magazine Co.

[d] Nixdorf, E., and Bruggeman, P. (1988). Biomechanical analysis of the long jump. In *Scientific Report on the II World Championships in Athletics, Rome 1987* (Book 2, pp. D/2–D/53). London: International Athletic Foundation.

[e] Hay, J. G., and Miller, J. A. (1985). Techniques used in the transition from approach to takeoff in the long jump. *International Journal of Sport Biomechanics,* 1:174–84.

[f] The values in this column are those that yield a maximum horizontal displacement when the position of the athlete's center of gravity at takeoff is 60 cm above its position on landing. (The effects of air resistance have been ignored in these computations.)

In still air, the effects of air resistance are probably so small that they can safely be disregarded. Under windy conditions, air resistance can have a profound effect on the distances recorded. A tailwind of 2.0 m/s (the legal limit for record purposes) might so influence the approach velocity, and the air resistance encountered during the flight phase of the jump, that the distance of the jump is increased by more than 20 cm compared with what it would have been under still conditions.[2]

The landing distance depends on the athlete's body position at touch-down in the pit and on the actions employed to avoid falling backward and reducing the measured length of the jump. The principal factors influencing the body position at touchdown are the initial body position (that is, its position as the athlete leaves the ground), the rotation imparted to the body during the run-up and takeoff, and the movements made in the air to minimize the effects of this rotation and to position the body for landing. Whether the athlete sits back in the sand or rotates forward over the feet depends primarily on the magnitude and direction of the ground-reaction forces exerted on the athlete during the landing. If the feet land beneath or just slightly forward of the center of gravity, the athlete is subjected to a ground-reaction force that passes behind the center of gravity and thus serves to increase the forward angular momentum. This results in the athlete rotating quickly forward over the feet, often sprawling headlong in an effort to regain control. If the athlete lands with the legs fully extended and in a near-horizontal position, the ground-reaction force passes in front of the center of gravity, and thus acts to decrease the forward angular momentum—usually to such an extent that the athlete sits back. The athlete's task, therefore, is to strike the best possible compromise between these two extremes.

Summary

The relationships between the distance with which a long jumper is credited and the factors that determine that distance are summarized in Fig. 16-2.

Techniques

For the purposes of analysis the long jump may be considered to consist of four consecutive parts: the run-up, the takeoff,* the flight, and the landing.

Run-Up

The purpose of the run-up is to get the athlete to the optimum position for takeoff with as much speed as he (or she) can control during that part of the jump.

The length of run-up that an athlete should use depends on the percentage of top sprinting speed that he (or she) can control at takeoff and

* The term *takeoff* is used here to mean the whole period during which the athlete's takeoff foot is in contact with the ground immediately prior to leaving the ground. The term *instant of takeoff*, on the other hand, refers to the exact moment at which contact with the ground is broken.

on the athlete's ability to maintain a consistent pattern of striding from one jump to the next. Considering only the first of these factors, the findings of Henry[3] (p. 405) suggest that if an athlete is capable of controlling 100 percent of his (or her) maximum sprinting speed, a run-up equal in length to the distance he (or she) can sprint in 6 s—some 45-55 m—should be used. However, if the athlete can handle "only" 95 percent of his (or her) top speed, Henry's findings suggest that a run-up as short as 20 m might be sufficient. (*Note:* Because most long jumpers do not use a crouch start and do not run with maximum effort from the very beginning of the run-up—as did the subjects in Henry's study—and since allowance should be made for an additional 2 to 3 strides during which the athlete prepares both physically and mentally for the takeoff, these figures are some 4-7 m less than the theoretical lower limits for the respective cases.) As the length of the run-up (and thus the number of strides taken) increases, the scope for errors also increases. For this reason, the long jumper must weigh carefully the gains that may be expected from a long run, and the extra speed it affords, against the losses that may be incurred as a result of the increased opportunity for errors in striding. In practice, most top-class long jumpers use run-ups between 40 m and 45 m (or 17 to 23 running strides) in reaching a compromise between these conflicting requirements of speed and accuracy.

The transition from the run-up to the takeoff is widely regarded as being one of the most important parts in the technique of long jumping. During the last two strides of the approach the athlete makes a series of adjustments in body position in preparation for the takeoff to follow. In elite athletes, these adjustments consist of:

- a decrease of about 4 cm in the height of the center of gravity at touchdown and an increase of 5–7 cm in the landing distance at the end of the second-last stride;

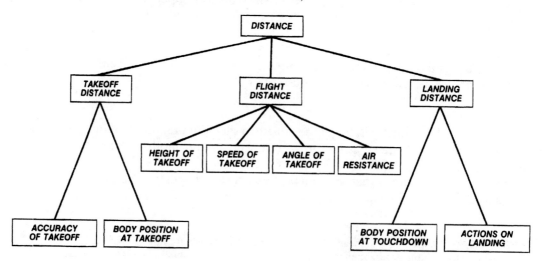

Figure 16-2. Basic factors in long jumping.

- a decrease of 38–46 cm in the flight distance of the last stride; and
- an increase of 27–34 cm in the landing distance at the end of the last stride, compared with the corresponding measures for the preceding 2 to 3 strides.[4]

Takeoff

The purpose of the takeoff is to obtain vertical velocity (or lift) while retaining as much horizontal velocity as possible. As the athlete's foot strikes the ground at the end of the last stride of the approach, very large forces are exerted upon it. (Fischer[5] has reported peak vertical impact forces of 7,160–11,770 N—or 11.1–16.4 times body weight, and others[6,7] have reported similar values.) Despite strong extensor muscle activity, the hip, knee and ankle joints are forced to flex a little under the large loads imposed on them at this time. The associated forced lengthening (or eccentric action) of the extensor muscles serves to augment the athlete's ability to exert large forces against the ground when the muscles shorten (concentric action) a moment later. The reaction to this extension drives the athlete into the air and, if it acts eccentrically, as is usually the case, causes the athlete to rotate about a transverse axis through the center of gravity. While it is possible to obtain either a backward or forward rotation (or, indeed, no rotation at all) at this time, in good jumping the rotation imparted is almost invariably in a forward direction.

Flight

Once in the air, the athlete's sole objective should be to assume the optimum body position for landing. This would be a relatively easy task were it not for the fact that the athlete will almost certainly have acquired some forward angular momentum during the run-up and takeoff. This forward angular momentum tends to bring the feet beneath the center of gravity at the very time (that is, the instant of landing) when the athlete wants them to be well forward of this point. The athlete's principal problem is thus to minimize the undesirable effects of this forward angular momentum.

There are three in-the-air techniques in common use—the sail, the hang, and the hitch-kick.

In the sail technique (Fig. 16-3) the athlete brings both legs together shortly after takeoff and continues the remainder of the flight in a sitting position, either with both legs fully extended or with the knees bent at about a right angle. While the virtue of this technique lies in its simplicity—it is the technique that most people would use naturally—it has the great weakness of placing the mass of the body close to its transverse axis and thus of facilitating the forward rotation that the athlete needs to inhibit to obtain a good landing position.

In the hang technique (Fig. 16-1) the athlete reaches forward with the leading leg and then sweeps it downward and backward until both legs are together and somewhat behind the line of the body. This sweeping move-

Figure 16-3. The in-the-air position adopted in the sail technique.

ment of the leading leg (and the downward and backward swing of the opposite arm that usually accompanies it) produces a contrary reaction in the athlete's upper body. It also has the effect of extending the body, thereby increasing the moment of inertia about its transverse axis and lessening the rate at which the athlete rotates forward. The circular swing of the arms continues until both are high overhead, at about which time the athlete bends the knees and begins the forward movement of the legs in preparation for landing. It is important that the legs be well bent as they are brought forward under the body, for otherwise the forward and downward reaction of the trunk, which their movement evokes, might well be large enough to bring the trunk into a position where it limits the height to which the legs can be raised. Some athletes, generally those with good hip and trunk flexibility, keep their legs fairly straight and swing them wide on each side of the body as they bring them through. This serves the same purpose as bending them (that is, it keeps their moment of inertia about a transverse axis relatively small) and may also assist in overcoming the problem of the trunk restricting the lifting of the legs by having them outside the trunk rather than under it.

There are two main variants of the hitch-kick or "running-in-the-air" technique, named according to the number of in-the-air strides involved. Unfortunately, to the general confusion of those interested in the event, there is some lack of agreement as to when the counting of strides should begin. Some coaches and athletes count the "stride" from the takeoff foot to the lead foot, which begins the instant the athlete leaves the ground, as the first stride, and describe the two variants as the 2½ and the 3½ hitch-kick. Others commence the count one stride later. To them these same two variants are the 1½ and the 2½ hitch-kick. The former of these counting systems is used here.

The first part of the action in the hitch-kick (Fig. 16-4) is similar to that in the hang in that once the athlete has left the ground, he (or she) extends the leading leg forward and then sweeps it downward and backward. Coordinated with this movement is a pulling through of the takeoff leg (knee well bent, heel passing close to the buttocks) and a downward and backward swinging of the arm on the side opposite the lead leg.

Because of the difference between the moments of inertia of the legs, the angular momentum of the lead leg as it swings downward and backward far exceeds that of the takeoff leg that is simultaneously moving in the opposite direction. A similar situation exists with respect to the athlete's arms. Therefore, to provide the necessary "balance" between the angular momentum of the body parts moving in one direction (the action) and the angular momentum of the parts moving in the opposite direction (the reaction), the athlete's trunk rotates backward as the lead leg and arm swing downward and backward. And this, of course, is the whole purpose of the exercise—to move the athlete's trunk into a position from which an optimum landing position can later be obtained.

At the end of this in-the-air stride, the athlete's legs are in a position that is essentially the reverse of that at takeoff. Then, in a 2½ hitch-kick, the leg that is to the rear at this point is brought forward to join the other in preparation for landing. To minimize the undesirable forward rotation of the trunk, in reaction to this movement, this rear leg should be brought forward with the knee fully flexed. In a 3½ hitch-kick, a further full stride is taken before both feet are brought together for landing. In other words, once the athlete has reached that point at which the positions of the legs at takeoff have been reversed, the takeoff leg (the leg in front at this time) is swept downward and backward while the opposite leg is brought forward close under the buttocks. At the completion of this second reversal of the leg positions, the rear leg is brought forward for the final half stride to complete the sequence.

The question of which in-the-air technique a given jumper should use has been investigated by El Khadem and Huyck.[8] They concluded that "Because of the time involved in the execution of the various in-flight techniques, it seems that the optimum technique for the individual is determined by his own abilities." Their suggested optimum techniques for performers of various abilities are as follows:

Figure 16-4. Technique in the execution of a hitch-kick—Carl Lewis (U.S.A.).

Under 6 m	sail
6.0–6.5 m	sail or hang
6.5–7.0 m	hang
7.0–7.5 m	2½ hitch-kick
Over 7.5 m	3½ hitch-kick

Throughout any discussion of the flight phase in long jumping it is important to recognize that whatever the athlete does while in the air can have no effect whatsoever on the path followed by the center of gravity. This latter is determined at the instant of takeoff and can only be altered by the introduction of some force *external* to the jumper. And, ignoring air resistance, the conditions that normally apply in long jumping do not allow for such an external force. Certainly the assertion, occasionally found in coaching texts, that use of the hitch-kick aids in propelling the jumper forward through the air is completely without foundation.

Landing

Two sets of factors must be taken into account in deciding the optimum body position at the instant the athlete touches down in the pit:

- those that influence the distance between the takeoff board and the athlete's heel marks in the pit,
- those that determine whether the athlete passes forward over the feet or falls back in the sand.

With each of these, the most important single feature of the body position is the inclination of the athlete's trunk.

If the athlete deliberately leans well forward during the final moments of the flight, the legs are lifted in reaction to this movement and the touchdown is slightly delayed. This increase in the time of flight allows the athlete to be carried farther along the parabolic flight path than would otherwise be the case. On the other side of the ledger, the forward inclination of the trunk reduces the landing distance (assuming the athlete doesn't fall backward) by moving the center of gravity nearer to the feet than it would be if the trunk were in a more upright position. If the athlete assumes a position in which the trunk is erect, or inclined slightly backward, these various effects are reversed—the time of flight is decreased while the landing distance is increased.

If the athlete leans well forward just before landing, the angle at which the legs are inclined to the horizontal at touchdown is less than it would be if the athlete maintained a more upright body position. Under such circumstances, the magnitude and direction of the reaction force evoked from the ground are generally such as to make it considerably more difficult for the athlete to avoid sitting back.

It is clear therefore that the athlete must strike a compromise between (1) obtaining the maximum distance between the takeoff board and the marks of the heels in the sand; and (2) preserving the ability to rotate forward over the feet.

Once the heels have cut the sand, the athlete flexes the knees to cushion the shock of the impact and begins to rotate forward, thrusting the head and shoulders over (or between) the knees to facilitate this forward rotation. If at the instant of landing the athlete's arms have been level with, or behind, the trunk, these actions are supplemented by a forward and upward swing of the arms—an action that evokes a contrary angular reaction in the rest of the body and thus assists in rotating the athlete forward over the feet.

TRIPLE JUMP
Basic Considerations

The distance with which an athlete is credited in the triple jump may be broken down into a series of consecutive parts in much the same way as has already been described in the long jump. However, whereas distance in the long jump may be considered simply as the aggregate of one takeoff, one flight, and one landing distance, in the triple jump the distance achieved is equal to the sum of three different takeoff distances, three different flight distances, and three different landing distances—with the landing distances measured to the toe of the support foot in the first two cases, and as in the long jump in the third.

While the basic factors influencing each of these distances in each phase of the triple jump are essentially the same as those that apply in the case of the long jump, in the triple jump the takeoff and landing for each of the first two phases (the hop and the step) must be modified somewhat to allow for the phase or phases that follow. For example, a triple jumper who obtained the maximum (takeoff plus flight plus landing) distance of which he (or she) was capable in the hop phase would not produce his (or her) best effort simply because the distances obtained in the succeeding two phases would be very much below what could otherwise be achieved. In other words, the distance gained with a maximum effort in the hop would be more than lost in the step and jump phases.

The optimum distribution of effort over the three phases of the triple jump has been the subject of much discussion. This discussion has focussed on how the distance of the hop (measured from the board to the toe), the distance of the step (from toe to toe), and the distance of the jump (from toe to the nearest mark made in the sand)—each expressed as a percentage of the distance of the jump—should compare. Triple jump techniques in which the distance of the hop phase is at least 2 percent greater than the distance of the next longest phase are said to be *hop-dominated*, those in which the distance of the jump phase is at least 2 percent greater than the distance of the next longest phase are said to be *jump-dominated*, and those in which no one phase is at least 2 percent longer than the next longest are said to be *balanced*.[9 10]

Distances and ratios of the three phases recorded for world-record jumps are shown in Table 16-3. These data show that there have been major shifts in the techniques used in world record jumps over the past 80 years. The data also show that the contribution of the step to the distance of world-record jumps has increased substantially since the earliest records were set and now appears to have stabilized in the 28-30% range. The search for the best combination of contributions from the other two phases appears to be still in progress. In this last respect, it is now generally

TABLE 16-3 Phase Distances and Ratios for World Record Performances in the Triple Jump[a]

Athlete	Year	Hop Distance (m)	Step Distance (m)	Jump Distance (m)	Ratio[b]	Technique	Total Distance (m)
Dan Ahearne (U.S.A.)	1911	6.09	3.34	5.83	39%:22%:37%	Balanced	15.52
Nick Winter (Australia)	1924	6.09	3.34	5.83	39%:22%:37%	Balanced	15.52
Mikio Oda (Japan)	1931	6.50	3.50	5.56	41%:22%:36%	Hop-dominated	15.58
Chuhei Nambu (Japan)	1932	6.40	4.42	4.93	41%:28%:31%	Hop-dominated	15.72
Naoto Tajima (Japan)	1936	6.20	3.99	5.81	39%:25%:36%	Hop-dominated	16.00
Adhemar da Silva (Brazil)	1950	5.51	4.82	5.64	34%:30%:35%	Balanced	16.00
Adhemar da Silva (Brazil)	1952	6.20	4.59	5.42	38%:28%:33%	Hop-dominated	16.22
Leonid Sherbakov (USSR)	1953	6.01	4.96	5.24	37%:30%:32%	Hop-dominated	16.23
Adhemar da Silva (Brazil)	1955	6.27	4.98	5.31	38%:30%:32%	Hop-dominated	16.56
Olyeg Ryakhovskiy (USSR)	1958	6.46	4.96	5.15	39%:30%:31%	Hop-dominated	16.59
Olyeg Fyedoseyev (USSR)	1959	6.50	4.82	5.38	39%:29%:32%	Hop-dominated	16.70
Josef Schmidt (Poland)	1960	6.00	5.01	6.01	35%:29%:35%	Balanced	17.03
Victor Saneyev[c] (USSR)	1968	6.30	5.05	6.04	36%:29%:35%	Balanced	17.39
Victor Saneyev[c] (USSR)	1972	6.50	4.93	6.01	37%:28%:34%	Hop-dominated	17.44
Joao Carlos de Oliveira (Brazil)	1975	6.08	5.37	6.43	34%:30%:36%	Jump-dominated	17.89
Willie Banks[d] (U.S.A.)	1985	6.32	4.96	6.69	35%:28%:37%	Jump-dominated	17.97

[a] Adapted from McNab T. (1977). *Triple Jump* (p. 7). London: British Amateur Athletic Board.

[b] According to McNab, "All ratio distances must be treated with a 'pinch of salt', since in the heat of competition they are rarely accurately measured. This particularly relates to the distance of the hop, where the jumper's toe is rarely completely up to the edge of the take-off board. Distances are measured board to toe (hop), toe to toe (step) and toe to heels (jump)."

[c] Adapted from Kreer, V. (1973). The world record of Victor Saneyev. *Track and Field*, p. 11. Translated by Michael Yessis and reported in *Yessis Review of Soviet Physical Education and Sports*, IX, June 1974, p. 39.

[d] Miller, J. A., and Hay, J. G. (1986). Kinematics of a world record and other world-class performances in the triple jump. *International Journal of Sport Biomechanics*, 2:272-88.

regarded by authorities on the triple jump that there is no single phase ratio that is optimal for all jumpers. Instead, it is thought that the best phase ratio for a given jumpers depends on the athlete's speed, strength, and other characteristics. There is, however, little other than anecdotal data to support or refute this notion.

Techniques

The run-up serves the same function and is performed in essentially the same manner as in the long jump. The only difference of any real consequence occurs in the final three to four strides before takeoff where, because the emphasis on gaining height is less than in the long jump, the adjustments in stride length and frequency are generally less pronounced.

An example of the sequence of movements performed by a top-class triple jumper, from the instant of takeoff from the board until the final touchdown in the pit, is shown in Fig. 16-5. The following points should be noted:

(a)* The athlete's body position at the instant of takeoff is very similar to that of a long jumper—a near-erect position of the trunk; a full extension of the hip, knee, and ankle joints of the takeoff leg, reflecting a forceful downward and backward drive against the board; and a high position of the leading knee and of both elbows, reflecting the vigorous action of the free limbs and their contributions to the forces exerted via the athlete's takeoff leg. The athlete's attention is focused more directly forward than it would be at this point in a long jump. Because an angle of takeoff as great as that used in a long jump would produce a high, long hop and forces at touchdown that the jumper would be unable to control sufficiently to make an effective takeoff into the step phase, the angle of takeoff here is somewhat less than that normally used in long jumping. For example, an analysis of seven jumps by world-record holder Willie Banks (U.S.A.) yielded a mean angle of takeoff into the hop of 13.1°.[11]

(b) The left leg has been lowered and is moving backward while the flexed right leg is being brought forward in preparation for the next landing. Because of the difference in the moments of inertia of these two limbs, some slight backward rotation is imparted to the athlete's trunk as a result of their motion (see hitch-kick, pp. 430–432). The athlete's trunk is in an erect position and remains so throughout the hop—a markedly forward or backward lean is generally to be avoided, as this impairs the athlete's ability to land and drive upward and forward into the next phase.

The athlete's arms are now moving outward and backward in unison. With both arms moving like this in roughly the same plane, the action of one serves to balance the contrary action of the other, and the remainder of the body is unaffected except for its slight forward movement to compensate for (or "balance") the weight that has been shifted backward.

---

* The letters in parentheses refer to the corresponding positions in Fig. 16-5.

(a)   (b)   (c)

(f)   (g)   (h)

(k)   (l)   (m)

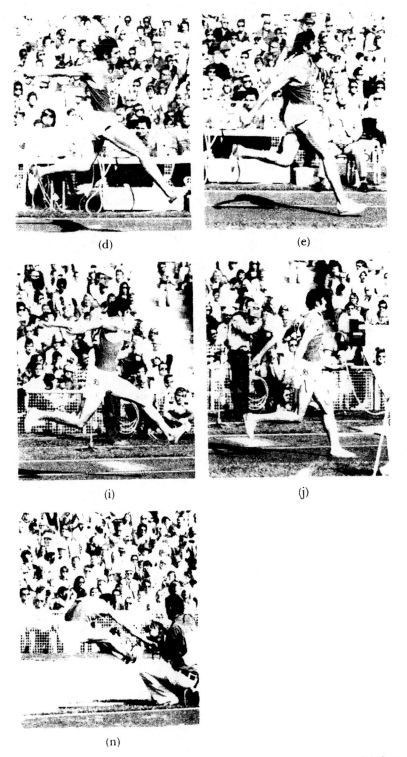

(d)　　　　　　(e)

(i)　　　　　　(j)

(n)

Figure 16-5. Technique in the triple jump.

(c) The arms are now approaching the backward limit of their range and the right leg is being swung forward in preparation for landing.

(d) The arms have reached their backward limit and are about to be swung forward. The right foot, having first been reached well forward, is now being swept forcefully downward and backward to ensure a so-called "active landing." The purpose of this action is to try to ensure that the backward speed of the foot relative to the athlete's center of gravity is relatively large and that the inevitable retarding horizontal forces evoked as the foot lands will, therefore, be correspondingly small (See Sprinting, pp. 407–408). In this way, they will allow the athlete to maintain as much of his horizontal velocity as possible.

An analysis of 16 elite male triple jumpers[12] revealed that the forward velocity of the center of gravity declined from phase to phase and that, for each landing, the forward velocity of the foot was much less than the forward velocity of the center of gravity. This latter finding indicated that an active landing was used in all cases. Data from this study are summarized in Fig. 16-6.

In attempting to maximize the benefits to be derived from using an active landing, some of the world's best triple jumpers swing the leading leg to a much higher position than shown in Fig. 16-5. These athletes bring the leg to a horizontal (or near-horizontal) position before sweeping it forcefully downward and backward for landing (Fig. 16-7).

The other leg is left well behind during these latter stages of the hop so that once the athlete touches down, the amplitude of its swing forward and then upward can be as great as possible.

(e) The landing to complete the hop has just been effected. The hip, knee, and ankle joints are about to flex—to cushion the shock of the impact and to place these joints in the optimum position for the leg drive preceding the takeoff into the step.

The forward swing of the arms and left leg is well advanced at this point. Since the time the athlete spends on the ground is small—approximately 0.17 s according to a study of 12 Olympic finalists[13]—this forward movement of the arms and free leg must start early (almost certainly before touchdown) and be fast if it is to be completed in time for takeoff.

The right shoulder is slightly lower than the left as the athlete leans to his right to bring his center of gravity over his supporting foot. This lateral shifting of the trunk to one side at the end of the hop and to the other at the end of the step can readily be observed by watching a triple jumper from in front or behind.

(f) Another strong takeoff position, similar to that shown in (a).

(g) The knee lift evident in the previous position is increased, the trunk is held near erect, and the arms are used for balance.

(h) The right leg has been flexed and brought forward, and in reaction to this movement the athlete's trunk has acquired some forward lean. The arms are beginning to sweep backward for the second time.

(i), (j), and (k) The landing at the conclusion of the step and the takeoff

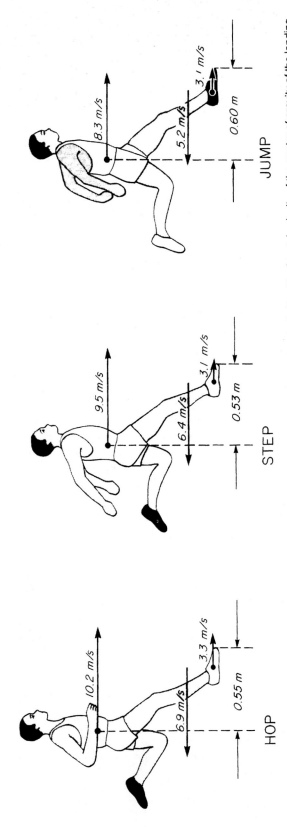

Figure 16-6. Average values for the forward horizontal velocity of the center of gravity; the forward horizontal velocity of the athlete's center of gravity; the backward horizontal velocity of the landing foot *relative to the center of gravity of the athlete*; and the horizontal distance from the hip to the toe of the landing leg, at touchdown beginning each of the three phases. (Based on data in Koh, T.J., and Hay J.G. [1990]. Landing leg motion and performance in the horizontal jumps II: The triple jump. *International Journal of Sport Biomechanics*, 6:361–73.)

Figure 16-7.
An active landing at the end of the
hop phase.

into the jump appear to be almost identical to the corresponding actions at the end of the hop phase (compare, [d], [e], and [f]).

Because the athlete's horizontal velocity is decreasing, the time he spends on the ground at each successive takeoff gets progressively longer—for example, Kreer[14] reported successive takeoff times of 0.133 s, 0.155 s, and 0.180 s for two world-record jumps by V. Saneev (USSR). Thus many jumpers who feel they have too little time to complete the lengthy double-arm swing as they go into the hop and step find they can do so comfortably and to their advantage as they take off for the jump.

(l) and (m) Except that the athlete has much less speed with which to work, the techniques employed in the jump phase are essentially the same as those used in the long jump. This relative lack of speed limits the time in the air and the movements that can be performed. The sail and hang techniques are those most widely used in this final phase. (*Note:* Since the distances achieved in this final jump range between 5.50 m and 6.70 m for top performers, the use of these techniques is in accord with the findings of El Khadem and Huyck[15] mentioned earlier, p. 431–432).

(n) Approaching the landing, the athlete is in an excellent position with his legs fully extended and his feet well forward of his center of gravity.

HIGH JUMP
Basic
Considerations

In high jumping, the height that an athlete clears may be regarded as the sum of three separate heights:

- the height of the athlete's center of gravity at the instant of takeoff (the takeoff height, H_1 in Fig. 16-8);

Figure 16-8.
Contributions to the height recorded in the
high jump.

- the height that the athlete raises the center of gravity during the flight (the flight height, H_2 in Fig. 16-8); and
- the difference between the maximum height reached by the center of gravity and the height of the crossbar (the clearance height, H_3 in Fig. 16-8).

Values obtained for four world-class high jumpers who used the Fosbury flop style are presented in Table 16-4. These values give some indi-

TABLE 16-4 Relative Contributions to Height in the High Jump

	Height of Athlete (m)	Height of Bar (m)	Height (m)	Percentage of Height of Bar
Louise Ritter (U.S.A.)	1.78	2.03		
			H_1 1.23	60.6
			H_2 0.88	43.3
			H_3 −0.08	−3.9
Stefka Kostadinova (Bulgaria)	1.80	2.01		
			H_1 1.19	59.2
			H_2 0.89	44.3
			H_3 −0.07	−3.5
Genadi Avdeyenko (USSR)	2.02	2.38		
			H_1 1.43	60.1
			H_2 1.07	45.0
			H_3 −0.12	−5.0
Hollis Conway (U.S.A.)	1.84	2.34		
			H_1 1.30	55.6
			H_2 1.26	53.8
			H_3 −0.22	-9.4

Adapted from Conrad, A., and Ritzdorf, W. (1990). Biomechanical analysis of the high jump. In *Scientific Research Project at the Games of the XXIVth Olympiad—Seoul 1988* (pp. 177–217). Monaco: International Athletic Foundation.

cation of the relative importance of the separate heights to the total performance.

Takeoff Height. The height of the center of gravity at the instant of takeoff depends on the athlete's body position at that instant. Although in practice the style of jumping employed may make it impossible to obtain (or even undesirable to attempt), the optimum body position in terms of the height of the center of gravity at takeoff is one with the trunk erect, both arms high, lead leg extended and high, and jumping leg fully extended and vertical.

Flight Height. The height that the center of gravity rises in flight is governed by the athlete's vertical velocity at takeoff. This in turn is governed by the vertical velocity at the instant the jumping foot touches down, and the change in the vertical velocity that takes place during the takeoff.

The athlete's vertical velocity at touchdown depends primarily on the actions during the last one to two strides of the run-up. If at the end of the second-last stride the athlete has sunk low over the supporting leg and then taken a low, fast stride onto the takeoff foot, the center of gravity is likely to have little or no downward vertical velocity at the instant this foot touches down. On the other hand, if by failing to sink low at the end of the second-last stride the athlete makes the last stride like those that preceded it, the downward vertical velocity at touchdown is likely to be relatively large. And, since the athlete must first arrest this downward motion before he (or she) can begin to drive the body upward, this large downward velocity is a liability. In fact, although it has yet to be convincingly demonstrated in practice, the ideal may well be to have the athlete's center of gravity moving upward (and forward, of course) at the instant the takeoff foot contacted the ground. (*Note:* An upward vertical velocity at touchdown necessarily implies a reduction in the vertical distance through which the athlete can exert forces once the takeoff foot is grounded. This, in turn, can lead to a reduction in the vertical impulse exerted during the takeoff itself. A zero or upward vertical velocity at touchdown is only desirable, therefore, if it does not lead to a corresponding [or more than corresponding] reduction in this vertical impulse.)

The change in vertical velocity during the takeoff depends on the magnitude of the vertical impulse that the athlete exerts against the ground and that the ground in reaction exerts against the athlete, and on the mass of the athlete (impulse-momentum relationship, p. 79). The vertical impulse, in turn, is dependent on the magnitude of the forces involved and the length of time during which they act.

The forces involved are those resulting from the swing of the athlete's arms and leading leg and from the extension of the hip, knee, and ankle joints of the jumping leg. The magnitude of these forces depends on such factors as the speed with which the free limbs are moved, the strength of the muscles of the jumping leg, and the manner in which the various movements are coordinated or timed.

One other very important factor influences the magnitude of the vertical forces. It is the amount of rotation (or angular momentum) that the athlete must acquire at takeoff in order to assume the required position by the time he (or she) reaches the peak of the jump. In some styles which require that the athlete obtain a considerable amount of rotation at takeoff, the vertical forces that can be exerted are somewhat smaller than if the athlete were to use a style requiring less rotation. In other words, the athlete acquires the layout position at the expense of some vertical lift. And what the athlete must try to do, of course, is to see that whatever is gained by being in a good layout position at the peak of the jump is not more than offset by losses incurred at takeoff.

The time during which the athlete's foot is in contact with the ground at takeoff, and thus the time during which it is possible to exert vertical forces, has been studied by a number of investigators. These studies have resulted in a number of important conclusions:

- The duration (or time) of takeoff is a function of the style of jumping employed. Athletes who use the flop style popularized by Fosbury in the late 1960s (Fig. 16-9) tend to have takeoff times in the 0.12-0.17 s range.[16][17][18] Those who used the straddle style popularized by Soviet athletes in the late 1950s and early 1960s (Fig. 16-10) generally had takeoff times in the 0.17-0.23 s range.[19][20][21]
- The time of takeoff is a function of the action of the free limbs and, in particular, of the leading leg. Irrespective of the style employed, athletes who use a straight-lead-leg action generally have longer times of takeoff than do those who use a bent lead leg.[22][23] There is also some evidence that those athletes who use a double-arm action at takeoff have longer takeoff times than those who use an alternate arm action.[24]
- Given the style and the specific actions of the free limbs, there appears to be an optimum time of takeoff for each athlete. Further, within limits that are specific to the athlete concerned, it appears that the shorter the time of takeoff the greater the vertical lift (H_2) the athlete obtains. At first glance this finding seems to be in direct conflict with the notion that the greater the vertical impulse at takeoff, the greater the vertical velocity at takeoff and therefore the greater the height attained. (*Note:* Impulse = force × time.) However, if the athlete is somehow able to increase the magnitude of the vertical forces he (or she) exerts by decreasing the takeoff time, and if these increases in force are effectively greater than the decreases in time, the conflict is dispelled. Under such circumstances the vertical impulse increases as the height of the jump increases, even though the takeoff time is meanwhile decreasing. How an athlete achieves these increases in vertical force while simultaneously decreasing the time of takeoff has yet to be completely explained. It appears though that following the forced eccentric action of the muscles of the jumping

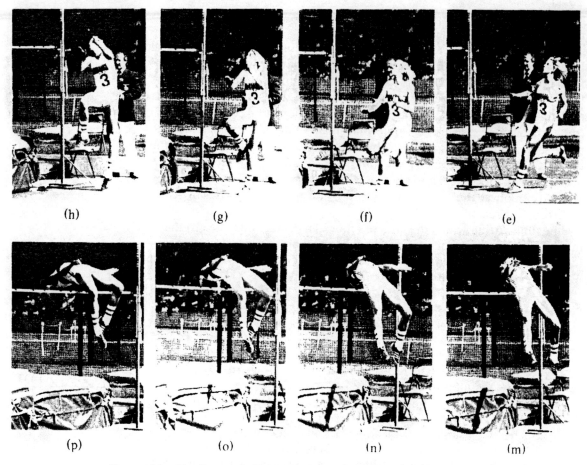

(h) (g) (f) (e)

(p) (o) (n) (m)

Figure 16-9. The Fosbury flop style. (Photographs courtesy of Howard Payne.)

leg. (during the first part of the takeoff) the elastic components of these muscles and/or a stretch reflex mechanism serve to enhance the explosive concentric action of the same leg (during the final part of the takeoff).[25].

Clearance Height. The difference between the maximum height reached by the athlete's center of gravity and the height cleared (often referred to as the efficiency of the bar clearance) depends on the athlete's body position at the peak of the jump and on the movements that he (or she) makes in crossing the bar.

The body position depends primarily on the style of jumping used—and here there are no less than six named styles (scissors, modified scissors or back layout, Eastern cutoff, Western roll, straddle, and Fosbury flop) and several unnamed ones which might be used.

The simplest of these, the first to evolve historically and the one most

(d)   (c)   (b)   (a)

(l)   (k)   (j)   (i)

(t)   (s)   (r)   (q)

Figure 16-10. The straddle style.

widely used by beginners, is the scissors. In this style the athlete takes off from the foot farther from the bar and rises to cross the bar with the trunk erect and the legs in a near-horizontal position (Fig. 16-11). In this body position the distance between the athlete's center of gravity and the greatest height cleared is generally something like 25–30 cm.

If the athlete rotates backward or sideways in rising to the bar, he (or she) can arrive in a clearance position in which this distance of 25–30 cm is substantially reduced—and this is exactly what some of the early high jumpers did. Some rotated backward to arrive in a position in which they were stretched out on their backs as they passed over the bar. This modified scissors or back layout style was especially hazardous because the rotation that carried the athlete into a horizontal position at bar level also tended to carry him (or her) into an inverted landing position and this, coupled with the meager pits in use at the time, discouraged most jumpers from using the style. The jumpers who rotated sideways as they rose to the bar evolved a style that later became known as the Eastern cutoff, owing to the popularity it enjoyed among jumpers in the Eastern United States (Fig. 16-12). Although in theory this style could allow the jumper to reduce the distance between the center of gravity and the bar to a mere 2–5 cm (perhaps even to zero), in practice it made such heavy demands on trunk and hip flexibility and on gymnastic ability that its exponents rarely achieved differences much less than 15-20 cm.

The next style to evolve historically was the Western roll—so named because a jumper from California developed it and popularized it among athletes on the West Coast of the United States. In this style the athlete took off from the foot nearer the bar and, with something closely akin to a

Figure 16-11.
The scissors style.

Figure 16-12. The Eastern cutoff style.

hopping motion, rose to cross the bar lying on the side with the knee of the takeoff leg tucked in against the chest (Fig. 16-13). At its best, the Western roll probably allowed the athlete to reduce the difference between the peak height of the center of gravity and the bar to approximately 15 cm.

In the straddle style the athlete takes off from the foot nearer the bar and rises to a clearance position "lying" face down along its length. If the body is stretched out, the center of gravity may be as little as 10 cm above the bar. On the other hand, if the body is wrapped around the bar (in a so-called drape- or dive-straddle), this distance may be reduced by as much as 5–10 cm.

The latest of this long line of styles, the Fosbury flop, incorporates a takeoff from the foot farther from the bar and a clearance position in which the athlete is arched backward over the bar (Fig. 16-10). Such a position affords the possibility of the center of gravity being outside the

Figure 16-13. The Western roll style.

body and perhaps even passing through or below the bar while the jumper passes over it (p. 129).

The extent to which the six styles described in the preceding paragraphs are used in practice varies considerably. The scissors is still widely used by beginners; the modified scissors, Eastern cutoff, Western roll, and straddle are rarely used in competition; and the Fosbury flop is used almost exclusively at all but the lowest levels of competition.

In most of the styles just described, the athlete performs certain movements in the air so that the various parts of the body can pass over and around the bar without dislodging it. Because the body's angular momentum is conserved during this time, each of these movements or actions that the athlete initiates in the air is accompanied by an equal and opposite reaction in some other part of the body.

Summary

The relationships between the height that an athlete clears and the factors that determine that height are summarized in Fig. 16-14.

Techniques

For the purposes of analysis the techniques in high jumping are considered here under four subheadings—the run-up, the takeoff, the bar clearance, and the landing.

Run-Up

The purpose of the run-up is to bring the athlete into the optimum position for takeoff, moving at a velocity consistent with the athlete's strength and skill.

The length of run-up employed depends primarily on the athlete's ability to use the speed generated during the run-up. This in turn depends

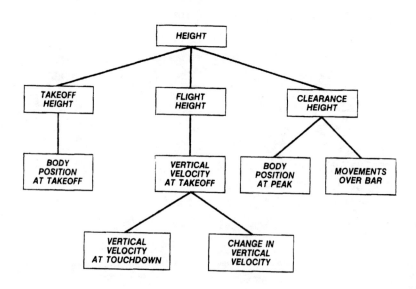

Figure 16-14.
Basic factors in high jumping.

mainly on the strength of the leg muscles and on the ability to coordinate the movements required at takeoff. If, by using too long a run-up, the athlete develops more speed than the legs have the strength to "control" at takeoff, the height of the resulting jump will inevitably be less than the athlete is capable of producing. Similarly, if the athlete arrives at the take-off traveling so fast that there is insufficient time to complete the required sequence of movements, the performance again suffers.

In view of this relationship between strength and skill on the one hand and the length and speed of the run-up on the other, most teachers and coaches recommend that beginning high jumpers use a short run of 5 to 7 strides and more experienced jumpers use one of 7 to 11 strides.

The angle at which the bar is approached is subject to considerable variation both between styles and between athletes using the same style. In general, however, most athletes make the last stride of their approach at an angle somewhere between 20° and 40°, irrespective of the style they employ.

Although a straight-line approach to the bar is generally used with most other styles, exponents of the Fosbury flop commonly use a J-shaped approach. That is, they start by running along a straight line and finish running around a circular arc. An athlete who uses such an approach acquires angular momentum about an axis parallel to the bar when moving up from the inward-leaning position (required to negotiate the curve) to the vertical position (desired at the instant of takeoff). An athlete who used a straight approach would generally acquire the same angular momentum by leaning toward the bar during the takeoff. This leaning toward the bar has a detrimental effect on the athlete's ability to generate lift.[26 27]

During the last few strides of the run-up, the athlete adjusts his (or her) body position in preparation for the takeoff. These adjustments take the following form:

- The trunk is brought from a position in which it is inclined forward to one in which it is inclined backward. With top-class jumpers, the greater part of this change in the inclination of the trunk occurs as a result of a forward movement of the hips at the beginning of the last stride of the run-up.

  With the trunk inclined backward at the end of the last stride, the athlete's center of gravity has greater horizontal and vertical distances to travel, from the instant of touchdown to the instant of takeoff, than it would if the trunk were erect. The athlete is therefore able to take more time to coordinate the takeoff movements or to take the same time and approach the takeoff at a slightly higher speed.

- The center of gravity is gradually lowered by the athlete increasing the flexion of the knee of the supporting leg as the body passes forward over the grounded foot at the end of each stride,

  There is some evidence to suggest that the amount the center of gravity is lowered is related to the height that the athlete jumps. For example, Nigg[28] analyzed the performances of Dwight Stones (U.S.A.) during a competition in which he set a world record of 2.30

m using the Fosbury flop style and found that the peak height attained by the athlete's center of gravity increased as the height of his center of gravity at touchdown of the takeoff foot decreased (Fig. 16-15).

- The lowering of the center of gravity—variously referred to as the "squat," "sink," or "gather"—is accompanied by a decrease in the degree to which the knee of the supporting leg is extended as the athlete "takes off" into the next stride. This incomplete extension of the leg assists in keeping the athlete's center of gravity low.

The stick-figure diagrams in Fig. 16-16 illustrate the extent of these various adjustments in body position in the case of a world-class high jumper.

As in the case of the long jump, the changes in body position during the final few strides before takeoff produce concomitant changes in the length of the strides involved. Most important of these is a gradual increase in length up until the second-to-last stride (almost invariably the longest of all the strides in the run-up) and a decrease in length of the final stride.

Takeoff

The takeoff begins with the grounding of the heel of the jumping foot at the end of the last stride of the run-up. At this instant the athlete's body is usually inclined backward, with the foot of the leading leg close to the

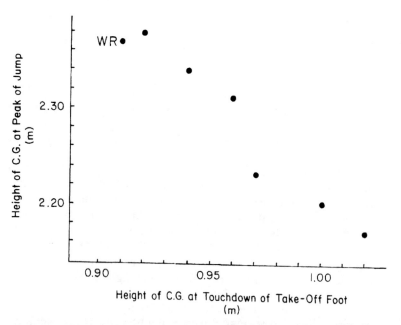

Figure 16-15. The height of the center of gravity (C.G.) at the touchdown of the takeoff foot and at the peak of the jump for Dwight Stones, U.S.A. WR = World Record. (Adapted from data in Nigg, B.M. [1974]. *Sprung, Springen, Sprunge* [pp. 56–74]. Zurich: Juris Verlag.)

Figure 16-16.
Adjustments made during the last stride of the approach and takeoff by an athlete using the Fosbury flop style. (Data courtesy Jesus Dapena, Indiana University.)

ground and well behind the body, and both arms behind the body or one forward and one backward "balancing" the respective legs.

Once the sole of the jumping foot has been grounded, the knee of the jumping leg flexes to reduce the effect of the impact and to put the leg into the optimum position for the forceful extension to follow.

During the initial movements of the takeoff, the lead leg, which has been deliberately left well behind the body during the last stride of the run, begins to swing forward and upward in unison with the arm or arms that accompany it. This forward and upward swing of the lead leg and arm(s) serves three principal functions:

- It increases the magnitude of the vertical forces exerted against the ground, the vertical forces that the ground exerts on the athlete in reaction, and thus the athlete's vertical velocity at takeoff.
- It imparts angular momentum to the athlete's body.
- It increases the height of the athlete's center of gravity at the instant of takeoff.

There are two main types of lead leg swing—the *bent leg* and the *straight leg*. The bent-leg swing is used by most exponents of the Fosbury flop. In using the Fosbury flop style, an athlete must acquire a certain amount of angular momentum at takeoff to get the body into the desired layout position at the peak of the jump. A vigorous straight-leg action imparts a large amount of backward angular momentum to the body and makes it difficult to acquire angular momentum in the opposite direction. For this reason, athletes who use the Fosbury flop style usually employ a bent-leg action. With this action, the lead leg makes a contribution to the vertical velocity at takeoff and to the height of the takeoff—although probably not as much as a straight lead leg would in either case—and, at the same time, keeps the backward angular momentum that must be overcome within acceptable limits.

With the straight-leg technique the athlete brings the leading leg forward with a bend at the knee just sufficient to allow the foot to clear the ground. Then, once the foot has passed forward of the supporting (jumping) leg, the knee is extended and the lead leg continues forward and upward as one unit.

Once the lead leg and the upper arm(s) reach the horizontal or near-horizontal, the athlete drives down vigorously against the ground by extending the hip, knee, and ankle joints of the jumping leg. The reaction to this leg drive propels the athlete into the air. In addition, if it acts eccentrically, as is usually the case, it also contributes to the angular momentum that the athlete acquires at takeoff.

Bar Clearance

Most of what takes place while the athlete is in the air may be directly attributed to the nature of the takeoff (that is, to the athlete's center-of-gravity height, velocity, and angular momentum at that instant). Nonetheless, the athlete does make use of a judicious interplay between the action of one part of the body and the reaction it evokes in some other part to effect a clearance of the bar.

In the Fosbury flop style, the athlete quickly extends the knees as soon as the legs reach the point at which they are in imminent danger of dislodging the bar (Fig. 16-17). This motion, which lifts the athlete's legs and feet clear of the bar, is accompanied by a contrary reaction in the athlete's upper body. Since one of the side effects of this combined action and reaction is a lowering of the athlete's hips relative to the rest of the body, it is important that the extension of the knees not be initiated before the hips have themselves crossed the bar. If it is initiated too soon, the athlete lessens the danger of dislodging the bar with one part of the body merely to increase it with another.

Figure 16-17. Stick-figure diagram showing bar-clearance action in the Fosbury flop style. The diagram is based on a 2.25-m clearance by Leo Williams (U.S.A.). (Data courtesy Jesus Dapena, Indiana University.)

Landing

The landing is generally made on either the foot of the leading leg (scissors), the foot of the jumping leg (Eastern cutoff), the hands and the foot of the jumping leg (Western roll), the side or back (straddle), or the back (Fosbury flop). The part of the body on which the landing is made in the back layout style is not easily predicted!

POLE VAULT
Basic
Considerations

For the purposes of analysis, the height that a pole-vaulter clears may be regarded as the sum of four separate parts:

- the height of the vaulter's center of gravity at the instant of takeoff (the takeoff height, H_1 in Fig. 16-18),
- the height that the center of gravity is raised while he is on the pole (the swing height, H_2 in Fig. 16-18),
- the height that the center of gravity is raised once the vaulter has released the pole (the flight height, H_3 in Fig. 16-18), and
- the difference between the height of the crossbar and the maximum height reached by the center of gravity (the clearance height H_4 in Fig. 16-18).

The contribution that each of these heights makes to the total height of a vault is shown for three top-class vaulters in Table 16-5.

The factors that influence the magnitude of H_1, H_3, and H_4 are identical to those that determine the magnitude of the corresponding heights in

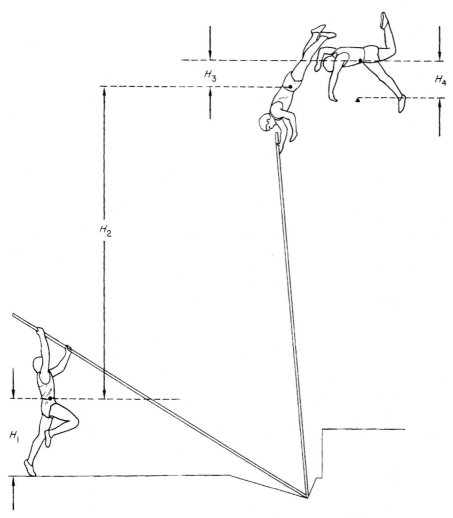

Figure 16-18. Contributions to the height recorded in the pole vault.

TABLE 16-5 Relative Contributions to Height in the Pole Vault

	Height of Athlete (m)	Height of Bar (m)	Height (m)		Percentage of Height of Bar
Sergei Bubka (USSR)	1.83	5.85			
			H_1	1.30	22.2
			H_2	4.45	76.1
			H_3	0.37	6.3
			H_4	−0.27	−4.6
Earl Bell (USA)	1.91	5.61			
			H_1	1.25	22.3
			H_2	4.22	75.2
			H_3	0.11	2.0
			H_4	0.03	0.5
Billy Olson (USA)	1.88	5.50			
			H_1	1.38	25.1
			H_2	3.92	71.3
			H_3	0.44	8.0
			H_4	−0.24	−4.4

Data courtesy Peter M. McGinnis, State University of New York at Cortland.

high jumping—body position (H_1), vertical velocity at release (H_3), body position and movements initiated in the air (H_4).

The factors that determine the magnitude of H_2 are perhaps best considered in terms of mechanical energy changes. At the instant of takeoff the vaulter has a large amount of kinetic energy (equivalent to speeds of 6.5-8.5 m/s) and a relatively small amount of potential energy (equivalent to a center-of-gravity height of 1.15–1.35 m). In addition. it is likely that the vaulter has already "stored" some energy in the pole by bending it. At the instant he releases the pole. the vaulter has a large amount of potential energy (equivalent to a height of up to 6.00 m) and a relatively small amount of kinetic energy. The difference between the mechanical energy that the vaulter possesses as he releases the pole and that at takeoff is equal to the algebraic sum of the work he does during the ascent and the losses in mechanical energy to other energy forms (heat, sound, and so on) incurred en route. (*Note:* Whereas the mechanical energy of an athlete in flight remains constant throughout the flight, the vaulter's mechanical energy is subject to change, whenever he retains contact with the ground via the pole.)

These various energy changes may be summarized in the following equation.*

---

* The kinetic and potential energies possessed by the pole at takeoff and at release are very small and have been disregarded.

Potential | kinetic | kinetic | potential | strain | work done | mechanical
energy at + energy at = energy at + energy at + energy at + during − energy
release | release | takeoff | takeoff | takeoff | ascent | losses

This equation can be rearranged to yield the following expression for ΔPE, the difference between the potential energies at release and takeoff:

kinetic | strain | work done | mechanical | kinetic
ΔPE = energy at + energy at + during − energy − energy at
takeoff | takeoff | ascent | losses | release

Since this difference is equal to the product of the vaulter's weight (a constant) and H_2, an examination of the five terms on the right-hand side of this equation should reveal the basic factors upon which the magnitude of H_2 depends.

Kinetic Energy at Takeoff

The kinetic energy that the vaulter possesses as he leaves the ground derives from the work he does to build up speed during the run-up and from the additional work he does at takeoff to add a vertical component to his motion.

Strain Energy at Takeoff

The amount of energy "stored" in the pole at the instant of takeoff is a function of the materials and construction of the pole and of the forces that are exerted upon it.

Poles of fiberglass, bamboo, or any similarly flexible material can more readily be deformed than the aluminum and steel poles in widespread use 30–35 years ago. Thus it is more likely that a vaulter can usefully "store" energy in a modern fiberglass pole than in one of the earlier metal poles. This, of course, is one of the advantages that present-day vaulters have over their predecessors.

The forces that the vaulter exerts on the pole at takeoff are transmitted to the pole via his hands. To examine how these forces may be used to deform the pole, and thus to invest in it a certain amount of strain energy, it is desirable to resolve the forces into components acting perpendicular and parallel to the long axis of the pole.

In good vaulting, the two perpendicular components act in opposite directions—the one applied by the lower hand in an upward and slightly forward direction, the other in a downward and forward direction (Fig. 16-19). The perpendicular component of the force exerted by the lower hand tends to rotate the pole upward about a transverse axis through the butt end of the pole. The perpendicular component of the force exerted by the upper hand tends to rotate the pole in the opposite direction. At the same time, the downward perpendicular component exerted by the upper hand effectively combines with an equal part of the upward perpendicular component exerted by the lower hand to form a couple. With the butt end

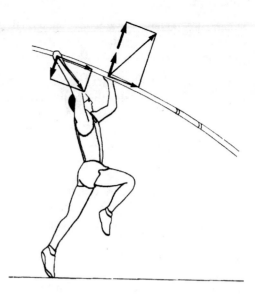

Figure 16-19.
Forces exerted on the pole via the hands.

of the pole firmly fixed in the box, this couple causes the pole to bend upward. The extent to which the pole is bent in this process is governed by the magnitude of the perpendicular forces exerted and by the distance between their lines of action, that is, the distance between the vaulter's hands.

The components acting parallel to the long axis of the pole may be regarded as eccentric forces that, like all eccentric forces, tend to both translate and rotate the body upon which they act. In this case, the tendency to translate the body is thwarted by the contrary forces exerted by the back of the box on the butt of the pole, and the pole merely becomes more firmly "fixed" in the box than before. With this "fixing" of the butt end of the pole, the only way in which the eccentric parallel forces can produce a rotation of the body on which they act is by causing the pole to bend—and this is exactly what happens. The amount that the pole is bent in this way is determine primarily by the magnitudes of the parallel forces involved, and these, in turn, are governed by the athlete's actions at takeoff. If the athlete drives upward and forward across the line of the pole, the magnitudes of the parallel forces are relatively small and their tendency to bend the pole, is minimal. On the other hand, if the vaulter drives forward into the pole, the magnitudes of the parallel forces and the resulting bending of the pole are both correspondingly greater.

Work Done During Ascent

Once the vaulter leaves the ground, he and the pole form what has frequently been referred to as a *double pendulum*. At the same time as the vaulter is swinging on the pole about an axis that passes transversely through the hands (the man pendulum), he and the pole together are rotating about a transverse axis through the base of the pole (the man-and-pole pendulum).

The vaulter's first objective, upon leaving the ground, is to bring the pole to a position in which he can most effectively do work to lift his body. To achieve this objective, the vaulter endeavors to bring his center of gravity* as close as he can to the axis about which the man-and-pole pendulum is rotating, thus decreasing its moment of inertia about that axis and facilitating the rotation of this pendulum toward the vertical. For a given height at which the vaulter grips the pole, there are basically two ways in which he may bring his center of gravity toward the axis through the end of the pole: (1) he can straighten his arms, lower his leading leg, and assume a fully extended body position; and (2) he can exert forces to increase the bend of the pole.

The forces that the vaulter can exert on the pole to increase its bend derive from two principal sources. If the vaulter keeps his lower arm firm (or perhaps even actively pushes with this lower arm), the force thus exerted, together with part of the component of his weight applied via the upper hand in the opposite direction, forms a couple that acts to increase the bend of the pole (Fig. 16-20[a]). The moment of this couple, and thus the effect it has on the magnitude of the pole bend, depends primarily on the force exerted via the lower hand. The vaulter may also exert force to increase the bend of the pole by vigorously swinging the legs upward. The reaction to the centripetal force that the pole exerts on the vaulter to make this angular motion possible is a force that the vaulter exerts on the pole in a forward and downward direction (Fig. 16-20[b]). This force, like the parallel forces referred to earlier, acts eccentrically to increase the bend of the pole.

There is a third way in which a vaulter can adjust the moment of inertia of the man-and-pole pendulum during the hang phase—he can alter the position at which he initially grips the pole. If he lowers his grip, he will decrease the moment of inertia; if he raises it, he will produce the reverse effect.

The position on the pole at which a vaulter grips with the upper hand is governed by his ability to bring the pole to the vertical (or near-vertical) position required to complete the vault effectively. If the vaulter holds too high (that is, too far from the butt end of the pole), the moment opposing the motion of the man-and-pole toward the vertical (that is, the weight of the man-and-pole times the horizontal distance from their combined center of gravity to the base of the pole) is such that the vaulter is unable to bring the pole to the vertical. As a direct consequence, the quality of his performance suffers. If the vaulter holds too low, his performance is also likely to suffer, for then the pole tends to come to the desired final position before he has time to complete the sequence of movements designed to project his body upward into the air. It should be clear, therefore, that there is an optimum height at which a vaulter should grip in any given case. Furthermore, since the higher the vaulter can grip and still bring the pole to the

---

* Strictly speaking, the center of gravity of the man and pole considered together.

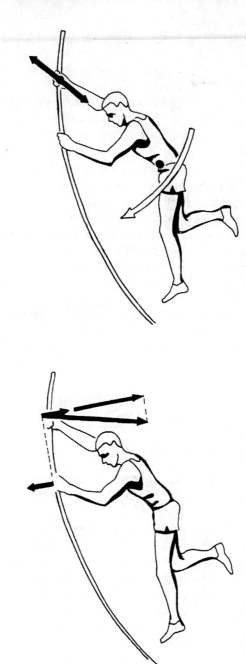

Figure 16-20. Components of the force that the vaulter exerts on the pole during the swing due to (a) the action of his left arm; and (b) the vigorous upward swing of his legs.

required final position, the better his overall performance is likely to be, the good vaulter continually strives to increase the height of the grip that he can use effectively.

The effects produced by changing the height at which a vaulter grips the pole have been very nicely summarized in a figure originally presented by Morawski, Wilclik, and Sliwinski[29]—Fig. 16-21. These investigators calculated the path that would be followed by the center of gravity of a vaulter who varied the height of his grip from 4.60–5.00 m while maintaining the same velocities at takeoff. (A horizontal velocity of 9 m/s and a vertical velocity of 2 m/s—which yield a takeoff angle of 12.5°—were used in the example of Fig. 16-21). The figure shows that the greatest height could be achieved in this case if the vaulter gripped the pole somewhere between 4.75 and 4.80 m from the end. With grip heights less than this, the vaulter would reach his peak height well past the bar. (*Note:* The bar can be placed anywhere within a range of ± "0.60 metres from the prolongation of the inside edge of the top of the stopboard"—that is, the back of the box.) With grip heights of 4.80 m and greater, the vaulter would fail to bring the pole to the vertical and would, as a result, be thrown back on the runway rather than towards the pit.

One major advantage that fiberglass poles have over the metal poles used previously lies in the higher grip heights that they permit. If a vaulter using a metal pole gripped the pole with his top hand at a distance of, say, 4 m from

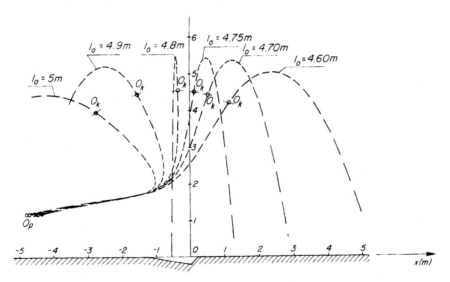

Figure 16-21. The path followed by the center of gravity of a vaulter with the top of the top hand at distances from the butt end of the pole (l_o) ranging from 4.60 to 5 m. The vaulter's horizontal and vertical velocities at takeoff are, respectively, 9 m/s and 2 m/s; O_p and O_k are the position of the vaulter's center of gravity at the instant the pole hit the back of the box and at the instant the vaulter released the pole, respectively. (Adapted from Morawski, et al. *Badania Modelowe Skoku o Tyczce.*)

the end of the pole, this distance would remain essentially unaltered throughout the vault. On the other hand, if the vaulter gripped a fiberglass pole 4 m from the end of the pole, this distance might be markedly reduced during the early stages of the vault due to the pole being bent. If, for example, this distance was reduced to 3.5 m at some instant during the vault, the pole would behave at that instant as if it were a straight pole being gripped at 3.5 m. Thus a vaulter who would normally grip at 4 m on a metal pole would find the same grip too low when he used a fiberglass pole.

Once the vaulter has used one or more of these methods to assist the upward motion of the man-and-pole pendulum, he concentrates on raising his body on the pole. To do this, he swings his legs forward, upward, and backward, flexing at the hips and knees as he does so. This process, which reduces the moment of inertia and increases the angular velocity of the man pendulum, also, regrettably results in an increase in the moment of inertia of the man-and-pole pendulum and a consequent slowing in the rate at which the pole approaches the vertical. (*Note:* Extension of the vaulter's body immediately after takeoff produces the reverse effect, slowing the vaulter as it speeds the pole.)

Having thus reached an inverted tuck position, the vaulter next exerts forces down the line of the near-vertical pole to raise his center of gravity above the level of his hands. This lifting of the center of gravity—aided by a returning to the vaulter of the energy "stored" in the pole—culminates in the vaulter pushing off from the pole and projecting himself into the air.

Mechanical Energy Losses

During the course of a vault, forces acting between the pole and the box and forces within the pole itself result in a conversion of mechanical energy to other nonmechanical forms (for example, heat and sound). Thus, if the vaulter did not work at all between the instants of takeoff and release of the pole, the total mechanical energy possessed by the vaulter and the pole at that latter instant would be less than they possessed at the instant of takeoff.

Kinetic Energy at Release

The vaulter's kinetic energy at the instant he releases the pole is determined primarily by his velocity at that time. Here the optimum velocity is one with a large vertical component (to carry the vaulter's center of gravity high into the air and maximize the value of H_3) and a small horizontal component (to ensure the vaulter a safe passage across the bar).

Summary

The relationship between the height that an athlete clears and the factors that determine that height are summarized in Fig. 16-22.

Techniques

For the purposes of analysis, pole vaulting may be subdivided into the following parts—the run-up, the plant, the takeoff, the hang, the swing-up and rock-back, the pull-turn-and-push, the clearance, and the landing.

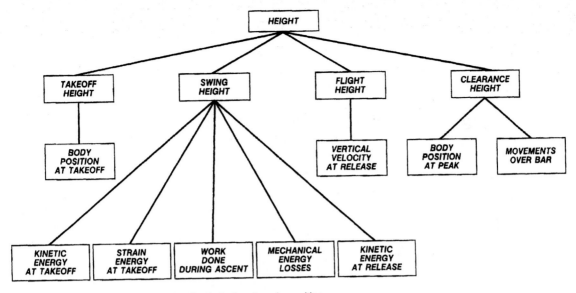

Figure 16-22. Basic factors in pole vaulting.

Run-up*

During the run-up the pole is carried close to the vaulter's right hip with the thumb of his left (lower) hand under the pole supporting its weight and the thumb of his right (upper) hand pressing down to hold the tip of the pole up—Fig. 16-23. Taking the vaulter's left thumb as the fulcrum, the moment of the downward force exerted via the right hand must be equal to the contrary moment of the weight of the pole, if the pole is to be held steady. The fingers of each hand are wrapped loosely around the pole and supplement the work done by the thumbs.

The height at which the tip of the pole is held as the vaulter runs toward the box is subject to some variation between vaulters. Some use a high carry with the tip of the pole well above head height. This permits the right elbow to be more fully extended than otherwise and makes it easier for the vaulter to apply the required downward force via his right hand. For this reason a high carry is often favored by vaulters using heavy poles and/or high grips, both of which require that a considerable force be exerted via the right hand.

The principal disadvantages in the use of a high carry are the large frontal area presented to the air through which the pole is moved—this can be particularly troublesome on a windy day—and the considerable distance through which the tip of the pole must be lowered during the plant. This latter increases the scope for error beyond that which exists when a lower carry is used. When the tip of the pole is carried at head height (a medium carry), or still lower at approximately hip height (a low or parallel carry), the advantages and disadvantages associated with a high carry tend to become reversed—difficulty in applying the required downward force in-

---

* Throughout the ensuing discussion of pole-vault techniques, it is assumed that the vaulter is right-handed.

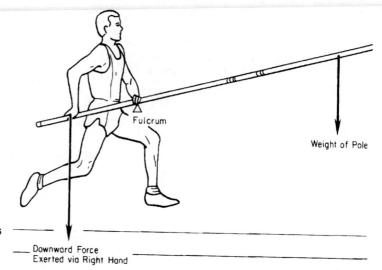

Fulcrum

Weight of Pole

Figure 16-23.
During the carry, the moment of the
downward force exerted by the vaulter's
top hand balances the moment of the
weight of the pole.

Downward Force
Exerted via Right Hand

creases as problems with air resistance and the potential for errors in planting the pole decrease.

The length, speed, and accuracy of a pole-vaulter's run-up are subject to precisely the same influences that operate in the case of a long or triple jumper, for athletes in all three events seek the same objective—to obtain the maximum speed that they can use effectively during the takeoff.

The remaining parts of the vault—the plant, the takeoff, the hang, the swing-up and rock-back, the pull-turn-push, the clearance, and the landing—are probably best considered with reference to a sequence that shows these movements being performed (Fig. 16-24, pp. 464–465).

(a)* With almost one full stride remaining before takeoff, the vaulter is partway through the plant—the process of lowering the tip of the pole into the box and raising the hands overhead in preparation for takeoff.

Although there are other techniques that might be used in planting the pole, the one most commonly used is the sidearm plant (Fig. 16-25). In this technique, the vaulter moves his right hand forward and upward to a position high above his head, using a predominantly sidearm action. Viewed from the rear, the path that the hand follows appears to be an arc of a circle in the plane of the athlete's trunk. Viewed from the side, it becomes apparent that the plane in which his hand moves is inclined slightly forward relative to the plane of the athlete's trunk.

(b) The completion of the last stride before takeoff. The vaulter has his top hand overhead and is stepping in under the pole as it slides the last few centimeters before striking the back of the box. Well-executed pole plants, regardless of type, result in the vaulter passing through this position.

(c) The takeoff. The vaulter drives vigorously upward with his leading

* The letters in parentheses refer to the corresponding positions in Fig. 16-24.

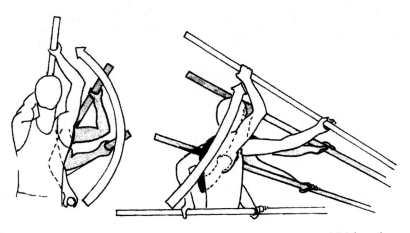

Figure 16-25. The sidearm plant as viewed (a) from the rear; and (b) from the side. Initial and final positions are in white, intermediate positions in gray.

knee and forcefully extends the hip, knee, and ankle joints of his takeoff leg. The takeoff foot is directly below the vaulter's top hand and, although not evident from this figure, on the line of his run-up, which also passes through the butt of the pole.

The position of the vaulter's left (takeoff) foot at this time is critical to the success of the vault. If the foot is too far forward of a perpendicular line through the top hand, the vaulter experiences a marked loss in horizontal velocity and some difficulty in generating vertical velocity as he leaps forward against the restraint imposed by his right arm. (*Note:* McGinnis[30] reported that the toe of the takeoff foot was forward of the top of the top hand an average of 16 cm in vaults by 16 elite pole vaulters [5.50–5.81 m in the vaults analyzed]; and an average of 21 cm in vaults by 16 non elite pole vaulters [5.19–5.40 m].) If the takeoff foot is placed well behind a perpendicular line through the top hand, the vaulter may develop more momentum in his swing than he is able to control later in the vault. The distant takeoff may also result in a reduction in the vertical force he can exert at takeoff and a concomitant difficulty in bringing the pole to the vertical. Serious though these problems are, even greater ones are likely to be experienced if the vaulter places his takeoff foot off-line in a lateral sense, for then he will almost certainly initiate a rotation of his body about the long axis of the pole and thus reduce the height of his vault. This fault, particularly common among beginning vaulters, who tend to "step around the pole" instead of driving straight forward onto it, usually results in the vaulter rotating around the pole to a position parallel (or near-parallel) to the bar. The same type of rotation is often initiated if the vaulter fails to bring the pole directly overhead at takeoff.

The distance between the vaulter's hands and the positions of his arms are such as would permit him to exert perpendicular forces to initiate the bending of the pole. Ganslen[31] reported the "hand spreads" used by 19

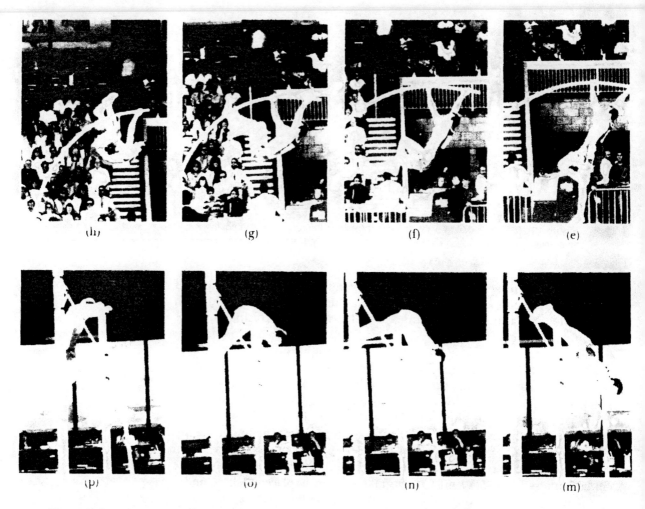

(h) (g) (f) (e)

(p) (o) (n) (m)

Figure 16-24. An example of good technique in vaulting with a fiberglass pole. (Photographs courtesy of Howard Payne.)

leading fiberglass-pole vaulters. They ranged from 20 cm to 76 cm and averaged 41 cm.

(d)-(e) The so-called hang phase of the vault. The vaulter has extended his arm to cushion the shock as his hands take over their weight-bearing role. This extension, together with the extension and lowering of the right knee, decreases the moment of inertia of the man-and-pole pendulum, thereby facilitating its passage toward the vertical. By increasing his moment of inertia relative to the transverse axis through his hands, it also slows the man pendulum and keeps the vaulter behind the pole.

(f)-(h) The vaulter is swinging his legs upward by flexing at the hips. To increase the speed of this action, he decreases the moment of inertia of his legs by bending his knees.

(i)-(k) As the pole straightens, the vaulter brings his knees back still

(d)   (c)   (b)   (a)

(l)   (k)   (j)   (i)

farther toward his hands and then, with an extension at the hips and knees, drives his feet high into the air, in the process passing through the so-called L, J, and I positions (Fig. 16-24[i], [j], and [k]).

(k)-(m) The pull-up and turn are delayed until the pole is very nearly vertical and then executed at considerable speed. The rotation of the vaulter's body about its long axis is facilitated if he assumes a position—body extended, legs straight and together—that minimizes his moment of inertia relative to this axis.

The timing of the pull is of some importance, for if it is initiated too soon—as is frequently the case with beginners—the pole is less likely to reach the desired final position, due to the premature increase in the moment of inertia of the man-and-pole pendulum. It is also important that the vaulter's center of gravity remain in line with the pole and not pass forward of this line prior to the pull, for if it is permitted to get away from the pole in this fashion, the reaction to the force that the vaulter exerts on the pole will be an eccentric one and will tend to cause his legs to drop at the very time he most wants to keep them moving upward.

(n) With the push-up completed and the left hand already removed from the pole, the vaulter releases the grip of his right hand and pushes the pole back away from the bar.

(o)-(p) The bar clearance. There are three basic methods of clearing the bar—the jackknife, the arch, and the flyaway. A combination of two of these (the arch-flyaway) has been more widely used than any other.

In the jackknife method, the vaulter actively swings both legs downward once they have cleared the bar and then, as his body begins to fall, extends his hips to lift his trunk and arms clear (Fig. 6-18). The objective here is to elevate the hips by lowering the legs and perhaps, too, to have the vaulter's body pass over the bar while his center of gravity passes below it. The principal disadvantage with this method lies in the fact that since his body is piked around the bar, the vaulter's timing must be highly precise if he is to avoid dislodging the bar with one of the many body parts in close proximity to it. As a direct consequence of this serious disadvantage, few top-class vaulters of recent years have used this method except as a last resort on otherwise poor vaults.

In the arch method, the vaulter arches his body around the bar and lets the angular momentum he acquired as he left the pole rotate his feet down toward the pit and his trunk and arms up clear of the bar.

With the flyaway method, the vaulter projects himself off the pole at such a speed that he is able to fly upward and across the bar while retaining his body in what is essentially a straight position. His arms, which would otherwise be the lowest parts of his body as he crossed the bar, are flung upward and backward before they endanger the success of the vault.

The arch-flyaway, the method used in the sequence of Fig. 16-24, involves an arching of the body around the bar, followed, once the chest has passed across the bar, by a lifting upward and backward of the vaulter's arms. This final action, which clears the arms, results in the vaulter's legs coming upward and backward (in reaction) and his chest and abdomen being moved in the opposite direction. The latter, however, is unimportant if the movement is timed correctly, for then these parts of the body have already passed safely over the bar. It might be noted here that dislodging the bar with the chest or abdomen, as a result of a premature flinging up of the arms, is a very common fault at this stage of the vault, even among relatively experienced vaulters.

Long Jump

Hay, J. G. (1985). In H. Payne (Ed.), *Athletes in Action*. London: Pelham Books, pp. 165–78 (Long jump).

Hay, J. G. (1986). *Exercise and Sport Sciences Reviews*. New York: Macmillan, pp. 401–46 (The biomechanics of the long jump).

Hay, J. G., Miller, J. A., and Canterna, R. W. (1986). The techniques of elite male long jumpers. *Journal of Biomechanics*, 19:855–66.

Nixdorf, E., and Brüggemann, G-P. (1990). *International Amateur Athletic Foundation Scientific Research Project at the Games of the XXXIV Olympiad—Seoul 1988 Final Report*. London: International Athletic Foundation, pp. 263–301 (Biomechanical analysis of the long jump).

Triple Jump

Brüggemann, G-P. (1990). *International Amateur Athletic Foundation Scientific Research Project at the Games of the XXXIV Olympiad—Seoul 1988 Final Report*. London: International Athletic Foundation, pp. 303–62 (Biomechanical analysis of the triple jump).

Hay, J. G. (1990). *Techniques in Athletics: Conference Proceedings* (pp. 296–308). Köln, Federal Republic of Germany: Deutsche Sporthochschule Köln (The biomechanics of triple jump techniques).

Hay, J. G. (1992). The biomechanics of the triple jump: A review. *Journal of Sports Sciences*, 10:343–78.

Muraki, Y. (1985). In H. Payne (Ed.), *Athletes in Action*. London: Pelham Books, pp. 179–97 (Triple jump).

High Jump

Ae, M., and others (1986). Biomechanical analysis of the preparatory motion in the Fosbury Flop. *International Journal of Sport Biomechanics*, 2:66–77.

Conrad, A., and Ritzdorf, W. (1990). *International Amateur Athletic Foundation Scientific Research Project at the Games of the XXXIV Olympiad—Seoul 1988 Final Report*. London: International Athletic Foundation, pp. 177–217 (Biomechanical analysis of the high jump).

Dapena, J. (1987). *Medicine and Sport Science: Current Research in Sports Biomechanics*. Basel, Switzerland: S. Karger, vol. 25, pp. 19–33 (Basic and applied research in the biomechanics of high jumping).

Dapena, J. (1990). *Techniques in Athletics: Conference Proceedings*. Köln, Federal Republic of Germany: Deutsche Sporthochschule Köln, pp. 309–22 (Introduction to the biomechanics of high jumping).

Wagner, B. (1985). In H. Payne (Ed.), *Athletes in Action*. London: Pelham Books, pp. 115–33 (High jump).

Pole Vault

Dyson, G. H. C. (1977). *The Mechanics of Athletics*. New York: Holmes & Meier, pp. 198–208 (Pole vaulting).

Gros, H. J. (1990). *Techniques in Athletics: Conference Proceedings*. Köln, Federal Republic of Germany: Deutsche Sporthochschule Köln, pp. 323–30 (Biomechanical aspects of pole vaulting).

Gros, H. J., and Kunkel, V. (1990). *International Amateur Athletic Foundation Scientific Research Project at the Games of the XXXIV Olympiad—Seoul 1988 Final Report*. London: International Athletic Foundation, pp. 219–60 (Biomechanical analysis of the pole vault).

Houvion, M. (1985). In H. Payne (Ed.), *Athletes in Action* London: Pelham Books, pp. 134–64 (Pole vault).

McGinnis, P. (1989). Pete's pointers for perfect pole vaulting. *Track Technique*, 109:3472–74.

Notes

1. Nigg, B. M. (1974). *Sprung, Springen, Sprünge* (pp. 56–74). Zurich: Juris Verlag.
2. Ward-Smith, A. J. (1985). The influence on long jump performance of the aerodynamic drag experienced during the approach and aerial phases. *Journal of Biomechanical Engineering*, 107:336–40.
3. Henry, F. M. (1952). Research on sprint running. *Athletic Journal*, 32:32.
4. Hay, J. G., and Nohara, H. (1990). Techniques used by elite long jumpers in preparation for takeoff. *Journal of Biomechanics*, 23:229–39.

5. Fischer, R. (1975). Weitsprung: Biomechanische Untersuchungen am Schweizerischen Weitsprungkader mittels Filmanalyse und Messungen mit der Mehrkomponentenmessplattform. Diplomarbeit in Biomechanik, ETH, Zurich.

6. Luhtanen, P., and Komi, P. V. (1979). Mechanical power and segmental contribution to force impulses in long jump take-off. *European Journal of Applied Physiology*, 41:267–74.

7. Mikhailov, N. G., Yakunin, N. A., and Aleshinsky, S. Y. (1981). Biomechanical assessment of take-off in the long jump (Russian). *Theory and Practice of Physical Culture (Moscow)* 5:13–15.

8. El Khadem, A., and Huyck, B. (1966). Long jump technique analysis. *Track Technique*. 24:758.

9. Hay, J. G. (1990). The biomechanics of triple jump techniques. In G-P. Brüggeman and J. K. Rühl (Eds.), *Techniques in Athletics: Conference Proceedings* (pp. 296–308). Köln, Federal Republic of Germany: Deutsche Sporthochschule Köln.

10. Hay, J. G. (1992). The biomechanics of the triple jump: A review. *Journal of Sports Sciences*. 10:343–78.

11. Hay, J. G. Unpublished data.

12. Koh, T. J., and Hay, J. G. (1990). Landing leg motion and performance in the horizontal jumps II: The triple jump. *International Journal of Sport Biomechanics*. 6:361–73.

13. Hay, J. G., and Miller, J. A. (1985). Techniques used in the triple jump. *International Journal of Sport Biomechanics*, 1:185–96.

14. Kreer, V. (1973). The world record of Victor Sancev. *Track and Field*, p. 11. Trans. by Michael Yessis and reported in *Yessis Review of Soviet Physical Education and Sports*, IX, June 1974, p. 39.

15. El Khadem and Huyck. Long jump technique analysis. p. 758.

16. Ozolin, N. (1973). The high jump takeoff mechanism. *Track Technique*. 52:1671.

17. Nigg. *Sprung, Springen, Sprünge*, (pp. 75–104).

18. Dapena, J. (1980). The mechanics of translation in the Fosbury flop. *Medicine and Science in Sports and Exercise*. 12:37–44.

19. Dyatchkov, V. M. (1968). The high jump. *Track Technique*, 34:1070.

20. Ozolin, The high jump takeoff mechanism, p. 1671.

21. Nigg, *Sprung, Springen, Sprünge* (pp. 75–104).

22. Dyatchkov. The high jump, p. 1070.

23. Nigg, *Sprung, Springen, Sprünge* (p. 92.)

24. Dapena, J. Personal communication, December 16, 1973.

25. Dapena, J. (1987). Basic and applied research in the biomechanics of high jumping. In B. van Gheluwe and J. Atha (Eds.), *Current Research in Sports Biomechanics* (pp. 19–33). Basel, Switzerland: Karger.

26. Dapena. The mechanics of translation in the Fosbury flop.

27. Ibid., pp. 45–53.

28. Nigg. *Sprung, Springen, Sprünge* (p. 90)

29. Morawski, J., Wilclik, K., and Sliwinski, M. (1977). *Badania Modelowe Skoku o Tyczce. Czesc III: Badania wstepne. Raport w Problemie Restowym 105/07/25*. Miedzyuczelniany Instytut Nanukowy Sportu/Pracownia Naukowo-Techniczna/12/77, Warszawa.

30. McGinnis, P. M. (1987). Performance limiting factors in the pole vault. Report to the United States Olympic Committee.

31. Ganslen, R. V. (1965). *Mechanics of the Pole Vault* (6th ed.). St. Louis: John Swift & Co.

TRACK AND FIELD: THROWING

The standard throwing events in track and field are the shot put, the discus throw, the javelin throw, and the hammer throw.

In each of these events, the athlete's objective is to obtain as large a displacement of the implement as possible, without infringing the rules governing the recording of a legal throw. The principal rules with which the athlete is concerned are those prescribing the manner in which the implement is to be thrown, the sector in which it must land, the manner in which it is to land (javelin throw), and the forward limits of the area from which the throw must be made.

SHOT PUT
Basic
Considerations

Assuming the athlete does not violate any of the rules just referred to, the distance with which he (or she) is credited is equal to the sum of (1) the horizontal distance that the shot is in front of the inside edge of the stop-board at the instant it is released; and (2) the horizontal distance it travels during the time it is in the air.

The first of these distances (as much as 17 cm for the men finalists and 11 cm for the women finalists in the 1987 World Championships[1]) is governed by the athlete's body position at the instant of release. The second is

469

governed by the speed, angle, and height at which the shot is released and by the air resistance encountered during its flight.

The speed of release, unquestionably the most important of these factors (see pp. 39–41), is determined by the magnitude and direction of the forces applied to the shot and by the distance over which these forces act (see work-energy relationship, pp. 101–105).

The angle of release is also fixed by these same three factors of magnitude, direction, and distance. The optimum angle of release is always somewhat less than 45°, because the point at which the shot is released is above the point at which it lands (p. 38). The extent to which the optimum angle differs from 45° depends on the magnitude of the release speed obtained and, to a lesser extent, on the height of release—the less the speed and the greater the height of release, the lower the optimum angle of release (pp. 37–38).

The height of release is governed by the athlete's body position at that instant. If all else is equal, an athlete who attains a position in which the legs, trunk, and throwing arm are fully extended at the instant of release will achieve greater distances than an athlete who is in some other less effective position.

As already indicated elsewhere (p. 178), the effects of air resistance in shot-putting are sufficiently small (and effectively beyond the control of the athlete) that they can be ignored in all but the most precise analysis.

Summary

The relationships between the distance with which a shot-putter is credited and the factors that determine that distance are summarized in Fig. 17-1.

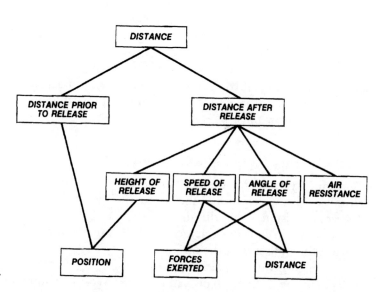

Figure 17-1.
Basic factors in shot-putting.

The techniques currently used by shot-putters are the result of a continuing series of developments aimed at increasing the speed with which the shot can be released.

The first major step in this process was the addition, in the very early days of the event, of some form of movement across the circle. By permitting the legs to make two contributions and by increasing the distance over which forces were exerted on the shot, this enabled athletes to obtain greater release speeds than they had hitherto with standing throws.

Although many variations were tried initially, the preliminary movement across the circle eventually evolved into a side-facing hopping (or gliding) motion (Fig. 17-2). This became the generally accepted technique and remained so for several decades until, in the early 1950s, James Fuchs (U.S.A.) developed a modification that substantially increased the contribution made by the muscles responsible for lateral flexion of the trunk and, in addition, permitted an increase in the distance over which the athlete exerted force on the shot. The technique used by Fuchs is shown in Fig. 17-3.

In an attempt to further increase the speed of the shot at release (by increasing the number of forces involved and the distances over which they acted) a number of athletes carried Fuchs's initial away-from-the-neck position of the shot to its logical conclusion and held it low and at arm's length behind the circle. However, this method yielded no marked success, before the rules were altered to make such a procedure illegal.

The next major development in shot-putting techniques was introduced

Techniques

Figure 17-2. Technique in the old side-facing style of shot-putting.

Figure 17-3. The shot-putting style of James Fuchs (U.S.A.).

by Parry O'Brien (U.S.A.), also in the early 1950s (Fig. 17-4). The O'Brien technique, used by almost every shot-putter of note during the next 25 years, made provision for a further increase in the distance through which force could be exerted on the shot and also allowed for an increase in the contribution of force from the muscles of the back.

The most recent and most radical development in shot-putting technique is the rotational (or discus-style) technique—Fig. 17-5—used by an increasing number of top-class throwers including current world-record holder Randy Barnes (U.S.A.). While the advantages and disadvantages of the rotational technique (vis-à-vis that of O'Brien) have been the source of much speculation, there is, as yet, little research on the subject. However, what research evidence is available has been quite helpful in clarifying the issues involved.

At about the same time as Fuchs was developing his new technique, other athletes were experimenting with weight training as a means of increasing their strength and thereby the magnitude of the forces they could exert against the shot. The successes enjoyed by these athletes and those that followed them have led to the recognition of weight training as an essential part of the training of shot-putters. To what extent recent advances in shot-putting performances are due to the development of improved techniques and to what extent they are due to the weight-training regimes followed by present-day champions may never be known. It seems likely, though, that the influence of weight training far exceeds that attributable to improvements in technique.

While athletes differ markedly in the routine (or ritual) undertaken in assuming the initial position at the back of the circle, the position finally adopted differs relatively little from one athlete to the next.

In adopting this initial position the athlete places the toes of the right foot pointing away from the direction of throw and close to the rear edge of the circle.* The athlete then moves the center of gravity over the right foot so that it is supporting the full weight of the body and the shot. The athlete holds the trunk erect, the left foot on the ground a short distance to the rear, and the left arm in a relaxed near-vertical position. These positions of the left arm and left foot are used to assist the athlete in maintaining a state of equilibrium—the former by minor adjustments in position and the latter by adjustments in the force exerted against the ground.

The shot is supported on the base of the fingers of the right hand and, in accord with the rules, against the athlete's neck. The manner in which the shot is held influences the forces that can eventually be applied to it. If it is held in the palm of the hand, as tends to be the case with beginners, the forces that can be applied to it as a result of wrist and finger flexion are severely reduced. Thus, although a beginner may initially feel more comfortable holding the shot in the palm of the hand, he (or she) will ultimately achieve greater distances supporting it on the base of the fingers.

From this preliminary position the athlete initiates a series of movements designed to help in assuming the optimum position from which to begin the movement across the circle. These generally consist of an upward and backward swing of the left leg accompanied by a lowering forward of the upper body—bringing the athlete into the so-called T position—followed by a flexion of the hip, knee, and ankle joints of the right leg and a downward and forward motion of the left leg. The lowering of the trunk carries the shot to a position slightly outside the circle and thereby increases the distance through which the athlete may exert force on it. It also places the trunk in a position that will later permit the muscles of the back to make a substantial contribution to the release speed of the shot. The flexion of the joints of the supporting leg serves some of these same purposes—it aids in bringing the shot to a low position, thereby increasing the distance over which force may be applied before the shot is released, and it puts the leg in a position to contribute force to accelerate the shot (and the athlete) across the circle.

The downward and forward swing of the left leg, together with the flexion of the right leg, puts the athlete into a low and compact position. As soon as the athlete reaches this position—a light touch of the left foot to the ground or to the right foot is often used as a cue that the position has been

---

* Throughout this chapter it is assumed that the athlete under discussion throws or puts with the right hand.

(a) (b) (c)

(g) (h) (i)

Figure 17-4. The O'Brien back-facing style of shot-putting. (Photographs courtesy of Howard Payne.)

reached—the athlete begins the drive across the circle. This consists of a well-coordinated combination of three separate movements:

- A shifting of the athlete's center of gravity beyond the backward limit of the base provided by the right foot (Fig. 17-4[a]). This shift, brought about by the downward and forward swing of the left leg and an accompanying pushing backward of the hips, sets the body in motion across the circle.

- A vigorous backward swing of the left leg toward the front of the circle (Fig. 17-4[b]).

- An extension of the knee and ankle joints of the right leg (Fig. 17-4[c]). The greater part of this extension is delayed until the previous

(d)　　　　　　　　　(e)　　　　　　　　　(f)

(j)　　　　　　　　　(k)　　　　　　　　　(l)

two movements have placed the athlete's center of gravity in a position that will allow it to be driven toward the front of the circle rather than upward.

As soon as the drive from the right leg has been completed, the right foot is whipped low across the circle (Fig. 17-4[d]) to a position near the center of the circle and beneath the athlete's center of gravity (Fig. 17-4(e)]. Shortly after the right foot has landed—times from 0.04-0.15 s have been reported for the finalists at the 1987 World Championships[2]—the left foot is grounded close to the stopboard and a little to one side of the direction line (Fig. 17-4[g]).

The extent to which the right leg is extended as the athlete drives across

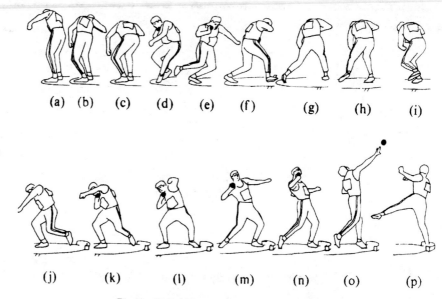

(a) (b) (c) (d) (e) (f) (g) (h) (i)

(j) (k) (l) (m) (n) (o) (p)

Figure 17-5. The rotational shot-putting style.

the circle varies between athletes. Some use an almost complete extension of both knee and ankle joints, while others confine the extension almost entirely to the knee joint. In the former case the athlete's toes are usually the last part of the foot to break contact with the ground, while in the latter the heel has this distinction (Fig 17-4[c]). Which of these two methods, if either, is generally the better has yet to be resolved.

The distance that the right foot travels, its orientation as it lands, and the manner in which it is grounded also vary considerably from one athlete to the next. The distance that the right foot travels distinguishes between two variants of the O'Brien technique. In the first, the right foot lands close to the center of the circle and the glide and delivery "strides" are of approximately the same length. In the second, the right foot lands in the rear half of the circle and the glide stride may be as much as 30–35 cm less than the delivery stride. Proponents of this latter short-long technique contend that the loss in the contribution that the right leg is able to make during the delivery, due to its relatively unfavorably position, is more than made up for by the increase in the distance over which the shot may be accelerated by virtue of the wider delivery stance.[3]

The orientation of the athlete's right foot on landing at the completion of the glide varies from the pointing-to-the-back-of-the-circle position used by Fuchs to the position at right angles to the direction line advocated by Tschiene.[4] However, most top-class athletes—presumably compromising between (1) the difficulty in coordinating the various movements of the delivery inherent in the position used by Fuchs and (2) the dangers of prematurely rotating the hips and trunk to the front inherent in that proposed by Tschiene—use a position roughly midway between the two (Fig. 17-4[e]).

Authorities on shot-putting technique differ with respect to the manner in which the right foot should be grounded at the end of the glide. Some contend that the landing should be flat-footed—either because the extension of the right ankle can then proceed without the delay associated with having to first flex the ankle by lowering the heel[5] or because the weak muscles crossing the ankle joint limit the extensor forces that the stronger muscles of the leg can exert.[6] Others contend that a landing on the ball of the foot is essential if the athlete is to obtain the well-known benefits of stretching the extensor muscles immediately prior to their shortening, as the athlete drives forward and upward into the delivery.[7] Although it may yet be some time before this matter is resolved, it is perhaps of interest to note that a landing on the ball of the foot is more common among outstanding exponents of the event than is a flat-footed landing.

The position of the upper body during the glide has a considerable bearing on the final result. If the athlete allows the head and trunk to turn toward the front—and the backward swing of the left leg tends to encourage this—the magnitude of the forces subsequently exerted on the shot and the distances over which these forces act are markedly reduced. To avoid these undesirable effects of turning to the front too soon, experienced athletes endeavor to maintain a back-facing (or "closed") position throughout the glide (Fig. 17-4[c] to [e]).

Delivery

As soon as the right foot lands near the center of the circle, the athlete begins the delivery, the final coordinated sequence of actions that culminates in the release of the shot.

The delivery begins with the lifting action produced by the contraction of the extensor muscles of the athlete's hip, trunk, and right knee.

The importance of the contribution of the legs during the initial phases of the delivery has been alluded to by Fischer and Merhaupt[8] following an electromyographic analysis of the actions of experienced and inexperienced shot-putters. They found that the leg muscles were active up to 72 percent of the time in the delivery of the experienced shot-putters and only 28 percent of the time in the case of the inexperienced ones. Furthermore, an analysis of the films taken in conjunction with the electromyographic recordings revealed that the inexperienced athletes threw "from a vertical position, bringing to bear only the body turn and the forward thrust of the shoulders." In other words, they made little or no use of the powerful lifting action that their legs were capable of producing.

This lifting movement is followed by a rotation of the athlete's body toward the front as the extension of the right leg continues and is supplemented by the contraction of the muscles producing trunk rotation—Fig. 17-4(g) to (i). (*Note:* The athlete shown in Fig. 17-4 deemphasizes the initial lifting action and the forceful extension of the right leg—so evident in the techniques of other top throwers—in favor of a very strong rotation of the trunk.)

The left arm, which has been held back throughout the glide is swung upward and backward, thereby contributing to the rotation of the trunk (Fig. 17-4 to [i]).

As the extension of the right leg and the rotation of the trunk to the front near completion, the shot moves away from its position against the athlete's neck, and the right arm begins to make its contribution to the release speed of the shot (Fig. 17-4[i]). This involves a coordinated forward rotation of the upper arm, a forceful extension of the right elbow, and a final flexion and pronation (or "snap") of the wrist.

The question of whether the athlete should retain contact with the ground during the release (Fig. 17-4[k] to [l]) has been the subject of some debate. Dyson[9] for example, has stated that "Theoretically, . . . the front foot should be firmly in contact with the ground, providing the necessary resistance for the hand to exert maximum force both vertically and horizontally." He concedes, however, that ". . . a majority—if not all—of the world's 60-ft [18. 29-m] shot putters *do* in fact break contact with this front foot fractionally before the missile leaves the hand." Nett[10] has produced photographic evidence that tends to confirm this latter point and has concluded that "the old idea of insisting that the feet be planted at the moment of release was simply an application of a 'brake' to the total effort." Herein, it seems, lies the crux of the matter—must the athlete reduce the magnitude of the vertical forces that he (or she) can exert to retain contact with the ground and, if so, is the resulting loss in the release speed of the shot larger or smaller than would result from being off the ground as the final "wrist snap" is executed? (*Note:* Only the vertical forces are of importance here, for these alone tend to cause the athlete to be projected into the air.) While to date there appears to be no objective basis for an answer to these questions, the empirically derived methods of the world's leading exponents of the shot put would seem to suggest that an athlete must reduce the vertical forces he (or she) exerts to remain on the ground and that the resulting loss in the release speed of the shot is probably greater than that due to being in the air during the concluding stages of the delivery.

Reverse

Once the shot has been released, the athlete's right foot comes forward to support his (or her) weight while the left leg swings back toward the center of the circle. This reversing of the feet is employed to assist the athlete to remain in the circle once the shot has left the hand. The swinging back of the left leg (and, in extreme cases, the flexion of the hips and downward-backward-upward swing of the arms—Fig. 17-6) serves to produce a contrary angular reaction that tends to move the athlete's center of gravity back from the forward limit of the base.

Figure 17-6.
Action and reaction in the reverse.

Rotational (or Spin) Technique

The rotational technique is essentially a combination of the techniques used in the first half of an orthodox discus throw with those used in the second half (or delivery phase) of an O'Brien-style shot put.

The argument most frequently advanced in favor of the rotational technique is that, because of the greater distance through which the shot travels, its velocity at the instant when the thrower lands in the front of the circle is greater than it would be if the thrower used the O'Brien style. This seemingly logical contention is not supported, however, by the available data. In a comparison of the techniques employed by Baryshnikov (who set a world record using the rotation technique) and Al Feuerbach (a former world-record holder who used the O'Brien style), Kerssenbrock[11] reported that, although both achieved similar release speeds of the shot (13.47 m/s and 13.81 m/s, respectively), the speeds at the instant when the final putting stance was reached (that is, when the left foot was grounded near the front of the circle) were vastly different (1.40 m/s and 2.50 m/s, respectively). Further, the difference was contrary to what the prevailing argument would suggest.

The reason for this discrepancy between theory and practice is not hard to find—the theory is at fault. When an athlete using the rotational technique moves across the circle, his (or her) body is simultaneously translated in the general direction of the throw and rotated about a vertical or near-vertical axis. In the first part of the turn (Fig. 17-5[d] to [f]) the shot moves forward relative to the athlete's center of gravity, which is itself moving forward across the circle. The effects of the rotation and translation thus complement each other and the shot moves forward at a relatively high speed. During the second part of the turn (Fig. 17-5[g] to [k]) the shot moves backward relative to the athlete's center of gravity while the latter continues to move forward across the circle. The respective contributions that the athlete's rotation and translation make to the speed of the shot thus tend to offset each other and the speed of the shot is relatively low. Indeed. if the shot is traveling backward relative to the athlete's center of gravity at a greater rate than the latter is traveling forward, the shot will actually be moving in a direction opposite to the ultimate direction of the throw! (These various effects are clearly evident in Fig. 17-7, which shows how the speed of the shot varies during the course of a throw using the rotational technique.)

On the basis of all this, it may reasonably be concluded that, if the rotational technique is as good or better than the O'Brien technique, it is *not* because the speed of the shot is greater when the athlete lands in the front of the circle. Instead, it seems likely that the success enjoyed by leading exponents of the rotational technique is due to the athlete being able to assume a favorable position from which to begin the final putting action.

The results of Soviet research, reported by Zatsiorsky[12] tend to support this conclusion. These results showed that, at the beginning of the delivery phase, the difference between the line of the shoulders and the line of the hips (as viewed from a position looking along the long axis of the trunk) may be up to 68 degrees when the rotational technique is used, and only up to 49 degrees when the O'Brien technique is used. Or, in other words, that the final putting action can be initiated from a more twisted position of the trunk when the rotational technique is used than when the O'Brien technique is used.

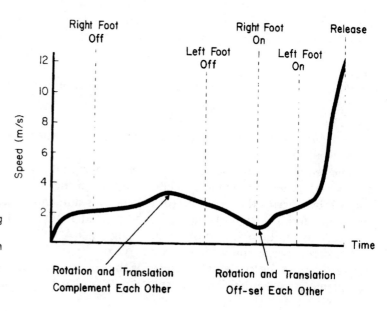

Figure 17-7.
Variations in the speed of the shot during the execution of a throw using the rotational technique. (Based on data in Geese, R. [1974]. Uberlegungen zur Kugelstoss-Drehtechnik. *Die Lehre der Leichtathletik*, 25.)

Assuming the throw conforms with the rules governing the event, the distance with which a discus thrower is credited is determined by the speed, height, and angle at which he (or she) releases the implement and by the aerodynamic factors that influence its flight.

The speed and angle of release are determined by the magnitude and direction of the forces exerted on the discus and the distance over which these forces are applied.

The height of release is governed by the athlete's body position at that instant. Although the height of release is a factor of relatively minor importance compared to the speed and angle of release, if all else is equal, a thrower who releases the discus from an erect position with the legs and trunk fully extended will have an advantage over other throwers who release the implement with their bodies in a less effective position.

In addition to the ever-present gravitational force, a discus in flight is subjected to forces exerted upon it by the air through which it passes (p. 184 and following).

These forces can have a significant effect on the distance of a throw (Table 17-1).

The magnitude of the forces exerted by the air on the discus, and hence the extent of their influence, is governed by:

- The speed of release.
- The angle of release—that is, the angle between the direction in which the center of gravity of the discus moves immediately after release and the horizontal.

TABLE 17-1 The Influence of Air Resistance on the Distances Recorded by the First Six Competitors in the Men's Event at the 1976 Olympic Games

Athlete	Distance of Throw (m)	Theoretical Distance If No Air (m)	Gain or Loss Due to Air (m)	Percent Gain or Loss
Wilkins (U.S.A.)	67.50	68.87	−1.37	−2.0
Schmidt (East Germany)	66.22	72.93	−6.71	−10.1
Powell (U.S.A.)	65.70	63.20	2.51	3.8
Thiede (East Germany)	64.30	57.29	7.01	10.9
Pachale (East Germany)	64.20	64.07	0.13	0.2
Kahma (Finland)	63.12	68.19	−5.07	−8.0

Adapted from Terauds, J. (1978). Computerized biomechanical cinematography analysis of discus throwing at the 1976 Montreal Olympiad. *Track and Field Quarterly Review*, 78:25–28.

- The angle that the discus is inclined to the horizontal—the so-called *attitude angle* or *angle of tilt*—at the instant it is released. (*Note:* Contrary to what might be expected, the angle at which a discus is released is generally not the same as that at which it is inclined to the horizontal. Most good throwers, in fact, throw slightly upward "across the line" of the discus and thus obtain an angle of release that is greater than the attitude angle—Fig. 17-8[a].)
- The velocity of the wind.
- The angular velocity of the discus at release.

The problem of establishing the role played by each of these factors (like most such problems in fluid mechanics) is exceedingly complex. Several attempts have been made to solve the problem by placing a men's discus in a wind tunnel and measuring the forces exerted upon it under varying conditions.

Ganslen[13][14][15] conducted an extensive series of studies into the aerodynamic factors influencing the flight of the discus. Among the various conclusions he reached as a result of these studies were the following:

- A relatively poor thrower will benefit more from a head wind of a given velocity than will a good thrower. This is because the percentage increase in the relative wind will be greater for the poor thrower than for a thrower who is attaining a high speed of release.
- There is no such thing as an optimum wind velocity for maximum distance.
- The discus stalls (that is, experiences a marked reduction in lift) at angles of attack between 27° and 29°.

(*Note:* The *angle of attack* is the angle between the central plane of the discus and the relative wind. If the discus is thrown in still air, the relative wind is

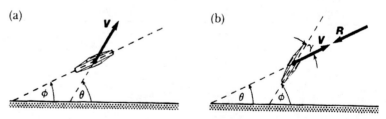

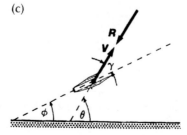
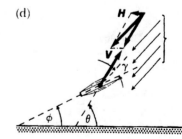

Figure 17-8. Relationships between the angle of release (Θ), the attitude angle (φ), and the angle of attack (γ) under differing conditions. (The release velocity of the discus is designated by *V*, the relative wind by *R*, and a head wind by *H*.)

equal in magnitude and opposite in direction to the velocity of the implement. The angle of attack at the instant of release is therefore equal to the attitude angle minus the angle of release—Fig. 17-8[b]. A positive angle of attack means that the underside of the discus is exposed to the oncoming airflow, while a negative angle of attack—by far the more common in good throwing—means that the upper side is thus exposed, Fig. 17-8[c]. If the discus is thrown in other than still air, the velocity of the wind must also be taken into account to determine the magnitude and direction of the relative wind and the angle of attack—Fig. 17-8[d]).

Kentzer and Hromas[16] used a wind tunnel to examine the aerodynamic characteristics of a spinning discus and found that at an air velocity of 30.5 m/s the maximum value of the lift/drag ratio was obtained with an angle of attack of 9°, a finding in close accord with those of Ganslen for speeds between 24 m/s and 29 m/s (see Table 7-2, p. 192).

Cooper, Dalzell, and Silverman[17] (introduced to the problem by Hromas) attempted to determine the attitude angle and angle of release at which a men's discus should be thrown to obtain the maximum possible distance for a given initial speed. Using lift and drag values obtained by Ganslen and a computer program designed for the purpose, they obtained the results depicted in Fig. 17-9. From these they concluded:

- The speed of release is the most important factor in determining the length of a throw.
- For any given speed of release, the angle of release is of prime importance. Good throwers (that is, those who throw in the 45–60-m range) should use an angle of release of between 35° and 40°, while throwers of lesser ability should increase this slightly but never beyond 45°.
- The attitude angle should be between 25° and 35°.

These conclusions are supported by the findings of Soong,[18] who reported that the optimum angles of release and the optimum attitude angle for a men's discus released at 25.5 m/s in still air are, respectively, 35° and 26°. (*Note:* At first glance these findings—implying, as they do, an angle of attack of from 0° to 15°—appear to be in conflict with those of Kentzer and Hromas and Ganslen, who have indicated that the angle of attack that yields the best lift/drag ratio is of the order of 9°–10°. The reason for this apparent conflict lies in the fact that while the attitude angle may remain essentially constant throughout the flight—a point attested to by Taylor[19] following an examination of slow-motion films of the discus in flight and by Soong[20] using mathematical techniques—the direction of the relative wind and hence the angle of attack is constantly changing as the discus rises to its peak height and then falls toward the ground. The angle of attack obtained at release should therefore be the one that will yield the best results overall rather than the one that merely happens to be the optimum for that instant.)

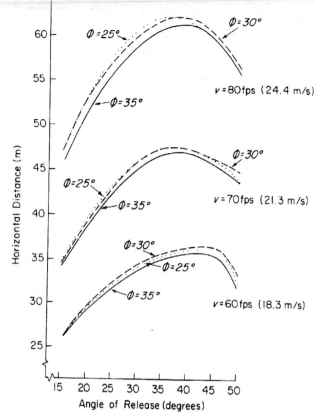

Figure 17-9.
The effect of variations in release speed
(*v*), the angle of release, and the attitude
angle (φ), on distances achieved in the
discus throw. (Based on data in Cooper,
L., Dalzell, D., and Silverman, E. [1959].
Flight of the discus. Division of
Engineering Science, Purdue University.)

The influence that the velocity of the wind has on the distance of a throw has been studied by Frohlich[21] using methods similar to those employed by Cooper, Dalzell, and Silverman. He found that "the worst possible conditions to obtain long throws is to throw with a wind of 7.5 m/sec, and that if the wind velocity is less than about 20 m/sec, longer throws can always be obtained by throwing against the wind." Frohlich concluded, therefore, that "under all conditions under which a discus competition could conceivably be held, discus throwers desiring record performances are correct in their preference for throwing in the face of stiff wind."

Information on the angles of release, attitude angles, and so on, used in practice is very limited indeed. What is available indicates, however, that the experimental results cited here are in excellent accord with those recorded in practice. Lockwood,[22] for example, studied slow-motion films of 10 experienced athletes throwing between 160 ft and 190 ft [48.8 m and 57.9 m] and found that all used angles of release between 30° and 45° and that 6 used angles between 34° and 37°. The angles of attack varied between 0° and 10°.

Terauds[23] obtained similar values for the angle of release and larger negative values for the angle of attack when he analyzed the best throws by the top six male throwers in the 1976 Olympic Games (Table 17-2); and Gregor, Whiting, and McCoy[21] reported average angles of release for each of the medallists in the men's and women's events at the 1984 Olympic Games ranging from 33.6–36.3°.

Summary

The relationships between the distance with which a discus thrower is credited and the factors that determine that distance are summarized in Fig. 17-10.

Techniques

Techniques in discus throwing have developed along much the same lines as those in shot-putting with the emphasis on increasing the distance through which force may be applied to the discus and on increasing the magnitude of the forces exerted by increasing the strength of the athlete through weight training.

Initial Stance

The first of these emphases has been most clearly apparent in the initial stance adopted by the thrower.

From the mid-1920s to the late 1930s the initial stance adopted by most leading exponents of the event was one in which the athlete stood at the back of the circle with the body sideways to the direction of the throw. From this position the athlete pivoted on the ball of the left foot and executed a one-and-one-quarter turn to bring him (or her) to the point in

TABLE 17-2 The Angle of Release, Angle of Attack, Attitude Angle, Release Velocity, and Distance Recorded in the Best Throw of the First Six Competitors in the Men's Discus Event at the 1976 Olympic Games

Athlete	Angle of Release (deg)	Angle of Attack (deg)	Attitude Angle (deg)	Release Velocity (m/s)	Distance of Throw (m)
Wilkins (U.S.A.)	37.0	−19.0	18.0	25.9	67.50
Schmidt (East Germany)	34.0	−12.0	22.0	27.3	66.22
Powell (U.S.A.)	36.5	−27.5	9.0	25.0	65.70
Thiede (East Germany)	33.0	−15.5	17.5	24.2	64.30
Pachale (East Germany)	36.5	−12.5	24.0	25.2	64.20
Kahma (Finland)	39.5	−10.5	29.0	25.7	63.12

Adapted from Terauds, J. (1978). Computerized biomechanical cinematography analysis of discus throwing at the Montreal Olympiad. *Track and Field Quarterly Review*, 78:25–28.

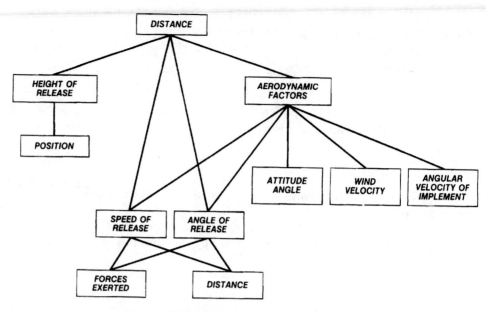

Figure 17-10. Basic factors in discus throwing.

the front of the circle from which the implement was released (Fig. 17-11[a]).

Since that time, the initial positioning of the feet relative to the direction of the throw has been progressively modified in an attempt to increase the distance through which force may be applied to the discus. Figure 7-11(b) to (d) shows the initial foot placements and the path followed by the discus in those modifications that have gained some measure of support among top-class throwers. Many other possibilities have been explored—some being used occasionally in competition by top-class performers (Fig. 17-11[e][25] and [f])[26] and others seemingly far too fanciful to attract much support (Fig. 17-11[g]).[27]

With regard to the initial placement of the feet it is well to recognize that, because the only reason a thrower adds a preliminary turn (or turns) before executing the final delivery is to increase the speed of release of the discus beyond what he (or she) can achieve with a standing throw, the efficacy of a given initial placement of the feet can be judged only in terms of the effect produced on the speed of release of the implement. (*Note:* Because the speed of the discus at release is a function of the forces exerted upon it during the turn[s] and delivery and the distance over which these forces act, it is often supposed that any initial stance that allows an increase in distance through which the discus travels before it is released is necessarily better than one for which the distance traveled is less. This is a fallacy. Only if the forces exerted in the case where the longer distance is involved do not decrease by an amount comparable, or more than comparable, to the gain in distance—in other words, only if the work done on the discus is greater—will there be an increase in the speed of release.)

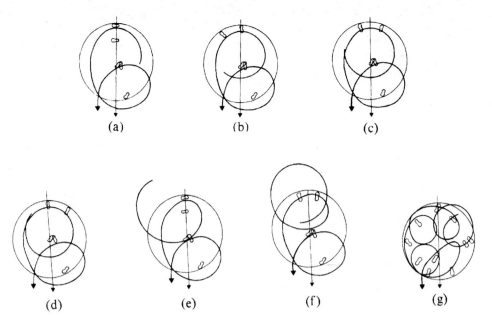

Figure 17-11. Variations in the placement of the feet and the path followed by the discus. (a) Side-facing 1¼ turn used by leading throwers from mid-1920s to late 1930s. (b) Oblique back-facing, slightly less than 1½ turn. (c) Back-facing 1½ turn currently used by most leading throwers. (d) Oblique, back-facing, slightly more than 1½ turn used by some leading throwers. (e) Side-facing 1¾ turn advocated by Bosen and used by Neu (East Germany) in 1968 Olympic Games final. (f) Back-facing 2¾ turn throw developed by Bob Humphreys (U.S.A.). (g) Multiturn method suggested by Davenport.

Studies of the manner in which the speed of the discus changes in the course of a throw have revealed the following:

- The speed of the discus at release is not the result of a steady acceleration from the end of the backswing to the point of release.[28,29,30,31]
- There is an initial increase in the speed of the discus until the athlete's right foot breaks contact with the ground[28,29,30,31] and, for elite throwers, a further increase until the left foot breaks contact with the ground.[29,30,31] Changes in the speed of the discus during the short period in which both feet are off the ground differ from thrower to thrower and, occasionally, from trial to trial by the same thrower. In some cases the speed increases, in some it decreases, and in some it remains essentially constant.[30] With elite throwers, the speed of the discus generally decreases during the period between the right foot landing near the center of the circle and the left landing at the front. Finally, once the left foot has been grounded, there is a marked acceleration of the discus that continues up until the instant the implement is released.

Thus, to be advantageous, any change in an athlete's initial position must accomplish one or more of the following without producing a comparable, or more than comparable, loss in speed at some other point in the throw:

- increase the speed attained by the discus before the right foot is lifted,
- increase the speed of the discus during the period after the right and before the left foot leaves the ground,
- reduce the loss in speed that occurs between the time the left foot breaks contact with the ground at the back of the circle and the time it regains contact in the front of the circle.
- increase the gain in the speed of the discus during the delivery.

Preliminary Swings

From an erect standing position with the discus held over the left shoulder or just in front of the chest, the athlete begins the throw with one or two preliminary swings. The aim of these swings is to relax the athlete and get him (or her) mentally "set" for the throw. On the completion of these preliminary swings (which, incidentally, are subject to considerable variation between throwers), the athlete moves into position to commence the turn. This involves a swinging of the discus downward and backward to a position behind the body and somewhere between hip and shoulder level, a twisting of the trunk to the right that carries the discus still farther back, a flexing of the knees in preparation for the movements to follow, and a shifting of the athlete's weight over the right foot (Fig. 17-12[a] to [c]).

Transition

As the discus nears the limit of its backward swing (or just as it begins to come forward again), the athlete adjusts the position of the left foot by rotating it (usually heel raised and pivoting on the ball of the foot) toward the direction of the throw—Fig. 17-12(d). This movement is accompanied by a shifting of the center of gravity to the left and over the left foot, a movement that is of considerable importance in determining the ultimate success of the throw. If the athlete fails to shift the weight sufficiently to the left, a moment (weight times distance from line of gravity to foot) is established that tends to rotate the athlete sideways when the right foot is lifted from the ground. In an effort to offset or correct the unbalancing effects of this moment, the athlete usually drives rather more to the side than is desirable, when pushing off from the left foot into the turn. This leads to a final placement of the left foot well to the left of the direction line and a correspondingly poor throw. (*Note:* The shifting of the athlete's center of gravity to the left during the transition and the resulting position with the center of gravity "balanced" over the left foot for the drive across the circle, are shown in Fig. 17-13[a] to [c] and Fig. 17-13[d], respectively.)

Turn

A discus turn is a combination of angular motion (the angular motion of the athlete rotating about his [or her] longitudinal, or a near-longitudinal, axis) and horizontal motion (the horizontal motion of the athlete's center of gravity as it moves forward across the circle).

To initiate the turn, the athlete pivots on the ball of the left foot until facing in the direction of the throw and then, lifting the knee of the right leg high, drives vigorously forward across the circle (Fig. 17-12[g]). The drive from the left leg, augmented by the quick lifting action of the right knee, projects the athlete forward (and slightly upward) toward the center of the circle.

The instant at which the right foot is lifted from the ground, and the action of the right leg prior to the initiation of the left leg drive, have been the subject of some discussion. Some authorities[32 33 34] maintain that the right foot should be kept in contact with the ground for as long as possible—reasoning presumably, that by so doing the athlete can exert small forces via the right foot to aid in controlling balance—and should then be brought close to the left foot as it is moved forward for the drive across the circle. Others,[35 36] prefer the right foot to be lifted much earlier and the near-straight leg to be brought around to the front in a wide-sweeping action (Fig. 17-12[f]). This action increases the athlete's moment of inertia relative to the axis about which he (or she) is rotating and, providing there is not a comparable or more than comparable loss in angular velocity, enables the athlete to increase the angular momentum of the lower body. This gain in angular momentum can then be used to advantage later in the throw. The question as to which of these two techniques should be used by a given athlete is probably best viewed from the standpoint of experience—an inexperienced thrower is likely to fare better with the technique that emphasizes control; and the experienced thrower, who has already achieved a high degree of control, is likely to benefit more from the method that affords the greater momentum.

During the short time that the athlete is in the air the hips move ahead of the shoulders which in turn maintain their "lead" over the right arm and the discus. Knicker[37] reported values for the angles (a) between the line of the hips and the line of the shoulders, and (b) between the line of the shoulders and the line of the throwing arm, at the instant the left foot broke contact with the ground and at the instant the right foot landed in the center of the circle, for the best throws of eight, elite male throwers. The distances of the throws analyzed ranged from 60.42–67.20 m. On average, the angle between the hips and the shoulders increased from 26.5° to 53.3°—with the hips moving farther "forward" of the shoulders; and the angle between the shoulders and the arm remained essentially unchanged, decreasing slightly from 32.5° to 28.8°. The movement of the hips to a position ahead of the shoulders is facilitated if the athlete:

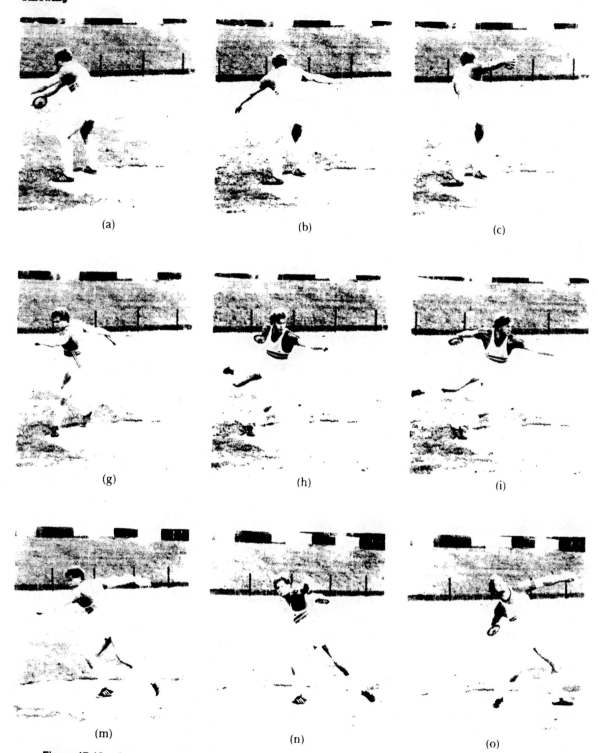

(a)   (b)   (c)

(g)   (h)   (i)

(m)   (n)   (o)

Figure 17-12. An example of good technique in the discus throw. (Photographs courtesy of Howard Payne.)

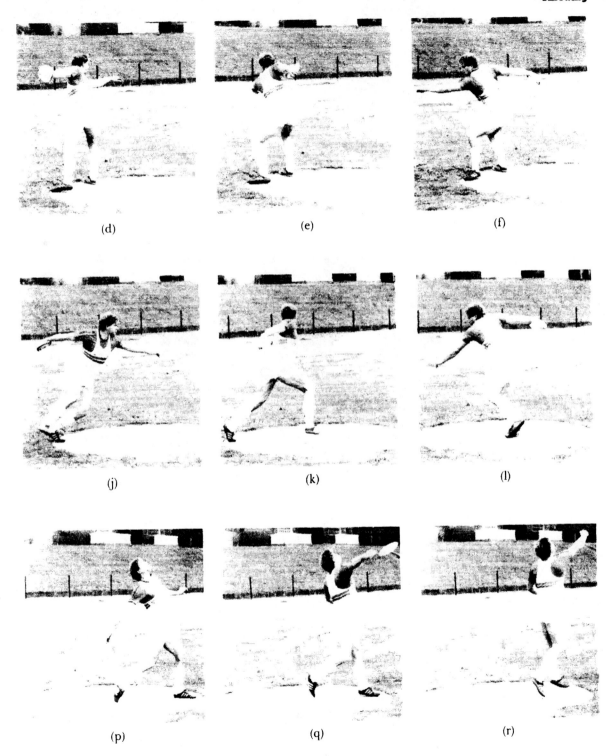

(d)   (e)   (f)

(j)   (k)   (l)

(p)   (q)   (r)

(a)

(b)

(c)

(d)

Figure 17-13. The shifting of the athlete's center of gravity to the left during the transition from the last preliminary swing to the turn. (Photographs courtesy of Howard Payne.)

- keeps the thighs fairly close together, thereby decreasing the moment of inertia and increasing the angular velocity of the legs.
- holds the right arm and the discus some distance away from the axis of rotation to increase the moment of inertia of the upper body and thus reduce its angular velocity.
- holds the left arm across the body in a deliberate attempt to keep the

shoulders back—an angular action that yields a contrary reaction of the lower body. (*Note:* The athlete in Fig. 17-14 makes good use of all three of these techniques.)

Delivery

At the conclusion of the flight phase of the turn, the athlete lands near the center of the circle on the ball of the right foot and with the center of gravity directly above or slightly behind the right foot. If the athlete has correctly executed the preceding movements, the hips are well ahead of the shoulders and the shoulders are well ahead of the throwing arm at this instant (Fig. 17-12[k]). The athlete's next task is to get the left foot grounded in the appropriate position as quickly as possible. This is of critical importance because the discus is being decelerated at this time (presumably as a result of [1] a frictional couple applied via the right foot; and [2] a decrease in the body's angular velocity as the left leg moves progressively farther from the axis of rotation), and the longer this deceleration is permitted to continue, the worse the final result is likely to be. In addition, the stretching of the musculature of the upper body to allow the hips to get ahead of the shoulders and the shoulders to get ahead of the throwing arm cannot readily be maintained unless powerful forces are exerted via the legs. Such forces can be exerted only if both feet are on the ground. In short, therefore, unless the athlete gets the left foot grounded quickly, he (or she) loses both the momentum that has been built up in the turn and the strong throwing position that is needed for the final, all-important acceleration of the discus.

Once the right foot has landed, and before the left foot is grounded in the front of the circle, the right leg drive initiating the delivery begins. This consists of a turning inward of the right knee, accompanied by a pivoting on the ball of the foot and an outward turning of the heel (Fig. 17-12[k] to

Figure 17-14.
The hips move ahead of the shoulders during the brief time the thrower is in the air. (Photograph courtesy of Howard Payne.)

[m]). This is followed, once the left leg is in position to provide resistance, by an extension of the hip, knee, and ankle joints that drives the athlete's hips forward and around toward the front (Fig. 17-12[n] to [p]). Well before the hips reach the front, the muscles that rotate the trunk, and which have been stretched by the preceding movements, contract forcefully to bring the shoulders around (Fig. 17-12[n] to [q]). Finally, the right arm—left well behind by these strong rotary movements of the hips and trunk—is swept forcefully outward and forward; the near-straight left leg is extended in a short forceful movement that brings the athlete to maximum height and adds to the vertical velocity of the implement; and the discus is brought around to the point where it is released (Fig. 17-12[o] to [q]). This point is usually somewhere between 1.72 m and 2.02 m above the ground for elite male throwers and at the maximum distance possible from the axis of rotation—the latter to ensure the maximum linear velocity of the implement at release.

The question of whether the athlete should retain contact with the ground throughout the delivery (a question already discussed here with reference to shot-putting techniques—p. 478) is also the subject of some debate among those interested in discus throwing.

Basically the athlete has three methods of imparting the necessary vertical velocity to the implement:

- by lifting the arm relative to the shoulder as the implement is swung forward,
- by driving off the right leg and rotating forward and upward over the left,
- by vigorously extending both legs (but particularly the left) immediately before the discus is released.

Which of the last two is given the greater emphasis would appear to determine whether the athlete completes the delivery while retaining contact with the ground or with both feet in the air. Throwers who stress driving up and over the firmly planted left leg generally release the implement with the left foot, and occasionally the toes of the right foot, in contact with the ground. Others who emphasize the vigorous driving action of both legs usually have both feet in the air at that instant. According to Lockwood, throwers in this second group tend to have their feet closer together during the delivery than do those in the first group. He also states that "There does not seem to be any correlation with the type of turn employed; there may be some correlation with build—the bigger and heavier men seem to favor the first style, probably because they have more bodyweight to lift into the air."[38]

Reverse

To prevent fouling, most throwers use some form of reverse once the implement has been released. There are basically two types in common use: the orthodox reverse, which is essentially the same as that used in shot-putting (Fig. 17-12[r]); and the spinning reverse, which involves one or more rotations on the ball of the right foot to dissipate angular momentum left over from the turn and throw. The former is unquestionably the easier to learn and execute; the latter is probably essential for a few highly skilled throwers.

JAVELIN THROW
Basic Considerations

The basic factors determining the distance with which an athlete is credited in the javelin throw—as always, assuming that the throw conforms with the various rules governing the event—are the same as those that apply in the case of the discus throw: the speed, height, and angle at which the implement is released and the aerodynamic factors that influence its flight. Although the techniques used in the two events are vastly different, the only one of these basic factors that warrants further consideration here is the last, the aerodynamic factors.

The aerodynamic factors that influence the flight of a javelin are greatly influenced by its design, which is limited (but not completely determined) by the rules governing the event.

In the mid-1980s, concerns over the increasingly longer throws being recorded—the men's world record had reached a distance of 104.80 m—and the limited space available inside modern athletics stadia, led the International Amateur Athletic Federation to change the rules governing the design of the men's javelin. (The corresponding rules for the women's javelin were not altered.)

This change in the rules rendered many of the findings from previous research on the aerodynamics of javelin flight—for example, Ganslen and Hall,[39] Terauds,[40 41] and Soong[42]—no longer applicable. It also spurred a revival of interest in the subject and a series of studies on the basic issues involved.[43 44 45 46]

Several conclusions have been reached concerning the aerodynamic behavior of the so-called new-rules javelin, and of the women's javelin, as a result of this research. These include the following:

- For both the new-rules javelin and the women's javelin, the flight distance—that is, the horizontal distance traveled by the center of gravity of the javelin from release to landing—is less than it would be if the javelin were thrown in a vacuum. In other words, the air resistance encountered by the javelin in flight serves to reduce the distance of the throw.
- The speed of release is by far the most important single factor in determining the distance of a throw.
- The optimum angle of release appears to lie within the 30–40° range. The angles of release for the finalists in the men's javelin at the 1987 World Championships ranged from 31-38°, and those for the finalists in the women's event from 32–41 deg.[47]

- The optimum angle of attack at release for the new-rules javelin is as yet unclear. A computer simulation study by Best and Bartlett[48] indicated that the optimum angle is negative—that is, the angle of release is greater than the attitude angle of the javelin; while analyses by Menzel[49] of the world's best male and female throwers yielded positive angles of attack in every case.

- The angle of release and angle of attack have relatively little influence on the distance of a throw with either the new-rules or the women's javelin.

- A tail wind is beneficial when throwing a new-rules javelin or a women's javelin, but the benefits in terms of increased distance of the throw are small. For example, a computer simulation study by Best and Bartlett[50] revealed that a strong tailwind of 7.5 m/s resulted in an increase of only 0.67 m in the distance of a throw with a new-rules javelin.

Techniques
Grip

Three grips are in common use:

- the thumb-and-first-finger grip—Fig. 17-15 (a);
- the thumb-and-second-finger grip—Fig. 17-15(b); and
- the first-and-second-finger grip—Fig. 17-15(c).

Of these, the third has been reported to be the most popular—70 percent of the leading throwers surveyed by Paish[51] used this grip; 25 percent used the thumb-and-second-finger grip, and 5 percent used the thumb-and-first-finger grip.

Although opinions abound on the relative merits of the three grips, there is little, if any, scientific evidence to indicate that any one of them is significantly better than another.

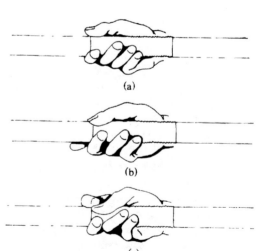

Figure 17-15.
Grips used in javelin throwing: (a) the thumb-and-first-finger grip; (b) the thumb-and-second-finger grip; and (c) the first-and-second-finger grip.

During the approach run the javelin is usually carried in an over-the-shoulder position with the hand moving back and forth close to the ear and in unison with the athlete's leg action. **Carry**

To reach the maximum speed that they are capable of controlling during the transition from run to throw and during the throw itself, most good throwers use a run-up of some 6 to 10 steps (approximately 9–15 m). This, together with (1) the short walking or jogging steps often used at the start; (2) the 5 to 7 steps used in the transition from run to throw; and (3) the recovery step used to bring the thrower to a halt after the implement has been released, generally results in a total run-up length of some 12 to 18 strides (approximately 20–30 m). **Run**

As the thrower's right foot is grounded 5 strides before the final throwing position is reached, the withdrawal of the javelin begins. Although there are several ways in which this movement may be executed, the simplest, and the most widely used by top throwers, is a direct pushing back of the throwing hand to a position in which the arm is fully extended and the hand is at approximately shoulder height. This movement, accompanied by a turning of the shoulders to maintain the javelin in line with the intended direction of the throw, occupies the first 1½ to 2 strides of the transition. Throughout these strides and, indeed those that follow, the athlete's hips are kept essentially "square" to the front and the feet are grounded pointing directly forward—both measures aimed at maintaining the momentum developed in the approach run. (*Note:* Techniques that involve the placement of the feet across the line of the run-up almost inevitably result in some loss of forward momentum.) **Withdrawal**

An example of the sequence of movements performed by a top-class thrower, from the withdrawal of the javelin at the start of the transition to the recovery stride following the release, is shown in Fig. 17-16. The following points should be noted: **Cross-Step**

(a)–(d)* The cross step. The step preceding that in which the athlete adopts the final throwing position has been given this name because in the early techniques the legs actually crossed, one in front of the other, at this time. Although the term is no longer appropriate, at least for the majority of good throwers, it appears to have been retained by most writers on the subject.

The objective of the cross step is to get the feet forward of the upper body so that, as the athlete lands on the right foot at the end of this step,

---

* The letters in parentheses refer to the corresponding positions in Fig. 17-16.

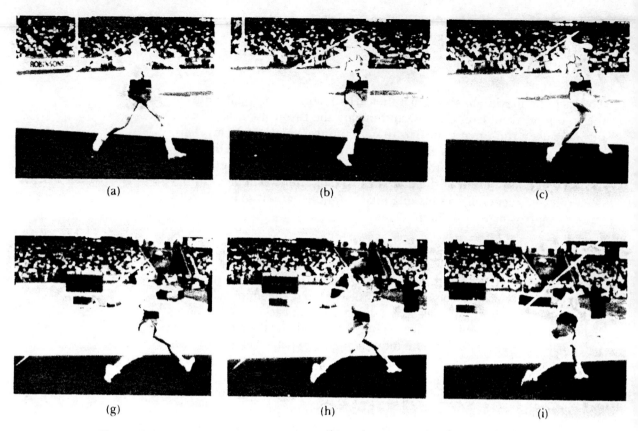

Figure 17-16. Good technique in throwing the javelin. (Photographs courtesy of Howard Payne.)

he (or she) is able to move into the optimum position from which to execute the throw.

This is accomplished with a forceful drive from the left foot and a fast action of both legs during the flight phase of the stride. This fast leg action brings the left foot level with (or forward of) the right foot at the instant the latter is grounded and thus facilitates a rapid transition to the throwing position. (*Note:* In a normal running stride the foot of the recovery leg is well behind the grounded foot at the instant the latter touches down.)

(e) The landing at the end of the cross step. The athlete has landed on the ball of the right foot with the trunk inclined backward at a angle of about 115° to the forward horizontal direction. (Menzel[52] has reported angles of inclination of 104–126° and 110–118°, respectively, for the finalists in the men's and women's events at the 1987 World Championships.)

Compared with a more erect position, this backward inclination allows the athlete more time to exert force on the javelin before it reaches the point at which it should be released. It also increases the distance through

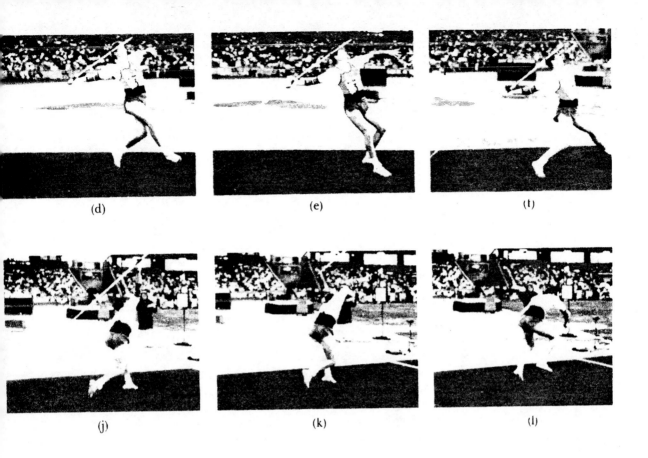

(d)　　　　　(e)　　　　　(f)

(j)　　　　　(k)　　　　　(l)

which force may be exerted on the javelin—a distance which, according to Pugh,[53] may be as much as 14 ft (4.27 m) in the case of a great thrower.

From this position, the hip, knee, and ankle joints of the right leg flex (1) to cushion the shock of the landing—up to 9.1 times the athlete's bodyweight in the vertical direction and up to 6.4 times bodyweight in the backward horizontal direction;[54] (2) to speed the rotation of the body over the right foot; and (3) to put the right leg in the optimum position to exert force downward and backward against the ground.

(f) The athlete's center of gravity has passed forward over and beyond the right foot and a forceful extension of the right leg has begun to drive the hips forward. The trunk and the throwing arm are held in essentially the same position as before, awaiting the appropriate moment to make their contribution to the release velocity of the implement.

(g) The left foot has been grounded, heel first, and some distance to the left of the direction line.

(h) The right leg has completed its drive and the toes of the right foot are being dragged forward across the ground; and, with the rotation of the

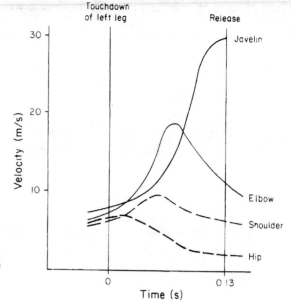

Figure 17-17.
The hip, shoulder, elbow, and javelin
attain their peak velocities in that order.
(Adapted from Arbeit, et al. [1988]. The
javelin. *New Studies in Athletics*,
1:57–74.)

hips toward the front almost completed, the muscles responsible for the rotation of the trunk have begun to make their contribution, aided by an outward and backward swing of the left elbow.

The length of the stride at this instant (that is, the horizontal distance between the toe of the right foot and the toe of the left foot, at the instant the latter makes contact with the ground) is a function of the athlete's stature and technique. Values for the best throws by the finalists in the 1987 World Championships ranged from 1.42-1.57 m (men) and 1.33-1.62 m (women).[55]

(i) The left leg, after bending somewhat under the large force to which it has been subjected, is now firmly braced. For top-class throwers, the time during which the knee of the left leg is flexing should be as short as possible, and the extent to which it is flexed should not be less than 155°.[56]

The hips are now "square" to the front, driven in that direction by the extension of the right leg and by the resistance provided later by the left leg; the trunk is also "square" to the front, chest well forward, and back arched slightly; and the throwing arm is being whipped forward with the elbow high, and the hand trailing.

(j) The release. The left leg has been extended a little to increase the height of release and, by contributing to the vertical component of the velocity, to increase both the speed and the angle of release. The extension of the elbow is complete and the javelin has been released from the fingers spinning about its long axis.

According to Arbeit and colleagues,[57] the optimum coordination of the movements of the individual parts of the body is achieved if the hip, shoulder, elbow, and javelin reach their peak velocities in the order shown in Fig. 17-17.

(k)–(1) The athlete takes a roughly 1.5–2.0-m long recovery step to dissipate the momentum left over from the preceding movements.

As in each of the other throwing events, the horizontal distance with which a hammer thrower is credited (assuming, that the throw is executed in strict accord with the rules) is governed by (1) the speed; (2) the height; and (3) the angle at which the implement is released; and (4) the air resistance encountered in flight.

HAMMER THROW
Basic Considerations

Speed of Release

Since the hammer is initially at rest, the velocity that it possesses some time later clearly depends on the forces exerted on it to produce its subsequent motion (Newton's second law). These forces are its weight acting downward through the center of gravity of the hammer; the air resistance encountered during the preliminary swing(s) and the turns; and the forces exerted on it by the thrower.

The weight of the hammer can be resolved into three components—a centripetal (or radial) component acting toward the center of rotation of the hammer, a tangential component acting along the path of the center of gravity of the hammer, and a component acting at right angles to these two. Of these three components, it is only the tangential component that influences the speed of the hammer along its path. From the high point of its path to the low point in each swing or turn, the tangential component of the weight tends to increase the speed of the hammer. And, conversely, from the low point to the high point, it tends to decrease the speed of the hammer.[58]

The air resistance encountered by the hammer during the preliminary swing(s) and the turns is generally considered to be negligible compared to the other forces involved.

The forces that the thrower exerts on the hammer are applied at the grip or handle and transmitted via the wire to the head of the hammer. Since the wire is light and flexible, only forces exerted along its length and toward the handle are effective in influencing the motion of the hammer-head. If the wire is aligned so that an imaginary extension of it passes through the axis about which the hammer is rotating, any force exerted by the thrower acts inward toward the axis and thus may correctly be described as a centripetal force. Such a force (like all centripetal forces) serves only to change the direction in which the body is moving (Fig. 17-18[a]). If the wire of the hammer is aligned at an angle to a line joining the head of the hammer and the axis, the forces exerted along its length have both a centripetal (or radial) and a tangential component (Fig. 17-18[b]). Such forces change both the direction in which the hammerhead is moving and the speed with which it is moving. The speed of release is determined in

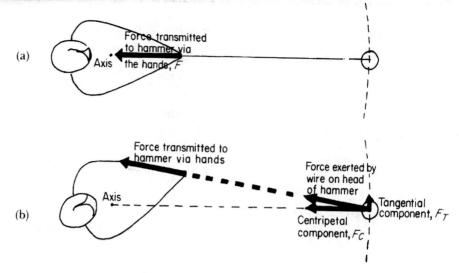

(a)

(b)

Figure 17-18. Forces exerted in the hammer throw.

large measure by the thrower's ability to repeatedly get "ahead" of the hammer and into positions from which he can exert forces of this latter kind—forces that serve to increase the speed at which the hammer is moving.*

The forces exerted on the hammer have been studied by Dapena[59] who reported a maximum centripetal force of 2750 N and values for the tangential component ranging between − 130 N and + 340 N, for a 67.50-m throw by a top American thrower. (The minus and plus signs refer to tangential components that, respectively, decreased and increased the speed of the hammer.)

The factors influencing the speed of release can also be considered from a purely kinematic standpoint by means of Eq. (4-5):

$$v_T = \omega r$$

From this equation the following conclusions can be drawn:

- If the angular velocity is constant, the greater the radius, the greater the linear velocity of the hammer.
- If the radius is constant, the greater the angular velocity at which the hammer is rotated, the greater its linear velocity.
- In practice, the greatest linear velocity is obtained when the combination of radius and angular velocity is optimal.

---

* The forces exerted along the length of the hammer wire—and the effects that they produce—are occasionally analyzed in terms of their horizontal and vertical components. Such analyses, although proceeding along slightly different lines from that presented here, invariably give rise to the same conclusions.

As the linear velocity of the hammer increases, so too does the magnitude of the centripetal force that the athlete must exert to keep the hammer moving on a circular path relative to the axis of rotation (see Eq. [6-12]). This increase in centripetal force is accompanied by an identical increase in the centrifugal force that the hammer exerts, in reaction, on the athlete. This buildup in centrifugal force necessitates that the athlete continually modify his body position to retain balance in a forward and backward sense. The athlete in Fig. 17-19 is acted on by three forces—W, the gravitational force, acting through his center of gravity; F_c, the centrifugal force, applied to his hands by the hammer; and R, the ground-reaction force, applied to his feet. The first two of these forces tend to rotate the athlete about a transverse axis through his feet—W with a moment Wx in a counterclockwise direction and F_c with a moment $F_c y$ in the opposite direction. As the speed with which the athlete rotates increases, F_c and the moment $F_c y$ increase accordingly, while the contrary moment Wx remains the same—unless, of course, some adjustment in the athlete's position alters the magnitude of the moment arm, x. Now, if the athlete makes no adjustment in x as his rate of rotation increases, he is subjected to a resultant clockwise moment *over and above that necessary to retain the body position he had initially* (that is, at the slower rate of rotation). To overcome the serious problem that this excess moment represents, a good hammer thrower progressively modifies his body position by "sitting back against the hammer."

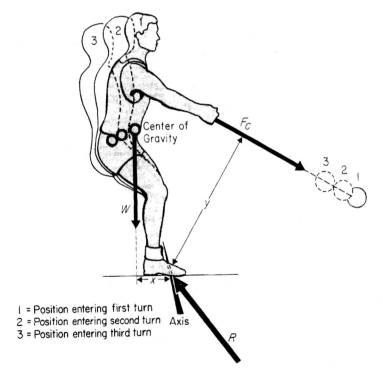

I = Position entering first turn
2 = Position entering second turn
3 = Position entering third turn

Figure 17-19.
To maintain his balance, the hammer thrower must "sit back against the hammer" as the centrifugal force it exerts on him gets progressively larger.

This action, incorporating a lowering and a backward movement of the center of gravity as the hips and knees are flexed, decreases the moment arm of the centrifugal force and increases the moment arm of the body weight to ensure the appropriate relationship between the two influences (Fig. 17-19).

Height of Release

The height of release depends primarily on the thrower's body position at that instant. The differences that exist, however, between one throw and another are generally so small as to be of little practical significance.

Angle of Release

Because the hammer is generally released at about shoulder level, a height of about 1.6-1.9 m above the level at which it will land, the optimum angle of release is slightly less than 45°—approximately 43°–44° for throws in excess of 45 m. (Values obtained by Otto[60] for the angles of release in world-class throws of 77.06–83.06 m ranged from 38°–44°.)

Air Resistance

The effects of air resistance on the distances achieved in hammer throwing are generally regarded as negligible. Payne,[61] for example, has reported that air resistance reduces a 200-ft (61-m) throw by 2-3 ft (0.6-0.9 m) at sea level—a reduction of 1-1.5% in the total length of the throw.

Techniques

An example of the techniques employed by a top-class hammer thrower is shown in Fig. 17-20. The following points should be noted:

(a)* The preliminary swing. In his initial stance the athlete has his feet a little more than shoulder width apart and close to the rim of the circle, his legs flexed and his weight over his right foot, his upper body twisted around approximately 90° to the right, and his arms extended behind him in line with the hammer wire. From this position he sweeps the hammer forward and around into a preliminary swing, shifting his center of gravity to the left and bringing his trunk into an upright position in the process (a_1). As the hammerhead passes in front of him and then out to his left (a_2 and a_3), the athlete shifts his center of gravity back toward the right. These adjustments in the position of the center of gravity are necessary to ensure that the moment of the athlete's weight is sufficient to offset the "overbalancing" moment of the centrifugal force. At the same time, however, the athlete endeavors to ensure that the hammerhead is moved through the largest arc possible, that is, that its radius of rotation is as large as he can make it. To do this, he leans his upper body to the side (a_2) and slightly backward (a_3)—a movement known in hammer throwing as *countering*.

As the hammer swings out to the thrower's left and before it begins to

* The letters in parentheses refer to the corresponding parts of the throw shown in Fig. 17-20.

move around behind him, he quickly pulls his hands across the top of his head, turning his hips and shoulders well to the right in the process (a_3 and a_4). This places the athlete in a "wound-up" position in which his hips, his shoulders, and the hammer wire are each progressively farther around to the right. From this position, reached shortly after the hammerhead passes through the high point of its swing, the thrower exerts force along the hammer wire by contracting those muscles that rotate the hips and shoulders around to the front. This force, acting downward and inward along the length of the hammer wire, is supplemented by the component of the weight of the hammer acting in that direction (a_4).

(b) The first turn. Immediately after the hammerhead passes through the low point of its swing, the thrower starts to move into the first turn by pivoting on the heel of his left foot and the ball of his right foot (b_2). This action continues (b_3) as increasingly larger forces are exerted via the right foot to drive the thrower around to the left. Throughout this phase of the action the thrower's arms serve as passive extensions of the hammer wire (as indeed they do throughout all three turns), his shoulders are relaxed and pulled well forward, his trunk is inclined slightly forward in the direction of the hammer, and his center of gravity is low and well behind the heel of his left foot. Such a body position ensures that the radius of the arc through which the hammerhead swings is as large as it can be without upsetting the thrower's balance.

As the hammer continues upward toward the high point, the thrower's right foot is lifted quickly from the ground (b_4). Then, as the hammer moves through the high point and begins to descend (b_5), the right foot is whipped quickly around the left leg to land about shoulder width away from the left foot (b_6). This movement, aimed at getting the thrower's feet ahead of his hips and his hips ahead of his shoulders, is facilitated if the right foot is kept close to the ground as it is brought around (thereby minimizing the distance it must travel) and if the right leg is kept close to the left leg (thus minimizing the moment of inertia of the thrower's lower body). Meantime, the pivot on the heel of the left foot (b_2 and b_3) blends smoothly into a rolling movement on the outside border of the foot (b_4) and concludes with a pivot on the ball of the foot (b_5 and b_6). (Note: The position of the right foot in [b_6]—and, too, in [c_4]—is indicative of a relatively recent development in the technique of hammer throwing. Leading exponents of the event previously attempted to place the right foot parallel with the left and pointing to the rear of the circle. According to Bondarchuk,[62] a former Olympic champion and a national coach for the event, "The earlier [the right foot] is placed on the ground, the greater can be the acceleration of the hammer completed by the thrower at the beginning of the double support phase of each turn."

With the right foot grounded, the thrower is once again in a wound-up position and, as before, he powerfully accelerates the hammer as the muscles that rotate his hips and shoulders to the front are contracted forcefully.

(c) The second turn. The completion of the first turn and the start of the

(a₁)   (a₂)

(b₁)   (b₂)

(b₅)   (b₆)

Figure 17-20. Good technique in the hammer throw. (Photographs courtesy of Howard Payne.)

(a₃)

(a₄)

(b₃)

(b₄)

(c₁)

(c₂)

(c₃)   (c₄)

(d₂)   (d₃)

(e₃)   (e₄)

(c₅)   (d₁)

(e₁)   (e₂)

(e₅)   (e₆)

second blend smoothly into one another as the right foot starts to drive the athlete's hips and trunk once more around to the left (b_6 and c_1). This action is accompanied by a strong lifting action of the legs and trunk (compare the leg and trunk positions in b_6 and c_2) that serves to further accelerate the hammer as it passes through the low point and begins to ascend. The remainder of the second turn (c_3 to c_5) follows much the same pattern as in the first turn.

(d) The third turn. Aside from the modifications in body position to ensure that balance is maintained as the centrifugal force to which he is subjected increases, the thrower's actions during the third turn (d_1 to d_3) are essentially the same as those in the preceding two turns.

(e) The delivery. The marked acceleration of the hammer during the delivery begins as the hammer passes through the high point of the third turn (d_2) and continues with a strong rotation of the hips and trunk—facilitated by a placement of the right foot slightly farther around to the left than in the previous two turns—and a strong upward and slightly backward drive from the legs and back (e_1 to e_4).

The extent to which the hammer may be accelerated during the delivery depends very largely on the thrower's body position as his right foot is grounded at the completion of the third turn. If he is in a strongly wound-up position at this time (that is, with his feet rotated to a position ahead of his hips, his hips leading the shoulders in similar fashion, and the hammer trailing well behind all three), he can make optimum use of the various muscular forces at his disposal. On the other hand, if he has failed to get his feet, hips, and shoulders progressively farther ahead of the hammer in this manner, the extent to which the available muscular forces can contribute to the speed at which the hammer is ultimately released is severely limited by the relatively short distance over which they can act.

Once the hammer has been released (somewhere between the positions shown in e_4 and e_5), the thrower's weight moves over his right foot (e_6) and the left foot is lifted and moved toward the left as he strives to recover his balance and avoid fouling.

Recommended Readings

DYSON, G. H. C. (1977). *The Mechanics of Athletics.* New York: Holmes & Meier. pp. 209–52 (Throwing).

HUBBARD, M. (1989). *Biomechanics of Sport.* Boca Raton, FL: CRC Press, Inc., pp. 213–38 (The throwing events in track and field).

Shot Put

TSCHIENE, P. (1985). Shot. In H. Payne (Ed.), *Athletes in Action.* London: Pelham Books, pp. 198–211 (Shot).

ZATSIORSKY, V. M., LANKA, G. E., AND SHALMANOV, A. A. (1981). *Exercise and Sport Sciences Reviews.* Philadelphia: The Franklin Institute Press. pp. 353–89 (Biomechanical analysis of shot putting technique).

Discus Throw

BARTLETT, R. M. (1990). *Techniques in Athletics: Conference Proceedings.* Köln, Federal Republic of Germany: Deutsche Sporthochschule Köln, pp. 126–45 (The biomechanics of the discus throw).

Lenz, G., and Ward, P. (1985). In H. Payne (Ed.), *Athletes in Action*. London: Pelham Books, pp. 212–36 (Discus).

Javelin Throw

Bartlett, R. M., and Best, R. J. (1988). The biomechanics of javelin throwing: a review. *Journal of Sports Sciences*, 6:1–38.

Koltai, J. (1985). In H. Payne (Ed.), *Athletes in Action*. London: Pelham Books, pp. 263–93 (Javelin).

Hammer Throw

Dapena, J. (1984). The pattern of hammer speed during a hammer throw and influence of gravity on its fluctuations. *Journal of Biomechanics*, 17:553–59.

Dapena, J. (1986). A kinematic study of center of mass motions in the hammer throw. *Journal of Biomechanics*, 19:147–58.

Dapena, J., and Feltner, M. E. (1989). Influence of the direction of the cable force and of the radius of the hammer path on speed fluctuations during hammer throwing. *Journal of Biomechanics*, 22:565–76.

Pedemonte, J. (1985). In H. Payne (Ed.), *Athletes in Action*. London: Pelham Books, pp. 237–62 (Hammer).

Notes

1. Stepanek, J. (1990). Findings of the IAAF biomechanical research concerning shot put. In G-P. Brüggeman and J. K. Rühl (Eds.), *Techniques in Athletics: Conference Proceedings* (pp. 625–28). Koln, Federal Republic of Germany: Deutsche Sporthochschule Koln.
2. *Ibid.*
3. Zatsiorsky, V., Lanka, G. E., and Shalmanov, A. A. (1981). Biomechanical analysis of shot putting technique. In D. I. Miller (Ed.), *Exercise and Sport Sciences Reviews* (pp. 353–89). Philadelphia: Franklin Institute Press.
4. Tschiene, P. (1969). Perfection of shot put technique. *Track Technique*, 37:1187–89.
5. Pearson, G. F. D. (1966). The shot put—I. In T. Ecker and F. Wilt (Eds.), *Illustrated Guide to Olympic Track and Field* (pp. 123–24). West Nyack, N.Y.: Parker Publishing.
6. Fidelus, K., and Zienkowicz, W. (1965). Sila i predkosc rozwijane podczas pchniecia kula. *Kultura Fizyczana (Warsawa)*, 18:83–95. (Cited in Zatsiorsky, Lanka, and Shalamanov, Biomechanical analysis of shot putting.)
7. Tschiene, P. (1985). Shot. In H. Payne (Ed.), *Athletes in Action* (pp. 198–211). London: Pelham Books, Ltd.
8. Fischer, A., and Merhaupt, J. (1962). Foot contact at the instant of release in throwing. *Track Technique*, 9:272.
9. Dyson, G. H. (1977). *The Mechanics of Athletics* (p. 247). London: University of London Press Ltd.
10. Nett, T. (1962). Foot contact at the instant of release in throwing. *Track Technique*, 9:274.
11. Kerssenbrock, K. (1974). Potential of the rotation shot put. *Track Technique*, 58:1848.
12. Zatsiorsky, V. (1990). The biomechanics of shot putting techniques. In G-P. Brüggeman and J. K. Rühl (Eds.), *Techniques in Athletics: Conference Proceedings* (pp. 118–25). Köln, Federal Republic of Germany: Deutsche Sporthochschule Köln.
13. Ganslen, R. V. (1958). *Aerodynamic Factors Which Influence Discus Flight*. Research report, University of Arkansas.
14. Ganslen, R. V. (1959). Aerodynamic forces in discus flight. *Scholastic Coach*, 28:46, 77.
15. Ganslen, R. V. (1964). Aerodynamic and mechanical forces in discus flight. *Athletic Journal*, 64:50,52,68, and 88–89.
16. Kentzer, C. P., and Hromas, L. A. (1958). Research report, School of Aeronautical Engineering, Purdue University.
17. Cooper, L., Dalzell, D., and Silverman, E. (1959). *Flight of the Discus*. Division of Engineering Science, Purdue University.
18. Soong, T. C. (1976). The dynamics of discus throw. *Journal of Applied Mechanics*, 43:531–36.
19. Taylor, J. A. (1932). Behavior of the discus in flight. *Athletic Journal*, 12:9–10, 45–47.
20. Soong. The dynamics of discus throw, p. 534.
21. Frohlich, C. (1981). Aerodynamic effects on discus flight. *American Journal of Physics*, 49:1125–32.

22. Lockwood, H. H. (1963). Throwing the discus. In G. F. D. Pearson (Ed.), *Athletics* (p. 206). Edinburgh: Thomas Nelson & Sons Ltd.

23. Terauds, J. (1978). Computerized biomechanics cinematography analysis of discus throwing at the 1976 Montreal Olympiad. *Track and Field Quarterly Review*, 78:25–28.

24. Gregor, R. J., Whiting, W. C., and McCoy, R. W. (1985). Kinematic analysis of Olympic discus throwers. *International Journal of Sport Biomechanics*, 1:131–38.

25. Bosen, K. O. (1963). Discus throw points to ponder. *Track Technique*, 11:335.

26. Lockwood, B. (1969). The double-turn throw. *Track Technique*, 35:110–14.

27. Davenport, H. (1961). A new discus technique. *Modern Athletics*, 5:11.

28. Finanger, K. E. (1969). An electromyographic study of the function of selected muscles involved in the throwing of the discus. Ph.D. dissertation, The University of Iowa, 126.

29. Lockwood. Throwing the discus, p. 189.

30. Knicker, A. (1988). Identifikation von leistungsbestimmenden Technikmerkmalen beim Diskuswurf von Hochleistungsathleten. Diplomarbeit, Deutsche Sporthochschule Köln, pp. 63–64.

31. Schluter, W., and Nixdorf, E. (1984). Kinematische Beschreibung und Analyse der Diskuswurftechnik. *Leistungssport*, 14:17–22.

32. LeMasurier, J. (1975). *Discus Throwing* (p. 16). London: The Amateur Athletic Association.

33. Ryan, F. (1962). Teaching the discus throw. *Scholastic Coach*, 32:25.

34. Pryor, D., and Lockwood, H. H. (1970). The discus throw. In F. Wilt and T. Ecker (Eds.), *International Track and Field Coaching Encyclopedia* (p. 264). West Nyack, N.Y.: Parker Publishing.

35. Ecker, T. (1971). *Track and Field Dynamics* (p. 55). Los Altos, Calif.: Tafnews Press.

36. Maughan, R. B. (1964). Jay Silvester's discus form. *Track Technique*, 15:477–78.

37. Knicker. Identifikation von leistungsbestimmenden Technikmerkmalen beim Diskuswurf, p. 66.

38. Lockwood, H. H. (1963). *Throwing the Discus.* In G. F. D. Pearson (ed) *Athletics* (p. 214). Edinburgh: Thomas Nelson and Sons Ltd.

39. Ganslen, R. V., and Hall, K. G. (1960). *Aerodynamics of Javelin Flight*. Fayetteville. Ark.: University of Arkansas.

40. Terauds, J. (1974). Optimal angle of release for the competition javelin as determined by its aerodynamic and ballistic characteristics. In R. C. Nelson and C. A. Morehouse, (Eds.), *Biomechanics IV* (p. 180). Baltimore: University Park Press.

41. Terauds, J. (1974). Wind tunnel tests of competition javelins. *Track and Field Quarterly Review*, 74:88.

42. Soong, T. C. (1975) The dynamics of javelin throw. *Journal of Applied Mechanics*, 42:257–61.

43. Hubbard, M., & Alaways, L. W. (1987). Optimum release conditions for the new rules javelin. *International Journal of Sport Biomechanics*, 3:207.

44. Bartlett, R. M., & Best, R. J. (1988). The biomechanics of javelin throwing: A review. *Journal of Sport Sciences*, 6:1–38.

45. Best, R. J., and Bartlett, R. M. (1988). Computer flight simulation of men's new-rules javelin. In G. de Groot, A. P. Hollander, P. A. Huijing and G. J. van Ingen Schenau (Eds.), *Biomechanics XI-B* (pp. 588–94). Amsterdam: Free University Press.

46. Hubbard, M. (1989). The throwing events in track and field. In *Biomechanics of Sport* (pp. 213–38). Boca Raton. Fla.: CRC Press, Inc.

47. Menzel, H-J. (1987). Biomechanical analysis of the javelin. In *Scientific Report on the II World Championships in Athletics—Rome 1987* (p. 20). Monaco: International Athletic Foundation.

48. Best and Bartlett. Computer flight simulation of the men's new rules javelin, p. 591.

49. Menzel, H-J. (1990). Biomechanical analyses of the javelin throw of top class athletes. In G-P. Bruggeman and J. K. Rühl (Eds.), *Techniques in Athletics: Conference Proceedings* (pp. 662–68). Koln: Federal Republic of Germany, Deutsche Sporthochschule Köln.

50. Best and Bartlett. Computer flight simulation of the men's new rules javelin, p. 592.

51. Paish, W. (1967). *Javelin Throwing* (p. 43). London: Amateur Athletic Association.

52. Menzel. Biomechhanical analysis of the javelin, pp. 9–10.

53. Pugh, D. L. (1960). *Javelin Throwing* (p. 11). London: Amateur Athletic Association.

54. Deporte, E., and van Gheluwe, B. (1988). Ground reaction forces and moments in javelin throwing. In G. de Groot, A. P. Hollander, P. A. Huijing and G. J. van Ingen Schenau (Eds.), *Biomechanics XI-B* (pp. 575–81). Amsterdam: Free University Press.

55. Menzel. Biomechanical analysis of the javelin. p. 13.

56. Ibid., p. 667.

57. Arbeit, E., and others (1988). The javelin. *New Studies in Athletics*, 1:57–74.

58. Dapena, J. (1984). The pattern of hammer speed during a hammer throw and influence of gravity on its fluctuations. *Journal of Biomechanics*, 17:553–59.

59. Dapena, J. (1982). Tangential and perpendicular forces in the hammer throw. *Hammer Notes*, 5:40–42.

60. Otto, R. M. Biomechanical analysis of the hammer throw. In *Scientific Report on the II World Championships in Athletics—Rome 1987* (p. 34). Monaco: International Athletic Association.

61. Payne, H. (1969), *Hammer Throwing* (p. 53). London: Amateur Athletic Association.

62. Bondarchuk, A. (1977). Uri Sedikh Throws the Hammer. *Track and Field*, 1:32–33. (Translated by M. Yessis and reported in *Yessis Review of Soviet Physical Education and Sports*, (1977) 12:67.)

ELEMENTARY
TRIGONOMETRY

A knowledge of elementary trigonometry—the branch of mathematics that deals with the relationships between the sides and angles of triangles—is essential to a complete understanding of many of the basic concepts in biomechanics.

Consider the right-angled triangle ABC in Fig. A-1. If the lengths of the three sides of this triangle are measured, a total of six fractions (or ratios) can be obtained by putting the length of one side in the numerator and the length of another in the denominator:

$$\frac{AC}{AB}, \frac{AC}{BC}, \frac{BC}{AB}, \frac{BC}{AC}, \frac{AB}{BC}, \frac{AB}{AC},$$

In trigonometry, these ratios are given special names according to how the sides are located relative to one of the acute (that is, less than 90°) angles in the triangle. For example, if the angle ABC is designated by the Greek letter β (beta), the ratio formed by placing the side opposite β (that is, AC) over the hypotenuse (that is, AB, the side opposite the right angle) is called the sine of β. Thus:

$$\text{sine } \beta = \frac{\text{opposite}}{\text{hypotenuse}} = \frac{AC}{AB}$$

Although there are five other such ratios, only two of these need be considered here. These are:

$$\text{cosine } \beta = \frac{\text{adjacent}}{\text{hypotenuse}} = \frac{BC}{AB}$$

and

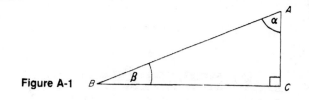

Figure A-1

$$\text{tangent } \beta = \frac{\text{opposite}}{\text{adjacent}} = \frac{AC}{BC}$$

The sine, cosine, and tangent ratios (normally abbreviated to sin, cos, and tan) for the angle BAC (here designated by the Greek letter α [alpha]) are similarly

$$\sin \alpha = \frac{\text{opposite}}{\text{hypotenuse}} = \frac{BC}{AB}$$

$$\cos \alpha = \frac{\text{adjacent}}{\text{hypotenuse}} = \frac{AC}{AB}$$

and

$$\tan \alpha = \frac{\text{opposite}}{\text{adjacent}} = \frac{BC}{AC}$$

Now, for an angle of a given size (say, 30°) the sine of that angle is a constant value regardless of the size of the right-angled triangle. In other words, the ratio formed by placing the length of the side opposite the 30° angle over the hypotenuse will always be the same—whether these sides be appropriately measured in millimeters or kilometers. The same holds true for each of the other trigonometrical ratios.

The values of the sine, cosine, and tangent of angles ranging from 0° to 90° are presented in Table A-1. Thus, if the angle β (in Fig. A-1) is 30°,

$$\sin \beta = \frac{AC}{AB} = 0.5000$$

$$\cos \beta = \frac{BC}{AB} = 0.8660$$

$$\tan \beta = \frac{AC}{BC} = 0.5774$$

A simple rearrangement of these equations shows clearly the relationships between the various sides of the triangle ABC:

TABLE A-1 Trigonometric Functions

Degrees	Sines	Cosines	Tangents	Degrees	Sines	Cosines	Tangents
0	0.0000	1.0000	0.0000	46	0.7193	0.6947	1.0355
1	0.0175	0.9998	0.0175	47	0.7314	0.6820	1.0724
2	0.0349	0.9994	0.0349	48	0.7431	0.6691	1.1106
3	0.0523	0.9986	0.0524	49	0.7547	0.6561	1.1504
4	0.0698	0.9976	0.0699	50	0.7660	0.6428	1.1918
5	0.0872	0.9962	0.0875	51	0.7771	0.6293	1.2349
6	0.1045	0.9945	0.1051	52	0.7880	0.6157	1.2799
7	0.1219	0.9925	0.1228	53	0.7986	0.6018	1.3270
8	0.1392	0.9903	0.1405	54	0.8090	0.5878	1.3764
9	0.1564	0.9877	0.1584	55	0.8192	0.5736	1.4281
10	0.1736	0.9848	0.1763	56	0.8290	0.5592	1.4826
11	0.1908	0.9816	0.1944	57	0.8387	0.5446	1.5399
12	0.2079	0.9781	0.2126	58	0.8480	0.5299	1.6003
13	0.2250	0.9744	0.2309	59	0.8572	0.5150	1.6643
14	0.2419	0.9703	0.2493	60	0.8660	0.5000	1.7321
15	0.2588	0.9659	0.2679	61	0.8746	0.4848	1.8040
16	0.2756	0.9613	0.2867	62	0.8829	0.4695	1.8807
17	0.2924	0.9563	0.3057	63	0.8910	0.4540	1.9626
18	0.3090	0.9511	0.3249	64	0.8988	0.4384	2.0503
19	0.3256	0.9455	0.3443	65	0.9063	0.4226	2.1445
20	0.3420	0.9397	0.3640	66	0.9135	0.4067	2.2460
21	0.3584	0.9336	0.3839	67	0.9205	0.3907	2.3559
22	0.3746	0.9272	0.4040	68	0.9272	0.3746	2.4751
23	0.3907	0.9205	0.4245	69	0.9336	0.3584	2.6051
24	0.4067	0.9135	0.4452	70	0.9397	0.3420	2.7475
25	0.4226	0.9063	0.4663	71	0.9455	0.3256	2.9042
26	0.4384	0.8988	0.4877	72	0.9511	0.3090	3.0777
27	0.4540	0.8910	0.5095	73	0.9563	0.2924	3.2709
28	0.4695	0.8829	0.5317	74	0.9613	0.2756	3.4874
29	0.4848	0.8746	0.5543	75	0.9659	0.2588	3.7321
30	0.5000	0.8660	0.5774	76	0.9703	0.2419	4.0108
31	0.5150	0.8572	0.6009	77	0.9744	0.2250	4.3315
32	0.5299	0.8480	0.6249	78	0.9781	0.2079	4.7046
33	0.5446	0.8387	0.6494	79	0.9816	0.1908	5.1446
34	0.5592	0.8290	0.6745	80	0.9848	0.1736	5.6713
35	0.5736	0.8192	0.7002	81	0.9877	0.1564	6.3138
36	0.5878	0.8090	0.7265	82	0.9903	0.1392	7.1154
37	0.6018	0.7986	0.7536	83	0.9925	0.1219	8.1443
38	0.6157	0.7880	0.7813	84	0.9945	0.1045	9.5144
39	0.6293	0.7771	0.8098	85	0.9962	0.0872	11.43
40	0.6428	0.7660	0.8391	86	0.9976	0.0698	14.30
41	0.6561	0.7547	0.8693	87	0.9986	0.0523	19.08
42	0.6691	0.7431	0.9004	88	0.9994	0.0349	28.64
43	0.6820	0.7314	0.9325	89	0.9998	0.0175	57.29
44	0.6947	0.7193	0.9657	90	1.0000	0.0000	∞
45	0.7071	0.7071	1.0000				

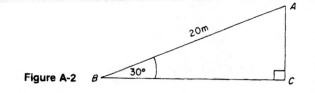

Figure A-2

$$AC = 0.5000 \times AB$$

$$BC = 0.8660 \times AB$$

$$AC = 0.5774 \times BC$$

Suppose now, that $\beta = 30°$, $AB = 20$ m, and nothing else is known about the right-angled triangle ABC (Fig. A-2). The length of the remaining sides can readily be determined using the trigonometrical ratios defined here:

$$\frac{AC}{AB} = \sin 30°$$

$$\frac{AC}{20 \text{ m}} = 0.5000$$

$$AC = 0.5000 \times 20 \text{ m}$$

$$= 10 \text{ m}$$

Similarly,

$$\frac{BC}{AB} = \cos 30°$$

$$\frac{BC}{20 \text{ m}} = 0.8660$$

$$BC = 0.8660 \times 20 \text{ m}$$
$$= 17.32 \text{ m}$$

Finally, suppose that the lengths of two sides of the triangle ABC are known (for example, $AB = 30$ cm, $AC = 27$ cm, as in Fig. A-3) and it is desired to find the size of the angles α and β. Now it is apparent that β is an angle, whose sine is given by the ratio AC/AB.* In the present example,

---

* This statement may be written in abbreviated form:

$$\beta = \arcsin \frac{AC}{AB}$$

in which the word *arcsin* is read "an angle whose sine is." Similar words (arccos and arctan) are used where the ratio involved is the cosine or tangent.

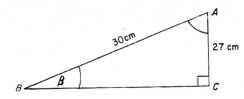

Figure A-3

$$\sin \beta = \frac{27}{30} = 0.9000$$

An examination of the sine values listed in Table A-1 reveals that

$$\sin 64° = 0.8988$$

and

$$\sin 65° = 0.9063$$

Thus, β is an angle just slightly larger than 64°. (*Note:* Tables that give values for fractions of a degree can be used if a more precise measure of β is required.)

Since the sum of the three angles in any triangle is 180°, α may be found simply by subtraction or, if preferred, by a similar use of trigonometry:

$$\cos \alpha = \frac{AC}{AB} = 0.9000$$

$$\alpha \approx 26°$$

B

EQUATION NUMBER	EQUATION	PAGE NUMBER
3-1	$\bar{s} = \dfrac{l}{t}$	15
3-2	$\bar{v} = \dfrac{d}{t}$	15
3-3	$\bar{a} = \dfrac{v_f - v_i}{t}$	18
3-4	$C = \sqrt{A^2 + B^2}$	24
3-5	$\theta = \arctan\left(\dfrac{A}{B}\right)$	24
3-6	$C = \sqrt{A^2 + B^2 + 2AB \cos \beta}$	25
3-7	$\theta = \arctan\left(\dfrac{A \sin \beta}{B + A \cos \beta}\right)$	25
3-8	$v_f = v_i + at$	28
3-9	$d = v_i t + \tfrac{1}{2}at^2$	28
3-10	$v^2_f = v^2_i + 2ad$	28
3-11	$R = v \cos \theta \times T$	33
3-12	$t_{up} = \dfrac{v \sin \theta}{g}$	34
3-13	$t_{down} = \sqrt{\dfrac{2d_{down}}{g}}$	34
3-14	$d_{up} = \dfrac{(v \sin \theta)^2}{2g}$	34
3-15	$t_{down} = \dfrac{v \sin \theta}{g}$	35
3-16	$T = \dfrac{2v \sin \theta}{g}$	35
3-17	$d_{down} = \dfrac{(v \sin \theta)^2}{2g} + h$	36
3-18	$t_{down} = \sqrt{\dfrac{(v \sin \theta)^2 + 2gh}{g}}$	36

521
Equations

EQUATION NUMBER	EQUATION	PAGE NUMBER
5-14	$v_1 = \sqrt{\left[\dfrac{m_2 u_2(1 + e) + u_1 \cos \alpha(em_2 - m_1)}{m_1 + m_2}\right]^2 + (u_1 \sin \alpha)^2}$	91
5-15	$\beta = \arctan\left[\dfrac{(u_1 \sin \alpha)(m_1 + m_2)}{m_2 u_2(1 + e) + u_1 \cos \alpha(em_2 - m_1)}\right]$	91
5-16	$\text{Pressure} = \dfrac{\text{force}}{\text{area}}$	95
5-17	$W = Fd$	97
5-18	$P = \dfrac{W}{t}$	98
5-19	$E_k = \tfrac{1}{2}mv^2$	99
5-20	$E_p = Wh$	100
5-21	$Fd = \tfrac{1}{2}mv_f^2$	103
5-22	$Fd = \tfrac{1}{2}mv_f^2 + Wd$	105
6-1	$M = Fx$	113
6-2	$x = \dfrac{1.8(R_2 - R_1)}{W}\ \text{m}$	135
6-3	$x = \dfrac{(R_{B2} - R_{B1})h}{W}$	136
6-4	$y = \dfrac{(R_{A2} - R_{A1})h}{W}$	136
6-5	$I = \Sigma\, mr^2$	149
6-6	$I_O = \dfrac{WhT^2}{4\pi^2}$	149
6-7	$I_A = I_{CG} + md^2$	150
6-8	$H = I\omega$	153
6-9	$H_S = I_S \omega_{S/G_S} + m_S r^2 \omega_{G_S/G}$	153
6-10	$H = \displaystyle\sum_{S=1}^{S=N} (I_S \omega_{S/G_S} + m_S r^2 \omega_{G_S/G})$	154
6-11	$T = I\alpha$	158
6-12	$F_R = m\dfrac{v_T^2}{r}$	169
6-13	$F_R = mr\omega^2$	169
7-1	$F_D = C_D\,\rho\,A\,\dfrac{v^2}{2}$	185
7-2	$F_L = C_L\,\rho\,A\,\dfrac{v^2}{2}$	185

AUTHOR INDEX

SUBJECT INDEX